Simply Heavenly!
The Monastery Vegetarian Cookbook

Brother Simeon and Father Philaret prepare "simply heavenly" dishes in the kitchen of Holy Protection Orthodox Monastery in Geneva, Nebraska.

Simply Heavenly!

The Monastery Vegetarian Cookbook

Abbot George Burke

Saint George Press
Geneva, Nebraska

ISBN 0-932104-07-X

CONTENTS

Foreword

ORIGINALLY Christians–like their Jewish spiritual antecedents, the Essenes–were vegetarians, but in time the insistence on a vegetarian diet became confined to the monasteries. One of the most interesting monastic "relics" of the early Christian era is a letter written by a monk of Egypt to one of his disciples who had gone to Alexandria on some project and there had begun to eat meat. Learning of this, the monk immediately wrote to him, exhorting him to return to his vegetarian ways, reminding him that in Paradise Adam and Eve had been told: "Behold, I have given you every herb bearing seed, which is upon the face of all the earth, and every tree, in the which is the fruit of a tree yielding seed; to you it shall be for meat" (Gen. 1:29). This being so, the monk wrote, those who aspire to return to that pristine state of purity and communion with God must eat the diet of Paradise while on the earth in order to prepare themselves to regain that lost blessedness.

Although at times–especially in the West–this ideal was forgotten, whenever there was a resurgence of spiritual consciousness and reform among the monastics the absolute first principle would be that of total abstinence from animal flesh (including eggs) in all forms. Usually this abstinence would be extended to dairy products as well.

In the Eastern and Oriental Orthodox Churches this principle is still evident in the requirement for all Orthodox Christians–lay as well as monastic–to totally abstain from meat, fish, eggs, and dairy products on nearly all Wednesdays and Fridays as well as all days in the seasons of abstinence such as the forty days of Lent and Advent. In the Oriental Orthodox Churches these days of abstinence comprise more than half of the calendar year.

But many of the Eastern Christian monastics–and some non-monastics as well–prefer to observe this abstinence all the time. This is because in the Eastern Church such abstinence is not regarded as penitential self-denial or "mortification of the flesh," but rather as an aid to interior prayer (*Hesychia*–The Silence). The Fathers of the East taught that diet had a formative influence on the mind–which they saw as a field of energy, not merely the physical brain, which they considered to be only the organ of the mind. They observed that some foods made the mental processes (movements of noetic energies) heavy, whereas other foods made the mind light and quick in movement. Topping the list of "heavy" foods were all animal proteins, including dairy. In contrast, vegetables, grains, and fruits–the food of Paradise–were seen to make the mind fluid and able to grasp the subtleties of spiritual thought and experience (*theoria*).

In this approach to vegetarianism they were maintaining the principle to be found in the Aramaic text of the *Evangelion Da-Mepharreshe*, the oldest text of the Gospels known to exist. There, in the Gospel of Luke (21:34), Jesus says most forthrightly: "See that you do not make your minds heavy, *by never eating meat* or drinking wine." In our own century, Saint John of Kronstadt (+1908) wrote that the more we live in the spirit the less will we live on animal flesh–the implication being that those who live fully in the spirit abstain completely from animal food. Saint John, a non-monastic parish priest, insisted that his spiritual children abstain at all times from animal foods, thus keeping a perpetual lent. Those priests who were under his spiritual aegis did the same in relation to those under their spiritual care.

Now that more detailed–and honest–research and information regarding diet and health are becoming widely spread, many clergy and laity of the Orthodox Church who had previously held an indifferent attitude toward observance of the traditional rules of abstinence are realizing the wisdom of the ancient ways.

So much excellent material has been written on the material and spiritual "why" of vegetarianism that I will not add any more here. (I would, though, like to recommend four publications: *What's Wrong With Eating Meat*, by Vistara Parham, *Diet For A New America*, by John Robbins, and my two booklets–*The Four Soul Killers*, and *Spiritual Vegetarianism*.)

But I do want to say a word about the quality of vegetarian food–at least what I think it should be.

From the first day I became a vegetarian I have been convinced that vegetarian food should not just be healthy in a theoretical sense and eaten like medicine, but that it should be really *good* food–in taste and appearance. In fact, since it is better for us than non-vegetarian food, it should taste even *better* than non-vegetarian food. Accomplishing that is not so simple. This cookbook is a result of more than twenty years' endeavor to do so.

One of the best ways to motivate others to consider becoming vegetarian is to feed them good vegetarian food. I am glad to say that by means of the recipes in this book our monastery has done so for many years. And so can you. Every recipe in this book has been put to the ultimate test: eating!

We always eat together with those who attend our Sunday church service, so we cook several experimental dishes for the Sunday lunch. Then we vote on whether or not to pass them on to you. This way I can make sure that each recipe that goes into this book is one that produces really good food, and not just some mediocre mess that can get by merely because it does not nauseate the eaters. That may seem strong language, but I am increasingly unhappy with the low quality of the recipes that usually appear in vegan publications. Why a vegan should be subsisting on fare that would have been dished up in the Cro-Magnon era when dad's spear missed the bison is beyond me.

When I quit eating meat the quality of my food got better–not just from the health aspect, but from the flavor aspect as well. No longer relying on a main dish of death to distract the attention of the diners from the insipidity of the vegetables, I had to get competitive with the carnivore cooks–of which I had been one. And I easily surpassed them, much to their and my

surprise. Things went along quite well for years until it became evident that a vegetarian had to be just that–and dairy needed to be eliminated. The result was that we "ate better" than ever before.

So much has been written on the subject of vegetarian and vegan diet that there is no need for it here. The proof is in the eating and in the resulting health benefits.

APPLES

We prefer to use Granny Smith apples in the recipes that call for apples. They are a bit tart, and the recipes reflect this in the amount of Sucanat used, so you might want to experiment with cutting it down when you use other kinds of apples.

CHEESE SUBSTITUTES

This book has three wonderful cheese alternatives: Yeast Cheez, Pimento Cheez, and Notzarella Cheez. We use them frequently and find them more than satisfactory. However some may not care to bother with making them or may want a more "melty" or "cheesey" type of ingredient. Most soy-based cheese substitutes are awful, but I can wholeheartedly recommend Soy Kaas, made by Soy Kaas, Inc., Atlanta, Georgia, and distributed by American Natural Snacks, St. Augustine, Florida 32085. Soy Kaas comes in several types: Mozzarella, Cheddar, Smoked Cheddar, Jalapeño, Garlic and Herb, and Monterey Jack. All contain sodium caseinate but the Monterey Jack, which is also fat-free.

There are some recipes in which the Parmesan Cheez given in this book just does not work, giving too lemony a taste to the dish. But I have just discovered a perfect Parmesan made from tofu that tastes exactly like the real thing, but has nowhere the amount of sodium. So it is a double-plus. The brand is Lite and Less made by Soyco. For information write to: Soyco Foods, 2441 Viscount Row, Orlando, FL 32809.

FLOUR

Most recipes in this book call for unbleached white flour. This may be surprising to some, but whole wheat flour is often simply too strong in its taste and interferes with the desired flavor. Although unbleached white flour does not contain all the nutrients of whole wheat flour, it is not devoid of food value. Bleached flour, however, is both worthless and poisonous.

GLUTEN SUBSTITUTE

Those who have trouble with gluten can make just about all of the meat substitutes given in this book by using an equal amount of tofu that has been frozen, thawed, pressed, and cut into slices or pieces and then cooked in the flavoring broth.

JALAPEÑO PEPPERS

You will often find jalapeño peppers listed as an ingredient. If you don't like them, just leave them out. Also, keep in mind that throughout the growing season jalapeños vary in their degree of hotness, so the amount may have to be adjusted some. You may find it simpler to use cayenne pepper instead since it is consistent. But the distinctive taste of jalapeños is worth the trouble in my opinion.

KITCHEN BOUQUET

Kitchen Bouquet has been around for many decades. I know, because as a child attracted by the name and the smell I took a gigantic swig from my "aunt" Suzy Snow's bottle! Brown lightning! It was my first introduction to flavorings that no kidding are supposed to be used sparingly! Only when I was a seasoned vegetarian did I drop my trauma and agree to try it in cooking.

Kitchen Bouquet imparts a richer flavor (and color) to dishes that accommodate a beef-like flavor. While it is no substitute for beef-like broth or other "beef" flavorings, it does sometimes give that added touch and body that makes a recipe just right.

You can buy Kitchen Bouquet at just about any grocery store.

LEA & PERRINS STEAK SAUCE

Many recipes need the boost that Worcestershire sauce can give, but when this cookbook was first printed the only two vegetarian versions I knew of (unnamed out of Christian charity) tasted terrible. Now I am glad to tell you that there is one source of a really good sauce: Harvest Direct, P.O. Box 4514, Decatur, Illinois 62525 (1-800-835-2867). When using Harvest Direct instead of Lea & Perrins Steak Sauce in a recipe from this book, cut the amount in half.

But I still somewhat prefer Lea & Perrins Steak Sauce (their Worcestershire sauce contains anchovies) as an excellent substitute. When you are cooking from another book and a recipe calls for Worcestershire sauce, use *twice* the amount of Lea & Perrins sauce as it is not as pungent as Worcestershire.

LIQUID SMOKE

I only recommend Wright's Liquid Smoke, as it alone is made from all natural ingredients.

LOUISIANA HOT SAUCE & TABASCO SAUCE

When the recipe calls for Louisiana Hot Sauce I mean the real Louisiana Hot Sauce made by Bruce Foods Corporation in New Iberia, Louisiana, not any of the imitations–all of which are poor. The purpose of this sauce is both to impart a red pepper "heat" and a good vinegary tang that brings out the other flavors in the dish. (If you are watching your salt intake, be aware that all hot pepper sauces of this type contain large amounts of salt.) Also, Louisiana Hot Sauce (the real thing, remember) does not mask any flavors, but only adds a dimension of its own.

Tabasco is of course known throughout the world, and rightly so. Tabasco, however, is much hotter than Louisiana Hot Sauce and tends to impart the heat of red pepper more than any tangy flavor. Yet there are times when that is needed in preference to the effect of Louisiana Hot Sauce. Therefore in these recipes the two are not interchangeable, but each is called for according to its characteristic effect on the dish. If you are in a pinch, however, use what you have, but remember: if the recipe calls for Louisiana Hot Sauce, use only *half* the amount of Tabasco; if the recipe calls for Tabasco, use *twice* the amount of Louisiana Hot Sauce.

MEASUREMENTS

One of my pet peeves is encountering of a recipe in which I find terms like "a large bell pepper," "a medium potato," and "a small onion"–not to mention "a scant cup" or a "heaping spoon." Grrrrrrr! So I have not done this to you–unless it has slipped by me or refers to packages of frozen vegetables, raw grains, or pasta. However, this may mean that you will have a little of some ingredient left over in the measuring. Put it in. Live!

MEASUREMENTS AND INGREDIENTS–ANOTHER WORD

God did not write this cookbook. Nor can I claim to be His instrument in the writing lest that prove me to be slightly bent if not broken. So don't think these recipes are infallible or inflexible. Feel free to use them as a basis for your own creativity. As Justin Wilson says, good cooking is a combination of imagination and common sense.

MILK SUBSTITUTES

In this book I give formulas for soy milk, cashew milk, and almond milk. But in the recipes you will see that I always recommend cashew milk. This is because I feel that soy and almond milks do not have the body or flavor I prefer in cooking. But go ahead and try the other two if cashew milk does not appeal to you. Try soy milk if you have an allergy to nuts.

For those who want the easy way I suggest two excellent products: Vitamite and Solait. In some places Vitamite is available in the dairy sections of stores, packaged just like milk. It is the nearest thing to milk we have found, and when cold is a delicious drink plain. However it does contain sodium caseinate. It is made by Diehl Specialties International, 24 N. Clinton Street, Defiance, Ohio 43512 (1-419-782-8219). Solait is a soymilk powder that is beyond excellent and is also wonderful by itself when cold. It also works perfect (as does Vitamite) in recipes that call for Cashew Milk. Solait makes by far the best soymilk we have ever tasted. It is available from Devansoy Farms, Inc., P.O. Box 885, Carroll, Iowa 51401 (1-800-747-8605.

MOLASSES

Barbados molasses is recommended in these recipes–unless you like the heavier taste of Blackstrap molasses. This really must be obtained from health food stores or suppliers. (Be warned: a very famous "natural" brand of "unsulphured molasses" found in regular supermarkets contains a high percentage of white sugar, but is not required to be so labeled since white sugar is considered "natural.")

MONOSODIUM GLUTAMATE (MSG)

Now here is something really important. A vegan friend of ours with a Doctorate in chemistry provided the following information:

"MSG is a flavor enhancing food product made from *gluten*, usually *wheat* gluten. The gluten is simply hydrolized with hot, dilute hydrochloric acid, about in the same concentration as stomach acid. After digestion is complete, the gluten has been broken down into its main amino acid component, glutamic acid, whereupon the glutamic acid is simply neutralized with baking soda, filtered, and crystallized from the solution by slow evaporation.

"Monosodium glutamate is a natural food product, but a number of people react badly to it mainly because they are sensitive to wheat gluten and while they may not react to wheat all the time, the highly soluble MSG gets into the bloodstream very rapidly and causes them problems.

"*To most adults, MSG acts as a brain nutrient and actually improves brain function such as concentration and memory.* However, babies are not adults and their systems usually cannot handle glutamates, and soluble glutamates may cause brain lesions in severe cases. Of course all mothers know babies should not be fed wheat products until after the first year, so they should be doubly careful of soluble wheat derivatives such as MSG.

"And all this goes without saying that for some people the sodium part must cause this food to be used somewhat sparingly."

So people with MSG problems should find out if they might actually have a problem with wheat gluten itself.

Our friend who wrote us the above was intrigued as to how oriental people can eat so much MSG and have no problems at all–actually be in better health than most of us in the West. His investigations revealed that even infants are not harmed by it *unless they are also being fed adulterated foods*. The combination with the adulterants produce an allergy which persists into adulthood and causes them to experience "Chinese restaurant syndrome." So the culprit is not MSG but the adulteration of our food!

Our experience has carried his research one step further. When we used dairy products we, too, would sometimes get "MSG hangovers" after eating in a oriental restaurant. *But after becoming vegans we never had any such reactions.* In fact we eat more oriental food than before, since we are safe. Apparently animal protein of any kind–including that from eggs and milk–is considered an adulterant by the body and causes an allergic reaction when MSG meets any residue of it in the body of the eater.

Realizing how tricky this whole matter of MSG can be, it is only listed in a recipe when the flavor desired cannot be obtained any other way. If you want, in the soups you can substitute salt, but in a couple of the flavoring broths it is just not possible to get a satisfactory flavor without it. Even in the recipes that contain MSG, not much really goes into a serving since it is diluted in the broth which flavors the dish. And also it will usually only be in one dish at a meal.

MUSHROOMS–A SUBSTITUTE

Those who do not care for mushrooms will find that in most recipes sliced or chopped black olives will substitute quite well.

NON-DAIRY MARGARINE

Read the labels of supposedly non-dairy margarine carefully, keeping in mind that ingredients such as sodium caseinate are really elements taken from milk.

Oil can be used if you do not have non-dairy margarine or prefer not to use it.

NON-OIL COOKING

Some of these recipes just will not work without some oil, but most of them will do just fine. Simply leave the oil out! But in cases where sautéeing can really enhance the flavor, use Heavenly Broth instead of oil. Here is a table for substitutions.

1 T. oil: ¼ c. Heavenly Broth
2 T. oil: ⅓ c. Heavenly Broth
3 T. oil: ½ c. Heavenly Broth
4 T. oil: ⅔ c. Heavenly Broth
5 T. oil: ¾ c. Heavenly Broth
6 T. oil: 1 c. Heavenly Broth

When a recipe says to fry something, instead broil or grill it.

NUTRITIONAL YEAST

First of all, Nutritional Yeast is NOT Brewers Yeast. I put this in because friends of ours have wanted to try the recipes in this book and been told at health food stores that it is, and their culinary attempts were disasters! (Recently "Betty Crocker" assured readers of "her" column that the two were the same.) Nutritional Yeast (*Saccharomyces Cerevisiae*) is a food yeast grown in a molasses solution. It gives a "cheesy" taste to food, and is the basis for the Yeast Cheez recipe given in the Dairy Substitutes section. It can be stirred into or sprinkled on many things, and is especially good in adding flavor to soups. It contains several B Vitamins, including the elusive B12 that is so important for those who eat no dairy products.

Nutritional Yeast can be obtained from a health food store or by mail from: The Farm, Summertown, Tennessee, 38483, or from the Red Star Yeast Company. There may be other sources, as well.

OIL

Once a Theravadin Buddhist monk, commenting on a rival school of Buddhism, said to me: "It is a jungle!" So is the world of "healthy eating"! More so, I expect. The question of oil–how much, if any, and what kind–is a truly "vexed" question. Especially so since I have had the vexation of going through every recipe in this book and looking carefully at the quantities of oil prescribed!

As an Orthodox monk I have had much experience of totally oilless cooking, and am not interested, for I can say with Huck Finn: "I've done been there." However, I have tried to reduce the oil to the minimum that will still (to my palate) produce something that tastes good yet is not (to my mind) unhealthy. Some "ethnic" dishes, such as Indian ones, demand oiliness–otherwise they are just not the dish. But I have done what I could without violating their basic nature. There is also quite a good chance that I have managed to skip or overlook a recipe. If so, cut down the oil and forgive (and if you would let me know about it I would be most appreciative.) But believe me, I have gone through the jungle of this book with an oil-hacking machete and done my best.

Olive oil is an excellent food. It is the only monosaturate among oils, and has been found to actively remove cholesterol deposits from arteries. It is best used raw as in salad dressings, and in cooked dishes where its distinctive flavor is desired.

Corn oil is excellent in cooking, since it loses very little of its nutritional value from the heat. Mazola is the best brand beyond a doubt.

ONIONS

Onions, despite some medicinal elements, do contain some toxins that can affect the heart action. This is why the yogis of India avoid them. Red onions, however, contain the least of these elements and are also easier to digest, so I recommend that you try them. However, you can use any type of onions you prefer in the recipes. Chives, leeks, scallions, or shallots are good substitutes for onions.

RECIPE COMMENTS

Under the heading of many recipes I have put some comments on the dish. This is because I am aware how easy it is to pass up a really good dish simply because it does not sound interesting. But please do not think that those without comments are not as good as those with them—they are! Sometimes I just could not think of anything clever to say about them. Often I have been tempted to put " Please try this! Please!" under many headings, because I know how much you will like it if you do.

RED PEPPER FLAKES

When the ingredients list says "red pepper flakes" I mean crushed *hot* red pepper flakes, not red *bell* pepper flakes.

RICE

Whenever a recipe in this book calls for rice, natural white rice is intended—not the white rice usually found in grocery stores which has neither fragrance nor taste. True natural rice has a definite fragrance and a distinct though delicate taste. The best sources for rice are Indian or Oriental grocery stores. The best rice from India is Basmati Rice, but my favorite is Jasmine Rice from Thailand. "Jasmine" is a type of rice, not a brand name, and don't be disturbed if the bag says the rice is "scented." The producers (whose English is not the best) only mean that it smells good when cooked. Also be assured that the rice does *not* smell or taste like Jasmine—a pretty awful idea.

If you have no Indian or Oriental stores in your town from which to obtain good quality rice, there are quite a few Oriental food companies that will sell to you through the mail. Oriental cookbooks often list such companies, or your local library should be able to help you locate them.

Those who prefer brown rice can substitute it, but should keep in mind that cooking time will need to be adjusted since brown rice takes about four times longer to cook. This is because brown rice is really white rice that has been steamed in the husk before its removal. This causes some of the nutrients and color from the husk to enter the grain. But when the partially-cooked grain dries out it becomes very hard—much like what occurs when beans are dried—so longer cooking time is needed.

SALT

Sea salt is always recommended in these recipes as being more easily assimilated by the body.

SOVEX AND VEGEX

Sovex and Vegex are the brand names for a dark, saltish paste that is a yeast extract used for flavoring. Some large grocery stores carry it in the section where they have bouillon cubes, but usually it must be bought from health food stores.

SOY SAUCE

In the recipes calling for soy sauce I prefer to use *low sodium* soy sauce, for not only is it better for us (it has been estimated that in the "normal" American diet we eat twenty to thirty times more salt than we need), I find that the low sodium soy sauce has a stronger-bodied—and better—flavor. If possible a naturally brewed sauce should be used rather than the "common garden variety" brands we grew up with.

Angostura Low Sodium Soy Sauce is lower in sodium than any others I know of, and the flavor is incomparably better. Also, some other brands are much less flavorful, so the amount will have to be increased in the recipe to get the desired taste. However, this will increase the overall amount of sodium. So get Angostura if you can.

Not all soy sauces, low sodium or regular, are equal in strength, so you may need to adjust the amounts used according to the brand—which can vary from batch to batch.

SPICES

Spices and herbs are important ingredients in cooking, both for flavor and health. But not all brands are the same in quality. I recommend that you use the excellent products produced by the Watkins company. They have been around for generations and deserve their fine reputation. We have found no other Poultry Seasoning that "delivers" like theirs—especially in making UnChicken and UnChicken Broth. So many of their products are good that I can't list them all. (Be aware, though, that not everything made by Watkins is animal-free.)

SWEETENERS

The latest—and best—word on sweeteners is a product called "granulated sugar cane juice" which, despite the odd name, is actually a sweetener made by dehydrating sugar cane juice. Completely unrefined, the resulting powder contains all the nutrients of the sugar cane juice with none of the negative qualities of refined sugar. The brand I am familiar with and use is Sucanat, which is produced by Nutra-Cane, Inc., 58 Meadowbrook Pkwy., Milford, NH 03055 (Phone: 603-672-2801). In the Etc. Section I give the formula for making powdered Sucanat when powdered sugar is needed in a recipe.

Since Sucanat can give a "brown sugar" taste to recipes, you might want to try a couple of alternatives that are not as healthy, however. One is Turbinado sugar that is not as refined as white sugar, and is filtered through wood charcoal, not bone char. The other is Palm sugar which, as its name indicates, comes from the sap of the palm tree. It usually comes in a soft but solid form (sometimes not so soft!) that looks like crystallized honey. Turbinado can be gotten at a health foods store, and palm sugar from either health food or oriental stores.

TAHINI

Tahini is a paste made from sesame seeds. It has a "smoky" or "bacon" taste that adds much to recipes. You can buy it in health food and import grocery stores.

TOMATOES

Our ancestors thought tomatoes were deadly poison. They were mistaken, but tomatoes do contain some elements that are toxic to a degree. It has been my experience that these elements are not in Italian (sometimes called Roma) tomatoes, and that Italian tomatoes are better in flavor when cooked. Nor are they as acidic as other tomatoes. As with the onions, if you prefer—or do not have Italian tomatoes—simply use whatever is available.

VITAMIN B12

There is far more misinformation than fact being given out regarding Vitamin B12, and as vegans it is important that we get the straight facts.

Vitamin B12 is *not* available from vegetable sources, but is made only by bacteria. Those who ingest animal proteins can get the vitamin that way, but do not be misled by the fear propaganda by the carnivores. The truth is, *most cases of severe Vitamin B12 deficiency develop in non-vegetarians.* But we vegans are the ones who get pointed at.

How to get Vitamin B12? Well, have you heard the old adage "eat dirt"? That's pretty good advice in this case. People with their own gardens used to get plenty of B12 from the dirt that was on the vegetables they ate. Go out, pull up a radish or carrot (from an *organic* garden, please), knock off the more obvious dirt, and eat it up. You will get plenty of B12—or would have, in a normal ecology. Fermented soyfoods at one time supplied plenty of B12, but there, too, it was the dirt involved. Now that governments have imposed stringent sanitation measures in their manufacture they no longer contain the vitamin to any significant degree. Cleanliness is obviously not always next to healthiness.

What to do, then? We do two things. First, Nutritional Yeast is always on the table, and we sprinkle it generously on our food (if it is not already in the dish). Here, too, because of sanitation the yeast can vary from batch to batch in its B12 content. But if you eat a lot you will surely manage. The second thing we do is to take a vitamin supplement three times a week. We prefer MEGA B-150 made by Nature's Plus. We suspect that the Nutritional Yeast alone would do the needful, but prefer to be sure.

If you want more information on Vitamin B12, Dr. Michael Klaper's books *Vegan Nutrition: Pure and Simple* and *Pregnancy, Children, and the Vegan Diet* give the whole and true picture.

ZATARAIN'S CRAB BOIL

"Crab Boil" is a mixture of spices put in the water used to boil crab or shrimp in Louisiana Creole and Cajun cooking. While it is not absolutely necessary to have it in making UnShrimp according to the recipe given in the UnSeafood section, I greatly recommend it.

There are several brands of Crab Boil available in supermarkets, but I have found that Zatarain's is by far the best, and more than a century of satisfied users agree with me. If you cannot find it in a local store, telephone: 504-367-2950 and ask where it might be sold near you. If there is no store "within reach" that stocks it, don't worry—Zatarain's will sell it directly to you through the mail (UPS, actually) by the case. That may seem like a lot to buy, but when you taste "shrimp" made with it you will make so much that it won't take long to use it up. Or you can split a case with friends.

Zatarain's sells three forms of Crab Boil: dry (whole spices in a bag), liquid, and preseasoned (powdered in a box). *Get the dry whole spices in the bag.*

Salad Dressings

ALFALFA SPROUT DRESSING

½ c.	Alfalfa sprouts
2 tsp.	Celery seed
2 T.	Olive oil
2 T.	Water
⅓ c.	Lemon juice or white vinegar
½ tsp.	Soy sauce
1 tsp.	Onion powder or 1 T. scallion, shallot, or leek
1 T.	Sesame seeds

Mix well by hand or blend in a blender–according to your taste.

ALMOND DRESSING

¼ c.	Almonds
¼ tsp.	Garlic powder
½ tsp.	Sea salt
½ c.	Tomato, chopped
2 T.	Lemon juice or white vinegar
3 T.	Olive oil

Mix well by hand or blend in a blender–according to your taste.

AVOCADO-CASHEW DRESSING

Blend until smooth:

½ c.	Raw cashews
1 ½ c.	Hot water

Add and continue to blend:

2	Avocados
2 tsp.	Lemon juice or white vinegar
¼ c.	Onions, chopped
½ tsp.	Sea salt

Cool before using.

AVOCADO DRESSING-1

1	Avocado, in chunks
1	Tomato, chopped
¼ tsp.	Sea salt
2 T.	Lemon juice
¼ c.	Onions, chopped
1 T.	Nutritional yeast
1 T.	Olive oil

Mix well by hand or blend in a blender–according to your taste.
Variation: Add ⅔ cup of Tofu Mayonnaise, Cashew Mayonnaise, or Miraculous Whip.

AVOCADO DRESSING-2

½ tsp.	Garlic powder
½	Medium avocado
2 T.	Lemon juice
4 T.	Tofu Mayonnaise, Cashew Mayonnaise, or Miraculous Whip

Mix well by hand or blend in a blender–according to your taste.
Variation: Add ¼ tsp. of dill weed.

AVOCADO DRESSING-3

This does not keep well. Use up at one meal, if possible.

4	Avocadoes, mashed
1 T.	Olive oil
1 ½ T.	Soy sauce
¼ tsp.	Onion powder
¼ tsp.	Oregano
¼ tsp.	Basil
¼ tsp.	Garlic powder
¼ tsp.	Sea salt

Mix well by hand or blend in a blender—according to your taste.

AVOCADO DRESSING-4

3	Avocados, mashed
1 c.	Cashew or Tofu Sour Cream
1 tsp.	Sea salt
2 T.	Lemon or lime juice

Mix well by hand or blend in a blender—according to your taste.

AVOCADO DRESSING-5

2	Avocados, mashed
1 ⅓ c.	Cashew or Tofu Sour Cream
1 tsp.	Sea salt
½ tsp.	Chives
⅛ tsp.	Onion powder
4 tsp.	Lemon juice or white vinegar

Mix well by hand or blend in a blender—according to your taste.

AVOCADO DRESSING-6

1	Avocado
1 T.	Lemon juice or white vinegar
2 T.	Onions, minced
2 T.	Bell pepper or pimento, chopped
½ tsp.	Sea salt
2 T.	Cashew or Tofu Sour Cream
¼ tsp.	Dill

Mix well by hand or blend in a blender—according to your taste.

AVOCADO-OLIVE DRESSING

1	Medium avocado, mashed
¼ c.	Ripe olives, sliced or chopped
1 c.	Tofu Mayonnaise, Cashew Mayonnaise, or Miraculous Whip or Cashew or Tofu Sour Cream

Mix well by hand or blend in a blender—according to your taste.

AVOCADO MAYONNAISE

¼ c.	Avocado, mashed
1 ½ tsp.	Lemon juice or white vinegar
1 T.	Corn oil

Mix well by hand or blend in a blender—according to your taste.

SIMPLE AVOCADO DRESSING

Mash avocado(s) and gradually add lemon juice (or white vinegar, or tomato juice), beating until it is creamy. Mix well by hand or blend in a blender—according to your taste.

BITTERS DRESSING

¾ c.	Lime juice
3 T.	Olive oil
¼ tsp.	Garlic powder
1 ½ tsp.	Sea salt
1 tsp.	Aromatic bitters

Mix well by hand or blend in a blender—according to your taste.

CAPER FRENCH DRESSING

1 c.	French Dressing
⅓ c.	Capers, minced

Mix well by hand or blend in a blender—according to your taste.

CARAWAY DRESSING

⅓ c.	Tofu Mayonnaise, Cashew Mayonnaise, or Miraculous Whip or Tofu Sour Cream or Cashew Sour Cream
¾ tsp.	Caraway seeds
1 T.	Sesame seeds
1 ½ tsp.	Lemon juice or white vinegar
¼ tsp.	Sea salt
¼ tsp.	Paprika

Mix well by hand or blend in a blender—according to your taste.

CARROT DRESSING

4	Carrots, grated
2 T.	Olive oil
½ tsp.	Garlic powder
½ tsp.	Onion powder
1 c.	Water
1 T.	Soy sauce
2 T.	Tahini or nut butter

Mix well by hand or blend in a blender—according to your taste.

CASHEW CHEEZ DRESSING

Superb!

¾ c.	Cashews
½ c.	Water

¾ tsp.	Sea salt
¾ tsp.	Onion powder
2 T.	Lemon juice or white vinegar
¼ c.	Canned pimentos
4 ½ tsp.	Olive oil

Put the nuts in a blender (Vita-Mix is best) and grind them as fine as possible. Add the rest of the ingredients and continue blending until everything is smooth–about 1 minute.
Variation: Add 3 tablespoons of Nutritional Yeast.

CASHEW MAYONNAISE

2 c.	Water
6 T.	Cornstarch or arrowroot powder
2 c.	Hot water
2 c.	Raw cashews
⅓ c.	Lemon juice or white vinegar
1 tsp.	Garlic powder
2 tsp.	Onion powder
1 T.	Sea salt
1 T.	Sucanat
⅛ tsp.	Paprika

Mix the 2 cups of water with the cornstarch or arrowroot and boil on the stove until it thickens. Cool slightly. Blend the hot water and cashews well. Add the rest of the ingredients to the cashew liquid. Add this to the cornstarch mixture and combine thoroughly. Cool before using.

CHIVE DRESSING

⅔ c.	French Dressing
¼ c.	Chives, chopped

Mix well by hand or blend in a blender–according to your taste.
Variation: Add ¼ c. Tofu Mayonnaise, Cashew Mayonnaise, Miraculous Whip, Tofu Sour Cream, or Cashew Sour Cream.

CREAM FRENCH DRESSING

When French Dressing-1 is used this is marvellous: good enough to eat by the spoonful.

½ c.	French Dressing
¼ c.	Cashew or Tofu Mayonnaise, Miraculous Whip, or Cashew or Tofu Sour Cream

Mix well by hand or blend in a blender–according to your taste.

CRUNCHY CREAM DRESSING

½ c.	Cucumber, finely chopped
2 T.	Bell pepper, finely chopped
2 T.	Chives, finely chopped
2 T.	Radishes, thinly sliced
1 c.	Cashew or Tofu Sour Cream
½ tsp.	Sea salt
¼ tsp.	Paprika

Mix well by hand or blend in a blender–according to your taste.
Variation: Add 1 or 2 teaspoons of soy sauce.

CUCUMBER DRESSING

1 c.	Cucumbers, chopped
½ tsp.	Sea salt
1 T.	Lemon juice
1 T.	Dill, minced or 1 tsp. dry
1 c.	Cashew or Tofu Mayonnaise, Miraculous Whip, or Cashew or Tofu Sour Cream

Mix well by hand or blend in a blender–according to your taste.
Variation: Add 2 or 3 tablespoons of finely chopped onions.

CURRY MAYONNAISE

1 ½ c.	Cashew or Tofu Mayonnaise, or Miraculous Whip
1 ½ tsp.	Curry Powder

Mix well by hand or blend in a blender–according to your taste.

DILL DRESSING

Outstanding!

¾ c.	Tofu, mashed
2 T.	Corn oil
2 T.	Wine vinegar
½ tsp.	Sea salt
1 tsp.	Sucanat
1 tsp.	Dill weed
⅛ tsp.	Black pepper
1 T.	Onion, minced

Blend in a blender until smooth and creamy.

DRIED BEAN DRESSING

Unusual, but equally tasty.

1 c.	Dried beans, cooked
2 T.	Onions, minced

1 c.   UnBeef Broth
1 tsp.   Garlic powder
½ tsp.   Oregano
½ tsp.   Basil
½ tsp.   Paprika

Mix well by hand or blend in a blender–according to your taste.

FRENCH DRESSING–1

3 T.   Olive oil
3 T.   Corn oil
2 T.   Water
3 T.   Lemon juice
½ tsp.   Sea salt
¼ c.   Raw cashews
½ tsp.   Paprika
¼ tsp.   Garlic powder
½ tsp.   Onion powder
¼ tsp.   Dill weed
¼ tsp.   Basil

Mix well by hand or blend in a blender–according to your taste.

FRENCH DRESSING–2

⅓ c.   Corn oil
2 T.   Vinegar
2 T.   Lemon
2 tsp.   Sucanat
½ tsp.   Sea salt
½ tsp.   Dry mustard
½ tsp.   Paprika

Mix well by hand or blend in a blender–according to your taste.

FRENCH DRESSING–3

1 ½ c.   Tomatoes, chopped
½ c.   Tahini
⅛ c.   Soy sauce
¼ tsp.   Oregano
¼ tsp.   Garlic powder
¼ tsp.   Parsley
¼ tsp.   Sea salt
¼ tsp.   Basil

Mix well by hand or blend in a blender–according to your taste.

FRESH HERB DRESSING

1 T.   Garlic, minced
½ c.   Chopped fresh herbs:
          Chives or green onions

Basil or oregano
Spearmint or peppermint
⅔ c.   Corn oil
⅓ c.   Lemon juice
2 T.   Soy sauce
¼ tsp.   Sea salt

Put everything in a blender and blend for 10 to 15 seconds.

FRESH TOMATO DRESSING

1 ½ c.   Tahini/Oil Dressing
¾ c.   Tomatoes, chopped
2 T.   Bell peppers, chopped
3 T.   Black olives, chopped
2 T.   Onions, minced

Mix well by hand or blend in a blender–according to your taste.

FRESH VEGETABLE DRESSING

1 c.   Fresh tomatoes, pureed
¼ c.   Spinach or other greens, chopped
2 T.   Squash, chopped
2 T.   Bean sprouts, minced

Mix well by hand or blend in a blender–according to your taste.

GARLIC DRESSING

1 c.   Tofu, mashed
2 T.   Corn oil
2 T.   Lemon juice
½ tsp.   Sucanat
¾ tsp.   Sea salt
2 tsp.   Garlic, minced

Blend in a blender until smooth and creamy.

GARLIC AND DILL DRESSING

¼ c.   Red wine vinegar
3 T.   Water
1 tsp.   Sucanat
3 T.   Olive oil
⅛ tsp.   Garlic powder
2 T.   Chopped parsley
2 T.   Chopped chives
2 T.   Parmesan Cheez
½ tsp.   Dill weed
½ tsp.   Sea salt
⅛ tsp.   Black pepper

Put all ingredients in a glass jar with a tight-fitting lid and shake until blended. Refrigerate.

GREEN DRESSING–1

1 ½ c.	Tahini/Oil Dressing
2 T.	Bell peppers
¼ c.	Spinach or bok choy
1 T.	Parsley

Mix well by hand or blend in a blender–according to your taste.

GREEN DRESSING–2

¼ c.	Bell pepper, finely chopped
¼ c.	Parsley, finely chopped
2 T.	Celery, finely chopped
1 T.	Onions, finely chopped
1 T.	Pimento, finely chopped
1 T.	Capers, finely chopped
½ tsp.	Sea salt
⅛ tsp.	Basil
2 T.	Olive oil

Mix well by hand or blend in a blender–according to your taste.

GREEN GAZPACHO DRESSING

2 T.	Onions, chopped
1 tsp.	Garlic powder
¼ c.	Bell pepper, chopped
1 T.	Fresh basil, or ¾ tsp. dried
2 tsp.	Parsley, chopped
1 c.	Tomatoes, quartered
3 T.	Lemon juice or white vinegar
2 T.	Olive oil
½ tsp.	Sea salt

Mix well by hand or blend in a blender–according to your taste.

GREEN GODDESS DRESSING

For those who love both flavor and tang!

1 c.	Cashew or Tofu Mayonnaise, Miraculous Whip, or Cashew or Tofu Sour Cream
2 T.	Corn oil
½ T.	Dried chives
½ c.	Parsley, fresh
2 T.	Tarragon vinegar
1 tsp.	Onion powder
⅛ tsp.	Black pepper
⅛ tsp.	Garlic powder
½ tsp.	Sea salt

Put all in a blender and blend until smooth and creamy.

GREEN ONION SALAD DRESSING

1	Bunch green onions, ends and dark tops removed, sliced as thin as possible
2 ¼ tsp.	Garlic, chopped
3 T.	Lemon juice
1 tsp.	Sea salt
½ tsp.	Black pepper
¾ c.	Tofu Yogurt

Put everything in a blender and purée until very smooth. Chill thoroughly.

HERB DRESSING–1

3 T.	Olive oil
2 T.	Lemon or lime juice
½ tsp.	Chervil
½ tsp.	Thyme
½ tsp.	Oregano
½ tsp.	Savory
¼ tsp.	Coriander
⅛ tsp.	Sage
½ tsp.	Sea salt
1 T.	Cashew or Tofu Sour Cream

Mix well by hand or blend in a blender–according to your taste.

HERB DRESSING–2

¼ c.	Celery, chopped fine
3 T.	Onions, chopped fine
2 T.	Parsley, chopped
½ tsp.	Sea salt
1 tsp.	Paprika
¼ tsp.	Basil
⅛ tsp.	Marjoram or rosemary
⅔ c.	Olive oil
⅔ c.	Lemon juice or white vinegar

Mix well by hand or blend in a blender–according to your taste.

HERB MAYONNAISE DRESSING

1 ½ c.	Cashew or Tofu Mayonnaise, or Miraculous Whip
¼ tsp.	Paprika
1 tsp.	Herbs
¼ tsp.	Onion powder
⅛ tsp.	Curry powder

Mix well by hand or blend in a blender–according to your taste.

HOT CHEEZ AND CIDER DRESSING

Something special!

½ c.	Apple cider
1 c.	Yeast or Pimento Cheez
½ tsp.	Sea salt
⅛ tsp.	Cayenne pepper
¼ tsp.	Parsley or chives, finely chopped
Pinch	Garlic salt

Heat the cider to the boiling point, then reduce to a simmer. Stir the cheez gradually into the cider until all is well blended. Add the seasonings.

HUMMUS DRESSING

An excellent way to boost protein when eating salad! Tastes good, too!

1 ⅓ c.	Dry garbanzos
2 T.	Olive oil
1 T.	Sea salt
1 T.	Garlic, minced
¼ c.	Lemon juice or white vinegar
1 c.	Tahini
	Water from cooking the garbanzos

Pressure-cook the garbanzos, drain and mash them. Add the remaining ingredients except the garbanzo water. Using the garbanzo water, blend all in a blender until smooth and of the consistency of a medium-thick sauce.

ITALIAN DRESSING–1

½ c.	Olive oil
½ c.	White vinegar or lemon juice
½ tsp.	Sea salt
¼ tsp.	Celery seed
¼ tsp.	Basil
¼ tsp.	Oregano
¼ tsp.	Onion powder
⅛ tsp.	Garlic powder

Mix well by hand or blend in a blender–according to your taste.

ITALIAN DRESSING–2

½ c.	Olive oil
½ c.	White vinegar or lemon juice
½ tsp.	Sea salt
¼ tsp.	Basil
¼ tsp.	Oregano
2 T.	Onions, minced

Mix well by hand or blend in a blender–according to your taste.

LEMON DRESSING

Combine:

1 tsp.	Sea salt
⅛ tsp.	Black pepper
	Pinch of Cayenne pepper
¼ tsp.	Paprika

Add slowly and beat thoroughly:

1 ½ T.	Lemon juice
3 T.	Olive oil

Chop until fine and add:

1 T.	Pimento
1 T.	Cucumber
¾ T.	Bell pepper
½ T.	Parsley
¼ c.	Onions

Mix well by hand or blend in a blender–according to your taste.

LEMON GARLIC DRESSING

⅓ c.	Olive oil
6 T.	Lemon juice
2 T.	Red wine vinegar
⅓ c.	Finely chopped green onions
2 T.	Chopped parsley
1 T.	Garlic, minced
1 tsp.	Dijon-style mustard
¼ tsp.	Sea salt
⅛ tsp.	Black pepper

Combine all ingredients in a jar with a tight lid. Shake vigorously until the mixture is blended. Store in the refrigerator.

LORENZO DRESSING

1 c.	French Dressing
4 T.	Tomato Relish, semi-liquefied
4 T.	Parsley, chopped

Mix well by hand or blend in a blender–according to your taste.

MARINADE DRESSING

2 T.	Olive oil
¼ c.	Lemon juice or white vinegar
½ c.	Water
2 tsp.	Soy sauce
3 T.	Nutritional Yeast
2 T.	Tahini
¼ tsp.	Onion powder
¼ tsp.	Garlic powder

½ tsp. Sea salt

Mix well by hand or blend in a blender–according to your taste.

MAYONNAISE DRESSING

1 c.	Cashew or Tofu Mayonnaise, or Miraculous Whip
1 T.	Cucumber, chopped
1 T.	Pimento, chopped
1 T.	Bell pepper, chopped
1 T.	Parsley, chopped
2 T.	Black olives, chopped
2 T.	Onions, chopped
	Salt to taste

Mix well by hand or blend in a blender–according to your taste.

MEXICAN TOMATO DRESSING

1 c.	Tomato, chopped
2 T.	Onions, minced
2 T.	Lemon juice or white vinegar
2 T.	Olive oil
1 tsp.	Cayenne
1 tsp.	Nutritional Yeast

Mix well by hand or blend in a blender–according to your taste.

MEXICAN TOMATO VINAIGRETTE

½ T.	Tomato paste
2 T.	Onions, minced
1 T.	Lemon juice or white vinegar
2 T.	Olive oil
½ tsp.	Chili powder

Mix well by hand or blend in a blender–according to your taste.

"MIRACULOUS WHIP"

Tastes as much like the real thing as the real thing itself!

1 ½ c.	Firm tofu
3 T.	Corn oil
1 T.	Apple cider vinegar
½ c.	Water
1 ½ tsp.	Prepared yellow mustard
1 tsp.	Garlic, minced
¼ c.	Onion, minced
¼ tsp.	White pepper
1 ¼ tsp.	Sea salt
1 T.	Lemon juice or white vinegar
1 T.	Cashew nuts ground fine

Put everything in a blender and blend until completely smooth. Refrigerate.
Variation: For dishes such as fruit salads in which you do not want the flavors of onion, garlic, and mustard, leave them out.

NUT BUTTER DRESSING–1

½ c.	Nut Butter
1 c.	Water
1 T.	Lemon juice or white vinegar
¼ tsp.	Sea salt

Mix well by hand or blend in a blender–according to your taste.
Variation: Add ¼ cup of Tofu Mayonnaise, Cashew Mayonnaise, Miraculous Whip, or Cashew Cream.

NUT BUTTER DRESSING–2

¼ c.	Nut butter
¼ c.	Cashew or Tofu Sour Cream
1 tsp.	Lemon juice or white vinegar
¼ tsp.	Basil or parsley

Mix well by hand or blend in a blender–according to your taste.

NUT BUTTER DRESSING–3

¼ c.	Nut butter
2 T.	Corn oil
2 T.	Lemon juice or white vinegar
2 T.	Water
½ tsp.	Sea salt
⅛ tsp.	Paprika

Mix well by hand or blend in a blender–according to your taste.

NUT BUTTER DRESSING–4

¼ c.	Nut butter
⅓ c.	Tomato juice
2 T.	Corn oil
¼ tsp.	Sea salt

Mix well by hand or blend in a blender–according to your taste.

NUTRITIONAL YEAST DRESSING

½ c.	Nutritional Yeast
2 T.	Corn oil
½ c.	UnBeef Broth
½ tsp.	Onion powder
½ tsp.	Garlic powder

¼ tsp.   Basil
¼ tsp.   Oregano
¼ tsp.   Paprika

Mix well by hand or blend in a blender–according to your taste.

OIL AND LEMON JUICE DRESSING

½ c.   Lemon juice
½ c.   Olive oil
¼ tsp.   Sea salt

Mix well by hand or blend in a blender–according to your taste.

OIL AND VINEGAR DRESSING

½ c.   Olive oil
¼ c.   Red wine vinegar
1   Garlic clove, minced
¼ tsp.   Basil
1 tsp.   Sucanat
1 tsp.   Dijon style mustard
½ tsp.   Sea salt
¼ tsp.   Black pepper

Combine all ingredients in a jar with a tight lid. Shake vigorously until the mixture is blended. Store in the refrigerator.

OLD FASHIONED BOILED DRESSING

1 T.   Non-dairy margarine
2 T.   Unbleached white flour
1 c.   Cashew Milk
1 tsp.   Dry mustard
⅛ tsp.   Cayenne pepper
¼ c.   Cider vinegar

Heat the margarine in a saucepan until it melts. Sprinkle in the flour, stirring carefully until it is smoothly blended with the margarine. Add the cashew milk, ¼ cup at a time, stirring briskly to avoid lumping. Stir in the mustard and cayenne pepper. Let the sauce bubble gently until it is thick, about 8 to 10 minutes. Slowly stir in the vinegar and bring the mixture to a gentle boil. Let the dressing cool before using. Makes about 1 cup.

OLIVE DRESSING

¾ c.   French dressing
¼ c.   Ripe olives

Mix well by hand or blend in a blender–according to your taste.

OREGANO-MINT DRESSING

3 T.   Olive oil
¼ c.   Lemon juice or white vinegar
¼ tsp.   Mint, chopped
¼ tsp.   Oregano
⅓ c.   Cashew or Tofu Mayonnaise, Miraculous Whip, or Cashew or Tofu Sour Cream

Mix well by hand or blend in a blender–according to your taste.

PARSLEY DRESSING

2 T.   Olive oil
2 T.   Lemon juice or white vinegar
¼ tsp.   Sea salt
¼ tsp.   Onion powder
2 T.   Parsley, chopped

Mix well by hand or blend in a blender–according to your taste.

POTATO DRESSING–1

½ c.   French Dressing
⅓ c.   Potato, baked and mashed

Mix well by hand or blend in a blender–according to your taste.

POTATO DRESSING–2

1 c.   Cashew or Tofu Sour Cream
1 c.   Potato, baked and mashed
2 T.   Onions, minced

Mix well by hand or blend in a blender–according to your taste.

POTATO DRESSING–3

½ c.   Onions, chopped
5 c.   Potatoes, mashed
1 ½ c.   Flavoring Broth or water from cooking the potatoes
3 T.   Olive oil
2 T.   Lemon juice or white vinegar

Mix well by hand or blend in a blender–according to your taste.
Variations: Use 4 tsp. of garlic powder instead of onions. Add ½ to 1 cup of chopped ripe olives.

POTATO MAYONNAISE

1 c.   Cashew or Tofu Mayonnaise, or Miraculous Whip

1 c.   Potato, baked and mashed

Mix well by hand or blend in a blender–according to your taste.

RUSSIAN DRESSING–1

1 c.   Cashew or Tofu Mayonnaise, Miraculous Whip, or Cashew or Tofu Sour Cream
2 T.   Bell pepper, finely chopped
2 T.   Celery, finely chopped
2 T.   Black olives, finely chopped
1 T.   Pimento, finely chopped
4 T.   Tomato Relish

Mix well by hand or blend in a blender–according to your taste.

RUSSIAN DRESSING–2

1 c.   Tomatoes
2 T.   Olive oil
1 T.   Lemon juice or white vinegar
2 T.   Onions, minced fine
½ tsp.   Sea salt
1 tsp.   Paprika
1 tsp.   Garlic powder

Mix well by hand or blend in a blender–according to your taste.

"SOUR CREAM" DRESSING–1

½ c.   Cashew or Tofu Sour Cream
3 T.   Corn oil
½ c.   Wine vinegar
2 T.   Sucanat
½ tsp.   Sea salt
2 T.   Onions, minced

Mix well by hand or blend in a blender–according to your taste.

"SOUR CREAM" DRESSING–2

1 c.   Cashew or Tofu Sour Cream
1 T.   Pimento, chopped
1 T.   Bell pepper, chopped
1 T.   Parsley, chopped
2 T.   Lemon juice or white vinegar
2 T.   Chopped black olives
2 T.   Onions, minced
       Sea salt to taste

Mix well by hand or blend in a blender–according to your taste.

SWEET BASIL DRESSING

1 c.   Hot water
½ c.   Raw cashews
¼ c.   Onions, chopped
½ tsp.   Sea salt
1 tsp.   Basil
2 T.   Lemon juice or white vinegar
¼ c.   Black olives, minced

Blend well in a blender.

TAHINI DRESSING–1

3 T.   Tahini
3 T.   UnChicken, UnBeef Broth, or Soy sauce

Mix well by hand or blend in a blender–according to your taste.

TAHINI DRESSING–2

¼ c.   Tahini
2 T.   Lemon juice or white vinegar
2 T.   Olive oil
¼ c.   UnBeef Broth
⅛ tsp.   Sea salt
1 T.   Parsley, chopped

Mix well by hand or blend in a blender–according to your taste.

TAHINI DRESSING–3

¼ c.   Celery, chopped as finely as possible
½ c.   Tahini
1 T.   Lemon juice or white vinegar
       Water, if needed, to thin the dressing

Mix well by hand or blend in a blender–according to your taste.

TAHINI DRESSING–4

1 tsp.   Garlic powder
1 c.   Tahini
¾ c.   Water
¼ c.   Lemon juice or white vinegar
1 tsp.   Sea salt

Mix well by hand or blend in a blender–according to your taste.

TAHINI DRESSING–5

½ c.   Tahini
⅔ c.   Water

1 T.   Soy sauce
¼ tsp.   Garlic powder
⅓ tsp.   Paprika
⅛ tsp.   Basil
⅛ tsp.   Oregano
1 tsp.   Onion powder

Mix well by hand or blend in a blender–according to your taste.

TAHINI DRESSING–6

1 c.   Tahini
1 c.   Water
1 tsp.   Sea salt
2 T.   Onion, chopped very fine
¼ c.   Lemon juice or white vinegar
¼ tsp.   Basil
¼ tsp.   Oregano

Mix well by hand or blend in a blender–according to your taste.

TAHINI/OIL DRESSING

2 c.   Tahini or olive oil
1 tsp.   Sea salt
3 T.   Onions
¼ c.   Black olives
⅛ tsp.   Cayenne pepper
2 T.   Bell pepper, chopped very fine
1 T.   Lemon juice or white vinegar
½ tsp.   Basil
½ tsp.   Oregano
1 ½ c.   Water

Mix well by hand or blend in a blender–according to your taste.

TARTAR DRESSING

1 c.   Cashew or Tofu Mayonnaise, Miraculous Whip, or Cashew or Tofu Sour Cream
2 T.   Ripe olives, chopped very fine
1 T.   Cucumber, chopped very fine
1 T.   Pimento, chopped very fine
1 T.   Bell pepper, chopped very fine
2 T.   Onions, chopped very fine
1 T.   Parsley, chopped very fine
¼ tsp.   Sea salt

Mix well by hand or blend in a blender–according to your taste.
Variations: Add 1 tablespoon of capers, chopped very fine. Add 2 tablespoons of lemon juice or white vinegar.

THOUSAND ISLAND DRESSING–1

3 c.   Cashew or Tofu Mayonnaise, Miraculous Whip, or Cashew or Tofu Sour Cream
½ c.   Catsup or Tomato Relish (liquefied)
¼ c.   Bell pepper, chopped fine
4 tsp.   Pimento, chopped
2 T.   Onions, minced
2 T.   Black olives, minced

Mix well by hand or blend in a blender–according to your taste.

THOUSAND ISLAND DRESSING–2

1 c.   French Dressing
2 T.   Bell pepper, chopped
3 T.   Pimento, chopped
2 T.   Black olives, chopped
½ tsp.   Soy sauce

Mix well by hand or blend in a blender–according to your taste.

THOUSAND ISLAND DRESSING–3

1 c.   Cashew or Tofu Mayonnaise, or Miraculous Whip
3 T.   Catsup
1 T.   Bell pepper, chopped
1 tsp.   Pimento, chopped
1 tsp.   Chives

Mix well by hand or blend in a blender–according to your taste.

TOFU MAYONNAISE-1

Adding the lemon in stages, and the oil as slowly as possible, is the secret of making good thick mayonnaise with this recipe.

1 c.   Firm tofu
1 tsp.   Dijon mustard
½ tsp.   Sea salt
Pinch   Paprika
1 T. & 1 ½ tsp. Lemon juice or white vinegar
2 T.   Corn oil

Put the tofu, mustard, salt, and paprika in a blender with 1 tablespoon of the lemon juice (or vinegar). Blend at high speed, stopping frequently to scrape down the sides of the jar, until all is well combined. Still blending, add the oil a few drops at a time, increasing to a steady stream, until about ⅓ of the oil is used. Slowly add another teaspoon of lemon juice while blending. Dribble in another ⅓ of the oil. Add the rest of the lemon juice in the same way as before. Continue adding the oil until it is gone.

TOFU MAYONNAISE-2

1 ½ c.	Firm tofu
2 T.	Corn oil
1 T.	Cider vinegar
2 T.	Water
1 ½ tsp.	Prepared mustard
½ tsp.	Garlic, minced
¼ c.	Onion, minced
¼ tsp.	White pepper
1 ¼ tsp.	Sea salt
1 T.	Lemon juice or white vinegar
1 T.	Cashew nuts, ground fine

Put everything in a blender and blend until smooth. Refrigerate.

TOFU MAYONNAISE-3

1 ½ c.	Firm tofu
½ tsp.	Garlic powder
1 tsp.	Prepared mustard
1 ½ T.	Lemon juice or white vinegar
2 T.	Corn oil
1 tsp.	Sea salt
⅛ tsp.	White pepper

Put everything in a blender and blend until smooth. Refrigerate.

TOFU MAYONNAISE DRESSING–1

3 T.	Tofu Mayonnaise
3 T.	UnChicken, UnBeef Broth, or soy sauce

Mix well by hand or blend in a blender–according to your taste.

TOFU MAYONNAISE DRESSING–2

¼ c.	Tofu Mayonnaise
2 T.	White vinegar
3 T.	Water
¼ c.	UnBeef Broth
⅛ tsp.	Sea salt
1 T.	Parsley, chopped

Mix well by hand or blend in a blender–according to your taste.

TOFU MAYONNAISE DRESSING–3

¼ c.	Celery, chopped as finely as possible

½ c.	Tofu Mayonnaise
1 T.	White vinegar

Water, if needed, to thin the dressing
Mix well by hand or blend in a blender–according to your taste.

TOFU MAYONNAISE DRESSING–4

1 tsp.	Garlic powder
1 c.	Tofu Mayonnaise
¾ c.	Water
¼ c.	White vinegar
1 tsp.	Sea salt

Mix well by hand or blend in a blender–according to your taste.

TOFU MAYONNAISE DRESSING–5

½ c.	Tofu Mayonnaise
⅔ c.	Water
1 T.	Soy sauce
¼ tsp.	Garlic powder
⅓ tsp.	Paprika
⅛ tsp.	Basil
⅛ tsp.	Oregano
1 tsp.	Onion powder

Mix well by hand or blend in a blender–according to your taste.

TOFU MAYONNAISE DRESSING–6

2 c.	Tofu Mayonnaise
1 tsp.	Sea salt
3 T.	Onions
¼ c.	Black olives
⅛ tsp.	Cayenne pepper
2 T.	Bell pepper, chopped very fine
1 T.	White vinegar
½ tsp.	Basil
½ tsp.	Oregano
1 ½ c.	Water

Mix well by hand or blend in a blender–according to your taste.

TOFU MAYONNAISE DRESSING–7

1 c.	Tofu Mayonnaise
1 c.	Water
1 tsp.	Sea salt
2 T.	Onion, chopped very fine
¼ c.	White vinegar
¼ tsp.	Basil
¼ tsp.	Oregano

Mix well by hand or blend in a blender–according to your taste.

TOMATO DRESSING–1

½ c.	Tomato puree (or blend raw tomatoes well)
1 T.	Dill weed
2 T.	Onion, minced
2 tsp.	Bell pepper, minced
2 T.	Lemon juice or white vinegar
¼ tsp.	Tarragon
1 T.	Soy sauce
½ tsp.	Basil
½ tsp.	Garlic powder

Mix well by hand or blend in a blender–according to your taste.

TOMATO DRESSING–2

2 qts.	Tomatoes, chopped
1 c.	Celery, chopped
½ c.	Bell pepper, chopped
1 c.	Onions, chopped
¼ tsp.	Garlic powder
2 tsp.	Sea salt
1 c.	Lemon juice or white vinegar

Blend all ingredients. Use up in a few days.

TOMATO-CASHEW DRESSING

½ c.	Raw cashews
½ c.	Onions, chopped
1 tsp.	Garlic powder
1 tsp.	Celery salt
1 tsp.	Paprika
1 tsp.	Marjoram
2 c.	Tomato juice
2 T.	Olive oil
	Sea salt, if needed

Blend well in a blender.

TOMATO MAYONNAISE

1 c.	Cashew or Tofu Mayonnaise, Miraculous Whip, or Cashew or Tofu Sour Cream
⅓ c.	Tomato juice or puree
1 tsp.	Onions, minced
⅛ tsp.	Garlic powder
½ tsp.	Sea salt

Mix well by hand or blend in a blender–according to your taste.

TOMATO FRENCH DRESSING

1 c.	French Dressing
½ c.	Tomato juice
	OR
2 or 3	Tomatoes, chopped

Mix well by hand or blend in a blender–according to your taste.

"VINAIGRETTE" DRESSING–1

2 ½ T.	White vinegar or lemon juice
2 ½ T.	Olive oil
1 T.	Parsley, chopped
½ tsp.	Sea salt

Mix well by hand or blend in a blender–according to your taste.

"VINAIGRETTE" DRESSING–2

2 T.	Olive oil
2 T.	White vinegar or lemon juice
¼ c.	UnBeef Broth
1 tsp.	Basil
1 tsp.	Oregano
½ tsp.	Garlic powder

Mix well by hand or blend in a blender–according to your taste.

ZESTY FRENCH DRESSING

1	Garlic clove, crushed
¼ tsp.	Sea salt
2 T.	Olive oil
1 T.	Lemon juice
¼ c.	Wine vinegar
4 tsp.	Lea & Perrins Steak Sauce
½ tsp.	Louisiana Hot Sauce

Blend together in a blender.

Salads

I HAVE NOT GIVEN any recipes for fruit salad, simply because fruit looks, smells and tastes wonderful just as it is. To my way of thinking, the trouble of cutting it up and mixing it seems pointless. Also, since the fruits have such natural good taste and juiciness it seems a shame to mask them with some kind of dressing—whereas vegetables need a dressing since they are so dry.

Another big "absent" in most of these recipes is lettuce. We should indeed eat lettuce, but a lot of people (including me) consider a salad that is mostly lettuce just plain uninteresting. Therefore I have listed the non-lettuce ingredients only, and you can put in the amount of lettuce you like, or leave it out altogether. But when you do use lettuce, be sure it is not iceberg or "head" lettuce. That stuff is wet cellulose not worth the trouble, a waste of time for your stomach which deserves something real. Romaine lettuce is the staple, but other types are good, too. I always prefer spinach to lettuce in salad, and I recommend it.

Consider sometimes using cabbage instead of lettuce. Bok choy, "Chinese cabbage," is excellent, too.

Also, I have not listed lettuce so you can exercise the option of using the recipes to make salads with grains—an option well worth the trying. Instead of lettuce, mix the salad ingredients with rice, tabouli wheat, cracked wheat, barley or millet. Tabouli wheat need not be cooked, just soaked adequately, but cracked—or bulghur—wheat must be cooked (see section on Grains).

In case you prefer your grain in another form, put the salad in pocket bread. Any salad goes well stuffed in fresh pocket bread. Haters of lettuce salad often find they like it very much when eaten this way as a sandwich.

So you can use these recipes four ways: (1) just as given, (2) with lettuce, (3) with grains, and (4) in pocket bread.

Except for potatoes, grains, and beans, all the vegetables listed in these recipes should be raw.

Peas should be frozen first, as this makes them soft and easy to eat–as well as especially delicious. But be sure to drain them or put them on paper towels so they won't be wet and clammy. To get them at room temperature in a hurry, run tap water over them, then drain and dry them.

Corn, if not frozen, may need to be lightly steamed before using.

If you are not familiar with the different types of bean sprouts, start out using alfalfa sprouts.

When good avocadoes are not available, substitute mashed green peas.

Most of these salads should be served with a dressing from the Salad Dressings section. Those that have their own dressing or one recommended can be varied by substituting another dressing.

❖ ❖ ❖

ANNE GOLDSTEIN'S TABOULI

Gourmet simplicity!

1 c.	Bulgur wheat, uncooked
1 ¼ c.	Parsley, chopped
1 c.	Mint, chopped
1 c.	Onion, chopped
2	Bunches of green onions, chopped fine
2 c.	Canned tomatoes, chopped

½ c.   Lemon juice
⅓ c.   Olive oil
1 tsp.   Sea salt
1 tsp.   Pepper

Wash the wheat, then soak it in enough water so there are 2 inches of water above the wheat. Soak until the wheat is soft. Drain and squeeze dry. Combine with the rest of the ingredients. Refrigerate 2 to 8 hours.

AVOCADO SALAD–1

2   Large avocados, diced
2   Large tomatoes, diced
¼ c.   Bell pepper, chopped rather fine
¼ c.   Onions, chopped fine
2 T.   Lemon juice
1 tsp.   Olive oil
½ tsp.   Sea salt

AVOCADO SALAD–2

2   Avocados, mashed
¼ c.   Onions, chopped
¼ c.   Parsley, chopped
½ tsp.   Sea salt
2 T.   Lemon juice
1 ¼ c.   Cashew or Tofu Sour Cream
1 tsp.   Soy sauce

BARBECUE BEAN SALAD

Mix together 1 part of Barbecue Beans and 2 parts of Cottage Cheez Salad-1.

BEAN SALAD

6 c.   Water
1 c.   Corn
1 c.   Carrots, diced fine
1 c.   Celery, diced fine
2 ½ c.   Cooked beans or black-eyed peas
1 c.   Bell pepper, diced fine
1 ½ tsp.   Red onion, minced
⅓ c.   Balsamic vinegar
2 tsp.   Corn oil
½ c.   Parsley, chopped
1 tsp.   Sea salt
½ tsp.   Black pepper

Bring the water to a boil. Add the corn, carrots, and celery. Blanch for 1 minute or until just tender. Drain and rinse under cold water. Drain well. Combine the beans, blanched vegetables, bell pepper, and onion. Pour the vinegar and oil over all and toss well. Let stand at least 30 minutes

at room temperature. Half an hour before serving, add the parsley, pepper, and salt and toss well.

BEAN SPROUT SALAD–1

½ c.   Celery, chopped fine
½ c.   Bell pepper, chopped
2 ½ c.   Bean sprouts
¼ c.   Onions, chopped
½ c.   Cucumber, chopped
2 c.   Tomatoes, chopped
2 c.   Garbanzos, cooked
1 c.   French Dressing

BEAN SPROUT SALAD–2

2 c.   Bean sprouts
1 c.   Carrots, shredded
1 c.   Avocado, diced

BROCCOLI, POTATO, AND GARBANZO SALAD

3 c.   Potatoes, cut into 1-inch cubes, steamed, and drained
2 T.   Tarragon vinegar
2 ½ tsp.   Corn oil
½ tsp.   Black pepper
1 tsp.   Sea salt
6 c.   Broccoli florets, steamed, drained, and rinsed under cold running water and drained
1 c.   Cooked garbanzos
½ c.   Tofu yogurt
3 T.   Lemon juice
1 T.   Balsamic vinegar
1 tsp.   Dijon mustard
¾ tsp.   Garlic, minced

Toss the potatoes with the vinegar, oil, pepper, and salt. Toss the broccoli with the rest of the ingredients (not the potatoes). Combine the potatoes and broccoli mixture and toss gently to mix completely. Serve warm or at room temperature.

CABBAGE-PINEAPPLE SALAD

3 c.   Cabbage, shredded
1 c.   Pineapple chunks
1 c.   Carrots, shredded
¼ c.   Raisins
¼ c.   Sunflower seeds (unsalted)
¾ c.   Miraculous Whip made according to the variation for fruit salad

Combine everything well.

CABBAGE AND PEPPER SALAD

1	Red bell pepper, seeded and thinly sliced
1	Green bell pepper, seeded and thinly sliced
1	Onion, thinly sliced and pushed out into rings
1	Cucumber, cut into ½-inch cubes
2	Tomatoes, thinly sliced
½	White cabbage, thinly sliced
2 T.	Sucanat
3 T.	Lemon juice
½ c.	Olive oil
4 T.	Red wine vinegar
2 tsp.	Sea salt
1 tsp.	Black pepper

Combine the vegetables in a large bowl. Put the other ingredients in a blender or jar and blend or shake until well mixed. Pour over the vegetables and toss well.

CABBAGE AND LIMA BEAN SALAD

1	Small head of cabbage, shredded
½ c.	Radishes, sliced
½ c.	Parsley, finely chopped
1	10 oz. pkg. of frozen green lima beans, thawed
½ c.	Scallions, shallots or leeks
½ tsp.	Sea salt

CABBAGE SLAW–1

4 c.	Cabbage, shredded
1 ½ c.	Carrots, shredded
1 c.	Bell pepper, chopped
1 c.	Celery, chopped
½ c.	Onions, chopped
1 ½ c.	Cashew or Tofu Sour Cream
1 ¼ T.	Lemon juice
½ tsp.	Dill
½ tsp.	Sea salt

Variations: Slice tomatoes and put the slaw on top of the slices. Sprinkle with chopped ripe olives. Add 3 cups of cooked beans to the slaw. Add ½ tsp. caraway seed.

CABBAGE SLAW–2

5 c.	Cabbage, shredded
1 c.	Carrots, shredded
1 c.	Cashew or Tofu Mayonnaise, or Miraculous Whip
2 ½ T.	Vinegar
1 T.	Prepared mustard
1 T.	Celery seed
1 tsp.	Sea salt

Combine cabbage and carrots. Blend the mayonnaise, vinegar, mustard, celery seed, and salt, and mix with the cabbage and carrots. Let sit for an hour or so for flavors to blend.
Variation: For extra zest, add ½ to 1 teaspoon of Louisiana Hot Sauce.

CAJUN COLE SLAW

Fun on the bayou, I tell you!

½ c.	Cashew or Tofu Mayonnaise, or Miraculous Whip
3 T.	Prepared mustard
1 T.	Olive oil
2 T.	Lea & Perrins Steak Sauce
1 tsp.	Louisiana Hot Sauce
2 T.	Catsup
2 tsp.	Sea salt
1 tsp.	Garlic salt
1 T.	Wine vinegar
2 T.	Lemon juice
1	Large head of cabbage, very finely shredded
4	Bell peppers, shredded fine
2	Medium onions, shredded very thin

Put the mayonnaise and mustard in a bowl. Beat together with a fork until combined. Slowly add the olive oil, beating all the time, until the mixture has returned to the thickness of the original mayonnaise. Still beating, add the steak sauce, then the hot sauce, then the catsup, then the salt and garlic salt, then the vinegar, and then the lemon juice. Place the cabbage, peppers, and onion in a large bowl, pour the sauce over all and toss well. This should sit at least an hour before serving, and tastes even better the next day.

CHEF'S BEAN SALAD

5 c.	White beans
½ tsp.	Garlic, minced
½ c.	Italian dressing
¼ c.	Onions, minced
½ c.	Celery, diced
½ c.	Dill pickles, diced
¼ c.	Cashew or Tofu Mayonnaise, or Miraculous Whip

½ c.   Pimento Cheez
1 tsp.   Jalapeños, minced
4 tsp.   White vinegar.

Combine all and chill for several hours or overnight.

CORN SALAD-1

2 c.   Corn
½ c.   Bell pepper, chopped fine
⅓ c.   Onions, chopped
1 c.   Tomatoes, chopped fine

Variations: Add 1 to 2 cups of shredded cabbage. Omit the tomatoes and put the Mexican Tomato Dressing over it.

CORN SALAD-2

3 c.   Corn
1 ½ c.   Tomatoes, chopped
¼ c.   Onions, chopped
⅓ c.   Cashew or Tofu Sour Cream
1 T.   Lemon juice
½ tsp.   Sea salt
¼ tsp.   Mustard seed
¼ tsp.   Celery seed

CORN, RICE, AND BEAN SALAD

1 ½ c.   Corn
½ c.   Dried beans, pressure-cooked and drained
2 c.   Tomatoes, chopped
2 T.   Parsley, chopped
¼ c.   Bell pepper, chopped
1 tsp.   Sea salt
½ c.   Cashew or Tofu Mayonnaise, or Miraculous Whip
1 ½ tsp.   Lemon juice
1 ½ tsp.   Olive oil
¼ tsp.   Cayenne pepper
2 c.   Rice, cooked

Mix the corn, beans, tomatoes, parsley, bell pepper, and salt. Let this sit for 30 minutes at room temperature. Combine the mayonnaise or sour cream, lemon juice, olive oil, and pepper. On a serving plate, place the rice, then the corn-bean mixture, and spoon the dressing over all.

COTTAGE CHEEZ SALAD-1

4 ½ c.   Tofu Cottage Cheez
3 c.   Tomatoes, chopped small
¼ c.   Onions, chopped

½ c.   Black olives, chopped
½ c.   Bell pepper, finely chopped
1½ tsp.   Jalapeños, minced
¼ tsp.   Basil
⅛ tsp.   Dill weed
1½ t.   Sea salt

COTTAGE CHEEZ SALAD-2

2 c.   Tofu Cottage Cheez
1 c.   Cashew or Tofu Sour Cream
1 c.   Frozen mixed vegetables, steamed and cooled
⅓ c.   Onions, minced fine
½ tsp.   Jalapeños, minced fine
½ tsp.   Sea salt
¼ tsp.   Dill or Basil

COUNTRY RICE SALAD

Dressing:
½ c.   Miraculous Whip
¼ c.   Prepared mustard
2 T.   Sucanat
1 tsp.   Balsamic vinegar
¼ tsp.   Sea salt
⅛ tsp.   Black pepper
1-2 T.   Cashew Milk (if needed)

Salad:
3 c.   Cooked rice, chilled
¼ c.   Sweet pickle relish
1   2 oz. jar of pimentos, drained and chopped
⅓ c.   Green onions, finely chopped (tops, too)
¼ c.   Bell pepper, finely chopped
¼ c.   Celery, finely chopped
    Parsley
    Cherry tomatoes

Combine the dressing ingredients except for the "milk" and set aside. Combine the salad ingredients. Pour the dressing over them and stir gently, adding the "milk" if it is too dry. Chill several hours before serving. Top with parsley and cherry tomatoes.

CUCUMBER SALAD-1

3 c.   Cucumbers, sliced about ⅛-inch thick
1 tsp.   Sea salt
2 tsp.   Lemon juice
1 c.   Cashew or Tofu Sour Cream
¼ tsp.   Dill weed

CUCUMBER SALAD–2

4 c.	Cucumbers, thinly sliced
2 c.	Tomatoes, chopped
⅓ c.	Onions, chopped
¼ c.	Fresh basil (or 1 tsp. dried)
1 ½ tsp.	Olive oil
1 T.	Lemon juice
¼ tsp.	Sea salt

Variations: Substitute dill or parsley for the basil. Add ¼ or ½ cup of chopped ripe olives.

COUSCOUS SALAD

2 ½ c.	Couscous, cooked
2 c.	Tomatoes, diced
½ c.	Onion, minced
½ c.	Cucumber, diced
¾ c.	Parsley, chopped
4 T.	Lemon juice
2 tsp.	Corn oil
¾ tsp.	Garlic, minced
½ tsp.	Ground cumin
½ tsp.	Ground coriander seed
¾ tsp.	Sea salt
½ tsp.	Black pepper

Combine everything. Let sit for a while to develop the flavors.

DILLED CUCUMBERS

2 c.	Cucumbers, peeled and sliced thin
½ tsp.	Sea salt
½ c.	Cashew or Tofu Sour Cream
1 T.	Lemon juice
2 T.	Green onion, chopped fine
⅛ tsp.	Black pepper
¼ tsp.	Sucanat
½ tsp.	Dried dill weed

Toss the cucumbers with the salt. Let stand for 10 minutes. Meanwhile, combine all the other ingredients. Drain the cucumbers and combine with the other ingredients. Chill until ready to serve.

DRIED BEAN SALAD

4 c.	Cooked dried beans (one type or more), drained
¼ c.	Onions, chopped
2 T.	Lemon juice
2 tsp.	Olive oil
½ tsp.	Oregano
¼ tsp.	Cumin

½ tsp.	Sea salt
2 T.	Parsley, minced
¼ c.	Bell pepper
2 c.	Tomatoes, diced
½ c.	Cucumbers, peeled and diced

Combine and let sit for a few hours.

GARBANZO BEAN SALAD–1

½ tsp.	Olive oil
4 T.	Lemon juice
½ tsp.	Sea salt
1 c.	Garbanzo beans, cooked
2 T.	Parsley, chopped
1 c.	Celery, chopped
¼ c.	Onions, chopped

GARBANZO BEAN SALAD–2

2 ½ c.	Cooked garbanzos, drained
2 T.	Parsley, finely chopped
2 T.	Onions, chopped
⅛ tsp.	Garlic powder
1 T.	Lemon juice
½ tsp.	Olive oil
½ tsp.	Sea salt

GARBANZO AND CABBAGE SALAD

2 c.	Cabbage, shredded
1 c.	Garbanzos, cooked
3 T.	Onions, chopped
¼ c.	Pimento, chopped
2 tsp.	Fresh basil, or ½ tsp. dried
½ tsp.	Sea salt
3 T.	Lemon juice
1 tsp.	Olive oil
¼ c.	Cashew or Tofu Sour Cream

GARBANZO SALAD–1

1 c.	Garbanzos, pressure-cooked and drained
2 T.	Onions, chopped
1 T.	Parsley, minced
2 tsp.	Lemon juice
¼ tsp.	Olive oil
¼ tsp.	Cumin, ground
½ tsp.	Sea salt

In a glass or enamel bowl combine the beans, onions, and parsley. In a separate bowl, whisk the lemon juice with the oil, cumin, and salt. Pour over the bean mixture.

GARBANZO SALAD–2

1 c.	Garbanzos, cooked and drained
1 T.	Green onions (not the tops)
¼ tsp.	Cumin, ground
1 T.	Parsley, minced
2 tsp.	Lemon juice
¼ tsp.	Olive oil
½ tsp.	Sea salt

In a glass or enamel bowl combine the beans, onions, cumin seeds and parsley. In a separate bowl, whisk the lemon juice with the oil and salt. Pour over the bean mixture.

GARBANZO-TOMATO SALAD

1 tsp.	Olive oil
2 T.	Lemon juice
1 tsp.	Sea salt
½ tsp.	Oregano
1 c.	Garbanzos, cooked
2 c.	Tomatoes, chopped
¾ c.	Bell pepper, chopped
12	Ripe olives, sliced
¾ c.	Onions, chopped
¼ c.	Parsley, chopped

GAZPACHO SALAD

1 c.	Bell peppers, chopped
4 c.	Tomatoes, chopped
2 c.	Cucumbers, chopped
⅓ c.	Onions, chopped
½ tsp.	Sea salt

Dressing:

3 T.	Olive oil
2 T.	Lemon juice
2 T.	Chopped parsley
¼ tsp.	Garlic powder

Variation: Add 3 cups of mashed avocado to the dressing and mix thoroughly.

GLUTEN SALAD

You can trust this to please every time!

2 ½ c.	Flavored gluten, ground or chopped
¼ c.	Celery, chopped fine
¼ c.	Bell pepper, chopped fine
⅓ c.	Onions, chopped fine
¾ c.	Dill or sweet pickle, chopped fine
1 T.	Parsley, chopped fine
2 c.	"Mayonnaise" or "sour cream"
¼ tsp.	Louisiana Hot Sauce
⅛ tsp.	Garlic powder

⅛ tsp.	Black pepper
1 T.	White vinegar

Combine and chill for a few hours to let flavors mix.

Variation: Use frozen tofu that has been flavored beef, chicken, ham, sausage, or fish.

GREEN PEA SALAD–1

2	10-oz. packages of frozen peas, thawed
1 ½ c.	Medium tomatoes, coarsely chopped
1 c.	Cashew or Tofu Mayonnaise, Miraculous Whip, or Cashew or Tofu Sour Cream
⅓ c.	Onions, chopped
1 ½ T.	Lemon juice
1 tsp.	Sea salt

GREEN PEA SALAD–2

2	10-oz. pkgs. of frozen green peas, thawed
1 c.	Celery, thinly sliced
½ tsp.	Dill weed (dried)
⅓ c.	French or Italian Dressing

GREEN VEGETABLE SALAD

1 c.	Peas
1 c.	Lima beans, cooked
1 c.	Celery, chopped
½ c.	Bell pepper, chopped
½ c.	Onions, finely chopped

I doubt that guacamole is really holy—but every one of these certainly is heavenly!

GUACAMOLE–1

2	Large, ripe avocados, peeled, seeded and mashed
¼ c.	Onions
½ c.	Tomatoes, chopped
½ tsp.	Sea salt
⅛ tsp.	Pepper
2 ½ tsp.	Lemon juice

GUACAMOLE–2

3	Avocados, mashed
⅓ c.	Cashew or Tofu Mayonnaise, Miraculous Whip, or Cashew or Tofu Sour Cream
1 tsp.	Sea salt
¼ tsp.	Garlic powder

2 T.   Lemon juice
1   Tomato, chopped
¼ c.   Onions, chopped
⅓ c.   Celery, sliced
½ c.   Bell pepper, chopped

GUACAMOLE–3

2   Avocados, mashed
¼ c.   Cashew or Tofu Mayonnaise, Miraculous Whip, or Cashew or Tofu Sour Cream
2 T.   Onions, chopped
½ tsp.   Sea salt
½ tsp.   Garlic powder
4 tsp.   Lemon juice
2   Tomatoes, chopped

GUACAMOLE–4

4   Avocados, mashed
½ tsp.   Sea salt
2 T.   Lemon or lime juice
½ tsp.   Soy sauce
1 tsp.   Garlic powder

GUACAMOLE–5

2   Large ripe avocados, mashed to a puree
1 T.   Onions, finely chopped
½ c.   Tomatoes, chopped
½ tsp.   Sea salt
⅛ tsp.   Black pepper (freshly ground is best)
2 tsp.   Lemon juice
3 T.   Salsa or Taco Sauce

KIDNEY BEAN SALAD–1

This is almost a meal in itself, and is excellent in pocket bread.

5 c.   Kidney beans, cooked and drained
¼ c.   Apple cider vinegar or lemon juice
2 ½ tsp.   Olive oil
1 T.   Sea salt
½ tsp.   Dry mustard
¼ tsp.   Black pepper
⅛ tsp.   Cayenne pepper
¼ tsp.   Dill weed
¾ c.   Onions, chopped
2 c.   Cucumbers, chopped
2 c.   Tomatoes, chopped
½ c.   Celery, chopped
½ c.   Bell pepper, chopped

Blend the vinegar (or lemon juice), oil and spices. Mix all ingredients. Serve cold.
Variations: Use some other type of beans other than kidney. Use mayonnaise instead of vinegar (or lemon juice) and olive oil. Add 1 cup of cooked lentils.

KIDNEY BEAN SALAD–2

2 c.   Kidney beans, cooked and drained
1   Lemon–juiced and the peel grated
½ tsp.   Corn or olive oil
¼ tsp.   Sage
3 T.   Parsley, chopped
½ tsp.   Sea salt
¼ tsp.   Cayenne pepper

Combine everything, cover, and marinate for several hours.

LENTIL SALAD–1

3 c.   Lentils, pressure-cooked and chilled
3 T.   Onions, chopped
1 c.   Tomatoes, chopped
¼ c.   Bell pepper, chopped
½ c.   Peas
2 T.   Lemon juice
½ c.   Cashew or Tofu Mayonnaise, Miraculous Whip, or Cashew or Tofu Sour Cream
¼ tsp.   Celery seed
¼ tsp.   Sesame seed
¼ tsp.   Sea salt
¼ tsp.   Garlic powder
¼ tsp.   Marjoram
¼ tsp.   Basil

LENTIL SALAD–2

2 c.   Lentils, pressure cooked
½ c.   French Dressing
¼ c.   Bell pepper, chopped
¾ c.   Onions, chopped
½ c.   Celery, chopped
2 T.   Parsley, chopped

LENTIL SALAD–3

2 c.   Lentils, cooked and chilled
¼ c.   Onions, chopped
1 c.   Carrots, grated
½ c.   Radishes, chopped

Dressing:
1 T.   Lemon juice
2 T.   Olive oil

1 tsp.   Sea salt
⅛ tsp.   Garlic powder

LENTIL SALAD–4

1 c.	Lentils
1	Small yellow onion
3 ¾ c.	Tomatoes, chopped very fine and drained in a fine sieve over a bowl
½ c.	Celery, chopped fine
½ c.	Carrot, chopped fine
¼ c.	Red onion, chopped fine
¼ tsp.	Ground ginger
1 ½ T.	Lemon juice
1 ½ T.	Soy sauce
¼ tsp.	Black pepper
¼ tsp.	Cayenne
¾ tsp.	Sea salt
1 ½ c.	Cucumber, peeled, seeded, and diced
1 ½ tsp.	Balsamic vinegar
1 T.	Corn oil
¾ tsp.	Dried dill weed
½ tsp.	Dijon mustard

Wash and gently cook the lentils with the whole onion for 45 minutes or until done. Drain, discard the onion, and cool. Combine the lentils with the tomatoes, celery, carrots, red onion, ginger, lemon juice, soy sauce, pepper, cayenne, and salt. Mix well and set aside. Put the cucumbers in a blender with the vinegar, oil, dill, and mustard. Process until very smooth. Season to taste with black pepper and salt. Combine everything and serve.

LIMA BEAN SALAD–1

2 c.	Green lima beans, cooked, drained, and cooled
1 c.	Celery, chopped
2 c.	Frozen green peas, thawed
¼ c.	Onions, chopped

Good with Potato Dressing-1.
Variations: Add 1 cup of chopped tomatoes and ½ cup of chopped bell pepper. Add 2 cups of corn.

LIMA BEAN SALAD–2

2	Pkgs. of frozen lima beans, cooked, drained, and cooled
1 T.	Lemon juice
¼ tsp.	Garlic powder
1 ½ tsp.	Olive oil
2 T.	Parsley

½ tsp.   Sea salt
1 c.   Cashew or Tofu Sour Cream

Variations: Add ½ cup of chopped celery. Add ½ cup of chopped bell pepper.

LIMA BEAN AND GARBANZO SALAD

1 ½ c.	Cooked garbanzos
1 ½ c.	Cooked lima beans
¼ c.	Onions, chopped
¼ c.	Pimento, chopped

LIMA BEAN GAZPACHO SALAD

2 c.	Cooked lima beans, fresh, frozen, or dried (cooked)
2 c.	Tomatoes, chopped
½ c.	Cucumber, chopped
½ c.	Bell pepper, chopped
½ c.	Celery, chopped
½ c.	Onions, chopped
½ tsp.	Garlic powder
½ tsp.	Oregano
½ tsp.	Basil
⅛ tsp.	Cumin
2 c.	French or Italian Dressing

MACARONI AND CHEEZ SALAD

2 c.	Macaroni, cooked and drained
1 ½ c.	Peas, cooked and drained
2 c.	Yeast or Pimento Cheez
½ c.	Black olives, chopped
½ c.	Cashew or Tofu Mayonnaise, Miraculous Whip, or Cashew or Tofu Sour Cream
2 T.	Onions, chopped
½ tsp.	Sea salt

MARINATED ZUCCHINI SALAD

3 c.	Zucchini, sliced thin
½ c.	Bell pepper, chopped
½ c.	Celery, diced
½ c.	Onion, diced
¼ c.	Pimentos, diced
¾ c.	Balsamic vinegar
⅓ c.	Olive or corn oil
½ c.	Sucanat
½ tsp.	Sea salt
½ tsp.	Black pepper

Combine the zucchini, bell pepper, celery, onion, and pimento and set aside. Combine the rest of the ingredients in a jar, cover, and shake well. Pour over the vegetables and toss gently. Cover and chill 8 hours or overnight.

MEXICAN CORN SALAD

2 ½ c.	Corn
½ c.	Pimento, chopped
1 c.	Onions, chopped
½ c.	Bell pepper, chopped
1 c.	Cucumber, chopped

MEXICAN BEAN AND CORN SALAD

1 c.	Corn
1 ½ c.	Kidney or pinto beans, cooked and drained
2 c.	Lettuce, shredded
¼ c.	Black olives, sliced or chopped
2 T.	Bell pepper, chopped fine
3 T.	Onions, minced
½ c.	Mexican Tomato Vinaigrette

MIXED VEGETABLE SALAD–1

¾ c.	Carrots, grated
¾ c.	Cauliflower, chopped
1 c.	Peas
¼ c.	Ripe olives, sliced

MIXED VEGETABLE SALAD–2

2 c.	Potatoes, cooked and cubed
2 c.	Peas
2 c.	Corn
2 c.	Lima beans
2 c.	Carrots, cubed
½ c.	Sunflower seeds

Variation: Add 2 or 3 cups of chopped tomatoes.

MONASTERY TOMATO SALAD

4 c.	Tomatoes, diced
1 c.	Non-dairy soy cheese (Soy Kaas), cubed
1 ½ c.	Bell peppers, chopped
¾ c.	Onions, chopped
2 T.	Lemon juice
2 T.	Balsamic vinegar
4 tsp.	Basil, fresh and chopped (1 tsp. if dried)
1 c.	Olives, sliced
1 ½ tsp.	Sea salt
¼ tsp.	Pepper
1 tsp.	Paprika
½ tsp.	Celery seed
2 tsp.	Olive oil

Put tomatoes, cheese, bell pepper, and onion into

a bowl. Combine the remaining ingredients, pour into the bowl and toss well.

Variation: Use flavored gluten instead of cheese.

MUSHROOM SALAD

Fantabulous!

4 ⅔ c.	Mushrooms, sliced
½ c.	Bell pepper (red preferred), sliced thin
4 T.	Green onions, chopped
3 T.	Parsley, chopped
½ c.	Olive oil
4 T.	Raspberry vinegar
1 tsp.	Sea salt
½ tsp.	Black pepper

Combine the mushrooms, bell pepper, onions, and parsley. Whisk together the oil, vinegar, salt, and pepper until well blended. Add to the mushroom mixture and toss thoroughly to coat.

PASTA SALAD VINAIGRETTE

2 c.	Vermicelli, cooked and chilled
2 c.	Black olives, sliced
1 ¼ tsp.	Olive oil
4 tsp.	Wine vinegar
1 T.	Lemon juice
1 tsp.	Sea salt
2 tsp.	Sucanat
1 tsp.	Dill weed
½ c.	Peas
½ c.	Bell pepper, cut in strips
	Lettuce or spinach

Toss together all the ingredients except the peas, bell pepper, and greens. Let it marinate for 20 minutes in the refrigerator. Mix in the peas and bell pepper. Serve on the lettuce or spinach.

PEANUT PASTA SALAD

2 c.	Dry pasta (bow-tie or macaroni, etc.)
4 c.	Chinese cabbage (bok choy), chopped coarsely
¼ c.	Bell pepper (red preferred), cut into ¼-inch dice
4 T.	Green onion, sliced thin
½ c.	Peanut butter
¼ c.	Vinegar
3 T.	Low sodium soy sauce
2 T.	Genuine maple syrup
1 T.	Oriental sesame oil
¼ c.	Water

¾ tsp.   Cayenne
¾ c.   Roasted peanuts

Cook the pasta, drain, rinse with cold water, and drain again. Put into a large bowl and add the bok choy, bell pepper, and onions and toss well. Whisk together the peanut butter, vinegar, soy sauce, maple syrup, and sesame oil until smooth. Whisk in the water and cayenne. Pour this dressing over the salad, add the peanuts, and toss well.

PECOS BEAN SALAD

4 c.   Cooked dried beans, drained
⅓ c.   Onions, chopped
¼ tsp.   Garlic powder
½ c.   Bell pepper, chopped
1 ½ tsp.   Olive oil
1 T.   Lemon juice
½ tsp.   Oregano
½ tsp.   Basil
1 tsp.   Sea salt

PIQUANT CAULIFLOWER

2 c.   Cauliflower flowerets
½ tsp.   Corn oil
3 T.   White vinegar
⅓ c.   Tomatoes, chopped
4 tsp.   Pimento, chopped
2 tsp.   Green olives, chopped
1 T.   Dill pickle, chopped
1 tsp.   Sucanat
1 tsp.   Sea salt
1 tsp.   Paprika
⅛ tsp.   Cayenne

Separate the cauliflower into flowerets and cook in boiling water until tender–about 10 minutes. Combine the rest of the ingredients and pour over the cauliflower. Chill 2 to 3 hours, stirring occasionally. At serving time drain off the excess liquid.

PINK BEANS AND RED CABBAGE SALAD

3 c.   Pink or pinto beans, cooked
1 c.   Celery, grated
1 c.   Radishes, grated
1 c.   Cucumber, grated
2 c.   Red cabbage, shredded
¼ c.   Onions, chopped fine

RICE SALAD–1

Basic, but never dull!

2 c.   Rice, cooked
1 tsp.   Sea salt
1 ¼ tsp.   Olive oil
1 ½ T.   Lemon juice
¼ c.   Parsley, chopped
⅓ c.   Onions, chopped
1 c.   Tomatoes, chopped
1 c.   Total of one or more of the following (singly or in combination):
         Lima beans, cooked
         Dried beans, cooked
         Thin carrot slices
         Peas
         Corn
         Celery, diced
         Cucumber, diced
         Bell pepper, chopped
         Cabbage, shredded
         Green beans, cooked
         Radishes, sliced or chopped
         Bean sprouts
         "Greens" of any type, chopped

Combine everything. If it seems too dry, add more oil and lemon. Let stand to develop flavor. *Variation:* Cook the rice in a Flavoring Broth.

RICE SALAD–2

2 c.   Cooked rice
½ c.   Corn
½ c.   Bell pepper (red preferred), diced
½ c.   Tomatoes, chopped
¼ c.   Cooked peas
¼ c.   Red onion, diced
¼ c.   Green beans, cut into pieces and cooked
2 T.   Balsamic vinegar
2 tsp.   Corn oil
2 T.   Basil, chopped, or ¼ tsp. dried
2 T.   Parsley, chopped
1 T.   Lime juice
⅛ tsp.   Black pepper
¼ tsp.   Sea salt

Combine everything and toss well.

RICE AND AVOCADO SALAD

1 c.   Avocado, mashed
½ tsp.   Garlic, crushed
1 tsp.   Sea salt

1 ½ tsp.	Olive oil
2 tsp.	Lemon juice
2 tsp.	Wine vinegar
2 tsp.	Louisiana Hot Sauce
4 tsp.	Lea & Perrins Steak Sauce
1 T.	Poupon mustard
½ c.	Parsley, chopped
1 c.	Tomatoes, chopped
3 c.	Rice, cooked and chilled

RICE AND BEAN SALAD

½ c.	Onions, chopped
½ c.	Cucumber, chopped
½ c.	Bell pepper, chopped
½ c.	Black olives, halved
1 ½ c.	Beans, cooked
2 ½ c.	Rice, cooked
½ tsp.	Sea salt
2 T.	Lemon juice
1 ½ tsp.	Olive oil

RICE SALAD ESPECIAL

1 ½ c.	Rice, uncooked
1 c.	Black olives, chopped
1 tsp.	Olive oil
¼ c.	Pimentos
1 c.	Tomatoes, chopped
2 T.	Wine vinegar
½ tsp.	Oregano
½ tsp.	Marjoram

Cook the rice. Add the remaining ingredients, mixing well. Chill at least 2 hours.

RICE SALAD SOUTHERN STYLE

Even Yankees will like this!

2 c.	Rice, uncooked
1 c.	Green onions, chopped
1 c.	Dill pickles, chopped
1 c.	Sweet pickles, chopped
1 c.	Celery, chopped
1 c.	Bell pepper, chopped
1 c.	Green olives, stuffed with pimentos, chopped
1 ¼ c.	Cashew or Tofu Mayonnaise, or Miraculous Whip
3 T.	Prepared mustard
¼ tsp.	Cayenne pepper
2 tsp.	Olive oil
2 tsp.	Wine vinegar

Cook the rice, cool, and then combine with the vegetables. Combine the mayonnaise, mustard,

pepper, oil, and vinegar. Mix well with the rice mixture. Refrigerate.

RICE SALAD WITH BLACK-EYED PEAS

5 c.	Black-eyed peas, cooked
1 T.	Olive oil
⅛ c.	Lemon juice
1 tsp.	Sea salt
3 c.	Rice, cooked
½ c.	Onions, finely chopped
¾ c.	Celery, chopped
¾ c.	Carrot, grated
½ c.	Bell pepper, chopped
⅓ c.	Pimento, chopped

RICE SALAD WITH OLIVES AND CAPERS

4 ½ tsp.	Dijon-style mustard
¼ c. & 1 ½ tsp.	Balsamic vinegar
½ tsp.	Sucanat
½ tsp.	Sea salt
½ tsp.	Black pepper
¼ c. & 1 ½ tsp.	Olive oil
3 c.	Cooked rice, warm
1 c.	Bell pepper (different colors, if possible), cut into strips
½ c.	Onion (red preferred), diced
½ c.	Capers, rinsed and drained
4 T.	Green onions, sliced thin
½ c.	Black olives, chopped
¼ c.	Parsley, chopped
¼ c.	Fresh dill (1 T. dried), chopped

Combine the mustard, vinegar, and Sucanat. Whisk in the salt and pepper, then the oil. Pour this over the rice and toss well. Add the rest of the ingredients and toss again. Serve warm or cold.

RUSSIAN POTATO AND BEET SALAD

2 ½ c.	Beets, peeled, cooked, and diced
2 ½ c.	Potatoes, peeled, cooked, and diced
1 c.	Cucumber, peeled and seeded
6 T.	Green onions, chopped fine
½ tsp.	Dry mustard
1 tsp.	Sucanat
1 tsp.	Sea salt
½ tsp.	Black pepper
2 T.	Balsamic vinegar
1 c.	Tofu Yogurt
⅓ c.	Tofu Sour Cream
2 T.	Dill, chopped

Mix everything thoroughly and refrigerate for a
few hours before serving.

SALAD NICOISE–1

Outstanding!

2 T.	Lemon juice
1 tsp.	Garlic, crushed
1 T.	Olive oil
½ tsp.	Sea salt
1 tsp.	Chives, minced
2 c.	Potatoes, cooked and sliced
1 c.	Tomatoes, chopped
¾ c.	Onions, chopped
¾ c.	Celery, chopped
½ c.	Bell pepper, chopped
¼ c.	Black olives, chopped or sliced
4 c.	Romaine lettuce, chopped

Blend the lemon juice, garlic, oil, and salt. Toss
with all the ingredients except the lettuce. Just
before serving, mix in the lettuce.
Variation: Add 1 cup of cooked white or northern
beans.

SALAD NICOISE–2

You must!

4 T.	Lemon juice or balsamic vinegar
¼ c.	Olive oil
½ tsp.	Sea salt
½ tsp.	Chervil
1 tsp.	Garlic, crushed
2 c.	Potatoes, peeled, cooked and sliced
2 c.	Green beans, cooked and cut into 1-inch pieces
1 c.	Tomato, chopped
1 c.	Onion, sliced
¼ c.	Black olives
4 c.	Romaine lettuce, chopped

Blend the lemon juice/vinegar, oil, salt, chervil,
and garlic. While the potatoes and beans are still
warm, combine them and mix in the dressing.
Let sit for a few hours or overnight (refrigerate).
When ready to serve add the rest of the
ingredients and mix well.

SUMMER CROCK SALAD

Ideal!

8	Bell peppers, sliced
6 c.	Tomatoes, sliced thin
8 c.	Onion, sliced and separated into rings

3 c.	Apple cider vinegar
1 c.	Sucanat
2 T.	Sea salt
2 tsp.	Celery seed
3 c.	Corn oil

Put the vegetables in layers in a deep glass bowl,
jar, crock, or enamelware pan. In another bowl
combine the vinegar, Sucanat, salt, and celery
seed until the Sucanat is dissolved. Then stir in
the oil. Pour this over the vegetables, cover and
marinate overnight in the refrigerator.
Variation: Use fresh dill or basil instead of celery
seeds.

SUMMER TOMATO SALAD

2 c.	Tomatoes, cut into wedges
¼ c.	Onion, sliced
2 T.	Olive or corn oil
2 T.	Balsamic vinegar
½ tsp.	Garlic salt
¼ tsp.	Coarse ground black pepper
1 T.	Fresh basil

Combine everything.

SUNSHINE SALAD

2 c.	Garbanzos, cooked
2 c.	Corn
1 c.	Celery, diced
¼ c.	Onions, chopped
¼ c.	Bell pepper, chopped
3 T.	Pimento, diced

TABOULI SALAD

Put this in pocket bread and you have magic!

3 c.	Tabouli wheat (this is not cracked wheat–see Grains section)
½ c.	Lemon juice
1 T.	Olive oil
2 c.	Cucumbers, diced small
½ c.	Bell pepper, minced
¼ c.	Parsley, chopped fine
4 c.	Tomatoes, diced
1 c.	Onions, chopped fine
½ tsp.	Cayenne pepper
2 tsp.	Sea salt

Place the cracked wheat in a bowl and cover with
water. Let it soak for 15 minutes, then drain. Add
the lemon juice to the wheat and combine all
the ingredients and mix well.

THREE-BEAN SALAD–1

1 c.	Lima beans or green beans, cooked
1 c.	Kidney or pinto beans, pressure-cooked, drained, and cooled
1 c.	Garbanzos or white beans, pressure-cooked, drained, and cooled
⅓ c.	Onions, chopped
½ tsp.	Jalapeños, minced
2 T.	Lemon juice
1 tsp.	Olive oil
¼ tsp.	Sea salt

Combine the beans, onions, and jalapeños. Blend the lemon juice, oil, and salt. Pour over the beans and let them marinate at room temperature for 30 minutes.

THREE-BEAN SALAD–2

2 c.	Garbanzo beans, cooked
1 c.	Kidney beans, cooked
1 c.	Lima beans or green beans, cooked
¼ c.	Bell pepper, chopped
½ c.	Celery, chopped
½ c.	Black olives, chopped
¾ c.	Onions, chopped
1 ½ tsp.	Olive oil
3 T.	Lemon juice
1 tsp.	Sea salt
1 tsp.	Celery seed
1 tsp.	Lemon peel, grated
1 tsp.	Mustard seed
1 tsp.	Garlic powder
1 tsp.	Dill seeds

THREE-BEAN SALAD–3

2 c.	Kidney beans, cooked and drained
2 c.	Garbanzo beans, cooked and drained
2 c.	Green beans, cooked and drained
½	Small red onion, chopped
2-4 T.	Parsley, finely chopped
½ c.	Balsamic vinegar
⅓ c.	Olive oil
3	Garlic cloves
½ tsp.	Basil
½ tsp.	Oregano
½ tsp.	Marjoram
½ tsp.	Black pepper
1 tsp.	Sea salt

Combine beans, onion, and parsley. Combine the dressing ingredients, add to beans and mix. Refrigerate for 2 to 3 hours.

TOMATO SALAD

As a lover of tomatoes this is my favorite!

4 c.	Tomatoes, diced
1 ½ c.	Bell peppers, chopped
¾ c.	Onions, chopped
2 tsp.	Olive oil
2 T.	Lemon juice
2 T.	Red wine vinegar
4 tsp.	Basil, fresh and chopped (1 tsp. if dried)
1 c.	Cucumber, thinly sliced
1 ½ tsp.	Sea salt
¼ tsp.	Pepper
1 tsp.	Paprika
½ tsp.	Celery seed

Put tomatoes, bell pepper, and onion into a bowl. Add the olive oil and toss to coat evenly. Add the remaining ingredients and toss well. Refrigerate 30 minutes before serving.

TOMATO AND BEAN SALAD

1 ½ tsp.	Olive oil
4 ½ tsp.	Lemon juice
1 tsp.	Sea salt
½ tsp.	Oregano
2 c.	Cooked dried beans
1 ½ c.	Tomatoes, chopped
¾ c.	Bell pepper, chopped
12	Black olives, sliced
3 T.	Onions, chopped
2 T.	Parsley, chopped

TOMATO SLAW

2 c.	Cabbage, shredded
1 c.	Tomatoes, diced
¼ c.	Bell pepper, chopped
¼ c.	Cucumber, chopped
1 tsp.	Sea salt

TOSSED SALAD

2	Tomatoes, chopped
1	Bell pepper, chopped
1	Carrot, chopped
1	Celery stalk, chopped
1	Cucumber, chopped
1	Head of Romaine lettuce

Variation: Put in whatever you please. Experiment!

UNSHRIMP SALAD

3 c.	Macaroni
5 c.	UnShrimp
2 c.	Onion, chopped fine
1 c.	Celery, chopped fine
2 c.	Black olives, chopped fine
2 c.	Dill pickles, chopped
1 qt.	Miraculous Whip
4 tsp.	Olive oil
2 tsp.	Louisiana Hot Sauce
	OR ½ tsp. cayenne pepper
2 T.	Lemon juice
2 T.	Lea & Perrins Steak Sauce
1 T.	Mustard
2 T.	Seafood Cocktail Sauce

Cook the macaroni, drain it, and let it cool. In a large bowl combine the macaroni, gluten, onions, celery, olives, and pickles, and toss well. Combine the mayonnaise, oil, hot sauce, lemon juice, steak sauce, mustard, and cocktail sauce. Pour this over the macaroni mixture and mix well. If the salad seems too dry, make some more sauce and mix it in. Refrigerate for 1 hour before serving.

WHITE BEAN SALAD–1

1 c.	Dried white beans, soaked overnight in cold water
¼	Onion (yellow preferred), peeled
½ c.	Carrot, peeled and cut into large chunks
½ tsp.	Basil
Pinch	Oregano
¼	Bay leaf
	Enough UnChicken Broth to cover the beans
8	Garlic cloves

1 tsp.	Sea salt
¾ tsp.	Black pepper
1 c.	Celery, chopped
1 ¼ c.	Tomatoes, diced
2 T.	Basil, chopped, or 1 tsp. dried
2 T.	Balsamic vinegar
2 tsp.	Corn oil
4 T.	Green onion, sliced
2 T.	Parsley, coarsely chopped
1 T.	Lemon juice
1 T.	Capers, rinsed and chopped

Drain the beans and cover them with cold water in a saucepan. Bring to a boil, drain, return to the pan and add the onions, carrot, basil, oregano, bay leaf, broth, garlic, a pinch of the salt and ½ tsp. of the black pepper. Bring to a boil, reduce heat, cover, and simmer gently until the beans are tender–about 2 hours–adding more broth if needed. Drain and cool. Combine the rest of the ingredients in a bowl and then mix with the beans.

WHITE BEAN SALAD–2

5 c.	White beans, pressure cooked and cooled
¾ c.	Italian Dressing
½ c.	Onions, chopped
½ c.	Bell pepper, chopped
¼ c.	Parsley, chopped
¼ c.	Cashew or Tofu Mayonnaise, Cashew or Tofu Sour Cream, or Miraculous Whip
1 tsp.	Sea salt
½ tsp.	Louisiana Hot Sauce

Variation: Add 3 cups of Pimento Cheez.

Potato Salads

AUSTRIAN POTATO SALAD

2 c.	Potatoes, cooked, sliced and chilled
⅓ c.	Onions, minced
½ tsp.	Garlic, minced
½ tsp.	Sea salt
¼ tsp.	Cayenne or black pepper
1 T.	Parsley, minced
½ tsp.	Olive oil
4 tsp.	Tarragon vinegar
½ tsp.	Prepared mustard

Combine the potatoes in a bowl with the onion, garlic, salt, pepper, and parsley. Bring the oil, vinegar, and mustard to a boil and pour over the salad. Mix and serve cold.

CAJUN POTATO SALAD

A real zinger!
It is best to make this a day ahead of time so the flavor will develop.

10 c.	Potatoes
1 ½ c.	Cashew or Tofu Mayonnaise, or Miraculous Whip
¼ c.	Prepared yellow mustard (the "American" type)
2 tsp.	Sea salt
¼ c.	Louisiana Hot Sauce
1 c.	Dill relish
½ c.	Sweet relish
1 c.	Green olives, chopped
1 c.	Onions, chopped fine
½ c.	Celery, chopped fine
½ c.	Parsley, chopped fine

Boil the potatoes in their skins, cool them, peel them, and chop them in large chunks. Mix the mayonnaise, mustard, salt, and hot sauce. Add this to the potatoes along with the rest of the ingredients and mix well.

DILLED POTATO SALAD

1 lb.	Potatoes, cut into chunks and cooked
2 c.	Brussels sprouts (or a 10-oz. pkg. frozen, thawed), halved and cooked
1 c.	Cherry tomatoes, halved, or regular tomatoes, chopped
2 T.	Green onion, sliced
½ c.	Balsamic vinegar
2 T.	Olive or corn oil
2 tsp.	Fresh dill, snipped, or ¼ tsp. dried
1 tsp.	Sucanat
¼ tsp.	Sea salt

Cook the potatoes and brussels sprouts together, covered, in a small amount of boiling water for about 12 minutes, or until the potatoes are tender. (If you are using frozen sprouts, then add them after 7 minutes of cooking the potatoes.) Drain and transfer to a bowl. Add the tomatoes and onion. Put the vinegar, oil, dill, Sucanat, and salt together in a jar and shake well to combine. Pour over the potatoes and toss everything to mix and coat well. Serve warm or cold.

FRENCH-STYLE POTATO SALAD–1

4 c.	Potatoes, cooked and diced
½ c.	Onions, chopped
1 c.	French Dressing
4 T.	Parsley

½ tsp.   Sea salt
½ tsp.   Paprika

Combine, cover, and chill—except for the parsley. Just before serving, stir in the parsley.

FRENCH-STYLE POTATO SALAD–2

2 lb.	Potatoes, peeled
¼ c.	Tarragon vinegar
¾ tsp.	Sea salt
½ tsp.	Black pepper
1 T.	Dijon-style mustard
¼ c.	Onion, minced
6 T.	Olive oil
3 T.	Fresh parsley, minced
1 T.	Fresh tarragon, minced

Put the potatoes in a pot and cover with water. Bring to a boil, cover, and simmer, sitrring once or twice to ensure even cooking, until a thin-bladed paring knife or a metal cake tester inserted into a potato can be removed with no resistance. Drain, cool the potatoes slightly, and cut them into slices while still warm, rinsing the knife occasionally in warm water. Layer warm potato slices in medium bowl, sprinkling with 2 tablespoons of the vinegar and the salt and pepper as you go. Let stand at room temperature while preparing the dressing. Combine the rest of the vinegar, mustard, and shallot. Gradually whisk in the oil. Pour over potatoes and toss lightly. Refrigerate until ready to serve. Bring to room temperature and toss with the parsley and tarragon and serve.

GERMAN POTATO SALAD–1

½ c.	Onions, chopped
1 ¾ tsp.	Corn oil
2 T.	Unbleached white flour
1 tsp.	Celery seed
2 T.	Sucanat
1 ½ tsp.	Sea salt
½ c.	Wine vinegar
1 c.	Water
6 c.	Potatoes, cooked and sliced
¼ c.	UnBacon, chopped fine, or imitation bacon bits
½ tsp.	Paprika
¼ c.	Canned pimento, diced
1 T.	Fresh parsley, chopped

Sauté the onions in the oil until tender. Blend in the flour, celery seed, Sucanat, and salt. Add the vinegar and water. Cook and stir until thickened and bubbly. Add the potatoes and gluten and heat thoroughly, tossing lightly. Garnish with paprika, pimento, and parsley.

GERMAN POTATO SALAD–2

As good as it is simple!

¾ c.	Onion, chopped
2 T.	Corn oil
2 T.	Unbleached white flour
⅔ c.	Cider vinegar
1 ⅓ c.	Water
¼ c.	Sucanat
1 tsp.	Sea salt
⅛ tsp.	Black pepper
10 T.	UnBacon ground
6 c.	Potatoes, cooked, peeled, and sliced

Sauté the onion in the oil until soft. Stir in the flour and blend well. Add the vinegar and water. Cook and stir until bubbly and slightly thick. Add the Sucanat and stir until it dissolves. Add salt and pepper. Gently stir in the gluten and potatoes. Heat through, stirring carefully to coat the potato slices. Serve warm.

GERMAN POTATO SALAD–3

7	Medium potatoes, peeled, cooked, drained, and sliced
1 c.	UnBacon, chopped
2 T.	Corn oil
½ c.	Onion, chopped
½ c.	Celery, diced
3 T.	Unbleached white flour
3 T.	Sucanat
¾ c.	Water
¾ c.	Vinegar
1 tsp.	Sea salt
½ tsp.	Black pepper

Put the potatoes in a large bowl. Brown the gluten in the oil and take out with a slotted spoon. In remaining oil sauté the onion and celery until tender. Add the flour, Sucanat, water, vinegar, salt, and pepper. Cook and stir until it bubbles and thickens. Add the gluten and sauce to the potatoes. Toss gently to coat. Serve warm or at room temperature.

GRANDMA'S POTATO SALAD

When I was growing up in a small town in Illinois, THIS was potato salad!

3 c.	Miraculous Whip

2 ½ T.	Sucanat
¾ tsp.	Vanilla
¼ tsp.	Prepared mustard
¼ c.	Cashew Milk
5 lb.	Potatoes, cooked, peeled, and cubed
1 c.	Celery, chopped
3	Radishes, sliced
½ c.	Onion, chopped
3 T.	Bell pepper, chopped
2 ¼ tsp.	Sea salt
½ tsp.	Black pepper
½ tsp.	Paprika
1 ½ T.	Parsley, chopped

Combine the Miraculous Whip, Sucanat, vanilla, and mustard. Stir in the "milk." Gently fold in the potatoes, celery, radishes, onion, bell pepper, salt, and pepper. Chill for several hours or overnight. Before serving sprinkle the paprika and parsley over the top.

HERBED POTATO SALAD

Salad:

6 c.	Potatoes, cooked, peeled, and cubed
¼ c.	Parsley, chopped
½ c.	Celery, chopped
2 T.	Green onions, chopped
½ c.	Bell pepper, diced

Combine well.

Dressing:

¾ c.	Fresh Herb Dressing
¼ c.	Miraculous Whip
½ tsp.	Prepared mustard
¼ tsp.	Sea salt
Dash	Black or white pepper

Combine everything thoroughly, pour over the salad ingredients, and fold in.

HOT POTATO SALAD

4 c.	Potatoes, quartered lengthwise and cut crosswise into ¾-inch pieces
½ c.	Onion, chopped fine
2 tsp.	Corn oil
1 c.	Sausage Gluten of choice, cut in ¼-inch cubes
½ c.	White vinegar
½ c.	UnBeef Broth
½ tsp.	Sea salt
¼ tsp.	Black pepper
⅓ c.	Parsley, minced

Steam the potatoes until they are just tender. Put in a bowl and let them cool to room temperature. While steaming the potatoes, in a skillet sauté the onion in the oil until soft. Remove the skillet from the heat and add the gluten, vinegar, broth, salt, and pepper. Bring this to a boil until the liquid is reduced to about ⅔ cup. Add this to the potatoes with the parsley and combine well. Let sit for a few hours. Reheat before serving.

MEXICAN POTATO SALAD

½ c.	Salsa
¼ c.	Lime juice
2 T.	Corn oil
½ tsp.	Sea salt
¼ tsp.	Cayenne pepper
2 lb.	Potatoes, cut into chunks and cooked until tender
2 ½ c.	Tomato, chopped
1 c.	Mushrooms, sliced
½ c.	Green onions, sliced
2 T.	Parlsey (or cilantro), chopped

Combine the salsa, lime juice, oil, salt, and cayenne. Cook, uncovered, until heated through. Add to the cooked potatoes along with the rest of the ingredients and toss together to coat well.

PARSLEYED POTATO SALAD

4 c.	Potatoes, cooked and diced
¼ c.	Celery, chopped
¼ c.	Parsley, chopped
¼ c.	Bell pepper, chopped
½ c.	Onions, chopped
¼ c.	Dill pickle, chopped
1 ¾ c.	Miraculous Whip or other "mayonnaise"
¾ c.	French Dressing–1
2 tsp.	Prepared mustard
1 ½ tsp.	Sea salt

POTATO-CUCUMBER SALAD

Vegetables:

| 5 c. | Potatoes, peeled, cubed, and boiled in UnChicken Broth until just cooked |
| ¼ c. | Bell pepper, chopped fine |

Dressing:

1 c.	Tofu yogurt
1 tsp.	Garlic, minced
¼ tsp.	Ground ginger
½ tsp.	Ground cumin

1 ½ c.   Cucumbers, peeled, quartered, and
          sliced ¼-inch thick
1 c.   Tomatoes, diced
¼ c.   Onions, chopped
1 T.   Jalapeño, seeded and minced
2 T.   Parsley (or 1 T. parsley and 1 T.
          mint), chopped
3 T.   Nutritional Yeast
¼ c.   Balsamic vinegar, lemon juice, or
          juice from some type of pickles
1 tsp.   Sucanat
¼ tsp.   Black pepper
½ tsp.   Sea salt

Put everything in a blender or food processor and
blend until smooth, but not liquefied. Toss with
the vegetables.

POTATO SALAD–1

6 c.   Potatoes, cooked and cubed
1 c.   Cucumber, chopped
½ c.   Celery, finely diced
¾ c.   Onions, chopped
½ c.   Bell pepper, finely chopped
¼ c.   Chopped black olives
2-3 T.   Chopped fresh parsley or dill, or
          some of both
1 tsp.   Sea salt

Good with Cashew or Tofu Sour Cream or
French Dressing.
Variation: Add ½ head of cabbage.

POTATO SALAD–2

4 c.   Potatoes, boiled and sliced
1 c.   Celery, chopped
½ c.   Onions, chopped
1 T.   Pimento, chopped
2 T.   Parsley, chopped
1 tsp.   Sea salt
          Caper French Dressing

POTATO SALAD–3

8 c.   Potatoes, cooked and cubed
6 T.   Parsley, chopped fine
½ c.   Bell pepper, chopped fine
⅓ c.   Black olives, chopped fine
¼ c.   Pimentos, chopped fine
3 T.   Onions, chopped fine
¼ tsp.   Cayenne pepper
3 c.   Cashew or Tofu Sour Cream
2 ¼ tsp. Corn oil
1 T.   Wine vinegar
1 ½ tsp. Sea salt

Variation: Use French Dressing, Cashew or Tofu
Mayonnaise, or Miraculous Whip instead of
"sour cream."

POTATO SALAD–4

3 T. & 1 tsp. Balsamic vinegar
¼ tsp.   Sea salt
1 tsp.   Fresh thyme, chopped, or ½ tsp.
          dried
2 tsp.   Dijon-style mustard
1 T.   Corn oil
⅛ tsp.   Black pepper
¼ c.   Water
1 T.   Green onions, chopped
4 ½ c.   Potatoes, sliced and cooked in
          salted water

Whisk everything but the potatoes together, pour
over the potatoes and toss to coat well.

POTATO SALAD WITH MUSTARD DRESSING

4 c.   Potatoes, quartered lengthwise and
          cut crosswise into ¾-inch pieces
1 T.   Balsamic vinegar
2 T.   Dijon-style mustard
½ tsp.   Sea salt
¼ tsp.   Black pepper
¼ c.   Olive oil
¼ c.   Onion, chopped fine
¼ c.   Bell pepper, chopped fine
2 T.   Sweet gherkin, chopped fine

Steam the potatoes until they are just tender. Put
in a bowl and let them cool to room temperature.
Whisk together the vinegar, mustard, sea salt, and
pepper. Add the oil in a stream, whisking, and
whisk until it is emulsified. Add the dressing to
the potatoes along with the onion, bell pepper,
and gherkin, and combine well.

POTATO SALAD WITH PEAS

2 c.   Peas
3 c.   Potatoes, cubed and cooked
¼ c.   Onions, chopped
¾ tsp.   Sea salt
1 T.   Parsley
⅓ c.   Ripe olives, sliced or chopped
1 ½ tsp. Olive oil
2 tsp.   Lemon juice

RED POTATO SALAD

¾ c.   Cashew or Tofu Sour Cream

½ c. Miraculous Whip
2 T. Herb or balsamic vinegar
1 ½ tsp. Sea salt
1 tsp. Celery seed
4 c. Red potatoes, peeled, cooked, and cubed
¾ c. Green onions, sliced
⅓ c. Radishes, sliced
¼ c. Celery, chopped

Combine the "sour cream," mayonnaise, vinegar, salt, and celery seed, and set aside. Combine the rest of the ingredients. Add the dressing and toss lightly. Cover and chill.

ROAST POTATO SALAD WITH GREEN BEANS AND ONIONS

6 c. Potatoes, halved and cut into 1-inch wedges
⅔ c. Olive oil
¾ tsp. Garlic, minced
¼ c. Red wine vinegar
2 tsp. Rosemary
1 ½ tsp. Sea salt
1 ½ c. Onions, halved lengthwise and sliced thin lengthwise
6 c. Green beans, cut into 1-inch pieces
24 Black olives, pitted and halved

Heat ⅓ cup of the oil in a large roasting pan in a 425° oven for 5 minutes. Add the potatoes, tossing them to coat them with the oil. Roast them, stirring every 10 minutes, for 30 minutes, or until they are tender. Let the potatoes cool in the pan. In a blender purée the garlic, vinegar, rosemary, and salt. Add the other ⅓ cup of the oil in a stream and blend the dressing until it is emulsified. Soak the onion in a small bowl of ice and cold water for 5 minutes. Drain it well and pat dry. Bring some water to a boil and boil the beans for 5 minutes or until crisp-tender, and drain in a colander. Rinse the beans under cold water and pat dry. Combine everything and toss gently. Serve at room temperature.

TANGY POTATO SALAD

Genteel fare!

12 Medium red potatoes
1 c. Onion, chopped
2 Dill pickles, chopped fine
2 T. Parsley, minced
¾ c. UnChicken Broth
¾ c. Miraculous Whip

1 ½ tsp. Sea salt
½ tsp. Black pepper
¼ tsp. Garlic powder
2 c. Tomatoes, cubed
¾ c. Bacon Gluten, chopped fine

Cook the potatoes in boiling salted water until tender. Drain and let cool slightly. Peel and slice. Combine with the onion, pickles, and parsley. Set aside. Heat the broth to warm, not hot. Take from heat and add the Miraculous Whip, salt, pepper, and garlic powder. Mix until smooth. Pour over the potato mixture and mix lightly. Cover and chill. Just before serving, gently stir in the tomatoes and gluten.

TUNISIAN POTATO SALAD

Truly Something Completely Different!

3 c. Potatoes, peeled and cut into ¼-inch cubes
¾ tsp. Cayenne
¼ tsp. Cumin, ground
4 ½ tsp. Lemon juice, strained
4 T. Olive or corn oil
1 tsp. Caraway, ground
¾ tsp. Sea salt

Put the diced potatoes in lightly salted boiling water (enough to cover the potatoes completely), and cook briskly, uncovered, until they are tender but still intact. Drain off the water and, sliding the pan back and forth constantly, cook over low heat for a minute or so until the potatoes are dry. Combine the cayenne, cumin, and lemon juice thoroughly. Heat the oil in a skillet, then add the lemon juice mixture, caraway, and salt. Stirring occasionally, cook until most of the liquid has evaporated. Remove from heat, add potatoes and turn them about gently with a spoon until they are evenly coated. Transfer to a serving bowl and cool to room temperature before serving.

WARM POTATO SALAD WITH GARLIC UNSAUSAGE

4 ½ c. Potatoes, peeled
        UnSausage Broth—enough to cover the potatoes
2 c. Garlic UnSausage, cubed
4 tsp. Balsamic vinegar
2 tsp. Dijon-style mustard
⅓ c. Olive oil
4 T. Sausage-Like Broth (use some of what the potatoes were cooked in)

¼ tsp.	Sea salt
⅛ tsp.	Black pepper
4 tsp.	Fresh tarragon, chopped fine
2 tsp.	Fresh chives, chopped fine
2 tsp.	Parsley, chopped fine
2 T.	Parmesan Cheez

Put the potatoes into a saucepan of broth, bring to a boil, and simmer until the potatoes are tender–about 15 minutes. Remove the potatoes, let them cool, and slice them thinly. Combine with the cubed gluten. Whisk all the rest of the ingredients together. Pour over the potatoes and mix thoroughly. Serve at room temperature, or warm in an oven before serving.

Breads and Such

ANADAMA BREAD

You might as well know—I did not like bread. Then one day I tried this. Revelation! It was so good that we began baking and selling it in stores and from that came a successful bakery which we operated for several years.

½ c.	Corn meal
3 T.	Corn oil
¼ c.	Barbados molasses
2 tsp.	Sea salt
¾ c.	Boiling water
1 pkg.	Yeast
¼ c.	Warm water
3 c.	Flour

Combine the corn meal, oil, molasses, salt and boiling water. Let stand until lukewarm. Sprinkle yeast over the ¼ cup of warm water to dissolve. Stir yeast and half of the flour into the corn meal mix. Beat. Stir in remaining flour. Knead until smooth and elastic (about 10 minutes). Transfer to a greased loaf pan, cover with a cloth, and set in a warm place until dough is 1 inch above the top of the pan. Sprinkle with a little corn meal and salt, if desired. Bake at 350° for 50 to 60 minutes.

APPLE AND BANANA BREAD

1	Apple
4 c.	Unbleached white flour
2 ½ tsp.	Dry yeast
½ c.	Warm water
1 c.	Sucanat
1 tsp.	Sea salt
1 tsp.	Ground cinnamon
1 tsp.	Ground nutmeg
⅓ c.	Golden seedless raisins, soaked in apple juice
2	Bananas, mashed
⅛ tsp.	Grated lemon peel

Chop and steam the apple until tender. Press through a sieve to make a puree and let cool. Mix together 1 cup of flour, yeast, and warm water until smooth. Leave in a warm place until frothy. Combine remaining flour, Sucanat, salt, spices, and raisins in a bowl. Stir in yeast mixture, apple puree, mashed banana, and lemon rind and beat well. Divide the mixture between 2 greased loaf pans. Let rise in a warm place until mixture reaches top of pans. Bake at 375° for about 35 minutes.

APPLE ICING BREAD

¾ c.	Warm water
2 ½ tsp.	Sucanat
1 T.	Yeast
1 tsp.	Sea salt
1 T.	Corn oil
2 ½ c.	Unbleached white flour
6 c.	Applesauce, slightly warm
¼ c.	Unsweetened coconut

Mix the water, Sucanat, and yeast together and let it sit for 10 to 15 minutes. Add in the rest of the salt, oil, and flour. Squeeze between your fingers until all is mixed and the dough begins to stop sticking to your fingers. (You may need to add more flour, but do not be too quick to do so.) Turn onto an oiled board and knead well. Roll the dough out ½" thick. Place in a large, flat baking pan, lining it, including the sides. Prick the dough with a fork. Pour in the warm applesauce. Sprinkle with the coconut. Cover with a flat pan or kneading board. Let rise until the dough is double in thickness. Bake 1 ¼ hours at 350°. Leave in the pan for one or more days. Heat before serving. Slice as a pie.

BAKING POWDER BISCUITS

4 c.	Unbleached white flour
2 T.	Baking powder
1 tsp.	Sea salt
1 c.	Corn oil
1 ½ c.	Water

Sift the dry ingredients into a bowl. Cut in the oil until the whole thing is like coarse crumbs. Make a depression in the mass and put in the water all at once. Stir quickly with a fork just until the dough follows the fork around the bowl. *Do not overmix!* The dough should be soft. Turn onto a lightly floured surface. Knead gently 10 to 12 strokes. Roll or pat the dough into a ½-inch thickness. Dip a cutter in flour and cut the dough straight down–no twisting! Bake on an ungreased baking sheet at 450° for 12 to 15 minutes.

BISCUIT DUMPLINGS

2 ¼ c.	Biscuit Mix (see below)
⅔ c.	Cashew milk or water

Mix into a soft dough. Drop by spoonfuls into boiling liquid. Cook uncovered over low heat for 10 minutes. Cover and cook 10 minutes more.

BISCUIT MIX

6 c.	Unbleached white flour
3 T.	Baking powder
3 T.	Sucanat
1 T.	Sea salt
1 c.	Non-dairy margarine

In a large mixing bowl combine thoroughly the dry ingredients. Sift it all together 6 to 8 times. Work in the margarine with your fingers until the mixture is the consistency of very fine gravel. Store in a tightly covered container at room temperature for up to 4 months. Tape 2 or 3 whole bay leaves to the inside of the lid to keep away any bugs.

BISCUITS

2 c.	Unbleached white flour
1 T.	Baking powder
½ tsp.	Sea salt

¼ c.	Corn oil
¾ c.	Cashew Milk

Sift the dry ingredients into a bowl. Cut in the oil until the mixture is like coarse crumbs. Make a well in the mixture and add the cashew milk all at once. Stir quickly with a fork just till dough follows the fork around the bowl. Turn onto a lightly floured surface. (The dough should be soft.) Knead gently 10 to 12 strokes. Roll or pat the dough ½-inch thick. Dip a cutter in flour and cut the dough straight down–no twisting. Bake on an *ungreased* baking sheet at 450° for 12 to 15 minutes.

BREADSTICKS

A satisfying change from ordinary bread or crackers. Also a great crunchy snack when you want that little something that is also good for you!

2 T.	Yeast
1 c.	Warm water
1 tsp.	Sucanat
¼ c.	Corn oil
3 c.	Unbleached white flour
½ tsp.	Garlic powder
1 ½ tsp.	Sea salt
¼ c.	Nutritional Yeast
½ c.	Onions, minced fine

Mix the yeast, water, and Sucanat. Let stand in a warm place for 10-15 minutes until risen and foamy. Whisk in the oil. In another bowl sift together the flour, garlic powder, salt, and nutritional yeast, and mix well. Add this, in small amounts at a time, with a whisk, to the yeast mixture, alternating with onion pieces. Continue to mix it with a spoon till it is smooth. Knead it for a while, just until it is a nice soft ball. Roll it out to about pencil thickness, and cut in strips with a pizza cutter. Put strips in lightly oiled baking pans with some space between. Let stand in a warm place until they rise. Bake in a 400° oven for about 10 to 15 minutes, or until golden brown on both sides, turning them over once. *For hard breadsticks:* Put breadsticks in a warm oven overnight or in a 200° oven for 2 to 3 hours, or until hard.

"BUTTERED" BREAD CRUMBS

Sauté 1 cup of bread crumbs in ⅓ cup of non-dairy margarine. You may add minced onions, if you like.

CHEEZ BREAD

Make the recipe for White Bread, except put in 1 cup of Nutritional Yeast.

CORN BREAD–1

All as for White Bread, except for these ingredients:

4 c.	White flour
1 ¾ c.	Corn flour
2 ¾ c.	Water

The kneading time must be 15 minutes.

CORN BREAD–2

2 c.	Corn meal
2 c.	Unbleached white flour
5 tsp.	Baking powder
1 ½ tsp.	Sea salt
2 T.	Sucanat
2 ¾ c.	Water
⅓ c.	Corn oil

Mix all dry ingredients, then add all liquid ingredients and mix. Pour into greased and floured pan. Bake at 425° for about 45 minutes or until top is browned.
Variation: For crispy corn bread, add water until a thin batter is formed, pour out until batter covers the bottom of the pan or cookie sheet, and then bake.

CORN BREAD–3

½ c.	Onions, chopped fine
1 ¼ c.	Unbleached white flour
¾ c.	Cornmeal
2 T.	Sucanat
1 T.	Baking powder
1 tsp.	Sea salt
1 T.	Nutritional yeast
3 T.	Non-dairy margarine
1 c.	Cashew Milk
½ c.	Bacon Gluten, chopped fine

Sauté the onion in as little corn oil as possible. Mix the flour, cornmeal, Sucanat, baking powder, salt, and yeast together. Melt the margarine and add the cashew milk to it. Stir that into the dry ingredients. Stir in the onions and gluten. Pour into greased and floured pan. Bake at 425° for about 45 minutes or until top is browned.

CORN CHIPS

The commercial cardboards just cannot equal these!

½ c.	Cashew Milk or water
3 T.	Corn oil
½ c.	Yellow cornmeal
½ c.	Toasted cornmeal
½ c.	Unbleached white flour
¾ tsp.	Sea salt
¼ tsp.	Baking soda
⅛ tsp.	Cayenne pepper
½ tsp.	Chili powder
¼ tsp.	Onion powder

Combine the cashew milk and oil. Stir the dry ingredients together in a mixing bowl. Add the cashew milk mixture and stir until the dough forms a ball. Knead on a floured board (adding a little more flour if necessary) about 5 minutes. Divide the dough in half. Roll each half into a 12-inch square. Cut into 1-inch squares. Sprinkle with salt or paprika. Bake on a lightly oiled baking sheet for 15 minutes or until lightly brown around the edges. Cool slightly before removing from the baking sheet, and transfer to a wire rack.

CORN TORTILLAS

3 c.	Unbleached white flour
3 c.	Corn *flour* (not meal)
1 tsp.	Sea salt
1 tsp.	Baking powder
¼ c.	Corn oil or non-dairy margarine, melted
1 ¾ c.	Warm water

Mix the flours, salt, and baking powder. Make a depression and put in the oil (or margarine). Mix with a spoon. Add ½ cup of warm water and mix again. Add about ¾ cup more warm water, or enough to knead it into bread dough consistency. Let it rest for about 5 minutes. Form into balls about 1 ½ inches in diameter and dip each ball into flour before rolling it out on a lightly floured board. Cook on a hot, dry griddle until bubbly and brown-flecked on each side. (This will not take long—only a few seconds on a really hot griddle.)
Variation: For deep-fried tortillas, omit the baking powder.

CRANBERRY BREAD

This makes a special gift, but bake some for yourself, too!

2 c.	Unbleached white flour, sifted

1 tsp.	Sea salt
½ tsp.	Baking soda
1 ½ tsp.	Baking powder
1 ¼ c.	Sucanat, or genuine maple syrup
¼ c.	Corn oil
1	N'egg
¾ c.	Orange juice
1 T.	Grated orange rind (optional)
½ c.	Chopped nuts
1 c.	Chopped cranberries

Sift together the dry ingredients. Cut in the oil. Pour the n'egg, orange juice, and grated rind all at once into the dry ingredients, mixing just enough to dampen. Carefully fold in the nuts and cranberries. Spoon into a greased loaf pan. Spread the corners and sides slightly higher than the center. Bake at 350° about 1 hour.

DROP BISCUITS

| 2 ¼ c. | Biscuit Mix |
| ⅔ c. | Cashew Milk or water |

Mix into a dough and beat for 30 seconds. Drop by spoonfuls onto an ungreased baking sheet. Bake at 450° 8 to 10 minutes until golden brown.

FLAT BREAD

This doesn't look like much on the page, but it is excellent! We much prefer this to chapattis or puris when eating Indian food.

1 c.	Rye flour
2 c.	Unbleached white flour
⅔ c.	Soy flour
⅓ c.	Wheat bran
1 tsp.	Sea salt
¼ c.	Corn oil
1 ¼ c.	Boiling water

Mix the flours, bran, and salt in a bowl. Add the oil. Stir in only enough of the boiling water to make a stiff dough. Knead to mix thoroughly. Roll out small pieces of dough paper-thin to about 8 inches in diameter. Bake directly on top of an ungreased griddle, or place on an ungreased cookie sheet in an oven set at 250° until thoroughly dried and slightly browned.

FLOUR TORTILLAS

6 c.	Unbleached white flour
1 tsp.	Sea salt
1 tsp.	Baking powder
¼ c.	Corn oil or non-dairy margarine, melted
½ c.	Warm water
¾ c.	Warm water

Mix together the flour, salt, and baking powder. Make a well and pour in the oil or margarine and mix again with a spoon. Add ½ cup of warm water and mix again. Add about ¾ cup more warm water—enough to knead it into bread dough consistency. Let it rest for 5 minutes. Form into balls about 1 ½ inches in diameter and dip each ball into flour before rolling it out very thin on an unfloured board. Cook on a hot, dry griddle until bubbly and brown-flecked on each side.

FRENCH BREAD

1 pkg.	Dry yeast
1 tsp.	Sucanat
½ c.	Warm water (100-103°)
1 ½ c.	Warm water (100-103°)
3 ⅓ c.	Unbleached white flour
1 ½ tsp.	Sea salt
1 T.	Corn Oil

In a glass measuring cup, stir together the yeast, Sucanat, and ½ cup of warm water. Allow it to stand until foamy. In a large bowl of an electric mixer, place the yeast mixture, additional water, flour, and salt, and beat for about 5 to 7 minutes or until the dough is smooth and elastic. It should be very soft and sticky. Drizzle the oil evenly over the dough. Cover the bowl with plastic wrap and then a towel and set it in a warm place (75-80°) until it is doubled in bulk. With a spatula, scrape the dough down into the bowl, cover it as before and let it rise again until doubled. Grease a 3-loaf baguette pan, 8 ½x17 inches. With a large kitchen spoon, scoop out ⅓ of the dough into each section and spread it out evenly. Brush the tops with a little oil. Cover the pan loosely with plastic wrap and allow the dough to rise again until almost doubled. Remove the plastic wrap and bake in a preheated 425° oven about 25 minutes, until the tops are a beautiful golden brown and the bread sounds hollow when thumped. Remove the bread from the pan and cool on a rack.

FRIED CHEEZ BALLS

1 c.	Biscuit Mix
1 ½ c.	Yeast or Notzarella Cheez
⅓ c.	Onions, chopped

Mix everything together, adding a little water if needed, and form into balls and fry them in oil.

FRIED CORNMEAL CAKES

Versatile. Can be a side dish to themselves or can take the place of cornbread, regular bread, biscuits, etc. Good with syrup, too!

2 T.	Non-dairy margarine, softened
2 c.	Cashew Milk
2 c.	Water
1 T.	Corn oil
1 ⅓ c.	Yellow cornmeal
1 tsp.	Sea salt

Spread the margarine over the bottom and sides of a shallow baking dish with a pastry brush. Set aside. In a saucepan bring the "milk," water, and corn oil to a boil. Stirring constantly with a wooden spoon, pour in the cornmeal in a slow, thin stream so the water continues to boil as the cornmeal is absorbed. Stir in the salt, reduce heat to low and, stirring frequently, simmer for 15 to 20 minutes, or until the cornmeal is so thick that the spoon will stand unsupported in the middle of the pan. While the cornmeal is still hot, spoon it into the baking dish, spreading it out to ½-inch thickness, smoothing the top with a spatula. Cover with wax paper and refrigerate overnight or for at least 6 hours, or spread the cornmeal into a pan with sides and cool in a freezer for 15 or more minutes—until the cornmeal is firm to the touch. With a pastry wheel or sharp knife, divide the chilled cornmeal into 2-inch squares and carefully lift them out of the pan with a small metal spatula. In a skillet melt 2 tablespoons of non-dairy margarine. Fry 4 or 5 of the cornmeal squares for 2 or 3 minutes on each side, turning them over gently with a spatula until brown. Fry the remaining squares, adding more margarine as needed.

GARLIC BREAD

Melt two cups of non-dairy margarine with 1 tablespoon of garlic powder. Spread on bread slices. Toast the bread in the oven under the broiler.

GARLIC CROUTONS

1	Loaf of bread
2 c.	Non-dairy margarine
1 T.	Garlic powder

Cube the bread (about ½-inch cubes). Toast in the oven at 550°, turning often until the edges brown—about 10 minutes. Melt the margarine with the garlic powder. Roll the toasted bread cubes in the margarine.

HAMBURGER BUNS

Make Whole Wheat or White Bread recipe. Roll out dough thickly on a lightly floured surface and cut into six 4-inch rounds. Place on a baking sheet, brush lightly with apple juice, and bake at 400° for 20 to 25 minutes.

HERB BREAD

Make the recipe for White Bread, except put in 1 teaspoon of oregano, 1 ½ teaspoon of rosemary, 1 teaspoon of tumeric, and ½ teaspoon of sage.

HERB AND ONION BREAD

Make the recipe for White Bread, except put in 1 cup of finely chopped onion and ½ teaspoon of dill weed.

HUSH PUPPIES

Even Yankees can like these!
Try using different kinds of chopped vegetables.

2 c.	Cornmeal
1 c.	Unbleached white flour
1 tsp.	Baking powder
1 tsp.	Sea salt
½ tsp.	Baking soda
½ tsp.	Garlic powder
½ c.	Parsley, finely chopped
¼ tsp.	Cayenne pepper
2	N'eggs
1 c.	Cashew Milk or Tofu Buttermilk
1 c.	Green onions, finely chopped
2 T.	Corn oil

Combine the cornmeal, flour, baking powder, salt, baking soda, and garlic powder. Add the rest of the ingredients and mix well. Drop by the spoonfuls into hot oil and deep fry until brown on all sides. Remove and drain on paper towels.

MEXICAN BREAD

1 pkg.	Yeast
¼ c.	Warm water
3 c.	Unbleached white flour
¾ c.	Yellow cornmeal
½ c.	Corn
1 T.	Jalapeños, chopped
1	N'egg
1 T.	Non-dairy margarine
½ tsp.	Sea salt

4 tsp. Sucanat
1 c.   Warm water

Dissolve yeast in warm water until it starts to foam. Combine the rest of the ingredients except for the cup of water. Add the yeast and water. Knead into a dough. Place in a nonstick loaf pan and allow to rise until double. Bake at 400° until golden brown.

MEXICAN CORNBREAD

1 c.   Unbleached white flour
1 ½ c.   Cornmeal
3 tsp.   Baking powder
1 tsp.   Sea salt
½ tsp.   Baking soda
1 tsp.   Sucanat
1 c.   Corn
2   N'eggs
2   Jalapeño peppers, chopped
2 T.   Bell pepper, chopped fine
1 c.   Tofu Sour Cream or Tofu Buttermilk
1 c.   Yeast Cheez
2 tsp.   Corn oil

Mix everything together and pour into a hot skillet. Bake at 400° for 1 hour or until brown.

OATCAKES

Something truly different. I like these just by themselves, but they can be used in place of crackers, biscuits, and regular bread. A backpacker's delight!

1 ¾ c.   Oatmeal
¼ tsp.   Baking powder
¼ tsp.   Sea salt
1 T.   Non-dairy margarine, melted
5-8 tsp. Hot water

Half a cup at a time, pulverize 1 cup of the oatmeal by blending at high speed in a blender until you have a gritty "flour." Combine the pulverized oatmeal, baking powder, and salt in a bowl. Stir in the melted margarine. When all the margarine has been absorbed, add the hot water, a teaspoon at a time, stirring constantly, to make a smooth but firm paste. Gather the mixture into a ball and place it on a board or table lightly sprinkled with ¼ cup of the remaining oatmeal. Roll the ball into the oatmeal until it is completely covered with the flakes. Spread another ¼ cup of oatmeal evenly over the board and, with a rolling pin, roll the ball out into an 8-inch circle about ⅛-inch thick. With a pastry wheel or sharp

knife, cut the circle into 8 pie-shaped wedges. Scatter the remaining ¼ cup of oatmeal on a baking sheet and, with a large metal spatula, carefully transfer the wedges to the sheet. Bake the cakes in the middle of the oven for about 15 minutes at 350°. When the wedges are light brown, turn off the heat and open the door of the oven. Leave the oatcakes in the oven for 4 or 5 minutes, or until they become firm and crisp. Serve at once.

ONE-HOUR WHOLE WHEAT BREAD

Everything—including the flour—must be measured, warm, and ready to go. (Warm the flour by putting it in a 275° oven for 3 to 5 minutes.)

1 c.   Warm water
3 pkg.   Yeast
1 T.   Molasses (unsulphured)
3 c.   Hot water
⅓ c.   Sucanat
1 ½ c.   Whole wheat flour
1 ½ T.   Salt
4 T.   Oil
          Approximately 7 ½ cups whole wheat flour—just enough to make a soft dough consistency

Combine the 1 cup of warm water, yeast, and molasses, and let it stand for 10 minutes. While the yeast mixture is standing, combine the 3 cups of hot water, Sucanat, and 1 ½ c. of whole wheat flour. After the 10 minutes—or when this has cooled to lukewarm—add the yeast mixture and let it stand for 15 minutes. Add the salt, oil, and flour. Mix so it makes a soft dough—not too stiff. If you want, you can knead it for up to 10 minutes, but you may knead it just until it is smooth. Put directly into loaf pans (3 or 4, according to the size of loaf you want.) Let sit in a warm place until doubled in bulk. Bake at 350° until done.

ONION BREAD

Make the recipe for White Bread, except put in 1 ½ cups of chopped onions.

POCKET BREAD

We struggled for years to succeed in making pita (pocket) bread. And here is the success!

1 ½ tsp. Dry active yeast
1 ½ c.   Warm water

1 T.	Sucanat, genuine maple syrup, or Barbados molasses
¼ c.	Corn oil
4 c.	Unbleached white flour
½ tsp.	Sea salt

Preheat your oven to 550°. Dissolve the yeast in warm water, and add the sweetener and oil. Set aside for a few minutes. It will (should) foam up. Sift together the flour and salt. Add the yeast mixture to the flour and salt and knead 5 minutes. Shape the dough into a ball and place it in an oiled bowl. Coat the dough ball lightly with oil. Cover the bowl with a dry towel and place it in a warm place until it is doubled in bulk—about one hour.

Again knead for 5 minutes. Separate the dough into 4 parts. Divide each of those parts into 6 small balls, so you have 24 total. (If you desire a larger size pocket bread, divide the parts into larger balls.) Roll all of the balls out into round shapes about ⅛ to ¼ inch in thickness. Then beginning again—in the order you originally rolled them out–roll the rounds out slightly thinner (somewhere between ¼ and ⅛ inches thick). This may seem unnecessary, but it is important. Cover them all with a dry cloth and then with a damp cloth over the dry. Let the rounds rise for 20 minutes.

While the rounds are rising, put your *ungreased* baking pans (or cookie sheets) in the oven so they will get hot. After twenty minutes, take the pans out of the oven and quickly *and gently* transfer the rounds to the pans. Place the pans on the bottom rack of the oven for about 2 minutes. Then transfer the pans to the middle of the oven for 1 to 2 minutes more. Remove the pans, cool the rounds and cut in half. If you are not going to serve the bread immediately, cover the rounds with a damp cloth so they will not dry out.

Tips: If you wish the tops of the bread to be more browned, transfer the pans to a rack in the middle of the oven and leave them there for two more minutes. If the bread is a day or more old, you can steam it to soften it before serving.

PUMPERNICKEL BREAD

1 qt.	Water, warm enough to warm up the molasses
1 c.	Barbados molasses
1 T.	Oil
1 T.	Salt
1	Package of yeast
3 c.	Rye flour

6 c.	Whole wheat flour

Mix the water, molasses, oil, salt, and yeast, and let them stand for 10 minutes. Slightly warm the flour in the oven. Add the flour to the other ingredients. Mix. Let stand for 15 minutes. Knead until smooth and elastic. Cover and put in a warm place until it is doubled in bulk. Form into small loaves and place in pans. Let rise again until doubled in size. Bake for one hour at 350°.

PURIS

½ tsp.	Sea salt
1 c.	Whole wheat flour
1 c.	Unbleached white flour
1 ½ tsp.	Non-dairy margarine
1 ½ tsp.	Corn oil
1 c.	Warm water (all this may not be used)

Combine the salt, flour, margarine, and oil and mix until it looks like coarse meal. Add the minimum amount of water and knead well, adding water slowly. Use only enough water so as to form a firm compact ball. Knead about 7 minutes, or until the dough becomes smooth and elastic. Cover the dough with a damp towel and let it sit for at least 30 minutes. Break off pieces about 2 tablespoons in size. Roll out each piece on a lightly floured surface into a 5-or-6-inch circle. Deep fry until it starts to brown, turning occasionally. They will puff up some. Set to drain in a colander or on paper toweling. Keep them covered if they are to sit for any length of time. Taste-test the first few. If they are raw, either the oil is too hot or the puri is rolled too thick. If it is too crisp, then it has been rolled too thin.

"SOURDOUGH" BREAD

Use one of the recipes for whole wheat or white bread, but instead of water use Tofu Yogurt–in the same amount as the recipe calls for water.

SOY BREAD

7 c.	Warm water
2 T.	Barbados molasses
3 T.	Yeast (dry; or 2 yeast cakes)
½ c.	Barbados molasses
½ c.	Corn oil
2 T.	Sea salt
14 c.	Unbleached white flour
4 c.	Soy flour

Combine the water, 2 tablespoons of molasses,

and yeast. Let it stand until dissolved. Add the ½ cup of molasses, oil, and salt. Stirring, slowly add the flours. Mix with a spoon and then knead for 10 minutes. Let rise in warm place until doubled. Shape into loaves. Brush with oil and let rise till very light. Bake at 350° for 1 hour or until brown on top.

SWEET MUFFINS

2 c.	Biscuit Mix
⅓ c.	Sucanat
⅔ c.	Cashew Milk
2 T.	Corn oil

Mix all ingredients together until just moistened. Spoon into greased muffin pans and bake at 400° for about 15 minutes, until brown.
Variation: After mixing muffin batter, fold in ¾ cup blueberries.

TOAST POINTS

Trim the crust from thin slices of bread. Cut the bread slices diagonally in half. Brush one side of each slice with melted margarine. Put the bread, margarine side up, on a baking sheet. Bake at 450° for 3 minutes. Turn the bread over and bake 2 to 3 minutes or until golden brown.

WHITE BREAD

1 pkg.	Dry yeast
¼ c.	Warm water
2 c.	Warm water
2 tsp.	Sea salt
2 T.	Corn oil
1 T.	Sucanat, genuine maple syrup, or Barbados molasses
6 ¼ c.	Unbleached white flour (or a combination of white and whole wheat flours)

Soften the yeast in the ¼ cup of warm water. Combine all the rest of the ingredients with the yeast. Turn out on floured board and knead until smooth and satiny—about 10 minutes. Cover and let sit in a warm place for about 20-30 minutes. Punch down and separate into three equal parts. Put the dough into loaf pans and shape. Wipe their tops with more oil and let rise 30-45 minutes. Bake in 400° oven until well brown so there will be a heavy crust.

WHOLE WHEAT BREAD

A lot of whole wheat bread ought to be sold to the roads department to fill holes in the pavement. But THIS is what it ought to be!

3 c.	Warm (105°-110°) water
3 T.	Yeast
3 T.	Sucanat, genuine maple syrup, or Barbados molasses
3 tsp.	Sea salt
3 T.	Corn oil
8 c.	Whole wheat flour (warmed in a 275° oven for 3 to 5 minutes)

Mix the water, yeast, and sweetener together. Add the salt, oil, and flour. Knead for 10 minutes. Let rise in the bowl in a warm place, covered, until double in bulk. Cut into 3 parts with a sharp knife, place in loaf pans, and shape. Allow to rise until doubled in bulk. Bake in a 425° oven for 15 minutes. Reduce heat to 350° and bake about 30 minutes more. Remove from pans and cool on a wire rack so the air can circulate around them.
Variations: For Raisin Bread, add 1 ½ cups of raisins to the dough. For a single loaf, use only ⅓ of the ingredients, except use 2 ½ cups of flour.

WHOLE WHEAT BUNS

Make the Whole Wheat Bread recipe. Roll out the dough thickly on a lightly-floured surface and cut into 6 4-inch rounds. Put on a baking sheet, brush lightly with apple juice, and bake at 400° for 20 to 25 minutes.

YEAST BISCUITS–1

A good idea!

1 ⅓ c.	Warm water
1 T.	Yeast
4 c.	Unbleached white flour
1 tsp.	Sea salt
2 T.	Sucanat
¼ c.	Corn oil

Mix all ingredients, but only BARELY ENOUGH to get them wet, as over-handling makes the biscuits more like rolls. Oil your hands and shape the biscuits. Place on an oiled pan ½ inch apart. Let them rise only about ¼ inch or the texture will resemble buns instead of biscuits. Bake at 400° for 20 to 30 minutes.

YEAST BISCUITS–2

1 T.	Dry yeast
½ c.	Warm water
1 T.	Sucanat or Barbados molasses
2 ½ c.	Unbleached white flour
1 tsp.	Sea salt
5 T.	Non-dairy margarine or corn oil
½ c.	Warm water

Dissolve the yeast in the ½ cup of warm water with the sweetener. Sift together the flour and salt. Cut shortening and one more ½ cup of warm water into the flour and salt. Add the yeast mixture and mix *lightly*. Roll out 1-inch thick. Cut with biscuit cutter. Place on an oiled pan ½ inch apart. Let rise 20 minutes. Bake at 400–425° for 25 to 30 minutes.

Crackers

CRACKERS

This makes good pizza dough, too.

1 ½ T.	Yeast
1 c.	Warm water
1 tsp.	Sucanat
⅓ c.	Corn oil
1 tsp.	Sea salt
3 ½ c.	Unbleached white flour

Combine the yeast, water, and Sucanat in a medium-sized bowl. Let sit until foamy. Add the oil, salt, and flour to the yeast mixture and knead lightly together. Let rise at least 5 minutes. Roll out thin. Put in a baking pan that has NOT been oiled. Cut or score into squares or diamonds. Bake at 450°–500° until light brown.

CHEEZ CRACKERS

My favorite cracker to eat straight or in soup. Make these good and crispy.

2 c.	Unbleached white flour
2 tsp.	Baking powder
½ tsp.	Sea salt
2 T.	Corn oil
¾ c.	Water
½ c.	Nutritional yeast
1 tsp.	Garlic powder
1 tsp.	Chili powder (optional)

Mix all ingredients into a stiff dough, adding more water as needed. Knead lightly. Roll dough as thin as possible. Oil the top of the dough and sprinkle with salt. Cut into squares. Bake 5–7 minutes at 375° or until brown on both sides.

COCONUT CRACKERS

As good as they are unusual.

⅓ c.	Coconut
¼ c.	Barbados molasses
1 tsp.	Sea salt
3 T.	Corn oil
¾ c.	Water
3 c.	Unbleached white flour

Blend the coconut, molasses, salt, oil, and water in a blender until the coconut is chopped. Pour this into the flour and mix into a dough. Roll out very thin on cookie sheets. Score and prick. Bake at 275° until well browned–about 45 minutes.

GRAHAM CRACKERS

Better than the "real thing"!

2 c.	Whole wheat flour
1 ½ c.	Unbleached white flour
2 T.	Cornstarch or arrowroot
½ tsp.	Sea salt
½ c.	Water
⅓ c.	Corn oil
½ c.	Barbados molasses

Mix all the dry ingredients. Mix all the wet ingredients in a blender. Combine. Knead a little. Roll out to ¼-inch thick. Cut, and prick with a fork. Bake at 275° for 35 minutes.

RYE CRISPS

          3 c.   Rolled oats
          1 c.   Rye flour
        ½ tsp.   Sea salt
          ¼ c.   Corn oil
          1 c.   Water

Grind the oats to a course flour in a blender. Mix the dry ingredients. Add the oil to the water in a blender and whirl to emulsify. Pour it over the dry mixture while stirring to distribute the moisture evenly. Divide into three equal portions and place each on an ungreased cookie sheet. Press out flat with your fingers. Sprinkle lightly with flour to prevent sticking to the rolling pin, and then roll out until thin and even. Cut into squares or diamond shapes. Bake at 300° for 50 minutes. Watch carefully when nearly done. OR: Bake at 250° for 1 ¼ hours to be sure the crisps do not burn.

Soups

ABBOT GEORGE'S LOW CALORIE SOUP

9 c.	Tomato juice
3 c.	Potatoes, cubed
1 c.	Onion, chopped
½ c.	Bell pepper, chopped
6 T.	Jalapeños, chopped fine
1 c.	Lima beans
1 T.	Fresh parsley, minced
1 ¼ c.	Gluten (plain or flavored), cubed
⅓ c.	Carrot, chopped
¾ tsp.	Sea salt
¼ tsp.	Basil
⅛ tsp.	Garlic powder

Combine and cook until potatoes are good and soft–about 30 minutes or more.
Variation: For 2 cups of the tomato juice substitute 2 cups of Snap-E-Tom.

"ALMOST INSTANT" VEGETABLE SOUP-1

6 c.	Frozen vegetables of choice, thawed
⅛ tsp.	Black pepper
¼ tsp.	Onion powder
⅛ tsp.	Garlic powder
1 ½ tsp.	Corn oil
½ tsp.	Sea salt
1 tsp.	MSG
½ tsp.	Poultry seasoning
3 T.	Nutritional yeast
4 c.	Water

Combine all ingredients, heat, and serve.
Variations: Include 3 cups of canned tomatoes, blended slightly to break them up (in which case use 2 tsp. of oil). Omit the MSG and add 1 teaspoon of salt.

"ALMOST INSTANT" VEGETABLE SOUP-2

¾ c.	Onions, chopped
2 tsp.	Corn oil
4 c.	Frozen Vegetables
3 c.	Canned tomatoes, chopped (reserve liquid)
1 tsp.	Basil
3 T.	Soy sauce
½ tsp.	Cayenne pepper
4 c.	UnBeef Broth

Sauté the onions in the oil. Combine all ingredients and cook together for 20 to 30 minutes. If more liquid is needed, use the tomato liquid or more broth.

AVOCADO AND TOMATO SOUP

6	Medium tomatoes, chopped and pureed
⅔ c.	Tofu Sour Cream or Cashew Sour Cream
½ c.	Cashew Milk
3 T.	Lemon juice
2 T.	Italian tomato paste
1 ½ tsp.	Olive oil
3 T.	Fresh parsley, chopped
1 ½ tsp.	Sea salt
¼ tsp.	White pepper
1	Small ripe avocado, pureed or mashed

Combine everything–except the avocado–until well blended. Cover tightly and refrigerate for at least 2 hours, until thoroughly chilled. Just before serving, blend the avocado into it.

BAKED BEAN SOUP

3 c.	Barbecue Baked Beans
½ c.	Canned tomatoes, blended
2 c.	Water
1 T.	Soy sauce
¼ tsp.	Cayenne pepper

Combine everything and simmer for 30 minutes. Add more water or tomato juice if it gets too thick.

BASQUE VEGETABLE SOUP

2 ½ c.	Onion, chopped
¾ tsp.	Garlic, minced
1 T.	Corn oil
1 ½ c.	Sausage Gluten of choice, sliced
2 c.	UnChicken, cubed
1 c.	Carrots, sliced
1	Large turnip, peeled and cubed
1 ¼ c.	Potatoes, peeled and cubed
1 ½ tsp.	Sea salt
½ tsp.	Black pepper
1 T.	Parsley, chopped
1 tsp.	Thyme
1 c.	Cabbage, shredded
2 c.	Cooked navy or great northern beans
6 c.	UnChicken Broth

Sauté the onion and garlic in the oil until soft. Combine everything, bring to a boil, reduce heat, cover, and simmer for 30 minutes.

BLACK BEAN AND SPINACH SOUP

⅔ c.	Black beans
3 T.	Onion, chopped
2 T.	Celery, chopped
1 tsp.	Garlic, chopped fine
2 tsp.	Corn oil
¼ tsp.	Ground ginger
½ tsp.	Sea salt
¼ tsp.	Black pepper
4 c.	Water
5 oz.	Spinach leaves, stemmed and rinsed
4 T.	Tofu yogurt

Sort, wash well, and drain the black beans. Sauté the onion, celery, and garlic in the oil until soft. Combine with the beans, ginger, salt, pepper, and water and bring to a boil, stirring occasionally. Reduce heat and simmer, covered, for 1 hour or

until the beans are fully cooked. Meanwhile, wash the spinach leaves to remove all sand and grit. Put them in a skillet and sauté in a small amount of corn oil until they are wilted but still bright green–2 to 3 minutes. Cool. Mince the spinach and set aside. Put ⅓ of the beans into a blender or food processor. Purée until completely smooth and transfer back to the soup. Stir the spinach into the soup, return to a simmer. Take from the heat and stir in the yogurt.

BLACK BEAN SOUP–1

2 ½ c.	Dry black beans
1 c.	Bell pepper, chopped
3 T.	Onions, chopped
2 tsp.	Corn oil
6 c.	UnBeef or UnChicken Broth
¾ tsp.	Sea salt
⅛ tsp.	Cayenne pepper
2 c.	Tomatoes, chopped
¼ tsp.	Summer savory

Pressure-cook the beans. Sauté the bell peppers and onions in the oil. Combine with rest of ingredients and cook about 30 minutes more. If needed, add more broth or water to keep a soup consistency.

BLACK BEAN SOUP–2

2 c.	Dry black beans
⅓ c.	Onions, chopped
½ c.	Celery, chopped
½ tsp.	Garlic, minced
2 tsp.	Corn oil
⅛ tsp.	Italian Herb Seasoning
¼ tsp.	Sage
1	Bay leaf
¼ tsp.	Cayenne pepper
2 c.	Potatoes, cooked and diced
1 c.	Carrots, cooked and sliced into rounds
1 c.	UnBacon, chopped fine
4 c.	UnChicken Broth

Pressure-cook the beans. Sauté the onions, celery, and garlic in the corn oil. Combine all ingredients and cook for 30 minutes.
Variations: Omit the gluten and use UnBeef Broth instead.

BLACK BEAN SOUP–3

1 c.	Dry black beans
¾ c.	Onions, chopped

1 tsp.   Non-dairy margarine
2 c.   UnBeef or UnChicken Broth
¼ tsp.   Cayenne pepper

Pressure-cook the beans. Sauté the onions in the margarine. Combine all ingredients and simmer for 1 hour.

BORSCHT–1

Peeling the beets ensures that they will not have their usual "earthy" taste that many people dislike.

2 c.   Beets, peeled and diced
1 c.   Carrots, peeled and diced
4 c.   Potatoes, peeled and diced
½ c.   Celery, diced
½ c.   Onions, chopped
½ c.   Tomatoes, chopped
1   Bay leaf
1 tsp.   Sea salt
¼ tsp.   Black pepper
4 c.   UnBeef Broth
1 T.   Corn oil

Combine everything, bring to a boil, reduce heat, and simmer until the potatoes start to fall apart. Serve with Cashew or Tofu Sour Cream.

BORSCHT–2

1 c.   Onions, chopped
1 T.   Corn oil
½ c.   Carrots, chopped
¼ c.   Celery, chopped
¼ tsp.   Black pepper
1 c.   Tomato purée
1 tsp.   Dill weed
2 c.   Beets, peeled and grated
1 c.   Potatoes, peeled and grated
2 ½ c.   Cabbage, shredded
8 c.   UnBeef Broth
2 T.   Lemon juice

Sauté the onions in the oil until they are transparent. Add the carrots, celery, and pepper, and sauté until they are soft. Add the tomato purée and dill and simmer 10 minutes. Add the beets, potatoes, cabbage, and broth. Bring to a boil, reduce heat, and simmer until the vegetables are tender. Add the lemon juice.

BROCCOLI, BEAN, AND SPAGHETTI SOUP

⅓ c.   Onions, chopped
½ tsp.   Garlic, minced

3 ½ tsp. Corn oil
2 c.   Cooked dried beans
4 c.   Broccoli, chopped
6 c.   Tomatoes, chopped
½ tsp.   Basil
½ tsp.   Oregano
⅛ tsp.   Cayenne pepper
½ tsp.   Sea salt
2 c.   UnChicken Broth
1 c.   Spaghetti, uncooked, broken in pieces

Sauté the onions and garlic in the oil. Combine all the ingredients–except the spaghetti–and cook for 30 minutes. While this is being done, cook and drain the spaghetti. When the soup has cooked for 30 minutes, add the spaghetti and cook for 5 minutes more.

BUDAPEST BEAN SOUP

Every spoonful of this is a delight!

1 lb.   Dried white beans
9 c.   UnChicken Broth
1   Bay leaf
½ tsp.   Oregano
1 c.   Onion, chopped
½ c.   Celery, chopped
1 T.   Olive oil
2 T.   Paprika (or ½ tsp. hot paprika)
¼ tsp.   Cayenne pepper
4 c.   Zucchini, cubed
½ tsp.   Black pepper

Pressure-cook the beans in 6 cups of the UnChicken broth with the bay leaf and oregano. Put half the beans through a food mill or purée them in a food processor and mix back in with the rest of the beans. Sauté the onion and celery in the oil until the onion is translucent. Stir in the paprika, cayenne, zucchini, and rest of broth. Cook for 5 minutes. Combine with the beans and add the black pepper. Cook 5 more minutes, adding more broth or water if it gets too thick.

CABBAGE AND CHEEZ SOUP–1

1 c.   Cabbage, shredded
1 ½ c.   Potatoes, grated
2 c.   Cashew Milk
¾ tsp.   Non-dairy margarine
2 c.   Water
½ tsp.   Sea salt
¼ tsp.   Black or cayenne pepper
¼ c.   Pimento, Yeast, or Notzarella Cheez

Cook the cabbage and potatoes together until soft. Drain off the cooking liquid and reserve 2 cups of it. If it is not 2 cups, add enough water to complete that measure. Mash the cooked cabbage and potatoes with the "milk" and margarine. Gradually add the reserved liquid, salt, and pepper. Cook slowly for 15 minutes, stirring occasionally. Stir in the cheez just before serving. *Variation:* Make the cashew milk with UnChicken or UnBeef Broth and cut the salt in half.

CABBAGE AND CHEEZ SOUP-2

⅓ c.	Onions, chopped
1 c.	Cabbage, shredded
1 ½ c.	Potatoes, grated
2 c.	Cashew Milk
¾ tsp.	Non-dairy margarine
2 c.	UnChicken Broth
¼ tsp.	Sea salt
¼ tsp.	Cayenne pepper
¼ c.	Pimento, Yeast, or Notzarella Cheez

Cook the onions, cabbage, and potatoes together until soft. Drain. Mash them with the "milk" and margarine. Gradually add the broth, salt, and pepper. Cook slowly for 15 minutes, stirring occasionally. Add the cheez and stir in well.

CABBAGE AND POTATO SOUP

1 c.	Onion, chopped
1 T.	Corn oil
4 c.	Cabbage, coarsely shredded
2 c.	Potatoes, cut into ½-inch pieces
4 c.	Canned tomatoes, chopped, with juice
3 T.	Lemon juice
2 T.	Sucanat
¼ tsp.	Thyme
1 tsp.	Sea salt
½ tsp.	Black pepper

Sauté the onion in the oil until soft. Combine everything and simmer 1 hour or until the potatoes and cabbage are tender.

CABBAGE AND TOMATO SOUP

1 c.	UnBeef, chopped or ground
2 c.	Cabbage, grated or coarsely cut
½ c.	Sauerkraut, drained
1 c.	Canned tomatoes, drained and chopped
2 c.	UnChicken Broth
½ c.	UnBeef Broth
1 ½ tsp.	Soy sauce
1 ¼ c.	Onions, chopped
¾ tsp.	Garlic, minced
⅓ c.	Carrot, finely grated
⅛ tsp.	Black pepper
1 ½ tsp.	Corn oil

Combine all the ingredients, bring to a boil, lower the heat, and simmer with the lid slightly off for about 1 hour.

CABBAGE BORSCHT

Although a long-standing beet-hater, I love this, and I think you will, too!

¾ c.	Beets, peeled and chopped
⅔ c.	Red onion, chopped
¾ c.	Carrots, grated
2 ½ c.	Cabbage, thinly sliced
1 T.	Non-dairy margarine
8 c.	UnBeef broth
1 ¼ c.	Tomatoes, chopped
⅛ tsp.	Sea salt
¼ tsp.	Cayenne pepper
2 c.	Potatoes, peeled and diced

Combine everything and simmer for 1 ½ hours. This is good served with Cashew or Tofu Sour Cream.

CABBAGE SOUP-1

⅓ c.	Onions, chopped
2 T.	Non-dairy margarine
2 T.	Unbleached white flour
4 c.	UnBeef Broth
1 c.	Potatoes, diced
8 c.	Cabbage, shredded
1 c.	Cashew or Tofu Sour Cream

Sauté the onions in the margarine until light yellow-not brown. Add the flour, mix well, and then add the broth, potatoes, and cabbage. Cook until the potatoes are soft. Add a bit of the hot soup liquid to the "sour cream" and mix well. Add this to the soup (it should not curdle).

CABBAGE SOUP-2

Not What You Might Expect!

1 c.	Onion, chopped
1 ½ tsp.	Garlic, minced
2 T.	Corn oil
4 c.	Unbeef, cubed

1 c.	Carrots, pared and coarsely chopped
1	Bay leaf
1 tsp.	Thyme
½ tsp.	Paprika
4 c.	UnBeef Broth
4 c.	Water
8 c.	Cabbage, chopped coarsely
4 c.	Canned tomatoes
2 tsp.	Sea salt
½ tsp.	Tabasco
¼ c.	Parsley, chopped
3 T.	Lemon juice
3 T.	Sucanat
2 c.	Sauerkraut

Sauté the onion and garlic in the oil until soft. Combine everything and cook until the vegetables are tender.

CALSOUP

½ c.	Bell pepper, chopped
⅓ c.	Onions, chopped
2 T.	Corn oil
6 c.	Tomatoes
4 T.	Flour
1-2 T.	Lemon juice
½ tsp.	Sea salt

Sauté the bell peppers and onions in the oil. Combine with rest of ingredients and cook.

CARROT SOUP

¾ c.	Onions, chopped
1 tsp.	Garlic, minced
1 ¾ tsp.	Non-dairy margarine
2 c.	Carrots, chopped
2 c.	Potatoes, chopped
¼ tsp.	Sage
¼ tsp.	Thyme
4 c.	UnBeef or UnChicken Broth
¼ tsp.	Sea salt
¼ tsp.	Cayenne pepper

Sauté the onions and garlic in the margarine until the onions are transparent. Add the rest of ingredients. Bring to a boil, reduce heat, and simmer, covered, 30 minutes. Cool a bit, then blend in a blender. Reheat if need be.

CHEEZ SOUP–1

½ c.	Bell peppers, chopped fine
1 c.	Mushrooms, sliced or chopped
3 T.	Onions, chopped
⅛ tsp.	Cayenne
½ tsp.	Non-dairy margarine
1 ½ c.	UnChicken Broth
3 c.	Cheez sauce, warm

Combine everything but the cheez sauce and cook until the vegetables are done. Sir in the cheez sauce.
Variations: Add 1 cup of chopped canned tomatoes. Add ⅓ cup of Cooked Tomato Salsa. Add Tofu Sour Cream.

CHEEZ SOUP–2

¾ c.	Onions, chopped
1 c.	Potatoes, chopped
1 c.	Carrots, chopped
¾ tsp.	Non-dairy margarine
2 c.	UnBeef Broth
¼ tsp.	Thyme
1 c.	Cashew Milk
1 ½ c.	Yeast or Pimento Cheez
¼ tsp.	Sea salt
¼ tsp.	Cayenne pepper

Combine the vegetables, broth, margarine, and thyme. Bring to a boil, reduce heat, cover, and simmer for 25 minutes. Add the rest of the ingredients and allow to cool slightly. Blend until smooth. Reheat, if need be, but do not boil.

CHEEZ AND ONION SOUP

1 ½ c.	Onions, chopped coarsely
½ tsp.	Garlic, minced
½ tsp.	Non-dairy margarine
2 T.	Unbleached white flour
2 c.	Cashew Milk
1 tsp.	Sea salt
¼ tsp.	Black or cayenne pepper
½ c.	Pimento, Yeast, or Notzarella Cheez

Combine everything but the cheez and cook till the onions are soft. Stir in the cheez.

CHILI POTATO SOUP

6 c.	Potatoes, peeled and diced
3 c.	UnChicken Broth
1 ½ c.	Onion, chopped
¼ c.	Green onions, finely chopped, including the tops
½ tsp.	Sea salt
½ tsp.	Cumin, ground
1 tsp.	Basil
½ tsp.	Black pepper

2 Garlic cloves, minced
¾ c. Bell pepper, finely diced
2 T. Jalapeños, chopped, or 1 ½ tsp. hot pepper flakes
2 c. Cashew Milk made with UnChicken Broth

Combine everything but the "milk" and cook for 15 minutes or until the potatoes start to fall apart. Add the "milk" and cook 15 more minutes.

CHILLED TOMATO AND BELL PEPPER SOUP

4 Red bell peppers
2 tsp. Corn oil
1 c. Onion, chopped
2 tsp. Garlic, chopped
5 c. Tomatoes, chopped
Pinch Thyme
8 Basil leaves
1 tsp. Genuine maple syrup
¼ tsp. Black pepper
½ tsp. Sea salt
6 c. Vegetable Consommé
1 T. Balsamic vinegar
¾ c. Tofu yogurt

Put the bell peppers on a baking sheet and roast them in the top third of the oven at 500°, turning them frequently, until they blacken and blister. Immediately put them in a bowl and seal it, airtight, with plastic wrap. Let them steam for 30 minutes. Remove and discard the skin, stem, and seeds. (For difficult spots, use a paring knife.) As you do this, dip your fingers occasionally in water. Keep any juice that may be released from the peppers. Chop them and set aside in their juice (if any). Heat the oil in a pan and sauté the onion until translucent. Add the garlic, tomatoes, bell peppers, thyme, basil, syrup, pepper, and salt. Cook slowly for 5 minutes. Add the vegetable consommé and bring to a boil. Reduce the heat and simmer for 15 to 20 minutes. Put in a blender or food processor and purée until completely smooth—in batches if necessary. Cool to room temperature and refrigerate. Just before serving stir in the vinegar and yogurt. Thin with more yogurt if needed.

COLD CREAM OF SQUASH SOUP

1 ½ tsp. Non-dairy margarine
3 T. Onions, finely chopped
¾ c. Carrot, finely chopped
1 T. Bell pepper, finely chopped
3 ½ c. Yellow crookneck squash, cut into ½-inch dice
1 c. Potato, peeled and cut into ½-inch dice
4 c. UnChicken Broth made with Cashew Milk
½ tsp. Dill weed
¼ tsp. Cayenne pepper

Melt the margarine and sauté the onions, carrot, and bell pepper, and cook for 5 to 6 minutes until the vegetables are soft but not brown. Stir in the diced squash and potato, and pour in the broth. Bring to a boil, reduce heat and simmer, partially covered, for about 20 minutes, or until the squash is tender and offers no resistance when pierced with the tip of a sharp knife. Strain through a fine sieve set over a large mixing bowl, and purée the vegetables through a food mill or by pushing them through the sieve with the back of a large wooden spoon. Combine the purée and the soup liquid and, when the soup has cooled to room temperature, stir in the dill and cayenne. Cover tightly with plastic wrap and refrigerate for at least 2 hours, or until thoroughly chilled.

COLD CREAM OF TOMATO SOUP

Unusual—and unusually good!

2 tsp. Olive oil (do not use "extra virgin" olive oil, as the taste will be too strong in this dish)
1 ½ c. Onion, chopped
1 ½ tsp. Garlic, minced
¼ tsp. Ground mace
3 T. Unbleached white flour
3 c. UnChicken Broth
4 c. Tomatoes, coarsely chopped
½ tsp. Sucanat
½ c. Tofu Sour Cream or Cashew Sour Cream
½ tsp. Sea salt
⅛ tsp. Black pepper

Heat the oil in a heavy saucepan over low heat. Add the onion, garlic, and mace. Cook, covered, for 5 minutes. Do not let brown. Sprinkle the flour over the onion mixture, and cook while stirring for 2 minutes. Whisk in the broth. Add the tomatoes and Sucanat. Bring to a boil, reduce heat, and simmer, uncovered, for 20 minutes. Let cool to room temperature. Purée in batches in a blender or food processor. Combine and stir together until smooth, then pour through a sieve into a bowl. Whisk in the sour cream, salt, and pepper. Chill thoroughly. Sprinkle with chopped chives before serving.

"COOL-AS-A-CUCUMBER" SOUP

1 T.	Cornstarch
1 c.	Cold Cashew Milk
¾ tsp.	Sea salt
⅛ tsp.	Black pepper
2 c.	Cucumbers, peeled and finely diced
¼ c.	Onion, chopped fine
1 T.	Corn oil
1 c.	UnChicken Broth
1 tsp.	Dried mint
1 c.	Cashew or Tofu Sour Cream

Combine the cornstarch, "milk," salt, and pepper. Bring to a boil, stirring constantly. Boil for 1 minute. Sauté the cucumbers and onion in the oil for 5 minutes. Combine with the sauce, broth, and mint. Cool. Blend 2 cups of this on high for 30 seconds until smooth. Mix with the rest. Stir in the "sour cream." Chill.

CORN AND POTATO CHOWDER–1

½ c.	Onions, chopped
1 ¼ tsp.	Corn oil
6 c.	UnChicken Broth
2 c.	Potatoes, cooked and cubed
2 ½ c.	Corn
⅛ tsp.	Cayenne pepper
½ tsp.	Savory

Sauté the onions in the oil. Combine with rest of ingredients and cook.

CORN AND POTATO CHOWDER–2

½ c.	Onions, diced
½ c.	Celery, diced
¼ c.	Bell pepper, chopped
1 tsp.	Corn oil
1 c.	Potatoes, raw and cubed
¾ c.	UnBeef Broth
2 c.	Creamed style corn
1 ½ c.	UnBeef Broth made with Cashew Milk

Sauté the onions, celery, and bell pepper in the corn oil. Stir in the potatoes and plain broth. Heat to boiling. Reduce heat and simmer until tender, but do not overcook. Add the corn and milk-broth and heat to the boiling point.

CORN AND TOMATO CHOWDER

½ tsp.	Non-dairy margarine
2 T.	Onions, chopped
2 T.	Unbleached white flour
1 c.	Tomato juice
2 c.	Canned tomatoes
1 ½ c.	Corn
½ tsp.	Sea salt
Pinch	Cayenne pepper
½ c.	Yeast , Pimento, or Notzarella Cheez

Melt the margarine. Sauté the onions. Blend in the flour. Gradually add the tomato juice. Stir in the rest of the ingredients except for the cheez. Simmer for 10 minutes. Stir in the cheez well.

CORN CHOWDER–1

¼ c.	Bell peppers, chopped
3 T.	Onions, chopped
1 tsp.	Corn oil
1 c.	Potatoes, cooked and cubed
Pinch	Cayenne pepper
½ c.	UnChicken Broth
2 c.	Creamed corn
1 ½ c.	Corn milk (equal parts of corn and UnChicken Broth well blended in a blender)
¼ tsp.	Sea salt

Sauté the bell peppers and onions in the oil. Combine with rest of ingredients and cook until it thickens.

CORN CHOWDER–2

½ c.	Onions, chopped
2 tsp.	Corn oil
6 c.	UnChicken Broth
2 c.	Potatoes, cooked and cubed
5 c.	Corn
⅛ tsp.	Cayenne pepper
½ tsp.	Savory

Sauté the onions in the oil until soft. Combine all ingredients and cook until the potatoes start to fall apart–about 30 minutes.

CORN CHOWDER DELUXE

1 c.	Mexican Chorizo UnSausage, cubed
2 T.	Corn oil
1 c.	Onion, chopped
½ c.	Celery, chopped

1 c.	Red bell pepper, chopped
½ c.	Green bell pepper, chopped
3 c.	Corn
1	Bay leaf
4 c.	UnChicken Broth
2 ½ c.	Potatoes, peeled and cut into ½-inch cubes
1 c.	Cashew Cream
½ tsp.	Sea salt
¼ tsp.	Black pepper

Brown the gluten in the oil. Add the onion, celery, and bell pepper and cook until the vegetables are softened. Add the corn and bay leaf, and cook, stirring, for 1 minute. Add the broth and simmer, stirring occasionally, for 30 minutes. Add the potatoes, "cream," salt, and pepper, and simmer, stirring occasionally, for 25 minutes, or until the potatoes are tender. Discard the bay leaf.
Variation: Use Italian UnSausage.

CORN SOUP

1 c.	Bell pepper
3 T.	Onions, minced
1 tsp.	Non-dairy margarine
4 c.	Corn
3 c.	UnChicken Broth
¼ tsp.	Cayenne pepper
½ tsp.	Sea salt

Sauté the bell peppers and onions in the margarine. Combine corn and broth in a blender, and blend slightly till "cream corn" consistency. Combine everything and cook for 20 minutes.
Variations: When done, add 2 cups of Yeast or Pimento Cheez and stir over low heat until the cheez is mixed in. Add 3 cups of cubed potatoes and 2 more cups of UnChicken broth to ingredients. Add 2 cups of squash or pumpkin to ingredients.

CREAM OF BROCCOLI SOUP

This tastes very much like oyster soup!

¾ tsp.	Non-dairy margarine
4 c.	Cashew milk
¼ tsp.	Garlic powder
¼ tsp.	Onion salt
Dash	Cayenne pepper
3 c.	Broccoli, cooked in UnChicken Broth and drained

Purée all ingredients together in a blender. Simmer for 5 minutes.

Variation: During the 5 minutes of simmering, stir in 1 cup of Yeast or Pimento Cheez.

CREAM OF CARROT SOUP

1 ½ c.	Onions, chopped
1 tsp.	Garlic, minced
1 tsp.	Corn oil
3 c.	Carrots, chopped and cooked
4 c.	UnChicken Broth made with Cashew Milk
½ tsp.	Sea salt
¼ tsp.	Cayenne pepper

Combine all ingredients, cook, and run through a blender until smooth. Heat just to the boiling point.

CREAM OF CAULIFLOWER SOUP

2 c.	Cauliflower, broken or cut into flowerets
2 T.	Onions, chopped
¼ tsp.	Garlic, minced
1 c.	Celery, chopped
¾ tsp.	Non-dairy margarine
¼ c.	Unbleached white flour
4 c.	UnChicken Broth
2 c.	Cashew Milk

Cook the cauliflower in boiling salted water until barely tender. Reserve ⅓ of the flowerets. Chop the rest of the cauliflower fine or run through a sieve or purée strainer. Sauté the onion, garlic, and celery in the margarine. Add the flour. Slowly add the broth. Add all the cauliflower and "milk" and heat through.

CREAM OF CELERY SOUP

1 ½ c.	Celery, diced
⅓ c.	Onions, chopped
¼ tsp.	Garlic, minced
1 c.	Salted boiling water
3 ½ c.	Medium White Sauce, made with UnChicken Broth

Cook the celery, onion, and garlic, covered, in the cup of boiling water until tender–about 13 minutes. Drain off the water, stir in the white sauce, and heat through.

CREAM OF CORN SOUP

1 c.	Cooked corn
2 c.	Thin White Sauce
1 T.	Onions, chopped

2 tsp.   Non-dairy margarine
¼ tsp.   Sea salt
¼ tsp.   Paprika
⅛ tsp.   Cayenne

Blend together in a blender, heat and serve.

CREAM OF MUSHROOM SOUP

¼ c.   Onions, chopped
2 c.   Mushrooms, chopped
1 tsp.   Garlic, minced
1 T.   Non-dairy margarine
1 T.   Cornstarch
2 c.   UnBeef Broth made with Cashew Milk

Sauté the onions, mushrooms, and garlic in the margarine until the onions are soft. Combine the cornstarch and broth. Add to the vegetables and cook until it thickens.

CREAM OF ONION SOUP

1 ½ c.   Onions, sliced
2 tsp.   Non-dairy margarine
5 c.   Thin White Sauce made with UnChicken Broth

Sauté the onions in the margarine. Add the White Sauce and cook slowly for 30 minutes.

CREAM OF PEA SOUP–1

4 c.   Peas (if frozen, thawed; if fresh, lightly steamed)
2 c.   UnChicken or UnBeef Broth made with Cashew Milk
4 ½ tsp. Non-dairy margarine

Blend the peas with the broth and margarine. Heat and serve.
Variation: Use 2 cups of Thin White Sauce made with UnChicken or UnBeef Broth.

CREAM OF PEA SOUP–2

1 tsp.   Non-dairy margarine
1 T.   Onions, chopped
2 c.   Peas, fresh or frozen, cooked
½ tsp.   Sea salt
1 tsp.   Sucanat
3 c.   Thin white sauce
       Paprika

Sauté the onions in the margarine. Combine all ingredients and process in a blender, then heat through.

CREAM OF PINTO BEAN AND TOMATO SOUP

¼ c.   Onions, sliced
1 tsp.   Corn oil
1 c.   Pinto beans, cooked
1 c.   Canned tomatoes, chopped
3 c.   Thin white sauce

Sauté the onions in the oil. Combine with beans and tomatoes and heat together. Put through a sieve or blender. Combine with the white sauce just before serving.

CREAM OF POTATO SOUP–1

1 c.   Onions, chopped fine
1 tsp.   Garlic, minced
2 T.   Bell pepper, chopped fine
2 T.   Celery, chopped fine
2 tsp.   Non-dairy margarine
1 T.   Unbleached white flour
4 c.   UnChicken Broth made with Cashew Milk
3 c.   Potatoes, peeled, cooked, and cubed
¼ c.   UnBacon, minced, or imitation bacon bits
1 T.   Parsley, minced
⅛ tsp.   Black or cayenne pepper

Sauté the onions, garlic, bell pepper, and celery in the margarine until soft. Stir in the flour well. Combine everything and cook until the soup thickens–about 15 minutes.

CREAM OF POTATO SOUP–2

1 c.   Mashed potatoes
2 c.   Thin White Sauce made with UnBeef or UnChicken Broth
       Paprika

Combine and heat through.

CREAMED LENTIL-CELERY SOUP

2 c.   Onion, diced
1 c.   Celery, chopped
2   Garlic cloves, mashed
1 T.   Corn oil
1 ½ c.   Lentils, sorted through and rinsed well
2   Bay leaves
¼ c.   Parsley, chopped
1 ½ tsp. Sea salt
2 tsp.   Dijon mustard

1 T.   Balsamic vinegar

Sauté the onion, celery, and garlic in the oil until soft. Combine everything but the mustard and vinegar. Bring to a boil, reduce heat, and simmer, partially covered, until the lentils are competely tender–about 45 minutes–stirring occasionally. Let cool a bit, purée in batches in a blender, then pass the purée through a food mill to remove the lentil skins. Put back in the pot, return to the heat, and stir in the mustard and vinegar. Thin with some water if necessary.

CREAMY ONION SOUP

2 ¾ c.	Onions, chopped
1 ½ tsp.	Garlic, minced
1 tsp.	Non-dairy margarine
1 c.	Potato, chopped
2 c.	Cashew Milk
1 c.	UnBeef, UnChicken, UnHam, or UnSausage Broth
1	Bay leaf
¼ tsp.	Sea salt
¼ tsp.	Cayenne pepper

Combine everything, bring to a boil, reduce heat, cover, and simmer for 20 minutes. Remove the bay leaf. Cool slightly, then run through a blender. Reheat if need be.

CREOLE SOUP

This really is Something Different!

1 T.	Bell pepper, chopped
1 T.	Red onions, chopped
1 tsp.	Non-dairy margarine
2 T.	Unbleached white flour
1 c.	Italian tomatoes, cooked
3 c.	UnBeef Broth
⅛ tsp.	Sea salt
⅛ tsp.	Cayenne pepper
½ tsp.	Balsamic vinegar

Sauté the bell pepper and onions in the margarine for 5 minutes. Stir in the flour and add the tomatoes and broth. Simmer for 15 minutes, then strain and add the salt, pepper, and vinegar.

CURRIED MUSHROOM SOUP

This is best made one day before so the flavors will mingle!

¼ c.	Unbleached white flour
2 c.	Onions
2 tsp.	Garlic, minced or crushed
2 tsp.	Corn oil
3 c.	Mushrooms, cleaned, stemmed, and sliced or chopped
4 ½ tsp.	Curry powder
¼ tsp.	Cayenne pepper
¼ tsp.	Sea salt
4 c.	UnChicken or UnBeef Broth

Put the flour in a heavy skillet, spreading it out. Put it on low heat. Stir with a wooden spoon occasionally. Within a few minutes the flour will turn a slightly darker shade and begin to smell "nutty." Then begin stirring continuously to prevent burning. When the flour has toasted and developed a rich aroma, remove it from the pan immediately and set aside. Sauté the onions and garlic in the oil over medium heat for 3 to 5 minutes. Add the mushrooms and sauté 2 to 3 minutes more. Sprinkle the curry powder, cayenne, and salt over the vegetables and stir gently. Add the toasted flour and stir to coat all the vegetables. Stir in the broth. Bring to a boil, lower the heat, and simmer for 15 to 20 minutes. When the vegetables are soft, transfer the soup– 2 cups at a time–to a blender and purée it. *Variations:* Instead of mushrooms, try cauliflower, broccoli, or zucchini. Stir in ⅓ cup of Cashew Milk before serving.

CURRIED SPLIT PEA SOUP

1 c.	Onion, minced
2 tsp.	Garlic, minced
1 T.	Curry powder
½ tsp.	Tumeric
1 tsp.	Mustard seeds (black preferred)
1 T.	Corn oil
8 c.	UnChicken Broth
2 c.	Yellow split peas
1	Bay leaf
2 tsp.	Sea salt
1 tsp.	Cayenne
½ c.	Tofu Yogurt
2 ½ T.	Lemon juice

Sauté the onion, garlic, curry powder, tumeric, and mustard seeds in the oil until the onion is soft. Combine everything but the yogurt and lemon juice. Bring to a boil, reduce heat and simmer, covered, 45 to 60 minutes, until the peas are tender. Cool a bit, take out bay leaf, then process in a blender or food processor to a coarse purée. Return to the saucepan. Just before serving, heat through and stir in the yogurt and lemon juice.

CURRY STEW

Our version of a Vietnamese-Indian recipe!

1 ½ c.	Onions, cut in large chunks
1 tsp.	Garlic, crushed
1 ¼ tsp.	Corn oil
3 T.	Curry powder
3 c.	UnChicken Broth
2 c.	Potatoes, cubed small
1 ½ c.	Carrots, sliced
1 ½ c.	Coconut milk

Sauté the onions and garlic in the oil. When the onions are transparent, add the curry powder and sauté for 2 more minutes, stirring constantly. Add the rest of ingredients EXCEPT the coconut milk and cook until the vegetables are done. Add the coconut milk and cook for 10 more minutes.

DAL SOUP

¼ c.	Bell pepper, chopped fine
3 T.	Onions, chopped
1 ½ tsp.	Corn oil
2 c.	Dal, dry
¾ tsp.	Sea salt
⅛ tsp.	Crushed red pepper
1 c.	Tomatoes
4 ½ c.	UnChicken Broth

Sauté the bell peppers and onions in the oil. Combine with rest of ingredients and cook.

DIETER'S BROTH

This is a tremendous help for those wanting to cut down on calories. However, if water retention is also a problem you might want to omit either the salt or soy sauce.

¼ c.	Soy sauce
½ c.	Tomato juice
1 ½ tsp.	Sea salt or salt substitute
½ tsp.	Garlic powder
4 c.	Cabbage
1 ½ c.	Celery
2 c.	Onions
¾ c.	Bell peppers
2 c.	Tomatoes
3 qt.	Water
¼ tsp.	Cayenne pepper
1 ½ tsp.	Nutritional Yeast

Combine everything except the nutritional yeast in a pot. Cook for 40 minutes. Take from heat and stir in the yeast. Purée in a blender or food processor if you like.

EASY DAYS VEGETABLE SOUP

1	10-oz. pkg. frozen cut green beans
1	10-oz. pkg. frozen peas and carrots
1	10-oz. pkg. frozen lima beans
1	10-oz. pkg. frozen corn
1	10-oz. pkg. frozen chopped spinach
4 c.	Canned tomatoes
1 ¼ c.	Cooked kidney beans, drained and rinsed
1 c.	Tomato sauce
1 T.	Minced onion flakes
1	Bay leaf
½ tsp.	Thyme
1 ½ tsp.	Basil
¼ tsp.	Garlic powder
1 ½ tsp.	Sea salt
½ tsp.	Black pepper
5 c.	UnBeef or UnChicken Broth, or water
1 T.	Corn oil
1 c.	Orzo, or other small pasta

Put everything but the pasta in a pot and bring to a boil, stirring occasionally, using a spoon to break up any clumps of frozen vegetables as well as the tomatoes. Cover, reduce heat, and simmer 45 minutes or until the vegetables are tender. Add the pasta, cover, and cook 10 to 15 more minutes, until the pasta is tender. Remove and discard the bay leaf before serving.

FRESH TOMATO SOUP

1 ½ c.	Onions, chopped
1 ¼ tsp.	Non-dairy margarine
1 c.	Potatoes, chopped
2 c.	Tomatoes, chopped
½ tsp.	Basil
1	Bay leaf
2 T.	Tomato paste
2 c.	UnBeef Broth
½ tsp.	Sea salt
¼ tsp.	Cayenne pepper
2 c.	Cashew Milk, hot

Sauté the onions in the margarine until transparent. Add the rest of the ingredients except for the "milk." Cover and simmer for 20 minutes. Remove from the heat, take out the bay leaf, and stir in the "milk."

Variation: Instead of Cashew Milk, use UnBeef, UnChicken, or UnSausage Broth, or plain water. If broth is used, cut the salt in half.

GARBANZO AND CABBAGE SOUP

3 T.	Onions, chopped
1 T.	Corn oil
1 ½ c.	Tomatoes, diced
2 c.	Cabbage, finely shredded
1 ½ c.	Potatoes, diced
4 c.	Water
5 c.	Cooked garbanzos
	Juice of half a lemon
1 tsp.	Paprika
½ c.	Parsley, minced
1 tsp.	Sea salt

Sauté the onions in the oil until soft. Add tomato and cabbage, stir well, then cover and simmer until the cabbage is cooked–about 10 minutes. Set aside. In a pot cook the potatoes in the water until tender–about 15 minutes. Strain off 2 cups of the liquid and purée the potatoes in a blender with 1 cup of the garbanzos until smooth. Add the blended beans and sautéed vegetables to the potatoes. Stir in the remaining beans. Add lemon juice, paprika, parsley, and salt. If needed, thin the soup with extra water to the desired consistency.

GARBANZO SOUP

2 T.	Corn oil
1 c.	Onion, chopped
1 c.	Celery, chopped
1 c.	Carrots, sliced
2 tsp.	Garlic, minced
1 c.	Potatoes, diced
5 c.	UnChicken Broth
½ tsp.	Sea salt
¼ tsp.	Cayenne
3 ¾ c.	Cooked garbanzos, drained

Sauté the onion, celery, and carrots in the oil until soft. Add garlic and sauté 2 more minutes. Put everything together and simmer until everything is well cooked. Purée half of this in a blender or food processor before serving.

GAZPACHO–1

3 T.	Onions, minced
2 tsp.	Corn oil
3 T.	Soy sauce
1 tsp.	Kitchen Bouquet
1 T.	Nutritional Yeast
⅛ tsp.	Sage, rubbed
2 c.	Tomato juice
2 c.	Tomatoes, finely chopped
2 c.	Tomatoes, chopped and then puréed
3 T.	Onions, finely chopped
¼ c.	Bell pepper, finely chopped
½ c.	Celery, finely chopped
¼ c.	Cooked Tomato Salsa
¼ tsp.	Sea salt

Sauté the onions in oil until transparent. Add soy sauce, Kitchen Bouquet, nutritional yeast, sage, and tomato juice. Simmer for 5 minutes. Cool to room temperature. Combine all ingredients and chill for a few hours. Serve with Cashew or Tofu Sour Cream.

GAZPACHO–2

1 c.	Canned tomatoes, crushed–or chopped fresh tomatoes
4 c.	Tomato juice
½ c.	Onions, finely chopped
½ c.	Cucumbers, finely chopped
½ c.	Bell pepper, finely chopped
½ c.	Salsa
4 tsp.	Soy sauce
⅛ tsp.	Garlic powder

Combine all (you may need to blend the garlic powder with some of the tomato juice in a blender to make sure it mixes) and chill for a few hours.

GAZPACHO–3

2 c.	Canned tomatoes with juice
¾ c.	Tomato juice
¾ tsp.	Garlic, minced
½ c.	Bell pepper, chopped
2 T.	Green onion, minced
3 T.	Parsley, chopped
¼ c.	Watercress, chopped
⅓ c.	Celery, chopped fine
2 tsp.	Olive oil
2 T.	Low sodium soy sauce
3 T.	Lemon juice
⅓ c.	Black olives, sliced

In a blender purée the tomatoes, juice, and garlic. Add the rest of the ingredients and blend thoroughly.
Variation: Serve with Nutritional Yeast so each one can mix in to taste.

GOLDEN CORN SOUP

¾ c.	Onions, chopped
1 tsp.	Non-dairy margarine

2 c.	Corn
¾ c.	UnChicken Broth made with Cashew Milk
½ tsp.	Sea salt
Pinch	Cayenne pepper
1 c.	Tomatoes, chopped
¾ c.	UnChicken Broth
½ tsp.	Oregano

Sauté the onions in the margarine, put all together and cook.

GREEN PEA SOUP

⅓ c.	Onions, coarsely chopped
½ tsp.	Garlic, minced
¾ tsp.	Non-dairy margarine
1 ½ c.	Green peas (if frozen, thawed, if fresh, lightly steamed)
1 c.	Potatoes, coarsely chopped
2 ½ c.	UnChicken or UnBeef Broth
⅛ tsp.	Sea salt
⅛ tsp.	Cayenne pepper
½ c.	Cashew Milk

Sauté the onions and garlic in the margarine until the onions are transparent. Add the peas, potatoes, broth, salt, and pepper, and bring to a boil. Reduce heat, cover and simmer for 20 minutes. Remove from heat and stir in the "milk." Cool a bit, then blend in a blender. Reheat if need be.
Variation: May be served chilled. If so, chill before adding the "milk," which should also be cold.

HUNGARIAN UNCHICKEN STEW

⅓ c.	UnBacon, chopped fine
2 c.	Onions, sliced thin
4 c.	UnChicken, cubed
2 T.	Paprika
½ tsp.	Sea salt
½ tsp.	Caraway seeds
1 tsp.	Garlic, crushed
½ c.	Tomato slices
1 c.	Bell pepper slices (half red and half green if possible)
4 c.	Potatoes, cut into small chunks
2 c.	UnChicken Broth

Brown the UnBacon in some oil and set aside. Sauté the onions until soft and set aside. Brown the UnChicken. Add the rest of the ingredients and simmer, covered, for 20 minutes or until the potatoes are done, adding extra broth if needed.

LENTIL AND TOMATO SOUP

½ c.	Lentils, dry
¾ c.	Onions, chopped
1 tsp.	Garlic, minced
1 ½ tsp.	Corn oil
4 c.	Tomatoes, chopped
1 c.	Tomato juice
3 ¾ c.	UnBeef Broth
¼ tsp.	Sea salt
¼ tsp.	Cayenne pepper

Pressure-cook the lentils. Sauté the onions and garlic in the oil until the onions are transparent. Add the rest of ingredients, cover, and simmer for 30 minutes.

LENTIL SOUP–1

2 ½ c.	Dry lentils
	Enough UnBeef or UnChicken Broth to cover the lentils with 2 inches of broth
1 c.	Bell pepper, chopped
3 T.	Onions, chopped
2 tsp.	Corn oil
¾ tsp.	Sea salt
⅛ tsp.	Cayenne pepper
2 c.	Tomatoes, chopped
¼ tsp.	Summer savory

Cook the lentils in the broth for about 30 minutes until they are soft. Sauté the bell peppers and onions in the oil. Combine with rest of ingredients and cook about 30 minutes more. If needed, add more broth or water to keep a soup consistency.

LENTIL SOUP–2

2 c.	Dry lentils
⅓ c.	Onions, chopped
½ c.	Celery, chopped
½ tsp.	Garlic, minced
2 tsp.	Corn oil
⅛ tsp.	Italian Herb Seasoning
¼ tsp.	Sage
1	Bay leaf
¼ tsp.	Cayenne pepper
2 c.	Potatoes, cooked and diced
1 c.	Carrots, cooked and sliced into rounds
1 c.	UnBacon, chopped fine
4 c.	UnChicken Broth

Pressure-cook the lentils. Sauté the onions, celery, and garlic in the corn oil. Combine all

ingredients and cook for 30 minutes.
Variation: Omit the gluten and use UnBeef Broth instead.

LENTIL SOUP–3

1 c.	Dry lentils
¾ c.	Onions, chopped
1 tsp.	Non-dairy margarine
2 c.	UnBeef or UnChicken Broth
¼ tsp.	Cayenne pepper

Pressure-cook the lentils. Sauté the onions in the margarine. Combine all ingredients and simmer for 1 hour.

LENTIL SOUP–4

1 c.	Lentils, dry
¾ c.	Onions, chopped
¾ c.	Celery, chopped
¼ tsp.	Garlic, minced
1 ½ tsp.	Corn oil
¾ c.	Carrots, chopped
1 c.	Tomatoes, chopped
⅛ tsp.	Basil
⅛ tsp.	Oregano
1	Bay leaf
1 tsp.	Sea salt
¾ c.	Potatoes, diced
3 c.	UnBeef or UnChicken Broth

Pressure-cook the lentils for 5 minutes. Sauté the onion, celery, and garlic in the oil. Put everything together and cook for 30 minutes.

LIMA BEAN SOUP

2 T.	UnBacon, minced
1 T.	Corn oil
½ c.	Onion, chopped fine
2 c.	UnChicken Broth
1 ¾ c.	Lima beans, fresh or frozen (thawed)
	Sea salt
	Pepper
⅓ c.	Green onion, sliced thin

Brown the gluten in some oil until crisp, and drain on paper towels. In the 1 tablespoon of oil sauté the onion until soft. Add the broth and beans and simmer for 8 minutes or until the beans are tender. Add the salt and pepper. Purée the soup in a food processor or blender, return to the pan, and heat until hot. Serve with the gluten and green onions to be sprinkled on the soup as desired.

MASHED POTATO AND CHEEZ SOUP

1 c.	Bell pepper, chopped fine
¼ c.	Onions, chopped
1 tsp.	Non-dairy margarine
3 c.	Mashed potatoes
4 c.	UnBeef or UnChicken Broth
⅛ tsp.	Cayenne pepper
¼ tsp.	Sea salt
1 c.	Yeast , Pimento, or Notzarella Cheez

Sauté the bell pepper and onions in the margarine. Combine all ingredients except the cheez, and simmer 30 minutes, adding more broth if needed. Add the cheez and stir in well.
Variation: Make the broth with Cashew Milk instead of water.

MEXICAN SUMMER STEW

2 c.	Onions, sliced ¼-inch thick
2 tsp.	Garlic, minced
2 T.	Corn oil
1 qt.	Water or UnChicken or UnBeef Broth
4 c.	Zucchini, sliced ½-inch thick
2 ⅔ c.	Yellow squash, sliced
⅔ c.	Bell pepper, cut into ½-inch dice
2 c.	Peas
3 c.	Tomatoes, chopped
3 T.	Soy sauce
3 T.	Chili powder
1 T.	Ground cumin
3 c.	UnBeef, UnChicken, or UnPork, chopped
1 T.	Catsup
2 c.	Corn
1 T.	Cornstarch or arrowroot
¼ c.	Cold water

Sauté the onions and garlic in the oil until soft. Combine everything but the cornstarch and water. Simmer 30 minutes. During the final minutes, dissolve the cornstarch in the water and add to the stew. Stir until thickened.

MINESTRONE–1

1 ½ tsp.	Non-dairy margarine
¼ c.	Onions, chopped
1 ½ tsp.	Garlic, minced
½ c.	Peas
½ c.	Zucchini or other squash, scrubbed and sliced (not peeled)

½ c.   Potatoes, diced
½ c.   Carrots, diced
3 T.   Celery, thinly sliced
1 ½ c. Tomatoes, coarsely chopped
4 c.   UnChicken Broth
½ tsp. Basil, dried
1   Bay leaf
1 ½ tsp. Parsley, dried
⅛ tsp. Sea salt
Dash   Black or cayenne pepper
2 T.   Uncooked spaghetti broken in
        1-inch pieces
¼ c.   Cooked dried beans of choice,
        drained
⅛ c.   UnBacon, chopped fine
2 c.   UnHam or UnSausage, ground
        and fried

Melt the margarine in a skillet and sauté the onions and garlic until the onions are soft and lightly browned. Stir in the peas, zucchini, potatoes, carrots, celery, tomatoes, broth, basil, bay leaf, parsley, salt, and pepper. Bring to a boil, reduce heat and simmer partially covered for 25 minutes. Add spaghetti, beans, and gluten and cook for 15 to 20 more minutes until the spaghetti is done.

MINESTRONE–2

1 c.   Cooked white beans
¼ c.   Green split peas
¼ c.   Yellow split peas
½ c.   Cabbage, shredded
1 c.   Onion, chopped
1 c.   Mushrooms, diced
1 tsp. Garlic, minced
⅓ c.   Tomato paste
4 ½ c. UnChicken or UnBeef Broth
2 T.   Low sodium soy sauce (omit if using
        UnBeef Broth)
2 tsp. Corn oil
¼ c.   Macaroni, small

Combine everything but the macaroni and cook for 30 minutes. Add the macaroni and simmer until it is done.

MOCK "CREAM OF MUSHROOM" SOUP

1 c.   Celery, minced
½ c.   Onions, minced
2 tsp. Corn oil
2 T.   Unbleached white flour

2 c.   Garbanzos, cooked
4 c.   Thin White Sauce
½ tsp. Sea salt
¼ c.   Parsley, minced
1 T.   Nutritional Yeast

Sauté the celery and onion in the oil until tender. Stir in the flour well. Add the remaining ingredients and heat through.

MONASTERY POTATO SOUP

¾ c.   Onions, chopped
1 tsp. Garlic, minced
1 ¼ tsp. Corn oil
¼ c.   Celery, chopped fine
1 c.   Mushrooms, chopped
1 ½ tsp. Jalapeños, minced
2 c.   Potatoes, cubed
1 c.   Carrots, chopped small
½ tsp. Sea salt
2 c.   Water
¼ c.   Nutritional yeast

Sauté the onions and garlic in the oil until the onions are transparent. Combine with rest of ingredients, bring to a boil, reduce heat, and simmer for 30 minutes. Take off the heat and stir in the nutritional yeast.
Variation: When sautéing the vegetables, add 2 tablespoons of curry powder, and do not add the nutritional yeast at the end.

MONASTERY VEGETABLE SOUP

1 c.   Onions, chopped
¼ c.   Celery, chopped fine
½ c.   Bell pepper, chopped
1 c.   Mushrooms, chopped
3 c.   UnBeef or UnChicken, cubed
4 tsp. Corn oil
2 tsp. Garlic, minced
3 c.   Potatoes, cubed
1 ½ c. Yellow squash, cubed
1 c.   Green beans
¾ c.   Lima beans
¾ c.   Carrots, chopped small
¾ tsp. Crushed red pepper flakes
6 c.   Water
3 c.   Canned tomatoes, mashed
        (use juice)
¼ c.   Tomato paste
3 T.   Parsley, chopped
¼ tsp. Basil
¼ tsp. Oregano
1 ½ tsp. Sea salt

Sauté the onions, celery, bell pepper, mushrooms, and gluten in the oil until the onions are transparent. Add the garlic and sauté a little more. Combine with rest of ingredients, bring to a boil, reduce heat, and simmer for 45 minutes or until the potatoes begin to fall apart.

MULLIGATAWNY SOUP

1 ½ c.	Onions, chopped
1 tsp.	Garlic, minced
2 tsp.	Curry powder (Madras style preferred)
2 tsp.	Corn oil
1 c.	Carrots, chopped
2 c.	Potatoes, chopped
1 c.	Tomato juice
5 c.	UnBeef Broth
½ tsp.	Sea salt
¼ tsp.	Cayenne pepper

Sauté the onions, garlic, and curry powder in the oil until the onions are transparent. Add the rest of the ingredients and bring to a boil. Reduce heat, cover, and simmer for 30 minutes. Cool a bit, then blend in a blender. Reheat if need be.

ONION SOUP

1 tsp.	Corn oil
4 c.	Onions, thinly sliced
2 tsp.	Garlic, minced
1 qt.	UnBeef, UnChicken, UnHam, or UnSausage Broth

Combine everything and cook uncovered over low heat, stirring occasionally, for 20 to 30 minutes. Add the broth and cook for 20 minutes or more—until done.

PEASE PORRIDGE

Remember the nursery rhyme? Well, here it is!

2 c.	Dry green split peas
2 c.	Water
1 tsp.	Sea salt
2 tsp.	Non-dairy margarine
¼ tsp.	Paprika

Pick over the split peas and discard any discolored ones. Wash them thoroughly under cold running water and continue to wash until the draining water runs clear. In a heavy 3 to 4-quart saucepan, bring the water to a boil. Drop in the peas slowly so the water continues to boil. Reduce the heat and simmer, partially covered, for 1 ½ hours, or until the peas can be easily mashed against the side of the pan with a spoon. Drain the peas in a colander and purée them in a food mill or force them through a fine sieve set over a large bowl. Return the peas to the pan, stir in salt, margarine, and paprika, and cook over low heat, stirring constantly, until the purée is heated through. Serve at once from a heated dish.

POTATO SOUP

¾ c.	Onions, chopped
1 tsp.	Garlic, minced
3 T.	Bell pepper, chopped
1 tsp.	Corn oil
3 c.	Potatoes, cubed
Pinch	Cayenne pepper
¼ tsp.	Sea salt
3 c.	UnBeef Broth

Sauté the onions, garlic, and bell pepper in the oil. Combine ingredients and cook until the vegetables are done.
Variation: Add 2 cups of corn and omit the garlic.

PORTUGUESE BEAN SOUP

Goodness with a difference!

4 c.	Cooked beans (usually red beans)
¼ c.	Red onions, sliced
1 ½ c.	Potatoes, diced
1 ½ tsp.	Sea salt
1 tsp.	Paprika
¼ tsp.	Cayenne
1 T.	Corn oil
½ c.	Uncooked macaroni
1 c.	Tomato sauce
5 c.	Water
2 c.	Cabbage, chopped
2 T.	Lemon juice

Combine and cook 25 to 30 minutes.

POTATO AND MUSHROOM SOUP

6 c.	Potatoes, diced
2 qt.	Water
2 tsp.	Sea salt
1 c.	Red onions, chopped well
2 tsp.	Garlic, minced
2 c.	Mushrooms, sliced
2 ½ tsp.	Non-dairy margarine
2 T.	Unbleached white flour
½ tsp.	Black pepper
2 tsp.	Poultry seasoning
3 T.	MSG

| ⅔ c. | Nutritional yeast flakes |
| ½ tsp. | Caraway seed |

Begin to boil the potatoes in the water with the salt. Sauté the onions, garlic, and mushrooms in the margarine. Add the flour and stir it in well. Add this and all the rest of the ingredients to the boiling potatoes. Cook until the potatoes start to fall apart.

POTATO SOUP WITH GARLIC AND GREENS

2 c.	Onion, diced
4	Garlic cloves, peeled
2 T.	Jalapeño, seeded and minced
4 tsp.	Corn oil
5 c.	Potatoes, cubed
3 c.	Swiss chard or spinach, coarsely chopped
3 c.	Tomatoes, coarsely chopped
2 c.	Canned tomatoes
1 qt.	UnChicken or UnBeef Broth
1 tsp.	Sea salt
½ tsp.	Black pepper
3 T.	Balsamic vinegar

Sauté the onion, garlic, and jalapeños in the oil until the onion is soft. Combine everything in a big pot and cover. Bring to a boil over high heat, reduce heat, and simmer, covered, for 35 minutes, or until the potatoes are soft. Cool slightly and purée in blender or food processor.

POTATO-CABBAGE SOUP

½ c.	Bell pepper, chopped
¼ c.	Onions, chopped
1 ¼ tsp.	Corn oil
2 c.	Cabbage, chopped
2 c.	Potatoes, peeled and chopped in pieces no bigger than 1 inch
¼ tsp.	Sea salt
⅛ tsp.	Cayenne pepper
2 ¼ c.	UnBeef or UnChicken Broth

Sauté the bell pepper and onion in the oil until the onion is soft. Combine with the rest of the ingredients and cook for about 30 minutes or until the potatoes are done.
Variation: Use squash instead of cabbage.

POTATO-ONION SOUP

3 c.	Onions, cubed
1 T.	Non-dairy margarine
2 tsp.	Garlic, minced
4 c.	Potatoes, cubed
7 c.	UnChicken Broth made with Cashew Milk
¼ tsp.	Cayenne pepper

Sauté the onions in the margarine until soft. Add the garlic and sauté 1 more minute. Add everything else and cook until the potatoes start to fall apart.

POTATO-SPINACH SOUP

1 ½ tsp.	Garlic, minced
1 c.	Onion, chopped
3 c.	Potatoes, peeled and cut into 2-inch pieces
2 T.	Corn oil
2 ½ c.	Mexican Chorizo UnSausage, cubed
1	Bay leaf
¾ tsp.	Sea salt
¼ tsp.	Cayenne
4 c.	Mexican Chorizo UnSausage broth
2 c.	Water
2 c.	Spinach

Sauté the garlic, onion, and potatoes in the oil until the onion is soft. Add the gluten, bay leaf, salt, pepper, UnSausage broth, and water, and bring to a boil. Simmer, uncovered, stirring occasionally, for 45 minutes. Stir in the spinach and simmer 10 more minutes.

ROASTED TOMATO SOUP

Something different and worthwhile!

6 lb.	Tomatoes, cored
¼ c.	Olive oil
2 ¼ tsp.	Garlic cloves, minced
1 tsp.	Thyme
1 ½ c.	Onion, chopped
2 tsp.	Olive oil
2 ¼ tsp.	Dried basil
2 c.	UnChicken Broth
½ c.	Cashew Cream
3 ½ tsp.	Sea salt
¼ tsp.	Black pepper
¼ c.	Fresh basil

Put the tomatoes in a baking pan large enough to hold them in one layer. Drizzle them with ¼ cup of the oil and sprinkle them with the garlic and thyme. Roast the tomatoes at 350°, turning them occasionally, for 1 hour. Sauté the onions in the 2 teaspoons of oil until they are soft. Add the tomatoes and dried basil, and cook, stirring, for 5 minutes. Add the broth, bring to a boil, and simmer, stirring, for 5 minutes. Force the mixture through a food mill (medium disk) into a bowl, or process in a blender or food processor for 10 seconds (in batches) and return it to the cooking pot. Stir in the "cream," salt, and pepper. Keep the soup warm. Put a little broth or water with the fresh basil in a blender and blend thoroughly. Stir into the soup.

RUSSIAN VEGETABLE SOUP

⅓ c.	Onions, chopped
½ c.	Cabbage, shredded
1 ¼ tsp.	Non-dairy margarine
2 c.	Potatoes, chopped
1 c.	Parsnips, chopped (carrots, if none are available or you don't like parsnips)
1 c.	Carrots, chopped
2 T.	Parsley, chopped
¼ tsp.	Basil
¼ tsp.	Oregano
5 c.	UnBeef Broth
¼ tsp.	Sea salt
¼ tsp.	Cayenne pepper

Sauté the onions and cabbage in the margarine until they are transparent. Add the rest of the ingredients, bring to a boil, reduce heat, cover, and simmer for 30 minutes. Let cool a bit, then run through a blender until smooth.

SAVANNAH UNBEEF AND OKRA STEW

2 c.	UnBeef, cubed
3 T.	Olive oil
1 ½ c.	Onion, chopped
2 tsp.	Garlic, minced
2 c.	Canned tomatoes, drained (keeping back 1 cup of juice) and chopped
3 c.	UnBeef Broth
½ tsp.	Sea salt
1	Bay leaf
½ tsp.	Oregano, crumbled
2 tsp.	Louisiana Hot Sauce
1 ½ c.	Okra, cut into ¾-inch pieces

Brown the gluten in the oil. Add the onions and sauté until soft. Add the garlic and sauté 1 more minute. Combine everything but the okra and simmer together, stirring occasionally, for 30 minutes. Add the okra and simmer 15 more minutes, stirring occasionally, until the okra is tender.

SHCHI-1

1 can	Loma Linda "Big Franks"
1 qt.	Sauerkraut, drained
1 c.	Onions, finely minced
4 c.	UnBeef Broth
2 ½ tsp.	Corn oil
1	Bay leaf
¼ tsp.	Black pepper
2 c.	Potatoes, diced
½ tsp.	Caraway seeds
	Liquid from the "Big Franks"

Pour off the liquid from the Big Franks and reserve it. Grind the Franks in a food processor or grinder. Add all the ingredients, including the Big Frank liquid, and cook for 45 minutes.
Variation: Instead of Big Franks use 2 cups of UnSausage, but retain the UnBeef Broth.

SHCHI-2

2 c.	Cabbage, coarsely shredded
⅓ c.	Wine vinegar
1 tsp.	Sea salt
2 c.	Water
½ c.	Onions, chopped
2 tsp.	Corn oil
2 c.	Canned tomatoes
5 c.	UnBeef Broth
1	Bay leaf
½ c.	Carrot, grated
1 tsp.	Caraway seeds
⅛ tsp.	White pepper
2 c.	Potatoes, diced

Combine the cabbage, vinegar, salt, and water. Bring to a boil and cook, partially covered, for 20 minutes. While cabbage is cooking, sauté onions in the oil. Add tomatoes, broth, bay leaf, carrot, caraway, and pepper. Simmer. When cabbage is done, drain it, saving the liquid. Add it to simmering soup along with the potatoes. Simmer at least 30 to 45 minutes. If soup is not tart enough, add some of the reserved cabbage juice. Serve with Cashew or Tofu Sour Cream.

SMOKY BLACK BEAN AND VEGETABLE SOUP

This delivers!

1 ½ c.	Onions, coarsely chopped
¾ c.	Celery, sliced thin
¾ c.	Carrots, chopped
2 T.	Olive oil
1 T.	Garlic, minced

1 ½ T.	Canned or dried Chipotle chilies, seeded and minced
2	Bay leaves
2 tsp.	Ground cumin
2 tsp.	Basil
1 tsp.	Chili powder
1 tsp.	Oregano
4 c.	Cooked black beans
3 ½ c.	Canned tomatoes, chopped, with liquid
4 c.	UnChicken Broth
4 c.	Water
1 tsp.	Sea salt

In a large soup pot sauté the onions, celery, and carrots in the oil until the onions are soft. Add the garlic and sauté 1 more minute. Add the chilies, bay leaves, cumin, basil, chili powder, and oregano and sauté 2 more minutes. Stir in the rest of the ingredients and bring to a boil. Lower heat and cook, partially covered, for 1 to 2 hours.

SOUP THICKENER

For each 2 cups of soup, melt 1 tablespoon of margarine and stir in 1 tablespoon of unbleached white flour or 1 teaspoon of potato flour (this is best). Cook slowly until smooth, stirring constantly–about 5 minutes. Add a little of the hot soup, stir well and pour into the rest of the soup. Reheat the soup, stirring constantly.

SOUR CREAM TOMATO SOUP

2 T.	Onions, minced fine
1 tsp.	Corn oil
2 c.	Tomato juice
¼ tsp.	Sea salt
Pinch	Cayenne pepper
Pinch	Dill weed
1 c.	Tofu Sour Cream or Cashew Sour Cream

Sauté the onions in the oil. Add rest of ingredients except the "sour cream" and simmer for 30 minutes. Just before serving blend in the "sour cream."

SPICY TOMATO SOUP

¼ c.	Onions, chopped
¼ tsp.	Garlic, minced
1 tsp.	Jalapeños, minced
2 T.	Bell pepper, chopped
1 tsp.	Non-dairy margarine
1 T.	Unbleached white flour
2 c.	Hot water
1 c.	Tomatoes, chopped
¼ tsp.	Sea salt

Sauté the onions, garlic, jalapeños, and bell pepper in the margarine for 6 minutes. Add flour and blend, then add the hot water gradually while stirring. Add tomatoes and salt. Simmer for 15 minutes.

SPICY VEGETABLE SOUP

2 ½ c.	Onion, sliced
2 T.	Corn oil
1 T.	Garlic, minced
3 c.	Cooked garbanzos or white beans, drained
1	Bay leaf
6 c.	UnChicken Broth
3 c.	Tomatoes, canned or fresh, coarsely chopped
1 T.	Jalapeño, sliced
2 ¼ c.	Carrots, coarsely chopped
2 ¼ c.	Potatoes, coarsely chopped
½ tsp.	Sea salt
¼ tsp.	Black pepper
3 c.	Zucchini, sliced thick
¼ tsp.	Cayenne
1 c.	Parsley, chopped

Sauté the onion in the oil until soft. Add the garlic and cook 1 more minute. Combine everything in a pot. Bring to a boil, reduce heat, and simmer, covered, for 30 minutes.

SPINACH SOUP

¾ c.	Onions, chopped
1 tsp.	Garlic, minced
1 ½ tsp.	Non-dairy margarine
½ c.	Potatoes, chopped
¼ c.	Carrots, chopped
1 c.	Tomatoes, chopped
2 T.	Parsley
1	Bay leaf
2 ½ c.	UnBeef or UnChicken Broth
⅛ tsp.	Sea salt
¼ tsp.	Cayenne pepper
2 c.	Spinach, finely shredded

Sauté the onions and garlic in the margarine until transparent. Add everything else except the spinach. Bring to a boil, reduce heat, cover and simmer for 30 minutes. Let cool a bit, then run through a blender until smooth. Return to saucepan, add the spinach and simmer for 10 minutes.

SPLIT PEA SOUP–1

Now this does what it is supposed to!

2 ½ c.	Dry split peas
	Enough UnBeef or UnChicken Broth to cover the peas with 2 inches of broth
1 c.	Bell peppers, chopped
3 T.	Onions, chopped
2 tsp.	Corn oil
¾ tsp.	Sea salt
⅛ tsp.	Cayenne pepper
2 c.	Tomatoes, chopped
¼ tsp.	Summer savory

Cook the peas in the broth for about 30 minutes until they are soft. Sauté the bell peppers and onions in the oil. Combine with rest of ingredients and cook about 30 minutes more. When done the peas will be "dissolved." If needed, add more broth or water to keep a soup consistency.

SPLIT PEA SOUP–2

2 c.	Split peas
⅓ c.	Onions, chopped
½ c.	Celery, chopped
½ tsp.	Garlic, minced
2 tsp.	Corn oil
⅛ tsp.	Italian Herb Seasoning
¼ tsp.	Sage
1	Bay leaf
¼ tsp.	Cayenne pepper
2 c.	Potatoes, diced and cooked in water
1 c.	Carrots, sliced into rounds and cooked in water
1 c.	UnBacon, minced or chopped fine
4 c.	UnChicken Broth

Pressure-cook the split peas. Sauté the onions, celery, and garlic in the corn oil. Combine all ingredients and cook for 30 minutes.
Variations: Omit the UnBacon and use UnBeef broth instead. Use lentils instead of split peas.

SPLIT PEA SOUP–3

1 c.	Green split peas, dry
¾ c.	Onions, chopped
1 tsp.	Non-dairy margarine
2 c.	UnBeef or UnChicken Broth
¼ tsp.	Cayenne pepper

Pressure-cook the split peas. Sauté the onions in the margarine. Combine all ingredients and simmer for 1 hour.

"THREE SISTERS" SOUP

The American Indians understood the nutritive value of combining dried beans, corn, and squash–so much so that they referred to them as "the three sisters." I think you will agree.

3 T.	Onions, chopped
1 ½ tsp.	Corn oil
2 c.	Cooked beans
2 c.	Corn
2 c.	Squash, chopped
½ tsp.	Sea salt
⅛ tsp.	Cayenne pepper
3 c.	UnBeef Broth

Sauté the onions in the oil. Combine with rest of ingredients and cook.

TOFU GUMBO

2 c.	Yellow onions, diced
1 c.	Celery, sliced ¼-inch thick
4 ½ tsp.	Garlic, sliced
1 T.	Corn oil
1 ½ c.	Canned crushed tomatoes
½ c.	Carrots, sliced ¼-inch thick
4 c.	Okra, sliced ¼-inch thick
1 c.	Red bell pepper, diced
1 c.	Green bell pepper, diced
1 c.	Yellow squash, sliced
¾ c.	Corn
1 T.	Cajun Spice
1 tsp.	Paprika
½ tsp.	Fenugreek
¼ tsp.	Hot pepper flakes
½ tsp.	Sea salt
¼ tsp.	Black pepper
10 oz.	Tofu, frozen, pressed and cubed

Sauté the onions, celery, and garlic in the oil until soft. Combine everything but the tofu, bring to a boil, and simmer for 20 minutes. Add the tofu and simmer 10 more minutes.

TOFU STEW

12 oz.	Tofu, frozen, pressed, and cubed
1 c.	Onion, chopped
½ c.	Celery, chopped
3 T.	Corn oil

1 T.	Garlic, sliced
2 ¾ c.	Heavenly Broth
2 c.	Potatoes, cut into ½-inch chunks
½ c.	Button mushrooms, quartered
½ c.	Turnips, cut into ½-inch chunks
½ c.	Parsnips, cut into ½-inch chunks
½ c.	Carrots, sliced
½ c.	Soy sauce
½ tsp.	Ground ginger
½ c.	Yellow squash, sliced ¼-inch thick
½ c.	Zucchini, sliced ¼-inch thick
½ tsp.	Szechuan peppercorns
⅛ tsp.	Black pepper
½ tsp.	Sea salt
4 T.	Green onions, chopped

Sauté the tofu, onion, and celery in the oil until the onion is soft. Add the garlic and sauté 1 more minute. Add everything else but the green onions, bring to a boil, reduce heat, and simmer until the potatoes and turnips are very soft. Serve garnished with the green onions.

TOMATO BEAN CORN CHOWDER

1 tsp.	Garlic, minced
½ c.	Onion, cut into ¼-inch dice
¼ c.	Celery, cut into ¼-inch dice
2 tsp.	Corn oil
3 ¾ c.	Tomatoes, cut into ¼-inch dice
4 c.	Water
1 ¼ c.	Potatoes, peeled and cut into ¼-inch dice
1 c.	Cooked white beans
1 c.	Corn
3	Dashes of Tabasco Sauce
Pinch	Black pepper
¾ tsp.	Sea salt

Sauté the garlic, onion, and celery in the oil until soft. Combine everything, bring to a boil, reduce heat, and simmer 30 minutes.

TOMATO CONSOMMÉ

Unusual…and unusually good!

1 lb.	Tomatoes, quartered
3 c.	Tomato juice
1 T.	Corn oil
¾ c.	Celery, chopped
¾ c.	Onion, chopped
½ c.	Parsley, chopped
1	Whole clove
1	Garlic clove
½	Bay leaf

1 ½ T.	Tomato paste
¼ tsp.	Thyme
½ tsp.	Coriander seeds
2 c.	UnBeef Broth
¼ tsp.	Cayenne
½ tsp.	Sea salt

Put the tomatoes, tomato juice, oil, celery, onions, parsley, cloves, garlic, bay leaf, tomato paste, thyme, and coriander seeds. Purée thoroughly. Pour into a nonreactive pot and add the broth, cayenne, and salt. Bring to a boil, reduce heat, and simmer, covered, for 15 minutes. Uncover and simmer 10 more minutes.

TOMATO SOUP–1

This is fabulous the first day and legendary a day or so later when the flavors have blended to perfection.

1 tsp.	Non-dairy margarine
¼ tsp.	Rosemary
¼ tsp.	Basil
¼ tsp.	Sea salt
⅛ tsp.	Cayenne pepper
2 c.	Tomatoes, chopped
1 c.	Tomato sauce
⅓ c.	Onions, chopped
1 tsp.	Garlic, minced
½	Bay leaf
1 c.	Frozen lima beans, thawed
2 c.	Water

Combine all ingredients and cook for 30 minutes.

TOMATO SOUP–2

¼ c.	Onions, chopped
1 tsp.	Non-dairy margarine
1 ½ tsp.	Unbleached white flour
2 ½ c.	Water
2 c.	Tomatoes, chopped
1 c.	Carrots, chopped
½ tsp.	Basil
2 T.	Parsley, minced
1 tsp.	Sea salt
¼ tsp.	Black or cayenne pepper

Sauté the onions in the margarine until they are soft. Add the flour and stir in well. Gradually add the water, stirring constantly. Add the rest of the ingredients and cook together for 30 minutes.

TOMATO SOUP–3

1 ½ c.	Onion, chopped
⅛ tsp.	Thyme

½ tsp.	Basil
¼ tsp.	Oregano
¼ tsp.	Black pepper
2 tsp.	Non-dairy margarine
5 c.	Tomatoes, diced
3 T.	Tomato paste
¼ c.	Unbleached white flour
3 ¾ c.	UnChicken Broth
1 tsp.	Sucanat
1 c.	Cashew Cream

Sauté the onion, thyme, basil, oregano, and pepper in the margarine until the onion is soft. Add the tomatoes and tomato paste, blending well. Simmer for 10 minutes. Put the flour and ¼ cup of the broth in a blender, blend thoroughly, and stir into the tomato mixture. Add the rest of the broth and simmer 30 more minutes, stirring frequently. Let this cool, then purée in a blender or food processor. Return to the pot and add the Sucanat and "cream." Heat through, stirring occasionally.

TOMATO SOUP-4

4 c.	Tomatoes, chopped
1 ¼ c.	Potatoes, peeled and diced
2 tsp.	Sucanat
1 tsp.	Sea salt
¼ tsp.	Black pepper
1 T.	Basil, dried
1 c.	UnChicken Broth
½ c.	Cashew or Tofu Sour Cream

In a saucepan put the tomatoes, potatoes, Sucanat, salt, pepper, and basil. Cook, covered, for 20 minutes until the potatoes are tender, stirring frequently. Add the broth and cook for another 2 to 3 minutes. Put through a sieve or food mill, and return to the pan. Just before serving take out 1 cup of the soup and mix it with the "sour cream," then put it back into the soup and mix it in well.

TOMATO SOUP WITH RICE

½ c.	Bell pepper, chopped
⅓ c.	Onion, chopped
½ tsp.	Garlic, minced
2 tsp.	Corn oil
5 c.	Tomatoes, chopped
1 ½ c.	Okra, sliced, or green beans, cut in 1-inch pieces
¾ tsp.	Sea salt
½ tsp.	Basil
⅛ tsp.	Dill weed
¼ tsp.	Cayenne pepper
1 ½ c.	Cooked rice or barley
1 c.	UnBeef or UnChicken Broth

Sauté the bell peppers, onions, and garlic in the oil. Combine with rest of ingredients and cook.

TOMATO-MUSHROOM SOUP

First Class!

1 c.	Onion, chopped
¾ tsp.	Garlic, minced
1 T.	Non-dairy margarine
4 c.	Mushrooms (fresh only), sliced
2 ½ c.	UnChicken Broth
¼ c.	Water
6 T.	Tomato paste
½ tsp.	Sea salt
¼ tsp.	Black pepper

Sauté the onion and garlic in the margarine until the onion is soft. Add the mushrooms and cook, covered, about 5 minutes or till the mushrooms are tender. Stir in the broth, water, tomato paste, salt, and pepper. Bring to boiling, reduce the heat, and simmer, covered, for 20 minutes.

TOMATO VEGETABLE CREAM SOUP

3 T.	Onions, chopped
½ tsp.	Garlic, minced
1 tsp.	Non-dairy margarine
1 c.	Tomatoes, chopped
1 ½ c.	Mixed vegetables, chopped if need be
2 c.	Thin White Sauce
⅛ tsp.	Basil
Pinch	Dill weed
1 ½ tsp.	Corn flour (not meal, though it can be used)
¼ tsp.	Sea salt

Sauté the onions and garlic in the margarine. Combine all and cook.
Variation: Make the white sauce with UnBeef or UnChicken Broth and cut the salt in half.

UNBEEF MINESTRONE SOUP

2 c.	UnBeef, cubed
½ c.	Onion, chopped
1 c.	Celery, sliced
2 T.	Corn oil
1 tsp.	Sea salt
¼ tsp.	Black pepper
2 c.	Canned tomato sauce

2 ½ c.	UnBeef Broth
2 c.	Cooked kidney beans
¼ tsp.	Oregano
Pinch	Thyme
¼ c.	Uncooked macaroni
¼ c.	Parsley, chopped

Sauté the gluten, onion, and celery together in the oil until the gluten is browned and the vegetables are soft. Add everything else except the macaroni and parsley. Cover and simmer for 20 minutes. Add the macaroni and cook for 10 more minutes–until tender. Stir in the parsley.

UNCHICKEN NOODLE SOUP

1 c.	Onions, chopped
1 tsp.	Garlic, minced
2 T.	Bell pepper, chopped
1 ½ tsp.	Corn oil
1 c.	UnChicken or Soy Grits UnChicken
3 c.	Mixed vegetables, chopped if need be
3 c.	UnChicken Broth
¼ tsp.	Black pepper
½ c.	Spaghetti or other noodles

Sauté the onions, garlic, and bell pepper in the oil. Combine with the rest of the ingredients–except for the pasta–and cook together for 30 minutes. Meanwhile cook the pasta and drain it. At the end of the 30 minutes, add the pasta and cook for 5 more minutes.
Variation: For UnChicken Rice Soup use 2 ½ cups of cooked rice instead of pasta.

UNFISH SOUP

1 c.	Green onions, chopped fine
⅓ c.	Celery, chopped fine
1 ½ tsp.	Corn oil
1 c.	Unbleached white flour
3 qt.	Chicken-like Broth
1 c.	Canned tomato sauce
1 T.	Lemon juice
2 c.	UnFish, cut in 1-inch cubes
1 bag	Zatarain's Crab Boil
½ tsp.	Cayenne pepper

Sauté the onions and celery in the oil. Brown the flour and add it to the onions and celery. Combine everything and cook for 20-30 minutes. Remove the bag of crab boil before serving.

UNSHRIMP AND CORN SOUP

3 ½ c.	Water
3 ½ c.	UnShrimp Broth
½ tsp.	Cayenne pepper
1 c.	Onion, finely chopped
½ c.	Parsley, finely chopped
1 ½ tsp.	Garlic, minced
1 ½ tsp.	Non-dairy margarine
2 c.	Tomatoes, chopped or mashed
2 c.	Corn
4 c.	UnShrimp

Combine the water, broth, and pepper in a pot and bring it to a boil. Sauté the onions, parsley, and garlic in the margarine until the onions are soft. Add this along with the tomatoes and corn to the broth and bring it back to a boil. Lower heat to a simmer and add the gluten. Cook on low heat for 30 to 40 minutes, stirring occasionally.

UNSHRIMP SOUP

2 qt.	Chicken-like Broth
1 c.	Green onions, chopped
½ c.	Celery, chopped
1 T.	Garlic, diced
1 c.	Parsley, chopped
2 c.	Water
2 tsp.	Louisiana Hot Sauce OR ½ tsp. cayenne pepper
2 T.	Lea & Perrins Steak Sauce
3 c.	UnShrimp

Put the ingredients–except for the UnShrimp–in a pot. Bring to a boil and lower the heat. Cover and simmer for 45 minutes. Add the UnShrimp and simmer for 30 more minutes.

UNSHRIMP STEW-1

Eat it up and call for more!

2 ½ tsp.	Olive oil
¼ c.	Unbleached white flour
3 c.	Onion, chopped
½ c.	Bell pepper, chopped
½ c.	Celery, chopped
½ tsp.	Garlic, minced
1 c.	Parsley, chopped OR ½ c. dried parsley
4 c.	Water
4 c.	UnShrimp
¼ tsp.	Sea salt
¼ tsp.	Cayenne pepper

Heat the oil, add the flour, and cook to a dark

brown over low heat, stirring constantly. Add the onion, bell pepper, celery, garlic, and parsley and cook for 10 minutes. Slowly add the water, stirring, and simmer over low heat for 30 minutes. Add the UnShrimp, salt, and pepper. Cover and simmer for 30 more minutes, keeping the heat low. Serve over rice or pasta.

Variation: Instead of the water, use 6 cups of canned tomatoes, crushed (without the liquid).

UNSHRIMP STEW-2

1 ½ c.	Onion, minced
2 T.	Garlic, minced
1 ¼ c.	Bell pepper (half red and half green, if possible)
1 T.	Olive oil
½ tsp.	Lemon peel, freshly grated
4 ½ c.	UnShrimp, cubed or chopped
4 c.	Tomatoes, chopped, or 2 c. canned, drained and chopped
1	Bouquet garni made of 5 parsley sprigs, 3 thyme sprigs, and 2 bay leaves tied in cheesecloth
⅛ tsp.	Cayenne
2 c.	UnShrimp Broth (can be the broth used in making the Unshrimp)
1 T.	Capers, drained
1 tsp.	Black pepper

Sauté the onion, garlic, and bell pepper in the oil. Combine everything and cook for 30 minutes. Remove the bouquet garni.

VEGETABLE CONSOMMÉ

1 qt.	Cold water
2 tsp.	Corn oil
2 ½ c.	Onions, chopped
1 c.	Celery, peeled and diced
1 ½ c.	Tomato, peeled, seeded, and diced
1 c.	Carrots, diced
2 tsp.	Garlic, coarsely chopped
3	Parsley sprigs
1 ½ tsp.	Basil leaves
2 c.	Mushrooms, chopped
⅛ tsp.	Thyme
2	Bay leaves
2	Pinches of chervil
¼ tsp.	Black pepper
1 tsp.	Sea salt

Combine everything in a pot. Bring to a boil, reduce heat, and simmer lightly, covered, for 20 minutes. Turn off the heat, keep covered, and set aside to steep for 20 more minutes. Strain carefully through a fine strainer.

WHITE BEAN AND TOMATO SOUP

1 c.	Onions, chopped
1 tsp.	Garlic, minced
½ c.	Celery, chopped
¼ c.	Bell pepper, chopped
1 T.	Corn oil
5 c.	Cooked white beans
2 tsp.	Sea salt
¼ tsp.	Basil, dried
¼ tsp.	Black or cayenne pepper
1 c.	Tomatoes, chopped
1 c.	Carrots, chopped or sliced
2 c.	Water

Sauté the onions, garlic, celery, and bell pepper in the oil until soft. Combine everything, bring to a boil, reduce heat, and simmer 20 to 30 minutes, adding more water if needed.

WINTER HOT POT

⅓ c.	Onions, chopped
1 ½ tsp.	Non-dairy margarine
5 c.	Mixed vegetables, chopped if need be
¼ c.	Barley, soaked
3 ¾ c.	UnBeef Broth
1	Bay leaf
½ tsp.	Sea salt
¼ tsp.	Cayenne pepper

Sauté the onions in the margarine until transparent. Add the rest of the ingredients. Bring to a boil, reduce heat, and simmer 15 to 20 minutes or until the vegetables are just tender.

ZUCCHINI SOUP

3 c.	UnChicken Broth
2 c.	Zucchini, scrubbed, trimmed, and chopped
1 ½ c.	Onion, sliced thin
2 tsp.	Corn oil
1 T.	Curry powder

Bring the broth to a boil. Add the zucchini, reduce heat, and simmer for 12 to 15 minutes, or until the zucchini is tender. Sauté the onion in the oil until soft, then add the curry powder and sauté for 3 more minutes. In a blender or food processor, purée the onion and zucchini mixtures, combine, and season with salt and pepper. Serve hot, chilled, or at room temperature.

Variation: Use other types of squash.

ZUCCHINI-CARROT SOUP

2 T.	Non–dairy margarine
3 c.	Zucchini, quartered lengthwise and then sliced
1 c.	Carrots, quartered lengthwise and then sliced
1 c.	Potatoes, cut in eighths lengthwise and then sliced
3 ¼ c.	UnChicken or UnBeef Broth
½ c.	Green onions, sliced thin

Sauté the zucchini, carrots, and potatoes in the margarine for 5 minutes. Add the broth and onions and bring to a boil, lower the heat and simmer 5 to 7 more minutes.

ZUCCHINI-TOMATO STEW

¾ c.	Onions, sliced
¾ tsp.	Garlic, minced
¾ c.	Bell pepper, chopped
1 ½ tsp.	Corn oil
¼ c.	UnChicken Broth or water (add ½ tsp. salt if water)
2 c.	Zucchini, in ½-inch slices
2 ½ c.	Tomatoes, chopped
1 tsp.	Basil
¼ tsp.	Cayenne pepper

Sauté the onions, garlic, and bell pepper in the oil. Combine everything and cook over low heat, covered, 20 minutes or until the squash is tender.

Chili

BLACK BEAN CHILI-1

2 c.	Dry black beans
2 c.	Onions, chopped
2 tsp.	Garlic, minced
1 T.	Corn oil
1 T.	Jalapeños, minced
1 tsp.	Cumin seeds
½ tsp.	Cayenne pepper
½ tsp.	Paprika
1 tsp.	Oregano
1 tsp.	Sea salt
4 c.	Canned tomatoes, chopped

Pressure-cook and drain the beans, reserving the cooking water. Sauté the onions and garlic in the oil until onions are transparent. Add the jalapeños and spices and sauté for 1 more minute. Add rest of ingredients and simmer for 1 hour–adding bean water if more liquid is needed. Serve with vinegar on the side to be added to taste.

BLACK BEAN CHILI-2

2 c.	Dried black beans
1 ½ tsp.	Cumin seed
1 ½ tsp.	Oregano
1 tsp.	Paprika
½ tsp.	Cayenne pepper
1 ½ c.	Onion, chopped
2 tsp.	Corn oil
½ c.	Bell pepper, diced
1 ½ tsp.	Garlic, minced
1 ½ c.	Italian tomatoes, chopped
1 c.	Tomato juice
½ tsp.	Sea salt
¼ c.	Green onion (including the tops), chopped

Wash the beans thoroughly and pressure-cook them. In a small dry skillet, heat the herbs, and toss them until they are fragrant. Sauté the onion in the oil for 2 to 3 minutes. Stir in the bell pepper, garlic, and herbs until the onion is soft and golden. Add to the cooked beans, along with the tomatoes, juice, and salt. Simmer for 30 or more minutes. Serve with the green onion on the top.

CHILI

More than you can eat at one sitting, but the rest is terrific the second day in Chili-Mac!

2 c.	UnBeef or Soy Grits UnBeef
1 ½ c.	Onions, coarsely chopped
3 T.	Chili powder
1 tsp.	Garlic powder
1 T.	Corn oil
3 ¼ c.	UnBeef Broth
1 c.	Tomato paste
5 c.	Cooked kidney beans (other beans may be used)
1 qt.	Tomatoes, chopped
½ tsp.	Cayenne pepper
½ tsp.	Sea salt

Sauté the gluten (or grits), onions, chili powder, and garlic powder in the oil. Combine the broth and tomato paste (you might want to blend the paste in a blender with some of the broth). Combine all ingredients and cook for 1 hour.

CHILI SUPREME

What else?…Supreme!

3 c.	Onion, chopped

1 T.	Garlic, minced
2 T.	Jalapeños, minced (with the seeds)
2 T.	Corn oil
7 c.	Canned tomatoes, drained (keep the juice)
½ c.	Tomato paste
1 c.	Bell peppers, chopped
¾ c.	Carrots, chopped
1 T.	Cumin, ground
¾ tsp.	Sea salt
½ tsp.	Cayenne pepper
2 c.	Kidney beans, cooked
2 c.	Pinto beans, cooked
2 c.	Zucchini, diced

Sauté the onions, garlic, and jalapeños in the oil until the onions are translucent–about 6 minutes. Add the tomatoes, 1 cup of the reserved tomato juice, tomato paste, bell peppers, carrots, cumin, salt, and cayenne. Simmer for 20 minutes, stirring frequently. Add the beans and cook 15 more minutes, thinning with more tomato juice if needed so the chili will not be too thick. Add the zucchini and cook 5 more minutes, stirring occasionally.

CHILI WITH MUSHROOMS

Distinctively good. But be sure you use Mexican oregano, not Italian. It is not the same at all.

2 c.	Onions, coarsely chopped
½ c.	Bell pepper, chopped
1 T.	Corn oil
2 tsp.	Garlic, minced
1 ½ c.	Mushrooms, shredded
¾ tsp.	Cumin, powdered
1 ½ tsp.	Sea salt
5 c.	Tomatoes, chopped
½ c.	Canned tomato sauce
2 tsp.	Dried cilantro
¾ tsp.	Mexican oregano, powdered
1 tsp.	Cayenne pepper
4 c.	Cooked dried kidney beans, cooking liquid reserved

Sauté the onions and bell pepper in the oil. When the onions are transparent add the garlic and mushrooms and cook a little bit longer. Add the rest of the ingredients except for the beans–but including the bean cooking liquid. Simmer together for 45 minutes. Add the beans and simmer 30 more minutes.

COUNTRYSIDE CHILI

For those who like mild chili–and for everybody else, too!

4 tsp.	Corn oil
3 c.	UnBeef, ground
2 c.	Onions, chopped
¾ c.	Bell pepper, chopped
¼ c.	Celery, chopped
6 c.	Canned whole tomatoes, undrained
½ c.	Canned tomato paste
1 T.	Dried parsley flakes
2 T.	Chili powder
½ tsp.	Sea salt
½ tsp.	Cayenne pepper
½ tsp.	Garlic powder
2 c.	Cooked kidney beans
1 c.	Cooked pinto beans

Heat the oil in a large skillet and brown the gluten. Add the onions, bell pepper, and celery, and sauté until the onions are soft. Add the rest of the ingredients except for the beans, reduce heat, cover, and simmer for 1 hour. Stir in the beans (if needed, add tomato juice at this point to make it soupy) and cook, uncovered, for 30 more minutes.

DENVER CHILI

2 c.	UnBeef, ground
1 c.	Onion, diced
1 c.	Celery, sliced
1 c.	Carrots, sliced
1 ½ tsp.	Garlic, minced
2 T.	Corn oil
2 c.	Canned tomatoes
2 c.	Tomato sauce
2 c.	Cooked kidney beans, drained
2 c.	UnBeef Broth
1 T.	Dried parsley flakes
½ tsp.	Oregano
½ tsp.	Basil
½ tsp.	Sea salt
¼ tsp.	Black pepper
2 c.	Cabbage, shredded
1 c.	Green beans, cut into 1-inch pieces
½ c.	Small elbow macaroni

Sauté the gluten, onion, celery, carrots, and garlic in the oil until the vegetables are soft. Combine everything *except* the cabbage, green beans, and macaroni. Bring to a boil, lower heat, cover, and simmer 20 minutes. Add the cabbage, green beans, and macaroni. Bring back to a boil, lower the heat, and simmer until the vegetables are tender.

HALF-HOUR CHILI

3 c.	Onions, chopped
⅓ c.	Carrots, chopped
1 T.	Jalapeño, minced
1 ½ tsp.	Garlic, minced
1 T.	Corn oil
4 tsp.	Chili powder
1 tsp.	Ground cumin
3 ½ c.	Canned tomatoes, chopped, with juice
1 tsp.	Sucanat
4 c.	Cooked kidney beans, drained and rinsed
⅓ c.	Fine or medium-grain bulgur

Sauté the onions, carrots, jalapeño, and garlic in the oil until the onion is soft. Combine everything but the beans and bulgur and cook for 15 minutes. Stir in the beans and bulgur and cook 15 more minutes.

PINTO BEAN CHILI

2 c.	Onions, chopped
½ c.	Jalapeños, chopped
1 T.	Garlic, minced
1 T.	Corn oil
5 c.	Cooked pinto beans, drained
2 c.	Tomatoes, diced
2 tsp.	Ground cumin
1 tsp.	Oregano

½ tsp.	Thyme
¼ tsp.	Chili powder
⅛ tsp.	Hot pepper flakes
1	Bay leaf
Pinch	Sucanat
1 c.	Corn
¼ c.	UnBeef or UnSausage, diced fine
1 T.	Soy sauce
1 ½ tsp.	Balsamic vinegar
1 ½ tsp.	Lemon juice
1 T.	Parsley, chopped
5 c.	Water or UnBeef Broth

Sauté the onions, jalapeños, and garlic in the oil until soft. Combine everything and cook for 30 minutes.

UNCHICKEN CHILI

1 c.	Onion, chopped
1 c.	Bell pepper, chopped
1 ½ tsp.	Garlic, minced
1 T.	Corn oil
4 ½ c.	UnChicken, diced
4 c.	Canned stewed tomatoes
2 c.	Cooked pinto beans
⅔ c.	Salsa or Picante Sauce
2 tsp.	Chili powder
1 tsp.	Ground cumin
½ tsp.	Sea salt

Sauté the onion, bell pepper, and garlic in the oil until the onion is soft. Add the rest of the ingredients and bring to a boil. Reduce the heat and simmer for 20 minutes.

Dairy Substitutes

THE MILK SUBSTITUTES given here will keep only for two to three days, so it is best to make only as much as you need in a recipe or make sure to use the rest later that day or the next day.

Any other dairy substitutes that have vinegar or lemon juice in them will keep well for five days.

When storing these substitutes, use containers that will not have much "air space." This will ensure that they keep better and longer.

ALMOND MILK

This is very thin, but that is necessary to obtain the right flavor.

1 c.	Almonds
	Boiling water to cover
⅛ tsp.	Salt
1 ½ tsp.	Vegetable oil
2 T.	Sucanat

Drop the almonds into boiling water. Boil for 10 seconds. Turn off the heat and let the almonds stand for 2 to 3 minutes. Drain water. Remove the skins and discard. Combine the almonds with the rest of the ingredients in a blender. Blend for 1 to 2 minutes. Strain through a cheesecloth.

CASHEW BUTTERMILK

For 1 cup of "buttermilk," put 1 tablespoon of lemon juice or vinegar (white or cider) in a cup measure and add enough cashew milk to make 1 cup. Stir and let stand about 5 minutes.

CASHEW CREAM

Make Cashew Milk, as below, but with only 2 cups of water.

CASHEW MILK

1 c.	Raw cashew nuts
4 c.	Water
¼ tsp.	Salt
1 ½ tsp.	Sucanat

In a blender put the cashews and 1 cup of the water. Blend until smooth. Add the rest of the ingredients and blend for 30 more seconds.

Note: If the "milk" is to be used in a dessert or other sweet dish—or even on breakfast cereal—make it with double the Sucanat (i.e., 1 tablespoon of Sucanat).

Variation: For use in some "salty" dishes, use Beef-like or Chicken-like Broth instead of water and leave out the Sucanat altogether.

CASHEW SOUR CREAM

2 c.	Water
6 T.	Cornstarch or arrowroot powder
1 c.	Hot water
2 c.	Raw cashews
⅓ c.	Lemon juice
1 tsp.	Garlic powder
1 T.	Sea salt
2 tsp.	Onion powder

Mix the 2 cups of water with the cornstarch or arrowroot and boil on the stove until it thickens. Cool slightly. Blend the hot water and cashews well. Add the lemon juice, garlic powder, salt, and onion powder to the cashew liquid. Add this to the starch mixture and combine thoroughly. Cool before using.

CHEEZCAKE

Filling:

3 c.	Pimento Cheez
4 T.	Green olives, chopped
1 T.	Dried chives, or 2 T. fresh chives, chopped
½ tsp.	Garlic powder
1 tsp.	Lemon juice
½ tsp.	Soy sauce
¼ tsp.	Paprika
½ tsp.	Sea salt
¼ tsp.	Louisiana Hot Sauce

Combine everything.

Crust:

1 ¼ c.	Cheez Cracker crumbs
¼ c.	Non-dairy margarine, melted

Combine crackers and margarine and press into a pie pan and bake at 375° for 6 to 8 minutes or until light brown. Put the filling in the crust and refrigerate until needed.

NOTZARELLA CHEEZ

I saw this adaptation of my Mozzarella Cheez in Vegetarian Voice. Bravo!!!

2 c.	Water
2 ¼ tsp.	Lemon juice
⅓ c.	Nutritional Yeast flakes
⅓ c.	Rolled oats
¼ c.	Arrowroot
¼ tsp.	Garlic powder
¼ tsp.	Italian seasoning
1 ½ tsp.	Onion powder
3 T.	Tahini
1 ½ tsp.	Sea salt

Put everything in a blender and blend for 1 minute. Pour into a saucepan and heat, stirring constantly, until thickened. Blend with electric mixer to remove any clumps.
Note: This can be frozen, then quickly grated and spinkled over dishes such as pizza.

PARMESAN CHEEZ–1

This both is and is not like parmesan cheese, but it adds a lot to a recipe where parmesan cheese is needed. It is very strong in flavor, so be cautious in its use. Refrigerated, this keeps at least one month.

1 c.	Sesame seeds
¼ c.	Lemon juice
1 ¼ c.	Nutritional Yeast
2 tsp.	Garlic Powder
1 T.	Onion Powder
3 T.	Schilling's Vegetable Supreme Seasoning

Mix all together. Sprinkle on a cookie sheet. Cover with a piece of waxed paper. Roll out thin. Remove the waxed paper. Put in a 200° oven for 2 hours. Grind fine and store in a covered container in a cool place.

PARMESAN CHEEZ–2

For those who find the first recipe too salty. To my taste this is more like powdered Yeast Cheez than Parmesan Cheese, but you may prefer it. Refrigerated, this keeps at least one month.

1 c.	Sesame seeds
2 tsp.	Sea salt
1 c.	Nutritional Yeast
2 tsp.	Onion powder
½ tsp.	Garlic powder
2 T.	Special Seasoning (see Etc. section)
2 T.	Lemon juice

Toast the sesame seeds in a dry skillet on medium-high heat, stirring constantly until they are slightly browned and beginning to crackle– about 5 minutes. Remove from heat, put in a blender, and blend on high until it is ground fine. Pour into a bowl, add the rest of the ingredients, and mix together well. Keep refrigerated.

PIMENTO CHEEZ-1

This Cheez should not be grainy from the ground (blended) cashews. If this happens to yours, then you did not blend long enough or your blender lacks the power to do the job. We use a Vitamix, and it works perfectly.

¼ c.	Agar
1 c.	Water
¾ c.	Cashews
¼ c.	Pimentos
1 tsp.	Salt
1 tsp.	Onion powder
½ tsp.	Corn oil

2 T. Lemon juice

Soak the agar in water about 5 minutes and boil gently until clear. While the agar is boiling, place the nuts, pimentos, salt, onion powder, and oil in a blender and whirl until smooth. Add the hot agar and whirl ½ minute. Add the lemon juice and mix for only a second. Pour immediately into a mold and set in the refrigerator to cool.
Variations: For a cheez sauce or spread, use only half the agar. Use cooked potatoes instead of cashews.

PIMENTO CHEEZ–2

See what I have written above about grainy cheez.

¼ c.	Agar
1 c.	Water
¾ c.	Cashews
¼ c.	Pimentos
1 ¼ tsp.	Salt
1 tsp.	Onion powder
2 T.	Sesame seed
3 T.	Nutritional Yeast
Dash	Garlic powder
Dash	Dill seed
½ tsp.	Corn oil
2 T.	Lemon juice

Soak the agar in water about 5 minutes and boil gently until clear. Place the other ingredients—except for the oil and the lemon juice—in a blender with the agar and whirl. Add slowly the oil. Add the lemon juice last of all. Pour immediately into a mold and set in the refrigerator to cool.
Variations: For a cheez sauce or spread, use only half the agar. Use cooked potatoes instead of cashews.

PIZZA CHEEZ

Makes 2 ½ cups.

½ c.	Nutritional Yeast
¼ c.	Cornstarch
1 tsp.	Sea salt
½ tsp.	Garlic powder
2 c.	Water
1 T.	Corn oil
1 tsp.	Prepared mustard

Mix the dry ingredients in a saucepan. Whisk in the water. Cook over medium heat while whisking until it thickens and bubbles. Cook 30 seconds more and remove from heat. Whip in the oil and mustard. Add 1 cup or more of water to make a thick, smooth sauce that will pour easily. Pour on pizza, and for the last few minutes of baking, broil the pizza for a few minutes until the cheez is speckled.

RICE CREAM

1 c.	White rice, cooked according to Basic Rice recipe
2 c.	Water
¾ tsp.	Sucanat
⅛ tsp.	Vanilla

Put all in a blender and blend on high speed for 5 minutes. Do not strain.
Note: For use in desserts, double the Sucanat.

RICE MILK

1 c.	White rice, cooked according to Basic Rice recipe
2 c.	Water
¾ tsp.	Sucanat
⅛ tsp.	Vanilla

Put all in a blender and blend on high speed for 3 minutes. Strain through a cheesecloth. Squeeze liquid out of pulp remaining in the cheesecloth.
Note: For use in desserts, double the Sucanat.

SOY MILK–BASIC

Sort dried soybeans and wash in cold water. Soak the beans until they double in size—about 4 hours. In warm weather, soak them in the refrigerator so they will not ferment and spoil. Using 2 ½ cups of water to 1 cup of beans, liquefy in a blender or grind in a food grinder. Heat the mixture to a boil in a double boiler or heavy pot. Simmer for 40 minutes, stirring occasionally. Strain through a clean cloth (nylon, folded cheesecloth, etc.) placed in a colander or strainer. This only lasts a couple of days.

SOY MILK

4 c.	Soy milk
1 tsp.	Corn oil
¼ & ⅛ tsp.	Sea salt
¼ c. & 3 T.	Sucanat

Blend together in a blender.

SOY WHIPPED CREAM

¾ c.	Soy milk
1 T.	Cornstarch

½ c.   Corn oil
¼ c.   Sucanat
⅛ tsp. Salt
2 tsp. Vanilla

Put the soy milk and cornstarch in a blender. While running on high, slowly add the oil in a thin stream until the spinning funnel of soy milk closes and the mixture stops blending–the blender blades changing speed. Add the Sucanat, salt, and vanilla to the blender and blend again until the mixture thickens as before. If necessary, add a small amount of oil. Allow to set in the refrigerator for at least one hour before using. This lasts only two or three days.

TOFU BUTTERMILK

Make Tofu Sour Cream and add ⅔ cup of water.

TOFU COTTAGE CHEEZ

1 ½ c. Firm tofu
¼ c.   Miraculous Whip or other "Mayonnaise" recipe
2 T. & 1 ½ tsp. Lemon juice
2 tsp. Soy sauce
¼ tsp. Garlic powder
Pinch   Paprika

Mash all together.

TOFU CREAM CHEEZ–1

1 ½ c. Tofu, squeezed
2 T.   Corn oil
½ tsp. Sea salt
Dash   White pepper
2 tsp. Lemon juice
Pinch   Onion powder

Purée in a blender until smooth and thick.

TOFU CREAM CHEEZ–2

1 c.   Tofu Cottage Cheez
¼ c.   Non-dairy margarine

Blend in a blender until smooth.

TOFU RICOTTA CHEEZ

6 c.   Firm tofu, pressed to remove excess water
½ c.   Lemon juice
4 tsp. Sucanat
2 tsp. Sea salt
¼ c.   Corn oil

4 tsp. Basil
1 tsp. Garlic powder

Mash the tofu. Mix the other ingredients into the mashed tofu–mixing well.

TOFU SOUR CREAM

1 c.   Tofu
¼ tsp. Corn oil
1 T.   Lemon juice
½ tsp. Salt
¼ tsp. Sucanat

Combine and blend till smooth. Can be used in place of mayonnaise.

TOFU WHIPPED CREAM

1 ½ c. Tofu
3 T.   Maple syrup
⅛ tsp. Sea salt
½ tsp. Vanilla
1 T.   Corn oil

Purée in a blender until smooth.

TOFU YOGURT

Make Tofu Sour Cream, using 1 ½ teaspoons more lemon juice, and add ⅓ cup of water.

YEAST CHEEZ

This is a bit like "process cheese," but is distinctively itself. Make it and see what I mean.
Makes 2 ½ cups.

½ c.   Nutritional Yeast flakes
½ c.   Unbleached white flour
1 tsp. Sea salt
½ tsp. Garlic powder
2 c.   Water
1 T.   Non-dairy margarine
½ tsp. Prepared mustard

Mix the dry ingredients in a saucepan. Whisk in the water. Cook over medium heat while whisking until it thickens and bubbles. Cook 30 seconds more and remove from heat. Whip in the margarine and mustard. This thickens when it cools, and thins when heated. Water can be added to thin it more. This keeps about five days.

Gluten–
For Goodness' Sake!

GLUTEN IS THE PROTEIN of wheat (flour) that remains when the starch is washed away in water. Gluten is sometimes referred to as "seitan," although that is a Japanese term properly applied only to gluten that has been flavored with soy sauce.

Gluten can be made into a variety of meat substitutes that are an ideal means of supplying healthy protein to the diet–something all vegetarians need just as much as non-vegetarians. Two-thirds of a cup of raw gluten supplies 56 grams of protein–a little more than the recommended daily allowance for a 167-pound man. Also they are a boon for those of us who are frustrated with the way so many commercial meat substitutes contain egg albumen. And they are much, much less in cost than the commercial substitutes, too!

Gluten is usually to be preferred to Textured Vegetable Protein (TVP), because TVP is made using a chemical process to separate the soy flour from the soybeans. I was told by the owner of a health food store (who refused to sell TVP) that Hexane–a poison–is used in the process. Organic TVP made in a non-chemical manner is available from: The Farm, Summertown, Tennessee, 38483.

Many vegetarians who feel an aversion for meat dislike the idea of eating non-meat substitutes that look or taste like meat. This is quite understandable, yet meat substitutes can be of great value. For one thing they can demonstrate to meat-eaters that there is an alternative to animal flesh. They also make it very easy for people to make the transition to vegetarianism, since they can keep on eating the kind of dishes they have been used to for much of their life.

Meat substitutes are often the only tactic a person has to convince spouse or children that vegetarianism does not mean grazing out in the back yard. For no matter how delicious and creative vegetarian dishes can be, there are some who just cannot believe they are eating "real food" if it does not include meat–or something very like it. I am not theorizing. Through the years we have helped many individuals and families to become vegetarian by means of these meat substitutes. Although our personal motives for diet are based on what we feel are bed-rock principles of health and spiritual development, not many share those ideals–at first. But serve them up a "meat" dish that is even better than "the real thing" and you have them more than halfway to taking what a friend of ours called "the first step to wisdom": a vegetarian diet. It is results that count.

With these recipes vegetarians can continue using the dishes they liked when they ate meat. As I have said, they are also excellent means of convincing non-vegetarians that they can "live" without meat, and they can help beginning vegetarians make the transition to a non-meat diet.

By using these meat substitutes the family cooks can also keep right on using the same recipes and the same cookbooks they have all along. When meat is called for–no problem!

Don't forget to look for other excellent recipes in the "beef," "pork," "poultry," and "seafood" sections as well as in this one.

Raw gluten, unflavored and uncooked, will keep only one day. It should not be frozen.

Once gluten is cooked, any that is not going

to be used right away should be frozen. It will keep indefinitely and can also be refrozen.

Unfrozen cooked gluten can be kept, refrigerated, for up to one week.

Dishes containing gluten can only be kept as long as the "life" of the other ingredients.

Gluten should be stored in airtight containers.

BASIC GLUTEN

Don't let this intimidate you. It is easy after you have done it once.
Do not use pastry flour in this because it does not have enough gluten to work.

8 c.	Whole wheat flour
8 c.	White flour
6 c.	Cold–not chilled–water

Mix the flour and water together and knead it for about 10 to 15 minutes, adding water or flour as (if) needed, until you have a very smooth ball of dough with no cracks in it. Kneading is what develops the gluten. It should bounce back when you punch it.

Put this ball of dough in a bowl large enough to hold it and add enough cold water to cover the ball completely. Let it soak under water for one-half hour at least, preferably one to two hours.

Then begin kneading it under water, kneading out all the starch and being careful to hold the gluten together. Change the water when it gets quite milky from the starch, and keep changing it until the water stays almost clear. The last part of the kneading should be done in a colander (not a strainer) under running water.

If the dough distintegrates in the kneading-washing you must try another brand of flour.

Cook according to one of the methods given below.

COOKING METHOD 1

Oil a loaf pan. Place the raw gluten in the pan and bake at 450° for 45 minutes. The gluten will rise just like a loaf of bread and when done will have a shiny golden brown "skin."

Slice the gluten "loaf" into slices ⅜-inch to ½-inch thick. If chunks are desired, cut the slices into cubes or strips.

Place the slices or cubes in boiling Gluten Broth (not Flavoring Broth) of the type that is prescribed in the recipe, and boil for 30 minutes.

A weight may be required to keep the gluten submersed while boiling.

If possible, let the cooked gluten soak overnight for best flavor, though it can be used right away if need be.

COOKING METHOD 2

The long, slow cooking time of this method permits the seasoning to penetrate the gluten and gives it a texture that enables it to be sliced very thin.

Shape 2 cups of raw gluten into an oval loaf and place it in an oiled loaf pan.

Pour 2 ½ cups of the prescribed Gluten Broth (not Flavoring Broth) over the gluten.

Cover *tightly* with aluminum foil and bake in a 250° oven for 10 hours or overnight–turning the gluten over after 5 hours of baking so the flavoring will be evenly absorbed.

For a larger quantity of gluten, increase the amounts of raw gluten and broth proportionately. You may need to increase the baking time to give the increased amount of gluten adequate time to absorb the broth. You should be sure to bake it in a pan or dish that will be of a size that ensures the broth covers the gluten at the beginning of the baking.

COOKING METHOD 3

We have found that pressure-cooking gluten is by far the best method. Not only is it much quicker, and therefore easier, the texture is perfect. Also, gluten cooked by other methods may have a "raw" taste even when cooked with other things in well-seasoned dishes. But pressure cooking eliminates this problem completely.

I have still given the other methods of cooking gluten in case someone does not have a pressure-cooker or would rather not use one.

To pressure-cook gluten: Put 2 cups of gluten in a pressure cooker with 6 cups of liquid (water for plain unflavored gluten, and one of the broths for flavored gluten) and a little sea salt and cook at 15 lbs. for 45 minutes.

"INSTANT" GLUTEN

I have good news for those who would like to cook with gluten but don't want to make it in the "old-fashioned" way. All you need do is obtain Vital Wheat Gluten (Instant Gluten Flour) from your local health foods store or order it from: The Farm, Summertown, Tennessee,

(continued on page 81)

How to make gluten

Fig. 1. Mix the flour and water together.

Fig. 2. Knead the flour and water for about 10 to 15 minutes.

Fig. 3. Add water or flour as (if) needed…

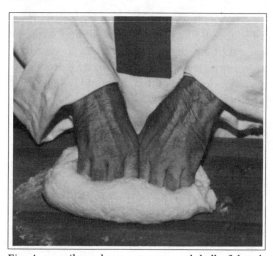

Fig. 4 …until you have a very smooth ball of dough with no cracks in it.

Fig. 5. Put this ball of dough in a bowl large enough to hold it and add enough cold water to cover the ball completely.

Fig. 6. Let is soak under water for one-half hour at least, preferably one to two hours.

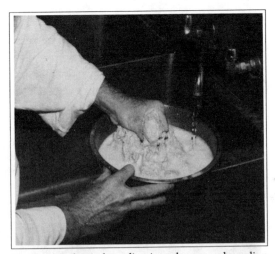

Fig. 7. Then begin kneading it under water, kneading out all the starch and being careful to hold the gluten together. Change the water when it gets quite milky from the starch, and keep changing it until the water stays almost clear.

Fig. 8. The last part of the kneading should be done in a colander (not a strainer) under running water.

Fig. 9. During the washing process—towards the end of gluten development—the gluten will separate into small pieces. Just continue to wash, and the gluten will soon come together.

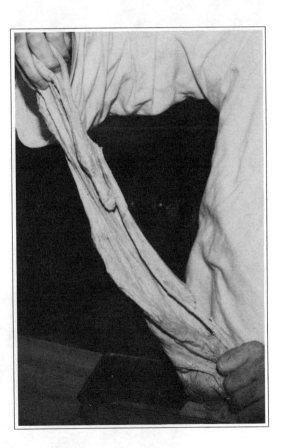

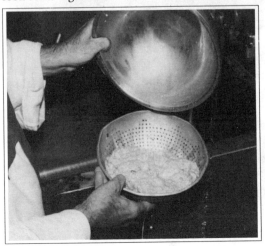

Fig. 10. (Left) Continue to wash in a colander until the water around the gluten becomes clear.

Fig. 11. (Above) When the gluten is finished it will be in one piece with a somewhat elastic consistency.

Fig. 12 (left). Cooking Method 1: Oil a loaf pan. Place the raw gluten in the pan and bake.

Fig. 13 (below, left). Slice the gluten "loaf" into slices 3/8-inch to 1/2-inch thick. If chunks are desired, cut the slices into cubes or strips.

Fig. 14 (below). To pressure cook gluten: Put 2 cups of gluten in a pressure cooker with 6 cups of liquid (water for plain unflavored gluten, and one of the broths for flavored gluten) and a little sea salt and cook at 15 lbs. for 45 minutes.

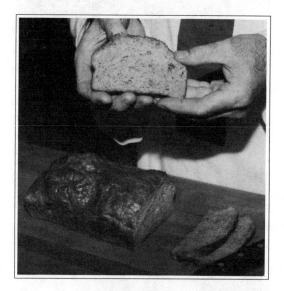

Fig. 15. Sliced gluten "UnBeef," made with the Pressure Cooker Method.

(cont.)
38483. Vital Wheat Gluten is pure gluten powder, it is *not* "high gluten flour." Don't mistake it!

Important: Gluten made in this way and immediately used will be somewhat less soft or tender than gluten made the regular way, but if you have time, put the gluten in a bowl and cover it with warm water and let it sit for 30 minutes and then bake it.

Here is the formula for making one "loaf" of gluten from Vital Wheat gluten.

1 c.	Vital Wheat Gluten
14 T.	Water (this is 7/8 cup–measure out 1 cup of water (16 tablespoons) and then remove 2 tablespoons)

Mix the gluten and water by hand until it forms a spongy "dough"–no kneading is required. Put into an oiled loaf pan and bake at 375° for 1 hour and 15 minutes–or until dark brown on top. The gluten will rise just like a loaf of bread and when done will have a shiny golden brown "skin." However, after about 30 minutes of baking, check the gluten, and if it is starting to puff up more than 2 inches above the sides of the pan, pierce the top in 3 places with a knife.

When it is done, slice the gluten "loaf" into slices ⅜-inch to ½-inch thick. If chunks are desired, cut the slices into cubes or strips.

Place the slices or cubes in boiling Gluten Broth (not Flavoring Broth) of the type that is prescribed in the recipe, and boil for 30 minutes. A weight may be required to keep the gluten submersed while boiling.

If possible, let the cooked gluten soak overnight for best flavor, though it can be used right away if need be.

BAKED GLUTEN

2 c.	Onions, chopped fine
1 c.	Bell pepper, chopped
1 tsp.	Garlic, minced
1 T.	Corn oil
1 tsp.	Sea salt
1 tsp.	Dried mint
½ tsp.	Cayenne pepper
4 c.	Canned tomatoes, crushed
2 T.	Parsley, chopped
¼ tsp.	Thyme, chopped
6 c.	Flavored gluten, sliced

Sauté the onions, bell pepper, and garlic in the oil until the onions and pepper are tender. Put in the salt, mint, cayenne, tomatoes, parsley, and thyme. Cook for 15 minutes. Put the gluten in a casserole and pour this mixture over it. Cover the casserole tightly and bake at 325° for 45 minutes. Serve with rice.

BAKED CUBED GLUTEN

Fantastic is the word for this recipe. And don't worry about the hot sauce–it blends into the rest of the flavors and loses its bite.

5 c.	Flavored gluten, cooked by Method 2 or 3, and cut in 1-inch cubes
2 T.	Corn oil
2 T.	Unbleached white flour
½ tsp.	Kitchen Bouquet
¾ c.	Onions, chopped
¾ tsp.	Garlic, minced
1 ½ c.	Flavoring Broth according to type of gluten being used
¼ tsp.	Sea salt
1 T.	Lea and Perrins Steak Sauce
1 ½ tsp.	Louisiana Hot Sauce

In a skillet brown the gluten in the oil and put it in a baking dish or pan. Stir the flour into the oil remaining in the skillet and turn the fire down so it will cook slowly. Add the Kitchen Bouquet and keep stirring the flour constantly, adding more oil if the mixture is too dry, until the mixture is a rich brown. Add the onions and garlic, stirring constantly. Add the broth and keep stirring until it starts to form a thick gravy. Add the salt, steak sauce, and hot sauce. Add more water if you need to, and bring all to a boil. Pour the sauce over the gluten cubes. Bake at 400° for 30 to 45 minutes, basting frequently and adding water if needed. This is good served on a bed of mashed potatoes.

BARBECUE GLUTEN

This is something special!

2 c.	Onions, chopped
¾ c.	Bell pepper, chopped
⅓ c.	Celery, chopped
2 tsp.	Garlic, minced
2 ½ tsp.	Corn oil
6 c.	Flavored gluten, cut in thin slices
6 c.	Barbecue Sauce of choice
1 tsp.	Hot pepper flakes

Sauté the onions, bell pepper, celery, and garlic in the oil until the onions just start to get soft.

Add the gluten and continue to sauté until the gluten begins to brown. Add the barbecue sauce and pepper flakes and simmer for 20 more minutes. If it gets too dry, add more barbecue sauce or some water.

GLUTEN AND GREEN BEANS STIR-FRY

2 c.	Flavored gluten of choice
½ tsp.	Sea salt
⅓ tsp.	Black pepper
2 tsp.	Corn oil
1 c.	Green beans, cut into 1–inch lengths
1 c.	Onions, chopped
1 tsp.	Garlic, minced
¾ c.	Flavoring Broth according to the type of gluten being used
1 tsp.	Basil (dried)
⅛ tsp.	Sea salt
1 T.	Cornstarch
2 T.	Water
1 ½ c.	Tomatoes, chopped
½ tsp.	Kitchen Bouquet

Thinly slice the gluten into 2 ½ x ½-inch strips and season them with the salt and pepper. Heat the oil in a skillet over medium heat until hot. Add the gluten and stir-fry 3 to 5 minutes. Remove the gluten from the skillet and put in 1 more teaspoon of oil and heat it until hot. Put the green beans, onions, and garlic in the skillet and sauté for a few minutes. Add the broth, basil, and salt. Cover and simmer for 15 minutes or until the beans are tender. Combine the cornstarch and water in a small bowl and stir until blended. Add the cornstarch mixture, gluten, and tomatoes to the skillet. Stir in the Kitchen Bouquet. Cook, stirring constantly, until the mixture boils and thickens–about 2 minutes.

GLUTEN AND POTATO HASH

1 ½ c.	Flavored gluten, ground
1 ½ tsp.	Non-dairy margarine
1 c.	Onions, chopped
1 tsp.	Garlic, minced
2 T.	Browned flour
1 c.	Flavoring Broth according to the type of gluten being used
3 c.	Cold, boiled potatoes, diced
⅛ tsp.	Black pepper

Sauté the gluten in the margarine until it is browned. Just before the gluten is done, add the

onions and garlic and sauté until the onions are soft. Add the flour. Gradually add the broth, stirring constantly. Add potatoes, gluten, and pepper and cook for 5 minutes. Transfer to a baking dish and bake at 375° about 30 minutes.

GLUTEN CHOW MEIN

1 ½ c.	Celery, chopped
½ c.	Onions, chopped
½ c.	Bell pepper, chopped
½ c.	Snow peas
1 tsp.	Hot pepper flakes
4 tsp.	Corn oil
⅓ c.	Cold water
⅓ c.	Cornstarch
1 c.	Flavoring Broth according to the type of gluten being used
⅓ c.	Soy sauce
1 c.	Bean sprouts, blanched at 160° for 10 seconds
½ c.	Bamboo shoots
½ c.	Water chestnuts, sliced
1 ½ c.	Flavored gluten, cubed

Sauté the celery, onions, bell pepper, peas, and pepper flakes in the oil until they are crisp-tender. Blend the water, corn starch, broth, and soy sauce together. Add the blended liquid to the vegetables along with the sprouts, bamboo shoots, water chestnuts, and gluten. Cook until thick–about 15 minutes.

GLUTEN CURRY

The aristocrat of curries!

½ c.	Onion, chopped fine
1 T.	Garlic, minced
½ tsp.	Ginger, powdered
1 tsp.	Corn oil
1½ tsp.	Garam Masala
2 tsp.	Chili powder
¾ tsp.	Tumeric
2 c.	Coconut milk
¾ c.	Tomato, chopped
1 ½ tsp.	Lemon juice
¼ tsp.	Sea salt
2 c.	Flavored or unflavored gluten, cubed

Sauté the onion, garlic, and ginger in the oil until the mixture is golden. Add the garam masala, chili powder, and tumeric, and sauté for 2 more minutes. Stir in the coconut milk, tomato, lemon juice, and salt. Boil, stirring occasionally, until thickened. Add the gluten and cook together for 1 minute.

GLUTEN DUMPLINGS

Unflavored gluten can often add a great deal to dishes that contain a lot of liquid for it will absorb the flavors of the vegetables and seasonings. When the dish is fully assembled or boiling, take the raw (uncooked) gluten, break off small ½-inch pieces, roll each between your thumb and fingers and drop them in. After dropping in 10 pieces stir so the gluten pieces will not stick to one another.

GLUTEN ENCHILADAS

You're always on target with this dish!

2 tsp.	Garlic, minced
2 c.	Onions, chopped
2 tsp.	Jalapeños, minced
1 T.	Corn oil
3 T.	Chili powder
¾ c.	Black olives, chopped
¼ tsp.	Sea salt
4 c.	Flavored gluten, ground
10 c.	Spanish Tomato Sauce
1	Recipe of Corn Tortillas or Flour Tortillas
	Yeast or Pimento Cheez to cover

Sauté the garlic, onions, and jalapeños in the oil until the onions are transparent. Add the chili powder and sauté for 2 more minutes, stirring constantly. Add olives, salt, gluten, and 3 cups of the tomato sauce and cook for another 5 minutes. Dip a tortilla in the remaining tomato sauce, put some of the filling on it and roll it up and put it in a casserole pan. Do this with all the tortillas until the filling is used up. Cover the enchiladas with the remaining sauce. Spread a layer of cheez over that. Bake at 350° for 30 minutes.
Variation: Use flavored soy grits instead of gluten.

GLUTEN HASH

Don't think this is just a way of using up leftovers! It can stand on its own!

1 T.	Non-dairy margarine
3 c.	Onions, chopped
2 c.	Mushrooms, sliced
½ c.	Unbleached white flour
2 c.	Flavoring Broth of the type of gluten used
½ c.	Cashew Cream

3 c.	Flavored gluten, diced
⅓ c.	Parsley, chopped fine
2 T.	Lea & Perrins Steak Sauce
⅛ tsp.	Cayenne Pepper

Melt the margarine and sauté the onions until they are soft. Add the mushrooms and cook until most of the liquid is evaporated. Stir in the flour and then the broth and "cream," stirring constantly. Cook until thickened. Stir in the gluten, parsley, steak sauce, and pepper. Heat through.
Serve over Toast Points (see Bread and Such section).

GLUTEN JAMBALAYA

This is worth swimming the bayou for!
Even if you are not a rice fan you will love it in this dish, I garontee!

1 T.	Corn oil
3 c.	Onions, chopped
1 T.	Bell pepper, chopped fine
1 T.	Celery, chopped fine
4 c.	Flavored gluten, sliced ¼-inch thick
1 c.	Mexican Chorizo Sausage Gluten, chopped fine
3 c.	Uncooked rice
1 ½ tsp.	Sea salt
	Black pepper
	Cayenne pepper
2 ½ c.	Flavoring Broth of gluten type
2 ½ c.	Water
⅛ tsp.	Liquid Smoke
2 tsp.	Garlic clove, chopped fine

Sauté the onions, bell pepper, and celery in the oil until the onions are transparent. Add the glutens, rice and salt. Cook over low heat for 15 minutes, stirring often. Add the broth, water, liquid smoke, and garlic. Stir and cover. *Do not stir any more.* Simmer over low heat for 20 or 30 minutes until the rice is done. Keep covered until served.

GLUTEN LOAF

2 ½ c.	Flavored gluten, ground
1 c.	Rolled oats
1 c.	Bread crumbs
1 c.	Nuts, ground
1 c.	Onions, ground
1 ¼ c.	Mushroom soup made by using Basic 'Cream of' Soup recipe
½ tsp.	Sea salt

¼ tsp.	Garlic, minced
2 T.	Water
2 tsp.	Corn oil

Mix the gluten, oats, crumbs, nuts, onions, soup, salt, and garlic together and form into a loaf. Put the loaf in a well-oiled baking dish or pan. Mix the water and oil and baste the loaf. Bake at 350° until the loaf is brown and firm.

Variation: Instead of gluten, use flavored soy grits.

GLUTEN PAPRIKA

You haven't lived until...

1 T.	Corn oil
1 c.	Onion
¾ tsp.	Garlic, chopped
3 tsp.	Paprika
5 c.	Flavored gluten, cut in 1-inch cubes
2 c.	Tomatoes, cubed
¾ c.	Bell pepper, chopped
3 T.	Water
1 tsp.	Sea salt
¼ tsp.	Cayenne pepper
3 T.	Unbleached white flour
1 ½ c.	Cashew or Tofu Sour Cream
1 c.	Cashew Milk

Sauté the onion and garlic in the oil until transparent. Stir in the paprika and cook a few more seconds. Add the gluten and sauté over high heat, lightly tossing, until it is lightly browned– about 15 minutes. Add the tomatoes and bell pepper along with the water, salt, and pepper. Mix well and cook over moderate heat for 12 to 15 minutes, stirring occasionally. Whisk in the flour. Combine the "sour cream" and "milk." Add to the gluten and stir. Cook for a few more minutes, stirring, until thickened.

GLUTEN PIQUANT

This is a "somewhat Cajun" recipe adapted for use by vegetarians from some recipes of Justin Wilson, the famous television Cajun cook.

2 tsp.	Olive oil
¼ c.	Unbleached white flour
1 c.	Mushrooms, chopped
1 c.	Onions, chopped
1 c.	Green onions, chopped
¼ c.	Bell pepper, chopped
2 T.	Celery, chopped
½ c.	Parsley, chopped
1 ½ tsp.	Garlic, minced

3 c.	Cold (i.e., not hot) Flavoring Broth according to the type of gluten being used
3 c.	Flavored gluten, cooked by Method 1 or 2, and cut in 1-inch cubes
2 T.	Olive oil
2 T.	Louisiana Hot Sauce
1 ½ c.	Canned tomato sauce
¼ c.	Canned tomatoes, mashed
1 tsp.	Dried mint OR 1 bay leaf
1 T.	Lemon juice
2 T.	Lea & Perrins Steak Sauce
½ tsp.	Sea salt

Heat the oil in the skillet, stir in the flour, and turn the fire down so it will cook slowly, stirring constantly, adding more oil if the mixture is too dry, until it is a rich brown. Add the mushrooms, onions (both kinds), and bell pepper, and sauté until they are tender. Add the celery and parsley, and sauté until the celery is tender. Add the garlic and sauté a bit longer. Add the broth, *which should be cold, not heated,* and stir in well. Let simmer. While the above is simmering, brown the gluten in the oil and put it in a cooking pot. Add all the rest of the ingredients and mix well. Cover and bring to a boil. Lower the heat and simmer for 2 ½ hours, adding more water if needed. Serve over spaghetti, rice, or potatoes.

GLUTEN POT PIE

This is a regular standby–but not dull!

½ c.	Pimentos or bell peppers, chopped
½ c.	Mushrooms, sliced
½ c.	Onions, minced
1 T.	Non-dairy margarine
½ c.	Unbleached white flour
3 c.	Flavoring Broth according to the type of gluten being used
6 c.	Mixed vegetables, cooked
3 c.	Flavored gluten
1 tsp.	Garlic, minced
¼ tsp.	Cayenne pepper

Sauté the pimentos (or peppers), mushrooms, and onions in the margarine. Stir in the flour. Gradually add the broth. Add rest of ingredients and cook until it is thick and bubbly. Serve over biscuits.

Variations: With ham gluten use chicken-like broth. Serve over rice instead of biscuits.

HEARTY GLUTEN BAKE

A sure thing.

2 c.	Mashed potatoes
2 tsp.	Non-dairy margarine, melted
2 c.	Flavored gluten of choice, cubed small
½ c.	Onions, chopped
4 tsp.	Lea & Perrins Steak Sauce
½ tsp.	Sea salt
⅛ tsp.	Cayenne pepper
1 c.	Tofu Cottage Cheez
2	Medium tomatoes, sliced
1 c.	Pimento Cheez

Mix the potatoes and margarine. Spread 1 ½ cups of this in the bottom of a casserole and set aside. In some corn oil, sauté the gluten and onions until the gluten begins to brown. Add the steak sauce, salt, and pepper. Spoon the gluten mixture onto the potatoes in the casserole. Spread the cottage cheez over the gluten mixture. Cover with the tomato slices. Spread the cheez over all. Spread the remaining potatoes over that. Bake at 350° for 20 to 30 minutes.

OVEN-FRIED GLUTEN

Good the first day but better the next. Cold it is very much like cold fried chicken.

1 c.	Onion, chopped fine
1 ½ tsp.	Garlic, crushed
1 ½ tsp.	Non-dairy margarine, melted
4 c.	Raw gluten, made from all white flour
½ tsp.	Sage
1 c.	Nutritional Yeast

4 ½ tsp.	Sea salt
1 tsp.	Black pepper
1 tsp.	Paprika
¼ c.	Tahini
	Non-dairy margarine for rolling up

Sauté the onions and garlic in the margarine. Add all the other ingredients along with the hot sautéed onion and garlic to the raw gluten and work them through with your fingers. Take about a ⅓ cup piece of gluten and pull and flatten it out until it is about ¼ inch thick and 3 to 4 inches long. Spread about 1 ½ teaspoons of margarine on this stretched piece and roll it up like a jelly roll, then flatten it out with your fingers. Next, roll it in a mixture made of:

1 ¾ c.	Cracker crumbs
1 tsp.	Garlic powder
½ tsp.	Sea salt
¼ tsp.	Black pepper

Pour 2 tablespoons of corn oil on a baking sheet or in a baking pan. Put the gluten pieces rolled in the crumbs on it. Bake at 375° for about 45 minutes, turning once when golden brown on the bottom. Be sure not to overcook.

SANTA FE GLUTEN

4 c.	Flavored gluten, cubed
2 T.	Corn oil
1 c.	Tomato Salsa
½ tsp.	Cumin, ground

Sauté the gluten in the oil until browned. Add everything else and simmer, covered, 5 or 6 minutes.

UnBeef
Substitutes & Dishes

UNBEEF

If you have regular soy sauce instead of low sodium soy sauce to use in this broth, then cut the amount you use in half.

Cook 2 cups of raw gluten according to Method 1, 2, or 3 in:

¼ c.	Soy sauce
2 tsp.	Kitchen Bouquet
2 T.	Nutritional Yeast
½ c.	Onions, chopped
¼ tsp.	Sage, rubbed
1 tsp.	Corn oil
2 c.	Water

Combine everything and simmer for 5 minutes.

UNBEEF SOY GRITS

½ c.	Soy grits
1 c.	Boiling UnBeef Gluten Broth (see UnBeef recipe)

Stir grits into the broth and cook for 5 minutes.

BARBECUED UNBEEF

½ c.	Onions, chopped
2 tsp.	Corn oil
1 c.	Catsup
3 T.	Cider vinegar
4 tsp.	Lemon juice
1 T.	Louisiana Hot Sauce
1 ⅓ c.	Lea & Perrins Steak Sauce
6 c.	UnBeef, sliced

Sauté the onion in the oil until transparent. Add everything else except the UnBeef and simmer for 10 minutes, stirring occasionally. Meanwhile brown the UnBeef in some oil. Pour half of the sauce into a baking dish or pan large enough so the UnBeef slices will make a single layer. Put in the UnBeef, pour the remaining sauce over it, and bake at 350° for 20 minutes.

CHIMICHANGAS

3 T.	Corn oil
2 c.	UnBeef, chopped
1 c.	Onion, diced
1 ½ tsp.	Garlic, minced
1 ½ c.	Tomatoes, chopped
2	4-oz. cans of green chilies, chopped
1 ¼ c.	Potatoes, peeled, boiled, and diced
1 tsp.	Sea salt
1 ½ tsp.	Oregano
2 tsp.	Chili powder
1 T.	Powdered coriander seed
12	Flour tortillas, warmed

Sauté the gluten, onion, garlic, tomatoes, chilies, and potatoes in the oil until the onions are soft. Add the salt, oregano, chili powder, and coriander. Simmer 2 to 3 minutes. Place ½ cup of filling on each tortilla, and fold into "envelopes." Fry, seam side down, in hot (360° to 375°) oil until crisp and brown on both sides. Drain on paper towels. Serve with cheez, "sour cream," guacamole, salsa, shredded lettuce, chopped tomatoes, and sliced black olives on the side for topping.

CHINESE PEPPER UNSTEAK

Simple as this is, it delivers.

3 c.	Unflavored gluten cooked by Cooking Method 2 or 3

2 tsp.   Corn oil
1 tsp.   Sea salt
1 c.   Celery, sliced
1 c.   Bell peppers, sliced
1 c.   Onion, sliced
2 tsp.   Garlic, minced
2 c.   Tomatoes, sliced

Cut the gluten in thin strips. Sauté it in the oil, until slightly brown or deep-fry it (this is best). Remove from the pan. Sauté the vegetables and seasonings in the skillet, mixing gently but thoroughly. Cook until just tender. Add the gluten. Serve over rice. You can season this with soy sauce or some other condiment.
Variation: Use gluten made with UnBeef or UnChicken Broth. Add 1 tablespoon of minced or sliced jalapeños.

COMPANY PRIDE HASH

Worthy of serving to guests—not just family!

1 tsp.   Non-dairy margarine
1 c.   UnBeef, chopped or ground
1 c.   Potatoes, cooked and diced
1 c.   Onion, diced
1 T.   Parsley, minced
½ c.   Cashew milk
¼ tsp.   Salt
⅛ tsp.   Black pepper

In a skillet (or on a griddle) melt the margarine. Add all the ingredients and mix well. Cover and cook until the mixture is crisp on the bottom. Then turn and brown the other side.

CONTINENTAL STROGANOFF

2 ½ c.   UnBeef, cut into strips
¼ c.   Onions, chopped
1 tsp.   Non-dairy margarine
3 T.   Unbleached white flour
⅛ tsp.   Black pepper
1 c.   Cashew Milk
½ c.   Tofu Sour Cream or Cashew Sour Cream

Sauté the gluten and onions in the margarine until the gluten is browned. Add the flour and pepper and gradually stir in the "milk." Add the "sour cream" and heat through. Serve over rice or pasta with more "sour cream" on the side.

GOULASH

2 c.   UnBeef, cut into ½-inch cubes

1 c.   Bell pepper, diced
1 c.   Onion, chopped
1 tsp.   Garlic, minced
1 c.   Spaghetti sauce
½ tsp.   Paprika
¼ tsp.   Sea salt
Pinch   Caraway seed, crushed
⅓ c.   Tofu Sour Cream or Cashew Sour Cream

Brown the gluten and set aside. Sauté the bell peppers, onion, and garlic until tender-crisp. Combine everything but the "sour cream" in a casserole and bake at 400° for 20 minutes. Stir in the "sour cream" and serve.
Variation: Use UnChicken.

ORIENTAL MARINATED UNSTEAK

2 T.   Corn oil
2 T.   Oriental sesame oil
¼ c.   Sucanat
⅓ c.   Low sodium soy sauce
⅓ c.   Balsamic vinegar
3 T.   Green onions, chopped
½ tsp.   Powdered ginger
1 T.   Garlic, minced
3 T.   Lemon juice
½ tsp.   Hot pepper flakes
⅓ c.   Water
4 c.   Beef Gluten, sliced

In a blender or food processor, blend everything but the gluten until smooth. Put the gluten in a shallow dish and pour the marinade over it, turning it to coat it well. Marinate the gluten, covered and chilled, for at least 6 hours or overnight. Discard the marinade and grill or broil the gluten on each side. Let it stand for 10 minutes.

ORIENTAL UNBEEF AND TOMATOES

1 T.   Cornstarch
2 T.   Low sodium soy sauce
1 T.   UnBeef Broth
1 ½ tsp.   Sucanat
2 c.   UnBeef, cubed
2 tsp.   Corn oil
1 c.   Onion, chopped coarsely
2 tsp.   Garlic, minced
¼ tsp.   Sea salt
1 ½ c.   Tomatoes, diced
1 tsp.   Sucanat
1 tsp.   Chili paste, or ¼ tsp. of cayenne

3 T.   Tomato sauce
2 T.   UnFish Broth

Combine the cornstarch, soy sauce, UnBeef Broth, and Sucanat. Add the gluten, toss well, and let marinate for 20 minutes. In 1 tsp. of the oil sauté the onion for 1 minute and transfer to a plate. Add the other teaspoon of oil and sauté the garlic until it is golden. Add the gluten and salt and sauté for 1 minute. Sprinkle the tomatoes with the Sucanat, add them to the gluten along with the chili paste (or cayenne), and sauté just until the tomatoes are heated through. Add the tomato sauce and bring to a boil. Add the onion and UnFish broth. Sauté for 1 minute. Serve with rice.

REUBEN CASSEROLE

4 c.   Mashed potatoes, warm
2 c.   Sauerkraut, rinsed and drained
4 T.   Green onions, sliced
2 c.   UnBeef or other gluten of choice, diced and browned in oil
1 c.   Notzarella or Yeast Cheez

Combine the potatoes, sauerkraut, and onions. Mix well. Spoon ⅔ of this into a nonstick casserole. Put the UnBeef over this. Spread the cheez over that. Top with the rest of the potato mixture. Sprinkle paprika over the top. Bake, uncovered, at 350° for 30 minutes or until heated through.

ROAST UNBEEF–1

A favorite. Excellent cold, and gets better with age. Chopped or ground this is a superb hamburger substitute.

6 c.   Raw gluten
2 tsp.   Corn oil
¾ c.   Soy sauce
1 ½ tsp.   Sea salt
1 ½ tsp.   Garlic powder
1 T.   Onion powder
¼ & ⅛ tsp.   Black pepper
1 ½ c.   Roasted unsalted peanuts, ground

Combine all the ingredients well. Put in an oiled casserole, and spread out to about 1-inch thick. Blend together equal parts of corn oil, soy sauce, and water–enough to cover the gluten well. Pour this into the loaf pan. Bake at 350°, covered, for 45 minutes. Uncover, and continue to bake until the gluten becomes dark brown on top.

ROAST UNBEEF–2

Make UnBeef cooked according to Method 3 given in the "Gluten–For Goodness' Sake!" section.

SALISBURY UNSTEAK

2 c.   UnBeef, sliced
2   N'eggs
⅓ c.   Dry bread crumbs
2 T.   Non-dairy margarine
1 ½ c.   Mushrooms, sliced
¼ c.   Onion, chopped fine
1 tsp.   Garlic, minced
1 ¼ c.   Cream of Mushroom Soup

Coat gluten slices with the n'eggs and coat with the crumbs. Brown on both sides in some oil (or grill on both sides) and set aside. Melt the margarine and sauté the mushrooms, onions, and garlic till soft. Add the soup and cook for 5 minutes. Cover the bottom of a casserole with a small amount of the sauce. Put in the gluten in a single layer. Cover with rest of the sauce. Bake, uncovered, at 400° for 20 minutes.

SAUCY GROUND UNBEEF CASSEROLE

You'll call for more!

1 c.   UnBeef, ground
1 c.   Onion, coarsely chopped
2 T.   Corn oil
3 c.   Eggplant, cubed and browned in oil
1 ½ tsp.   Garlic, minced
¾ tsp.   Oregano
½ tsp.   Sea salt
¼ tsp.   Pepper
1 ¼ c.   Zucchini, cut into 1-inch chunks
2 c.   Canned stewed tomatoes
¼ c.   Tomato paste

Sauté the UnBeef and onion in the oil until soft. Add the rest of the ingredients and continue to cook until the vegetables are almost tender, stirring occasionally. Bake at 375° for 30 minutes. *Variation:* Use some type of UnSausage instead of UnBeef.

SAUCY MEATLESS LOAF

2 ⅓ c.   Mushrooms, chopped
1 ½ c.   Onions, chopped fine
¾ tsp.   Garlic, minced
2 T.   Olive oil

3 ½ c.	Canned tomatoes, crushed
¾ c.	Tomato paste
1 tsp.	Sea salt
⅛ tsp.	Black pepper
2 tsp.	Sucanat
½ c.	Tomato juice
1	Bay leaf
2 tsp.	Basil
4 c.	UnBeef, ground (or a combination of UnBeef and UnPork)
1 c.	Seasoned dry bread crumbs
3 T.	Cashew Milk
2	N'eggs

In a skillet sauté the mushrooms, onion, and garlic in the oil. Add the tomatoes, tomato paste, salt, pepper, and Sucanat. Take out 1 ½ cups of this mixture and set aside. To the skillet add the tomato juice, bay leaf, and basil. Simmer, uncovered, for 45 minutes, stirring occasionally. Meanwhile, combine the gluten, crumbs, "milk," n'eggs, and the 1 ½ cups of the sauce that was set aside. Press into a loaf or casserole pan. Bake at 350° for 45 minutes. Take from the oven and spread the herb sauce over the top of the loaf. Return to the oven and bake 15 more minutes. Discard the bay leaf.

SAUCY UNSTEAK SKILLET

2 c.	UnBeef, cut into large pieces
½ c.	Unbleached white flour mixed with ¼ tsp. of black pepper
2 tsp.	Corn oil
1 c.	Onions, chopped
2 tsp.	Garlic, minced
1 c.	Potato water
¼ c.	Catsup
1 T.	Kitchen Bouquet
2 T.	Bell pepper flakes
1 tsp.	Soy sauce
½ tsp.	Marjoram
¼ tsp.	Black pepper
2 c.	Potatoes, peeled, boiled whole, and cut in chunks (reserving the cooking water)
1 ¼ c.	Green beans
¼ c.	Sliced pimento

Coat the gluten pieces with flour-pepper and pound it into the gluten. Brown the gluten in the oil. Add the onions and garlic and sauté until they are tender. Mix the potato water, catsup, Kitchen Bouquet, bell pepper flakes, soy sauce, marjoram and pepper and pour it over the gluten

and onions. Heat this to the boiling point, reduce heat, cover, and simmer 75 to 90 minutes. Add potatoes, beans, and pimento. Heat to boiling, reduce heat, cover, and simmer until the beans are tender–10 to 15 minutes.

SPICED UNBEEF POLENTA

4 c.	Water
½ tsp.	Sea salt
1 T.	Non-dairy margarine
1 c.	Corn meal
1 ½ c.	Onion, chopped fine
3 T.	Corn oil
½ c.	Bell pepper, chopped fine
2 c.	UnBeef, ground
1 ½ tsp.	Garlic, minced
2 c.	Canned tomato sauce
1 c.	Water
1 tsp.	Sucanat
1 tsp.	Chili powder
1 T.	Cider vinegar
1 T.	Peanut butter
1 tsp.	Prepared mustard
2 tsp.	Low sodium soy sauce

Bring the water and salt to a boil and stir in the margarine and cornmeal. Lower the heat and simmer, stirring frequently, until it becomes thick–about 10 minutes. Sauté the onion in the oil for 2 minutes. Add the bell pepper and sauté 3 more minutes. Add the gluten and cook for 5 more minutes. Add the garlic and sauté 1 more minute. Stir in the rest of the ingredients and cook, stirring frequently, until much of the liquid has evaporated. Spread the cornmeal on a platter and top with the gluten mixture.

STIR-FRY UNBEEF

Good on rice or pasta.

2 c.	UnBeef, thinly sliced
1 ½ tsp.	Corn oil
2 c.	Broccoli flowerets
½ c.	Green onions, sliced
½ c.	Mushrooms, sliced
1 ½ tsp.	Soy sauce
¼ tsp.	Powdered ginger
¼ tsp.	Black pepper

Sauté the gluten in the oil, take out, and set aside. Add 1 more tablespoon of oil to the skillet. Add the broccoli and sauté for 1 minute. Add the onions and sauté for 1 more minute. Add the mushrooms and sauté for 1 more minute. Add the gluten and the rest of the ingredients and sauté 2 or more minutes.

STUFFED MEATLESS LOAF

Stuffing:

2 c.	Mixed vegetables of choice, chopped or diced, and cooked
1	N'egg
2 T.	Dry bread crumbs

Combine all and set aside.

Meatless Loaf:

3 c.	Beef Gluten, ground
½ c.	Onion, chopped
¼ c.	Corn oil
¼ c.	Catsup
¼ c.	Rolled oats
¼ c.	Dry bread crumbs
1	N'egg
2 T.	Lea & Perrins Steak Sauce
1 tsp.	Black pepper
1 tsp.	Sea salt
½ tsp.	Garlic powder

Sauté the gluten and onions in the oil until the onions are soft. Combine with the rest of the loaf ingredients and spread half of it in a loaf pan. Spread the stuffing over that and top with the rest of the loaf mixture. Bake at 375° for 45 to 55 minutes.

SWISS UNSTEAK

This is an all-time favorite, the one that has won over the most meat-eaters to the idea that there is an alternative to meat. It's easy, too!

2 tsp.	Garlic, minced
2 c.	Onions, chopped
1 ½ c.	Celery, chopped
2 T.	Corn oil
2 qt.	Tomatoes, pureed
½ tsp.	Cayenne pepper (black, if you prefer)
1 tsp.	Basil
1 tsp.	Sea salt
2 c.	UnBeef Broth
6 c.	UnBeef sliced, cooked and flavored according to Method 2, and deep-fried
4 c.	Potatoes, peeled, sliced ½-inch thick, and boiled

Sauté the garlic, onions, and celery in the oil until the onions are transparent. Add the tomatoes,

pepper, basil, salt and broth, and simmer together for 1 hour. Cover the bottom of a casserole with a small amount of this sauce. Put in the gluten in a layer, covering the bottom of the casserole. Layer the potatoes over the gluten. Top with the remaining sauce. Bake at 375° for 30 to 45 minutes.

TAMALE PIE

Oh, yes!

2 c.	UnBeef, ground
1 c.	Onions, chopped
1 c.	Bell pepper, chopped
1 T.	Corn oil
2 ½ c.	Tomato sauce
1 ½ c.	Corn
½ c.	Black olives, chopped
1 ½ tsp.	Sucanat
1 tsp.	Sea salt
1 T. & 1 tsp.	Chili powder
½ tsp.	Garlic, minced
Dash	Cayenne pepper
1 c.	Yeast Cheez
¾ c.	Cornmeal (yellow)
½ tsp.	Sea salt
2 c.	Cold water
1 T.	Non-dairy margarine

In a large skillet, sauté the gluten, onions, and bell pepper in the corn oil until tender. Stir in the tomato sauce, corn, olives, Sucanat, salt, chili powder, garlic, and pepper. Simmer 20 to 25 minutes, or until thick. Stir in the cheez and mix thoroughly. Put in an oiled 9x9x2 baking dish. Stir the cornmeal and salt into the cold water. Cook and stir until it is thick. Add the margarine and mix well. Spoon this over the UnBeef mixture in the dish and bake at 375° about 40 minutes.

TANGY UNMEATBALLS

Flavoricious!

2 c.	UnBeef, ground
1	All-purpose n'egg
¼ c.	Chili sauce
¼ c.	Onion, chopped fine
½ tsp.	Sea salt
¼ tsp.	Cayenne pepper
1 ½ c.	Cheez Cracker crumbs
1 tsp.	Corn oil

Combine the gluten, n'egg, chili sauce, onions, salt, pepper, and 1 cup of the cracker crumbs and mix thoroughly. Shape into small balls and roll in the remaining crumbs. Put ½ inch of corn oil in a skillet and heat. Sauté the gluten balls 3 to 5 minutes, turning to brown on all sides.

UNBEEF AND BROCCOLI

1 ½ c.	UnBeef, cut into very thin strips
1 ½ tsp.	Corn oil
1 tsp.	Garlic, minced
1	Medium onion, cut into wedges
2 c.	Cream of Broccoli Soup (from this book)
1 T.	Soy sauce
¼ tsp.	Sea salt
½ tsp.	Cayenne
2 c.	Broccoli florets
1 c.	Pimento Cheez

Brown the gluten in the oil. Combine everything but the cheez and cook until the broccoli is tender. Stir in the cheez and serve over noodles or rice.

UNBEEF AND MUSHROOM ÉTOUFFÉE

4 c.	UnBeef, cubed
4 tsp.	Corn oil
½ c.	Unbleached white flour
3 ½ c.	Tomato juice
3 c.	Onions, chopped
6 c.	Mushrooms, thickly sliced
1 c.	Bell pepper, chopped
1 T.	Garlic, chopped
3 T.	Parsley, chopped
¼ tsp.	Cayenne pepper
4 ½ tsp.	Louisiana Hot Sauce
⅓ c.	Lea & Perrins Steak Sauce
1 tsp.	Sea salt

Deep-fry the gluten and set it aside. Combine the oil and flour and cook until dark brown. Add the tomato juice and mix until it is absorbed by the flour-oil mixture. Add the onions, mushrooms, bell pepper, and garlic and cook for 10 minutes or until the onions are soft. Add the rest of the ingredients, including the gluten, and cook for 15 more minutes, adding more tomato juice if necessary to keep it from getting too thick. Transfer to a casserole and bake, uncovered, at 350° for 30 minutes. Serve with rice, spaghetti, or mashed potatoes.

UNBEEF PARMESAN

1	N'egg
2 tsp.	Water
Pinch	Black pepper
1 c.	Crackers, finely crushed
½ c.	Parmesan Cheez
4	UnBeef slices
	Non-dairy margarine
2 c.	Pizza Sauce of choice

Combine the n'egg, water, and pepper. Put the crumbs and cheez on a plate. Dip each gluten slice into the n'egg mixture and then into the crumb mixture. Melt some margarine in a skillet and brown the gluten on both sides, adding more margarine to keep from burning. (Or broil or grill until brown on both sides). Put a thin layer of the pizza sauce in a casserole. Cover with the gluten slices. Add the rest of the sauce. Sprinkle the remaining crumb mixture over all. Bake, uncovered, at 400° for 20 minutes.

UNBEEF POT ROAST

6 c.	UnBeef, sliced or cubed
	Unbleached white flour
⅔ c.	Non-dairy margarine
1 ½ c.	Onions, chopped
1 ½ tsp.	Garlic, minced
¼ c.	Lea & Perrins Steak Sauce
¾ c.	Tomato sauce
2 c.	UnBeef Broth
1 tsp.	Paprika
1 ½ tsp.	Oregano, crumbled
½ tsp.	Thyme, crumbled
½ tsp.	Sea salt
½ tsp.	Black pepper

Coat the gluten with the flour, shaking off any excess. In the margarine brown the gluten and set aside. Add the onion and garlic and sauté until they are soft. Put the gluten back in and add the steak sauce, tomato sauce, broth, paprika, oregano, thyme, salt, and pepper. Bring to a boil, reduce heat, and simmer, covered, for 15 minutes. Turn the gluten and simmer 10 more minutes.

UNBEEF ROULADEN

As good as it is unusual! The pickle will surprise you!

4	UnBeef slices, ¼-inch thick
	Coarse-ground prepared mustard
	Sea salt
	Cayenne pepper

1	Medium dill pickle, quartered lengthwise
2	Carrots, cut into sticks
1	Small onion, cut into wedges
2 T.	Unbleached white flour
1 T.	Corn oil
3 c.	UnBeef Broth
6 T.	Canned tomato sauce
2 tsp.	Garlic, minced

On one side of each gluten slice spread the mustard and sprinkle on the salt and pepper. On each one, top one edge with a piece of pickle, carrot, and a wedge of onion. Roll up and secure with a toothpick. Coat each roll with flour. In a skillet brown the gluten rolls evenly in the oil and remove from the skillet. Put the remaining flour in the oil and cook, stirring, until it browns. Stirring constantly, add the broth, tomato sauce, and garlic. Cook, stirring, until it thickens. Put the gluten rolls in a nonstick casserole and cover with the sauce. Bake at 400° for 30 minutes, basting occasionally.

UNBEEF STEAKS WITH PEPERONATA TOMATO SAUCE

¼ c.	Dry bread crumbs
¼ c.	Parmesan Cheez
1 T.	Parsley, chopped
Dash	Pepper
4	N'eggs
6	UnBeef slices, ½-inch thick
2 tsp.	Garlic, minced
3 c.	Onions, sliced thin and separated into rings
1 ½ c.	Bell pepper, cut into bite-size strips
½ tsp.	Rosemary
3 T.	Olive oil
6 c.	Canned tomatoes, chopped, with liquid
2 T.	Balsamic vinegar
1 T.	Non-dairy margarine

Combine the crumbs, cheez, parsley, and pepper. Dip the gluten slices in the n'eggs and then coat with the crumb mixture. Set aside. In 2 tablespoons of the oil cook the garlic, onions, bell peppers, and rosemary until the onions are tender, stirring occasionally. Add the tomatoes and cook for 30 more minutes. Stir in the vinegar. Remove from heat and keep warm. Melt the margarine and rest of the oil. Brown the gluten slices, turning once. Cover the bottom of a casserole with a small amount of the tomato

mixture. Put in the gluten in a single layer. Cover with rest of tomato mixture. Bake, uncovered, at 400° for 20 minutes.

UNBEEF STROGANOFF

A more than pleasant surprise!

2 c.	UnBeef, cut into very thin strips
½ c.	Onions, chopped
1 T.	Non-dairy margarine
1 ¼ c.	Cream of Mushroom Soup
½ tsp.	Paprika
¼ tsp.	Sea salt
½ c.	Tofu Sour Cream

In a skillet sauté the gluten and onions in the margarine until the onions are soft. Stir in the soup, paprika, and salt and heat through, stirring occasionally. Reduce the heat to very low and stir in the "sour cream." Gently heat through. Serve over noodles.

UNBEEF WITH RICE AND TOMATOES

6	UnBeef slices, cut 1-inch thick
6	Large bell pepper rings
2 c.	Rice, cooked
6	Medium onion slices
6	Tomato slices
6 c.	Canned tomatoes with juice
½ tsp.	Sea salt
¼ tsp.	Cayenne pepper
1 tsp.	Louisiana hot sauce

Sprinkle the gluten on both sides with some salt and pepper, and brown it in a skillet. Put the gluten slices in a large baking dish so they do not overlap. Put a bell pepper ring on each gluten slice. With an ice cream scoop or large spoon take some of the rice and put it in the pepper ring, patting to make it firm. Put an onion slice on each mound of rice. Put a tomato slice on each onion slice. Empty the canned tomatoes into a bowl and chop or squeeze them until they are all broken up fine. Season the tomatoes with the salt, pepper, and hot sauce and pour them around the gluten slices. Cover and bake 1 hour at 375°.

UNSTEAK AND ONION PIE

1 c.	Onions, sliced
2 c.	UnBeef, cubed
2 tsp.	Corn oil
¼ c.	Unbleached white flour
2 tsp.	Sea salt

½ tsp.	Black pepper
½ tsp.	Paprika
Pinch	Ground ginger
Pinch	Ground allspice
2 c.	Potatoes, peeled and diced
1 c.	Carrots, diced
1 c.	Peas
2 c.	UnBeef Broth
1	Unbaked pie shell
1	Unbaked top crust

Sauté the onions and gluten in the oil until the onions are soft. Stir in the flour. Add rest of ingredients but the crusts, and cook until the potatoes are almost tender. Spoon the filling into the pie shell and top with the crust. Seal the edges. Bake at 450° for 20 to 25 minutes or until golden brown.

UNSTEAK ÉTOUFFÉE

7	UnBeef "steaks"
1 T.	Corn oil
1 ½ c.	Mushroom Gravy
1 c.	UnBeef Broth
1 c.	Onion, chopped
¼ c.	Pimento, chopped
1 T.	Garlic, minced
½ tsp.	Celery seed
1 T.	Parsley, dried
1 T.	Soy sauce
½ tsp.	Angostura bitters
½ tsp.	Sea salt
¼ tsp.	Black pepper
1 ½ tsp.	Louisiana hot sauce or ¾ tsp. Tabasco

Sauté the gluten in the oil. Combine the rest of the ingredients and pour over the gluten. Cover and let cook over low heat for 45 minutes.

Burgers

BARBECUE BURGERS

4 c.	Unbeef, ground
4	Slices of bread, crumbed
2	N'eggs
½ c.	Cashew milk
2 tsp.	Sea salt
1 T.	Onion, minced
1 T.	Celery, minced
½ tsp.	Chili powder
1 c.	Barbecue sauce
2 tsp.	Corn oil

Combine everything and shape into patties. Brown in oil or bake at 400° for 30 minutes, turning after 15 minutes.

BEAN BURGERS-1

6 c.	Pressure-cooked dried beans
3 c.	Rice cooked in UnBeef Broth
2 c.	Tomatoes
1 c.	Tomato sauce
1 c.	Bell pepper
⅓ c.	Onions, chopped
1 tsp.	Minced garlic
3 T.	Soy sauce
1 ½ tsp.	Sea salt
½ tsp.	Basil
¼ tsp.	Oregano
1 T.	Parsley
1 T.	Corn oil

Mash the cooked beans. Mix all ingredients together. Form into patties. Brown in oil, or place on an oiled sheet pan and bake at 400° until light brown, turning once, or cook on a griddle.

BEAN BURGERS-2

1 ¼ c.	Red onion, chopped
1 c.	Carrot, grated
1 ¼ c.	Celery
¾ c.	Bell pepper
1 ½ tsp.	Garlic, minced
4 tsp.	Corn oil
6 c.	Cooked beans
3 c.	Rice, cooked
1 ½ tsp.	Sea salt
¾ tsp.	Basil
¾ tsp.	Parsley
½ tsp.	Garlic powder
½ c.	Soy sauce

Sauté onions, carrot, celery, bell pepper, and garlic in the oil. Mix everything together well. Form into patties and brown in oil or place on a nonstick sheet pan and bake at 375° for 35 minutes or until light brown.

BEAN BURGERS-3

2 c.	Bread crumbs
2 c.	Refried beans
1 c.	Cooked rice
¼ c.	Quick rolled oats
¼ c.	Tomato paste
½ tsp.	Garlic powder
½ tsp.	Sea salt
1 T.	Arrowroot powder
3 T.	Onion (or parsley), minced fine
2 tsp.	Corn oil
⅓ c.	Water

Combine everything, form into patties, and brown on both sides.

BURGERS SUPREME

¼ c.	Onion, chopped
1 T.	Corn oil
8 T.	UnBacon, minced
1 ¼ c.	Mushrooms, chopped fine
2 c.	UnBeef, ground
2 c.	UnPork, ground
¼ c.	Parmesan Cheez
½ tsp.	Black pepper
¼ tsp.	Garlic powder
2 T.	Lea & Perrins Steak Sauce
⅓ c.	Unbleached white flour

Sauté the onions in the oil until soft. Combine everything and shape into patties. Brown in oil or broil or grill.

EGGPLANT BURGERS

This will surprise you! We know how to make a lot of "burgers," but this is far and away my favorite!

1	Eggplant, peeled and cut into ½-inch-thick slices
	Sea salt
4 c.	Unbleached white flour
¼ tsp.	Garlic powder
¼ tsp.	Onion powder
¼ tsp.	Basil
¼ tsp.	Black pepper
	Corn oil

Sprinkle a layer of sea salt on a counter top or other large surface, and lay the eggplant slices out on that. Sprinkle sea salt over the top of the slices. Let them sit for twenty minutes to draw out the moisture. Take each slice and pat it dry with paper towels and set aside. Mix the flour with the garlic powder, onion powder, basil, and black pepper. Lightly dust each slice of eggplant in the flour mixture, shaking off any excess. Deep fry in a skillet that has ¾-inch of hot corn oil until golden brown. Drain on paper towels. Put in buns just as you would "burgers."

GARBANZO BURGERS

2 T.	Green onions, chopped fine
¾ c.	Mushrooms, chopped fine
½ tsp.	Curry powder
2 tsp.	Corn oil
2 ½ tsp.	Garlic, minced
1 c.	Cooked garbanzos, drained (keep liquid)
¾ c.	Garbanzo liquid
¼ tsp.	Sea salt
½ c.	Bread crumbs
¼ c.	Dry bread crumbs

Sauté the onions, mushrooms, and curry powder in the oil until soft. Put the garlic, garbanzos, garbanzo liquid, and salt in a blender and blend until smooth. Combine everything and mix well. Shape into patties and brown in oil or grill or broil.

GLUTEN BURGERS

2 c.	Flavored gluten of choice, ground
½ c.	Bread crumbs
⅓ c.	Parsley, chopped fine
1	N'egg
1 T.	Unbleached white flour
½ tsp.	Sea salt
½ tsp.	Black pepper
½ c.	Onion, chopped fine
1 tsp.	Corn oil
1 tsp.	Garlic, minced

Combine the gluten, crumbs, parsley, n'egg, flour, salt and pepper well. Cover and refrigerate. Sauté the onion in the oil until soft. Stir in the garlic, and take from the heat and let cool to room temperature. Stir into the gluten mixture. Shape into patties and brown in oil or grill or broil.

OAT BURGERS

These are as good as they sound insipid! Try them!

4 ⅓ c.	Water
1 tsp.	Corn oil
½ c.	Low sodium soy sauce
1 ½ c.	Onion, chopped
1 tsp.	Garlic salt
¼ tsp.	Italian seasoning
¼ c.	Nutritional yeast
4 ½ c.	Rolled (not quick) oats

Combine everything but the oats and bring to a boil. Reduce the heat and add the oats. Stir in well. Cook about 5 minutes. Set aside to cool. Form or cut into patties and brown in oil or put them on a baking sheet and bake at 400° for 45 minutes, turning every 15 minutes.

OAT BURGERS WITH MUSHROOMS

You will not be ashamed of these!

½ lb.	Mushrooms, diced
1 ½ c.	Onion, diced
½ tsp.	Sea salt
2 T.	Corn oil

4 c.	Water
⅓ c.	Low sodium soy sauce
1 tsp.	Garlic powder
¼ tsp.	Oregano
½ tsp.	Basil
½ tsp.	Thyme
¼ c.	Nutritional Yeast
5 c.	Rolled oats

Sauté the mushrooms, onions, and salt in the oil. While sautéing, bring all the other ingredients, except for the oats, to a boil. Lower the heat, add the sautéed vegetables, and add the oats, 1 cup at a time, allowing each cupful to sink a little before stirring gently. Cook up to 5 minutes—until the mixture starts to stick to the bottom of the pot. Set aside to cool. Form into patties and brown in oil or place on a nonstick baking sheet and bake at 350° for 45 minutes, turning once after 20 minutes.

Variation: Instead of the mushrooms, use bell pepper or celery, or a combination.

SOYBURGERS

1 ½ c.	Onions, chopped
1 c.	Carrot, grated
1 ¼ c.	Celery, chopped fine
¾ c.	Bell pepper, chopped fine
1 ½ tsp.	Garlic, minced
4 tsp.	Corn oil
6 c.	Cooked soybeans (save the cooking water)
3 c.	Cooked rice
1 ½ tsp.	Sea salt
¾ tsp.	Basil
¾ tsp.	Parsley
½ tsp.	Garlic powder
½ c.	Soy sauce
⅓ c.	Tahini

Sauté onions, carrot, celery, bell pepper, and garlic in the oil. Mash beans, combine everything, and mix well. If too dry, add bean water or tomato juice. Form into patties and place on an oiled sheet pan. Bake at 400° until light brown, turning once, or fry on a griddle.

SUNBURGERS

3 c.	Water
½ c.	Soy sauce
2 tsp.	Corn oil
1	Onion, chopped, or ⅛ cup of dried onion flakes
⅛ tsp.	Garlic powder

1 tsp.	Thyme
¼ tsp.	Liquid smoke
¼ c.	Sunflower seeds
3 c.	Quick oats

Put all the ingredients except the oats in a large saucepan and bring it to a boil. Add the oats slowly, stirring constantly and gently, until it is mixed. Turn the heat to low and simmer for a few minutes, being careful that the oats do not burn. Remove from heat, cover and set aside until the mixture is cool enough to handle. Form into patties about ½ inch thick and 3 ½ inches in diameter. Bake at 350° on an oiled baking sheet for 20 minutes. Turn the patties over and bake for 20 more minutes.

Variation: Fry on a griddle.

TOFU-PEPPER BURGERS

1 lb.	Tofu, drained
1 c.	Bell pepper, finely chopped
½ c.	Red onions, finely chopped
1 T.	Low sodium soy sauce
1	Garlic clove, minced
½ tsp.	Ginger, powdered
1 T.	Corn oil
½ tsp.	Lemon juice
3 T.	Unbleached white flour

Wrap the tofu in a towel and place it under a weighted cutting board for 15 minutes. Combine all ingredients except the lemon juice and flour. Sauté in the oil until the vegetables begin to brown. Add the lemon juice and flour. Form into patties and brown in oil or broil or grill on both sides.

UNBEEF AND ZUCCHINI BURGERS

2 c.	UnBeef, ground
⅔ c.	Zucchini, shredded
⅓ c.	Onion, minced
¼ c.	Unbleached white flour
½ c.	Dried bread crumbs
½ tsp.	Sea salt
1	N'egg
2 tsp.	Corn oil
¼ tsp.	Black pepper
⅔ c.	Notzarella Cheez
⅛ tsp.	Garlic powder
½ tsp.	Basil
¼ c.	Cashew Milk

Combine everything well. Shape into patties. Brown in oil, grill or broil.

VEGEBURGERS

2 c.	Cooked soybeans, ground (save the cooking water)
1 c.	Cooked garbanzos, ground (save the cooking water)
1 ½ c.	Rice, cooked in UnChicken Broth
1 ½ c.	Onions, chopped
1 ½ tsp.	Sage
¾ tsp.	Celery salt
½ tsp.	Garlic powder
1 ½ tsp.	Corn oil

Combine all ingredients, adding bean water if too dry, or crumbs or oatmeal if too wet. Form patties and brown in oil or bake, covered with foil, for 25 minutes at 350° then turn and bake 10 minutes or more.

VEGETABLE BURGERS

1 c.	Onion, minced
1 c.	Carrots, grated
1 c.	Turnips, grated
1 c.	Zucchini, grated
1 c.	Beets, grated
1 ½ tsp.	Garlic, chopped
½ tsp.	Cumin, ground
1 tsp.	Dill weed, dried
¼ tsp.	Tarragon, dried
2 T.	Corn oil
¼ c.	Instant rolled oats
¼ c.	Water
1 ½ c.	Mashed potatoes
⅔ c.	Cooked rice
½ tsp.	Sea salt
½ tsp.	Pepper

Sauté the onion, carrots, turnips, zucchini, beets, garlic, cumin, dill, and tarragon in the oil until the vegetables begin to wilt–about 5 minutes. Let them cool slightly. Soak the oats in the water for 5 minutes, drain, and press out excess water. Combine all the ingredients and mix well. Shape into patties and brown in oil or grill or broil.

UnPork
Substitutes & Dishes

UNPORK–1

Cook 2 cups of raw gluten according to Method 1, 2, or 3 in:

UNPORK GLUTEN BROTH–1

½ c.	Onions, chopped
4 ½ tsp.	Monosodium glutamate
1 tsp.	Sea salt
⅓ c.	Nutritional Yeast
½ tsp.	Hot pepper flakes
¼ tsp.	Black pepper
3/4 tsp.	Sage
1 tsp.	Corn oil
2 c.	Water

Combine everything and simmer for 5 minutes.

UNPORK–2

Cook 2 cups of raw gluten according to Method 1, 2, or 3 in:

UNPORK GLUTEN BROTH–2

½ c.	Onions, chopped
4 ½ tsp.	Monosodium glutamate
1 tsp.	Sea salt
1 tsp.	Poultry seasoning
⅓ c.	Nutritional Yeast
1 tsp.	Corn oil
2 c.	Water
½ tsp.	Black pepper
½ tsp.	Mace

Combine everything and simmer for 5 minutes.

UNPORK–3

Cook 2 cups of raw gluten according to Method 1, 2, or 3 in:

UNPORK GLUTEN BROTH–3

½ c.	Onions, chopped
4 ½ tsp.	Monosodium glutamate
1 tsp.	Sea salt
1 tsp.	Poultry seasoning
⅓ c.	Nutritional Yeast
1 tsp.	Corn oil
2 c.	Water
½ tsp.	Black pepper
1 tsp.	Garlic, crushed
¼ tsp.	Marjoram, powdered

Combine everything and simmer for 5 minutes.

UNPORK CHOPS

Cook 2 cups of raw gluten according to Method 1, 2, or 3 in a broth made by combining and simmering together for 5 minutes:

½ c.	Onions, chopped
4 ½ tsp.	Monosodium glutamate
1 tsp.	Sea salt
⅓ c.	Nutritional Yeast
½ tsp.	Black pepper
¼ tsp.	Paprika
1	Bay leaf
½ tsp.	Ground sage
1 tsp.	Corn oil
2 c.	Water

Cut the gluten into "chops."

BARBECUE "SPARE RIBS"

1 c.	Onions, chopped
1 ½ tsp.	Non-dairy margarine or corn oil

⅓ c.	Nutritional Yeast flakes
½ c.	Tahini
2 T.	Paprika
2 tsp.	Sea salt
4 c.	Raw gluten
2 T.	Corn oil

Sauté the onions in the margarine (or oil) until soft. Combine the nutritional yeast, tahini, paprika, and salt in a bowl. Add the onions along with the sautéing margarine (or oil) to this and combine well. Take half of this seasoning mixture and half (2 cups) of the gluten (broken into several pieces) and blend together in a food processor using the metal blade, gradually adding the gluten. Set aside and repeat with the other half of the seasoning mixture and ingredients. Spread the corn oil over the bottom of a baking sheet.

Form into 2 by 3-inch patties one inch thick, and place in rows on the baking sheet. Bake, uncovered, at 350° for 45 minutes. Pour 1 to 2 cups of barbecue sauce over them. Put back in the oven and bake at 375° for 20 minutes or until well done. Serve with extra barbecue sauce on the side.

BARBECUE "SPARE RIB" SAUCE

½ c.	Onion, chopped
1 tsp.	Garlic, minced
2 tsp.	Corn oil or non-dairy margarine
2 ½ c.	Canned tomato sauce
¼ c.	Water
1 c.	Sucanat
2 T.	Barbados molasses
½ c.	Prepared mustard
1 ½ tsp.	Sea salt
1 tsp.	Allspice
2 tsp.	Hot pepper flakes
1 ½ tsp.	Dried parsley or 1 sprig of fresh parsley, chopped
¼ c.	Water
1 T.	Soy sauce
2 T.	Lemon juice
1 tsp.	Liquid smoke

Sauté the onion and garlic in oil or margarine until the onions become clear and golden. Add tomato sauce, the first ¼ cup of water, Sucanat, molasses, mustard, salt, allspice, pepper flakes, and parsley. Bring to a boil, reduce heat, and let simmer for about an hour. Add second ¼ cup of water, soy sauce, lemon juice, and liquid smoke. Cook 10-15 minutes longer.

CHILI UNPORK CHOP CASSEROLE

4	UnPork slices, ¾-to-1-inch thick
	Corn oil
1 c.	Onion, chopped
¼ c.	Jalapeños, chopped, or canned chilis, chopped
½ c.	Celery, chopped
2 ½ c.	Cooked rice
3 ½ c.	Cream of Mushroom Soup
3 T.	Low sodium soy sauce

Brown the gluten on both sides in the oil. Remove and set aside. Sauté the onion, jalapeños, and celery until the onion is tender–adding more oil if needed. Stir in the rice, soup, and soy sauce. Blend well. Put into a nonstick casserole. Top with the gluten and bake, covered, at 400° for 30 minutes.

CHINESE UNPORK WITH WATER CHESTNUTS AND MUSHROOMS

2 tsp.	Corn oil
2 c.	UnPork, minced fine
¼ c.	Mushrooms, minced
10	Water chestnuts, drained and minced
⅓ c.	Green onions, sliced
2 tsp.	Jalapeños, sliced
½ tsp.	Sucanat
½ tsp.	Powdered ginger
2 T.	Soy sauce
1 T.	Cornstarch, mixed in 3 T. of cold water

In the oil, sauté the gluten, mushrooms, water chestnuts, onions, jalapeños, Sucanat, and ginger until the gluten browns. Add the soy sauce and cornstarch-cold water mixture and cook for 5 more minutes. Serve with rice.

FRIED UNPORK

½ c.	Unbleached white flour
¼ tsp.	White pepper
4 c.	UnPork, sliced ¼-inch thick
¼ c.	Corn oil
1 ½ c.	UnChicken Broth
1 T.	White vinegar
2 T.	Green onion, sliced thin
1 tsp.	Fresh rosemary (or ¼ tsp. dried)
	Non-dairy margarine
½ tsp.	Black pepper

Combine the flour and white pepper. Lightly dredge the gluten in this, shaking off the excess.

Making your own Barbecue "Spare Ribs"

Left: Combine the sautéed onions, Nutritional Yeast, tahini, and spices with the gluten in a bowl and mix well (see recipe on page 98-99 for details).

Right: Form into 2 by 3-inch patties one inch thick, and place in rows on an oiled baking sheet. Bake, uncovered, at 350° for 45 minutes.

Above: Pour 1 to 2 cups of Barbecue "Spare Rib" Sauce (recipe on page 99) over them. Put back in the oven and bake at 375° for 20 minutes or until well done. Serve with extra barbecue sauce on the side.

Heat 2 tablespoons of the oil in a skillet, put in ⅓ of the gluten and brown it well then set it aside on a platter arranged in a single layer. Do the same with another ⅓ of the gluten, adding 1 tablespoon of the oil. Repeat this with the final ⅓ of the gluten, setting it aside on the platter, also. To the skillet add the broth, vinegar, onion, and rosemary. Bring to a boil and cook until slightly thickened–about 2 minutes. Return the gluten to the skillet briefly to heat it through–about 30 seconds. Put the gluten back on the platter. Stir the margarine into the sauce in the skillet and stir in the black pepper. Spoon this over the gluten.

GINGER-PEACH UNPORK

Top of the Class! You must try this!

1 T.	Sea salt
½ tsp.	Black pepper
1 tsp.	Ground ginger
2 T.	Water
2 T.	Cider vinegar
½ c.	Sucanat
3 T.	Chili sauce
3 ½ c.	Peaches, sliced
4 c.	UnPork

Combine everything but the gluten in a blender and blend until smooth. Marinate the gluten in this overnight in the refrigerator. Coat the bottom of a baking pan with oil, put in the gluten and pour in enough of the marinade just to cover the gluten. Bake at 425° for 45 minutes.

GLORIFIED UNPORK CHOPS

1 T.	Corn oil
6	UnPork "chops"
1 c.	Onion, sliced
1 ½ c.	Cream of Mushroom Soup

Brown the chops–3 at a time–in the oil. Stir in the onion and soup, transfer to a casserole, and bake, uncovered, at 350° for 20 minutes.

KRAUT-STUFFED UNPORK CHOPS

12	½-inch-thick slices of UnPork
2 T.	Corn oil
2	Bell peppers
1 c.	Onion, chopped
1 ½ c.	Carrots, peeled and shredded
1 tsp.	Sea salt
¼ tsp.	Cayenne pepper
¼ tsp.	Dried mint
1 T.	Sucanat
4 c.	Sauerkraut, drained

In a skillet brown the gluten slices on both sides in the oil. Remove and set aside. Slice 4 rings from the peppers and set aside. Dice the rest. Sauté the diced pepper and onions in the remaining oil until the onion is transparent. Stir in the carrots and sauté 1 minute. Add seasonings, Sucanat, and sauerkraut. Toss until combined. Layer ⅓ of this mixture in the bottom of a nonstick casserole. Put half the gluten over this in a layer. Layer another ⅓ of the sauerkraut mixture, and top with the rest of the gluten. Put the remaining sauerkraut mixture over all. Top with the pepper rings. Cover and bake at 400° for 45 minutes.

MEXICAN UNPORK CHOPS AND BEANS

2 T.	Unbleached white flour
1 c.	Salsa
2 T.	Lime juice
¾ tsp.	Chili powder
½ tsp.	Garlic powder
2 c.	Kidney beans, cooked and drained
1 c.	Bell pepper, cubed
4	UnPork slices, ½-inch thick

Blend the flour, salsa, lime juice, chili powder, and garlic powder in a blender. Combine this with the beans and bell pepper. Put the gluten slices in a baking dish, pour the other ingredients over them. Cover and bake at 350° for 30 minutes.

ORANGE UNPORK CHOPS

6	UnPorkchops ½-inch thick
1 T.	Corn oil
¾ c.	Water
½ tsp.	Paprika
½ tsp.	Pepper
1 ¼ tsp.	Sea salt
1	Orange
⅓ c.	Sucanat
1 T.	Cornstarch
½ tsp.	Cinnamon
4 or 6	Whole cloves
1 c.	Orange juice

Brown the gluten on both sides in the oil. Add the water, paprika, pepper, and 1 teaspoon of the salt. Bring to a boil, reduce the heat, cover, and simmer about 35 minutes, turning once. Grate

1 tablspoon of the orange peel from the stem end. Cut 6 slices from the other end. Set aside. In a saucepan combine the grated peel, Sucanat, cornstarch, cinnamon, cloves, and rest of the salt. Stir in the juice and cook and stir until thickened. Top the gluten with the sauce and serve.

ORIENTAL UNPORK CHOPS

1 c.	Unbleached white flour
½ tsp.	Sea salt
¼ tsp.	Cayenne pepper
6	UnPork chops, cut thick
½ c.	UnPork Broth
1 c.	Bell pepper, chopped
1 c.	Onion, chopped
1 c.	Mushrooms, sliced
¾ tsp.	Garlic, minced
3 T.	Low sodium soy sauce
1	15-oz. can pineapple chunks, drained, reserving the juice

Combine the flour, salt, and pepper in a bag. Toss the gluten in this until coated. Take out the gluten and shake off excess flour. Broil or grill on both sides. Set aside in a casserole dish. Put the UnPork broth, bell pepper, onion, mushrooms, and garlic in a skillet. Cover and simmer for 25 to 30 minutes. Add the soy sauce and juice from the pineapple. Stir until somewhat thickened. Add the pineapple chunks and bring to a boil. Pour over the gluten and serve.

OVEN-BARBECUED UNPORK CHOPS

6-8	UnPork slices, ¾-inch thick
2 T.	Lea & Perrins Steak Sauce
2 T.	Balsamic vinegar
2 tsp.	Genuine maple syrup
½ tsp.	Pepper
½ tsp.	Chili powder
½ tsp.	Paprika
¾ c.	Catsup
⅓ c.	Hot water

Put the gluten in a baking dish (single layer) or cast-iron skillet. Combine the rest of the ingredients and pour over the gluten slices. Bake, uncovered, at 375° for 1 hour.

SAUTÉED UNPORK CHOPS WITH TOMATO AND EGGPLANT SAUCE

4	UnPork Chops cut 1-inch thick
4 c.	Eggplant, peeled and cubed
2 tsp.	Olive oil
1 c.	Onion, chopped
1 ½ tsp.	Garlic, minced
2 c.	Canned tomatoes, chopped, with the juice
⅓ c.	Water
½ tsp.	Sea salt
¼ tsp.	Black pepper
⅓ c.	Parsley, chopped

Deep-fry the gluten and set aside. Deep-fry the eggplant and set it aside. In the oil sauté the onion and garlic for 9 minutes. Stir in the tomatoes, water, salt, pepper, and parsley. Bring to a boil and add the eggplant. Cook for about 20 minutes. Cover the bottom of a casserole with half of the sauce. Put the gluten over that. Cover with the rest of the sauce. Cover the casserole tightly and bake at 400° for 20 minutes.

SWEET AND SOUR UNPORK–1

¾ c.	Unbleached white flour
¾ c.	Cornstarch
4 ½ tsp.	Baking powder
¼ tsp.	Sea salt
1 c.	Cold water
4 ½ tsp.	Peanut oil

Combine the flour, cornstarch, baking powder, and salt. Slowly add the water, stirring with a fork until the batter is smooth. Stir in the oil very well. This should make the batter the consistency of pancake batter. If it is too thick, add up to 2 tablespoons more water, a bit at a time. Set aside.

⅔ c.	White vinegar
½ tsp.	Sea salt
6 T.	Canned tomato sauce, or 1 T. tomato paste mixed with 5 T. of water
2 T.	Lea & Perrins Steak Sauce
¾ c.	Sucanat
1 T.	Cornstarch

Combine everything and set aside.

4 c.	Peanut oil for deep-frying
1 ½ c.	UnPork, cut into 1-inch cubes
1 T.	Unbleached white flour
1 tsp.	Garlic, minced
4	Green onions, white part only, cut ½-inch-thick diagonally
½ c.	Bamboo shoots, cut into ¾-by-1-inch pieces
½ c.	Bell pepper (red preferred), cut into ¼-inch dice

Preheat the oven to 250°. Heat the oil to between 350° and 375°. Coat the gluten cubes with the flour. Coat ⅓ of the gluten with the batter and transfer them, using tongs, to the hot oil. Fry for 5 seconds and turn them over. Fry for a total of 3 minutes, turning several times, until light brown. Transfer with a slotted spoon to a strainer set over a bowl to drain. Repeat this process with the other ⅓'s of the gluten. Make sure the oil has come back up to temperature, put all the gluten back in and fry about 3 more minutes until a deep golden brown. With a slotted spoon, put the gluten on a warm platter and put it in the warm oven. Sauté the garlic and onions for 30 seconds on high heat. Add the bamboo shoots and bell pepper and sauté for 30 more seconds. Pour the sauce into this and, stirring, bring it to a boil and turn off the heat. Pour the sauce over the gluten.

SWEET AND SOUR UNPORK–2

2 T.	Unbleached white flour
3 T.	Corn oil
2 c.	UnPork Broth
⅓ c.	Vinegar
⅓ c.	Low sodium soy sauce
⅓ c.	Catsup or chili sauce
½ c.	Celery, chopped
¾ tsp.	Sea salt
¼ tsp.	Cayenne
1 c.	Carrot, sliced in rounds
1 c.	Bell pepper, cut into strips
1 c.	Pineapple chunks, drained
6 c.	UnPork, cut in strips or cubes

Brown the flour in 1 tablespoon of the oil in a small saucepan. Stir in the broth, vinegar, soy sauce, catsup, celery, salt, and cayenne, and cook, stirring frequently, until thick. Set aside. Heat the rest of the oil in a skillet and sauté the carrots for 1 minute, stirring constantly, then add the bell pepper and pineapple and heat through. Put everything together and simmer for 20 minutes. Serve over rice.

UNPORK AND SAUERKRAUT CASSEROLE

3 c.	UnPork, cubed
2 T.	Corn oil
1 c.	Onion, chopped
1 c.	Celery, chopped
1 c.	Fresh mushrooms, sliced
1	16-oz. can of sauerkraut, undrained
8 oz.	Noodles, cooked and drained

2 c.	Cream of Mushroom Soup, made with Cashew Cream
¼ tsp.	Sea salt
¼ tsp.	Black pepper

Sauté the gluten in the oil until light brown. Add the onions, celery, and mushrooms and sauté until the onions are soft. Stir in the rest of the ingredients. Put into a casserole. Bake, uncovered, at 400° for 30 minutes.

UNPORK CHOPS WITH CRUMB CRUST

Crunchalicious!

¼ c.	Dried bread crumbs
1 tsp.	Basil
¼ tsp.	Sea salt
¼ tsp.	Black pepper
4	N'eggs
4	UnPork slices, 1-inch thick

Combine the crumbs, basil, salt, and pepper. Dip the gluten in the n'eggs, then in the crumb mixture, coating both sides well. Oil a baking pan well and put the gluten on it. Broil until golden brown on both sides.

UNPORK WITH SAUERKRAUT

3 c.	Onions, chopped
1 T.	Corn oil
3 c.	UnPork, cubed
1 ½ tsp.	Paprika
½ tsp.	Caraway seeds (optional)
5 T.	Tomato paste
½ c.	UnPork Broth
1 c.	Water
2 c.	Sauerkraut, drained and washed
2 ½ c.	Potatoes, grated
1 c.	Cashew or Tofu Sour Cream

Lightly sauté the onion in the oil in a heavy pot. Add the gluten and sauté it until it is light brown. Add the paprika, caraway seed, tomato paste, broth, and water. Cover and simmer over low heat for 30 minutes. Add the sauerkraut and potatoes, cover, and simmer for 1 hour, adding extra water if you need it. Just before serving, stir in the "sour cream."

UNSAUSAGE AND SAUERKRAUT CASSEROLE

2 c.	Macaroni, uncooked
3 T.	Corn oil

2 c.	UnSausage of choice, chopped or ground
1 c.	Onion, chopped
2 c.	Canned tomatoes, chopped, with liquid
1 c.	Sauerkraut
1 tsp.	Sucanat
¼ tsp.	Sea salt
¼ tsp.	Cayenne
1 c.	Yeast Cheez

Cook the macaroni. Heat the oil in a skillet or pan and sauté the gluten and onion until the onion is soft. Add everything else but the cheez and macaroni and cook for 10 minutes. Drain the macaroni and stir it into vegetables along with the cheez. Put into a casserole and bake, uncovered, at 400° for 30 minutes.

ZESTY GRILLED UNPORK CHOPS

½ c.	Low sodium soy sauce
¼ c.	Water
¼ c.	Lemon juice
1 T.	Chili sauce
3 tsp.	Sucanat
1 tsp.	Barbados molasses
¾ tsp.	Garlic, minced
6	¾-inch-thick slices of UnPork

Combine the ingredients except for the gluten. Put the gluten slices in a baking dish and pour the marinade over them. Cover and refrigerate several hours or overnight. Remove the gluten from the marinade and grill or broil 4 inches from the heat until they are done, brushing occasionally with the marinade.

UnHam
Substitutes & Dishes

UNHAM

Cook 2 cups of raw gluten according to Method 1, 2, or 3 in:

¼ c.	Low sodium soy sauce
2 tsp.	Kitchen Bouquet
2 T.	Nutritional Yeast
½ c.	Onions, chopped
¼ tsp.	Sage, rubbed
½ tsp.	Black pepper
½ tsp.	Oregano
1 tsp.	Garlic powder
1 ¼ tsp.	Liquid smoke
1 tsp.	Corn oil
2 c.	Water
1 tsp.	Sea salt

Combine everything and simmer for 5 minutes.

BAKED UNHAM

Cook 2 cups of raw gluten according to Method 3 in:

BAKED UNHAM GLUTEN BROTH

½ c.	Onions, chopped
4 ½ tsp.	Monosodium glutamate
1 tsp.	Sea salt
1 tsp.	Poultry seasoning
⅓ c.	Nutritional Yeast
2 T.	All Purpose Seasoning (see Etc.)
1 tsp.	Corn oil
2 T.	Low sodium soy sauce
2 T.	Liquid smoke
2 T.	Barley malt syrup
2 c.	Water

Combine everything and simmer for 5 minutes.

SOY GRITS UNHAM

½ c.	Soy grits
1 c.	Boiling UnHam Gluten Broth (see Unham recipe)

Stir grits into the broth and cook for 5 minutes.

UNHAM LOAF

1 ½ T.	Cornstarch
1 c.	UnHam Broth, cold
½ c.	Sucanat
2 T.	Barbados molasses
¼ c.	White vinegar
1 T.	Dry mustard
3 c.	UnPork, ground
2 c.	UnHam, ground
1 c.	Cashew Milk
1 c.	Fine dry bread crumbs
¾ tsp.	Prepared mustard
2	N'eggs
2 T.	Bell pepper, chopped fine

In a saucepan, dissolve the cornstarch in the *cold* broth. Mix in the Sucanat, molasses, vinegar, and dry mustard. Bring to a boil, stirring often. Remove from the heat when it begins to thicken and set aside. Combine the glutens, "milk," crumbs, prepared mustard, n'eggs, and bell pepper. Press into a nonstick casserole or loaf pan. Pour a thin layer of sauce over it and bake at 325° for 2 hours. Serve the rest of the sauce with the loaf.

UnSausage
Substitutes & Dishes

A NOTE on cooking UnSausage that applies to all the types of UnSausage whose recipes are given here: If the UnSausage is to be used in a dish, the recipe will tell you if it needs any prior preparation. If you are going to eat it "straight," you can either fry it, using a small amount of oil, or spray or brush on a small amount of oil (both sides) and lightly broil.

BREAKFAST UNSAUSAGE

Nice and mild, yet flavorful.

Cook 2 cups of raw gluten according to Method 1, 2, or 3 in a broth made by combining and simmering together for 5 minutes:

½ c.	Onions, chopped
4 ½ tsp.	Monosodium glutamate
1 tsp.	Sea salt
1 tsp.	Poultry seasoning
⅓ c.	Nutritional Yeast
1 tsp.	Dried crushed sage leaves
½ tsp.	Ground ginger
¼ tsp.	Black pepper
1 tsp.	Liquid Smoke
1 tsp.	Corn oil
2 c.	Water

CAJUN UNSAUSAGE

This bites back!

Cook 2 cups of raw gluten according to Method 1, 2, or 3 in a broth made by combining and simmering together for 5 minutes:

½ c.	Onions, chopped
4 ½ tsp.	Monosodium glutamate
1 tsp.	Sea salt
1 tsp.	Cayenne pepper
⅛ tsp.	Garlic powder
1 tsp.	Cumin
1 tsp.	Poultry seasoning
⅛ tsp.	Sage
⅛ tsp.	Curry powder
1 tsp.	Dried mint
⅓ c.	Nutritional Yeast
1 tsp.	Corn oil
2 c.	Water

FARMER'S UNSAUSAGE

Flavor galore!

Cook 2 cups of raw gluten according to Method 1, 2, or 3 in a broth made by combining and simmering together for 5 minutes:

½ c.	Onions, chopped
4 ½ tsp.	Monosodium glutamate
1 tsp.	Sea salt
1 tsp.	Poultry seasoning
⅓ c.	Nutritional Yeast
¾ tsp.	Fennel seed
½ tsp.	Black pepper
2 T.	Soy sauce
1 ½ tsp.	Oregano
¼ tsp.	Cayenne
1 T.	Sucanat
1 T.	Garlic powder
1 T.	Prepared mustard
1 tsp.	Allspice
1 tsp.	Corn oil
2 c.	Water

GARLIC UNSAUSAGE

A garlic lover's delight!

Cook 2 cups of raw gluten according to Method 1, 2, or 3 in a broth made by combining and simmering together for 5 minutes:

1 c.	Onions, chopped
4 ½ tsp.	Monosodium glutamate
1 tsp.	Sea salt
1 tsp.	Poultry seasoning
⅓ c.	Nutritional Yeast
⅓ c.	Garlic powder
½ tsp.	Black pepper
1 tsp.	Corn oil
2 c.	Water

HERB UNSAUSAGE

This has been formulated for those who find the spices in regular UnSausage too hard to digest easily. But everybody will like it.

Cook 2 cups of raw gluten according to Method 1, 2, or 3 in a broth made by combining and simmering together for 5 minutes:

½ c.	Onions, chopped
4 ½ tsp.	Monosodium glutamate
⅓ c.	Nutritional Yeast
½ tsp.	Garlic salt
1 tsp.	Dried parsley
1 tsp.	Dried sage
⅛ tsp.	Thyme leaves
½ tsp.	Black pepper
1 tsp.	Corn oil
2 c.	Water
¼ tsp.	Allspice, ground

ITALIAN UNSAUSAGE

Pizza delight!

Cook 2 cups of raw gluten according to Method 1, 2, or 3 in a broth made by combining and simmering together for 5 minutes:

½ c.	Onions, chopped
4 ½ tsp.	Monosodium glutamate
1 tsp.	Sea salt
1 tsp.	Poultry seasoning
⅓ c.	Nutritional Yeast
½ tsp.	Sucanat
¼ tsp.	Garlic powder
¼ tsp.	Fennel seed
¼ tsp.	Lemon pepper seasoning
¼ tsp.	Paprika

⅛ tsp.	Celery salt
⅛ tsp.	Dried crushed sage leaves
⅛ tsp.	Cayenne pepper
1 ½ tsp.	Soy sauce
1 tsp.	Lea & Perrins Steak Sauce
1 tsp.	Corn oil
2 c.	Water

MEXICAN CHORIZO UNSAUSAGE

Good and spicy!

Cook 2 cups of raw gluten according to Method 1, 2, or 3 in a broth made by combining and simmering together for 5 minutes:

½ c.	Onions, chopped
4 ½ tsp.	Monosodium glutamate
1 tsp.	Sea salt
1 tsp.	Poultry seasoning
⅓ c.	Nutritional Yeast
1 ½ tsp.	Paprika
½ tsp.	Black pepper
¾ tsp.	Hot pepper flakes
¼ tsp.	Sucanat
¼ tsp.	Garlic powder
¼ tsp.	Dried oregano leaves
⅛ tsp.	Cumin seed, powdered
1 T.	White vinegar
1 tsp.	Corn oil
2 c.	Water

PIZZA UNSAUSAGE

This is a milder version of Italian UnSausage for those who prefer it.

Cook 2 cups of raw gluten according to Method 1, 2, or 3 in a broth made by combining and simmering together for 5 minutes:

½ c.	Onions, chopped
4 ½ tsp.	Monosodium glutamate
1 tsp.	Sea salt
1 tsp.	Poultry seasoning
⅓ c.	Nutritional Yeast
¼ tsp.	Black pepper
¼ tsp.	Red pepper flakes
½ tsp.	Fennel seeds
1 tsp.	Corn oil
2 c.	Water

ROSEMARY UNSAUSAGE

Different and delicious! Mild, too.

Cook 2 cups of raw gluten according to Method 1, 2, or 3 in a broth made by combining and simmering together for 5 minutes:

½ c.	Onions, chopped
4 ½ tsp.	Monosodium glutamate
1 tsp.	Sea salt
1 tsp.	Poultry seasoning
⅓ c.	Nutritional Yeast
½ tsp.	Black pepper
¾ tsp.	Rosemary, powdered
¼ tsp.	Thyme
¼ tsp.	Marjoram
¼ tsp.	Freshly grated nutmeg
1 tsp.	Corn oil
2 c.	Water

UNSAUSAGE AND CABBAGE

Not for food snobs—but the rest of us love it!

2 tsp.	Corn oil
1 ½ c.	UnSausage of choice, cut into 1-inch cubes
4 c.	Cabbage, chopped
2 c.	Onion, sliced thin
1 ½ c.	Broth of type of UnSausage used

Brown the gluten in the oil. Add the cabbage and onion and cook, stirring occasionally, until the cabbage is browned. Add the broth and simmer, partly covered, for 15 to 20 minutes, until the cabbage is tender. Serve over mashed potatoes.

SIMPLE UNSAUSAGE

Cook 2 cups of raw gluten according to Method 1, 2, or 3 in a broth made by combining and simmering together for 5 minutes:

2 T.	Soy sauce
1 tsp.	Kitchen Bouquet
1 T.	Nutritional Yeast
¼ c.	Onions, chopped
⅛ tsp.	Sage, rubbed
¼ tsp.	Black pepper
¼ tsp.	Oregano
½ tsp.	Garlic powder
1 tsp.	Liquid smoke
2 T.	Sausage seasoning
1 tsp.	Corn oil
2 c.	Water

SOY GRITS UNSAUSAGE

½ c.	Soy grits
1 c.	Boiling flavoring broth of UnSausage type desired

Stir grits into the broth and cook for 5 minutes.

WATKINS UNSAUSAGE

Cook 2 cups of raw gluten according to Method 1, 2, or 3 in a broth made by combining and simmering together for 5 minutes:

¼ c.	Soy sauce
2 tsp.	Kitchen Bouquet
2 T.	Nutritional Yeast
½ c.	Onions, chopped
¼ tsp.	Sage, rubbed
½ tsp.	Black pepper
½ tsp.	Oregano
1 tsp.	Garlic powder
2 tsp.	Liquid smoke
4 T.	Watkins Sausage Seasoning
1 tsp.	Corn oil
2 c.	Water

UnBacon

USE IN RECIPES as indicated. For crispy bacon, slice thinly, spray or coat lightly with oil and broil until it starts to turn brown. It gets crisp as it cools, so do not overbroil by having it get crispy under the broiler.

UNBACON–1

Cook 2 cups of raw gluten according to Method 3 in:

¼ c.	Soy sauce
2 tsp.	Kitchen Bouquet
2 T.	Nutritional Yeast
½ c.	Onions, chopped
¼ tsp.	Sage, rubbed
½ tsp.	Black pepper
½ tsp.	Oregano
1 tsp.	Garlic powder
1 ¼ tsp.	Liquid smoke
1 tsp.	Corn oil
2 c.	Water
1 tsp.	Sea salt

Combine everything and simmer for 5 minutes.

UNBACON–2

Cook 2 cups of raw gluten according to Method 3 in:

½ c.	Onions, chopped
4 ½ tsp.	Monosodium glutamate
1 tsp.	Sea salt
1 tsp.	Poultry seasoning
⅓ c.	Nutritional Yeast
½ tsp.	Black pepper
1 tsp.	Garlic, minced
1 tsp.	Coriander seed, ground
¼ tsp.	Mace
1 tsp.	Liquid smoke
1 tsp.	Corn oil
2 c.	Water

Combine everything and simmer for 5 minutes.

UnChicken
Substitutes & Dishes

UNCHICKEN

Cook 2 cups of raw gluten according to Method 1, 2, or 3 in:

UNCHICKEN GLUTEN BROTH

½ c.	Onions, chopped
4 ½ tsp.	Monosodium glutamate
1 tsp.	Sea salt
1 tsp.	Poultry seasoning
⅓ c.	Nutritional Yeast
1 tsp.	Corn oil
2 c.	Water

Combine everything and simmer for 5 minutes.

BRAISED UNCHICKEN AND "CHORIZO"

1 T.	Corn oil
3 c.	UnChicken, cubed
1 T.	Curry powder
1 c.	Onion, chopped
1 T.	Garlic, minced
2 ½ c.	Potatoes, cubed
1 ¼ c.	Tomatoes, minced
¼ c.	Unbleached white flour
2 T.	Lea & Perrins Steak Sauce
2 T.	Tomato paste
3 ½ c.	UnChicken Broth
¼ c.	UnHam, cubed
½ c.	Mexican Chorizo UnSausage, cubed
½ c.	Green olives, chopped
½ c.	Thick coconut milk
¼ tsp.	Cayenne pepper

In the oil brown the UnChicken, transferring it to a bowl as it is browned. To the remaining oil add the curry powder and stir for about 30 seconds. Then add the onion, garlic, potatoes, and tomatoes, and cook, stirring, until the vegetables are softened. Stir in the flour and cook, stirring for 3 more minutes. Stir in the steak sauce, tomato paste, broth, UnHam, "chorizo," olives, coconut milk, and pepper. Add the UnChicken, and simmer, stirring occasionally, for 45 to 60 minutes.

CAJUN UNCHICKEN BAKE

	Sea salt
	Cayenne pepper
	Black pepper
6 c.	UnChicken, sliced ¼-inch thick
	Corn oil
3 c.	Onions, chopped
½ c.	Green onions, chopped
½ c.	Bell pepper, chopped
½ c.	Celery, chopped
1 c.	Parsley, chopped
¼ c.	Pimentos, cut in strips
4 c.	Water
4 T.	Lea & Perrins Steak Sauce
2 tsp.	Louisiana Hot Sauce

Sprinkle the salt and peppers on the gluten slices—both sides. Fry the gluten in the oil until it begins to brown. Pour a small amount of oil into the bottom of a baking pan. Put the gluten in the pan in a layer. On top of the gluten put the onions (both types), bell pepper, celery, and parsley. Put the pimento strips over that. Mix the water, steak sauce, and hot sauce together and pour over all. Bake, covered, at 375° for 1 hour. Just before serving, take off the cover and broil for a few minutes.

CHICKARITOS

Make plenty, for these are GOOD!

3 c.	UnChicken, chopped fine
¼ c.	Jalapeños, minced
½ c.	Green onions, chopped fine
1 ½ c.	Yeast Cheez
1 tsp.	Louisiana Hot Sauce
1 tsp.	Garlic salt
¼ tsp.	Black pepper
¼ tsp.	Cumin, ground
¼ tsp.	Paprika
	Enough Convent Pie Crust for 2 10-inch pie crusts
	Water
	Salsa
	Guacamole

Combine the gluten, jalapeños, onions, cheez, and seasonings, and mix well. Roll out half of the crust into a 9x12-inch rectangle. Cut into 9 small rectangles. Put about 2 tablespoons of the filling across the center of each rectangle. Wet the edges of the pastry with water and roll it around the filling, crimping the ends with a fork to seal. Repeat with the rest of the pastry and filling. Place, seam side down, on an oiled or nonstick cookie sheet. Bake at 425° for 20 to 25 minutes—until golden brown. Serve with salsa and guacamole.
Variation: Use UnBeef instead for "Beefaritos."

CREAMED UNCHICKEN WITH MUSHROOMS AND HERBS

Amazingly flavorful!

1 c.	Mushrooms, cleaned and sliced
2 T.	Minced onion
⅛ tsp.	Thyme leaves
1 tsp.	Corn oil margarine
2 c.	UnChicken
⅓ c.	Ritz-style cracker crumbs (Hi-Hos are best—they do not contain animal fat)
1 c.	Tofu Sour Cream
½ c.	Cashew Cream
Pinch	Sea salt
Pinch	Cayenne pepper

Sauté the mushrooms, onion, and thyme in the margarine until the mushrooms are tender. Stir in the remaining ingredients until blended.

GLORIFIED UNCHICKEN

4 c.	UnChicken, sliced
1 T.	Corn oil
2 c.	Cream of UnChicken Soup made with the Basic Cream Of soup recipe
⅛ tsp.	Pepper
Pinch	Thyme

Brown the gluten on both sides in the oil. Combine the soup, pepper, and thyme. Put half of this in the bottom of a casserole. Put the gluten over that in a layer. Pour the rest of soup mixture over the gluten. Bake, uncovered, at 400° for 30 minutes.

HUNGARIAN UNCHICKEN

6 T.	Unbleached white flour
½ tsp.	Sea salt
½ tsp.	Black pepper
¼ c.	Non-dairy margarine
1 ½ c.	Onion, chopped
7 c.	UnChicken, cubed or in pieces or slices
2 c.	Tomato juice
2 T.	Paprika
¼ tsp.	Cayenne
1 tsp.	Sucanat
1 tsp.	Sea salt
1	Bay leaf
2 c.	UnChicken Broth
1 c.	Cashew or Tofu Sour Cream
	Cooked noodles

Combine the flour, salt, and pepper, and toss with the gluten until it is well coated. In 1 tablespoon of the margarine sauté the onion until soft. Take out the onion and set aside. Melt the rest of the margarine with the first and brown the gluten well. Combine the tomato juice, paprika, cayenne, Sucanat, and salt. Pour over the gluten. Add the bay leaf and broth, and simmer 45 minutes. Remove the gluten and put it on a platter of noodles. Take out the bay leaf and stir in the "sour cream." Heat through for 2 or 3 minutes (do not boil). Pour this sauce over the gluten.

ITALIAN UNCHICKEN CASSEROLE

2 T.	Olive oil
4	UnChicken slices
1 c.	Mushrooms, sliced

½ c.	Onion, chopped fine
¼ tsp.	Rosemary
¼ tsp.	Sea salt
¼ tsp.	Cayenne
2 c.	Canned stewed tomatoes
3 T.	Unbleached white flour

In half the oil brown the gluten on both sides. Heat the remaining oil in a skillet and sauté the mushrooms, onion, rosemary, salt, and pepper until the onions are soft. Add the tomatoes and cook 5 minutes. Blend in the flour well. Put half of this sauce over the bottom of a casserole. Layer the gluten over this. Pour the rest of the sauce over all and bake, uncovered, at 400° for 20 minutes. Good as is, or served over pasta or rice.

JAMBALAYA

2 c.	UnChicken, cut into pieces
2 c.	Rice, cooked
3 c.	Tomatoes, canned
1 ½ c.	Onion, chopped
⅓ c.	Green pepper, chopped
⅔ c.	Celery, chopped
1 T.	Non-dairy margarine
½ tsp.	Sea salt
½ tsp.	Basil
1 ½ c.	Bread crumbs

Mix the gluten, rice and tomatoes. Sauté the onion, green pepper and celery in the margarine. Add to the gluten mixture along with the salt and basil. Pour into a nonstick 2-quart casserole. Melt the rest of the margarine and toss with the bread crumbs. Spread the crumbs on top and bake, uncovered, for 1 hour at 350°.
Note: Other flavors of gluten may also be used in this dish.

MOROCCAN UNCHICKEN

¼ c.	Onion, minced
1 tsp.	Olive oil
½ c.	Zucchini, unpeeled, coarsely grated, squeezed dry in a paper towel, and packed tightly
2 T.	Pimento, chopped
½ c.	Yeast Cheez
¼ tsp.	Sea salt
¼ tsp.	Cayenne
1 ½ c.	UnChicken, cubed
1 T.	Olive oil
½ c.	UnChicken Broth

Sauté the onion in the teaspoon of oil until soft. Add the zucchini and cook, stirring, until tender. Stir in the pimento, cheez, salt, and cayenne. Mix well. Transfer to a small bowl and let cool slightly. Sauté the gluten in the tablespoon of oil until lightly browned. Combine everything and mix well.

OMELETS

2 ½ c.	Unbleached white flour
2 T.	Baking powder
2 T.	Sucanat
1 tsp.	Sea salt
2 ¾ c.	Nutritional yeast
1	N'egg
2 tsp.	Corn oil
2 c.	Cashew Milk
½ c.	Onions, chopped
½ tsp.	Garlic, minced
½ c.	Bell pepper, chopped
¾ c.	Pimento Cheez
¼ c.	Bacon Gluten, chopped fine

Mix the flour, baking powder, Sucanat, salt, and yeast. Add the n'egg, oil, and "milk" to that. This should be the consistency of pancake batter. Add water if needed to obtain this. Add onions, garlic, bell pepper, cheez, and gluten and mix well. Using ⅓ cup of mixture for each omelet, cook on an oiled griddle at about 350°, turning once, until golden brown on both sides. Serve with salsa, tomato sauce, mushroom sauce, or onion sauce.

ROASTED UNCHICKEN WITH POTATOES AND "CHORIZO"

4 c.	Potatoes, peeled and halved (or quartered, if large)
1 T.	Olive oil
2 c.	Onions, coarsely chopped
1 c.	Bell pepper (red preferred), cut into 1-inch squares
2 c.	Mexican Chorizo Sausage Gluten, or other spiced sausage-type gluten, chopped fine
1 T.	Garlic, minced
4 c.	UnChicken Broth
½ tsp.	Black pepper
3 c.	UnChicken slices, coated with oil and broiled until brown

Heat a little olive oil in a skillet and cook the potatoes until golden brown all over–about 20 minutes. Pour off the oil and set the potatoes aside in the skillet. Heat the tablespoon of oil in another skillet and sauté the onions and bell pepper until soft and starting to brown–about 12 or 15 minutes. Add the "sausage" and garlic and cook 5 more minutes. Add this to the potatoes. Add the broth and pepper and bring to a simmer. Cook, uncovered, until the potatoes are tender and the broth has reduced by half–about 10 minutes. Arrange the gluten slices in a baking dish, pour the potato mixture over them, and bake at 400° for 10 to 15 minutes to heat through.

SOY GRITS UNCHICKEN

½ c.	Soy grits
1 c.	Boiling UnChicken Broth

Stir grits into the broth and cook for 5 minutes.

SPANISH UNCHICKEN AU GRATIN

2 c.	Fresh mushrooms, sliced
1 ½ c.	Onions, chopped
1 T.	Garlic, minced
2 tsp.	Corn oil
4 c.	UnChicken, sliced
3 c.	Cream of Mushroom Soup
¼ tsp.	Cayenne pepper
2 T.	Parmesan Cheez

Sauté the mushrooms, onions, and garlic in the oil until the onions are soft. Add the gluten and cook 5 more minutes. Add the mushroom soup and cayenne and cook for another 5 minutes. Put in a casserole pan and sprinkle with the "parmesan." Bake at 400° for 20 minutes.

SPANISH UNCHICKEN WITH RICE

1 ½ c.	Onion, chopped fine
¾ tsp.	Garlic clove, crushed
½ c.	Bell pepper, chopped fine
1 T.	Olive oil
4 c.	Tomatoes, canned
½ tsp.	Sucanat
1 T.	Sea salt
2 T.	Paprika
½	Bay leaf
¼ tsp.	Basil (ground)
3 c.	Water
2 c.	Rice, uncooked
3 c.	UnChicken cut in pieces

Sauté the onion, garlic, and bell pepper in the oil until soft. Add the tomatoes and seasonings and cook for 15 minutes. Add the water, rice and gluten. Cook or bake for 40 minutes, or until the rice is done.

SUNDAY UNFRIED UNCHICKEN

Crunchelicious!

2 c.	Unbleached white flour
½ c.	Cornmeal
1 T.	Sea salt
2 T.	Dry mustard
2 T.	Paprika
2 T.	Garlic salt
1 T.	Celery salt
1 T.	Black pepper
1 tsp.	Ground ginger
½ tsp.	Thyme
½ tsp.	Oregano
6 c.	Chicken gluten, cut into frying-size pieces

Combine everything except the gluten. Put 1 cup of this mixture in a bag and shake a few pieces of the gluten at a time to coat them well. Heat ¼-inch of corn oil in a large skillet and brown the gluten on all sides and put into a shallow baking pan. Or you can broil or grill it until brown.

UNCHICKEN A LA KING

Truly worthy of a king!

4 c.	UnChicken, cubed
2 c.	Onions, chopped
4 c.	Mushrooms, sliced thick
2 ½ tsp.	Non-dairy margarine
4 ½ tsp.	Garlic, crushed
1 T.	Unbleached white flour
2 T.	Pimentos, chopped
¾ c.	Carrots, sliced thin and steamed
4 c.	UnChicken Broth made with Cashew Milk
⅛ tsp.	Coarse black pepper
⅛ tsp.	Cayenne pepper

Deep-fry the gluten and set it aside. Sauté the onions and mushrooms in the margarine until they are soft. Add the garlic and cook 2 more minutes. Add the flour, and stir it in well. Add the rest of the ingredients and simmer for 10 minutes, adding more broth if it gets too thick. Serve on toast points or biscuits–rice, too.

UNCHICKEN AND CHEEZ POT PIE

1 ½ c.	UnChicken Broth
2 c.	Potatoes, peeled and cubed
1 c.	Carrots, sliced

1 c.	Peas
½ c.	Celery, sliced
½ c.	Onion, chopped
⅓ c.	Pimentos, chopped
¼ c.	Unbleached white flour
1 ½ c.	Cashew Milk
1 c.	Yeast Cheez
4 c.	UnChicken, cubed
¼ tsp.	Watkins poultry seasoning
½ tsp.	Sea salt
¼ tsp.	Black pepper
1	Times the Convent Pie Crust, chilled

Bring the broth to a boil and add the vegetables. Simmer 10 to 15 minutes until tender. Blend the flour with the "milk" and stir into the broth mixture. Cook and stir over medium heat until slightly thickened and bubbly. Stir in the cheez, gluten, poultry seasoning, salt, and pepper. Mix well. Put into a casserole and set aside. Roll out the dough on a lightly floured surface to a size that will fit the casserole, trimming the edges as needed. Put in the casserole over the filling and seal the edges. Make a few slits in the center for steam to escape. Bake at 425° for 40 minutes—until the crust is golden brown.

UNCHICKEN AND DUMPLINGS

6 c.	UnChicken, cubed
4 ½ c.	UnChicken Broth
1 c.	Onion, chopped
1 ⅓ c.	Celery, sliced
1 c.	Carrots, sliced
1 tsp.	Sage
1 tsp.	Sea salt
¼ tsp.	Black pepper
3 c.	Biscuit Mix
¾ c. & 2 T.	Cashew Milk
1 T.	Parsley, minced

Simmer the gluten, broth, onion, celery, carrots, ½ teaspoon of the sage, salt, and pepper together for 45 minutes—until the vegetables are tender. Combine the biscuit mix, "milk," parsley, and rest of the sage to make a stiff batter. Drop by tablespoons into the simmering gluten mixture. Cover and simmer for 15 more minutes.

UNCHICKEN AND PASTA TOSS

1 ½ c.	Chicken Gluten, cut into thin strips
½ c.	Celery, sliced
½ c.	Bell pepper, cut into thin strips
¾ c.	Onion, chopped
½ tsp.	Garlic, minced
4 tsp.	Non-dairy margarine
¾ c.	UnChicken Broth
¼ tsp.	Dried tarragon
¼ c.	Parsley, chopped
¼ tsp.	Black pepper
8 oz.	Pasta, cooked

Sauté the gluten, celery, bell pepper, onion, and garlic in the margarine for 2 minutes. Add the broth, tarragon, parsley, and pepper. Simmer 15 minutes. Toss the pasta and gluten together to mix well.

UNCHICKEN AND POTATO SAUTÉ

Home food!

4 c.	Chicken Gluten, cubed
3 T.	Non-dairy margarine
1 c.	Onion, chopped
¾ tsp.	Garlic, minced
2 T.	Unbleached white flour
¼ tsp.	Thyme, dried
¼ tsp.	Sea salt
⅛ tsp.	Pepper
1 ¼ c.	UnChicken Broth
2 c.	Potatoes, cooked, peeled, and cubed

Sauté the gluten in the margarine until browned. Add the onion and garlic and cook 5 minutes. Combine the flour and seasonings, stir in the broth, pour it over the gluten, cover, and simmer for 20 minutes. Add the potatoes and heat through.

UNCHICKEN AND UNSAUSAGE GUMBO

This am Haut Cuisine, I garontee!

4 ½ tsp.	Corn oil
¾ c.	Unbleached white flour
5 c.	Onions, chopped
½	Bell pepper, chopped
1 T.	Celery, chopped
6	UnChicken slices, cut 1-inch thick
2 c.	UnSausage, sliced ¼-inch thick
5 c.	Canned tomatoes, crushed and drained
3 c.	Water
3 c.	Tomato juice
1 tsp.	Garlic clove, minced
1 T.	Parsley, chopped fine
¾ c.	Green onions, chopped fine
½ tsp.	Cayenne pepper

½ tsp. Sea salt
2 c. Okra, chopped

Heat the oil in a large heavy pot, stir in the flour and cook, stirring constantly, until the flour is very dark brown but not burned. Lower the heat and add the onion, bell pepper, and celery. Cover and simmer until the onions are transparent, stirring occasionally. Add all the gluten, the tomatoes, water, tomato juice, garlic, parsley, green onions, pepper, and salt. Cover, and simmer stirring frequently. While that is cooking, sauté the okra in a skillet until soft, then add it to the rest of ingredients. Bring to a boil, reduce the heat, and simmer, covered, 30 to 40 minutes until most of the water is evaporated. Serve on rice.

UNCHICKEN CACCIATORE–1

6 c.	UnChicken, cubed
1 c.	Unbleached white flour
	Corn oil
2 c.	Onion, chopped
1 T.	Garlic, minced
2 c.	Mushrooms, sliced
1 ½ c.	UnChicken Broth
3 c.	Canned tomato purée
1 tsp.	Oregano
¼ c.	Parsley, chopped
¾ tsp.	Sea salt
⅛ tsp.	Black pepper
⅛ tsp.	Cayenne pepper

Toss the gluten with the flour until coated and brown it in a skillet in the oil. Remove and set aside. In the same skillet sauté the onions until soft (add more oil if needed). Combine everything, cover, and simmer 30 minutes. Serve over spaghetti.

UNCHICKEN CACCIATORE–2

1 c.	Unbleached white flour
5 c.	UnChicken, cubed
2 c.	Onion, sliced and separated into rings
1 c.	Bell pepper, cut into strips
2 c.	Mushrooms, sliced
2 T.	Non-dairy margarine
2 tsp.	Garlic, minced
3 c.	Tomatoes, chopped
¾ c.	Cashew Milk
1 tsp.	Oregano
½ tsp.	Black pepper
¼ tsp.	Cayenne

½ tsp. Sea salt
¾ c. Yeast Cheez

Toss the gluten and flour together in a bag. Deep-fry and set aside. Sauté the onion, bell pepper, and mushrooms in the margarine until the onions are soft. Add everything else but the cheez and gluten. Bring to a boil, reduce heat, and simmer 15 minutes. Add the gluten and simmer until thick. Stir in the cheez and serve over spaghetti.

UNCHICKEN DIANE

4	Large slices of UnChicken
½ tsp.	Sea salt
½ tsp.	Black pepper
1 T.	Corn oil
1 T.	Non-dairy margarine
3 T.	Green onion, chopped
4 ½ tsp.	Lemon or lime juice
3 T.	Parsley, chopped
2 tsp.	Dijon-style mustard
¼ c.	UnChicken Broth

Sprinkle the gluten slices on both sides with the salt and pepper. Heat the oil and margarine in a skillet and cook the gluten–2 minutes on each side. Put on a warm serving platter. To the skillet add the onion, juice, parsley, and mustard, and cook for 15 seconds, stirring constantly. Stir in the broth and continue to stir until the sauce is smooth. Pour the sauce over the gluten and serve right away.

UNCHICKEN GUMBO

Wonderful flavor!

2 tsp.	Corn oil
⅔ c.	Unbleached white flour
1 ½ c.	Onion, chopped fine
¾ tsp.	Garlic, chopped fine
4 c.	UnChicken Broth
¼ c.	Lea & Perrins Steak Sauce
1 tsp.	Louisiana Hot Sauce or ½ tsp. Tabasco
4 c.	UnChicken, cubed
2 c.	UnSausage or UnHam, cubed

Heat the oil in a skillet, stir in the flour and cook until it is dark brown but not burned. Add all the ingredients and simmer for 30 minutes.

UNCHICKEN PAELLA

1 ½ c.	Onion, chopped
¾ tsp.	Garlic, minced

½ c.	Bell pepper, cut in strips
2 ½ tsp.	Olive oil
1 ½ c.	Tomatoes, chopped
2 T.	Tomato paste
1	Bay leaf
1 tsp.	Thyme
1 tsp.	Paprika
2 c.	Uncooked rice
4 c.	UnChicken Broth, boiling
5 c.	UnChicken, cubed

Sauté the onion, garlic, and bell pepper in the oil until the onion is transparent. Add the tomatoes, tomato paste, bay leaf, thyme, and paprika. Cook 10 minutes. Stir in the rice. Add the broth and cook for 5 or 6 minutes, stirring occasionally. Mix in the gluten. Put in a casserole and bake at 325° for 20 to 25 minutes until the broth is absorbed.

UNCHICKEN PAPRIKA-1

2 tsp.	Corn oil
1 ½ tsp.	Garlic, minced
1 T.	Paprika
1 c.	Tomato, chopped
½ c.	Bell pepper, sliced thin
1 c.	UnChicken Broth
¼ tsp.	Sea salt
¼ tsp.	Cayenne pepper
4	UnChicken slices, browned in a small amount of oil
1 c.	Cashew or Tofu Sour Cream

Put everything but the "sour cream" and gluten in a skillet and cook, stirring occasionally, until the tomatoes are soft. Add the gluten, turning the pieces over to coat them. Simmer 2 more minutes. Stir in the "sour cream." Serve with noodles or rice.

UNCHICKEN PAPRIKA-2

3 c.	Onions, sliced or chopped
2 T.	Corn oil
2 T.	Paprika
½ tsp.	Cayenne
6 c.	UnChicken slices, browned in a small amount of oil
½ tsp.	Sea salt
3 T.	Parsley, chopped
2 ½ c.	UnChicken Broth
2 c.	Cashew or Tofu Sour Cream
4 tsp.	Capers with juice

In a skillet sauté the onions in the oil until soft. Add the paprika, cayenne, gluten, salt, parsley,

and broth. Cover and cook over low heat for 10 minutes. Stir in the "sour cream" and capers with their juice and gently heat through.

Variation: UnBeef may be used instead of UnChicken.

UNCHICKEN POT PIE

Almost beyond superb!

¼ c.	Unbleached white flour
¼ tsp.	Sea salt
½ tsp.	Black pepper
½ tsp.	Garlic powder
3 c.	UnChicken, cut into ½-inch cubes
2 T.	Corn oil
1 ½ c.	Onion, chopped
1 c.	Carrots, sliced
1 c.	Celery, sliced
2 T.	Water
1 c.	Peas
3 T.	Non-dairy margarine
4 c.	Mushrooms, sliced
¼ c.	Unbleached white flour
1 tsp.	Sea salt
¼ tsp.	Sage, powdered
1 tsp.	Garlic powder
¼ tsp.	Thyme
½ tsp.	Paprika
¼ tsp.	Black pepper
3 ½ c.	UnChicken Broth
1	Unbaked pie crust shell, and a top crust (Convent Pie Crust recipe)

Combine the flour, salt, pepper, and garlic powder. Toss the gluten cubes in this and coat them well. Sauté the gluten in the oil until golden. Stir in the onion and cook 3 more minutes. Add the carrots, celery, and water. Cover and cook, stirring frequently, until the carrots are just tender. Remove from the heat and stir in the peas. In a saucepan sauté the mushrooms, covered, in the margarine until they are soft. Stir in the flour, salt, sage, garlic powder, thyme, paprika, and black pepper, and cook 3 minutes more. Whisk in the broth and simmer, uncovered, for 10 minutes or until thickened. Mix the gravy into the gluten and vegetable mixture and put the rest aside. Put the gluten-vegetable mixture into the pie shell, put on the top crust, seal it, and cut several slits in it so the steam can escape. Bake at 400° for 20 minutes, reduce the heat to 350° and bake 20 to 30 more minutes—until the crust is well browned.

UNCHICKEN TETRAZZINI

Something to sing—or crow—about!

½ lb.	Spaghetti
1 T.	Non-dairy margarine
¼ c.	Unbleached white flour
2 c.	Mushrooms, sliced
½ c.	Bell pepper (red or green)
¾ tsp.	Garlic, minced
3 ½ c.	UnChicken Broth made with Cashew Milk
⅛ tsp.	Tabasco sauce
½ tsp.	Black pepper
½ c.	Parsley, chopped fine
2 c.	UnChicken (made by Method 3 is best), cubed and browned in oil
1 c.	Parmesan Cheez

Cook the spaghetti, drain and blanch it. Set aside. Melt the margarine in a skillet, add in the flour and cook it, stirring, until it is dark brown but not burned. Add the mushrooms and bell pepper and sauté for 5 minutes. Add the garlic and sauté 2 more minutes. Add the broth, Tabasco, pepper, parsley, gluten, and ½ cup of the "parmesan." Cook until the mixture begins to thicken. Mix in the pasta, put in a casserole, sprinkle the rest of the "parmesan" on top, patting lightly to press it in. Cover and bake at 350° for 20 minutes. Uncover and broil until the top is brown.

UNCHICKEN WITH MUSHROOMS, TOMATOES, AND RICE

2 c.	Onions, chopped
2 tsp.	Garlic, mashed
1 T.	Corn oil margarine
2 ⅓ c.	Mushrooms
1 c.	Rice
2 c.	Tomatoes, coarsely chopped
2 c.	UnChicken Broth
¼ c.	Pimento strips
1 tsp.	Sea salt
½ tsp.	Cayenne pepper
3 c.	UnChicken
1 ¼ c.	Frozen green peas

Sauté onions and garlic in margarine until onions are transparent. Add mushrooms and continue sautéing until the mushrooms are tender. (Add a little more margarine, if necessary.) Add the rice and sauté for 5 minutes, tossing and turning. Now add the remaining ingredients and stir until blended. Simmer mixture until rice is cooked and liquid is absorbed. Stir and serve hot.

YANKEE UNFRIED UNCHICKEN

Good as is, but better with "Cream" Gravy or "Sour Cream" Mushroom Gravy.

1	N'egg
3 T.	Cashew Milk
1 c.	Soda crackers, crushed fine
1 tsp.	Thyme
½ tsp.	Paprika
⅛ tsp.	Pepper
6 c.	Chicken Gluten, cut into slices
3 T.	Corn oil
1 c.	Cashew Milk

Combine the n'egg and 3 tablespoons of "milk." Combine the crackers, thyme, paprika, and pepper and set aside. One at a time, dip the gluten slices in the n'egg mixture and then roll them in the cracker mixture. Heat the oil in a large skillet and evenly brown the gluten on both sides. Add the cup of "milk," reduce heat, cover tightly, and cook for 35 minutes. Uncover and cook 10 more minutes.

UnTurkey
Substitutes & Dishes

UNTURKEY

Cook 2 cups of raw gluten according to Method 1, 2, or 3 in:

UNTURKEY GLUTEN BROTH

2 T.	Soy sauce
1 tsp.	Kitchen Bouquet
⅛ tsp.	Sage, rubbed
½ c.	Onions, chopped
2 ¼ tsp.	Monosodium glutamate
½ tsp.	Sea salt
½ tsp.	Poultry seasoning
3 T. & 2 tsp.	Nutritional Yeast
1 tsp.	Corn oil
2 c.	Water

Combine everything and simmer for 5 minutes.

LISBON UNTURKEY

2 T.	Unbleached white flour
½ tsp.	Cumin, ground
1 tsp.	Paprika
½ tsp.	Cayenne pepper
¼ tsp.	Sea salt
3 c.	UnTurkey, in strips or cubes (or 4 slices of UnTurkey, ¼-inch-thick) Corn oil
½ c.	Bell pepper, chopped
¼ c.	Celery, chopped
¼ c.	Green onions, sliced
1 tsp.	Garlic, minced
¼ c.	Black olives, sliced
¼ c.	Green pimento-stuffed olives, sliced
½ c.	UnTurkey Broth
½ tsp.	Cornstarch

Combine the flour, cumin, paprika, cayenne, and salt. Coat the gluten with this mixture and brown in a skillet in the oil. (Or broil or grill until brown on both sides.) Remove and set aside, keeping warm. In the same skillet–adding more oil if needed–sauté the bell pepper, celery, onions, and garlic until almost tender. Stir in the olives. Combine the broth and cornstarch. Add this and cook and stir until bubbly, then continue to cook, stirring for 1 more minute. Pour over the gluten and serve.

UNTURKEY CUTLETS PICCATA

Something different.

1	N'egg
1 T.	Cashew Milk
4	UnTurkey "cutlets" ¼-inch thick
2 c.	Fresh bread crumbs
1 tsp.	Lemon juice
½ c.	UnTurkey Broth
Dash	Black pepper

Combine the n'egg and "milk." Melt some margarine in a skillet. Dip each cutlet into the n'egg mixture and then into the bread crumbs. Fry the cutlets, 2 at a time, until lightly browned on both sides, adding more margarine if needed. Set the cutlets aside. Put the lemon juice into the skillet. Add the broth and pepper. Return the cutlets to the skillet, cover, and simmer 10 to 15 minutes.

UNTURKEY CUTLETS WITH MUSHROOMS AND TOMATOES

2 T.	Non-dairy margarine
3 c.	Mushrooms, thickly sliced
1 T.	Lemon juice

2 T.	Prepared mustard
1 tsp.	Cornstarch
½ tsp.	Sea salt
⅛ tsp.	Black pepper
2 c.	UnTurkey, sliced ¼-inch thick
1 ½ c.	Tomatoes, coarsely chopped
2 T.	Green onion, or chives, chopped

Melt the margarine and sauté the mushrooms. Add the lemon juice, mustard, cornstarch, salt, and pepper, stirring until smooth. Put into a nonstick casserole, arrange the gluten slices over it. Sprinkle the tomatoes and onion over all. Bake at 350° for 30 minutes.

UNTURKEY HOLIDAY CASSEROLE

You can't do without it!

2	Times the UnTurkey recipe
1	Times the Bread Dressing recipe
3	Times the Mushroom Gravy recipe—made with UnTurkey Broth

Slice the gluten thin. Spray both sides of the slices lightly with oil and broil lightly–not letting it get crisp. Set aside. Put the dressing ingredients in a large casserole and cook according to the instructions given in the Bread Dressing recipe. When the dressing is done, cover it with ⅓ of the gravy. Put ½ of the gluten slices over that. Cover that with another ⅓ of the gravy. Cover with the rest of the gluten slices. Pour the rest of the gravy over all. Bake at 400° for 30 minutes.

UNTURKEY MEATLESS-BALLS WITH CAPER SAUCE

3 c.	UnTurkey, ground and browned in corn oil
½ c.	Onion, grated
1	N'egg
1 T.	Unbleached white flour
½ c.	Dried bread crumbs
	Non-dairy margarine

2 T.	Unbleached white flour
⅛ tsp.	Black pepper
½ tsp.	Sea salt
3 c.	Cashew Milk
2 T.	Capers, drained
1 T.	Parsley, chopped

Combine the gluten, onion, n'egg, flour, and crumbs. Shape into 1-inch balls. In the margarine brown the gluten balls–half at a time–removing them as they brown. Stir the flour, pepper, and salt into the remaining oil and cook 1 minute. Gradually stir in the "milk" and capers. Cook till slightly thickened, stirring constantly. Return the gluten to the skillet and bring to boiling. Reduce heat to low, cover, and simmer 10 minutes, stirring occasionally. Sprinkle with the parsley.

UNTURKEY SALAD BURRITOS

A masterpiece!

2 c.	UnTurkey, chopped
2 T.	Celery, chopped fine
½ c.	Onion, chopped fine
¼ c.	Black olives, sliced (add up to ¼ cup more if you like)
1 c.	Yeast, Pimento, or Notzarella Cheez
½ c.	Miraculous Whip
⅓ c.	Salsa
⅛ tsp.	Sea salt
6	Flour tortillas–7-8 inches in diameter

Combine the gluten, celery, onion, olives, and cheez. Whisk together the "Miraculous Whip," salsa, and salt. Pour this sauce over the gluten mixture and blend well. Spoon this filling onto the tortillas and wrap them burrito-style. Put in a baking dish or pan and bake at 350° for 20 minutes, until thoroughly warmed. Serve with extra salsa and olives.

UnSeafood
Substitutes & Dishes

UNFISH

These are the UnScallops in a different shape.
Feed them to fish lovers and turn them into gluten lovers!

Make Basic Gluten using all unbleached white flour. Use Cooking Method 2, and slice the gluten ¼ to ½-inch thick. Make a broth by combining and simmering together for 5 minutes:

4 c.	Water
2 T.	MSG
1 T.	Sea salt
2 tsp.	Corn oil

Boil the gluten in the broth for 30 minutes. Then let it soak overnight in the broth. Drain well. Dip each piece in a mixture of:

2 c.	Cashew milk
¼ tsp.	Cayenne pepper
¼ tsp.	Sea salt

Roll in a mixture of:

2 c.	Corn flour, corn meal, Cream of Wheat (Farina), Malto-Meal, or powdered cracker crumbs
¼ tsp.	Cayenne pepper
¼ tsp.	Sea salt

Deep fry at 350° until light brown.

Variation: Coat in Deep-Frying Batter (see Etc. section) and deep-fry at 400°.

DEEP-FRIED UNFISH

Drench:

2 c.	Cashew milk
¼ tsp.	Cayenne pepper
¼ tsp.	Sea salt

Dredge:

2 c.	Cracker crumbs OR corn flour
¼ tsp.	Cayenne pepper
¼ tsp.	Sea salt

Take slices of Unfish cooked by Method 2. Dip each slice in the drench and then in the dredge, coating well, but gently shaking off excess crumbs or flour. Deep fry.

UNSCALLOPS

Because these are so much better than either the real thing, or the dreary canned imitations, words fail me. But your appetite won't!

Make Basic Gluten using all unbleached white flour. Use Cooking Method 1, tearing the gluten into ¾-inch chunks. Make a broth by combining and simmering together for 5 minutes:

4 c.	Water
2 T.	MSG
1 T.	Sea salt
2 tsp.	Corn oil

Boil the gluten in the broth for 30 minutes. Then let it soak overnight in the broth. Drain well. Dip each piece in a mixture of:

4 c.	Cashew milk
¼ tsp.	Cayenne pepper
1 tsp.	Sea salt

Roll in a mixture of:

4 c.	Powdered cracker crumbs, corn flour, corn meal, Cream of Wheat (Farina), or Malto-Meal

½ tsp.   Cayenne pepper
½ tsp.   Sea salt

Deep fry at 350° until light brown.

Variation: Coat in Deep-Frying Batter (see Etc. section) and deep-fry at 400°.

UNSHRIMP

When I became a vegetarian thirty years ago the only thing I missed was shrimp, which I loved heartily. Now after thirty years I can enjoy it again–and so can you. This makes a lot of UnShrimp, but you can freeze it and it keeps just fine.
Be sure you use the Zatarain's Crab Boil which is whole spices in a bag.

Make Basic Gluten and cook by Method 2. Slice the cooked gluten ¼-inch thick and then cut into 1x2-inch pieces (or into shrimp-like shapes). Boil in a broth made by combining and simmering together for 5 minutes:

1 gal.   Water
½ c.   MSG
¼ c.   Sea salt
1 bag   Zatarain's Crab Boil
1 T.   Corn oil

(If you want to make less broth, break open the crab boil bag and use the quantity of spices proportionate to the amount of water you are using, tying them in a piece of cheesecloth. *Or:* If you do not have Zatarain's Crab Boil, use the broth given above for UnScallops and UnFish.) Boil the gluten in the broth for 30 minutes. Then let it soak overnight in the broth–keeping the crab boil bag in the broth as well. Drain before using.

BROILED UNSHRIMP

3 T.   Olive oil
3 T.   Non-dairy margarine
4 tsp.   Lea & Perrins Steak Sauce
1 tsp.   Louisiana Hot Sauce
6 c.   UnShrimp
          Cayenne pepper
1 c.   Water

Put the oil in a baking pan, slice the margarine into it, and heat it in an oven until the margarine is melted. Take the pan from the oven and add the steak sauce and hot sauce, mixing well. Put the gluten in a single layer into the mixture and sprinkle them generously with cayenne pepper. Pour the water into the pan, using just as much as is needed to half-cover the gluten. Bake at 350°

for 20 minutes, then place in a broiler, basting frequently and turning, until the gluten is well browned and dark around the edges.

FRENCH FRIED UNSHRIMP

Oh me, oh my, oh!
You won't believe how wonderful these are!

6 c.   UnShrimp
3 c.   Cashew Milk
½ c.   Parmesan Cheez
2 c.   Onion, sliced
1 tsp.   Garlic, sliced
½ c.   Bell pepper, sliced
2 T.   Lea & Perrins Steak Sauce
2 tsp.   Louisiana Hot Sauce

Place the gluten in a large bowl. Combine the "milk," "parmesan," onion, garlic, bell pepper, steak sauce, and hot sauce, and blend in a blender. Pour this over the gluten, adding more milk if needed to cover it. Stir a bit to mix everything evenly, and marinate overnight or at least 12 hours. When ready to fry the gluten, combine:

2 c.   Powdered cracker crumbs, corn
          flour, corn meal, Cream of Wheat
          (Farina), or Malto-Meal
¼ tsp.   Cayenne pepper
¼ tsp.   Sea salt

Put the "flour" mixture in a brown paper bag. Drain the UnShrimp a bit at a time, shake in the bag, and deep fry at 400°. (Or coat in Deep-Frying Batter–see Etc. section–and fry.)

GARLIC UNSHRIMP ESPAÑOL

1 c.   Olive oil
1 ½ c.   UnFish Broth
½ c.   Water
3 T.   Garlic, crushed
1 tsp.   Basil
1 tsp.   Oregano
¼ tsp.   Cayenne
6 c.   UnShrimp

Whisk together the oil, broth, water, garlic, herbs, and pepper. Add the gluten and let it marinate, turning them, for at least 4 hours or overnight. Broil, in the marinade, about 4 inches from the heat, turning them once, for 5 minutes or until pale golden.

MARINATED UNSHRIMP

This is delicious breaded and deep-fried, too.

6 c.	UnShrimp
3 c.	UnShrimp Broth
3 c.	Water
2 tsp.	Tabasco Sauce or 4 tsp. of Louisiana Hot Sauce
2 T.	Dry mustard
¼ c.	Vinegar
2 c.	Onion, sliced
3 T.	Sucanat
½ tsp.	Angostura Bitters

Combine everything, bring to a boil, let cool, and marinate for several hours.

MEXICAN UNSHRIMP

This is quite similar to UnShrimp Creole, but distinctive enough for me to include here for you to try. But be warned: this dish is HOT.

¾ c.	Onion, chopped
½ c.	Bell pepper, chopped
½ c.	Celery, chopped
1 ½ tsp.	Corn oil
¾ c.	Canned tomatoes
2 tsp.	Garlic, minced
½ tsp.	Cayenne pepper
½ tsp.	Sea salt
1 tsp.	Paprika
½ c.	Water
1 T.	Unbleached white flour
2 c.	UnShrimp

Sauté the onion, bell pepper, and celery in the oil. Add the tomatoes, garlic, pepper, salt, paprika, water, and flour. Blend well and simmer for 45 minutes. Add the UnShrimp and simmer 15 more minutes. Serve over rice and top with Yeast Cheez if desired.

UNOYSTERS BATON ROUGE

5 c.	Fresh mushrooms
¼ c.	Non-dairy margarine
½ c.	Unbleached white flour
¼ c.	Water
½ c.	Green onions, chopped
1 T.	Garlic, minced
2 c.	Cashew Milk
1 ½ c.	UnFish Broth
½ c.	Parsley, minced
4	Artichoke hearts, minced
⅛ tsp.	Sea salt

⅛ tsp.	Cayenne pepper
2 tsp.	Louisiana Hot Sauce

Stem the mushrooms, mince the stems, and set aside. Melt the margarine in a skillet, stir in the flour gradually, and cook until medium brown. Add the water, stir in the onions and garlic, and cook until the onions are soft, stirring constantly. Add the "milk" and broth—a little at a time—stirring constantly. Cook until thick, adding a little more broth if needed. Add the mushroom stems, parsley, artichoke hearts, salt, pepper, and hot sauce. Simmer for 20 minutes, stirring occasionally. Put the mushroom tops in a shallow baking dish. Cover with the sauce and bake at 400° for 20 minutes.

UNSHRIMP CREOLE

You can't eat this just once!

½ c.	Onion, chopped
½ c.	Celery, chopped
½ c.	Parsley, chopped
⅓ c.	Bell pepper, chopped
2 tsp.	Olive oil
2 c.	Water
2 c.	Okra, sliced
2 c.	Tomatoes, chopped
1 c.	Tomato purée or sauce
¾ tsp.	Garlic, minced
1 tsp.	Lea & Perrins Steak Sauce
½ tsp.	Louisiana Hot Sauce
⅓ tsp.	Sea salt
2 c.	UnShrimp
3 c.	Cooked rice

Sauté the onion, celery, parsley, and bell pepper in the oil until they are tender. Add the water, okra, tomatoes, tomato purée (or sauce), and garlic. Simmer for 5 minutes. Add the steak sauce, hot sauce, and salt. Cook for 30 minutes. Add the gluten and cook 30 more minutes until the mixture is thick. Serve over the rice.

UNSHRIMP CURRY–1

1 ½ c.	Unsweetened shredded coconut
1 ½ tsp.	Powdered coriander
1 ¼ c.	Warm water
¾ c.	Onions, chopped fine
1 T.	Garlic, minced
1 ½ tsp.	Corn oil
¾ tsp.	Ginger, powdered
1 tsp.	Tumeric
½ tsp.	Cumin, ground

¼ tsp.	Cayenne pepper
¼ tsp.	Black pepper
2 ½ c.	UnShrimp

Put the coconut, coriander, and water in a blender and purée on high. Sauté the onions and garlic in the oil until the onions are soft. Add the ginger, tumeric, cumin, cayenne, and black pepper, and sauté for 30 seconds. Add the gluten, stirring to coat well with the oil and spices. Add the coriander-coconut milk, bring to a simmer, and cook for 10 minutes. Serve over rice.

UNSHRIMP CURRY-2

¾ c.	Onion, chopped
2 tsp.	Non-dairy margarine
2 tsp.	Garlic, minced
1 T.	Curry powder
1 ¼ c.	Carrots, cut ¼-inch thick diagonally
½ c.	UnChicken Broth
1 ½ c.	Cashew Milk
¾ c.	Tofu Buttermilk
3 T.	Cornstarch
2 T.	Lemon juice
¼ tsp.	Sea salt
¼ tsp.	Cayenne pepper
⅛ tsp.	Black pepper
4 c.	UnShrimp
½ c.	Bell pepper, chopped

Sauté the onion in the margarine until soft. Stir in the garlic and curry powder, and sauté for 1 minute. Stir in the carrots and broth. Bring to a boil and cook, uncovered, about 10 minutes, or till the carrots are just tender. Combine the "milk," "buttermilk," and cornstarch. Add to the carrot mixture. Stir in the lemon juice, salt, and pepper. Cook and stir till thickened and bubbly. Add the gluten and bell pepper. Return to boiling. Cook, stirring, for 2 more minutes. Serve over rice or toast.

UNSHRIMP GUMBO

1 c.	Olive oil
1 ½ c.	Unbleached white flour
3 c.	Onions
1 ½ c.	Bell pepper, chopped
1 c.	Canned tomato sauce
3 T.	Garlic, minced
1 c.	Green onion, chopped
¾ c.	Parsley, chopped fine
10 c.	Water
4 T.	Lea & Perrins Steak Sauce

1 tsp.	Sea salt
1 tsp.	Cayenne pepper
1 c.	UnShrimp Broth
6 c.	UnShrimp

Heat the oil in a skillet, stir in the flour and cook until it is dark brown but not burned. Add the onions and bell pepper and sauté until the onions are transparent. Add the tomato sauce, garlic, and green onion and cook until the mixture is back to its original dark brown color. Add the parsley, water, steak sauce, salt, pepper, and broth. Cook for 45 minutes. Add gluten and cook for 30 minutes. Serve over rice.

UNSHRIMP IMPERIAL

2 T.	Green onion, chopped fine
2 T.	Celery, chopped fine
2 T.	Carrot, chopped fine
2 tsp.	Non-dairy margarine
2 T.	Unbleached white flour
1 c.	Cashew Cream
¼ tsp.	White pepper
¼ c.	UnFish Broth
Dash	Tabasco Sauce
1	N'egg
¼ c.	Cashew Cream
2 c.	UnShrimp, chopped or ground
2 T.	Parsley, chopped fine (leaves only)
½ c.	Bell pepper (red preferred), chopped fine
¼ tsp.	Grated orange peel
1 c.	Fine bread crumbs
½ tsp.	Paprika

Sauté the onion, celery, and carrot in the margarine for 1 minute. Stir in the flour and cook, stirring, for 3 minutes. Whisk in the 1 cup of the "cream" in a stream, add the pepper, and simmer, whisking, for 5 minutes. Take off the heat and stir in the broth and Tabasco. Separately, whisk together the n'egg and ¼ cup of "cream." Stir this into the vegetable mixture and combine well. Fold in the gluten, parsley, bell pepper, and orange peel. Put into a nonstick baking dish. Sprinkle with the bread crumbs and paprika, pressing in lightly. Bake at 425° for 12 to 15 minutes, or until the bread crumbs are golden and heated clear through.

UNSHRIMP MOLD

1 can	Campbell's Tomato Soup
1 ½ c.	Tofu Cream Cheez

2 pkg.	Unflavored *kosher* (non-animal) gelatin
½ c.	Water
1 c.	Miraculous Whip or other "mayonnaise"
4 or 5	Green onions
¼ tsp.	Sea salt
½ tsp.	Cayenne pepper
½ tsp.	Tabasco sauce
2 c.	UnShrimp

Heat the soup–direct from the can without adding milk or water–to a boil. Stir in the cream cheez. Dissolve the gelatin in the water and add it to the soup mixture. Let it cool. Add all other ingredients except the gluten. In a mold place alternating layers of sauce and gluten. Chill until the mold is set.

UNSHRIMP PIE

Remember the song about "Crawfish Pie"? UnShrimp Pie works just as well–maybe better.

¼ c.	Unbleached white flour
4 tsp.	Corn oil
4 tsp.	Olive oil
½ c.	Onions, chopped
½ c.	Mushrooms, chopped
½ c.	Green onions, chopped
1 tsp.	Garlic, minced
1 c.	Water
½ c.	Peas, cooked and drained
½ c.	Carrots, diced and cooked
¼ tsp.	Sea salt
1 ½ tsp.	Louisiana Hot Sauce
2 c.	UnShrimp

Combine the flour and oils in a skillet and cook, stirring, until the flour is dark brown but not burned. Add the onions, mushrooms, green onions, and garlic, stirring. Add the water and bring to a boil. Add the peas, carrots, salt, hot sauce, and gluten. Cook for 5 more minutes until it thickens. Put everything in a pie pan with crust and top it with more crust, cutting holes to let out the steam. Bake at 350° for 45 minutes until the crust is golden brown.

UNSHRIMP WITH CAPER SAUCE

"Memorable" is the word for this dish.
It is gourmet food, I garontee!

1 c.	Onion, chopped fine
½ c.	Parsley, chopped
1 ½ tsp.	Olive oil
1 T.	Garlic, minced
½ tsp.	Dried mint, crumbled
¼ c.	Lea & Perrins Steak Sauce
1 tsp.	Louisiana Hot Sauce or ¼ tsp. cayenne pepper
1 c.	Water
4 c.	UnShrimp
¾ c.	Miraculous Whip
1 T.	Lemon juice
1 T.	Creole or poupon mustard
2 T.	Capers, drained

Sauté the onions and parsley in the oil until the onions are tender. Add garlic, mint, steak sauce, hot sauce, water, and gluten. Cook, stirring all the time, for 20 minutes. Combine the Miraculous Whip, lemon juice, mustard, and capers, and mix well. Serve UnShrimp over rice or spaghetti and top with the sauce. Do not mix the sauce with the UnShrimp before serving.

UNSALMON LOAF

Unlikely as this recipe looks, it works beautifully.

1 c.	Tomato juice
1 c.	Water
1 c.	Soy flour
1 ½ tsp.	Onion salt
1 T.	Oil

Whirl everything in a blender until smooth and pour into an oiled baking dish. Bake at 400° about 40 minutes until a tan crust forms. Cool and turn onto a platter. Serve hot or cold.

Flavoring Broths

I THINK this is one of the most valuable sections in this cookbook. By using these formulas you can impart a richer taste to the food you cook.

These broths are also for flavoring the various dishes which need a meat-like taste without any actual gluten imitations. (They are not for flavoring the gluten substitutes. The recipes for those broths are given in the sections for those meat substitutes–some formulas are the same as these, however.)

Not only is the flavor given by these broths superior to any of the various powdered or cubed forms of "beef" or "chicken" flavoring, they are immensely more healthful.

UNCHICKEN BROTH

¼ c.	Onions, chopped
2 ¼ tsp.	MSG
½ tsp.	Sea salt
½ tsp.	Poultry seasoning
2 T. & 2 ½ tsp.	Nutritional Yeast
1 tsp.	Corn oil
2 c.	Water

Combine and simmer for 5 minutes.

UNBEEF BROTH

2 T.	Soy sauce
1 tsp.	Kitchen Bouquet
1 T.	Nutritional Yeast
¼ c.	Onions, chopped
⅛ tsp.	Sage, rubbed
1 tsp.	Corn oil

2 c.	Water

Combine and simmer for 5 minutes

UNFISH BROTH

2 c.	Water
1 T.	MSG
1 ½ tsp.	Sea salt
1 tsp.	Corn oil

Combine and simmer for 5 minutes.
Variation: Add ⅛ teaspoon of powdered kelp for 2 cups of broth and ¼ teaspoon for 4 cups of broth.

UNHAM BROTH

¼ c.	Soy sauce
2 tsp.	Kitchen Bouquet
2 T.	Nutritional Yeast
½ c.	Onions, chopped
¼ tsp.	Sage, rubbed
½ tsp.	Black pepper
½ tsp.	Oregano
1 tsp.	Garlic powder
1 ¼ tsp.	Liquid smoke
1 tsp.	Corn oil
1 tsp.	Sea salt
2 c.	Water

Combine and simmer for 5 minutes.

UNPORK BROTH

¼ c.	Onions, chopped
2 ¼ tsp.	Monosodium glutamate
½ tsp.	Sea salt
½ tsp.	Poultry seasoning
3 T.	Nutritional Yeast

1 tsp.	Corn oil
2 c.	Water
¼ tsp.	Black pepper
½ tsp.	Garlic, crushed
⅛ tsp.	Marjoram, powdered

Combine and simmer for 5 minutes.

UNSAUSAGE BROTH

2 T.	Soy sauce
1 tsp.	Kitchen Bouquet
1 T.	Nutritional Yeast
¼ c.	Onions, chopped
⅛ tsp.	Sage, rubbed
¼ tsp.	Black pepper
¼ tsp.	Oregano
½ tsp.	Garlic powder
2 T.	Watkins Sausage Seasoning
1 tsp.	Liquid smoke
1 tsp.	Corn oil
2 c.	Water

Combine and simmer for 5 minutes.

Heavenly Broth

THIS IS ONE of the most valuable recipes in this book, not only because it works very well for sautéing in oilless cooking, but because it is incredibly nutritious and is especially good for those who are ill to give a boost to the body as it battles the baddies. This is the vegan answer to chicken soup which, in my opinion, has never been good for anybody!

Watch the amount of jalapeños, as they vary in hotness from season to season. You might want to work up to the level best for your taste. But don't leave them out as they have valuable nutrients and antiseptics including a natural form of quinine.

I give three ways of making Heavenly Broth after the list of ingredients, but there is a much, much better way: by using a Mehu-Maija Juicer. I had heard of these juicers many years ago and was intrigued at the idea, but my interest in raw juices deflected me from following up and getting information about it. But when I discovered Heavenly Broth my memory revived and I tracked it down.

The Mehu-Maija Juicers are not juicers in the sense we are used to. They consist of three parts: a basket for the cut-up vegetables, a reservoir to collect their juice, and another reservoir which holds boiling water. By means of a double-boiler type of effect the pure juice flows out of the vegetables (or fruits) and into the top reservoir. The result is marvelous and extremely easy to digest. Although the instructions speak of "soft" fruits and vegetables being used in the juicer, we have tried "hard" vegetables and found that it works just as well on them. By using this method no water is mixed into the juice, but you get only the 100% real thing. The taste of Heavenly Broth made in this way is simply…heavenly.

Also excellent is tomato juice extracted this way (put in some onions with the tomatoes and it is really delicious). This, too, is especially good-tasting and easy on the digestion.

Mehu-Maija juicers can be obtained from Lehman's Hardware Store and Appliances (wonderful people), 1 Lehman Circle, P.O. Box 41, Kidron, OH 44636. Phone 216-857-5757.

HEAVENLY BROTH

4 c.	Potatoes
2 c.	Carrots
2 c.	Cauliflower
2 c.	Squash
2 c.	Cabbage
2 c.	Green beans
2 c.	Celery
3 c.	Onions
2 c.	Bell peppers
6 c.	Tomatoes
1 c.	Parsley
1/4 c.	Jalapeños
2 tsp.	Sea salt
14 c.	Water

Do one of the following:

1) Chop all vegetables. Combine everything, bring to a boil, reduce heat, and simmer for 3 hours. Strain.
2) Shred or mince all vegetables in a food processor. Combine everything, bring to a boil, reduce heat, and simmer for 1 ½ hours. Strain.
3) Chop all vegetables. Combine everything and pressure-cook at 15 lbs. for 35 minutes. Strain.

Vegetables

ANANDAMAYI KITCHURI

This recipe was formulated by Sri Sri Anandamayi Ma, a leading religious teacher of India. She recommended it to all her students, saying that if a person ate this dish always, varying the vegetables, they would never be ill. I have personally known many people who ate this every day. The Ajwan–a small black seed with a slightly sour tang that is available in most Indian grocery stores–was not in the original recipe, but was recommended to me by one of those who cooked it daily. In the original there were no onions or garlic, either.

This is very good served with Puris or Flat Bread (see Bread and Such section).

1 c.	Rice, uncooked
1 T.	Corn oil
1 c.	Onions, chopped
1 T.	Jalapeños, sliced or minced (in this dish sliced seems better)
1 ½ tsp.	Tumeric, ground
1 tsp.	Powdered ginger, OR 1 T. fresh ginger, grated
1 tsp.	Cumin, ground
1 tsp.	Fenugreek, ground
1 tsp.	Anise, ground
½ tsp.	Ajwan, ground
1 ¼ tsp.	Sea salt
¼ tsp.	Garlic powder
1 qt.	Vegetables, chopped
2 ½ c.	Tomatoes, fresh or canned (if canned drain well, and use the juice as part of the boiling water measure)
3 c.	Boiling water (and tomato juice if canned tomatoes are used)

Wash the rice over and over, changing the water, until there is no more starch in the water, and drain it well. Heat the oil until very hot. Sauté the onions and jalapeños, then add the spices and stir constantly as it all fries to a rich brown color of a heavenly fragrance. Add the vegetables, tomatoes, and rice and stir continually until all is covered with the hot oil/spice mixture. Add the boiling water and stir. Bring to a boil, cover and simmer until all vegetables are done.

Variations: Include 1 ½ cups of cooked dal, garbanzos, or other beans. Leave out the tomatoes. Include 2 cups of chopped Unbeef, UnChicken, or unflavored gluten. Fry the gluten in the spices until it browns before you add the vegetables and rice.

BAKED MASHED POTATOES

6 c.	Potatoes, peeled and cut into 1-inch pieces
1 ½ c.	Green onions, sliced thin
¾ c.	Onion, chopped
1 ¼ tsp.	Garlic, minced
2 tsp.	Non-dairy margarine
⅔ c.	Cashew Milk
1 ½ c.	Yeast, Pimento, or Notzarella Cheez
1 tsp.	Chives, dried
½ tsp.	Sea salt
⅛ tsp.	Cayenne

Cook the potatoes. While the potatoes are cooking, sauté the onions and garlic in the margarine until the onions are soft. Force the potatoes through a ricer or food mill, stir in the "milk," onion mixture, half the cheez, the chives, salt, and pepper. Put this in a nonstick baking dish, spread the rest of the cheez on top, and bake at 400° for 20 minutes.

BOILED CABBAGE

Take the outer leaves off a head of cabbage, cut it into sections and remove the core. Shred or chop it finely. Drop it into rapidly boiling UnBeef or UnChicken Broth. Cook until it is barely tender—7 or 8 minutes.

BOILED CABBAGE DINNER

This is real frontier log cabin food not to be confused with the bland New England version.

2 T.	Olive oil
1	Medium cabbage, quartered
4	Large onions, quartered
4	Medium whole potatoes, peeled and quartered
4	Large carrots, peeled and cut in large pieces
3 c.	UnHam Broth
3 c.	Water
1 T.	Louisiana Hot Sauce
1 tsp.	Sea salt
4 c.	UnHam or UnSausage, cubed

In a pot large enough to hold all the ingredients put everything except the gluten and bring to a boil. After it boils add the gluten—and more water if necessary. Cook until the potatoes are done.

BOILED OKRA

Sounds dull, but is good!

4 c.	Okra, whole
1 tsp.	Corn oil
2 c.	Flavoring Broth of choice
1 c.	Water
2 tsp.	Louisiana Hot Sauce
2 tsp.	Sea salt

Wash the okra. Cut off most of the okra stems but keep a small bit on each one so the okra "glue" will not leak out and make the dish slimy. Combine everything in a pot, bring to a strong boil, turn down the heat and simmer slowly until the okra is tender.

BROCCOLI

1 tsp.	Non-dairy margarine
1 ½ tsp.	Olive oil
2 c.	Onion, coarsely chopped
1 tsp.	Garlic, minced
¼ tsp.	Red pepper flakes
¾ c.	Celery, chopped
6 c.	Broccoli, the stems chopped and the tops broken into small flowerets
¾ c.	Bell pepper, chopped
1 ½ c.	UnChicken Broth
½ tsp.	Sea salt

Melt the margarine in the oil. Sauté the onion, garlic, pepper flakes, and celery until transparent. Add broccoli and bell pepper and sauté briefly. Then add the broth and salt and stir well. Cover and cook until tender, but do not overcook. *Variation:* Add 2 tablespoons of curry powder when sautéing.

BROCCOLI DIVAN

1 T.	Cornstarch
1 c.	Cold Cashew Milk
1 tsp.	Non-dairy margarine
¼ tsp.	Sea salt
⅛ tsp.	Black pepper
½ c.	Cashew or Tofu Sour Cream
½ c.	Yeast, Pimento, or Notzarella Cheez
¾ tsp.	Prepared mustard
4 c.	Broccoli, cooked tender-crisp

Bring the cornstarch, "milk," margarine, salt, and pepper to a boil, stirring constantly. Boil until thickened. Remove from heat and stir in the "sour cream," cheez, and mustard. Pour over the broccoli. Broil 4 inches from the heat for 3 to 5 minutes.

BROCCOLI, MUSHROOMS, AND TOMATOES

4 ⅔ c.	Mushrooms, halved
¼ tsp.	Sea salt
1 T.	Non-dairy margarine
5 c.	Broccoli, cut into 2 ½x1-inch pieces and steamed
2 c.	Tomatoes, chopped
¾ tsp.	Lemon-pepper seasoning salt

Sauté the mushrooms and salt in the margarine until tender and golden. Stir in the broccoli, tomatoes, lemon-pepper seasoning salt, and 1 more tablespoon of margarine. Heat through.

BROWNED POTATOES

Peel and boil potatoes in UnBeef or UnChicken Broth until they are nearly tender. Drain. Melt 2 tablespoons of non-dairy margarine in a pan and cook and turn the potatoes until they are light brown. Season with salt and pepper. Bake them in a 400° oven until they are crisp and brown. Add more margarine if required. Turn the potatoes to brown them evenly.

CABBAGE, TOMATOES, AND CHEEZ

3 c.	Cabbage, finely shredded, cooked and drained
¾ tsp.	Sea salt
¼ tsp.	Cayenne pepper
1 ½ c.	Canned tomatoes, crushed or chopped
1 c.	Yeast or Pimento Cheez
2 c.	Bread crumbs
2 tsp.	Non-dairy margarine

Cook the cabbage with the salt and pepper. In a nonstick casserove put alternating layers of tomatoes and cabbage, beginning with tomatoes. Spread with the cheez and then with the bread crumbs, pressing in lightly. Bake at 325° for about 30 minutes or until the crumbs are brown.

CABBAGE GOULASH

This may be the first time you taste anything like this— but you won't let it be the last!

1 ½ c.	Onion, chopped
5 tsp.	Corn oil
2 c.	Sausage UnBeef, ground
2 c.	UnBeef, ground
3 ½ c.	Canned tomatoes, chopped and drained (reserving liquid)
¾ c.	Tomato paste
2 T.	Balsamic vinegar
1 T.	Chili powder
1 tsp.	Garlic powder
¼ tsp.	Hot pepper flakes
10 c.	Cabbage, shredded

Sauté the onion in the oil until soft. Add the rest of the ingredients except the cabbage. Mix well. Stir in the cabbage and simmer 15 to 20 minutes, or until the cabbage is tender.

CAJUN PEAS OR FRESH BEANS

Without a doubt!

1 c.	UnHam, chopped
2 tsp.	Non-dairy margarine
6 c.	Peas or fresh (not dried) beans
2 c.	UnHam Broth
1 ½ c.	Onion, chopped
¾ tsp.	Garlic, minced
1 tsp.	Louisiana Hot Sauce

Sauté the gluten in the margarine for 5 minutes. Add everything else and cook until the peas are tender. Then salt to taste.

CARROTS AND PEAS

In salted water, cook carrots and peas separately— in any proportions desired. Drain well. Combine. Season with salt and pepper. Pour melted margarine (¼ tsp. to 1 cup of vegetables) over them, OR heat together in Thin or Medium White Sauce (one-half as much sauce as vegetables).

CHILI CORN AND ZUCCHINI

1 c.	Onion, sliced
1 ½ tsp.	Garlic, minced
2 tsp.	Corn oil or non-dairy margarine
2 c.	UnChicken Broth
4 c.	Zucchini, sliced thin
1 ½ c.	Corn
2 T.	Jalapeños, minced
1 tsp.	Sea salt
⅛ tsp.	Black pepper
½ c.	Yeast Cheez

Sauté the onion and garlic in the oil until soft. Combine everything but the cheez and cook until the vegetables are tender. Drain off most of the liquid and stir in the cheez.

COLONIAL GREEN BEANS

Quietly special!

¼ c.	UnBacon, chopped
2 c.	Green beans
2 c.	Carrots, sliced thin
1 ½ tsp.	Garlic, minced
½ tsp.	Pepper
⅛ tsp.	Sea salt
2 tsp.	Non-dairy margarine

Sauté everything in the margarine until the vegetables are crisp-tender.

COPONATINI EGGPLANT

6 c.	Eggplant, peeled and cubed
1 T.	Sea salt

3 T.	Olive oil
1 c.	Canned tomato sauce
¾ c.	Onions, chopped
⅔ c.	Celery, chopped
½ tsp.	Garlic, minced
3 T. & 1 tsp.	Green olives, quartered
1 tsp.	Vinegar
1 tsp.	Sea salt

Sprinkle the tablespoon of salt over the cubed eggplant and let it sit for 30 minutes, then squeeze out the moisture lightly. Cook the eggplant in the oil until it is tender. Add the tomato sauce. Separately sauté the onion, celery, garlic, and olives in a little olive oil, then add the vinegar to the mixture. Combine all ingredients with the salt. Cook together until the flavors are blended. Serve with rice.

COPPER PENNIES

Unusual! Can be a salad, an appetizer, or a regular dish!

2 tsp.	Corn oil
1 c.	Sucanat
¾ c.	Vinegar
1 ½ c.	Tomato soup
1 T.	Powdered mustard
2 T.	Lea & Perrins Steak Sauce
4 c.	Carrots, sliced
1 c.	Onions, sliced
1	Small bell pepper, sliced

In a saucepan simmer the oil, Sucanat, vinegar, tomato soup, mustard, and steak sauce. Boil the carrots until they are tender. In a casserole alternately layer the carrots, onions, and pepper slices. Pour the sauce over all and refrigerate.

CORN A LA KING

3 T.	Onions, minced
½ c.	Bell pepper, chopped
2 T.	Pimento, chopped
1 tsp.	Non-dairy margarine
2 ½ c.	Corn
½ c.	White sauce made with UnChicken Broth
¾ tsp.	Sea salt
⅛ tsp.	Cayenne pepper

Sauté the onions, bell pepper, and pimento in the margarine. Add the rest of ingredients and cook.
Variation: Use squash instead of corn.

CORN AND PEPPERS

¾ c.	Bell pepper
3 T.	Onions, chopped
⅛ tsp.	Cayenne
1 ½ tsp.	Non-dairy margarine
4 c.	Corn
½ tsp.	Sea salt

Sauté the bell peppers, onions, and cayenne in the margarine. Combine with rest of ingredients and cook.

CORN SPECIAL

2 T.	Bell pepper, chopped
3 T.	Onions, chopped
1 tsp.	Non-dairy margarine
2 c.	Corn
¼ tsp.	Sea salt

Sauté the bell peppers and onions in the margarine. Add the corn and salt and cook.

COTTAGE MASHED POTATOES

¼ c.	Onions, chopped
1 ½ tsp.	Margarine, melted
3 c.	Mashed potatoes
1 ½ c.	Cottage Cheez
1 ½ c.	Peas
⅛ tsp.	Cayenne pepper
¾ tsp.	Sea salt

Sauté the onions in margarine. Combine with rest of ingredients and serve.

COUNTRY CORN

Never ordinary!

2 tsp.	Non-dairy margarine
½ c.	UnHam Broth
½ tsp.	Salt
6 c.	Corn
1 ½ c.	UnSausage (any flavor), cubed small

Melt the margarine and add the broth and salt. Heat through. Add the corn and gluten. Cook for 5 minutes, stirring occasionally.

COUNTRY CORN AND OKRA

Even more so!

2 ½ tsp.	Non-dairy margarine
½ c.	Onion, chopped
1 ½ c.	UnSausage (any flavor), cubed small
3 c.	Corn

3 c.   Okra
2 c.   Canned tomatoes, mashed
½ c.   UnHam Broth
½ tsp. Salt

Melt the margarine and sauté the onions and gluten until the onions are soft. Add the rest of the ingredients, bring to a boil, and cook until the okra is done, stirring occasionally.

COUNTRY CORN CREOLE-1

This has character!

½ c.   Bell pepper, diced
3 T.   Onions, minced
2 ½ tsp. Non-dairy margarine
2 ½ c. Tomatoes, chopped
3 c.   Okra, sliced
1 tsp. Sea salt
½ tsp. Oregano
3 c.   Corn
⅛ tsp. Cayenne pepper

Sauté the bell peppers and onions in the margarine. Combine with rest of ingredients and cook.

COUNTRY CORN CREOLE-2

This, too!

2 c.   Onions, sliced
¼ c.   Jalapeños, minced
1 ½ c. Bell pepper, diced
1 T.   Corn oil
2 ½ c. Tomatoes, chopped
3 c.   Sliced fresh okra
1 tsp. Sea salt
1 tsp. Oregano
½ tsp. Cumin seed
⅛ tsp. Cayenne pepper
3 c.   Corn

In the oil sauté the onion, jalapeños, and bell pepper until the onion is transparent. Add the rest of the vegetables and seasonings. Add just enough water to not quite cover the vegetables. Cook for 20 minutes over medium-low heat.
Variation: Instead of water, cook with UnBeef or UnChicken Broth.

CREAM-STYLE CORN

Who can do without it?

1 ½ tsp. Non-dairy margarine
5 c.   Corn

¼ tsp. Sea salt

Melt the margarine, put in a blender with the corn and salt, and blend–using two or three short spurts to get the corn to begin to break up. Be careful not to liquefy the corn. Heat and serve.

CREAMED CARROTS

¾ c.   Onions, chopped
½ tsp. Garlic, minced
1 ½ tsp. Non-dairy margarine
4 c.   Carrots, cooked and chopped
1 c.   Cashew Milk
½ tsp. Sea salt

Sauté the onions and garlic in the margarine. Place the carrots and "milk" in a blender and process. Add sautéed onions and salt to the blender and blend until smooth.

CREAMED GREEN PEAS

In a way, no big deal, but oh, so good!

3 T.   Onions, chopped
1 tsp. Non-dairy margarine
2 c.   Green peas, cooked
½ tsp. Sea salt
⅔ c.   Thin White Sauce made with UnChicken Broth

Sauté the onions in the margarine, then combine all ingredients and heat.

CREAMED POTATOES

3 T.   Onions, chopped
½ tsp. Garlic, minced
1 tsp. Non-dairy margarine
3 c.   Potatoes, boiled, cooled, and diced
1 ½ c. Medium White Sauce
1 ½ tsp. Dried parsley
1 c.   Bread crumbs

Sauté the onions and garlic in the margarine. Combine the onions, potatoes, sauce, and parsley. Put in an oiled baking dish. Cover with bread crumbs, pressing in lightly. Bake at 400° until the crumbs are brown.
Variation: Add ½ cup of Yeast or Pimento Cheez to the white sauce and stir in well.

CREAMY POTATOES AND PEAS

¼ c.   Onions, chopped
½ tsp. Garlic, minced
1 ½ c. Peas

1 ½ tsp.	Non-dairy margarine
1 ¼ c.	Thick White Sauce made with UnChicken Broth
Pinch	Cayenne pepper
¼ tsp.	Sea salt
3 c.	Hot cooked potato slices

Sauté the onions, garlic, and peas in the margarine. Combine the white sauce, pepper, and salt, and cook over low heat, stirring until the sauce is smooth. Combine with the potatoes and peas.

CREOLE OKRA

Heaven on earth!

½ c.	Bell pepper, diced
1 c.	Onions, minced
2 ½ tsp.	Non-dairy margarine
4 c.	Okra, sliced
1 tsp.	Garlic, minced
⅛ tsp.	Cayenne pepper
4 c.	Tomatoes, diced
1 T.	Parsley
¼ tsp.	Basil
¼ tsp.	Sea salt
¾ c.	UnBeef Broth
1 c.	Cooked Tomato Salsa

Sauté the bell peppers and onions in the margarine. Combine with rest of ingredients–except the salsa–and cook until the okra is tender. Stir in the salsa.

CREOLE TOMATOES

⅓ c.	Onions, finely chopped
½ c.	Bell pepper, finely chopped
⅛ tsp.	Garlic, minced
¼ tsp.	Jalapeños, minced
1 tsp.	Non-dairy margarine
1 T.	Fresh parsley, chopped
3 c.	Tomatoes, chopped
1 ½ tsp.	Sea salt
⅛ tsp.	White pepper
1 T.	Non-dairy margarine
2 T.	Unbleached white flour
1 c.	Cashew Milk

Sauté the onions, bell pepper, garlic, and jalapeños in the margarine until the vegetables are soft but not brown. Add the parsley, tomatoes, salt, and pepper and cook for 10 minutes. In a separate pan melt the tablespoon of margarine and stir in the flour. Stirring constantly with a whisk, pour in the "milk" in a slow, thin stream.

Cook over high heat until the sauce comes to a boil, thickens slightly, and is smooth. Reduce heat and simmer for 2 or 3 minutes to remove the raw taste of the flour. Stir into the tomato mixture.

CURRIED BROCCOLI

2 c.	Onions, chopped
⅔ c.	Bell pepper, chopped
⅔ c.	Celery, chopped
1 tsp.	Garlic, minced
2 ½ tsp.	Non-dairy margarine
2 T.	Curry powder
6 c.	Broccoli, the stems chopped and the tops broken into small flowerets
1 c.	UnChicken Broth
¾ tsp.	Sea salt

Sauté the onion, bell pepper, celery, and garlic in the margarine until the onions are transparent. Add the curry powder and sauté for 30 seconds, stirring constantly. Add the broccoli and stir until all is coated with the hot oil. Add the broth and the salt.

CURRIED GREEN BEANS

Everybody here calls for more!

2 c.	Onions, chopped
1 ½ tsp.	Garlic, minced
¼ tsp.	Hot pepper flakes
2 tsp.	Corn oil
1 ½ tsp.	Curry powder
1 T.	Lemon juice
1 ½ c.	Water
¾ tsp.	Sea salt
6 c.	Green beans

Sauté onions, garlic, and pepper flakes in the oil until transparent. Add the curry powder and sauté 1 minute more, stirring constantly. Add the water, salt, and lemon juice and stir well. Stir in the beans. Cover and cook.

CURRIED PEAS

Whenever someone feels hungry around here, two times out of three they say: "How about some curried peas?"

½ c.	Onions, chopped
1 tsp.	Non-dairy margarine
1 T.	Curry powder
1 T.	Unbleached white flour
3 c.	Cashew Milk
⅛ tsp.	Cayenne pepper

½ tsp. Sea salt
3 c. Peas (if frozen, thawed; if fresh, lightly steamed)

Sauté the onions in margarine until transparent. Add the curry powder and sauté 30 seconds longer, stirring constantly. Add the flour and stir it in. Slowly add the "milk" as you stir continually. Add the cayenne and salt. Simmer for 10 minutes, stirring occasionally so it will not stick. Add the peas and cook for 5 more minutes. Serve with rice.

CURRIED PEAS, CARROTS, AND POTATOES

1 c. Onion, chopped
¾ tsp. Garlic, minced
1 ½ tsp. Curry powder
1 ½ tsp. Non-dairy margarine
3 c. Potatoes, cooked and cubed
1 c. Peas
1 c. Carrots, cooked
½ c. Boiling water
½ c. Coconut milk

Sauté the onion, garlic, and curry powder in the margarine until the onions are transparent. Add the potatoes, peas, and carrots and stir until coated with the hot oil. Add the water and cook for 5 minutes. Add the coconut milk and cook for 5 more minutes.

CURRIED POTATOES AND PEAS

When I was starving in India nearly thirty years ago some Kashmiri friends made this for me and watched in awe as I ate their shares as well as mine!

1 ½ tsp. Non-dairy margarine
½ tsp. Powdered ginger
1 tsp. Garlic, minced
⅓ c. Onions (red preferred), chopped
1 tsp. Sea salt
1 tsp. Cumin, ground .
½ tsp. Tumeric
1 tsp. Coriander, powdered
¼ tsp. Garam Masala
¼ tsp. Cayenne
1 ½ c. Tomatoes, chopped
2 c. Green peas
1 ½ c. Potatoes, peeled and cut into ½-inch cubes
½ c. Water

Heat the margarine over high heat until a drop of water flicked into it splutters instantly. Stir in the ginger and garlic. Add the onions and salt. Lower the heat to moderate and, stirring constantly, sauté the onions for 7 or 8 minutes, until they are soft and golden brown. Add cumin, tumeric, coriander, garam masala, and cayenne. Stir in the tomatoes. Still stirring, cook briskly for 5 minutes, until most of the liquid in the pan evaporates and the mixture is thick enough to draw away from the sides and bottom of the pan in a dense mass. Drop in the peas and potatoes and turn them about with the spoon until they are evenly coated with the tomato mixture. Stir in the water, bring to a boil over high heat, cover tightly, and reduce the heat to low. Simmer for 10 minutes, or until the peas and potatoes are tender but still intact.

DEEP-FRIED OKRA

If your only acquaintance with okra is from those strange little "wheels" in Campbell's soup, or if you have only had okra cooked until it is gooshy, be sure to try this.

5 c. Cashew Milk
1 T. Louisiana Hot Sauce
1 T. Soy sauce
3 c. Corn flour
1 tsp. Garlic powder
1 tsp. Onion powder
1 tsp. Sea salt
8 c. Okra, cut into ½-inch pieces.

Combine the "milk," hot sauce, and soy sauce. Combine the corn flour, garlic and onion powders, and salt. Dip the okra in the cashew milk mixture, remove and roll it in the corn flour mixture. Deep-fry at 350-365° until it is brown. Drain on paper towels and serve immediately.

DEEP-FRIED SQUASH

This tastes a goodly bit like fried oysters—but so much nicer to chew!

4-6 Yellow squash, cut into ¼-inch slices

Drench:

1 c. Water
½ tsp. Garlic powder
½ tsp. Onion powder
½ tsp. Cayenne pepper
1 tsp. Sea salt

Dredge:

2 c. Corn flour
¼ tsp. Sea salt
¼ tsp. Cayenne pepper

Combine the drench ingredients. Dip the squash in the drench and then in the dredge. Deep-fry for 1 minute at 350°. Sprinkle with Parmesan Cheez after frying. Serve immediately.

DUTCH SUCCOTASH

½ c.	Bell pepper, diced
⅓ c.	Onions, chopped
2 ½ tsp.	Non-dairy margarine
3 c.	Potatoes, cubed and cooked
2 c.	Corn, cooked
1 ½ c.	Lima beans, cooked
2 ¼ c.	Chopped tomatoes
¼ tsp.	Cayenne pepper
½ tsp.	Basil
1 tsp.	Sea salt

Sauté the bell peppers and onions in the margarine. Combine with rest of ingredients and cook.

EGGPLANT AND TOMATOES

Tastes like more!

4 c.	Eggplant, sliced ⅛ to ¼-inch thick
1 T.	Olive oil
1 ½ c.	Onions, chopped
1 ½ tsp.	Jalapeños, minced
1 ½ tsp.	Garlic, minced
3 c.	Tomatoes, chopped
1 ½ tsp.	Sea salt
⅛ tsp.	Cayenne pepper

Heavily salt both sides of the eggplant slices. Let sit for 1 hour and wipe off the salt and liquid. Press between absorbent towels, squeezing out as much liquid as possible. Sauté the eggplant in half the oil until it becomes soft. Set aside on paper towels to drain. In the rest of the oil sauté the onions and jalapeños until the onions are soft. Add the garlic and tomatoes and cook for 2 minutes. Add the eggplant, salt, and cayenne. Cook until most of the liquid is evaporated.

FRENCH-FRIED POTATOES

These are not particularly healthy, yet sometimes we (or children) get a yen for "junk" food, and it is better to make our own not-so-junk versions.
This recipe is based on the McDonald's method of making french fries, and although it is somewhat tedious I think you will find the results worth the extra trouble. The best type of potatoes for french fries are Russet

Burbanks from Idaho.

1 qt.	Cold water
½ c.	White vinegar
4 c.	Potatoes, sliced into ¼-inch thick sticks
2 qt.	Water
1 T.	Sea salt
	Ice water
	Corn oil
	Onion salt

Combine the quart of cold water and the vinegar. Put the potatoes in this, cover, and refrigerate for 2 hours. Drain in a colander. Bring the 2 quarts of water and salt to a boil. When the water is boiling hard, drop the potatoes into the water and cook for 1 minute. Put into the colander again and drain and IMMEDIATELY plunge them into ice water. Drain them on paper toweling as best you can to remove as much water as possible. Put corn oil in a heavy 2-to-3-quart saucepan to a depth of 4 inches. Using a french-frying basket, fry the potatoes at 400° for only 1 minute. Remove and turn into a paper towel lined bowl or basket. Repeat until all the potatoes have been fried, making sure the oil temperature never goes below 375° and can quickly come back up to 400°. Now start all over again and re-fry the potatoes till they are crisp and golden brown. Sprinkle with onion salt while they are hot and serve before they get cold. If you are frying a goodly number of potatoes and do not want the first ones to get cold, after salting a batch of fries transfer them to a pan lined with a double thickness of paper towels and put them in a 250° oven to keep them warm while you proceed with the remaining batches.
Note: Use only long white potatoes. The thicker the skin of the potato, the better the quality for frying.

FRIED GREEN TOMATOES

After seeing the movie, what else could we do? And we loved these almost as much as the movie!
Firm ripe tomatoes work very well too, for a variation!

3 T.	Non-dairy margarine
1 T.	Corn oil
1 T.	Sucanat
1 c.	Unbleached white flour
1	N'egg
¼ c.	Cashew Milk
4-6	Medium green tomatoes, sliced ½-inch thick

1 c. Dry bread crumbs mixed with
⅛ tsp. garlic powder, ¼ tsp. onion
powder, ¼ tsp. black pepper,
¼ tsp. powdered basil, and
¼ tsp. sea salt

Melt the margarine together with the oil in a
skillet. Combine the Sucanat and flour. Combine
the n'egg and "milk." Dip the tomato slices into
the flour mixture, then into the "milk" mixture,
and then into the crumbs. Fry on both sides until
brown but firm enough to hold their shape.
To make gravy for these if you wish: Combine the
leftover "milk" mixture with the leftover flour
and the remaining bread crumbs. Add 1 more
cup of cashew milk and 1 cup of UnBeef Broth.
Blend all together in a blender. Put in a skillet
and cook until thickened. Add extra broth if it
gets too thick.

FRIED MASHED POTATO BALLS

3 T.   Cornstarch
¼ c.   Water
2 c.   Mashed potatoes, hot
¼ tsp. Onion powder
¼ tsp. Garlic powder
1 tsp. Baking powder
¼ tsp. Sea salt
⅛ tsp. Cayenne pepper

Dissolve the cornstarch in the (cold) water. Add
the other ingredients and mix well. Form into
balls and fry in oil until brown. Place them to
drain on paper in a colander. If needed, keep them
hot in a 425° oven.

FRIED 'TATERS 'N ONIONS

Just what it is. Yum!

Corn oil
2 c.   Onions, sliced thin
1 qt.   Potatoes, sliced medium thick
Garlic salt
Pepper (black or cayenne), or
curry powder

Heat oil, put in onions and potatoes and fry,
turning regularly, until the potatoes brown.
Toward the end of the frying, sprinkle with garlic
salt and black or cayenne pepper as you fry, *or*
sprinkle with curry powder and salt as you fry.

GINGER CURRY

1 lb.   Firm tofu, frozen, thawed, and
pressed

½ tsp.   Powdered ginger
1 ½ tsp. Garlic, minced
6 T.   Water
2 T.   Almond or peanut butter
1 T.   Low sodium soy sauce
2 tsp.   Curry powder
¼ tsp.   Cayenne
1 T.   Corn oil
1 c.   Onion, chopped
2 c.   Cashew Milk
¾ tsp.   Sea salt
¼ tsp.   Black pepper
⅔ c.   Peas
⅓ c.   Almonds, toasted

Cut the tofu into thin strips about ¼-inch by ¾-
inch by 1 ½-inches and set aside. Put the ginger,
garlic, water, nut butter, soy sauce, 1 teaspoon of
the curry powder, and the cayenne in a blender
and blend. Pour this over the tofu strips. Gently
turn and press the tofu until the mixture is
absorbed. Heat the oil and sauté the onion until
translucent. Add the other teaspoon of curry
powder and sauté for about 1 minute. Add the
tofu and continue to sauté until the tofu starts to
brown. Add the "milk," salt, and pepper. Bring
to a simmer and add the peas. Cook about 3
minutes or until the peas are tender. Just before
serving stir in the almonds.

GOLDEN VEGETABLE LAYER

2 c.   Potatoes, chopped
2 c.   Carrots, chopped
1 ½ tsp. Non-dairy margarine
½ tsp.   Sea salt
¼ tsp.   Cayenne pepper
2 c.   Tomato Sauce (see recipes in
Sauces and Gravies), cooked
down into a thick purée and kept
warm

Steam or boil the potatoes and carrots until they
are just tender. Mash them coarsely–not letting
them become smooth as in mashed potatoes–
with the margarine, salt and pepper. Put the
mixture into a serving dish, top with the tomato
sauce, and serve at once.

GREEK GREEN BEANS

1 c.   Onions, chopped or thinly sliced
¾ tsp.   Garlic, minced
2 tsp.   Corn oil
½ tsp.   Oregano
¾ c.   Tomatoes, diced

1 T.	Tomato paste
½ tsp.	Sea salt
¼ tsp.	Black pepper
3 c.	Green beans, trimmed, cut into 2-inch lengths, and cooked

Sauté the onions and garlic in the oil until soft. Combine everything but the beans and simmer 5 minutes. Add the beans and simmer until tender and some of the sauce is absorbed.

GREEK POTATOES

Distinctive!

3 T.	Onions, chopped
1 ½ tsp.	Corn oil
1	Bay leaf
½ tsp.	Oregano
¼ tsp.	Thyme
½ tsp.	Basil
2 T.	Parsley, chopped
1 ½ c.	Tomatoes, fresh or canned
½ c.	Tomato paste
½ c.	Water or UnBeef Broth
¼ tsp.	Sea salt
1 tsp.	Garlic, minced
3 c.	Potatoes, cut in 1-inch chunks

Sauté the onions in the oil. Put all the ingredients—except for the potatoes—in a pot, stir and simmer for 15 minutes. Place the potatoes in an oiled baking dish or pan. Pour the sauce over the potatoes and toss until well covered. Bake at 375° for at least 1 hour, or until the potatoes test done when pierced with a fork. Check the potatoes near the end of the cooking time for moistness—the potatoes should soak up most of the sauce and be rather dry but not blackened. Add a little water if necessary.

GREEN BEAN, POTATO, AND TOMATO COMBO

This is always welcome!
Try olive oil as a variation!

3 T.	Onions, chopped
½ tsp.	Garlic, minced
1 ½ tsp.	Corn oil
1 ¼ c.	Green beans (if fresh, stem and cut them into 1-inch sections)
1 ¼ c.	Potatoes, cut in 1-inch chunks and cooked
2 ½ c.	Tomatoes, puréed in blender
⅛ tsp.	Basil
⅛ tsp.	Oregano

⅛ tsp.	Cayenne pepper
¾ tsp.	Sea salt
½ c.	UnBeef Broth (omit if you are using canned tomatoes)

Sauté the onions and garlic in the oil. Combine with rest of ingredients and cook until the beans are done–about 25 minutes. During the cooking time, you may have to add additional water to keep the combo at a consistency of thick stew.

GREEN BEAN SUCCOTASH

Combine equal parts of cooked corn and finely shredded and cooked green beans. Season with salt, paprika, and non-dairy margarine..

GREEN BEANS

String and shred green beans lengthwise. Drop the beans into boiling water to which onion salt (1 ½ teaspoon per quart) has been added. Cook the beans until they are barely tender–no longer– about 20 minutes. Drain the beans. Return to the pot and reheat them in melted non-dairy margarine *or* thin white sauce (half as much sauce as there are beans) to which Yeast or Pimento Cheez may be added.

GREEN BEANS AND UNHAM

1 c.	Baked UnHam, cubed
1 ½ tsp.	Olive oil
4 c.	Green beans
1 ½ c.	Onions, chopped
¾ tsp.	Garlic, chopped
2 ½ c.	Water
2 T.	Lea & Perrins Steak Sauce
2 tsp.	Louisiana Hot Sauce
1 tsp.	Sea salt

In the pot you are going to use for cooking, sauté the UnHam in the oil. Add the beans, onions, garlic, water, steak sauce, hot sauce, and salt. Cook until the beans are tender.
Variation: Use UnBacon or UnSausage instead of the UnHam.

GREEN BEANS AND MUSHROOMS

1 c.	Mushrooms, sliced
¼ c.	Green onions, sliced
2 tsp.	Corn oil
2 c.	Green beans, cut in 2-inch pieces
¾ c.	UnBeef or UnChicken Broth, or water
¼ tsp.	Sea salt

⅛ tsp.   Pepper
⅛ tsp.   Dried basil

Sauté the mushrooms and onions in the oil a few minutes, add the rest of the ingredients and cook 10 to 15 minutes until the beans are done.

GREEN BEANS STIR FRY

1 c.	Green beans, cut into 1-inch pieces
¾ c.	Onions, chopped
½ tsp.	Garlic, minced
2 tsp.	Corn oil
1 c.	UnBeef or UnChicken Broth
1 tsp.	Basil
¼ tsp.	Sea salt
1 ½ c.	Tomatoes, chopped
1	N'egg

Sauté the beans, onions, and garlic in the oil for 1 minute. Add the broth, basil, and salt. Cover and simmer for 15 minutes, or until the beans are tender. Add the tomatoes and n'egg. Cook, stirring constantly, until the mixture boils and thickens.

GREEN BEANS SUPREME

3 T.	Onions, chopped
½ tsp.	Garlic, minced
1 ½ tsp.	Non-dairy margarine
4 c.	Green beans
½ c.	UnBeef or UnChicken Broth
¼ tsp.	Lemon peel
⅛ tsp.	Cayenne pepper
⅛ tsp.	Dill weed
¼ tsp.	Sea salt
1 c.	Cashew or Tofu Sour Cream

Sauté the onions and garlic in the margarine. Combine all ingredients–except the sour cream–and cook until beans are cooked but not too soft. Mix in the "sour cream."

GREEN BEANS WITH GREEN ONION DRESSING

1 lb.	Green beans, ends removed
1	Times the recipe of Green Onion Salad Dressing

Cook the beans in plenty of rapidly boiling salted water until tender-crisp. Drain and plunge into ice water to chill. Drain well, wrap in a towel, and refrigerate. When ready to serve, take from the refrigerator and slice at an angle. Mix well with the chilled dressing.

GREEN BEANS WITH HAZELNUTS

This is Blue Ribbon cuisine!

¼ c.	Hazelnuts
2 c.	UnChicken Broth
3 c.	Green beans
2 T.	Olive or corn oil
1 T.	Balsamic vinegar
¼ tsp.	Sea salt
¼ tsp.	Black pepper

Heat the oven to 350°. Spread the nuts on a baking sheet and toast in the oven for about 8 minutes, until fragrant. Transfer to a kitchen towel and rub them together vigorously to remove most of the skins. Finely chop them and set aside. Bring the broth to a boil, add the beans, and cook until tender–about 6 minutes. Drain. Whisk the oil and vinegar together and pour over the beans and toss with the salt and pepper. Serve sprinkled with the hazelnuts.

GREEN BEANS WITH UNBACON

1 ½ tsp.	Non-dairy margarine
1 ½ tsp.	Corn oil
2 c.	Onions, chopped
1 ½ tsp.	Garlic, minced
¼ tsp.	Hot pepper flakes
6 c.	Green beans
⅓ c.	UnBacon, chopped fine
1 qt.	UnChicken or UnBeef Broth

Put the margarine and oil together and melt the margarine. Sauté the onions, garlic, and pepper flakes until the onions are transparent. Add the green beans and stir well until they are coated with the hot oil. Add the gluten. Add the broth and cook until the beans are done.

GREEN BEANS WITH GARLIC

2 c.	Green beans, trimmed and broken in half
2 T.	Garlic, minced
2 tsp.	Olive oil
½ tsp.	Sea salt
1 T.	Soy sauce

Sauté the beans and garlic for 5 minutes in the oil. Keep heat high to singe the beans. Add the salt and soy sauce. Cover, lower heat, and stew for 5 minutes.
Variation: Use broccoli instead of beans, the broccoli having been pared and sliced into thin sticks.

GREEN BEANS WITH SUMMER SAVORY

3 c.	Green beans, cut into 1 ½-inch pieces
2 T.	Olive or corn oil
1 tsp.	Garlic, minced
1 T.	Fresh summer savory, chopped
½ tsp.	Black pepper
¼ tsp.	Sea salt

Blanch the beans in salted boiling water for 3 minutes. Drain and run cold water over them. Drain and set aside. Heat the oil in a skillet. Stir in the garlic. Add the beans. Cook, stirring frequently, until the beans are quite tender and the garlic is translucent—12 to 14 minutes. Stir in the savory, pepper, and salt.

GREEN BEANS WITH TOMATOES

2 c.	Onions, chopped
1 ½ c.	Bell pepper, chopped
1 ½ c.	Celery, chopped
1 ½ tsp.	Garlic, minced
¼ tsp.	Hot pepper flakes
2 T.	Olive oil
6 c.	Green beans
3 c.	Canned tomatoes, drained (save the juice) and chopped
2 T.	Soy sauce
	Tomato juice as needed

Sauté the onions, bell pepper, celery, garlic, and pepper flakes in the olive oil until the onions are transparent. Add the green beans and stir until they are coated well with the hot oil. Add the tomatoes and soy sauce. Cook until the beans are done, adding tomato juice if it seems to be getting too dry.

GREEN LIMA BEANS WITH FINES HERBES

2 ½ c.	Lima beans, cooked in a little UnChicken Broth until tender
1 tsp.	Non-dairy margarine
1 tsp.	Lemon juice
3 T.	Onions, chopped
1 T.	Minced parsley
½ tsp.	Fines Herbes
½ tsp.	Sea salt

Combine everything and cook together for 5 minutes.

GREEN PEAS AND ONIONS

3 T.	Onions, chopped
1 tsp.	Non-dairy margarine
2 c.	Green peas, cooked
⅛ tsp.	Garlic powder
½ tsp.	Sea salt

Sauté the onions in the margarine, then combine all ingredients and heat.

HASHBROWN WAFFLES

4 c.	Raw potatoes, shredded
2 T.	Corn oil
3 tsp.	Onion powder
½ tsp.	Garlic powder
1 tsp.	Sea salt
4 tsp.	Nutritional Yeast
2 T.	Dried parsley
1	N'egg
1 T.	Unbleached white flour

Combine everything well. Press into a preheated and oiled waffle iron. Close and bake 12 to 15 minutes until browned.
Variation: Use crumbled or chopped cooked potatoes.

HOMINY AND BELL PEPPER SAUTÉ

1 ½ T.	Olive or corn oil
1 c.	Onion, sliced thin
1 c.	Red bell pepper, cut into ½-inch dice
1 c.	Yellow bell pepper, cut into ½-inch dice
2	16 oz. cans of cooked hominy, drained
4 T.	Water
½ tsp.	Sea salt
¼ tsp.	Black pepper

Heat the oil in a saucepan, add the onion and bell peppers, cover, and cook over low heat, stirring, until tender—about 8 minutes. Stir in the hominy and 2 tablespoons of the water, cover, and cook 5 minutes. Stir in the rest of the water, cover, and cook 5 more minutes, or until the hominy is tender. Stir in the salt and pepper.

JAMAICA RICE AND "PEAS"

3 c.	Onions, chopped
1 ½ tsp.	Garlic, minced
1 T.	Corn oil

3 c.	Red kidney beans, cooked and drained
1 T.	Sea salt
1 T.	Lemon juice
1 tsp.	Basil
1 tsp.	Oregano
2 ⅓ c.	Rice, cooked
2 c.	UnChicken Broth

Sauté the onions and garlic in the oil. Combine all ingredients, turn into a large casserole, and bake at 350° for 1 hour, adding a little more broth if necessary.

JAMAICAN VEGETABLES

Marinade:

½ c.	Green onions, diced
1 c.	Onion, diced
2 T.	Jalapeño peppers, seeded and minced
¾ c.	Low sodium soy sauce
½ c.	Balsamic vinegar
¼ c.	Corn oil
⅓ c.	Sucanat
1 tsp.	Dried thyme
½ tsp.	Ground cloves
½ tsp.	Nutmeg, ground
½ tsp.	Ground allspice or cinnamon

8	Cherry tomatoes, halved
1	Bell pepper, seeded and cut into 8 pieces
8	Large mushrooms
8	Broccoli flowerets
1	Onion, cut into 8 pieces

Combine the marinade ingredients in a food processor and process for 15 to 20 seconds at high speed. Pour this over the vegetables in a casserole and refrigerate 3 to 4 hours, occasionally spooning the marinade over the vegetables. Broil.

"KENTUCKY FRIED" GREEN BEANS

My Kentucky grandmother Burge used to make these in a non-vegetarian version. The memory clung to me through the years until one day I went in the kitchen determined to duplicate them. I did!

4 c.	Green beans, steamed
2 T.	Corn oil
¾ c.	Onions, chopped
1 T.	UnBacon, chopped fine
⅛ tsp.	Black pepper
¼ tsp.	Garlic powder

½ tsp.	Sea salt (or ½ tsp. salt and ½ tsp. Monosodium Glutamate)

Sauté the beans in the oil until nearly cooked. Add the rest of the ingredients and sauté until the beans are completely cooked.

LAZY KITCHURI

1 c.	Rice, uncooked
1 T.	Corn oil
1 c.	Onions, chopped
1 T.	Jalapeños, sliced or minced (in this dish sliced seems better)
¼ c.	Curry powder (madrasi style is best)
1 ¼ tsp.	Sea salt
¼ tsp.	Garlic powder
1 qt.	Vegetables of choice, chopped
2 ½ c.	Tomatoes, fresh or canned (drained well, using juice as part of the water measure)
3 c.	Boiling water (and tomato juice if canned tomatoes are used)

Wash the rice over and over, changing the water, until there is no more starch in the water, and drain it well. Heat the oil until very hot. Sauté the onions and jalapeños, then add the curry powder, salt, and garlic powder, and stir constantly as it all fries to a rich brown color of a heavenly fragrance. Add the vegetables, tomatoes, and rice and stir continually until all is covered with the hot oil/spice mixture. Add the boiling water and stir. Bring to a boil, cover and simmer until all vegetables are done.

Variations: Include 1 ½ cups of cooked dal, garbanzos, or other beans. Leave out the tomatoes. Include 2 cups of chopped flavored or unflavored gluten, frying the gluten in the spices until it browns before you add the vegetables and rice.

LIMA BEANS

Cover 1 quart of lima beans with boiling UnBeef or UnChicken Broth. Add 1 tablespoon of non-dairy margarine. Simmer for 15 minutes. Add 1 teaspoon of sea salt. Cook the beans over a good flame until the water evaporates. Add:

1 ½ T.	Lemon juice
1 T.	Parsley, chopped

Variation: Instead of the last three ingredients, add ½ cup of cashew milk and heat thoroughly, but do not boil.

LIMA BEANS AND TOMATOES

¾ c.	Onions, chopped
¼ c.	Bell pepper, chopped
½ tsp.	Garlic, minced
1 ½ tsp.	Corn oil
2 c.	Lima beans, dried-cooked, fresh, or frozen and thawed
¼ tsp.	Cayenne pepper
2 tsp.	Sea salt
1 ½ c.	Tomatoes, chopped
¼ c.	Celery, chopped

Sauté the onions, bell pepper, and garlic in the oil. Add the rest of the ingredients and cook gently until all are well done.

LIMA BEANS IN CHEEZ SAUCE

Add to cooked lima beans one-half as much cheez sauce.

LIMA BEANS IN PIQUANTE SAUCE

¼ c.	Onions, chopped
¼ c.	Celery, chopped
½ tsp.	Garlic, minced
2 tsp.	Non-dairy margarine
2 ½ T.	Unbleached white flour
1 ½ c.	UnBeef or UnChicken Broth made with Cashew Milk
½ c.	Yeast, Pimento, or Notzarella Cheez
2 ½ c.	Lima beans, cooked and drained
¼ tsp.	Sea salt
⅛ tsp.	Cayenne pepper
¼ tsp.	Dry mustard
⅛ tsp.	Basil

Sauté the onions, celery, and garlic in the margarine until the onions are light brown. Stir in the flour until it bubbles. Slowly stir in the broth. Reduce the heat and stir in the cheez. Add the rest of the ingredients and stir.

LIMA BEANS WITH CHEEZ

More than a touch of class!

⅓ c.	Onions, chopped
½ tsp.	Garlic, minced
1 tsp.	Non-dairy margarine
1 c.	Yeast, Pimento, or Notzarella Cheez
4 c.	Lima beans, cooked
1 tsp.	Soy sauce
½ tsp.	Sea salt
¼ tsp.	Cayenne pepper

Sauté the onions and garlic in the margarine. Stir in the cheez and stir over low heat until it melts. Add the rest of the ingredients. Put in a baking dish, cover with bread crumbs, dot with margarine, and bake at 350° for ½ hour or until crumbs are brown.

LIMA-CORN SUCCOTASH

The ultimate succotash, I guarantee!

1 ½ c.	Onions, chopped
½ c.	Bell pepper, chopped
1 ½ tsp.	Garlic, minced
¼ tsp.	Red pepper flakes
2 tsp.	Non-dairy margarine
3 c.	Corn (if fresh, cooked, if frozen, thawed)
3 c.	Green lima beans, cooked
¾ tsp.	Sea salt

Sauté the onions, bell pepper, garlic, and pepper flakes in the margarine until the onion is transparent. Then add the corn, limas, and salt, and cook 5 minutes more.
Variation: Add ½ cup UnBacon, chopped fine, and cut the salt in half.

LOUISIANA CORN AND TOMATOES

1 ¼ c.	Onions, coarsely chopped
⅛ tsp.	Garlic, minced
2 tsp.	Corn oil
4 c.	Corn
½ c.	Bell pepper, coarsely chopped
3 c.	Tomatoes, coarsely chopped
1 ½ c.	Water
½ tsp.	Cayenne pepper
1 ½ tsp.	Sea salt

Sauté the onions and garlic in the oil until the onions are soft and translucent but not brown. Stir in the corn, bell pepper, tomatoes, water, cayenne and salt. Bring to a boil over high heat. Reduce heat to low, cover partially, and simmer about 10 minutes, or until the corn is tender.

MASHED CARROTS

A worthy change from mashed potatoes.

Cook carrots, drain, and mash. Add non-dairy margarine, salt, and pepper to taste.

MASHED POTATOES–1

Peel potatoes and cut them in large chunks. Boil in salted water until they can be broken apart with a fork but have not started to fall apart. Mash the potatoes with enough potato water to give a good consistency. For each gallon of potatoes, mash in 1 stick of non–dairy margarine and 2 teaspoons of salt.

Variations: Use Cashew Milk instead of the potato water in the mashing. Use UnBeef or UnChicken Broth as the mashing liquid. Cook the potatoes in UnBeef or UnChicken Broth.

MASHED POTATOES-2

2 lb.	Potatoes, unpeeled, cut into large pieces, cooked until tender, and drained
¼ c.	Cashew Cream
½ c.	Tofu Yogurt, made without the water
½ tsp.	Sea salt
½ tsp.	Paprika
¼ tsp.	White pepper

Put the potatoes through a sieve or ricer. Mash with the rest of the ingredients.

MEDITERRANEAN RAGOUT

Couscous:

2 c.	Medium grain couscous
3 c.	Water
1 tsp.	Sea salt

Put the couscous in a shallow baking pan. Bring the water and salt to a boil and pour over it. Cover the pan with foil and let sit 5 to 10 minutes.

Ragout:

1 ½ c.	Onions
1 T.	Corn oil
2 c.	Water
1 c.	Carrots, sliced
1 c.	Green beans
1 T.	Garlic, minced
1 T.	Ground coriander
1 T.	Paprika
2 tsp.	Ground cumin
1 ½ tsp.	Black pepper
½ tsp.	Cayenne
6 T.	Parsley, chopped
1 c.	Tomatoes, chopped
1 c.	Zucchini, chopped
4 c.	Spinach, chopped
1 ½ tsp.	Sea salt
3 T.	Lemon juice

Sauté the onions in the oil until soft. Combine everything and cook until done. Serve over the couscous.

MUSHROOM STROGANOFF

2 c.	Onions, sliced
2 tsp.	Corn oil
4 c.	Mushrooms, sliced
1 tsp.	Paprika
Pinch	Cayenne
¼ tsp.	Lemon zest
1 T.	Low sodium soy sauce
½ tsp.	Kitchen Bouquet
1 ½ tsp.	Nutritional Yeast
⅛ tsp.	Sage, rubbed
½ c.	Water
½ tsp.	Sea salt
¼ tsp.	Black pepper
½ c.	Cashew or Tofu Sour Cream
2 T.	Dill or parsley, chopped

Sauté the onions in the oil until soft. Add the mushrooms and sauté 5 more minutes. Stir in the the rest of the ingredients except for the "sour cream" and dill. Simmer for 10 minutes. Take from the heat and let sit for 5 minutes. Stir in the "sour cream." Sprinkle with the dill or parsley. Serve with polenta, rice, or noodles.

MUSHROOMS IN CREAM SAUCE

Marvelous on toast, biscuits, or rice!

1 c.	Onions, chopped
1 ½ tsp.	Non-dairy margarine
6 c.	Mushrooms, cleaned, stemmed and sliced (save stems to use later in soup)
¾ tsp.	Sea salt
⅛ tsp.	Black pepper
⅛ tsp.	Nutmeg
Pinch	Paprika
2 ½ c.	Thin White Sauce
½ c.	Fresh dill weed, chopped
½ c.	Fresh parsley, chopped

Sauté the onions in the margarine until the onions are soft. Add the mushrooms, salt, pepper, nutmeg, paprika and white sauce, and cook together for 10 minutes. Add dill and parsley and cook for 2 more minutes.

Variations: Add 1 tablespoon of garlic. Add 1 tablespoon of jalapeños.

OKRA AND TOMATOES

1 T.	Olive oil
2 c.	UnBacon, cubed

2 c.	Onions, chopped fine
¾ tsp.	Garlic, minced
6 c.	Okra, sliced
3 c.	Tomatoes, diced
1 c.	Water or tomato juice
2 tsp.	Louisiana Hot Sauce
2 T.	Lea & Perrins Steak Sauce
½ tsp.	Sea salt

In the oil sauté the gluten, onions, and garlic for 10 minutes. Add the okra and tomatoes. Pour water or juice over all. Add the hot sauce, steak sauce, and salt. Cook until the okra is tender and no longer tastes "green."

OKRA WITH CUMIN

Tastes like you are in India!

3 c.	Okra
1 tsp.	Corn oil
⅓ c.	Onions (red preferred), sliced lengthwise into paper-thin slivers
1 tsp.	Sea salt
2 tsp.	Cumin
¼ tsp.	White pepper

Wash the okra under cold running water. With a small, sharp knife scrape the skin lightly to remove any surface fuzz. Pat dry with paper towels. In a heavy skillet heat the oil over moderate heat until a drop of water flicked into it splutters instantly. Add the onions and salt and stir for 7 to 8 minutes, or until they are golden brown. Add the okra, cumin, and pepper, and continue to sauté, lifting and turning the vegetables constantly, for 25 minutes, or until the okra is tender and most of the liquid in the pan has evaporated (frozen okra will still be somewhat sticky).

ORIENTAL EGGPLANT AND MUSHROOMS IN GARLIC SAUCE

4 c.	Eggplant, peeled and cut into small cubes
3 c.	Mushrooms, sliced thick
2 c.	Onions, chopped coarsely
3 T.	Garlic, crushed
¼ tsp.	Garlic powder
1 T.	Olive oil
1 ¼ c.	Canned tomato sauce
4 ½ tsp.	Soy sauce or Maggi
4 ½ tsp.	Red chili paste with garlic
¼ tsp.	Sea salt

Deep-fry the eggplant and set aside. Sauté the

mushrooms, onions, garlic, and garlic powder in the oil until soft. Add the rest of the ingredients—including the eggplant. Cook until most of the liquid is evaporated—about 15 minutes. Serve with rice.

OVEN-FRIED POTATOES

These are superb!

⅔ c.	Corn oil
8 c.	Potatoes, cut into 1-inch chunks
1 ½ tsp.	Dill weed
1 ½ tsp.	Oregano
1 ½ tsp.	Onion salt

Pre-heat oven to 450°. Put the oil in a baking pan. Put the potato chunks in the pan and roll them around to coat them with the oil. Sprinkle generously with dill, oregano, and onion salt. Bake for 1 hour or until done, basting and turning every 10 minutes. Drain in a colander.
Variations: Stir in ¼ cup of UnBacon, chopped fine, after 45 minutes. Use sea salt instead of onion salt with the dill and oregano, and stir in 1 cup of chopped onions after 45 minutes.

OVEN-ROASTED OKRA

At first this seems simple and bland—but then it reveals itself!

4 T.	Olive oil
½ tsp.	Cumin, ground
½ tsp.	Oregano, crumbled
¼ tsp.	Sea salt
¼ tsp.	White pepper
6 c.	Small whole okra, rinsed and patted dry

Combine oil and seasonings in a mixing bowl. Add the okra and toss to coat. Place okra in a heavy pan and roast at 500°, stirring occasionally, for 8 to 10 minutes, or until tender and evenly browned. May be served with lemon wedges.

OVEN UNFRIES

These non-oil fries are a surprise.

7 c.	Potatoes, cut into thin "French-fry" strips
1 T.	Soy sauce
¼ tsp.	Garlic powder
½ tsp.	Onion powder
1 ½ tsp.	Paprika
¾ tsp.	Sea salt

Combine everything until the potatoes are evenly coated. Spread onto a nonstick baking sheet and bake at 400° for 35 to 45 minutes or until browned, turning once.

PAELLA-LIMAS

1 c.	Green limas, frozen
2 c.	Rice, uncooked
1 c.	Carrots, sliced thin
1 c.	Onions, minced
1 tsp.	Garlic, minced
2 tsp.	Corn oil
4 ½ c.	Boiling water
1 ¾ tsp.	Sea salt

Steam the lima beans and set aside. Sauté the rice, carrots, onions, and garlic in the oil until the vegetables are soft. Spoon into the boiling water, being careful not to get burned when the rice "explodes." (If it does not explode, something is wrong.) Put the rest of the ingredients into the water and boil for 30 minutes. Pour the paella into a casserole, cover and bake at 350 degrees for 1 hour, uncovering it for the last 5 minutes.

PEAS AND CARROTS

1 ¼ c.	Onions, chopped
½ tsp.	Garlic, minced
⅓ tsp.	Hot pepper flakes
1 ½ tsp.	Corn oil
1 ½ c.	Peas
1 c.	Carrots, sliced or diced
⅔ c.	UnChicken Broth
¼ tsp.	Sea salt
1 T.	Nutritional yeast
1 T.	Non-dairy margarine
2 c.	Rice, cooked

Sauté the onions, garlic, and pepper flakes in the oil until onions are transparent. Add the peas and carrots and stir well until coated with the hot oil. Add the broth, salt, yeast, and margarine. Cover and cook. When done, add the rice and mix well. *Variation:* Add ½ cup of UnBacon, chopped fine.

PEPERONATA–1

1 ½ c.	Bell peppers, cut in strips
1 c.	Onions, sliced
2 ½ tsp.	Corn oil
4 c.	Potatoes, cubed and cooked
3 c.	Tomatoes, chopped
1 tsp.	Garlic, minced
⅓ tsp.	Sea salt
½ tsp.	Basil
1 c.	UnBeef Broth
⅛ tsp.	Cayenne pepper

Sauté the bell peppers and onions in the oil. Combine with rest of ingredients and cook.

PEPERONATA–2

Simple and heavenly!

4 tsp.	Non-dairy margarine
4 tsp.	Olive oil
6 c.	Onions, sliced ⅛ inch thick
6 c.	Bell pepper, cut in 1x½-inch strips
3 c.	Tomatoes, coarsely chopped
1 tsp.	Red wine vinegar
1 tsp.	Sea salt
¼ tsp.	White pepper

Melt the margarine in a skillet along with the olive oil. Sauté the onions for 10 minutes, or until they are soft and lightly browned. Stir in the peppers, reduce the heat, cover the skillet, and cook for 10 minutes. Add the tomatoes, vinegar, salt, and white pepper. Cover and cook for another 10 minutes. Cook the vegetables uncovered over high heat stirring gently, until almost all the liquid has boiled away. May be served hot or cold.

PIZZA-STYLE VEGETABLES

1 T.	Olive oil
2 ⅔ c.	Zucchini or yellow summer squash, sliced into ½-inch thick slices
1	Small onion, cut into ¼-inch-thick slices and separated into rings
¾ tsp.	Garlic, minced
½ tsp.	Italian seasoning, crushed
2 c.	Canned stewed tomatoes, *un*drained
½ c.	Notzarella Cheez
¼ c.	Parmesan Cheez

Heat the oil, add the zucchini, onion, garlic, and Italian seasoning, and cook, uncovered, for 5 minutes, stirring occasionally. Carefully add the undrained tomatoes. Cover and cook for 3 minutes or until the zucchini is crisp-tender. Take from the heat and stir in the cheezes.

POTATO CHIPS

What I said about French Fries applies to these. Yet there are times when a little splurge never hurts!

Take Idaho potatoes, slice them paper-thin, and

put them directly into salted (1 teaspoon of sea salt per quart) cold water to remove the starch and prevent discoloration. Heat oil to 400°. When ready to fry them, take the potato slices, a batch at a time, drain them in a colander, spread them out in a single layer on paper towels, and pat them thoroughly dry with more towels. Then fry them in the hot oil, turning them about with a slotted spoon, for 2 or 3 minutes, or until they are crisp and golden brown. Remove the chips from the oil, drain them in a colander, then transfer them to paper towels and sprinkle them, turning gently, with onion salt. Repeat until all the chips have been fried, making sure the oil temperature never goes below 375° and can quickly come back up to 400°. If you are frying a goodly number of chips and do not want the first ones to get cold, after salting a batch of chips transfer them to a pan lined with a double thickness of paper towels and put them in a 250° oven to keep them warm while you proceed with the remaining batches. To serve, put the chips in a heated bowl.

An easier and better way: I happily recommend to you the Chip Factory made by West Bend. This Chip Factory makes marvelous potato chips automatically. All you do is peel the potatoes, trim them to fit into the machine, and wait for the goodies. The machine slices, fries, and empties the chips down the chute to whomever waits. The chips made by the Chip Factory are super thin and delicious. (Use baking potatoes for best results.) You will discover that they need no salt, no nothing—just the eating! If you put a paper towel on the chip chute any excess oil will be absorbed. Although they are great as they are being made, they are still good the next day or so. The Chip Factory makes a little bit of chips at a time, but if you start making them about an hour before you will want chips, you will find that they add up in time. Get in the chips!

POTATO CHIPS–SPICED

1 T.	Chili powder
¾ tsp.	Sea salt
Pinch	Cayenne pepper

Combine these ingredients. Make potato chips as above, and sprinkle them with this instead of onion salt, or use onion salt instead of sea salt in this combination.

POTATO CURRY

½ c.	Onions, chopped
¼ c.	Bell pepper, chopped
½ tsp.	Hot pepper flakes
½ tsp.	Sea salt
½ tsp.	Garlic salt
1 ½ tsp.	Corn oil
1 T.	Curry powder
4 c.	Potatoes, cubed and boiled

Sauté the onion, pepper, pepper flakes, and salts in the oil. Add the curry powder and sauté for 30 seconds more. Add the potatoes. Simmer 10 minutes.

POTATO PANCAKES

Although these are good plain, with Tofu Sour Cream or Cashew Sour Cream, salsa, Yeast, Pimento, or Notzarella Cheez, Tofu Ricotta Cheez, or a gravy or sauce from the Gravies and Sauces section they are outstanding.

2 c.	Potatoes, peeled and put in cold water to prevent discoloration
½ c.	Unbleached white flour
½ tsp.	Sea salt
¼ c.	Cashew Milk
1 ½ T.	Non-dairy margarine, melted
½ tsp.	Dill weed
⅛ tsp.	Cayenne pepper

Stir together the flour, salt, "milk," melted margarine, dill weed, and pepper. Pat one of the potatoes dry and grate it coarsely into a sieve or colander. Press the grated potato firmly down into the sieve with the back of a large spoon to remove its moisture, then immediately stir the gratings into the flour and cashew milk mixture. Repeat this process with each potato until all have been grated and stirred into the cashew milk and flour. Heat a heavy skillet that has been lightly oiled. (After this initial oiling, the margarine in the pancake mixture will be sufficient for frying.) For each pancake drop about ⅓ cup of mixture into the skillet. Let it fry for about a minute until a skin forms on the bottom. Then turn over and press flat–not before. Cook 3 or 4 pancakes at a time, leaving enough space between them so that they can spread into 3 ½ to 4-inch cakes. Fry them about 3 minutes on each side, or until they are golden brown and crisp around the edges. Transfer the finished pancakes to a heated plate and cover them with foil to keep them warm while the rest are being cooked. Add more margarine whenever you need it.

POTATO POT PIE

⅓ c.	Onions, chopped
1 tsp.	Garlic, minced
⅓ c.	Celery, diced and steamed
1 ½ tsp.	Corn oil
¼ c.	Mushrooms, sliced
1 T.	Unbleached white flour
½ c.	UnChicken Broth
2 c.	Potatoes, diced and steamed
2 c.	Carrots, diced and steamed

Sauté the onions, garlic, and celery in the oil until transparent. Add the mushrooms and sauté 2 to 3 more minutes. Add the flour. Slowly add the broth, letting the mixture cook and thicken. Stir in the potatoes and carrots, and heat through. Serve over biscuits.

POTATOES–BAKED

These are unparalleled in the baked potato world! I liked baked potatoes before eating these, but now I love them!
The boiling enables you to bake them for the shortest time possible so the nutrients will not be destroyed by long baking. I think it markedly affects the flavor and texture, too, making them so good that you need not bother putting anything on them at all for flavoring.

Scrub the potatoes, but do not peel them. Put in water, bring to a boil and simmer *lightly* for 30 minutes. Take out of the water and bake in a 350° oven for 30 more minutes.

POTATOES–BOILED

6 c.	Potatoes, cubed
6 c.	UnBeef or UnChicken Broth
½ c.	Onion, chopped
1 tsp.	Garlic, minced or sliced
1 tsp.	Jalapeño peppers, minced or sliced
2 T.	Non-dairy margarine
½ tsp.	Sea salt

Boil the potatoes in the broth and drain them, keeping the broth. Sauté the onion, garlic, and jalapeños in the margarine. Add this and the salt to the drained potatoes, plus 1 cup of the broth.

POTATOES AND GREEN ONIONS

4 c.	Potatoes, peeled and cut into 1-inch cubes
1 ½ tsp.	Sea salt
2 T.	Non-dairy margarine
2 T.	Green onions, chopped fine
¾ tsp.	Garlic, minced
⅓ c.	Chives, minced
¼ tsp.	Black pepper

In a saucepan, combine the potatoes and 1 teaspoon of the salt. Add enough water to cover the potatoes with 2 inches of water. Bring to a boil and cook until just tender–about 12 minutes. Drain in a colander. Heat the margarine in the saucepan, add the onions and garlic and sauté until the onions are thoroughly softened but not browned. Increase the heat, add the potatoes, and toss them to coat well. Add the chives, pepper, and remaining ½ teaspoon of the salt. Cook, stirring occasionally, until heated through–about 5 minutes.

POTATOES AND GREENS

½ c.	Onions, diced
2 tsp.	Garlic, minced
2 tsp.	Hot pepper flakes
2 tsp.	Corn oil
2 c.	Potatoes, cut into 1-inch chunks and boiled
½ c.	Green beans, cooked
1 ½ c.	Tomatoes, diced, or canned tomatoes, chopped
½ c.	Tomato juice
¾ tsp.	Sea salt
4 c.	Greens (one type or assorted)

Saute the onion, garlic, and pepper flakes in the oil till the onion is soft. Combine everything but the greens and cook until the vegetables are tender. Add the greens and cook until wilted.

POTATOES IN BROTH

4	Large potatoes, peeled and cut in pieces
⅓ c.	Onions, minced
3 c.	UnBeef or UnChicken Broth
1 T.	Non-dairy margarine
1 T.	Flour
½ tsp.	Sea salt
¼ tsp.	Cayenne pepper

Simmer the potatoes with the onions in the broth until nearly tender. Drain, keeping the liquid. Make a sauce of the liquid with the margarine and flour. Add seasonings. Combine potatoes and the sauce and simmer until tender.
Variation: Add chopped chives to the sauce when

it is finished.

POTATOES IN THEIR OWN GRAVY

Nothing special—and yet…

5 c.	Potatoes, diced
2 ½ c.	Flavoring Broth of choice
¼ tsp.	Sea salt
½ c.	Onion, chopped
½ c.	Mushrooms, sliced
1 ½ tsp.	Non-dairy margarine
2 T.	Unbleached white flour
1 ½ tsp.	Nutritional Yeast
½ tsp.	Garlic powder
2 tsp.	Soy sauce
⅛ tsp.	Black pepper

Cook the potatoes in the broth and salt until they are tender and drain them, retaining the liquid. Sauté the onions and mushrooms in the margarine until the onions are transparent. Stir in the flour, yeast, and garlic powder. Whisk in the potato liquid until all is smooth. Add the soy sauce and pepper and cook until thickened. Combine with the potatoes and serve.

POTATOES O'BRIEN

½ c.	Bell pepper, chopped
1 tsp.	Garlic, minced
¾ c.	Onions, chopped
1 ½ tsp.	Non-dairy margarine
1 T.	Unbleached white flour
1 c.	Cashew Milk
½ tsp.	Sea salt
¼ tsp.	Cayenne pepper
¾ c.	Yeast or Pimento Cheez
4 c.	Potatoes, boiled, chilled, and diced
	Bread crumbs

Sauté the bell pepper, garlic, and onions in the margarine. Blend in the flour. Add the "milk" and bring to a boil. Add the salt, pepper, and cheez. Add the potatoes. Place in an oiled baking dish. Cover with bread crumbs. Dot with non-dairy margarine. Bake at 350° for 15 minutes, or until the crumbs are brown.

POTATOES PAPRIKA

1 c.	Onion, chopped
¾ tsp.	Garlic, minced
1 ½ tsp.	Corn oil
1 T.	Paprika
3	Medium-sized potatoes, peeled and cut into "French fries" 2 inches long
1 ½ tsp.	Sea salt
2 c.	Water
½ c.	Bell pepper, cut in strips
1 ¼ c.	Tomatoes, chopped

Sauté the onion and garlic in the oil until the onion is transparent. Stir in the paprika, add the potatoes and salt, and cook for a few seconds, stirring. Add the water, cover, and simmer for 10 minutes. Add the pepper strips and tomatoes. Cover and simmer until the potatoes are just tender—about 10 or 15 minutes.

QUICK SAUCY VEGETABLES

4 c.	Raw or frozen vegetables, cooked
2 c.	UnBeef or UnChicken Broth
3 T.	Onions, minced
1 tsp.	Garlic, minced
1 tsp.	Non-dairy margarine
¼ tsp.	Basil (if using UnBeef Broth)
¼ tsp.	Dill weed (if using UnChicken Broth)
¼ tsp.	Cayenne pepper
2 T.	Cornstarch or arrowroot
¼ c.	Water

Cook the vegetables in the broth until tender—about 15 minutes—and drain. Sauté the onions and garlic in the margarine. Add the vegetables. Add the seasonings. Mix the cornstarch or arrowroot in the water and add to the vegetable mixture while stirring. Cook and stir until thickened. Serve over grains or pasta.

QUICK SAUERKRAUT

I have a suspicion that this is a lot better for us than the canned stuff.

2 c.	Cabbage, coarsely shredded
⅓ c.	Wine vinegar
1 tsp.	Sea salt
2 c.	Water
1 ½ tsp.	Unbleached white flour
1 T.	Water

Combine the cabbage, vinegar, salt, and 2 cups of water in a 2-quart pot. Bring to a boil and cook, partially covered, for 20 minutes. Mix the flour into a paste with tablespoon of water. Stir into the hot cabbage and cook, stirring constantly, until thickened.

RATATOUILLE

Better than just good!

1	Small eggplant, peeled and cubed
1 T.	Olive oil
1 ½ c.	Italian tomatoes, cubed
¾ c.	Zucchini, chopped
½ c.	Bell pepper, chopped
⅔ c.	Onion, chopped
2 ½ tsp.	Garlic, minced
½ tsp.	Sea salt
⅛ tsp.	Cayenne pepper

Sauté the eggplant in the oil until it is soft, then add all the ingredients, and cook on low heat for 10 to 20 minutes.

RED CABBAGE-1

1 T.	Non-dairy margarine
3 T.	Onions, chopped
6 T.	Barbados molasses
3 T.	Wine vinegar
¼ tsp.	Sea salt
12 c.	Red cabbage, shredded

Melt the margarine and sauté the onions lightly. Add the molasses, vinegar, and salt. Add the cabbage and cook for 25 minutes, stirring frequently.

RED CABBAGE-2

10 c.	Red cabbage, shredded
1 tsp.	Caraway seeds
3 T.	Lemon juice
2 T.	Balsamic vinegar
4 T.	Corn oil
3 T.	Sucanat
½ c.	Onion, chopped fine
2 T.	Apple juice
2 T.	Lemon juice
1 c.	Apple, grated (Granny Smith is best because of its tartness)
1 ½ tsp.	Sea salt

In a large bowl, combine the cabbage, caraway seeds, 3 tablespoons of lemon juice, and vinegar. Marinate overnight–or at least 10 hours–in the refrigerator. Put the oil and Sucanat in a heavy saucepan on the stove, turn the heat to medium, and cook, stirring, until the Sucanat dissolves. Add the onion and stir it in. Add the cabbage (with the marinating liquid), apple juice, lemon juice, and apple. Stir and season with the salt. Lower the heat, cover, and simmer for one hour, stirring occasionally.

ROASTED EGGPLANT, ONION, AND GARLIC IN TOMATO SAUCE

1 lb.	Eggplant, cut in ¾-inch slices
3 c.	Onions (yellow preferred), sliced ½-inch thick
	Olive oil
6	Garlic cloves, peeled
1 c.	Onion, diced small
2 tsp.	Garlic, minced
2 T.	Basil
1 T.	Oregano
1 ½ tsp.	Cumin
¼ tsp.	Thyme
1	Bay leaf
4 ½ c.	Canned tomatoes, chopped
¼ tsp.	Sea salt
¼ tsp.	Cayenne

Salt the eggplant slices and let them sit 30 minutes. Brush the eggplant and onion slices with olive oil. Put them on separate baking sheets. Toss the garlic cloves in enough olive oil to coat them and put them in a baking dish and cover with foil. Bake all of these at 375°. The garlic should be done in 20 to 30 minutes, when tender and slightly brown. Allow the eggplant and onion to get brown as well–25 to 40 minutes. Meanwhile, sauté the diced onion in olive oil with a pinch of salt. Add the minced garlic and the herbs, and stir together. Add the tomatoes, salt, and cayenne. Simmer for 45 to 60 minutes. When the vegetables are roasted, cube the eggplant and onion and add to the sauce along with the whole cloves of roasted garlic. Stir the sauce and adjust the seasonings if necessary.

Note: If you have any of this left over, cook up some lasagna noodles and use this for a filling. Great!

ROASTED POTATOES AND ONIONS

3 c.	Potatoes, peeled and cut into chunks
3 c.	Onions (red preferred), chopped
½ c.	Olive oil
3 T.	Cider vinegar
⅛ tsp.	Dried thyme
1 T.	Garlic, minced
1 ½ tsp.	Sea salt
¾ tsp.	Black pepper

Combine everything and mix well. Put on a baking sheet and bake at 450°, turning occasionally, until the potatoes are soft and brown on the edges. Put in a colander and drain the excess oil.

SAUTÉED EGGPLANT IN TOMATO SAUCE WITH BASIL

¼ c.	Corn oil
2 lb.	Eggplant
1 T.	Sea salt
1 tsp.	Sea salt
¼ tsp.	Black pepper
1 T.	Garlic, minced
1 ¼ c.	Tomatoes, crushed
¼ c.	Fresh basil, shredded

Cut off the stem and bottom end of the eggplants. Cut them crosswise into ¾-inch slices, then cut the slices into ¾-inch strips. Put them into a colander, sprinkle with the tablespoon of salt, and toss. Set the colander over a bowl or in the sink and let it stand for at least 1 ½ hours–2 to 3 hours is better–stirring a couple of times. Rinse the eggplant under cold, running water, rubbing the strips lightly in your hands. Shake the colander to drain. Put the strips 1 inch apart on a triple thickness of paper towels. Cover with another triple layer of towels. With your palms press each eggplant strip very firmly until it looks green and translucent and feels firm and leathery when pressed between your fingertips. Repeat the pressing on fresh toweling if the eggplant has not yet reached this stage. Repeat with the rest of the eggplant strips. (After this step you can refrigerate the eggplant up to 3 hours before cooking.) Heat the oil in a skillet. Add the eggplant strips and cook, stirring occasionally, until the eggplant is fully tender. Stir in the salt, pepper, and garlic. Cook 1 more minute. Stir in the tomatoes and basil and simmer until they thicken slightly.

SAUTÉED SPINACH

1 lb.	Fresh spinach
2 T.	Olive oil
⅓ c.	Onions, finely chopped
⅛ tsp.	Ground sage
½ tsp.	Sea salt

Wash the spinach and pat dry with paper towels. Trim off and discard the stems. In a heavy saucepan, heat the oil and sauté the onions, stirring frequently, for about 5 minutes until soft and transparent, but not brown. Add the spinach, sage, and salt and, stirring, turning the leaves

about constantly, cook over moderate heat for 2 minutes or until tender.

SAUTÉED VEGETABLES

2 T.	Corn oil
6 c.	Vegetables, sliced
1 ½ c.	Onions, chopped
1 tsp.	Garlic, minced
¼ tsp.	Cayenne pepper
⅓ c.	Soy sauce

Heat the oil in a pan or skillet, add the rest of the ingredients, stir, and cook.

SCALLOPED CABBAGE

4 c.	Cabbage, chopped, cooked, and drained
2 T.	Bell pepper, chopped
2 T.	Pimento, chopped
1 c.	Yeast or Pimento Cheez
1 ½ c.	White Sauce
1 c.	Bread crumbs, tossed in 2 tablespoons of melted non-dairy margarine

Place the cabbage in an oiled baking dish. Sprinkle the bell pepper and pimento over the cabbage. Spread the cheez over that. Cover with the white sauce. Top with the bread crumbs. Bake at 365° for 40 minutes, or until the crumbs are browned.

SLUMGULLIAN

This is real "down home food" and I have adored it since the first time I ate it as a child!

⅓ c.	Onions, chopped
2 tsp.	Garlic, minced
½ c.	Bell pepper, chopped
⅛ tsp.	Cayenne pepper
1 tsp.	Non-dairy margarine
1 ½ c.	Canned tomatoes, drained and chopped
1 c.	UnBeef Broth
1 ½ c.	Corn

Sauté the onions, garlic, bell pepper, and cayenne in the margarine. Add the tomatoes and broth and continue to cook until the tomatoes break up. Add the corn and cook 5 minutes more. *Variation:* Use water instead of broth, but in that case add ½ tsp. of sea salt.

SPANISH VEGETABLES

1 tsp.	Corn oil
½ tsp.	Garlic, minced
2 c.	Tomatoes, chopped
¼ tsp.	Sucanat
1 tsp.	Sea salt

Sauté the garlic in the oil until it browns. Add the rest of the ingredients and cook until done.

1 ½ tsp.	Corn oil
½ c.	Bell pepper, chopped
¾ c.	Onions, chopped

Sauté the bell pepper and onions in the corn oil until tender. Add to the tomato sauce.

1 tsp.	Corn oil
1 c.	Vegetable(s), chopped or sliced
⅛ tsp.	Cayenne pepper

Sauté the vegetables and pepper until all are tender. Add to the tomato sauce. Stir well.

SPINACH AU GRATIN

Put a thin layer of cooked and drained spinach in a baking dish. Cover it with a layer of Yeast, Pimento, or Notzarella Cheez. Season with pepper and salt. Pour 3 tablespoons of Cashew Milk over it. Broil until the cheez is spotted brown.

SPINACH, TOMATOES, AND RICE

This is a real staple. A Greek dish adapted by me. In my much younger days I used to cook up a huge pot of this and eat on it the rest of the week. It was never boring!

1 ½ c.	Onions, chopped
1 T.	Garlic, minced
⅓ c.	Bell pepper, chopped
1 T.	Olive oil
2 T.	Corn oil
2 c.	Spinach
4 c.	Tomatoes, chopped
2 c.	Rice, uncooked
4 c.	Water
¾ c.	Tomato paste
2 tsp.	Sea salt

Sauté the onions, garlic, and bell pepper in the oils. Add the remaining ingredients and simmer till cooked and of the proper consistency.

SPINACH WITH TOMATOES

¼ c.	Onions, chopped
1 ½ tsp.	Garlic, minced
1 ½ tsp.	Corn oil
4 c.	Spinach, cooked, drained, chopped, or puréed
1 c.	Tomato paste or purée
½ tsp.	Sea salt
¼ tsp.	Cayenne pepper

Sauté the onions and garlic in the corn oil. Add the rest of the ingredients and mix.

SQUASH AU GRATIN

1 ½ tsp.	Non–dairy margarine
4 c.	Squash, thinly sliced
¼ c.	Onions, chopped
1 tsp.	Sea salt
⅛ tsp.	Cayenne pepper
1 c.	Tomatoes, sliced
¼ c.	Yeast or Pimento Cheez

Melt the margarine. Add the squash, onions, salt, pepper, and tomatoes. Cover and cook for 15 minutes or until tender, stirring occasionally. Add the cheez and heat through. Serve with rice.

SQUASH, BEANS, AND CORN

Just plain goodness!

3 c.	Squash, cubed
1 c.	Onion, chopped
¾ tsp.	Garlic, minced
2	Jalapeño peppers, minced
2 ½ c.	Tomatoes, chopped, or ½ c. canned tomatoes
2 c.	Lima beans, fresh or frozen
2 c.	Green beans, sliced
2 ½ tsp.	Corn oil
1 c.	Water
3 c.	Corn
1 tsp.	Sea salt
¼ tsp.	Black pepper

Sauté the squash, onion, garlic, jalapeños, tomatoes, and beans in the oil until the onions are transparent. Add the water and simmer until the beans are done, stirring frequently. Add the corn, salt, and pepper, and cook 10 minutes more.

SQUASH, GREEN BEANS, AND TOMATOES

⅓ c.	Onions, chopped
1 tsp.	Garlic, minced
1 ½ tsp.	Non–dairy margarine
2 c.	Squash, sliced and chopped

2 c.	Green beans
2 c.	Tomatoes, blended
½ tsp.	Sea salt
Pinch	Cayenne pepper
¼ tsp.	Basil
¼ tsp.	Savory
1 c.	UnBeef Broth

Sauté the onions and garlic in the margarine. Combine with rest of ingredients and cook.

SQUASH AND PEAS

3 c.	Squash, sliced and chopped
3 c.	Peas
1 ½ tsp.	Non-dairy margarine
¼ tsp.	Sea salt
3 T.	Onions, minced
½ tsp.	Garlic, minced
Pinch	Cayenne pepper
¼ tsp.	Basil
1 c.	UnChicken Broth

Cook over medium heat until the squash is done.

SQUASH, MUSHROOM, AND PASTA PIE

1 T.	Non-dairy margarine
3 T.	Unbleached white flour
2 T.	Onion, minced
4 c.	Mushrooms, sliced
1 ½ tsp.	Garlic, minced
2 c.	Cashew Milk
½ tsp.	Sea salt
¼ tsp.	Black pepper
2 T.	UnHam Broth
1 ¾ c.	UnHam, in ½-inch cubes
¼ c.	Parsley, minced
¼ tsp.	Thyme
½ tsp.	Basil
½ tsp.	Dried mint leaves
4 c.	Squash, sliced or chopped
10 oz.	Spinach pasta
2 c.	Notzarella Cheez
1	Pie Crust recipe for 2 crusts

In a heavy saucepan melt the margarine, add the flour, and cook, whisking, for 3 minutes. Add the onions, mushrooms, and garlic and cook until they are soft. Add the "milk" and bring to a boil, whisking, and simmer it–still whisking–for 5 minutes, or until it is of the consistency of a sauce. Add the salt, pepper, broth, gluten, parsley, thyme, basil, and mint. Cook for 5 more minutes,

adding more broth if it becomes too dry. Cut the squash lengthwise into ¼-inch-thick slices. Deep-fry the squash at 380° until golden, transferring the fried slices to paper towels to drain. Cook the spinach pasta according to the maker's instructions, drain it in a colander, and briefly rinse it with cold water. Combine the mushroom sauce, squash, and cheez, and mix well. Put half of this into the unbaked pie shell. Over that make a layer of all the pasta. Put the rest of the sauce-filling on top of the pasta. Put on the top crust and seal it all around. Mist the dough with oil and prick it with a fork. Bake at 425° for 20 to 30 minutes, or until the top is golden.

SQUASH WITH TOMATOES

¾ c.	Bell pepper, chopped
¼ c.	Onions, chopped
1 tsp.	Garlic, minced
1 ½ tsp.	Corn oil
3 c.	Squash, cut in half lengthwise and then cut into 1-inch chunks
⅛ tsp.	Cayenne pepper
3 c.	Tomatoes, chopped
4 ½ tsp.	Soy sauce
¼ tsp.	Basil
¼ tsp.	Sea salt

Sauté the bell peppers, onions, and garlic in the oil. Combine with rest of ingredients and cook.

STEWED SQUASH

½ c.	UnHam, cut in ½-inch cubes
1 T.	Corn oil
8 c.	Squash, chopped
2 tsp.	Louisiana Hot Sauce
3 c.	Onions, chopped coarsely
2 c.	UnChicken Broth
1 c.	Water
2 tsp.	Garlic, minced

Sauté the gluten in the oil, but do not brown. Put in everything else, and bring to a vigorous boil. Lower the heat and simmer slowly until the squash is well cooked.

SUPER OKRA

1 c.	Onion, sliced thin
1 ½ tsp.	Corn oil
2 ½ tsp.	Garlic, minced
¼ tsp.	Powdered ginger
1 tsp.	Jalapeños, minced
¼ tsp.	Tumeric

2 T.	Almonds, ground
1 c.	Tomatoes, chopped
10	Okra "fingers" cut into ¾-inch thick rounds
¼ tsp.	Sea salt
1 T.	Parsley, chopped

Sauté the onion in the oil until it turns reddish brown–10 to 12 minutes. Stir in the garlic, ginger, jalapeños, tumeric, and almonds. Add the tomatoes and cook for 1 minute. Add the okra, mix well, and simmer, covered, for 6 to 7 minutes, until the okra is barely tender. Stir in the salt. Sprinkle with the parsley just before serving.

SWEET AND SOUR CABBAGE

As a cooked-cabbage hater I recommend this wholeheartedly.
It is simply delicious and demands seconds!

¼ c.	Thinly sliced onions
1 T.	Olive oil
8 c.	Cabbage, cut into ¼-inch strips
2 c.	Italian tomatoes, coarsely chopped
2 T.	Wine vinegar
1 ½ tsp.	Sea salt
¼ tsp.	Cayenne pepper
1 T.	Sucanat

Sauté the onions in the oil for 2 or 3 minutes until they are transparent but not brown. Stir in the cabbage, tomatoes, vinegar, salt, and pepper. Simmer uncovered, stirring frequently, for 20 minutes or until the cabbage is tender. Stir the Sucanat into the cabbage and cook 1 or 2 minutes more.

SZECHWAN BRAISED EGGPLANT

This is the breath of the dragon!

4 tsp.	Corn oil
4 c.	Eggplant, peeled and chopped into bite-size pieces
3 tsp.	Garlic, minced
¼ tsp.	Ginger, powdered
⅔ c.	Green onions, minced
2 T.	Chili paste with garlic (from an Oriental grocery store)
⅓ c.	UnChicken Broth
2 T.	Soy sauce
½ tsp.	Sucanat
1 tsp.	Red wine vinegar

Heat the oil to very hot, and sauté the eggplant,

coating thoroughly with the oil. Add the garlic, ginger, and onions, and stir in well. Add all the rest of the ingredients, mix well, and cook for 3 minutes, stirring occasionally. Cover and let simmer 10 to 15 minutes until tender.

THAI STYLE VEGETABLES

This is not for the faint-hearted. It was cooked for me by two friends from Thailand. I ate it up and demanded more. So they made me more. I ate that and demanded even more. So they gave me this recipe–and I went into their kitchen and made my own "more"!

¼ c.	Garlic, sliced
⅓ c.	Jalapeño peppers, sliced
2 tsp.	Corn oil
6 c.	Vegetables, sliced thin (if the type to be sliced)
2 c.	Onions, sliced
⅓ c.	Soy sauce

Sauté the garlic and jalapeños in the oil, but do not let the garlic brown except slightly–if at all. Add the soy sauce and vegetables and cook.
Note: Frying the jalapeños takes away some of the "bite." So for full effect, do not sauté them, but add them along with the rest of the vegetables.

TOMATOES AND OKRA

¾ c.	Onions, finely chopped
2 tsp.	Non-dairy margarine
1 ½ tsp.	Garlic, minced
4 c.	Okra, sliced
2 ½ c.	Canned tomatoes, chopped
1 ¼ tsp.	Sea salt
¼ tsp.	Cayenne pepper

Sauté the onions in the margarine until brown. Add and sauté the garlic and okra for 5 minutes. Add the rest of the ingredients and simmer, covered, until the okra is tender.
Variation: Add ½ cup of chopped bell pepper and/or 2 cups of corn.

TOMATOES AND VEGETABLES

1 c.	Bell peppers, chopped
3 T.	Onions, chopped
2 tsp.	Non-dairy margarine
4 c.	Tomatoes, chopped
2 c.	Vegetables, chopped if need be
¼ tsp.	Cayenne pepper
1 tsp.	Sea salt
⅓ tsp.	Basil
⅓ tsp.	Oregano

Sauté the bell peppers and onions in the margarine. Combine with rest of ingredients and cook.

TOMATOES, CORN, AND CHEEZ

½ c.	Bell pepper, chopped
⅓ c.	Onions, chopped
1 tsp.	Non-dairy margarine
1 c.	Canned tomatoes, chopped
⅔ c.	Corn
⅛ tsp.	Cayenne pepper
½ tsp.	Sea salt
1 ⅓ c.	Yeast, Pimento, or Notzarella Cheez

Sauté the bell pepper and onions in the margarine until they are browned. In a pan, heat the tomatoes and corn. Add the sautéed vegetables and the rest of the ingredients except the cheez. Cook for 7 minutes, stirring frequently. Add the cheez, stir in well, and heat through.

TOMATOES CREOLE

Perfect on rice!

1 c.	Bell pepper, chopped
1 ½ c.	Onions, chopped
2 tsp.	Non-dairy margarine
3 c.	Canned tomatoes, chopped (or 4 large tomatoes, sliced)
¾ tsp.	Sea salt
¼ tsp.	Cayenne pepper
2 T.	Barbados molasses

Sauté the bell pepper and onions in the margarine. Add the remaining ingredients and cook until all is tender.

VEGETABLE CURRY

½ c.	Onions, chopped
1 ¼ c.	UnBeef, UnChicken, or unflavored gluten, chopped
1 tsp.	Curry powder
2 tsp.	Corn oil
2 ½ c.	Cashew Milk
½ c.	Coconut milk
1 T.	Cornstarch
¼ c.	Water
1 ⅓ c.	Potatoes, diced
1 ½ c.	Carrots, diced
⅔ c.	Green beans or green peas
1 tsp.	Sea salt

Sauté the onion, gluten, and curry powder in the oil until the onions are soft and the gluten is browned. Add the cashew milk and coconut milk. Dissolve the cornstarch in the water and add. Cook until slightly thickened. Cook the vegetables in water with the salt until tender. Drain them and add to the curry powder sauce. Serve over rice.

VEGETABLE PIE

2 c.	Potatoes, peeled, thinly sliced
2 c.	Carrots, thinly sliced
2 ½ c.	Broccoli, coarsely chopped
3 T.	Non-dairy margarine
¼ tsp.	Black pepper
3 T.	Unbleached white flour
1 ½ tsp.	Sea salt
1 ¾ c.	Cashew Milk
1 c.	Notzarella Cheez
2	Times the Convent Pie Crust recipe, divided into a top and bottom crust, the bottom put into a casserole dish or deep baking dish—not a pie pan or dish

Cook the potatoes in boiling salted water until tender. Remove with a slotted spoon to a bowl. In the same water that you cooked the potatoes, heat the carrots to boiling, reduce heat, cover, and simmer for 10 minutes or until they are tender. Remove them with a slotted spoon to their own bowl. In the same water heat the broccoli to boiling, reduce heat, and simmer for 5 minutes, or until tender. Drain. In a saucepan melt the margarine, stir in the pepper, flour, and salt until blended. Cook 1 minute. Gradually stir in the "milk." Cook, stirring constantly, until the mixture boils and thickens. Reduce heat to low and stir in the cheez well. Remove from heat. Spoon the potatoes into the unbaked crust. Spoon ⅓ of the cheez sauce over that. Spread the carrots over all. Spoon ½ of the remaining sauce over the carrots. Top with the broccoli, then the rest of the sauce. Top with the crust and cut slits in the top for steam to escape. Bake at 425° for 35 to 40 minutes, until the filling is bubbly and the crust is golden.

VEGETABLE POT PIE

1 ½ c.	Onions, chopped
2 tsp.	Corn oil
⅔ c.	Carrots, diced
1 ¼ c.	Potatoes, diced
½ tsp.	Paprika

½ tsp.	Basil
½ tsp.	Marjoram
½ c.	Bell pepper, diced
1 c.	Mushrooms, sliced
½ c.	Peas
½ c.	Corn
1 tsp.	Sea salt
½ tsp.	Black pepper
2 T.	Non-dairy margarine
2 T.	Unbleached white flour
1 c.	Cashew Milk
1 tsp.	Dijon-style mustard
¼ tsp.	Nutmeg
1	Unbaked pie shell and dough rolled out for top crust (Convent Pie Crust recipe)

Sauté the onions in the oil until soft. Add the carrots, potatoes, paprika, basil, and marjoram. Cook, covered, on medium heat, stirring frequently, for about 10 minutes. Stir in the bell pepper, mushrooms, peas, corn, salt, and pepper. Cover and cook until the carrots are tender—5 to 10 minutes. In a saucepan melt the margarine, add the flour, and stir constantly over low heat for 3 to 5 minutes. Whisk in the "milk," mustard, and nutmeg. Continue to stir over low heat till hot and slightly thickened, but do not boil. Remove from heat. If there is liquid in the sautéed vegetables, drain it off. Add the roux/sauce, and combine well. Put the vegetables into the unbaked pie shell. Cover with the top crust and bake at 375° for 40 minutes.

YELLOW SQUASH CREOLE

1 c.	Onions, chopped
1 ½ tsp.	Garlic, minced
¼ tsp.	Hot pepper flakes
1 ½ tsp.	Corn oil
3 c.	Yellow squash, sliced
1 c.	Creole Sauce
½ c.	Water

Sauté the onion, garlic, and pepper flakes in the oil until onion is transparent. Add the squash and stir well until all is coated with the hot oil. Stir in the creole sauce and water. Cover and cook until the squash is tender.

ZUCCHINI PLAIN

1 tsp.	Non-dairy margarine
1 tsp.	Olive oil
2 c.	Onions, coarsely chopped
1 tsp.	Garlic, minced

¼ tsp.	Hot pepper flakes
¾ c.	Celery, chopped
3 c.	Zucchini, cut in half lengthwise and then cut into 1-inch chunks
¾ c.	Bell pepper, chopped
1 ½ c.	UnChicken Broth
¼ tsp.	Sea salt

Melt the margarine in the olive oil. Sauté the onion, garlic, pepper flakes, and celery until transparent. Add the zucchini and bell pepper and sauté briefly. Then add the broth and salt and stir well. Cover and cook until tender, but do not overcook.

Variation: Use other kinds of squash.

ZUCCHINI SUPREME

Sauce:

1 T.	Cornstarch
1 c.	Cold Cashew Milk
1 tsp.	Non-dairy margarine
¼ tsp.	Sea salt
⅛ tsp.	Black pepper
4 tsp.	Lemon juice
3 T.	Fresh dill, or 1 tsp. dry
1 T.	Parsley, chopped

Bring the cornstarch, "milk," margarine, salt, and pepper to a boil, stirring constantly. Boil for 1 minute. Mix with the rest of the sauce ingredients.

Vegetables:

3 c.	Zucchini, cut into 3-inch strips
1 ½ c.	Onion, sliced
2 tsp.	Corn oil

Sauté the zucchini and onion in the oil until tender-crisp. Toss with the sauce.

ZUCCHINI WITH MUSTARD-DILL SAUCE

4 c.	Cashew Milk or Cashew Cream
¼ tsp.	Cayenne
½ c.	Unbleached white flour
Pinch	Sea salt
Pinch	Black pepper
3	Whole zucchini, ends cut off, and sliced lengthwise into ¼-inch to ½-inch-thick slices
½ c.	Onion, diced
2 c.	Water
4 T.	Dill, chopped
2 T.	Grainy mustard

2 T.   Dijon mustard
½ tsp.   Sea salt
½ tsp.   Black pepper
1 T.   Dill, chopped

Combine the "milk" and cayenne, and set aside. Mix together the flour, salt, and pepper, and set aside. Heat some corn oil in a large skillet. Dip the zucchini slices in the "milk"-cayenne mixture and dredge them in the flour, shaking off any excess. Brown the zucchini on both sides. Add the rest of the ingredients except for the tablespoon of dill, mix in, and bring to a boil. Reduce heat, and simmer, covered, for 20 minutes, until thickened.

ZUCCHINI WITH TOMATOES

2 c.   Onions, coarsely chopped
½ tsp.   Garlic, minced
½ tsp.   Jalapeños, minced, or ½ tsp. red pepper flakes
¾ c.   Celery, chopped
2 ½ tsp.   Olive oil
3 c.   Zucchini, cut in half lengthwise and then cut into 1-inch chunks
¾ c.   Bell pepper, chopped
3 c.   Tomatoes, chopped
1 T.   Soy sauce

Sauté the onion, garlic, jalapeños, and celery in the oil until transparent. Add the zucchini and bell pepper and sauté briefly. Then add the tomatoes and soy sauce and stir well. Cover and cook until tender, but do not overcook.
Variation: Use other kinds of squash.

Casseroles

APULIAN STYLE BAKED POTATOES, ONIONS, AND TOMATOES

2 c.	Onion, thinly sliced
1 ½ tsp.	Olive oil
1 ½ tsp.	Non-dairy margarine
2 tsp.	Garlic, minced
2 tsp.	Jalapeños, minced
6 c.	Potatoes, peeled and sliced crosswise ¼-inch thick
3 c.	Tomatoes, cut into ⅓-inch dice
1 ¼ c.	Yeast Cheez
1 tsp.	Oregano
1 tsp.	Sea salt
½ tsp.	Black pepper
¾ c.	UnChicken Broth

Sauté the onions in the oil and margarine until soft. Add the garlic and jalapeños and cook 1 more minute. Combine with the rest of the ingredients and put into an oiled or nonstick casserole. Cover and bake at 400° for 1 hour or until the potatoes are done. Uncover and bake 15 more minutes for the extra moisture to evaporate.

BAKED CUBED UNBEEF CASSEROLE

This cannot fail to be appreciated!

3 T.	Corn oil
5 c.	UnBeef, cooked by Methods 1, 2, or 3, and cut in 1-inch cubes
3 c.	Potatoes, cut into ½-inch slices and boiled
1 c.	Carrots, sliced and boiled
1 ⅓ c.	Onions, cut into ½-inch slices
¼ c.	Unbleached white flour
1 ¼ tsp.	Kitchen Bouquet
3 c.	Mushrooms (fresh preferred), sliced thick
1 ½ c.	Onions, chopped
1 ½ tsp.	Garlic, minced
3 c.	Flavoring Broth according to type of gluten being used
3 T.	Lea and Perrins Steak Sauce
1 T.	Louisiana Hot Sauce

Put the oil in a skillet, heat it, and fry the gluten cubes until they are browned on all sides. Take the gluten and put it in a baking dish along with the potatoes, carrots, and onion slices. Stir the flour into the oil in the skillet and turn the fire down so it will cook slowly. Add the Kitchen Bouquet and keep stirring the flour constantly, adding more oil if the mixture is too dry, until the mixture is a rich brown. Add the mushrooms, and onions, stirring constantly and cook till the onions are soft. Add the garlic and cook a little bit more. Add the broth and keep stirring until it starts to form a thick gravy. Add the steak sauce, and hot sauce. Add more water if you need to, and bring all to a boil. Pour the sauce over the gluten and vegetables in the casserole. Cover and bake at 400° for 30 to 45 minutes, basting frequently and adding water if needed.

BAKED CURRY

Don't judge by appearances!
This is one of those recipes that looks stupid on paper but cooks up a genius!

2 tsp.	Corn oil
2 tsp.	Curry powder
2 T.	Unbleached white flour
1 ½ c.	Broth of type of gluten being used

1 ½ c. Gluten, any flavor, cubed
¼ c. Onion, chopped
2 c. Broccoli–cut into flowerets, along with the stem that has been peeled and sliced–and steamed
2 c. Head of cauliflower cut into flowerets
1 c. Potato, cubed
1 ½ tsp. Lemon juice
1 T. Soy sauce
¼ tsp. Sea salt
1 c. Dry bread crumbs
¼ tsp. Paprika

Heat the oil, add the curry powder and stir for 1 minute over medium heat. Add the flour and stir for 1 more minute. Stir in the water and cook until thickened–about 5 minutes. Add the rest of the ingredients except the crumbs and cook until the onions are soft. Put in a nonstick casserole and sprinkle the bread crumbs over all, pressing in lightly. Bake, covered, at 350° for 10 to 15 minutes. Uncover and bake until the crumbs begin to brown.

BREAD AND CHEEZ PUDDING

Surprising Goodness!

½ c. Onion, minced
1 tsp Non-dairy margarine
1 c. Yeast or Notzarella Cheez
2 N'eggs
2 ½ c. UnChicken Broth
¼ tsp. Cayenne pepper
¼ tsp. Black pepper
½ tsp. Sea salt
8 Slices of bread, sliced thick, toasted, and cut or torn into small pieces

Sauté the onion in the margarine until soft. Combine everything and let sit for 15 minutes. Put into a nonstick casserole. Bake at 375° for 45 minutes–until the top is puffed up and golden brown and it tests done when a knife is inserted into it.

BREAD DRESSING

There's always room for this–forget Jello!

1 c. Carrots, grated
½ c. Fresh parsley, chopped
¾ c. Onions, chopped
1 ½ lb. Bread cut in ½-inch cubes
1 c. Celery, chopped
¼ c. Bell pepper, chopped fine

½ c. Mushrooms or black olives, sliced
¼ tsp. Black pepper
2 tsp. Non-dairy margarine, melted
5 ½ c. UnBeef Broth

Mix the dry ingredients together. Combine the melted margarine and broth and pour over the dry ingredients gradually, stirring well. Pack into a casserole dish. Cover with aluminum foil and bake at 350° for 45 minutes. Uncover and bake for 15 minutes more to brown the top.

BROCCOLI AND CORN SCALLOP

2 tsp. Non-dairy margarine
⅔ c. Onions, chopped
½ tsp. Garlic, minced
2 T. Flour
¾ c. Water
2 c. Yeast, Pimento, or Notzarella Cheez
1 c. Corn
1 c. Cracker crumbs
5 c. Broccoli, cooked and drained

Melt the margarine, sauté the onions and garlic, and blend in the flour. Gradually add the water and cook until thickened. Add the cheez and stir till it melts. Stir in the corn and ½ cup of the cracker crumbs. Arrange the broccoli in a nonstick casserole and pour the cheez sauce over it. Toss the remaining crumbs with 2 T. of melted margarine and sprinkle them over the casserole. Bake at 350° for 30 minutes.
Variation: Omit the broccoli and add 5 cups more corn; or omit the corn and add 1 cup more broccoli.

BROCCOLI AND POTATO CASSEROLE WITH CHIVES AND CHEEZ

2 c. Broccoli, chopped
2 c. Potatoes, cubed and boiled
¾ c. Cashew Milk
1 c. Yeast or Pimento Cheez
½ c. Parmesan Cheez
3 T. Chives, chopped
½ tsp. Garlic, minced
2 T. Parsley, chopped
1 c. Tofu, crumbled
½ c. Fresh bread crumbs
¾ tsp. Sea salt
⅛ tsp. Cayenne pepper

Combine all the ingredients in a bowl and stir until thoroughly mixed. Place the mixture into a nonstick 9x9-inch pan and spread evenly. Bake in a 350° oven for 40 minutes.

BROCCOLI CASSEROLE

½ c.	Onion, chopped
½ c.	Celery, chopped
2 tsp.	Corn oil
1 ¼ c.	Cream of Mushroom Soup
4 ½ c.	Frozen chopped broccoli, thawed
¾ c.	Yeast or Notzarella Cheez
1 ½ c.	Cooked rice
½ tsp.	Sea salt
¼ tsp.	Black pepper

Sauté the onion and celery in the oil until soft. Combine everything in a casserole. Bake at 350° for 30 minutes.

CABBAGE, TOMATOES, AND CHEEZ

3 c.	Cabbage, finely shredded, cooked and drained
¾ tsp.	Sea salt
¼ tsp.	Cayenne pepper
1 ½ c.	Canned tomatoes, crushed or chopped
1 c.	Yeast, Pimento, or Notzarella Cheez
2 c.	Bread crumbs

Combine the cabbage, salt, pepper, and tomatoes. Put in a nonstick casserole. Spread with the cheez and then with the bread crumbs, pressing them in lightly. Bake at 325° for about 30 minutes or until the crumbs are brown.

CORNBREAD DRESSING

6 c.	Cornbread, crumbled
2 c.	Cream-style corn
1 c.	Jalapeños, seeded and chopped
½ c.	Mushrooms or black olives, chopped
¾ c.	Yeast, Pimento; or Notzarella Cheez
½ c.	Onion, chopped fine
½ c.	Bell pepper, chopped
1 T.	Parsley, chopped
1	N'egg
1 T.	Non-dairy margarine, melted

Put the crumbled cornbread in a large baking pan and bake at 350° for 30 minutes or until toasted, stirring every 10 minutes. Take from the oven and cool. Combine the other ingredients. Mix well. Add the cornbread and toss to mix. Bake,

covered, in a nonstick casserole at 325° for 45 to 60 minutes or till heated through.

CABBAGE UN-ROLLS CASSEROLE

1	Cabbage head
4 c.	Ground flavored gluten
4 tsp.	Corn oil
2 c.	Onion, chopped
2 tsp.	Garlic, minced
¼ tsp.	Cayenne pepper
1 c.	Broth of the flavor of gluten used
2 c.	Cooked rice
2 c.	Yeast or Pimento Cheez
2 ½ c.	Canned tomato sauce

Separate the cabbage into leaves, trimming away the tough part of the stem on each leaf. Put the leaves in a pan of salted boiling water and boil them until they are slightly soft. Drain and set aside. Sauté the gluten in the oil until it just begins to brown. Add the onions, garlic, pepper, and broth, and continue cooking until the onions are soft and the liquid has been absorbed or evaporated—so the mixture is not mushy. Add the rice to the gluten mixture and cook for 2 more minutes. In a casserole put a layer of cabbage leaves. Spread the gluten mixture over the leaves. Cover with the remaining cabbage. Cover that with a layer of cheez. Pour the tomato sauce over the cheez. Bake at 375° for 30 minutes.

CARROT ROAST

4 c.	Carrots, grated
4 c.	Cooked rice, or cooked garbanzos
1 c.	Bread crumbs
½ c.	Water
2 ½ tsp.	Corn oil
⅓ c.	Onions, chopped
¼ tsp.	Thyme
½ tsp.	Sea salt

Mix all together and bake, covered, at 350° for 45 minutes, and uncovered for 15 minutes. Serve with gravy.

CAJUN EGGPLANT

This was originally a recipe for an appetizer. Ha! It was so good everybody demanded more, so it became a main dish as it deserves to be.

3	Small eggplants, peeled and sliced ¼-inch thick, and put in salted water
3 T.	Olive oil

3 T.	Unbleached white flour, sifted
1 ½ T.	Tomato paste
1 ¼ c.	Canned tomato sauce
¼ c.	Celery, chopped fine
2 T.	Chopped parsley
1 c.	Onions, chopped fine
⅓ c.	Bell pepper, chopped fine
1 tsp.	Garlic clove, minced
1 ½ c.	Water
1 T.	Lea & Perrins Steak Sauce
1 tsp.	Louisiana Hot Sauce
1 ¼ tsp.	Sea salt
2-2 ½ c.	Pimento Cheez
	Parmesan Cheez

Let the eggplant slices marinate in the salted water for 2 hours. Meanwhile, put 1 ½ tablespoons of the olive oil in a skillet or heavy pot, heat it well, and stir in the flour. Cook the flour, stirring frequently, until it is browned to a very dark brown, but not burned. (This can take some time.) Add the tomato *paste* to the flour and, stirring constantly, cook it until all is the dark color it was before the sauce was added. Then add the tomato *sauce* to the flour and, stirring constantly, cook it until all is the dark color it was before the sauce was added. Add the celery, parsley, onions, bell pepper, and garlic, and cook over a very low flame for 20 to 30 minutes, stirring constantly. Add the water, Lea & Perrins, hot sauce, and salt. Add more water if the mixture is too thick. Cook on a low flame for 1 hour. When the sauce is nearly done, rinse the eggplant and drain it in a colander. Put the remaining olive oil in a skillet and fry the drained eggplant slices to a deep brown, adding more oil if needed. Place the slices in a casserole and spread some pimento cheez over them. Sprinkle some "parmesan" over that. Spread some of the sauce liberally over all. Add another layer of eggplant and repeat. Do this until all the eggplant is used up, finishing with a layer of sauce. Bake at 375° for 20 minutes. Serve hot over rice or chill it in the refrigerator, cut it into squares, and serve.

CAULIFLOWER AU GRATIN

6 c.	Cauliflower flowerets
2 tsp.	Non-dairy margarine
½ c.	Onion, diced
1 ½ c.	Yeast, Pimento, or Notzarella Cheez
1 c.	Cashew or Tofu Sour Cream
¼ tsp.	Sea salt
½ c.	Dried bread crumbs

Cook the cauliflower flowerets in boiling salted water for 10 minutes. Drain well. Combine the cauliflower with 2 tablespoons of the margarine, the onion, cheez, "sour cream," and salt. Put into a casserole. Melt the rest of the margarine and toss with the crumbs. Sprinkle the crumbs over the cauliflower mixture. Bake at 350° for 30 minutes.

CAULIFLOWER BAKE

Sauce:

1 T.	Cornstarch
½ c.	Cold Cashew Milk
¾ tsp.	Sea salt
⅛ tsp.	Black pepper
¼ tsp.	Paprika
1 c.	Yeast, Pimento, or Notzarella Cheez

Bring the cornstarch, "milk," salt, pepper, and paprika to a boil, stirring constantly. Boil until it thickens. Add the cheez and stir over low heat until combined.

Vegetables:

½ c.	Celery, chopped
⅓ c.	Bell pepper, chopped
1 c.	Onion, chopped
2 tsp.	Non-dairy margarine
1 ½ tsp.	Garlic, minced
4 c.	Cauliflower flowerets, cooked
2	Tomatoes, sliced

Sauté the celery, bell pepper, and onion in the margarine until the onions are soft. Add the garlic and sauté 1 more minute. Add to the sauce. Put the cauliflower into a nonstick casserole. Cover with the tomato slices. Pour the sauce over all. Bake at 400° for 20 minutes.

CHEEZ AND POTATO BAKE

½ c.	Onions, sliced or chopped
1 tsp.	Garlic, minced
1 tsp.	Corn oil
4 c.	Potatoes, peeled, sliced, and boiled in salted water
1 tsp.	Celery salt
¼ tsp.	Cayenne pepper
¼ tsp.	Dill weed
2 ½ c.	Thin White Sauce made with UnChicken Broth
1 c.	Yeast, Pimento, or Notzarella Cheez

Sauté the onions and garlic in the oil until the

onions are soft. In a nonstick casserole pan put a layer of onions. Add a layer of potatoes. Add another layer of onion. Mix the seasonings with the white sauce and add it to the casserole. Top with the cheez. Cover and bake at 400° for 30 minutes, removing the cover for the last 10 minutes.

CHEEZ ENCHILADA CASSEROLE

¾ c.	Onions, chopped
¼ c.	Bell pepper, chopped
2 T.	Corn oil
¾ c.	Tomato Salsa (see relevant section for recipe)
¼ tsp.	Paprika
⅛ tsp.	Sage
15	Corn tortillas
6 c.	Tomato sauce
9 c.	Yeast Cheez

Sauté the onions and bell pepper in the oil. Add the tomato sauce, salsa, paprika, and sage. Dip the tortillas in hot oil to make them soft. Layer in a casserole as follows:

Tomato sauce
Tortillas
Cheez
Tomato sauce
Tortillas
Cheez
Tomato sauce
Tortillas

Spread a thin layer of cheez, salsa, and chopped onions on top. Bake for 15 minutes at 400°.

CHEEZ ENCHILADAS-1

Plenty good and good and plenty!

2 tsp.	Corn oil
3 T.	Onion, minced
3 T.	Bell pepper, minced
3 T.	Celery, minced
2 tsp.	Garlic, minced
3 c.	Canned tomatoes, drained and crushed
½ tsp.	Cumin, ground
½ tsp.	Sucanat
1 ½ tsp.	Paprika
¾ tsp.	Oregano, dried and crumbled
½	Bay leaf
½ tsp.	Sea salt
¼ tsp.	Cayenne pepper
½ c.	Onion, sliced thin
½ c.	Bell pepper (red preferred), sliced thin
8	Corn tortillas
2 ½ c.	Yeast, Pimento, or Notzarella Cheez

In 1 teaspoon of the oil sauté the onion, bell pepper, celery, and garlic until all is softened. Add the tomatoes, cumin, Sucanat, paprika, oregano, bay leaf, salt, and pepper. Bring to a boil, reduce the heat, and simmer, stirring occasionally, for 20 minutes. Discard the bay leaf. In the other teaspoon of the oil sauté the onion and bell pepper until they are softened, and transfer them with a slotted spoon to paper towels to drain. Dip the tortillas in the tomato sauce and set aside. To assemble, on each tortilla put some of vegetables on the bottom third, top with 3 tablespoons of of the cheez, and roll up. As each is done, put it in a nonstick casserole. When all are in the dish, spoon the sauce over them and spread the remaining cheez over all. Bake at 400° for 20 minutes.

CHEEZ ENCHILADAS-2

2 T.	Cornstarch
3 c.	UnChicken Broth
3 T.	Chili powder
¼ tsp.	Garlic powder
⅛ tsp.	Cumin, ground
⅛ tsp.	Cayenne pepper
½ tsp.	Sea salt
¼ tsp.	Onion powder
2 tsp.	Corn oil
¾ c.	Onions, chopped
4 c.	Pimento Cheez
¼ c.	Black olives, chopped
12	Corn tortillas

Dissolve the cornstarch in the broth. Add the chili powder, garlic powder, cumin, pepper, salt, onion powder, and 1 teaspoon of the oil, and simmer together for 10 minutes. This is the "sauce." Sauté the onions in the remaining teaspoon of oil. Add the cheez and olives to the onions. This is the filling. Put a small amount of the sauce in the bottom of a casserole pan or dish. Put a small amount of the filling in a tortilla, roll it up, and put it in the casserole. Do the same with the rest of the tortillas. Fifteen minutes before serving, put the rest of the sauce on the enchiladas and heat in a 350° oven for 15 minutes.

CHEEZ PIE

1 c.	Onions, chopped fine
1 tsp.	Garlic, minced
½ c.	Bell pepper, chopped fine
2 ½ tsp.	Non–dairy margarine
3 T.	Cornstarch
2 c.	Cashew Milk
4 c.	Pimento or Yeast Cheez
4 c.	Tofu Cottage Cheez
4 c.	Canned tomatoes, drained and chopped
1	Pie crust recipe for two crusts

Sauté the onions, garlic, and bell pepper in the margarine. Mix the cornstarch with the "milk." Combine all ingredients. Put in unbaked pie shell and cover with top crust, perforating it with a fork or making cuts with a knife for steam to escape. Bake at 425° for 1 hour.
Variation: Use other vegetables.

CHEEZEY ONION CASSEROLE

4 ½ c.	Onions, sliced
2 T.	Non–dairy margarine
1 c.	Yeast Cheez
1 c.	Notzarella Cheez
¼ tsp.	Pepper
1 ¾ c.	Cream of UnChicken Soup
1 tsp.	Low sodium soy sauce
	Enough slices of bread, "buttered" on both sides, to cover the casserole

Sauté the onions in the margarine until transparent and slightly brown. Combine the cheezes and pepper thoroughly. Layer the onions and cheez mixture in a nonstick casserole. Combine the soup and soy sauce and pour in the casserole and stir gently. Top with the bread slices. Bake at 350° for 15 minutes. Push the bread slices under the sauce. Bake for 15 more minutes.

CHILI-CHEEZ BAKE

1 c.	Onion, chopped
1 ½ tsp.	Garlic, minced
⅓ c.	Jalapeños, chopped
1 T.	Corn oil
3 c.	Cooked rice
1 T.	Chili powder
½ tsp.	Sea salt
2 c.	Cooked kidney beans, drained
2 tsp.	Ground cumin
1 tsp.	Oregano
2 c.	Yeast or Notzarella Cheez

Sauté the onion, garlic, and jalapeños in the oil until the onions are soft. In a casserole combine everything but the cheez. Top with the cheez. Bake, covered, at 400° for 25 to 35 minutes.

COMPANY CASSEROLE

1 ½ c.	Baked UnChicken, cubed
1 c.	Baked UnHam, cubed
2 ½ c.	Cooked rice
1 ¼ c.	Broccoli, chopped
1 ¼ c.	Yeast Cheez
½ c.	Mushrooms, sliced
1 ¼ c.	Miraculous Whip or other "mayonnaise"
1 ¼ tsp.	Prepared mustard
2 c.	Curried Mushroom Soup
2 T.	Parmesan Cheez

Fry the gluten (both kinds together) in a small amount of oil until browned. In a nonstick casserole, spread the rice over the bottom. Over the rice spread the broccoli. Over the broccoli spread the gluten. Over the gluten spread the cheez. Over the cheez spread the mushrooms. Combine the mayonnaise, mustard, and soup, and spread over the mushroom layer. Sprinkle with the parmesan cheez. Bake at 350° for 45 to 60 minutes or until the top is light golden brown.
Variation: If you don't care for the taste of curry powder, just substitute a plain cream of mushroom soup by making some from the Basic "Cream Of" Soup recipe.

CORN AND LIMA STEW CASSEROLE

Filling:

2 c.	Onion, chopped
1 ½ c.	Celery, diced
½ c.	Bell pepper, chopped
2 T.	Corn oil
2 tsp.	Jalapeño, minced very fine
1 ½ tsp.	Garlic, minced
1 tsp.	Ground cumin
3 T.	Chili powder
2 c.	Lima beans (not dried)
2 T.	Parsley, minced
3 c.	Fresh or canned tomatoes, chopped (with juice, if canned)
1 c.	Water
½ tsp.	Sea salt
¼ tsp.	Cayenne
2 c.	Corn

Sauté the onion, celery, and bell pepper in the oil in a large pan or Dutch oven until soft. Add the jalapeños, garlic, cumin, and chili powder and sauté 1 more minute. Add the rest of ingredients except the corn and simmer, covered, for 15 minutes. When the beans are tender, add the corn. Turn off the heat.

Crust:

5 c.	Water
1 tsp.	Sea salt
1 ½ c.	Cornmeal
2 T.	Corn oil
1 ½ tsp.	Cayenne
2 c.	Yeast Cheez

Bring the water to a boil. Add the salt and pour in the cornmeal in a steady stream, whisking constantly. Cook, stirring frequently at first, until the cornmeal is cooked–about 30 minutes. Stir in the oil, cayenne or chili powder, and the cheez. This should be thick but pourable–add more water if it is not.

Put ⅔ of this into an oiled or nonstick casserole and spread over the bottom. Let set about 5 minutes to get firm. Spoon the vegetables over the cornmeal mixture. Pour the remaining batter over the top. Set on a tray and bake at 375° for 25 minutes.

CORN AND SPINACH CASSEROLE

¼ c.	Onions, minced
½ tsp.	Garlic, minced
1 tsp.	Non-dairy margarine
2 c.	Cream-style corn
1 ½ c.	Frozen spinach, chopped
1 tsp.	Vinegar
½ tsp.	Sea salt
¼ tsp.	Black or cayenne pepper
¼ c.	Fine dry bread crumbs
2 T.	Parmesan Cheez

Sauté the onions and garlic in the margarine. Add the corn, spinach, vinegar, salt, and pepper. Put in a nonstick casserole. Blend the crumbs and cheez, and spread over the vegetables. Bake at 400° for 20 minutes.

CORN BAKE

3 c.	Corn, cooked and drained
¼ c.	Cashew milk
2 T.	Onions, finely chopped
1 tsp.	Corn oil
½ tsp.	Sea salt
½ tsp.	Paprika
¾ c.	Yeast, Pimento, or Notzarella Cheez

½ c.	Bread crumbs
2 T.	Non-dairy margarine, melted

Combine the corn, cashew milk, onions, oil, salt, paprika, and cheez. Turn into a nonstick casserole. Top with the bread crumbs, pressing in lightly. Bake at 350° for 25 minutes.

CORN CHIP CASSEROLE

1 ½ c.	Onions, chopped
¾ c.	Bell pepper, choppped
4 ½ tsp.	Chili powder
¼ tsp.	Garlic powder
2 T.	Corn oil
3 c.	UnBeef, ground
1 ½ c.	Salsa
1 ½ c.	Canned tomatoes with juice
¼ tsp.	Sea salt
6 c.	Corn chips
4 c.	Notzarella Cheez

Sauté the onions, bell pepper, chili powder, and garlic powder in the oil. Add the gluten and sauté until slightly brown. Combine everything but the chips and cheez in a skillet and cook until most of the liquid is evaporated. Layer the bottom of a casserole with half the chips. Spread half the cheez over that. Spread the gluten mixture over that. Repeat the chips and cheez layers. Bake at 400° for 30 minutes.

Variation: Instead of the salsa and chili powder use 1 jar of McIlhenny Seven Spice Chili Recipe.

CORN TAMALE PIE

More than worth the trying!

½ c.	Bell pepper, chopped
3 T.	Onions, chopped
2 tsp.	Corn oil
¾ c.	Corn meal
2 c.	Corn
3 c.	Canned tomatoes
½ c.	Ripe olives, chopped
¼ tsp.	Cayenne pepper
½ c.	Tomato sauce
1 tsp.	Sea salt
3 c.	Yeast or Pimento Cheez

Sauté the bell pepper and onions in the corn oil. Add the rest of the ingredients except the cheez and simmer, covered, for 5 minutes, stirring occasionally and adding a little water (up to ¾ cup) if it gets too thick. Put in a nonstick casserole. Bake at 350° for 45 minutes. Within the last 10 minutes put the cheez on the top and let it brown slightly.

CORN-BEAN PIE

Simple goodness!

> *Crust:*
> | | |
> |---|---|
> | 2 T. | Corn oil |
> | 2 c. | Cornmeal |
> | ½ c. | UnBeef Broth |

In a small mixing bowl, stir the oil into the cornmeal with a fork. Add enough broth to make a stiff batter. Pat into a nonstick casserole or pie plate.

Filling:

½ c.	Bell peppers, chopped
⅓ c.	Onions, chopped
1 tsp.	Garlic, minced
1 ½ tsp.	Corn oil
2 c.	Potatoes, cooked and cubed
3 c.	Cooked dried beans
1 c.	Tomatoes, chopped
Pinch	Cayenne pepper
1 c.	UnBeef Broth
¼ tsp.	Sea salt
	Yeast or Pimento Cheez

Sauté the bell peppers, onions, and garlic in the oil. Combine with the rest of the ingredients—except for the cheez—in a pot. Cook for 2 minutes. Pour the filling into the prepared crust and bake at 350° about 30 minutes. Remove the pie and cover with the cheez. Bake 10 more minutes.
Variation: Use squash instead of potatoes.

COUNTRY CASSEROLE

3 c.	Onions, chopped
4 tsp.	Corn oil
1 T.	Garlic, crushed
1 c.	UnChicken Broth
2 c.	Stewed tomatoes, chopped
¼ tsp.	Thyme flakes
½ tsp.	Sea salt
¼ tsp.	Cayenne pepper
2 c.	UnBeef, cubed
2 c.	UnPork, cubed
5 c.	Cooked white beans, drained

Sauté the onions in the oil until soft. Add the garlic and sauté 2 more minutes. Add the broth, tomatoes, thyme, salt, and pepper. Bring to a boil, reduce heat, and simmer, covered, for 10 minutes. Add the gluten and beans. Mix all

together well. Transfer to a nonstick casserole and bake at 350°, uncovered, for 30 minutes.
Variation: Any type of flavored gluten can be used singly or in combination.

CREAMED BROCCOLI

2 T.	Non-dairy margarine
¼ c.	Unbleached white flour
1 c.	Cashew Milk made with UnChicken Broth
¼ tsp.	Sea salt
Pinch	Cayenne pepper
½ tsp.	Paprika
½ c.	Onions, minced
½ tsp.	Garlic, minced
4 c.	Broccoli, cooked, drained, and chopped very fine
1 c.	Bread crumbs tossed in 2 tablespoons of non-dairy margarine

Melt the margarine and stir in the flour until well blended. Slowly stir in the cashew milk and add the salt, pepper, paprika, onions, and garlic. Add the broccoli and put in a nonstick casserole. Sprinkle with bread crumbs. Bake at 425° for 15 to 20 minutes.

CREAMED CABBAGE CASSEROLE

8 c.	Cabbage, shredded
1 ½ c.	Onions, sliced
½ tsp.	Garlic, minced
1 T.	Non-dairy margarine
⅛ tsp.	Black pepper
2 c.	Yeast, Pimento, or Notzarella Cheez
1 ½ c.	Thin White Sauce made with UnChicken Broth, boiling
2 c.	Bread crumbs

Boil cabbage in salted water. Sauté the onions and garlic in the margarine and mix with the cabbage and pepper. In a small nonstick casserole put a layer of half the cabbage. Spread 1 cup of cheez over that. Layer the rest of cabbage, with the rest of cheez over that. Pour the white sauce over all. Top with bread crumbs and dot liberally with non-dairy margarine. Bake at 400° until the crumbs are brown.

CREAMED POTATOES WITH CHEEZ

6 c.	Potatoes, diced and boiled
3 c.	Thin White Sauce, made with UnChicken Broth

¾ c.   Onions, chopped
1 tsp.   Garlic, minced
2 tsp.   Non-dairy margarine
3 T.   Parsley, chopped
3 c.   Yeast or Pimento Cheez
¾ tsp.   Sea salt
1 ½ c.   Bread crumbs

Combine the potatoes and sauce. Sauté the onions and garlic in the margarine. Combine all ingredients except the crumbs. Put in a nonstick casserole. Cover with bread crumbs. Dot with non-dairy margarine. Bake at 400° until the crumbs are brown.

CREAMED SPINACH, MUSHROOMS, AND ONIONS IN CHEEZ SAUCE

1 c.   Onions, chopped
1 T.   Garlic, minced
1 c.   Mushrooms, sliced
1 ½ tsp. Non-dairy margarine
3 c.   Cheez Sauce–1
3 ½ c.   Frozen spinach, defrosted, drained, and chopped
¼ tsp.   Sea salt
⅛ tsp.   Black pepper

Combine everything in a casserole, top with bread crumbs, pressing them in lightly, and bake at 350° for 20 minutes or until the crumbs have browned.

CREOLE RICE CASSEROLE

1 c.   Onions, chopped
2 tsp.   Garlic, minced
2 ½ tsp. Corn oil
6 c.   Rice, cooked in UnChicken Broth
3 c.   Okra, sliced
¼ tsp.   Cayenne pepper
4 c.   Creole Sauce
½ tsp.   Sea salt
         Yeast or Pimento Cheez

Sauté the onions and garlic in the corn oil. Combine with all other ingredients, put in a casserole, and bake for 25 minutes at 350°. Top with cheez and bake for 5 more minutes.

CRUNCH-TOP POTATOES

Try this!

3 T.   Non-dairy margarine
3 c.   Potatoes, peeled, cut in ½-inch slices, and boiled in UnBeef Broth

¾ c.   Corn flakes, crushed
1 ½ c.   Yeast or Pimento Cheez
½ tsp.   Sea salt
1 ½ tsp. Paprika

Melt the margarine in a pan in a 375° oven. Add a single layer of potatoes, turning them once in the margarine. Mix the remaining ingredients and sprinkle over the potatoes. Bake for ½ hour or until done and the top is crisp.

CURRIED POTATO AND ONION CASSEROLE

1 c.   Tofu Yogurt
2 tsp.   Corn oil
1 tsp.   Cayenne
1 T.   Garlic, chopped
½ tsp.   Ground ginger
1 T.   Curry powder
3 c.   Onions, sliced ¼-inch thick
6 c.   Potatoes, sliced ¼-inch thick
1 c.   UnChicken Broth

Combine the yogurt, oil, cayenne, garlic, ginger, and curry powder. Toss the onions and potatoes together. Add the yogurt mixture and spread the vegetables in an even layer in a shallow baking dish. Pour the broth over all. Bake at 350° for 1½ hours, until thoroughly cooked and browned on top.

EGGPLANT AND CHEEZ

This can be either a main dish (good on rice) warm, or an appetizer, cold.

2 c.   UnBacon or UnHam, cubed
¼ tsp.   Sea salt
⅛ tsp.   Cayenne pepper
1 c.   Unbleached white flour
6 c.   Eggplant, sliced
         Oil for deep frying
2 tsp.   Soy sauce
1 ½ c.   Notzarella Cheez
2 T.   Parmesan Cheez

Deep-fry the gluten in the oil and drain on paper towels. Salt, pepper, and flour the eggplant, then deep-fry it and drain well on paper towels. Put a layer of eggplant in a casserole dish or pan. Sprinkle soy sauce over the eggplant. Spread the notzarella over the eggplant. Sprinkle a layer of gluten over the eggplant. Sprinkle "parmesan" over that. Keep repeating this layering until all the eggplant is used up, finishing with a layer of cheez, gluten, and "parmesan." Bake at 350° for

20 minutes.

EGGPLANT CASSEROLE WITH TOMATOES, GARLIC, AND RICE

1	Small eggplant, peeled and cut into ¼-inch slices
4 c.	Zucchini, unpeeled and cut into ½-inch slices
2 c.	Onions, chopped
4 tsp.	Garlic, crushed
1 ¼ c.	Bell pepper, cut into strips
2 T.	Olive oil
6 c.	Canned tomatoes, drained and chopped
¼ c.	Parsley, chopped
¼ tsp.	Basil
¼ tsp.	Thyme
½ tsp.	Sea salt
¼ tsp.	Cayenne pepper
3 c.	Cooked rice–cooked in UnChicken Broth Yeast , Pimento, or Notzarella Cheez to cover
¼ c.	Parmesan Cheez

Deep-fry the eggplant and set aside. Steam the zucchini. Sauté the onions, garlic, and bell pepper in the oil until the onions are soft. Add the tomatoes, herbs, and seasonings and simmer the mixture for 25 minutes, adding water if the sauce gets too thick. Stir in the cooked rice and vegetables. Place the mixture in a casserole and top with the cheezes. Bake at 350° for 20 minutes.

EGGPLANT LASAGNE

A good idea and even better eating!

3 c.	Eggplant, peeled and sliced ⅓-inch thick
4 c.	Spanish Tomato Sauce
2 c.	Canned tomatoes, chopped
½ tsp.	Sucanat
1 tsp.	Garlic salt
½ tsp.	Basil
¼ tsp.	Oregano
1 c.	Frozen tofu, thawed and crumbled
1 ¼ c.	Mushrooms, chopped
¾ c.	Onions, chopped
1 T.	Olive oil
½ c.	Tofu Sour Cream or Cashew Sour Cream

Fry eggplant slices in a small amount of corn oil. Drain well on paper towels. Simmer the tomato sauce, canned tomatoes, and seasonings for about 5 minutes. Sauté the tofu, mushrooms, and onions in the oil. Add the "sour cream" and 1 cup of the tomato sauce. Layer ingredients in an 11x7x2-inch nonstick casserole in this order:

Tomato sauce
Eggplant slices
Tofu mixture

Repeat, ending with tomato sauce. Bake at 350° for 30 minutes.

EGGPLANT PARMESAN–1

A specialty of the house!

3 c.	Eggplant, peeled and cut in ½-inch slices
	Sea salt
	Unbleached white flour
	Corn oil
2 c.	Italian Tomato Sauce (Gravies and Sauces section)
	Notzarella, Pimento, or Yeast Cheez
	Parmesan Cheez

Sprinkle both sides of the eggplant slices with salt to draw out their moisture and spread them out in a single layer on a platter or board. After 20 to 30 minutes, pat the eggplant dry with paper towels. Dip each slice in flour, shaking or brushing off any excess. Heat the oil in a skillet and brown the eggplant a few slices at a time, working quickly to prevent them from soaking up too much oil. (If the oil cooks away, add more.) As the eggplant browns, transfer the slices to fresh paper towels to drain. Pour ½ cup of the tomato sauce into a nonstick casserole pan. Layer the eggplant slices over the sauce. Cover with cheez, and sprinkle the "parmesan" over that. Repeat 1 or 2 more layers, finishing with a layer of tomato sauce, cheez, and "parmesan." Cover with foil and bake at 400° on the middle shelf for 30 minutes. Remove the foil and bake, uncovered, for 10 minutes. Watch closely to avoid over-cooking.

EGGPLANT PARMESAN–2

1 T.	Olive oil
1 c.	Onion, chopped
2 ½ tsp.	Garlic, minced
½ c.	Bell pepper, chopped
½ tsp.	Cayenne
6 c.	Tomatoes, chopped
½ tsp.	Sea salt

1 T.	Fresh basil, minced
1 tsp.	Fresh oregano, minced
½ tsp.	Fresh thyme, minced
1 T.	Parsley (Italian preferred), minced
1	Large eggplant, peeled, sliced ½-inch thick, and slightly browned in olive oil
4 c.	Yeast Cheez
1 c.	Parmesan Cheez
1 c.	Dry bread crumbs

Heat 1 tablespoon of the oil in a large heavy pot and sauté the onion for several minutes. Add the garlic and bell pepper and sauté until all are soft. Add the cayenne and sauté briefly. Add the tomatoes, cover, and cook over low heat for 5 to 10 minutes until the juice has come out. Uncover, stir in the salt, and simmer gently for about 1 hour until the sauce thickens. Add the herbs and simmer a few more minutes. Take from the heat. In an oiled or nonstick 8-inch casserole spread a thin layer of sauce on the bottom and arrange half the eggplant slices on top. Spread ⅓ of the yeast cheez over the eggplant. Spread on a thicker layer of sauce than the first one, and sprinkle ½ cup of the "parmesan" over all. Repeat the layers, beginning with the eggplant and ending with the rest of the yeast cheez and "parmesan." Sprinkle the bread crumbs over the top and press in lightly. Bake at 350°, covered, about 30 minutes until heated through. Uncover and bake until the bread crumbs brown.

ENGLISH WARTIME "GOOSE"

This was developed during World War II in England and is delicious!

4 ½ c.	Potatoes, sliced thin
2 c.	Apples, sliced thin
1 ½ c.	Yeast or Notzarella Cheez
½ tsp.	Sage (dried)
¼ tsp.	Sea salt
¼ tsp.	Black pepper
1 ½ c.	UnChicken Broth
1 T.	Unbleached white flour

Put a layer of potatoes in an oiled or nonstick casserole. Cover with a layer of apples and a little sage. Sprinkle lightly with salt and pepper. Spread with a layer of cheez. Repeat the layers, ending with a layer of potatoes and a layer of cheez over that. Pour in 1 cup of the liquid and bake at 350° for 45 minutes. Blend the flour with the rest of the liquid, pour it into the casserole, and cook 15 more minutes.

FRESH CORN AND TOMATO CASSEROLE

This has endured the test of years to still be a favorite!

1 c.	Corn
1	N'egg
1 ½ tsp.	Corn oil
1 c.	Water
4 c.	Corn
1 c.	Bread crumbs
¾ tsp.	Sea salt
¼ tsp.	Cayenne pepper
3 T.	Onions, chopped
	Sliced tomatoes

Blend together the 1 cup of corn, n'egg, corn oil, and water to make "corn milk." Combine all the ingredients except the tomatoes and cook until it begins to bubble. Turn out into a casserole and bake at 350° for about an hour or until firm. Place the sliced tomatoes on top and sprinkle lightly with salt. Bake an additional 15 minutes.

GENOESE SQUASH

⅓ c.	Onions, chopped
2 T.	Corn oil
2 c.	Squash, sliced and lightly steamed
1 c.	Notzarella cheez
2 c.	Tomatoes, slightly pulverized in a blender
¼ tsp.	Dill weed
¼ tsp.	Sea salt
½ c.	Bread crumbs tossed with ¼ cup of melted non-dairy margarine.

Sauté the onions in the oil, then combine everything, top with the bread crumbs, and bake at 350° for 30 minutes.

GLUTEN AND CABBAGE CASSEROLE

1 c.	Celery, chopped
½ c.	Onions, chopped
½ tsp.	Garlic, minced
½ c.	Bell pepper, chopped
1 ½ c.	Flavored gluten of choice
1 T.	Corn oil
½ c.	Canned tomato sauce
1 T.	Parsley
¼ tsp.	Oregano
¼ tsp.	Sea salt
¼ tsp.	Italian Herb Seasoning
5 c.	Cabbage, chopped and parboiled until it is tender
½ c.	Pimento or Yeast Cheez

Sauté the celery, onion, garlic, bell pepper, and gluten in the oil. Add the tomato sauce, parsley, oregano, salt, and Italian seasoning. In a nonstick casserole alternate layers of cabbage and sauce mixture. Top with the cheez. Bake uncovered at 350° for 30 minutes.

GLUTEN AND CORN CASSEROLE

½ c.	Bell pepper, chopped
¼ c.	Onions, chopped
1 tsp.	Corn oil
1 c.	Flavored gluten or flavored soy grits
2 c.	Medium White Sauce
1 tsp.	Prepared mustard
2 c.	Corn
½ c.	Pimento or Yeast Cheez

Sauté the bell pepper and onion in the oil until tender. Add the gluten (or grits) and cook for 5 minutes. Blend the white sauce, mustard, and gluten mixture. Add the corn. Place in a casserole and top with cheez. Bake at 350° for 30 minutes.

GLUTEN AND EGGPLANT CASSEROLE

2 c.	Eggplant, peeled and cut into 1-inch cubes
1 ½ c.	Onion, chopped
1 ½ tsp.	Garlic, minced
1 T.	Corn oil
2 c.	Canned tomatoes, including the juice
1	Bay leaf
¼ tsp.	Rosemary
Pinch	Ground cloves
¾ c.	Broth of type of gluten being used
½ tsp.	Sea salt
¼ tsp.	Cayenne
½ lb.	Pasta
2 c.	Yeast or Notzarella Cheez
1 ½ c.	Flavored gluten, ground

Sauté the eggplant, onion, and garlic in the oil until the onion is soft. Stir in the tomatoes with the juice, bay leaf, rosemary, cloves, broth, salt and pepper. Bring to a boil, reduce the heat, and simmer, covered, stirring occasionally and breaking up the tomatoes, for 20 minutes. Discard the bay leaf. Cook the pasta and stir it into the gluten mixture. Spoon half of this into a nonstick baking dish and spread it with half of the cheez. Spoon the rest over that and top with the rest of the cheez. Bake at 350° for 25 to 30 minutes, or until it is bubbling.

GLUTEN AND RICE CASSEROLE

2 c.	Onions, chopped
2 c.	Celery, chopped
1 T.	Corn oil
4 ½ c.	Rice, cooked
3 c.	Tomato paste
4 c.	Pimento or Yeast Cheez
2 ½ c.	Flavored gluten, ground
1 tsp.	Bell pepper flakes
1 tsp.	Garlic powder

Sauté the onion and celery in the oil. Combine all and bake in a nonstick casserole or pan at 400° for 45 minutes, covered.
Variation: Use flavored soy grits instead of gluten.

GLUTEN-VEGETABLE CASSEROLE

2 c.	Potatoes, peeled and cut into ¾-inch cubes
1 c.	Carrot, coarsely grated
1 c.	Peas
3 c.	Flavoring Broth of the type of gluten being used
2 T.	Corn oil
3 T.	Unbleached white flour
2 T.	Non-dairy margarine
2 c.	Flavored gluten, cooked according to Method 2 or 3, and cubed
2 c.	Onions, chopped coarsely
3 c.	Mushrooms
2 tsp.	Garlic, minced
¼ c.	Parsley, chopped well
¼ c.	Lea & Perrins Steak Sauce
1 T.	Louisiana Hot Sauce

In a saucepan combine the potatoes, carrots, peas, and broth. Simmer for 10 minutes or until the potatoes are done, drain and set aside, saving the broth. Put the oil in a skillet, stir in the flour, and cook, stirring constantly, until the flour is dark brown but not burned. Slowly stir in the reserved broth. Add the steak sauce and hot sauce. Melt the margarine in a skillet and fry the gluten, onions, and mushrooms until the gluten starts to brown, adding more oil if necessary. Add the garlic and parsley and sauté 2 more minutes. Combine everything and simmer over low heat for 10 minutes. Put in a casserole and bake at 375° for 20 minutes.

GOLDEN VEGETABLE BAKE

2 T.	Non-dairy margarine, melted
2 T.	Unbleached white flour

1 c.	Cashew milk, scalded
1 tsp.	Sea salt
⅛ tsp.	Black or cayenne pepper
¾ tsp.	Paprika
1 ½ c.	Carrots, shredded
2 c.	Cream-style corn
2 T.	Onions, chopped
⅓ c.	Bell pepper, chopped

Blend the melted margarine and flour. Gradually add the cashew milk. Cook, stirring constantly, until thickened. Add seasonings. Cool slightly. Stir in rest of ingredients. Pour into a nonstick casserole dish or pan. Bake at 350° 50 to 55 minutes.

GREEN BEAN CASSEROLE

2 c.	Green beans
1 c.	Bell pepper, chopped
1 ½ c.	Onions, chopped
1 tsp.	Garlic, minced
1 T.	Non-dairy margarine
¼ tsp.	Paprika
2 T.	Soy sauce

Cook the green beans in salted water and drain. Sauté the bell pepper, onions, and garlic in the margarine. Mix with the beans, paprika, and soy sauce and put in a nonstick casserole "buttered" with margarine. Cover and bake at 350° for about 30 minutes.

GREEN BEANS IN TOMATO SAUCE

2 c.	Green beans
2 T.	Non-dairy margarine
2 T.	Unbleached white flour
2 c.	Tomato juice
2 T.	Soy sauce
¼ tsp.	Sea salt
¼ tsp.	Paprika
½ c.	Bread crumbs tossed in margarine

Cook the green beans in salted water. While the beans are cooking melt the margarine and stir in the flour. Gradually add the tomato juice, stirring constantly. Add the soy sauce, salt, and paprika, and cook for 5 more minutes. Drain the beans and place them in a nonstick casserole. Pour the sauce over the beans. Bake at 350° for about 20 minutes. Cover the top with the crumbs. Bake at 450° until the crumbs are brown–about 10 more minutes.

Variations: Instead of the crumbs tossed in margarine, use Yeast or Pimento Cheez and dry crumbs, dotted with margarine. Good over rice or toast.

GREEN BEANS SUPREME-1

Just what the name says!

¾ c.	Onions, sliced
½ tsp.	Garlic, minced
1 T.	Parsley, minced
2 tsp.	Non-dairy margarine, melted
2 T.	Unbleached white flour
½ tsp.	Sea salt
¼ tsp.	Paprika
4 c.	Green beans, julienned and steamed
1 c.	Cashew or Tofu Sour Cream
½ c.	Yeast or Pimento Cheez
½ c.	Dry bread crumbs

Sauté the onions, garlic, and parsley in half of the margarine. Add flour, salt, and paprika and mix well. Stir in the beans and heat. Take off the heat and mix in the "sour cream." Put all into a nonstick casserole. Top with cheez and press in the crumbs lightly. Bake in a 325° oven until the crumbs brown.

GREEN BEANS SUPREME-2

Ditto!

3 T.	Onions, chopped
¾ c.	Mushrooms, chopped
½ tsp.	Garlic, minced
2 tsp.	Non-dairy margarine
6 c.	Green beans, cooked
¼ tsp.	Lemon peel
¼ tsp.	Cayenne pepper
⅛ tsp.	Dill weed
½ tsp.	Sea salt
1 ½ c.	Yeast, Pimento, or Notzarella Cheez
1 ½ c.	Bread crumbs

Sauté the onions, mushrooms, and garlic in the margarine. Combine everything except the crumbs and the cheez. Put in a nonstick casserole and cover with cheez. Top with bread crumbs, pressing in lightly. Bake at 400° until the bread crumbs brown.

GREEN CHILI CORN CASSEROLE

| 12 | Tortillas |

Filling:

| 3 c. | Onions, diced |

1 T.	Corn oil
3 c.	Rice, cooked
2 ¼ c.	Corn kernels (thawed, if frozen)
⅔ c.	Red bell pepper, diced
⅔ c.	Green bell pepper, diced
½ tsp.	Oregano
1 tsp.	Coriander
1 tsp.	Salt
3 tsp.	Chili powder
2 T.	Soy sauce
½ tsp.	Curry powder
½ tsp.	Cumin, ground

Sauce:

4 c.	Potatoes, chopped and steamed
1 ½ c.	Green chilies (mild), diced
½ T.	Salt
3 c.	Water

Sauté the onion in the oil until transparent. Mix the onion and all the filling ingredients together and set aside. Blend together all the sauce ingredients and set aside. To assemble, dip 4 corn tortillas into the sauce and layer them on the bottom of a 9x12-inch pan. Spread 4 cups of filling over the tortillas. Spread 1 cup of sauce over the filling. Repeat this assembly procedure, ending with 4 tortillas. Pour 2 cups of sauce over the top. Cover the pan and bake at 350° for 50 minutes.

HARVEST VEGETABLE CASSEROLE

2 T.	Non-dairy margarine
3 c.	Onions, sliced
1 c.	Bell pepper, cut into 1-inch strips
½ c.	Uncooked barley
1 c.	UnBeef Broth
¾ c.	Carrots, cut into chunks
2	Large tomatoes, quartered
1 ½ c.	Zucchini, cut into 1 ½-inch chunks
2 ½ c.	Green beans (each bean cut in half)
1 c.	Peas
1 ½ c.	Cauliflower, separated into flowerets
2 T.	Lemon juice
1 ½ tsp.	Garlic, crushed
1 T.	Sea salt
1 tsp.	Paprika
2 T.	Parsley, chopped

Sauté the onion and bell pepper in the margarine until browned. In a nonstick casserole, combine the barley, UnBeef broth, carrots, tomatoes, zucchini, beans, peas, cauliflower, and onion mixture. Combine the lemon juice and garlic and

pour over all. Sprinkle the salt and paprika over all. Cover and bake at 400° for 1 ½ hours, or until the barley is tender. Stir in the parsley and serve.

HOT UNCHICKEN SALAD CASSEROLE

2 ½ c.	UnChicken, diced
1 c.	Celery, diced
1 c.	Mushrooms, sliced
½ c.	Onion, minced
1 tsp.	Lemon juice
⅛ tsp.	Rosemary, crushed
¼ tsp.	Black pepper
¾ c.	Water chestnuts, drained and sliced
2 c.	Cooked rice
¾ c.	Cashew or Tofu Mayonnaise, or Miraculous Whip
2 ½ c.	Cream of UnChicken soup made with the "Basic Cream of" soup recipe
3 T.	Non-dairy margarine, melted
¾ c.	Cornflakes, crushed into crumbs
¾ c.	Almonds, slivered

Combine the first 9 ingredients. Blend the mayonnaise with the soup and toss with the gluten mixture. Put into an oiled or nonstick casserole. Combine the margarine with the cornflakes and almonds. Top the casserole with this. Bake at 350° for 30 minutes.

ITALIAN EGGPLANT CASSEROLE

3 c.	Eggplant, sliced thin
1 ½ c.	Onions, chopped
½ tsp.	Garlic, chopped
2 tsp.	Olive oil
1 c.	Black olives, chopped
1 c.	Tofu, crumbled
1 ½ c.	Canned tomato sauce
1 c.	Golden Sauce (see Gravies and Sauces section)

Fry the eggplant in a small amount of olive oil. Drain well on paper towels. Sauté the onions and garlic in the 2 tablespoons of olive oil. Mix the onions with the olives and tofu. In a nonstick casserole, alternate layers of:

> eggplant
> tofu mixture
> tomato sauce
> Golden Sauce

Ending with Golden Sauce. Bake for 30-45

minutes at 350°.

ITALIAN UNSAUSAGE DRESSING

½ c.	Onion, chopped
2 tsp.	Corn oil
½ c.	Mushrooms, chopped
1 c.	Italian UnSausage
½ tsp.	Oregano
¼ tsp.	Sea salt
¾ tsp.	Garlic, minced
2	Slices of bread

Sauté the onion in the oil. Mix all the ingredients very quickly in a food processor or finely chop and blend them by hand. Set aside. Mix in a bowl and set aside:

¾ c.	Cashew or Tofu Sour Cream
½ c.	Notzarella Cheez
¼ tsp.	Thyme
½ tsp.	Rosemary

Combine everything, put into a casserole, and bake, covered, at 350° for 45 minutes. Uncover and bake 10 more minutes.

ITALIAN UNSAUSAGE, PASTA, AND BEAN CASSEROLE

2 c.	Italian UnSausage, ground
2 c.	Beef Gluten, ground
1 ½ c.	Onion, chopped
1 T.	Garlic, chopped
1 tsp.	Oregano
2 T.	Corn oil
½ tsp.	Thyme
3 ½ c.	Canned tomatoes, drained and chopped
2 T.	Tomato paste
½ tsp.	Sea salt
½ tsp.	Pepper
2 c.	Cooked kidney beans, drained
3/4 lb.	Macaroni, cooked and drained
⅓ c.	Parmesan Cheez
¼ c.	Parsley, chopped
2 c.	Yeast, Pimento, or Notzarella Cheez

Sauté the two types of gluten, onion, garlic, oregano, and thyme in the oil until the gluten is browned well. Add the tomatoes, tomato paste, salt, pepper, and beans, and heat through. Add the macaroni, "parmesan," and parsley and toss together well. Put into a nonstick casserole or pan. Spread the cheez on top and bake, uncovered, at 375° for 30 minutes.

LAYERED CASSEROLE

Plain goodness!

3 c.	Green beans, cooked in UnChicken or UnBeef Broth
4 c.	Potatoes, cooked with salt and sliced
¼ c.	Onions, chopped
½ tsp.	Garlic, minced
2 ½ tsp.	Corn oil
3 c.	Corn
1 c.	Water
	Cracker crumbs for topping, tossed in some melted margarine

Place the cooked green beans in a nonstick casserole. Cover with the potato slices. Sauté the onions and garlic in the oil. Blend with the corn, water, and margarine, and pour over all. Top with cracker crumbs, pressing in lightly. Bake at 350° until the cracker crumbs brown.
Variations: Instead of green beans use green peas, squash, pumpkin, or cooked dried beans. Put a layer of Yeast or Pimento Cheez on top of the corn and top with the cracker crumbs.

LEFT-OVER VEGETABLES WITH CHEEZ

Always the same but different!

Moisten the vegetables with one of the Flavoring Broths, soups, or tomato juice. Place them in a nonstick casserole. Cover them with Notzarella, Pimento, or Yeast Cheez. Top with bread crumbs and press them in lightly. Bake at 375° until well heated.

LIMA BEANS WITH CHEEZ

½ tsp.	Paprika
¾ c.	UnBeef Broth
1 tsp.	Non-dairy margarine
2 ½ c.	Lima beans, fresh, cooked (or frozen, thawed, and cooked)
½ c.	Yeast or Pimento Cheez
½ c.	Bread crumbs

Heat the paprika, broth, and margarine together until the margarine is melted. Mix in the lima beans. Place alternating layers of beans and cheez in a nonstick casserole. Cover the top with bread crumbs and press in lightly. Bake at 350° for 30 minutes.

MEXICAN LASAGNA

Si! Si!

1 c.	Onions, chopped
1 tsp.	Garlic, minced
2 tsp.	Corn oil
2 c.	Cooked pinto, red, pink, or kidney beans
2 c.	Corn
4 c.	Canned tomato sauce
¼ c.	Cooked Tomato Salsa
½ tsp.	Oregano
1 tsp.	Sea salt
20	Corn tortillas
3 c.	Yeast or Pimento Cheez

Sauté the onions and garlic in the oil. Combine all the ingredients except the tortillas and cheez. In a nonstick casserole pan, place a layer of tortillas. Over that put a layer of the filling. Over that spread 1 cup of the cheez. Repeat one more time. Cover with another layer of tortillas. Top with the third cup of cheez. Bake at 350° for 20 minutes.

MEXICAN LIMA BEAN CASSEROLE

⅓ c.	Onions, chopped
¼ c.	Bell pepper, chopped
Pinch	Cayenne pepper
1 ½ tsp.	Non-dairy margarine
½ tsp.	Garlic, minced
2 T.	Barbados molasses
2 c.	Canned tomatoes
1 tsp.	Sea salt
2 c.	Lima beans, cooked

Sauté the onions, bell pepper, and cayenne pepper in the margarine. Combine all ingredients and bake in a nonstick casserole dish at 375° for 45 minutes.
Variation: Add Yeast, Pimento, or Notzarella Cheez.

MUSHROOM AND ARTICHOKE PIE

½ lb.	Mushrooms, sliced (if fresh, clean first)
2	10-oz. pkgs. frozen artichoke hearts, thawed and chopped
3 T.	Lemon juice
2 T.	Olive oil
2 c.	Onion, chopped
1 ½ tsp.	Garlic, minced or mashed
¼ c.	Water
1 T.	Nutritional Yeast
½ tsp.	MSG
¼ tsp.	Poultry seasoning
½ c.	Parsley, chopped
1 ½ tsp.	Sea salt
½ tsp.	Black pepper
15 oz.	Tofu Ricotta Cheez
3	N'eggs
	Convent Pie Crust

Combine the mushrooms and artichokes. Sprinkle with the lemon juice. Heat the oil in a skillet, add the onions and garlic, and cook until lightly browned. Add the artichokes and mushrooms and cook 25 minutes, stirring occasionally. Add everything else, put into a 9x9 baking dish lined with unbaked pie crust, cover with more crust, and bake at 425° for 45 minutes, or until the crust is browned.

MUSHROOM AND BELL PEPPER QUICHE

3 T.	Corn oil
3 T.	Non-dairy margarine
2 lb.	Medium-firm tofu, mashed
1 c.	Onion, chopped
½ c.	Bell pepper, chopped
2 ½ c.	Mushrooms, sliced
2 c.	Tomatoes, chopped
½ tsp.	Garlic, minced
¼ tsp.	Sea salt
½ c.	Yeast Cheez
	Sliced tomatoes

Heat the oil and margarine together in a skillet and sauté the tofu until it begins to brown. Remove from the skillet with a slotted spoon and set aside. Add the onion, bell pepper, and mushrooms to the skillet–along with extra oil if needed–and sauté until they are soft. Add the tomatoes, garlic, and salt and sauté 5 more minutes. Put the tofu and cheez in a blender and blend until smooth. Combine everything well–except for the tomato slices–and press into a nonstick casserole. Cover with a layer of tomato slices. Sprinkle some salt and pepper over the tomato slices, cover, and bake at 350° for 30 to 40 minutes. Uncover and broil for a few minutes.

NOODLE CASSEROLE WITH ZUCCHINI, TOMATOES, AND CHEEZ

2 c.	Zucchini, grated and sprinkled with ½ teaspoon of salt and allowed to drain in a strainer and pressed dry

¾ c.	Onions, chopped
1 ½ tsp.	Garlic, minced
1 T.	Olive oil
3 c.	Canned tomatoes, drained and finely chopped
½ tsp.	Sea salt
⅛ tsp.	Cayenne pepper
1	8 oz. package of noodles, cooked, drained and tossed in 4 tablespoons of melted non-dairy margarine
1 c.	Yeast or Pimento Cheez
½ c.	Parmesan Cheez

Sauté the zucchini, onion, and garlic in the oil until the zucchini and onions are tender. Add the tomatoes, salt, and pepper and simmer for 10 minutes or until the sauce is thick. Toss the cooked noodles with the cheezes until blended. Toss the noodles with the sauce. Place in a casserole and heat in a 350° oven until heated through.

ONIONS IN TOMATO SAUCE

2 T.	Non-dairy margarine
2 T.	Unbleached white flour
2 c.	Tomato juice
2 T.	Soy sauce
¼ tsp.	Sea salt
¼ tsp.	Paprika
2 c.	Sliced onions
½ c.	Dry bread crumbs

Melt the margarine and stir in the flour. Gradually add the tomato juice, stirring constantly. Add the soy sauce, salt, and paprika, and cook for 5 more minutes. Put the sliced onions in a nonstick baking dish. Pour the sauce over the onions. Bake at 350° for about 20 minutes. Cover the top with the crumbs. Bake at 450° until the crumbs are brown—about 10 more minutes.
Variation: Instead of only crumbs as a topping, use Yeast or Pimento Cheez with crumbs over that. Good over rice or toast.

PAELLA-LIMAS

1 c.	Green limas, frozen
5 tsp.	Non-dairy margarine
2 c.	Rice, uncooked
1 c.	Onion, minced
1 c.	Carrot, sliced thin
4 ½ c.	Boiling water
1 tsp.	Sea salt

Steam the lima beans and set aside. Melt 3 teaspoons of the margarine in a heavy skillet, and stir in the rice. Continue stirring until the rice is slightly brown and popping (some rice does not pop). Sauté the onions and carrots together in the other 2 teaspoons of margarine for 3 minutes. Pour all the ingredients into the boiling water with the salt and boil for 30 minutes. Pour the paella into a casserole, cover and bake at 350° for 1 hour. Leave uncovered the last 5 minutes.

PIFFEL

I made this up, but couldn't think of a name for it. In disgust I said: "Piffel"—and it had a name!

¾ c.	Onions, chopped
½ c.	Bell pepper, chopped
2 tsp.	Corn oil
6 c.	Vegetables, chopped or sliced— fresh or frozen (thawed well)
1 ½ c.	Tomatoes, chopped
½ tsp.	Oregano
½ tsp.	Basil
3 c.	Yeast or Pimento Cheez
¼ tsp.	Garlic powder
1 ½ c.	UnChicken Broth

Sauté the onions and bell pepper in the oil. Combine all ingredients in a casserole dish and bake at 400° for 45 minutes.

CREAM OF PIFFEL

I wanted a variation on Piffel—and succeeded!

¾ c.	Onions, chopped
¼ c.	Bell pepper, chopped
2 ½ tsp.	Corn oil
4 c.	Thick White Sauce made with UnChicken Broth
6 c.	Vegetables, chopped or sliced— fresh or frozen (thawed well)
½ tsp.	Italian Herb Seasoning
¼ tsp.	Garlic powder
½ tsp.	Cayenne pepper
3 c.	Yeast or Pimento Cheez
2 c.	Dry bread crumbs

Sauté the onions and bell pepper in the oil. Combine with the sauce, vegetables, herb seasoning, garlic powder, and pepper, and pour into a casserole dish. Cover with the cheez. Top with bread crumbs, pressing in lightly. Bake at 400° for 30 minutes.

PIMENTO CHEEZ LOAF

1 c.	Pimento Cheez
1 tsp.	Cornstarch or arrowroot flour
2 c.	Cooked lima beans, mashed
¼ c.	Onions, chopped
2 T.	Parsley, chopped
½ tsp.	Sea salt
¾ c.	Dry bread crumbs

Mix all ingredients except the crumbs and shape into a loaf, adding a little water if needed. Put in a pan and sprinkle with the crumbs. Bake at 325° for 1 hour.

Variation: Instead of the pimento cheez, use 1 cup of Tofu Cream Cheez and 3 tablespoons of chopped pimentos.

POLENTA CASSEROLE

1 c.	Cornmeal
4 c.	UnBeef Broth
½ tsp.	Sea salt
3 T.	Onions, chopped
1 tsp.	Garlic, minced
1 tsp.	Non-dairy margarine
2 c.	Vegetable(s), cooked
½ c.	Yeast or Pimento Cheez
2 c.	Tomato Sauce (one of the recipes from Gravies and Sauces)

Mix the cornmeal with 1 cup of the broth until blended. Bring the remaining 3 cups of broth to a boil in a heavy saucepan. Add salt, then stir in the cornmeal paste and return to a boil, stirring continuously. Reduce heat to low and simmer, stirring occasionally with a wooden spoon, until the mixture is very thick. Add a little water if needed. Cook 15-20 minutes, depending on how fine or coarse the cornmeal is. Sauté the onions and garlic in the oil and add them to the cooked vegetables. Add the vegetables to the cooked cornmeal. Stir in the cheez and the margarine. Put the cornmeal mixture into a nonstick casserole. Top with the tomato sauce. Bake at 375° for about an hour.

POTATO-BROCCOLI CASSEROLE

2 tsp.	Non-dairy margarine, softened
1 c.	Onions, chopped
2 tsp.	Garlic, minced
2 ½ c.	Potatoes, cubed and cooked in UnChicken Broth
1 ½ c.	Broccoli, chopped and steamed
⅔ c.	Yeast Cheez
4 T.	Parmesan Cheez

¼ tsp.	Sea salt
⅛ tsp.	Black pepper
⅛ tsp.	Cayenne pepper
¼ c.	Cashew Cream
¼ c.	Parsley, chopped

Sauté the onions and garlic in the oil until the onions are soft. Mash the potatoes. Stir in the broccoli, ⅓ cup of the yeast cheez, 1 tablespoon of the parmesan cheez, salt, pepper, "cream," parsley, onions, and garlic. Put in a nonstick baking dish. Spread the rest of the yeast cheez on top, sprinkle with the remaining "parmesan," and bake at 350° for 30 minutes. Broil, 4 inches from the heat, for 1 to 2 minutes, until the top is golden.

Variation: Use carrots instead of broccoli.

POTATO-CHEEZ BAKE

¼ c.	Onion, chopped
½ c.	Non-dairy margarine
6 c.	Mashed potatoes
3 c.	Yeast, Pimento, or Notzarella Cheez
¼ tsp.	Cayenne
1 ½ tsp.	Sea salt
½ tsp.	Paprika

Saute the onions in the margarine. Combine everything well and put in a 1-inch layer in a casserole. Brush the top with melted margarine. Broil.

POTATO AND TOMATO GRATIN

1 c.	Onion, chopped
1 ½ tsp.	Garlic, minced fine
2 tsp.	Corn oil
2 c.	Tomatoes, diced
½ tsp.	Thyme, or 1 T. basil
2 ½ c.	Potatoes, peeled, sliced ⅛-inch thick, and cooked
½ tsp.	Sea salt
¼ tsp.	Black pepper

Sauté the onion and garlic in the oil until soft. Add the tomatoes, thyme, and broth. Cook, covered, stirring occasionally, until the onion is soft and translucent. Put ⅓ of this sauce on the bottom of a casserole. Top with potato slices and sprinkle them with a little salt and pepper. Layer another ⅓ of the sauce over all, then another layer of potatoes, also sprinkled with salt and pepper, the rest of the tomato sauce, then a layer of potatoes sprinkled with salt and pepper. Bake, covered, at 400° for 60 minutes, or until the potatoes are cooked through.

POTATO GRATIN

1 ½ c.	Onion, chopped fine
1½ tsp.	Garlic, minced
1½ tsp.	Non-dairy margarine
4 ½ c.	Potatoes, peeled and grated
2 T.	Cornstarch
1 c.	Yeast or Notzarella Cheez
¾ tsp.	Sea salt
¾ tsp.	Black pepper
1 ½ c.	Cashew Cream

Sauté the onions and garlic in the oil until soft. Add the rest of the ingredients except the cheez and "cream." Put into a nonstick casserole and pat it down. Drizzle the "cream" evenly over the top, sprinkle with the cheez, and bake at 400° 25 to 30 minutes–until the potatoes are done and the top is golden.

POTATO STUFFING

1 ½ c.	Onion, chopped fine
1 c.	Celery, chopped fine
1 T.	Corn oil
1 c.	UnBeef Broth
1 c.	White bread cubes
3 c.	Mashed potatoes
2 T.	Parsley, minced
¼ tsp.	Garlic powder
¼ tsp.	Sea salt
¼ tsp.	Cayenne

Sauté the onion and celery in the oil until soft. Take from heat. Add the rest of ingredients and mix well. Put into a casserole. Bake, uncovered, at 350° for 45 minutes or until the top is lightly browned.

POTATOES AND CARROTS AU GRATIN

2 ½ c.	Potatoes, peeled and sliced
1 ½ c.	Carrots, sliced thin
½ c.	Bell pepper, chopped
¼ c.	Onion, chopped
¾ c.	Yeast, Pimento, or Notzarella Cheez
½ tsp.	Sea salt
½ tsp.	Dry mustard
⅛ tsp.	Black pepper
2 c.	Cream of Celery Soup

Put the potatoes, carrots, bell pepper, and onion in a nonstick casserole. Combine half the cheez with the rest of the ingredients. Pour this over the vegetables. Toss gently. Bake at 350°, covered, for 35-40 minutes or until the potatoes are tender. Spread the rest of the cheez on top and bake, uncovered, for 10-15 more minutes.

POTATOES AU GRATIN

2 c.	Onions, sliced thin
1 tsp.	Garlic, minced
1 T.	Non-dairy margarine
⅛ tsp.	Cayenne pepper
⅛ tsp.	Black pepper
¼ tsp.	Sea salt
6 c.	Potatoes, sliced ½-inch thick and boiled in salted water
3 c.	Yeast, Pimento, or Notzarella Cheez Parmesan Cheez for sprinkling on top
⅔ c.	UnChicken, UnBeef, or UnHam Broth

Sauté the onions and garlic in the margarine until the onions are soft. Stir in the peppers and salt. Layer half of the boiled potato slices in a nonstick casserole, then a layer of one half of the onion-garlic mixture, and a layer of one half of the cheez. Repeat the layering as above. Sprinkle some "parmesan" over that. Pour the broth over that. Bake at 375° for 45 minutes or until brown on top.
Variation: Use cauliflower or broccoli instead of potatoes.

POTATOES SCALLOPED IN MARGARINE

Wash and peel the potatoes and cut them in slices ⅛-inch thick. Put them in cold water to cover for 15 minutes. Drain the potatoes and dry them between towels. Generously "butter" a baking dish with non-dairy margarine and sprinkle it with fine dry bread or cracker crumbs. Cover the bottom carefully with a layer of potato slices. Dot them generously with margarine and sprinkle them lightly with salt and paprika. Repeat this layering until the dish is filled. Cover and bake at 375° for 1 hour or until the potatoes are tender.

POTLUCK POTATOES

7 ½ c.	Potatoes, peeled and chopped
1 ¼ c.	Cream of UnChicken Soup

½ c.	Cashew or Tofu Sour Cream
1 c.	Tofu Cream Cheez
2 tsp.	Non-dairy margarine
¾ c.	Yeast Cheez
¼ c.	Green onions, sliced
¼ c.	Cashew Milk
1 T.	Parsley flakes
¼ tsp.	Garlic salt
¼ tsp.	Black pepper

Cook the potatoes in boiling water 10 to 12 minutes or until tender. Drain. Rinse with cold water. Drain again. Combine the soup, "sour cream," cream cheez and margarine. Add ¼ cup of the yeast cheez, 3 tablespoons of the green onion, "milk," parsley, garlic salt, and pepper. Stir to combine. Put into a nonstick casserole and bake, uncovered, at 350° for 30 to 35 minutes, or until heated through. Spread the rest of the cheez on top and bake 5 more minutes. Sprinkle with the rest of the green onion.

RATATOUILLE

3 T.	Olive oil
1 c.	Onion, chopped
1 ½ tsp.	Garlic, minced
1 ¼ c.	Bell pepper, sliced lengthwise ¼-inch thick (a mixture of green, red, and yellow, if possible)
1	Medium eggplant, sliced ¼-inch thick
1 c.	Mushrooms, sliced thin
¾ tsp.	Sea salt
½ tsp.	Black pepper
⅓ c.	Fresh basil leaves (lightly packed), chopped
4 c.	Tomatoes, halved lengthwise and sliced crosswise ⅓-inch thick
⅔ c.	Yeast, Pimento, or Notzarella Cheez

Heat the oil in a skillet and sauté the onion, garlic, bell pepper, eggplant, and mushrooms–adding more if needed–until softened (about 15 minutes). Add the salt, pepper, and basil. Stir in the tomatoes and cook for 1 more minute. Transfer to a nonstick casserole and spread the cheez on top. Cover with foil and bake at 400° for 30 minutes, until the vegetables are very tender. Can be served hot, warm, or cold.

RICE DRESSING

¼ c.	Onions, chopped
⅓ c.	Bell pepper, chopped

2 tsp.	Non-dairy margarine
4 c.	Rice cooked in UnChicken Broth
1 c.	Dry bread crumbs
⅔ c.	Black olives, chopped
¾ tsp.	Sea salt
1 c.	Thin White Sauce made with UnChicken Broth

Sauté the onions and bell pepper in the margarine. Combine all ingredients. Bake, uncovered, at 350° for 30 minutes.

RUMBLEDETHUMPS

A pity someone does not write a fairy story with this as a title! It is actually colcannon, a Scottish dish, adapted from an American version given in Gourmet *magazine.*

6 c.	Potatoes, peeled, diced, and cooked
1 T.	Non-dairy margarine, melted
2 T.	Fresh chives or green onions, minced
½ c.	Cashew Milk
4 c.	Cabbage, diced and cooked
1 tsp.	Sea salt
¼ tsp.	Black pepper
1 ½ c.	Yeast, Pimento, or Notzarella Cheez

Mash the potatoes, stir in the margarine, chives (or green onions), "milk," cabbage, salt, and pepper. Put into a baking dish, spread the cheez over the top, and bake at 400° for 30 minutes, or until heated through. Just before serving broil until the top browns lightly.

SAUERKRAUT CASSEROLE

2 T.	Corn oil
3 c.	UnPork, cubed
1 c.	Onion, chopped
1 c.	Celery, chopped
1	16-oz. can of sauerkraut, undrained
8 oz.	Noodles, cooked and drained
1 ¼ c.	Cream of Mushroom Soup
½ c.	Mushrooms
½ tsp.	Sea salt
¼ tsp.	Black pepper

Heat the oil in a skillet and brown the gluten. Add the onions and celery and sauté until the onions are transparent. Stir in the rest of the ingredients, put into a casserole, cover, and bake at 350° for 1 hour, stirring occasionally.

SCALLOPED BROCCOLI–1

3 c.	Cashew Milk
2 tsp.	Non-dairy margarine
½ c.	Onions, chopped
1 tsp.	Garlic, minced
2 T.	Unbleached white flour
1 ½ tsp.	Sea salt
⅛ tsp.	Black or cayenne pepper
1 ½ c.	Pimento or Yeast Cheez
6 c.	Broccoli, steamed and chopped

Preheat the "milk." Melt the margarine in a saucepan over low heat and sauté the onion and garlic. Blend in the flour, salt, and pepper. Add the "milk" slowly. Cook quickly, stirring constantly, until the mixture thickens and bubbles. Add the cheez and stir it in well. Put half the broccoli in a nonstick casserole. Cover with half of the sauce. Repeat this layering. Cover and bake at 350° for 1 hour. Uncover and bake 30 minutes longer.

SCALLOPED BROCCOLI–2

1 c.	Mushrooms, sliced
½ c.	Onions, chopped
1 ½ tsp.	Garlic, minced
½ tsp.	Crushed red pepper
2 tsp.	Corn oil
4 c.	UnChicken Broth
6 c.	Broccoli, steamed and chopped
3 c.	Notzarella Cheez
1 ½ c.	Bread crumbs

Sauté the mushrooms in the oil until the onions are soft. Combine everything but the cheez and crumbs and cook until the broccoli is tender. Drain off and discard 3 cups of the broth. Mix in the cheez and put in a nonstick casserole. Top with the crumbs, pressing in lightly. Bake, uncovered, at 350° for 45 minutes or until brown on top.

SCALLOPED CABBAGE

4 c.	Cabbage, chopped
3 T.	Corn oil
3 T.	Unbleached white flour
½ tsp.	Sea salt
Dash	Black pepper
1 c.	Cashew Milk
1 c.	Yeast Cheez
¾ c.	Bread crumbs

Put cabbage in a casserole and set aside. Heat the oil in a saucepan. Stir in the flour, salt, and pepper,

and cook until bubbly. Gradually stir in the "milk." Cook and stir until thickened. Fold in the cheez. Pour over the cabbage. Sprinkle the bread crumbs on top and press lightly into the cheez. Bake, uncovered, at 350° for 20 to 30 minutes or until bubbly.

SCALLOPED CARROTS AND POTATOES

1 c.	Onions, sliced
1 tsp.	Garlic, minced
2 tsp.	Non-dairy margarine, melted
4 c.	Potatoes, peeled, sliced, and boiled in salted water
2 c.	Carrots, peeled, sliced, and boiled in salted water
2 T.	UnBacon, minced
½ tsp.	Sea salt
⅛ tsp.	Black pepper
⅛ tsp.	Rosemary leaf, crumbled
¼ c.	Parsley, minced
2 c.	Thin white sauce

Sauté the onions and garlic in the margarine and mix with the cooked potatoes. Put a layer of the potato-onion mixture in a nonstick casserole. Put in a layer of carrots. Combine the gluten, salt, pepper, rosemary, and parsley, and sprinkle ½ of that over the carrots. Pour ½ the white sauce over all. Repeat. Bake at 350° for 20 minutes.

SCALLOPED CORN

½ c.	Bell pepper, chopped well
½ c.	Onions, chopped
2 ½ c.	Cheez Sauce of choice
10 c.	Corn

Combine the bell pepper, onions, and cheez sauce. Stir in the corn. Put into a casserole and bake at 350° until light brown on top.

SCALLOPED EGGPLANT

3 c.	Eggplant, peeled and sliced
2 T.	Bell pepper, chopped
2 T.	Onions, chopped
½ tsp.	Garlic, minced
1 T.	Non-dairy margarine
2 c.	Tomatoes, cooked or canned
1 tsp.	Sea salt
¾ c.	Bread crumbs

Heavily salt both sides of the eggplant slices. Let sit for 1 hour and wipe off the salt and liquid. Press between absorbent towels, squeezing out as much liquid as possible. Cut into small pieces. Sauté the bell pepper, onion, garlic, and eggplant in one-half of the margarine, adding some corn oil if needed. Add the tomatoes and salt. Simmer 20 to 30 minutes or until tender. Pour into a nonstick baking dish. Melt the remaining margarine, mix with bread crumbs, and spread over the top of the eggplant mixture. Bake at 350° for 20 minutes, or until the eggplant is tender and the bread crumbs are brown.

SCALLOPED PEAS AND SQUASH

⅓ c.	Onions, chopped
1 tsp.	Non-dairy margarine
2 c.	Squash, sliced or cubed
2 c.	Peas (if frozen, partially thawed)
3 c.	Medium white sauce
1 c.	Yeast, Pimento, or Notzarella Cheez

Sauté the onions in the margarine. Combine the squash and peas. Place in a nonstick baking dish. Pour the sauce over the vegetables. Top with the cheez. Bake at 375° for 45 minutes.
Variation: Use pumpkin instead of squash.

SCALLOPED POTATOES–1

Fill a nonstick casserole with layers of peeled and very thinly sliced raw potatoes, sprinkling each layer generously with unbleached white flour, salt, and soy sauce and spraying it with vegetable oil. Heat cashew milk that has been seasoned with salt and paprika. Pour it over the potatoes until it can be seen through the top layer. Bake at 350° for 75 minutes. (You may turn the potatoes with a spoon while cooking to ensure even baking.)

SCALLOPED POTATOES–2

3 c.	Cashew Milk
2 tsp.	Non-dairy margarine
½ c.	Onions, chopped
1 tsp.	Garlic, minced
2 T.	Unbleached white flour
1 ½ tsp.	Sea salt
⅛ tsp.	Black or cayenne pepper
1 ½ c.	Yeast, Pimento, or Notzarella Cheez
6 c.	Potatoes, peeled and thinly sliced

Preheat the "milk." Melt the margarine in a saucepan over low heat. Sauté the onion and garlic. Blend in the flour, salt, and pepper. Add the "milk" slowly. Cook quickly, stirring constantly, until the mixture thickens and bubbles. Add the cheez and stir it in well. Put half the potatoes in a nonstick casserole. Cover with half of the sauce. Repeat this layering. Cover and bake at 350° for 1 hour. Uncover and bake 30 minutes longer.

SCALLOPED POTATOES–3

½ c.	Miraculous Whip
2 T.	Unbleached white flour
1 c.	Cashew Milk
¼ tsp.	Sea salt
⅛ tsp.	Black pepper
1 c.	Yeast, Pimento, or Notzarella Cheez
4 c.	Potatoes, sliced

Combine the Miraculous Whip and flour. Gradually stir in the "milk," salt, and pepper. Cook, stirring constantly, until the mixture thickens and comes to a boil. Add the cheez and stir in well. Remove from heat. Put the potatoes in a baking dish and pour the liquid over them. Cover and bake at 350° for 45 minutes. Uncover and bake 15 more minutes or until the potatoes are tender.

SCALLOPED POTATOES AND MUSHROOMS

1 ½ c.	Onions, chopped
2 ½ c.	Mushrooms, stemmed and chopped coarsely
1 T. & 1 ½ tsp.	Jalapeños, chopped fine
2 tsp.	Garlic, minced
2 T.	Non-dairy margarine
4 c.	Medium White Sauce made with UnChicken Broth
6 c.	Potatoes, peeled, sliced 1-inch thick, and boiled in salted water

Sauté the onions, mushrooms, jalapeños, and garlic in the margarine. Add to the white sauce and cook for 5 minutes. Add the sauce to the potatoes and stir well. Place in a casserole pan and bake at 375° for 45 minutes.

SCALLOPED POTATOES AND SPINACH

⅓ c.	Onion, chopped
2 tsp.	Non-dairy margarine
3 T.	Unbleached white flour
2 c.	Cashew Milk
¼ tsp.	Sea salt

¾ c.   Yeast or Notzarella Cheez
½   10-oz. pkg. of frozen spinach,
       thawed and drained well
1 T.   Pimento, chopped
       Paprika
5 c.   Potatoes, peeled and sliced ¼-inch
       thick, and cooked with ⅛ tsp. of sea
       salt until just tender, and drained

Sauté the onion in the margarine until tender. Stir in the flour. Stir in the "milk" and salt. Cook over medium heat until thickened and bubbly, stirring occasionally. Add the cheez and stir in well. Combine this with the potatoes, spinach, and pimento in a nonstick casserole and bake at 350° for about 40 minutes. Sprinkle with the paprika and serve.

SHEPHERD'S PIE–1

I never tire of this.

2 c.   Peas or dried beans, cooked
2 c.   Corn
2 c.   Green beans, cooked
1 T.   Non-dairy margarine, melted
½ tsp.   Sea salt
2 c.   UnBeef Gravy 1 or 2
2 ½ c.   Mashed potatoes

Combine the peas, corn, beans, and margarine together in a deep casserole. Sprinkle them with the salt. Pour the gravy over the vegetables. Spread the mashed potatoes on top. Heat in oven about 30 minutes before serving until the peaks of the mashed potatoes are light brown.

SHEPHERD'S PIE–2

This merits a blue ribbon!

2 c.   Potatoes, cubed
         Just enough UnBeef Broth to
         cover the potatoes
⅓ c.   Onions, chopped
2 tsp.   Corn oil
1 c.   Tomatoes, chopped
1 c.   Vegetable(s) of choice, chopped
2 T.   Parsley, chopped
1 tsp.   Arrowroot
¼ tsp.   Sea salt
½ c.   UnBeef Broth
1 c.   Pizza Cheez
1   Pie Crust recipe for 2 crusts

Boil the potatoes in the broth for 5 to 10 minutes. Sauté the onions in the corn oil. Add the potatoes, tomatoes, vegetables, and parsley. Cover and cook 5 more minutes. Dissolve the arrowroot and salt in the half cup of broth, then add it and the cheez to the vegetables. Cook for 10 minutes, stirring occasionally. Oil a pie pan and put one of the unbaked crusts in it. Pour in the filling. Lay the other crust over the vegetable mixture. Seal the top. Cut steam holes or slits and brush the top with oil. Bake at 350° for 30 minutes or until the pastry is lightly browned.

SIMPLE GARDEN CASSEROLE

½ c.   Onion, chopped
1 tsp.   Garlic, minced
1 tsp.   Non-dairy margarine
1 c.   Zucchini, chopped
1 c.   Tomatoes, chopped
½ tsp.   Sea salt
¼ tsp.   Black pepper
½ c.   Cashew Milk
½ c.   Biscuit Mix
2   N'eggs
⅓ c.   Parmesan Cheez

Sauté the onions and garlic in the margarine until soft. Add the zucchini, tomatoes, salt, and pepper and cook until the zucchini is soft. Put into a nonstick casserole. Beat the "milk," biscuit mix, n'eggs and cheez together until smooth. Pour evenly over the vegetables. Bake at 400° for 30 to 35 minutes, or until a knife inserted in the center comes out clean. Let stand for at least 5 minutes before cutting.

SOY GRITS CASSEROLE

1 c.   Uncooked rice
1 ½ c.   UnBeef Broth
¼ c.   Bell pepper
1 ½ tsp. Non-dairy margarine
2 c.   Soy grits, soaked in 4 c. of UnBeef
         Broth
2 ½ c.   Tomatoes, chopped
¼ c.   Tomato paste
4 c.   Yeast or Pimento Cheez
¼ tsp.   Sea salt

Cook rice in the broth. Sauté the bell pepper in margarine. Combine all ingredients and put in baking dish. Bake at 350° for 20 minutes or until brown.

SOY GRITS ENCHILADA CASSEROLE

Hold on to your sombrero–this is GOOD!

1 c.	Soy grits
2 c.	UnBeef Broth, boiling hot
⅓ c.	Onions, chopped
2 T.	Bell pepper, chopped
½ tsp.	Garlic, minced
4 tsp.	Corn oil
⅛ tsp.	Cayenne pepper
3 c.	Tomato sauce
6 T.	Cooked Salsa
1 c.	Yeast, Pimento, or Notzarella Cheez
8	Corn tortillas

Soak the grits in the broth for at least 10 minutes, making sure the broth is enough for the grits to absorb, adding more if needed. Sauté the onions, bell pepper, and garlic in the oil. Add the grits and pepper and fry a few minutes more. Add the salsa. Dip the tortillas in hot oil to make them limp. Layer in a casserole pan as follows:

> Tomato sauce
> Tortillas
> Cheez
> Grits Filling
> Tomato sauce
> Tortillas
> Cheez
> Grits Filling
> Tomato sauce
> Tortillas

Spread a thin layer of cheez, salsa, and chopped onions on top. Bake for 15 minutes at 400°.

SPICY POTATOES

2 c.	Potatoes, thinly sliced
1 T.	Olive oil
½ tsp.	Garlic, minced
1 T.	Red onions, chopped
¼ c.	Parsley, chopped (2 T. dried)
1 tsp.	Unbleached white flour
¼ tsp.	Cayenne pepper
½ c.	Tomatoes, chopped
½	Bay leaf
¼ tsp.	Sucanat
¼ tsp.	Sea salt

Brush or spray the potato slices with olive oil. Place on a nonstick baking sheet and bake for 20 minutes, or until lightly browned and tender. Set aside. Heat the tablespoon of oil in a heavy skillet. Add garlic, onion, and parsley. Cook until the onion is transparent but not browned. Whisk in the flour and cayenne. Add the rest of the ingredients. Cook over low heat for 10 minutes, stirring occasionally. Remove bay leaf. Pour sauce over potatoes, and bake, uncovered, at 350° for 15 minutes.

SPINACH AND HERB POTATO CASSEROLE

I call this a "politician dish"–it stands on its record!

6 c.	Potatoes, peeled, boiled, and mashed
1 c.	Tofu Cream Cheez
1 c.	Cashew or Tofu Sour Cream
1 T.	Non-dairy margarine, softened or melted
2 tsp.	Sea salt
1 ½ tsp.	Dill weed
¼ tsp.	Black pepper
1	10-oz. pkg. frozen chopped spinach, cooked and well drained

Whip the potatoes, cream cheez, sour cream, and margarine together until smooth. Add all the rest and beat until well mixed. Put into a nonstick casserole and bake at 375° for 20 minutes.

SQUASH AND MACARONI BAKE

2 c.	Squash, chopped fine
½ c.	Onions, chopped
½ tsp.	Garlic, minced
1 ½ tsp.	Non-dairy margarine
¼ c.	Unbleached white flour
¼ tsp.	Sea salt
½ tsp.	Oregano
1 ¾ c.	Water
3 c.	Yeast or Pimento Cheez
2 c.	Macaroni, cooked and drained
1 c.	Tomatoes, chopped

Sauté the squash, onions, and garlic in the margarine. Blend in the flour and seasonings. Gradually add the water. Cook, stirring, until thickened. Stir in 1 ½ cups of the cheez. Stir in the macaroni and tomatoes. Pour into a nonstick casserole. Top with remaining cheez and bake at 350° for 25 minutes.
Variation: Use pumpkin instead of squash.

SQUASH BAKE

8 c.	Yellow squash, sliced
½ c.	Onion, chopped
¾ c.	Carrots, shredded

1 T.	Corn oil
1 ½ c.	Cream of UnChicken Soup
½ c.	Tofu Sour Cream
2 c.	Herb-flavored croutons

Cook the squash in lightly salted boiling water for 3 to 4 minutes, or until crisp-tender. Drain well. Sauté the onion and carrots in the oil until tender. Combine the onions, carrots, soup, "sour cream," and 1 ½ cups of the croutons. Add the squash and mix lightly. Put into a nonstick casserole. Sprinkle with the remaining croutons. Bake, uncovered, at 350° for 25 minutes or until heated through.

SQUASH CASSEROLE WITH TOMATOES, CHEEZ, AND RICE

¼ c.	Onions, chopped
1 T.	Non-dairy margarine
2 c.	Squash, sliced
2 c.	Tomatoes, chopped
⅛ tsp.	Cayenne pepper
1 ½ c.	Yeast or Pimento Cheez
½ tsp.	Sea salt
2 ½ c.	Cooked rice

Sauté the onions in the margarine. Combine all the ingredients and stir until nicely blended. Place the mixture in a nonstick casserole and bake at 350° for 45 minutes.

SQUASH CREOLE

You can rely on this!

2 ½ c.	Squash, sliced
2 tsp.	Corn oil
¼ c.	Bell pepper, chopped
⅓ c.	Onions, chopped
1 tsp.	Garlic, minced
3 T.	Unbleached white flour
1 c.	UnBeef Broth
2 c.	Canned tomatoes, chopped
1 T.	Barbados molasses
¼ tsp.	Cayenne pepper
1 tsp.	Sea salt
½	Bay leaf
¾ c.	Yeast, Pimento, or Notzarella Cheez
1 ½ c.	Dry bread crumbs

Steam the sliced squash until tender and put in a nonstick baking dish. Heat the oil; add bell pepper, onions, and garlic and sauté. Add flour and stir until blended. Add broth, tomatoes, molasses, and spices to this mixture. Cook these ingredients for 5 minutes, or until the peppers are tender. Pour this sauce over the squash. Cover with the cheez and top with the crumbs, pressing in lightly. Bake at 350° for 30 minutes or until crumbs are well browned.

SQUASH TAMALE BAKE

So easy and so good!

½ c.	Bell pepper, chopped
1 tsp.	Garlic, minced
⅓ c.	Onions, chopped
2 tsp.	Corn oil
⅔ c.	Corn meal
3 c.	Canned tomatoes
2 c.	Squash, cubed
¼ tsp.	Cayenne pepper
½ tsp.	Sea salt
2 c.	Water

Sauté the bell pepper, garlic, and onions in the oil. Place all the ingredients together in a saucepan and stir until the squash has released its juice well, and the corn meal has thickened. After partly cooking, turn out into a nonstick baking dish. Bake at 350° for about 1 hour.

TAMALE PIE

8 T.	Jalapeños, chopped
1 tsp.	Cayenne
1 ¾ c.	Cooked kidney beans, drained
3 c.	Onions, sliced thin and separated into rings
1 ½ tsp.	Garlic, minced
1 c.	Mushrooms, chopped
1 c.	Corn
2 c.	Yeast Cheez
2 c.	Cashew or Tofu Sour Cream
2 c.	Water
1 c.	Masa harina
2	N'eggs

Combine the jalapeños, cayenne, beans, onions, garlic, mushrooms, corn, cheez, and "sour cream," and put into a casserole. Bring the water to a boil and gradually add the masa while stirring constantly. Reduce the heat and cook until it thickens–about 10 minutes. Take from the heat and stir in the n'eggs. Spread this over the casserole and bake at 375° for 35 minutes.

TOMATO AND CORN SCALLOP

| 1 c. | Yeast or Pimento Cheez |
| 1 ½ c. | Corn |

¾ c.   Dry bread crumbs
        Sliced tomatoes–enough to make
        two layers in the casserole

Combine the cheez, corn, and ½ cup of the crumbs. In a nonstick casserole place half the corn mixture and cover with tomato slices. Repeat. Sprinkle the crumbs over the top and press in lightly. Bake at 350° for 30 minutes.

TOMATO EGGPLANT BAKE

As delicious as it is simple!

3 c.   Eggplant, cubed
1 c.   Onions, chopped
½ c.   Bell pepper, chopped fine
1 tsp.   Garlic, minced
2 tsp.   Olive oil
2 c.   Stewed Italian tomatoes
⅛ tsp.   Cayenne pepper
¼ tsp.   Sea salt

Deep-fry the eggplant until it begins to brown and transfer it to paper towels to drain. Sauté the onions, bell pepper, and garlic in the olive oil. When the onions are soft, add the tomatoes, pepper, and salt and cook for 15 minutes. Mix in the eggplant. Transfer to a nonstick casserole and bake at 350° for 20 minutes.

TOMATO RICE WITH CHEEZ

2 T.   Bell pepper, chopped well
3 T.   Onions, chopped
1 tsp.   Non-dairy margarine
1 ½ c.   Rice, cooked in UnBeef Broth
1 c.   Tomatoes, chopped
½ tsp.   Barbados molasses
½ tsp.   Sea salt
¼ tsp.   Paprika
1 c.   Yeast or Pimento Cheez
¼ c.   Dry bread crumbs

Sauté the bell pepper and onions in the margarine. Mix everything together–except the crumbs–and put in a nonstick casserole dish. Cover with the crumbs. Dot with 1 tablespoon of margarine. Bake at 350° for about 40 minutes.

TRIPLE LAYER CASSEROLE

A pot-luck staple!

3 c.   UnBeef or UnChicken, ground, or
         Baked Cubed UnSteak
2 T.   Corn oil
2 c.   Onions, chopped

2 tsp.   Garlic, minced
1 ½ tsp. Jalapeños, minced
3 c.   Potatoes, peeled, sliced, and boiled
¾ c.   Cashew Milk
Pinch   Black pepper
5 c.   Cream-style corn
1 c.   Cheez Cracker crumbs

Brown the gluten in half the oil. Set aside. Sauté the onions, garlic, and jalapeños in the remaining oil. When the onions are soft, add the gluten and cook for 5 more minutes. Put the gluten on the bottom of a nonstick casserole. On top of that put the cooked potatoes. Stir the "milk" and pepper into the corn and pour that over the potatoes. Sprinkle the cracker crumbs on top. Bake at 375° until the crumbs start to brown.

UNBACON AND CHEEZ POTATOES

8 c.   Potatoes, peeled, cooked, and
         cubed
½ c.   Onion, chopped fine
2 c.   Yeast, Pimento, or Notzarella
         Cheez
1 c.   Miraculous Whip
1 c.   UnBacon, chopped fine
¾ c.   Black olives, sliced

Combine the potatoes, onion, cheez, and Miraculous Whip. Put in a casserole. Sprinkle with the gluten and olives. Cover and bake at 350° for 30 minutes or until heated through.

UNHAM AND BROCCOLI CASSEROLE

¾ c.   UnHam, cubed
¾ c.   Yeast, Pimento, or Notzarella
         Cheez
1 ¾ c.   Cooked broccoli, drained and
         chopped
1 ¾ c.   Cream of Mushroom Soup
¾ c.   Biscuit Mix
⅓ c.   Cashew Milk
1 tsp.   Non-dairy margarine, melted
1   N'egg

Combine the gluten, cheez, broccoli, and soup in a nonstick casserole. Stir the rest of the ingredients together until a dough forms. Drop by spoonfuls evenly over the broccoli mixture. Bake, uncovered, at 350° for 40 to 45 minutes, or until the top is golden brown.
Variation: Use another type of gluten.

UNHAM AND POTATO CASSEROLE

Fundamentally good!

2 c.	Onions, chopped
1 T.	Garlic, minced
½ tsp.	Hot pepper flakes
1 T.	Non-dairy margarine
2 T.	Unbleached white flour
4 c.	UnPork Broth made with Cashew Milk
3 c.	UnHam, sliced and broiled on both sides
2 c.	Pimento Cheez
6 c.	Potatoes, sliced ¼-inch thick and boiled

Sauté the onions, garlic, and pepper flakes in the margarine. Add the flour and stir in well. Slowly add the broth and let it simmer for 15 minutes. Put a thin layer of this broth in a nonstick casserole pan, a layer of gluten, a layer of cheez, and a layer of potatoes. Repeat the layering once more. Put any remaining broth over the top to cover the potatoes. Bake at 400° for 30 minutes. Just before serving, broil for a few minutes to lightly brown the top.

UNHAM AND POTATOES AU GRATIN

2 c.	Potatoes, peeled, sliced, and cooked
1 c.	UnHam, diced
1 T.	Onion, minced
⅓ c.	Non-dairy margarine
3 T.	Unbleached white flour
1 ½ c.	Cashew Milk
1 c.	Yeast, Pimento, or Notzarella Cheez
¾ tsp.	Sea salt
Dash	White pepper

Combine the potatoes, gluten, and onion in an oiled or nonstick casserole and set aside. In a saucepan melt the margarine and stir in the flour until smooth. Gradually add the "milk," stirring constantly until it thickens and bubbles. Add the cheez, salt, and pepper. Stir until well combined and heated through. Pour over the mixture in the casserole and stir gently to mix. Bake at 350° for 35 to 40 minutes or until bubbly.

VEGETABLE CASSEROLE WITH TOMATOES AND RICE

½ c.	Bell pepper, chopped
¼ c.	Onions, chopped
1 tsp.	Garlic, minced
2 ½ tsp.	Corn oil
4 c.	Vegetables, cut in pieces and cooked
3 c.	Canned tomatoes, drained and chopped
1 T.	Parsley, chopped
¼ tsp.	Basil
2 ½ c.	Cooked rice
1 tsp.	Sea salt
1 c.	Yeast or Pimento Cheez

Sauté the bell pepper, onions, and garlic in the oil. Combine all ingredients in a nonstick casserole. Top with the cheez and bake for 20 minutes at 400°.

VEGETABLE CRUMBLE

Crumble:

2 T.	Non-dairy margarine
2 c.	Unbleached white flour
1 c.	Yeast, Pimento, or Notzarella Cheez

Rub the margarine into the flour until the mixture resembles fine crumbs. Add the cheez.

Base:

⅓ c.	Onions, chopped
½ tsp.	Garlic, minced
1 ½ tsp.	Non-dairy margarine
3 c.	Mixed vegetables, chopped if need be
¼ c.	Unbleached white flour
1 ½ c.	Tomatoes, chopped
1 c.	UnBeef Broth
½ c.	Cashew milk
3 T.	Parsley, chopped
½ tsp.	Sea salt
¼ tsp.	Paprika

Sauté the onions and garlic in the margarine until the onions are transparent. Add the vegetables and cook over gentle heat, stirring occasionally, for 10 minutes. Stir in the flour, then add the rest of the ingredients. Bring to a boil, reduce the heat, cover, and simmer about 15 minutes, or until the vegetables are just tender. Put in a nonstick casserole. Press the crumble topping over the vegetables. Bake at 375° about 30 minutes, or until golden brown.

VEGETABLE ENCHILADAS

1 ¼ c.	Potatoes, peeled and diced or cut into strips
¼ c.	Olive or corn oil

1 ½ c.	Onion, chopped fine
1 T.	Garlic, minced
1 c.	Zucchini, chopped
4 ⅔ c.	Mushrooms, sliced
4 c.	Canned tomatoes, drained and chopped
1 T.	Jalapeño, sliced
1 ¼ tsp.	Cumin, ground
1 tsp.	Sea salt
12	Corn tortillas, steamed until soft
1 c.	Salsa

Boil the potatoes in just enough water to cover until just tender–15 to 20 minutes. Drain and set aside. Heat the oil in a skillet and sauté the onion until it begins to soften. Add the garlic, zucchini, mushrooms, tomatoes, and jalapeño, and sauté until tender. Stir in the cumin and potato, and sauté several minutes. Add the salt. Coat one side of each tortilla with salsa, spread some of the filling down the center and roll up quickly, then put in an oiled or nonstick baking pan. When all are in the pan, blend the rest of the filling and the rest of the salsa together and spread over the top. Bake at 350° for 15 minutes.

VEGETABLE POT PIE

What can I say but…Yum!

1 ½ tsp.	Corn oil
1 c.	Onion, diced
1 c.	Celery, sliced thin
⅔ c.	Carrots, sliced thin
1 c.	Bell pepper, diced
⅔ c.	Frozen green beans
⅓ c.	Frozen peas
⅓ c.	Unbleached white flour
1 c.	Cashew Milk
2 c.	Flavoring Broth of choice
2 T.	Parsley, minced
1 tsp.	Sea salt
¼ tsp.	Sage
½ tsp.	Thyme
¼ tsp.	Black pepper
¼ tsp.	Cayenne
	Convent Pie Crust

Combine everything but the crust and cook, stirring often, until thickened. Put into a nonstick casserole. Lay the crust over the top of the mixture. Bake at 400° for 20 to 30 minutes, or until the crust is golden and the filling is bubbling.

VEGETABLES AND CHEEZ CASSEROLE

1 ½ c.	Tomato sauce
1 ½ c.	Yeast, Pimento, or Notzarella Cheez
4 c.	Vegetables, cut up and steamed
1 tsp.	Sea salt
⅓ tsp.	Cayenne

Combine the tomato sauce and cheez well. Combine everything, put into a casserole, and bake at 400° for 15 to 20 minutes. Serve with rice or pasta.

VEGETABLES PARMESAN–1

Excellent at all times!

⅓ c.	Onions, chopped
1 tsp.	Garlic, minced
3 c.	Vegetables, in ½-inch slices
4 tsp.	Corn oil
2 c.	Canned tomato sauce
1 ½ c.	Yeast or Pimento Cheez
½ c.	Parmesan Cheez

Sauté the onions, garlic, and vegetables in the oil. Oil a casserole dish. In the dish, pour ¼-inch of the tomato sauce. Over that put a layer of vegetables. Over that put a layer of cheezes. Repeat, ending with a layer *each* of tomato sauce, vegetables, and cheezes. Cover with foil and bake at 400° for 30 minutes. Remove foil and bake uncovered for 10 minutes. Watch closely to avoid over-cooking.

VEGETABLES PARMESAN–2

Fancier than Number 1, but worth all the making!

2 c.	Potatoes, cut into pieces
1 T.	Corn oil
2 c.	Vegetables, cut into pieces if needed
1 T.	Non-dairy margarine
⅓ c.	Onions, chopped
1 tsp.	Garlic, minced
1 c.	Tomatoes, chopped
2 T.	Unbleached white flour
½ c.	Cashew Milk
½ tsp.	Sage
½ tsp.	Basil
½ tsp.	Oregano
½ tsp.	Sea salt
¼ tsp.	Paprika
1 c.	Parmesan Cheez

1 c.   Bread crumbs

Boil the potatoes for about 10 minutes, or until just tender. Drain, keeping back 1 cup of liquid. Heat the oil and sauté the vegetables until they are tender. Melt the margarine and sauté the onions and garlic until the onions are transparent. Add tomatoes to onions, stir in the flour, and cook 1 minute. Add the potato liquid, "milk," herbs, and seasonings to this. Bring to a boil, reduce heat, and simmer 15 to 20 minutes. Put the potatoes and vegetables in a nonstick casserole. Pour the tomato sauce over that. Sprinkle the "parmesan" and then the bread crumbs over all, pressing in lightly. Put in the oven at 400° about 20 minutes, or until heated through.

Variation: Instead of using 2 cups of potatoes plus 2 cups of vegetables, use 4 cups of vegetables, including or excluding potatoes as one of the vegetables.

ZUCCHINI CASSEROLE–1

6 c.	Zucchini, sliced
2 c.	UnBeef, chopped or cubed
½ c.	Onions, chopped
1 tsp.	Garlic, minced
1 T.	Corn oil
1 c.	Rice, cooked
1 tsp.	Garlic salt
1 tsp.	Oregano
2 c.	Tofu Cottage Cheez
2 c.	White Sauce to which 3 T. soy sauce has been added
1 c.	Pimento or Yeast Cheez

Cook the sliced zucchini in salted water for 2 to 3 minutes and drain well. Place half the zucchini in a nonstick casserole. Sauté the gluten, onions, and garlic in the oil until the onions are transparent. Pour over the zucchini in the baking dish. Sprinkle the cooked rice and seasonings over the gluten layer. Spoon the cottage cheez over the rice layer, and cover with the remaining zucchini. Spread white sauce over all. Spread the cheez over that. Bake at 300° for 35 to 40 minutes.

ZUCCHINI CASSEROLE–2

½ c.	Onions, chopped
¾ tsp.	Garlic, minced
5 T.	Jalapeños, chopped
1 T.	Corn oil or non-dairy margarine
1 c.	Zucchini, chopped
½ c.	Tomato, chopped
1 tsp.	Fresh basil, chopped
⅓ c.	Green peas
2 c.	Yeast Cheez
¼ c.	Fine bread crumbs

Sauté the onions, garlic, and jalapeños in the oil until the onion is soft. Combine everything but the cheez and crumbs in a casserole and mix well. Spread the cheez over all and top with the crumbs, pressing them in lightly. Bake at 375° for 30 minutes.

ZUCCHINI CASSEROLE WITH TOMATOES, CHEEZ, AND RICE

1 c.	Mushrooms, sliced
½ c.	Onions, chopped
1 tsp.	Garlic, crushed
2 c.	Zucchini, unpeeled, thinly sliced
4 tsp.	Non-dairy margarine
1 ½ c.	Tomatoes, chopped
½ c.	Tofu Sour Cream or Cashew Sour Cream
1 c.	Yeast or Pimento Cheez
¼ tsp.	Sea salt
⅛ tsp.	Cayenne pepper
3 c.	Cooked rice

Sauté the mushrooms, onions, garlic, and zucchini in the margarine until the zucchini is soft. Place in a large bowl and add the tomatoes. Beat together the "sour cream," cheez, salt, and pepper. Combine all the ingredients and stir until nicely blended. Place the mixture in a casserole and bake at 350° for 45 minutes.

Variation: Cook the rice in UnBeef or UnChicken Broth.

ZUCCHINI CREOLE

Always welcome!

3 T.	Non-dairy margarine
3 T.	Unbleached white flour
1 ½ c.	Tomatoes, chopped
¼ c.	Bell pepper, chopped
¼ c.	Onions, chopped
½ tsp.	Sea salt
½ tsp.	Sucanat
½	Bay leaf
Pinch	Powdered cloves
2 ½ c.	Zucchini, sliced but not peeled, and steamed
1 c.	Bread crumbs
¾ c.	Yeast Cheez

Melt the margarine and stir in the flour until blended. Add the tomatoes, bell pepper, onion, and spices and cook for 5 minutes (if larger quantities are used, cook until the onion and pepper are tender). Place zucchini in a nonstick baking dish and pour the tomato mixture over it. Cover with cheez. Top with bread crumbs and dot with margarine. Bake at 350° until the crumbs turn light brown.

ZUCCHINI PARMIGIANA

4 ½ c.	Tomatoes, chopped
½ c.	Onion, minced
¼ c.	Parsley, minced
1 tsp.	Basil
2 ½ tsp.	Olive oil
½ tsp.	Sea salt
¼ tsp.	Cayenne pepper
5 c.	Zucchini, sliced lengthwise into ¼-inch-thick slices
	Unbleached white flour
5	All-purpose N'eggs
2 ½ c.	Notzarella Cheez

Cook the tomatoes over medium heat for 15 to 25 minutes–until they are falling apart. Put them through a food mill (medium disk) into a bowl. Cook the onion, parsley, and basil in the oil over medium heat, stirring occasionally, for 15 minutes. Add the tomatoes, salt, and pepper, and simmer, stirring occasionally, for 20 to 30 minutes–until it is thickened slightly. Put the flour and n'eggs in two separate bowls. Dip the zucchini slices in the n'eggs, letting any excess drip off, and then dip them in the flour, shaking off any excess. Deep-fry the zucchini at 380°, turning, for 2 minutes–until they are golden. When done, transfer them to paper towels to drain. Spread a thin layer of the tomato sauce in a nonstick casserole. Over that put half of the zucchini in a layer. Over the zucchini pour half of the remaining tomato sauce. Over that spread a layer of half of the cheez. Repeat this layering once more. Bake at 350° for 20 to 30 minutes. Put under a broiler, about 6 inches from the heat, for 2 to 4 minutes–until the top is slightly browned.

Dried Beans and Lentils

SEVERAL YEARS after the beginning of our Monastery—which was always vegetarian—we all began feeling low in energy and out of phase in general. I knew the problem was dietary, but not exactly what was wrong, and I began to wonder if we would have to modify our diet—a distasteful thought on all levels. Then it happened that a friend brought me a book on life in Medieval English monasteries. Most significant to me was the section on monastic diet. Research had revealed that in all monasteries the monks ate cooked dried beans at every meal without exception. The usual menu was: vegetable soup, bean soup, and bread.

Looking in books on nutrition I found that dried beans contained virtually all the needed amino acids. So we began eating beans every day and in less than a week we were out of the slump.

I urge you to consider making beans a frequent—if not daily—item in your diet. This seems essential for vegans.

But what about beans and gas? With the dawning of our bean era there did arise this question! The solution was found in the wonderfully wise and humorous *Carla Emery's Old Fashioned Recipe Book*. There was a whole section on beans. Carla Emery was what the English delicately called "a martyr to wind," and eating beans turned her into a holocaust! She tried all the recommended remedies, none of which worked. (I knew they wouldn't, for I had tried them all myself by the time I read her book.) Then some blessed and intelligent soul explained to her that when beans dry their nutrients become locked in something fierce. And only long cooking (or sufficient pressure-cooking)

will unlock them. Otherwise they will be indigestible and the result will be evident to all. Since most people undercook beans they assume that it is just the nature of beans to produce internal cataclysms. Not true. So forget the BEANO—just cook the beans thoroughly. They will take care of themselves.

To unlock the nutrients of beans it is best to pressure-cook them thoroughly. This applies to all dried beans, including lentils (whose "skins" will *not* clog the pressure cooker vent if enough water is used—as in the following instructions), soy beans, and whole dried peas. Cooking dried beans by boiling them the time required to fully release the nutrients is a tremendous waste of fuel-energy. Even cooking them for twelve to fourteen hours in a crock pot has not always proven to be sufficient, whereas pressure-cooking has proven completely effective.

Do not soak dried beans overnight before cooking as they will tend to ferment, especially in warm weather.

To cook beans/lentils in a pressure cooker use the following procedure.

1) Put the beans in the pressure cooker along with salt (1 tsp. per quart of dried beans) and enough water to cover the beans with water at least 2 inches deep.

2) Add 1 tablespoon of corn oil (this is so the skins will not clog the pressure cooker vent).

3) Cover—WITHOUT the weight—and bring them to the boil.

4) Continue to boil for 5 minutes.

5) Turn off the heat and let them rest for 1 hour.

6) Turn on the heat, put on the weight, and cook at 15 pounds of pressure.

Here is a list of times (minutes) recommended for pressure-cooking dried beans:

> Black–35
> Black-eyed peas-20
> Garbanzos-25
> Great Northern (White)-25
> Kidney–20
> Lentils–5
> Lima–25
> Navy–25
> Peas, whole–25
> Pinto–25
> Soy–45

Dal and split peas are cooked in water on the stove rather than pressure-cooked, as they foam up and tend to clog the cooker vent.

The amount that dried beans yield when cooked varies. Here is a listing of how much ONE CUP of dried beans will yield according to type.

> Black–2 cups
> Black-eyed peas-2 cups
> Garbanzos-2 ½ cups
> Great Northern (White)-2 ½ cups
> Kidney–2 ½ cups
> Lentils–2 cups
> Lima–2 ½ cups
> Navy–2 ½ cups
> Peas, whole–2 cups
> Pinto–2 ½ cups
> Soy–2 ½ cups

BAKED BEANS–1

5 c.	Cooked dried beans
3 T.	Onions, minced
1 tsp.	Garlic, minced
2 tsp.	Corn oil
⅛ tsp.	Cayenne pepper
¾ c.	Barbados molasses
2 c.	Canned tomato sauce
½ c.	UnBeef Broth
½ tsp.	Savory
½ tsp.	Sea salt

Pressure-cook and drain the beans. Sauté the onions and garlic in the oil. Combine all ingredients and simmer for 10 minutes, uncovered. Place in baking dish, cover with Yeast or Pimento Cheez. Bake at 400° 15 to 20 minutes.

BAKED BEANS–2

5 c.	Cooked dried beans
¾ c.	Onions, chopped
2 tsp.	Corn oil
¼ c.	UnBacon, minced
½ c.	Sucanat
¼ c. & 2 T.	Barbados molasses
1 T.	Dry mustard
1 tsp.	Salt
2 c.	Canned tomato sauce

Pressure-cook the beans and drain them. Sauté the onions in the oil. Combine everything in a covered casserole dish and bake, covered, at 350° for *at least* 90 minutes–the longer the better. *Variation:* Cut some Loma Linda Big Franks into pieces, and sauté with the onions.

BAKED BEANS BOSTON STYLE

2 ½ c.	Dried navy or kidney beans, soaked 5 hours
⅓ c.	Barbados molasses
¼ c.	Sucanat
1 T.	Dry mustard
¼ tsp.	Cayenne
2 tsp.	Soy sauce
½ c.	UnBacon, minced
1 T.	Corn oil
2 c.	Onions, coarsely chopped
2 ½ tsp.	Garlic, minced
2	Bay leaves
1 tsp.	Sea salt
¼ tsp.	Black pepper

Drain the beans, cover with fresh water, and bring to a boil for 5 minutes. Drain again. Whisk together the molasses, Sucanat, mustard, cayenne, and soy sauce in a bowl. Mix this with the beans. Add the rest of the ingredients. Put into a casserole and add enough water to cover the beans. Cover and bake at 300° 7 to 8 hours, or until the beans are very soft. Check periodically and add more water, if needed, to keep the beans from drying out. Uncover the last half hour of baking so a crust can form.

BAKED LENTILS

3 c.	Dried lentils
⅓ c.	Onions, chopped
½ tsp.	Garlic, minced
2 tsp.	Corn oil
2 tsp.	Sea salt
2 c.	Tomatoes, blended until smooth

½ c.   Bread crumbs tossed in melted
       non-dairy margarine

Pressure-cook the lentils. Sauté the onions and
garlic in the oil. Combine all the ingredients
except the bread crumbs and place in a baking
dish. Top with the crumbs. Bake at 350° until
the crumbs are golden brown.

BARBECUE BAKED BEANS

½ c.   Bell peppers, chopped
½ c.   Onions, chopped
2 tsp.   Garlic, minced
1 T.   Corn oil
4 c.   Cooked dried beans
½ tsp.   Cayenne pepper
3 c.   Tomato Sauce (one of the recipes
         from Gravies and Sauces)
¼ c.   Barbados molasses
¼ c.   Wine vinegar
1 T.   Sovex or Vegex (dissolve in the
         vinegar)
1 tsp.   Sea salt
         Yeast or Pimento Cheez

Sauté the bell pepper, onions, and garlic in the
corn oil. Combine all ingredients. Pour into a
large oiled casserole. Add more tomato sauce if
it is needed to cover the beans. Bake 30 minutes
at 400°, then cover with Yeast or Pimento Cheez
and bake 10 more minutes.

BARBECUE BEANS

Soybeans work well in this.

2 ¼ c.   Onions, chopped
2 tsp.   Garlic, minced
1 T.   Corn oil
1 c.   Tomato paste
3 c.   Water
½ c.   Sucanat
1 T.   Barbados molasses
2 T.   Soy sauce
½ tsp.   Allspice
1 tsp.   Sea salt
1 ½ tsp. Red pepper flakes
¼ c.   Vinegar or ½ c. lemon juice
4 c.   Beans, cooked and drained

Sauté the onions and garlic in the oil. Add the
tomato paste and stir in well. Add the rest of the
ingredients—except the beans—bring to a boil, and
simmer for 15 minutes. Stir in the beans and cook
for 15 to 20 more minutes.

BEAN AND POTATO LOAF

4 c.   Cooked beans, without salt
2 c.   Hot mashed potatoes, cooked
         without salt
1 T.   Non-dairy margarine, melted
1 ¾ c.   Tomato juice
2 T.   Tomato sauce
½ c.   Onions, minced
1 tsp.   Garlic
¼ tsp.   Cayenne
¼ tsp.   Black pepper
2 tsp.   Sea salt
2 T.   Bell pepper, chopped
2   N'eggs

Purée or mash the beans. Add rest of ingredients
and mix lightly. Pour into an oiled or nonstick
baking dish and bake slowly for 1 hour.

BEAN ENCHILADAS

8   6-inch corn tortillas made
         according to the recipe given in the
         Breads and Such section

Topping:

2 c.   Pimento or Yeast Cheez
½ c.   Onions, chopped
½ c.   Black olives, chopped

Sauce:

1 c.   Onions, chopped
1 ½ T.   Garlic, minced
2 tsp.   Corn oil
6 c.   Canned tomatoes, crushed
5 T.   Chili powder
1 ½ tsp. Sea salt
1 ½ tsp. Sucanat

Sauté the onions and garlic in the oil until the
onions are soft, then add the rest of the
ingredients and simmer for 45 minutes.

Filling:

4 c.   Cooked pinto beans, drained
2 tsp.   Onion salt
¾ tsp.   Garlic powder
½ tsp.   Cumin, ground
⅔ c.   Canned tomato sauce

Partially mash the beans in a bowl. Mix the rest
of filling ingredients together and add to the
beans. Mix well.

Assembly:

Cover the bottom of a casserole with some of
the sauce. Put some of the filling in each tortilla,

roll it up, and put in the casserole with the seam side down. Cover with the rest of the sauce. Spread the cheez over all. Sprinkle the onions and olives over that. Bake, uncovered, at 350° for 25 minutes.

BEAN LOAF

2 ½ c.	Dried beans, cooked and mashed
1 tsp.	Sea salt
½ c.	Bell pepper, chopped well
½ c.	Tomato pulp
½ c.	Corn flakes
⅓ c.	Onions, chopped
½ tsp.	Paprika
1 tsp.	Soy sauce
2 tsp.	Corn oil

Combine all ingredients in an oiled loaf pan. Bake at 350° for about 1 hour. Serve with Yeast or Pimento Cheez or tomato sauce.

BEAN POT–1

5 c.	Cooked dry beans
¾ c.	Onions, chopped
2 tsp.	Non-dairy margarine
1 ½ tsp.	Sea salt
½ tsp.	Minced garlic
½ c.	Pimento
½ tsp.	Paprika

Sauté the onions in the melted margarine for 5 minutes. Combine all ingredients and cook for 20-30 minutes.

BEAN POT–2

¾ c.	Onions, chopped
2 ½ tsp.	Corn oil
2 tsp.	Jalapeños, minced
1 ½ tsp.	Garlic, minced
5 c.	Cooked dried beans
4 c.	Water, including bean cooking water
2 tsp.	Sea salt
1	Bay leaf
2 c.	Potatoes, diced
1 ½ c.	Carrots, diced
½ tsp.	Basil
¼ tsp.	Oregano
1 T.	Soy sauce

Sauté the onions in the oil until soft. Add the jalapeños and garlic and sauté 2 more minutes. Add everything else and cook for 30 minutes or until the potatoes are done, adding more water if it gets too thick.

BEANS AND TORTILLAS

Tortillas:

1 c.	Rye flour
2 c.	Unbleached white flour
⅔ c.	Soy flour
⅓ c.	Wheat bran
1 ¼ c.	Boiling water
1 tsp.	Sea salt
2 T.	Genuine maple syrup
¼ c.	Corn oil

Put the flours and bran into a bowl. Mix everything else together and stir into the flour, adding only enough extra water to make a stiff dough. Knead well and roll out small pieces of dough to paper-thin rounds about 8 inches in diameter. Bake these directly on top of an ungreased griddle or put on an ungreased baking sheet and bake at 250° until thoroughly dried and slightly brown.

Filling:

8 c.	Cooked dried beans
2 c.	Salsa
2 c.	Cashew or Tofu Sour Cream
1 ⅓ c.	Tomatoes, chopped
⅓ c.	Onions, chopped
2 c.	Yeast, Pimento, or Notzarella Cheez

Combine the filling ingredients. Put about 1 cup of filling along one edge of a tortilla and roll up.

BEANS BOURGIGNONNE

¾ c.	Onions, chopped
2 tsp.	Corn oil margarine
½ c.	Carrot, sliced in half-rounds
1 ¼ c.	Potato, cubed
1 c.	UnChicken Broth
3 T.	Italian tomato paste
⅛ tsp.	Thyme
1	Bay leaf
2 c.	Mushrooms, sliced
4 c.	Pinto beans, cooked
2	Garlic cloves, crushed
1 tsp.	Sea salt

In a soup pot, sauté the onion in 1 tablespoon of the margarine. Add the carrot and potato. Stir in the broth, tomato paste, thyme, and bay leaf. Bring to a boil and simmer briskly until the potatoes and carrots are cooked–about 20 minutes–adding extra broth to keep the vegetables covered if necessary. Toward the end of the cooking time, sauté the mushrooms in the other tablespoon of margarine over low heat, then add them to vegetables along with the beans, garlic, and salt. Return to a boil, lower the heat, and simmer, uncovered, for another 10 minutes. Remove and discard the bay leaf.

BEANS WITH TOMATOES

¾ c.	Onions, chopped
1 tsp.	Garlic, minced
2 tsp.	Corn oil
2 c.	Dried beans, cooked and drained, reserving the liquid
3 c.	Canned tomatoes, chopped
1 tsp.	Sea salt
Pinch	Cayenne pepper

Sauté the onions and garlic in the oil. Combine all ingredients and cook for one hour, adding bean water if it gets too dry.

BLACK BEANS WITH TOMATOES

2 c.	Dry black beans
2 c.	Tomatoes, canned
1 c.	Onions, chopped
1 c.	Celery, chopped
2 tsp.	Corn oil
½ tsp.	Garlic powder
2 tsp.	Sea salt
½ tsp.	Black pepper

Pressure-cook the beans. Blend the tomatoes in a blender. Sauté the onion and celery in the oil. Combine everything and cook 20 to 30 minutes.

BUCKAROO BEANS

I can't describe these—but I sure can eat them!

2 c.	Pinto beans, dry
½ c.	Onions, chopped
1 tsp.	Garlic, minced
½ c.	Bell pepper, chopped
2 tsp.	Corn oil
1	Bay leaf (whole)
½ c.	UnBacon, minced or chopped fine
2 c.	Tomatoes, canned
2 tsp.	Chili powder
½ tsp.	Dry mustard
¼ tsp.	Oregano
1 tsp.	Sea salt

Pressure-cook the beans. Sauté the onions, garlic,

and bell pepper in the oil. Combine everything and cook until well done. Add more water if necessary.

CAMPFIRE RED BEANS

These taste more like they were cooked over a smoky hickory campfire than if they really were.
Mexican Chorizo UnSausage is especially good in this dish.

4 c.	Dry kidney beans
2 c.	UnHam or UnSausage, cubed
1 T.	Corn oil
1 c.	Onion, chopped
1 T.	Garlic, chopped
1 tsp.	Liquid smoke
1 T.	Louisiana Hot Sauce
2 T.	Lea & Perrins Steak Sauce
2 T.	Parsley flakes (dried)
1 T.	Bell pepper flakes (dried)
3 c.	UnHam or UnSausage Broth
3 c.	Water

Pressure-cook the beans according to the directions given in the Dried Beans section. Sauté the gluten in the oil. Add the onions and garlic and sauté until the onions are soft. Put everything together and cook for 15 minutes.

CHILI BEANS–1

Good by themselves or with cheez and tortillas.

¾ c.	Onions, chopped
1 c.	Bell pepper, chopped
2 tsp.	Corn oil
4 c.	Cooked dried beans
1 tsp.	Minced garlic
2 ½ c.	Tomatoes
¼ tsp.	Cayenne pepper
1 tsp.	Sea salt

Sauté the onions and bell pepper in the oil. Combine all ingredients with sufficient water and simmer together slowly for 45 minutes.

CHILI BEANS–2

Good by themselves or with cheez and tortillas.

4 c.	Cooked dried pinto or kidney beans
1 ½ c.	Onions, chopped
1 tsp.	Garlic, minced
1 ½ tsp.	Corn oil
2 tsp.	Sea salt
2 T.	Chili powder
2 tsp.	Cumin

Pressure-cook the beans. Sauté the onions and garlic in the oil. Combine everything and cook 10 to 15 minutes, adding any needed water.

CHIMICHANGAS

Never fails!

5 c.	Refried Beans (the recipe is given later in this section)
1	Time the recipe for Flat Bread (see Bread and Such section), uncooked

Put ½ cup of beans on an uncooked "bread." Fold in the two sides and then the top and bottom. Deep-fry at 375° until light brown, being careful to prevent them from unfolding. If not served immediately, refry *quickly* to reheat and recrisp the chimichungas shortly before serving. Serve with Tofu Sour Cream, Cashew Sour Cream, or Miraculous Whip, or some other type of vegan "mayonnaise," chopped tomatoes, and chopped lettuce.
Variation: Use Flour Tortillas instead of Flat Bread.

COWBOY BEANS

These are addicting!

2 c.	Dried pinto or pink beans
2 tsp.	Sea salt
¾ tsp.	Crushed red pepper
½ c.	Onions, chopped
2 tsp.	Garlic, minced
⅔ c.	UnBacon, minced
1 ½ tsp.	Corn oil

Pressure-cook the beans with the salt. Drain. Cover with water. Add rest of ingredients and bring to a boil. Simmer for 30 minutes.

DRIED BEAN PATTIES

2 c.	Cooked dried beans of choice, mashed
½ c.	Tomatoes, chopped
¾ c.	Onions, chopped
½ c.	Bell peppers, chopped
⅛ tsp.	Cayenne pepper
2 c.	Bread crumbs
2 tsp.	Sea salt
1 T.	Soy sauce
½ tsp.	Sage

Combine ingredients. Shape into balls and flatten. Dip them in flour. Chill the patties for one hour or more. Fry them slowly until brown on both sides.

GARBANZO CREOLE

¾ c.	Onions, chopped
1 tsp.	Minced garlic
½ c.	Bell peppers, chopped
1 ½ tsp.	Corn oil
3 c.	Cooked garbanzos
Pinch	Cayenne pepper
2 c.	Canned tomatoes
½ tsp.	Sea salt
1	Bay leaf
½ c.	Tomato Sauce
½ c.	UnChicken Broth

Sauté the onions, garlic, and bell pepper in the oil. Combine everything and cook for 30 minutes.
Variation: Use another type of dried bean.

GARBANZOS BOMBAY
(Kabuli Channa)

4 c.	Dry garbanzos
4 c.	Onions, chopped
4 tsp.	Garlic, minced
2 T.	Jalapeños, minced
4 tsp.	Tumeric
2 T.	Coriander, powdered
¾ tsp.	Ginger, powdered
1 T.	Garam masala
4 ½ tsp.	Non-dairy margarine
6 c.	Tomatoes
¼ c.	Lemon juice
1 T.	Sea salt

Pressure-cook the garbanzos, keeping back the water in which they are cooked. Sauté the onions, garlic, jalapeños, tumeric, coriander, ginger, and garam masala in the margarine. Add the cooked garbanzos and stir well until coated with the hot oil. Add the tomatoes, lemon juice and salt, stirring well. Add 1 quart of the garbanzo water (adding some plain water if there is less than a quart). Cover and cook for about one hour. You may want to add some more (garbanzo) water if it seems to be getting too dry.

GARBANZOS

2 c.	Garbanzos, dry
2 tsp.	Sea salt
1 ½ c.	Onions, chopped
2 tsp.	Corn oil

1 tsp.	Powdered ginger root
½ tsp.	Ground cumin
1 tsp.	Tumeric
1 tsp.	Ground coriander
¼ tsp.	Garam masala
½ tsp.	Chili powder
⅛ tsp.	Cayenne pepper
3 c.	Canned tomatoes, crushed, with juice

Cook the garbanzos in 1 teaspoon of the salt and reserve the liquid. Sauté the onions in the oil until they are tender. Add the ginger and cumin, and sauté for 2-3 minutes more. Add the rest of the spices and stir to blend together. Combine everything, including the garbanzo liquid, and simmer for 30 minutes.

HERBED BEANS

¾ c.	Onions, chopped
1 ½ tsp.	Corn oil
2 c.	Dried beans, pressure-cooked
2 tsp.	Sea salt
¼ tsp.	Fines herbes
Pinch	Cayenne pepper

Sauté the onions in the oil. Combine everything and cook for 1 hour.

HUMMUS–1

1 ⅓ c.	Dry garbanzos
2 T.	Olive oil
1 T.	Sea salt
1 T.	Garlic, minced
¼ c.	Lemon juice
1 c.	Tahini
¼ tsp.	Cayenne pepper
	Water from cooking the garbanzos

Pressure-cook the garbanzos, drain, and mash them. Add the remaining ingredients except the garbanzo water. Using the garbanzo water, blend all in a blender until smooth and of the consistency of a medium-thick sauce.

HUMMUS–2

2 ¼ c.	Cooked and drained garbanzos
¼ c. & 2T.	Tahini
1 T.	Garlic, coarsely chopped
1 lb.	Tofu
½ c.	Lemon juice
1 ¼ tsp.	Sea salt
½ tsp.	Black pepper
¼ c. & 2T.	Seasame seeds

2 tsp.	Ground cumin
3 T.	Green onions, minced
2 T.	Green onion tops, minced

In a food processor combine the garbanzos, tahini, and garlic. Purée until smooth and thick. Add the tofu, lemon juice, salt, and pepper, and process until creamy. Toast the sesame seeds in a heavy skillet over medium heat until they begin to pop–about 3 minutes. Cook, stirring, until lightly toasted and fragrant–about 3 more minutes. Add ¼ of the seeds to the food processor and pulse briefly to incorporate. Set the rest aside. Put the cumin in the skillet and cook over medium heat, stirring, until fragrant–about 1 minute. Add, along with the onions, salt, and pepper to the food processor and pulse briefly to incorporate. Remove to a bowl and stir in the rest of the sesame seeds and onion tops.

KERALA DAL

Kerala is the state at the southernmost tip of India where Saint Thomas the Apostle established the Indian Orthodox Church in 54 A.D. I expect he ate this very dish. If so, I hope he liked it as much as I do!

1 c.	Masur dal (the tiny orange kind that turns yellow when cooked)
3 c.	Water
½ tsp.	Sea salt
2 tsp.	Corn oil
1 T.	Black mustard seeds
½ tsp.	Cumin seeds
1 T.	Garlic, minced
1 tsp.	Tumeric
3 c.	Tomatoes, chopped
¼ tsp.	Hing (asafoetida), optional
¼ tsp.	Ground cumin
¼ tsp.	Cayenne pepper
½ tsp.	Sea salt

Cook the dal in the water and salt until it just begins to fall apart. Remove from heat and drain. Heat the oil in a very heavy, small pan. Add the mustard seeds, spreading them over the bottom of the pan evenly, and cook, stirring, until they turn black(er) and start to pop. Add the cumin and garlic and cook just one minute more. Stir in the tumeric and immediately remove pan from the heat. In a large saucepan, combine tomatoes, hing, cumin, cayenne pepper, salt, and the fried seed mixture. Bring to a boil and cook for 15 minutes. Add the dal and cook until it falls apart.

LENTIL LOAF

2 c.	Lentils, cooked
1 c.	Bread crumbs
½ c.	Squash, chopped
⅓ c.	Onions, chopped
2 T.	Corn oil
3 T.	Low sodium soy sauce
½ c.	Rice, cooked
1 tsp.	Sage
½ tsp.	Thyme
1 tsp.	Curry powder
⅔ c.	Water from cooking the lentils
1	Tomato, sliced
	Sesame seeds for garnish

Mix all ingredients together except for tomato and sesame seeds. Bake in a nonstick pan for 15 minutes at 375°. Remove loaf from oven and top with tomato slices and sesame seeds. Reduce heat to 350° and bake for another 15 minutes.

LENTIL PATTIES

These are really distinctive. Many who do not usually like lentils love these.

2 c.	Lentils cooked in UnBeef Broth, drained, and mashed
3 c.	Fine bread crumbs
¾ c.	Onions, minced
1 tsp.	Garlic, minced
1 tsp.	Sea salt
¼ c.	UnBeef Broth (can be that left over from cooking the lentils)
2 T.	Parsley, chopped

Mix the ingredients thoroughly and let sit for 15 minutes. Form into patties. Place on floured cookie sheet and bake at 350° for 20 to 30 minutes or until browned. Or dip the patties into flour and sauté in corn oil until brown. Good with Lentil Patty Sauce following.

LENTIL PATTY SAUCE

⅓ c.	Onions, chopped
1 tsp.	Corn oil
2 ½ c.	Cooked tomatoes
½ tsp.	Sea salt
3 T.	Cornstarch
3 T.	Water

Sauté the onions in the oil. Add to tomatoes and salt. Bring to a boil. Blend the cornstarch with the water and stir into the tomatoes. Bring to a boil again and remove from heat.

LENTIL POT

2 c.	Lentils
¾ c.	Onions, chopped
1 tsp.	Minced garlic
1 ½ tsp.	Wine vinegar
1 c.	Tomatoes
¾ c.	Bell pepper, chopped
1 ½ tsp.	Corn oil
1 ½ tsp.	Soy sauce
1	Bay leaf
½ tsp.	Sea salt

Pressure-cook the lentils. Add the rest of the ingredients–including sufficient water–and cook 30 more minutes.

MEXICAN BEAN POT

2 c.	Dried pinto beans
2 c.	UnSausage of choice (Mexican Chorizo is obvious)
1 ½ c.	Onions, chopped
1 tsp.	Minced garlic
¼ c.	Bell pepper
2 ½ tsp.	Corn oil
2 c.	Tomatoes, chopped
1 tsp.	Sea salt
1 tsp.	Oregano
½ tsp.	Ground cumin
½ tsp.	Black pepper

Pressure-cook the beans and retain the cooking water. Sauté the gluten, onions, garlic, and bell pepper in the oil. Combine everything and cook for 60 minutes, using the bean water and any extra water (or tomato juice) if it gets too dry.

MEXICAN GARBANZOS

¾ c.	Onions, chopped
1 tsp.	Minced garlic
1 ½ tsp.	Corn oil
4 c.	Garbanzos, pressure-cooked
½ c.	Bell pepper, chopped
1 T.	Barbados molasses
½ c.	Tomato paste
1 tsp.	Sea salt

Sauté the onions and garlic in the oil. Combine all ingredients and cook slowly for 30 to 60 minutes.

RED BEANS AND RICE

3 c.	UnSausage, sliced or cubed
2 T.	Corn oil

4 c.	Cooked kidney beans
1 c.	Corn
½ c.	Bell pepper, chopped
2 c.	Salsa

Sauté the gluten in the oil until browned. Add everything else and cook until the bell pepper is crisp-tender. Serve over rice.

RED BEANS WITH UNSAUSAGE

2 T.	Corn oil
4 c.	Onions, chopped
1 c.	Celery, chopped
1 c.	Bell pepper, chopped
1 T.	Garlic, minced
7 ½ c.	Cooked kidney beans
1 ½ c.	Ham Gluten, chopped
2	Bay leaves
½ tsp.	Thyme
2 c.	Italian UnSausage or Mexican Chorizo UnSausage, chopped and browned in some oil
1 ½ tsp.	White pepper
½ tsp.	Black pepper
½ tsp.	Cayenne pepper
4 c.	UnHam Broth

Sauté the onions, celery, and bell pepper until soft. Add the garlic and sauté 2 more minutes. Combine everything in a large pot and cook for 30 minutes.

REFRIED BEANS–1

Cannot be equaled much less surpassed by the canned stuff!

3 c.	Dried pinto beans
3 c.	Onions, chopped
4 tsp.	Garlic, minced
¼ c.	Jalapeños, chopped
2 T.	Corn oil
1 c.	Tomato paste
½ tsp.	Sea salt
	Bean water

Cook the beans and drain them, saving the water. Sauté the onions and jalapeños in the oil until the onions are transparent. While the onions are sautéing, put the beans through a food processor or mill and purée them, adding the tomato paste, salt, and enough bean water to get a smooth texture. Add the garlic to the onion and jalapeños and cook for 2 more minutes. Add the bean mixture and combine everything thoroughly. Continue cooking on high heat, stirring

frequently for 10 minutes. You may need to add more bean water if this gets too dry.

REFRIED BEANS–2

1 ½ c.	Onions, chopped
⅔ c.	Corn oil
¼ c.	Tomato paste
⅔ c.	UnBeef Broth
4 c.	Cooked kidney, pinto, or red beans, mashed
½ tsp.	Cayenne
½ tsp.	Sea salt

Sauté the onions in the oil. Combine the tomato paste and broth well. Mix everything together and cook for 10 minutes.

REFRIED BEANS–3

¾ c.	Onions, chopped
½ c.	Corn oil
1 ½ c.	Tomatoes, chopped
¼ tsp.	Ground sage
½ tsp.	Cayenne
¼ tsp.	Paprika
1 tsp.	Sea salt
5 c.	Cooked kidney, pinto, or red beans, mashed

Sauté the onions in ¼ cup of the oil until transparent. Add everything else but the beans and cook till well done, adding bean water if needed–but not too much. Fry the beans in a skillet with the rest of the oil, stirring frequently, adding more bean water if needed to keep the beans from getting too dry. Pour in the sauce and continue cooking and stirring until fairly dry again.

SIMPLE CASSOULET

½ c.	Onions, diced
1 c.	Carrots, diced
1 c.	Potatoes, diced
1 T.	Garlic, minced
1 T.	Olive oil
1 c.	UnChicken, UnHam, or UnSausage, cubed
¼ tsp.	Thyme
¼ tsp.	Basil
¼ tsp.	Marjoram
¼ tsp.	Rosemary
½ tsp.	White pepper
1 T.	Prepared mustard
½ tsp.	Sea salt

2 c.   White beans, cooked
2 c.   Water or broth of the type of gluten being used

Sauté the vegetables and garlic in the oil for about 5 minutes in a heavy ovenproof pot or casserole dish. Add the gluten, the seasonings, and the beans. Add enough of the water or broth to barely cover the mixture. Cover and bake at 350° for 45 minutes. Stir before serving.

SOUTHERN PINTO BEANS

This is what it's all about!

4 c.   Pinto beans, pressure-cooked and drained
1 ½ c.   Yeast or Pimento Cheez
2 c.   Corn
2 c.   Tomatoes, sliced (more, if needed for complete layer)
1 ½ tsp.   Sea salt
½ c.   Dry bread crumbs

In a casserole pan layer: beans, cheez, corn, cheez, tomatoes, salt, and bread crumbs. Bake at 350° for 30 minutes until heated through and brown on top.

SOY FRITTERS

4 c.   Soybeans, cooked and drained
1 ½ c.   Water from cooking the beans
2 c.   Unbleached white flour
1 ½ T.   Baking powder
1 tsp.   Sea salt
1 ½ tsp.   Garlic powder
1 ½ c.   Onions, chopped

Mash 3 cups of the soybeans. Combine everything to make a thick paste-batter. Drop into hot oil from a spoon and fry, turning them so they will brown all over. (Add more flour if the batter does not hold together in the frying.) Serve with a sauce such as Tartar Sauce, Tomato Sauce, Cheez Sauce, Tofu Sour Cream, or Cashew Sour Cream.
Variation: Use some other type of beans.

SOYTEENA

This is very much like some of the canned meat substitute commercially available, but I think it is better. It is very good fried—especially the next day.

1 c.   Dry soybeans
2 c.   Water
1 c.   Tomato juice
½ c.   Peanut butter
2 tsp.   Sea salt
⅓ c.   Celery, chopped fine
¼ c.   Nutritional Yeast
½ c.   Onions, chopped fine
4 T.   Soy sauce
½ tsp.   Garlic powder
1 c.   Cornmeal

Combine all the ingredients, except the cornmeal, and process them in a blender until smooth. Remove from the blender and mix in the cornmeal well. Pour into oiled Number 2 cans. Cover cans with metal foil and secure it with rubber bands. Steam for 2 hours or longer in a large kettle that is about ⅓ full of water when the cans are set in it. Keep the water simmering in the kettle with the lid on. When cooled, remove the cans.

SPECIAL GARBANZOS

¾ c.   Onions, chopped
2 tsp.   Garlic, minced
1 ½ tsp.   Corn oil
3 c.   Garbanzos, cooked
⅔ c.   Carrots or squash, sliced
1 c.   Bell peppers, chopped
1 tsp.   Sage, dried
2 T.   Parsley, chopped
½ tsp.   Louisiana Hot Sauce
1 ½ tsp.   Sea salt
¼ tsp.   Cayenne pepper

Sauté onion and garlic in the oil until soft. Combine everything and cook 10 minutes over low heat, stirring occasionally.
Variation: Use other types of beans.

SWEDISH BROWN BEANS

The only Swedish Brown Bean recipe I like—and love!

4 ⅔ c.   Pinto beans, DRY
¾ c.   Onions, chopped
½ tsp.   Garlic, sliced
1 T.   Corn oil
2 c.   UnBeef Broth
½ tsp.   Sea salt
¼ c.   UnBacon, chopped fine
¼ tsp.   Black or cayenne pepper
¼ c.   Barbados molasses
1 c.   Catsup or tomato sauce
1 tsp.   Louisiana Hot Sauce
½ c.   Wine vinegar
¼ tsp.   Dry mustard

Pressure-cook the beans and drain. Sauté the onions and garlic in the oil. Combine all ingredients and cook together for 30 minutes.

THREE-BEAN POT PIE

1 ½ c.	Onions, chopped
1 T.	Corn oil
1 tsp.	Garlic, minced
3 c.	Squash, sliced
½ c.	Bell pepper, chopped
1 c.	Italian tomatoes, chopped
1 c.	Garbanzos, cooked
1 c.	Kidney beans, cooked
1 c.	Pinto beans, cooked
¼ c.	Jalapeños, minced
1 c.	UnBeef Broth
1 tsp.	Cumin, ground
4 T.	Italian tomato paste
1 c.	Tomato sauce
2 T.	Nutritional Yeast
1 ¼ tsp.	Sea salt
½	Convent Pie Crust recipe, rolled out to fit over top of casserole dish

Sauté the onions in the oil until soft. Add garlic, squash, bell pepper, and tomatoes, and cook, stirring often, for 10 minutes, or until the squash is very soft. Remove from heat and add rest of ingredients. Pour into a nonstick casserole dish. Top with the crust and cut a few slits in it to let steam escape. Bake at 400° until the crust is golden brown.

TORTILLA AND TOSTADA FILLING–1

4 c.	Pressure-cooked dried beans, drained
2 c.	Salsa
2 c.	Cashew or Tofu Sour Cream
1 ⅓ c.	Tomatoes, chopped
⅓ c.	Onions, chopped
2 c.	Yeast or Pimento Cheez

Combine. Good rolled up in tortillas or spread on them. Add shredded lettuce if desired.

TORTILLA AND TOSTADA FILLING–2

⅓ c.	Onions, chopped
1 tsp.	Garlic, minced
1 ½ tsp.	Corn oil
1 tsp.	Sea salt
¼ tsp.	Cayenne pepper

1 c.	Tomatoes
4 c.	Cooked dried beans of choice, drained

Sauté the onions and garlic in the oil. Combine with the salt, pepper, and tomatoes and cook well. Blend with the beans.

TUSCAN WHITE BEAN CASSEROLE–1

1 c.	Dry white beans
½ c.	Onion, chopped
1 tsp.	Olive oil
2 c.	Tomatoes, chopped
3 T.	Tomato paste
½ tsp.	Sage (dried)
1	Bay leaf
3 T.	Parsley, chopped
½ tsp.	Sea salt
⅛ tsp.	Pepper

Pressure-cook the beans. Sauté the onion in the olive oil until transparent. Add the tomatoes, tomato paste, sage, bay leaf, salt, pepper, and parsley. Simmer for 15 minutes. Put the beans in a casserole. Stir in the tomato mixture. Cover and bake in a moderate oven for 20 to 25 minutes.

TUSCAN WHITE BEAN CASSEROLE–2

1 c.	UnHam, UnSausage, or UnBacon, cut into strips
1 c.	Onion, chopped
2 ½ tsp.	Garlic, minced
¼ tsp.	Black pepper
2 ½ tsp.	Olive oil
3 c.	Cooked white beans UnChicken Broth
1 c.	UnSausage–any flavor–sliced
4	Tomatoes, peeled, sliced, and soaked in olive oil and pepper
⅛ tsp.	Sage
⅛ tsp.	Black pepper Bread Crumb Topping (see Etc.)

Sauté the gluten strips with the onions, garlic, and pepper in the oil until the gluten is browned. Put all this into a saucepan with the cooked beans and enough broth to cover everything. Simmer for 20 minutes. Oil a nonstick casserole with garlic oil (plain olive oil if you have none). Put half of the beans in a layer in the casserole. Put the gluten slices on top of the beans. Put a layer of tomato slices and sage on top of the

UnSausages. Sprinkle with the pepper. Put the other half of the beans on top in a layer. Cover the beans with Bread Crumb Topping. Bake at 350° for 20 minutes in the upper half of the oven.

WHITE BEANS WITH TOMATOES–1

⅓ c.	Onions, chopped
1 ½ tsp.	Garlic, minced
1 ½ tsp.	Corn oil
3 c.	Cooked white beans
2 c.	Tomatoes
½ tsp.	Sea salt
⅛ tsp.	Cayenne pepper
1 T.	Wine vinegar

Sauté the onions and garlic in the oil. Stir in the rest of the ingredients. Cover and simmer over low heat for 10 minutes.

WHITE BEANS WITH TOMATOES–2

2 c.	Dry white beans
1 c.	Onions, chopped
1 tsp.	Garlic, minced
½ c.	Celery, chopped
¼ c.	Bell pepper, chopped
2 tsp.	Corn oil
2 tsp.	Sea salt
¼ tsp.	Basil, dried
¼ tsp.	Black or cayenne pepper
1 c.	Tomatoes, chopped
1 c.	Carrots, chopped or sliced

Pressure-cook the beans. Sauté the onions, garlic, celery, and bell pepper in the oil. Combine everything and cook together 20 to 30 minutes, adding any water as needed.

WHITE BEANS WITH UNBACON

2 c.	Dry white beans
1 c.	Onions, chopped
½ tsp.	Garlic, minced
1 ½ tsp.	Corn oil
½ tsp.	Sea salt
1 c.	UnBacon, chopped fine or ground
¼ tsp.	Black or cayenne pepper

Pressure-cook the beans. Sauté the onions and garlic in the oil. Combine everything and cook together 20 to 30 minutes, adding any water that might be needed.

Grains

BARLEY

Basic proportions for cooking barley are:

    1 c.   Barley
    2 c.   Water
    ¾ tsp.   Sea salt

Wash the barley well under cold running water while the cooking water is coming to a boil. Add the salt and the barley to the water and stir. Turn the flame down very low. Cover and cook for about 45 minutes–poor quality barley will cook faster than good quality.

BASIC RICE

Basic proportions for cooking Jasmine or Basmati rice are:

    1 c.   Rice
    1 ½ c.   Water
    1 tsp.   Sea salt

Wash the rice well under cold running water while the cooking water is coming to a boil. Add the salt and the rice to the water and stir. Turn the flame down very low. Cover and cook for about fifteen minutes.
This makes 2 ½ cups of cooked rice.

BROCCOLI RISOTTO

    ¾ tsp.   Garlic, sliced thin
    2 c.   Broccoli flowerets
    1 T.   Corn oil
    3 c.   UnChicken Broth, hot
    ¼ c.   Parsley, chopped
           Sea salt
           Black pepper
    ¼ c.   Onion, chopped
    ¾ c.   Uncooked rice
    1 tsp.   Lemon juice
    ¼ c.   Parmesan Cheez

Sauté the garlic and broccoli in 2 tsp. of the oil until the garlic is soft–about 3 minutes. Add ⅓ c. of broth, 3 T. of the parsley, and the salt and pepper. Simmer, uncovered, until the broccoli is just tender. Set aside. Sauté the onion in the rest of the oil until soft. Add the rice and stir until it is coated with the oil. Stir ⅔ c. of broth into the rice and cook, stirring constantly, until all the liquid is absorbed. Add the rest of the broth, ⅓ c. at a time, stirring constantly, allowing the liquid to absorb between additions. Cook, uncovered, until the rice is creamy and the grains are tender. Stir in the lemon juice and 3 T. of the cheez. Sprinkle with the rest of the parsley and cheez.

CHEEZ RICE

    1 c.   Rice that was cooked in UnBeef or UnChicken Broth
    ½ c.   Yeast or Pimento Cheez
    ¼ tsp.   Paprika

Cook the rice, and while it is still hot and in the pot, stir in the other ingredients.
Variation: Add 1 cup of tomato juice. Add ½ cup of Cashew or Tofu Sour Cream.

CRACKED WHEAT

Cracked wheat should not be confused with tabouli wheat which needs no cooking.

Basic proportions for cooking cracked wheat are:

1 ½ tsp.	Corn oil
1 c.	Cracked wheat
¾ tsp.	Sea salt
1 ½ c.	Boiling water

Heat the oil until it begins to smoke. Add the cracked wheat and stir rapidly and continuously to avoid burning and coat all the wheat with oil. Fry on high heat about 5 minutes until it starts to brown. Add the salt, then the wheat, to the boiling water and stir. Bring back to boil. Turn the flame down very low. Cover and cook for about fifteen minutes.

Variation: Use UnBeef or UnChicken Broth instead of water, and use only ⅓ teaspoon of salt.

CREOLE RICE

1 c.	Onions, chopped
2 tsp.	Garlic, minced
2 ½ tsp.	Corn oil
3 c.	Okra, sliced
¼ tsp.	Cayenne pepper
4 c.	Creole Sauce
½ tsp.	Sea salt
6 c.	Rice, cooked in UnChicken Broth

Sauté the onions and garlic in the corn oil. Combine with all other ingredients except the rice. Cook over medium heat for 20 minutes. Add the rice and cook for 10 minutes more, adding more Creole sauce if it becomes too dry.

DIRTY RICE

5 c.	UnBeef, UnPork, UnSausage, UnHam, or UnChicken–or a combination
1 T.	Olive oil
1 c.	Onion, chopped fine
1 c.	Green onions, chopped fine
½ c.	Bell pepper, chopped fine
½ c.	Parsley, chopped fine
½ c.	Celery, chopped fine
2 T.	Garlic, chopped fine
½ tsp.	Dry mint, crushed
½ tsp.	Cayenne pepper
1 tsp.	Louisiana Hot Sauce
4 ½ tsp.	Lea & Perrins Steak Sauce
1 c.	Flavoring Broth of the type of gluten used
3 c.	Cooked rice

Combine everything except the rice and cook together for 20 minutes, covered, stirring occasionally. Add the cooked rice and mix

thoroughly. Cook over low heat for another 20 minutes.

FLAVORED RICE

1 c.	Rice
1 ½ c.	Flavoring Broth of choice
½ tsp.	Sea salt

Wash the rice well under cold running water while the broth is coming to a boil. Add the salt and the rice to the water and stir. Turn the flame down very low. Cover and cook for about fifteen minutes.

FRIED RICE

3 c.	Rice, uncooked
1 T.	Non-dairy margarine
1 T.	Corn oil
4 ½ c.	UnBeef or UnChicken Broth
½ tsp.	Sea salt

Wash rice thoroughly and drain. Combine the margarine and oil in a skillet and melt the margarine. Add the washed rice and stir frequently until the rice becomes light brown– this takes quite a while, so don't give up. (Some of the rice kernels may even "pop" like popcorn.) If the rice becomes too dry add more margarine or oil to keep it shiny as it fries. Bring broth to a boil. Add the salt. Then add the rice–which must be coming directly from the skillet and be hot and frying–to the boiling water a little bit at a time, taking care because it will "explode." Cover the pot and turn the flame down. Simmer for 10 minutes.

GAZPACHO WITH COUSCOUS

6 oz.	Quick-cooking or instant couscous
¼ tsp.	Black pepper
¼ c.	Parsley
2 ⅔ c.	Canned tomatoes
¾ c.	Tomato juice
1 c.	Cucumber, peeled, seeded, and sliced
1 c.	Bell pepper (half red and half green, if possible), diced
½ c.	Onion, chopped
1 T.	Garlic, chopped
2 T.	Balsamic vinegar
1 T.	Jalapeño, seeded and diced
½ c.	Green onions, chopped

Cook the couscous and mix in the pepper and parsley. Set aside. Put everything else in a blender

or food processor and process just until coarse
and chunky in texture. Refrigerate until cold.
Mix in the couscous and serve.

GREEN RICE–1

1 c.	Rice that was cooked in UnChicken Broth
½ c.	Yeast or Pimento Cheez
½ c.	Parsley, finely chopped
1 c.	Tomato juice
Pinch	Cayenne pepper
⅓ c.	Onions, minced

Cook the rice, and while it is still hot and in the
pot, stir in the other ingredients.
Variation: Add Cashew or Tofu Sour Cream.

GREEN RICE–2

¾ c.	Mushrooms, sliced
¾ c.	Celery, chopped
¾ c.	Onions, chopped
½ tsp.	Garlic, minced
1 T.	Non-dairy margarine
2 c.	Broccoli, chopped and steamed
1 ½ c.	Rice, cooked

Sauté the mushrooms, celery, onions, and garlic
in the margarine until the onions and celery are
transparent. Carefully stir in the broccoli and rice
until all is heated through.

MILLET

Basic proportions for cooking millet are:

1 c.	Millet
1 ½ c.	Water
¾ tsp.	Sea salt

Wash the millet well under cold running water
while the cooking water is coming to a boil. Add
the salt and the millet to the water and stir. Turn
the flame down very low. Cover and cook for
about 30 minutes–poor quality millet will cook
faster than good quality.
Variation: Use UnBeef or UnChicken Broth
instead of water, and use only ⅓ teaspoon of salt.

OVEN–BAKED RICE WITH UNPORK AND GARBANZOS

2 tsp.	Olive oil
1 ½ c.	Tomatoes, peeled
1 T.	Garlic, minced
1 T.	Paprika
1 ½ c.	UnChicken Broth
1 ½ c.	UnPork Broth
1 ½ c.	Uncooked rice, washed well
1 ¼ c.	Cooked garbanzos, drained and rinsed
2 c.	UnPork, cut into ½-inch cubes and deep-fried
1 ¼ c.	Potatoes, peeled, sliced ¼-inch thick, and deep-fried

Heat the oil in a large skillet. Add the tomatoes
and garlic and sauté until the tomatoes release
their liquid and become "saucy." Stir in the
paprika and broths. Bring to a boil and add the
rice. Cook until the rice begins to soften. Add
the garbanzos and gluten. Transfer to a nonstick
casserole. Layer the potatoes on top, cover tightly
with foil, and bake at 400° for 30 minutes.

PILAF IMPERIAL

3 c.	Cracked wheat
4 ½ c.	UnBeef or UnChicken Broth, boiling
¼ c.	Soy sauce
1 tsp.	Paprika
1 ½ c.	Onions, chopped
1 tsp.	Minced garlic
1 ½ c.	Celery, chopped
1 ½ c.	Water chestnuts, sliced
⅓ c.	Bell pepper, chopped
2 T.	Non-dairy margarine

Combine the wheat, broth, soy sauce, and
paprika and bake in a covered casserole at 350°
for 45 minutes. Sauté the onions, garlic, celery,
chestnuts, and bell pepper in the margarine until
tender. Combine all and serve with Cashew or
Tofu Sour Cream.

RICE JAMBALAYA

½ c.	Bell pepper, chopped
¾ c.	Onions, chopped
1 tsp.	Minced garlic
1 c.	Squash or pumpkin, sliced
2 T.	Pimentos, chopped
1 c.	Tomatoes, cubed
1 T.	Corn oil
1 c.	Rice, uncooked
2 c.	UnChicken Broth
¼ tsp.	Cayenne pepper
1 tsp.	Sea salt

Sauté the vegetables in the oil until just tender.
Add rice, broth, pepper, and salt. Cook until rice
is tender.

RICE WITH PEAS

¼ c.	Onion, chopped fine
¾ tsp.	Garlic, minced
2 tsp.	Non-dairy margarine or corn oil
2 c. & 2 T.	UnChicken Broth
½ tsp.	Basil
1 c.	Rice
1 tsp.	Sea salt
½ tsp.	Black pepper
4 c.	Peas

Sauté the onion and garlic in the oil until soft. Combine everything but the peas. Cook, covered, for 5 minutes. Stir in the peas and cook until done–about 5 minutes more.

SIMPLE RISOTTO

⅓ c.	Onions, chopped
1 tsp.	Garlic, minced
¼ c.	Bell pepper, chopped
½ c.	Mushrooms or black olives, chopped
1 ½ tsp.	Non-dairy margarine
1 ½ tsp.	Corn oil
1 c.	Tomatoes, chopped
1 ⅓ c.	Rice that was cooked in UnChicken Broth
¼ tsp.	Sea salt
¼ tsp.	Paprika

Sauté the onions, garlic, bell pepper, and mushrooms (or olives) in the margarine and oil until the bell pepper is just tender. Add the tomatoes, rice, salt, and paprika. Continue stirring until the rice is heated through.

SPANISH RICE–1

½ c.	Bell peppers
¾ c.	Onions, chopped
1 T.	Garlic, minced
2 ½ tsp.	Corn oil
5 c.	Tomatoes, chopped
¼ tsp.	Cayenne pepper
1 tsp.	Sea salt
½ tsp.	Basil
Pinch	Dill weed, dried
1 ¼ c.	UnBeef Broth
3 ½ c.	Rice that was cooked in UnBeef Broth

Sauté the bell peppers, onions, and garlic in the corn oil. Combine with the rest of the ingredients except for the rice and cook for 20 to 30 minutes, until it gets thick. Add the cooked rice and cook for 5 more minutes.

Variation: Include 4 cups of eggplant, cubed, and sauté it along with the bell peppers and onions.

SPANISH RICE–2

1 c.	Onion, chopped
1 tsp.	Garlic, minced
2 T.	Jalapeños, minced
½ c.	Bell pepper, chopped small
2 tsp.	Olive oil
¾ c.	Tomato paste
2 c.	UnChicken Broth
2 T.	Unbleached white flour
¼ tsp.	Sea salt
3 c.	Rice that was cooked in UnChicken Broth
1 c.	Garbanzos, cooked

Sauté the onion, garlic, jalapeños, and bell pepper in the oil. Mix the tomato paste and the broth. Add the flour and salt to the sautéed vegetables. Add the tomato-broth mixture. Simmer gently until thickened, about 3-5 minutes. Add the rice and garbanzos. Bake in an oiled casserole 25 minutes at 350°.

Variation: Substitute other dried beans or dried green peas for the garbanzos.

SPANISH RICE–3

2 c.	UnBeef or Soy Grits UnBeef
1 ½ c.	Onions, chopped
½ tsp.	Garlic, minced
¼ c.	Bell pepper, chopped fine
1 T.	Corn oil
1 c.	Rice, cooked
4 ½ c.	Canned tomatoes
1 ½ tsp.	Sea salt
2 tsp.	Chili powder
½ c.	Salsa
½ c.	Black olives, sliced
½ c.	Mushrooms, sliced
1 c.	Pimento or Yeast Cheez

Sauté the gluten (or grits), onions, garlic, and bell pepper in the oil until tender. Add the rice, tomatoes, salt, chili powder, and salsa. Simmer at least 10 minutes. Stir in the rest of the ingredients, cover and bake 75 minutes at 350°.

SPANISH RICE–4

1 c.	Onion, chopped
4 tsp.	Garlic, minced
4 tsp.	Corn oil

4 c.	Canned stewed tomatoes
½ c.	Tomato sauce
1 c.	Green bell pepper, diced
1 c.	Red or yellow bell pepper, diced
1 c.	Mushrooms, sliced
2 c.	Corn
1 tsp.	Basil
½ tsp.	Italian seasoning
1 tsp.	Sea salt
½ tsp.	Black pepper
½ tsp.	Cayenne
4 c.	Cooked rice

Sauté the onion and garlic in the oil until soft. Combine with everything but the rice, bring to a boil, reduce heat, and simmer 15 minutes. Combine with the rice.

SPICY BULGUR PILAF

2 tsp.	Non-dairy margarine
¾ c.	Onion, chopped
1 ½ tsp.	Garlic, crushed
1 c.	Bulgur wheat
¼ tsp.	Cayenne pepper
¼ tsp.	Ground cumin
¼ tsp.	Celery seed
½ c.	Bell pepper, finely diced
¼ tsp.	Sea salt
2 ¼ c.	UnChicken or UnBeef Broth, boiling

Melt the margarine. Add the onion, garlic, and bulgur and cook 2 to 3 minutes, stirring occasionally. Stir in the cayenne pepper, cumin, and celery seed, and continue cooking for 3 to 5 more minutes. Add the bell pepper and salt. Pour in the boiling broth. Reduce to a simmer, cover, and cook until all liquid is absorbed.

SPINACH RISOTTO

2 c.	Rice, uncooked
2 tsp.	Non-dairy margarine
10 oz.	Frozen spinach, thawed and drained
3 ½ c.	UnChicken Broth
¼ tsp.	Black pepper

Sauté the uncooked rice in the margarine. Combine the other ingredients and bring them to a boil. Add the rice, lower the heat, and simmer, covered, until the rice is done–about 15 minutes.

TABOULI WHEAT

Put the wheat in a bowl and cover with warm

water–about two inches above the top of the wheat. Spring water takes fifteen minutes, distilled water takes about twice as long. Drain in a colander, pressing lightly to press out excess water.

VEGETABLE FRIED RICE–1

This is as delicious as it is simple and quick. Although it is worthy of serving at any time it is great as "emergency rations"!

2 tsp.	Corn oil
2 T.	Non-dairy margarine
2 c.	Onion, coarsely chopped
1 c.	Bell pepper, coarsely chopped
½ c.	Celery, chopped
3 c.	Mushrooms, sliced thick
2 tsp.	Garlic, minced
1 ½ tsp.	Hot pepper flakes
4 c.	Fresh tomatoes, chopped coarse
½ tsp.	Sea salt
5 c.	Cooked rice

Combine the oil and margarine. Sauté the onion, bell pepper, celery, mushrooms, garlic, and pepper flakes until the bell pepper is soft. Add the tomatoes and salt. Cook for 5 more minutes. Add the rice and continue to stir until most of the moisture is evaporated and the rice starts to brown.

VEGETABLE FRIED RICE–2

3 c.	Rice, uncooked
4 tsp.	Non-dairy margarine
4 tsp.	Corn oil
4 ½ c.	UnBeef or UnChicken Broth
½ tsp.	Sea salt
1 ½ c.	Onions, chopped
3 c.	Vegetables of choice, chopped if need be
1 T.	Corn oil

Wash rice thoroughly and drain. Combine the margarine and oil in a skillet and melt the margarine. Add the washed rice and stir frequently until the rice becomes light brown–this takes quite a while, so don't give up. (Some of the rice kernels may even "pop" like popcorn.) If the rice becomes too dry add more margarine or oil to keep it shiny as it fries. Bring broth to a boil. Add the salt. Then add the rice–which must be coming directly from the skillet and be hot and frying–to the boiling water a little bit at a time, taking care because it will "explode." Cover the pot and turn the flame down. Simmer for 10 minutes. While the rice is cooking, sauté the onions and vegetables until softened. When the rice is done, add the rice into the vegetables and continue to sauté until all excess water is evaporated.

VEGETABLE FRIED RICE–3

½ c.   Onion, chopped

4 tsp.   Corn oil
½ c.   Bell pepper, chopped
⅓ c.   Celery, chopped
1 c.   Mushrooms, chopped
½ c.   Squash, chopped
3 T.   Soy sauce
1 c.   Rice, cooked

Sauté the onions in the oil until transparent, then sauté the rest of the ingredients for 15 minutes.

Tofu Dishes

TOFU–especially when it is frozen, thawed, and pressed–can be used in many of the recipes that call for gluten, and can be flavored by simmering or soaking the tofu in the same broths as are used to flavor the gluten.

❖ ❖ ❖

TOFU

5 c.	Dry soybeans
2 ½ gal.	Boiling water
	One of the following:
2 T.	Nigari
2 T.	Epsom Salts
1 c.	Vinegar (any kind)
1 c.	Lemon juice

Wash the soybeans well and drain them.

Put them in a bowl, cover them with 12 cups of *cold* water, and let them soak 8 to 12 hours. (If the room temperature is below 65° then let them soak 16 to 20 hours.)

Drain off the water and wash again.

Put ⅓ of the beans in a blender or food processor, add 5 cups of the boiling water, and grind into a purée. Set aside.

Repeat this twice more.

Put the water-bean mixture into a large pot on the stove, add 15 more cups of boiling water, bring to a boil, and boil slowly for 10 minutes, stirring constantly.

Remove from the stove and strain through cheesecloth in a colander or large strainer, pressing hard to squeeze out all excess milk. (Use a rubber glove on your hand or the back of a large spoon for the pressing.)

Set the soy milk aside and return the soybean pulp to the pot. Add 10 cups of boiling water, put back on the stove, and bring to a boil again.

As soon as it comes to a boil, remove from the heat and press out as before, adding the milk to the first batch.

Let the milk cool to 185°. *This is important. A higher temperature will not work, and a cooler temperature will cause the tofu to be too soft.*

Dissolve the 2 tablespoons of nigari in 2 ½ cups of hot water.

Take ⅓ of the nigari mixture, hold it high above the surface of the soy milk, and while constantly stirring rapidly, add it all at once and continue stirring only 3 to 5 seconds more.

Take the second ⅓ of the nigari mixture and sprinkle it over the top of the soy milk.

Let it sit for 5 minutes.

Take the last ⅓ of the nigari mixture and sprinkle it over the top of the soy milk.

Let it sit for 5 minutes, then as gently and slowly as possible stir the mixture once to circulate the milk.

Let it sit for 5 more minutes, then a second time as gently and slowly as possible stir the mixture once to circulate the milk.

Let it sit for 5 more minutes, then a third time as gently and slowly as possible stir the mixture once to circulate the milk.

Let it sit for 5 minutes more.

The mixture should by now have turned into curds and whey. (If this is not the case, then something has gone wrong, and you should mix up 1 tablespoon of nigari in 1 cup of hot water and sprinkle it on the top of the soy milk, stirring very slowly for 3 seconds and then let it sit for 10 to 15 minutes, stirring every 5 minutes as previously described. But if the directions are followed correctly this should not be necessary.)

Pour or ladle the curds and whey slowly into a colander or large strainer lined with cheesecloth.

Transfer the curds in the cheesecloth to a tofu press and press lightly with a weight for 5 minutes.

Remove the weight and lift up the curds in the cheesecloth, and shake around gently to remove any folds that may have formed in the cheesecloth.

Put all back into the tofu press and press with heavy weights for 15 minutes for soft tofu and 30 minutes for firm tofu.

Cut into convenient size blocks.

For storage in the refrigerator, cover with cold water and put in an airtight container. Change the water every 24 hours. The tofu will keep for 7 to 10 days.

NOTES: Nigari (bittern) is the best coagulant to use in making your own tofu–both for flavor and for efficiency (amount of curds obtained). It is extracted from sea water.

Nigari and epsom salts make firm tofu. Vinegar and lemon juice make soft tofu.

If you want to use vinegar or lemon juice and yet get firm(er) tofu, then you must stir the curds for a few minutes longer.

OVEN METHOD TOFU

This recipe looks pretty silly, but it really works quite well. As you can see, the advantage of this method is the ability to add flavorings to the tofu beforehand. You can add other flavorings not given in this recipe, but some flavorings may keep the tofu from solidifying very well. So you must be willing to experiment.

4 c.	Water
2 ¼ c.	Soy flour
⅔ c.	Pimentos
2 ½ tsp.	Salt
2 ½ T.	Nutritional yeast
½ c.	Flour
⅓ c.	Lemon juice
¼ t.	Garlic salt
3 T.	Corn oil

Place everything in a blender and whirl until smooth. Pour into a small, greased loaf pan. Bake 2 hours at 275°. Turn off the oven, but keep it in the oven for one more hour. Chill before turning out of the pan. Peel off the brown skin on the top and trim the loaf to shape. Slice or cube for serving.

INDONESIAN-STYLE BAKED TOFU

You will love this!

1 ½ tsp.	Sesame oil (corn, if you do not have sesame)
½ tsp.	Garlic, minced
½ tsp.	Powdered ginger
Pinch	Cayenne (more, if you like)
¾ c.	UnChicken or UnPork Broth
3 ½ T.	Peanut butter
1 T.	Low sodium soy sauce
1 T.	Lemon juice
1 ½ tsp.	Vinegar
8 oz.	Tofu, frozen, thawed, and pressed
2 T.	Green onions, minced

Heat the oil and sauté the garlic for 1 to 2 minutes. Add the ginger and cayenne and sauté 1 more minute. Add the broth and bring to a simmer. Cover and simmer 10 minutes. Take from heat. Add the peanut butter and soy sauce and whisk until smooth. Bring back to a simmer and cook, stirring, for about 10 minutes until the sauce thickens. Whisk in the lemon juice and vinegar. Cook 5 more minutes. Take from heat. Cut the tofu lengthwise into ¼ to ⅜-inch-thick slices. Arrange in a lightly oiled baking dish. Drizzle the sauce evenly over the tofu, cover, and bake at 400° for 30 to 45 minutes. Sprinkle on the minced green onions and broil for 1 to 2 minutes.

STIR-FRY TOFU AND VEGETABLES

A standby you can count on!

2 c.	Tofu, cut in 1-inch cubes
1 ½ c.	Onions, cut in wedges
2 tsp.	Corn oil
1 c.	Carrots, sliced thin
½ c.	Green beans, cut in 1-inch pieces
½ c.	Mushrooms, sliced
½ c.	UnChicken Broth
¾ tsp.	Garlic, minced
½ tsp.	Dried basil
⅛ tsp.	Pepper

Deep-fry the tofu in corn oil and put on paper towels to drain. Sauté the onions in the 2 teaspoons of oil for 1 minute. Add the carrots and sauté for 1 more minute. Add the green beans and sauté for 1 more minute. Add the mushrooms and sauté for 1 more minute. Add the tofu and the rest of the ingredients and sauté 5 minutes, or until the vegetables are soft.

TOFU UNBEEF

Magnificently simple!
This sauce can be used to flavor 4 cups of gluten as well.

2 c.	Onions, coarsely chopped
1 tsp.	Garlic, minced
2 tsp.	Jalapeños, chopped
1 T.	Corn oil
3 T.	Cornstarch
1 ½ c.	Cold (not warm) water
¼ c.	Soy sauce
1 tsp.	Kitchen Bouquet
1 tsp.	MSG
1 ½ c.	Water
4 c.	Frozen tofu that has been thawed and pressed

Sauté the onions, garlic, and jalapeños in the oil. Mix the cornstarch and water together and add it, stirring constantly. Add the rest of the ingredients–except the tofu–and simmer until it starts to thicken. While this sauce is cooking, cut or slice the tofu into pieces about ½-inch thick. Deep-fry the tofu in corn oil–making sure the oil is very hot–until the tofu is brown. Drain in a colander and put on paper towels to absorb excess oil. When the sauce is done, add the tofu to it and cook for five minutes.

TOFU UNCHICKEN

What I have said about the recipe above applies to this one, too.

2 c.	Onions, coarsely chopped
2 tsp.	Jalapeños, chopped
3 T.	Corn oil
1 T.	Cornstarch
1 ½ c.	Cold (not warm) water
¼ tsp.	Poultry seasoning
1 ½ T.	Nutritional Yeast
½ tsp.	Salt
1 tsp.	MSG
1 ½ c.	Water
4 c.	Firm tofu, or frozen tofu that has been thawed and pressed

Sauté the onions and jalapeños in the oil. Mix the cornstarch and water together and add it, stirring constantly. Add the rest of the ingredients–except the tofu–and simmer until it starts to thicken. While this sauce is cooking, cut or slice the tofu into pieces about ½-inch thick. Deep-fry the tofu in corn oil–making sure the oil is very hot–until the tofu is brown. Drain in a colander and put on paper towels to absorb excess oil. When the sauce is done, add the tofu to it and cook for five minutes.

TOFU HUMMUS

Just as good as the chick pea type!

4 c.	Tofu
⅔ c.	Lemon juice
¼ c.	Olive oil
1 ⅓ tsp.	Sea salt
⅓ c.	Soy sauce
⅔ c.	Tahini
2 T.	Garlic, minced

Blend all in a blender or food processor.

TOFU "SCRAMBLED EGGS"

Extraordinary!

1 T.	Corn oil
½ c.	Onions, chopped
1 T.	Soy sauce
½ tsp.	Sea salt
¼ tsp.	Garlic powder
¼ tsp.	Tumeric powder
1 drop	Liquid smoke
2 T.	UnBacon, chopped fine
1 T.	Nutritional Yeast
2 tsp.	Jalapeños, chopped
2 c.	Soft tofu, crumbled

Put everything but the tofu in a skillet and stir well. Add the tofu and mix well with a fork until the seasonings are evenly distributed. Cook together until the water in the tofu evaporates and the mixture resembles scrambled eggs.
Variations: Add ¼ cup chopped bell pepper. Add ½ cup sliced mushrooms or other vegetables. Try green onions instead of regular ones. Serve with salsa or some kind of tomato sauce.

TOFU "SCRAMBLED EGGS" BREAKFAST CASSEROLE

1	Recipe of Tofu Scrambled Eggs made with bell pepper and mushrooms
1 c.	UnHam or UnSausage, ground and browned in corn oil
1 c.	Yeast or Pimento Cheez

Put the Tofu Scrambled Eggs in a casserole dish or a loaf pan, spread the gluten over that, spread the cheez over the gluten. Bake at 350° for 10 minutes.

UNBEEF ENCHILADAS

4 c.	Tofu, frozen, thawed, pressed and crumbled (or cut in small pieces)
2 T.	Corn oil
2 tsp.	Garlic, minced
2 c.	Onions, chopped
2 tsp.	Jalapeños, minced
3 T.	Chili powder
¾ c.	Black olives, chopped
¼ tsp.	Sea salt
10 c.	Spanish Tomato Sauce
1	Recipe of Corn Tortillas or Flour Tortillas
	Yeast or Pimento Cheez to cover

Sauté the tofu in 1 tablespoon of the oil until the edges begin to brown. Set aside. In the other tablespoon of oil, sauté the garlic, onions, and jalapeños until the onions are transparent. Add the chili powder and sauté for 2 more minutes, stirring constantly. Add olives, salt, tofu, and 3 cups of the tomato sauce and cook for another 5 minutes. Dip a tortilla in the tomato sauce, put some of the filling on it and roll it up and put it in a casserole pan. Do this with all the tortillas until the filling is used up. Cover the enchiladas with the remaining sauce. Spread a layer of cheez over that. Bake at 350° for 30 minutes.

Gravies

BROWN GRAVY

4 tsp.	Non-dairy margarine
3 T.	Onions, sliced
½ tsp.	Garlic, minced
2 T.	Unbleached white flour
1 c.	Tomatoes, puréed
¾ c.	UnBeef Broth
¼ tsp.	Sea salt
¼ tsp.	Paprika

Melt the margarine and sauté the onions and garlic until the onions are light brown. Remove the onions and stir in the flour and cook until it turns brown, as well. Slowly stir in the puréed tomatoes. Add the onions, broth, salt, and paprika. Stir and cook until the sauce is smooth and boiling.

CAJUN UNBEEF GRAVY

Get adventurous!

2 T.	Corn oil
1 c.	UnBeef, ground
¼ c.	Corn oil
¼ c.	Unbleached white flour
1 ¼ tsp.	Kitchen Bouquet
3 c.	Mushrooms (fresh preferred), stemmed and halved
1 c.	Onion, chopped
2 tsp.	Garlic, minced
4 c.	UnBeef Broth
3 T.	Lea & Perrins Steak Sauce
4 tsp.	Louisiana Hot Sauce

In a skillet heat 1 tablespoon of the oil and fry the gluten until it is browned on all sides. Remove the gluten and set aside. Put the other tablespoon of oil in the skillet and heat. Stir the flour into the oil and turn the fire down so it will cook slowly. Add the Kitchen Bouquet and keep stirring the flour constantly–adding more oil if the mixture is too dry–until the mixture is a rich brown. Add the mushrooms, onions, and garlic, stirring constantly. Continue to cook for 10 minutes, adding up to ½ cup of the broth if needed to keep it from sticking. Add the rest of the broth, steak sauce, and hot sauce, turn the heat down and continue cooking until it starts to thicken–about 20 minutes–stirring occasionally.

MUSHROOM GRAVY

Don't pass this by!

2 c.	Mushrooms, sliced
1 tsp.	Garlic, crushed
1 T.	Corn oil
¼ c.	Unbleached white flour
4 c.	UnBeef or UnChicken Broth

Sauté the mushrooms and garlic in the oil. Blend in the flour. Slowly add the broth. Cook for 15 minutes.

NUTRITIONAL YEAST GRAVY

⅓ c.	Unbleached white flour
⅓ c.	Nutritional Yeast
2 T.	Non-dairy margarine or corn oil
2 c.	Water
1 T.	Soy sauce
¼ tsp.	Sea salt
⅛ tsp.	Black or cayenne pepper

Toast the flour over medium low heat until it

starts to smell "toasty." Stir in the yeast. Add the margarine or oil and cook for a few minutes until it is bubbly. Add the water and cook, whisking until it thickens and bubbles. Add the soy sauce, salt, and pepper.

UNBEEF GRAVY–1

- ¼ c. Unbleached white flour
- 4 tsp. Corn oil
- 2 c. UnBeef Broth

In a skillet blend the flour in the heated oil. Slowly add the broth. Cook for 10 minutes.
Note: If potatoes have been boiled, use the potato water in making the broth.

UNBEEF GRAVY–2

- 4 tsp. Corn oil
- 4 T. Unbleached white flour
- 1 tsp. Kitchen Bouquet
- 1 ½ c. Onions, chopped
- 1 ½ tsp. Garlic, minced
- 3 c. UnBeef Broth
- ½ tsp. Sea salt
- 2 T. Lea & Perrins Steak Sauce
- 1 T. Louisiana Hot Sauce

Heat the oil in a skillet and stir in the flour. Turn the fire down so it will cook slowly. Add the Kitchen Bouquet and keep stirring the flour constantly, adding more oil if the mixture is too dry, until it is a rich brown. Add the onions and garlic, stirring constantly. Add the broth and keep stirring until it starts to form a thick gravy. Add the salt, steak sauce, and hot sauce. Add more water if you need to, and bring all to a boil and simmer for 10 minutes.

UNCHICKEN GRAVY

- ¼ c. Unbleached white flour
- 1 T. Corn oil
- 2 c. UnChicken Broth

In a skillet blend the flour in the heated oil. Slowly add the broth. Cook for 10 minutes.

Note: If potatoes have been boiled, use the potato water in making the broth.

UNHAM GRAVY–1

- 1 ⅓ c. Gluten Ham or Gluten Bacon, ground
- 1 ⅓ c. Onions, chopped
- 2 T. Corn oil
- ⅓ c. Unbleached white flour
- 1 qt. Cashew Milk
- ¼ tsp. Black pepper

Sauté the onions and "ham" in the oil. Add the flour and blend well. Gradually add the cashew milk, and then the rest of the ingredients. Cook for 10 minutes.

UNHAM GRAVY–2

- 1 T. Corn oil
- ¼ c. Unbleached white flour
- 2 c. Ham-like Broth

In a skillet blend the flour in the heated oil. Slowly add the broth. Cook for 10 minutes.
Note: If potatoes have been boiled, use the potato water in making the broth.

UNHAMBURGER GRAVY

We like this on mashed potatoes, though it goes just as well on bread and biscuits–even rice!

- 2 c. UnBeef, ground or chopped small, or soy grits soaked in UnBeef Broth
- ¼ c. Onions, chopped
- ½ tsp. Garlic, minced
- 1 T. Corn oil
- 6 T. Unbleached white flour
- 4 c. Cashew Milk made with UnBeef Broth

Sauté the gluten (or grits), onions, and garlic in the oil until it is lightly browned. Add the flour and mix well. Gradually add the "milk," stirring constantly. Cook and stir over medium heat until thickened.

Sauces

GET CREATIVE with these sauces! Use them in many ways: over bread, biscuits, grains, pasta, vegetables, as dips—whatever!

BARBECUE SAUCE–1

1 c.	Onions, chopped
1 T.	Corn oil
6 T.	Tomato paste
1 ¼ c.	Water
¼ c.	Sucanat
1 T.	Barbados molasses
¼ c.	Lemon juice
2 T.	Prepared mustard
2 tsp.	Sea salt
¼ tsp.	Cayenne pepper

Put all together and cook for 1 hour.

BARBECUE SAUCE–2

1 T.	Corn oil
2 c.	Onions
2	Garlic cloves
½ c.	Parsley
¾ tsp.	Louisiana Hot Sauce
1 c.	Water
1 T.	Lemon juice
4 T.	Lea & Perrins Steak Sauce
1 ½ tsp.	Sea salt
1 ½ c.	Canned tomato sauce
1 tsp.	Liquid smoke

Heat the oil in a large saucepan. Blend the onions, garlic, parsley, and hot sauce in a blender with just enough water so it will blend. Pour this into the saucepan and simmer for 30 minutes. Add the rest of the ingredients and simmer for 30 more minutes, covered, adding more water if it is needed.

BROWN SAUCE

4 tsp.	Non-dairy margarine
3 T.	Onions, sliced
½ tsp.	Garlic, minced
2 T.	Unbleached white flour
1 c.	Tomatoes, puréed
¾ c.	UnBeef Broth
¼ tsp.	Sea salt
¼ tsp.	Paprika

Melt the margarine and sauté the onions and garlic until the onions are light brown. Remove the onions and stir in the flour and cook until it turns brown, as well. Slowly stir in the puréed tomatoes. Add the onions, broth, salt, and paprika. Stir and cook until the sauce is smooth and boiling.

"BUTTER" SAUCE WITH HERBS

1 T.	Unbleached white flour
1 T.	Non-dairy margarine
2 T.	Cashew Milk
2 T.	Onions, minced
½ tsp.	Garlic, minced
1 ½ tsp.	Basil
1 ½ tsp.	Parsley
⅛ tsp.	Sea salt

Place all ingredients in a double boiler, cook and stir until smooth.

CAJUN CATSUP

This am delighteous, I garontee!

4 c.	Onion, chopped
1 c.	Celery, chopped
1 c.	Bell pepper, chopped
1 c.	Parsley, chopped
2 T.	Corn oil
2 T.	Garlic, chopped
3 c.	Lea & Perrins Steak Sauce
½ c.	Louisiana Hot Sauce
3 c.	Tomato sauce
3 tsp.	Sea salt

In a large skillet, sauté the onions, celery, bell pepper, and parsley in the oil until the onions are soft and transparent. Add the garlic and cook a little longer. Add the steak sauce, hot sauce, tomato sauce, and salt, and bring to a boil. Lower the heat and cover, and cook for 2 to 3 hours. This can be kept refrigerated for a few weeks.

CATSUP

1 c.	Tomato purée
2 tsp.	Corn oil
2 tsp.	Molasses
1 tsp.	Sea salt
2 T.	Wine vinegar
3 T.	Onions, chopped

Combine all the ingredients and cook for 15-30 minutes. While still warm, pour into a blender and blend until smooth as possible.

CHEEZ SAUCE–1

1 T.	Corn oil
½ c.	Flour
3 c.	Water
1 ½ tsp.	Sea salt
⅛ tsp.	Cayenne pepper
3 c.	Yeast or Pimento Cheez

Heat the oil. Slowly add the flour, blending it with a whisk. Slowly add the water, continuously blending with the whip. Cook until bubbly and thick. Add the salt, pepper, and cheez.
Variation: Use UnBeef Broth or UnChicken Broth instead of water, and cut the salt in half.

CHEEZ SAUCE–2

1 T.	Non-dairy margarine
2 T.	Unbleached white flour
1 ½ c.	Cashew Milk
1 c.	Yeast or Pimento Cheez
½ tsp.	Sea salt
⅛ tsp.	Paprika
Dash	Cayenne pepper
½ tsp.	Dry mustard

Melt the margarine in a saucepan. Stir in the flour until it is blended. Slowly stir in the "milk." When the sauce is smooth and boiling, reduce the heat and add the rest of the ingredients, stirring in well.
Variation: Make the "milk" with UnChicken Broth, and cut the salt in half.

CHEEZ SAUCE–3

1 c.	Cashew or Tofu Sour Cream
⅔ c.	Yeast or Pimento Cheez
2 T.	Onions, chopped
2 T.	Lemon juice
¼ tsp.	Sea salt

Combine everything well. Use over broccoli, brussels sprouts, spaghetti, etc.

CHEEZ SAUCE–4

½ c.	Yeast or Pimento Cheez
¼ c.	Miraculous Whip
½ c.	Cashew or Tofu Sour Cream
¼ tsp.	Paprika

Combine everything well. Use over broccoli, brussels sprouts, spaghetti, etc.

CHEEZ AND ONION SAUCE

1 ½ c.	Onions, chopped
1 tsp.	Garlic, minced
2 tsp.	Non-dairy margarine
2 T.	Unbleached white flour
2 c.	Cashew Milk, warm
1 tsp.	Sea salt
¼ tsp.	Paprika
½ c.	Yeast or Pimento Cheez

Sauté the onions and garlic in the margarine. Add the flour and blend. Add the "milk" slowly while stirring. Stir in the salt, paprika, and cheez.

CHILI SAUCE

1 c.	Catsup
2 T.	Prepared horseradish
2 T.	Lemon juice
1 tsp.	Chopped parsley
1 tsp.	Chopped chives

Combine all the ingredients and stir to blend.

Put in a container and refrigerate.

COCKTAIL SAUCE–1

1 ½ c.	Catsup
2 ½ T.	Lemon juice
1 T. & 1 ½ tsp.	Horseradish
2 T.	Lea & Perrins Steak Sauce
1 tsp.	Onions, grated
2 dashes	Louisiana Hot Sauce

Combine all the ingredients and stir to blend. Put in a container and refrigerate.

COCKTAIL SAUCE–2

½ c.	Miraculous Whip
1 T.	Olive oil
2 tsp.	Louisiana Hot Sauce
2 c.	Catsup
1 tsp.	Sea salt
2 T.	Lea & Perrins Steak Sauce
3 T.	Lemon juice
1 T.	Creamed style horseradish

Put the Miraculous Whip in a bowl, and while beating constantly with a fork, add the oil. Continuing to beat, add the hot sauce and then the catsup. Add the salt, steak sauce, lemon juice, and horseradish, mixing well. Cover and chill for at least 30 minutes. Beat just before serving.

CREOLE SAUCE

2 tsp.	Non-dairy margarine
⅓ c.	Onions, chopped
½ c.	Bell pepper, chopped
⅓ c.	Mushrooms, chopped
1 tsp.	Jalapeños, minced
1 ½ c.	Tomatoes, chopped
⅓ tsp.	Sea salt
1 tsp.	Barbados molasses
1 T.	Unbleached white flour
⅓ c.	Water

Melt the margarine, and sauté the onions, bell peppers, mushrooms, and jalapeños for 2 minutes. Add the rest of the ingredients and cook until the sauce is thick. Good over rice.

GOLDEN SAUCE

½ c.	Onion, chopped
½ tsp.	Garlic, minced
2 tsp.	Corn oil
¾ c.	Water
½ c.	Potatoes, cooked
¼ c.	Carrots, cooked
3 T.	Nutritional Yeast
½ tsp.	Sea salt
1 T.	Lemon juice

Sauté the onion and garlic in the oil. Liquefy all the ingredients together in a blender until smooth. Heat to serving temperature.

MAITRE D'HOTEL BUTTER SAUCE

¼ c.	Non-dairy margarine
½ tsp.	Sea salt
⅛ tsp.	Paprika
½ T.	Parsley, chopped
1 ½ tsp.	Lemon juice

Cream the margarine until it is very soft. Add the salt, paprika, and parsley. Very slowly add the lemon juice, stirring the sauce constantly.

OLIVE SAUCE–1

1 T.	Non-dairy margarine
3 T.	Onions, sliced
½ tsp.	Garlic, minced
2 T.	Unbleached white flour
1 c.	Tomatoes, puréed
12	Black olives, sliced
¾ c.	UnBeef Broth
¼ tsp.	Sea salt
¼ tsp.	Paprika

Melt the margarine and sauté the onions and garlic until the onions are light brown. Remove the onions and stir in the flour and cook until it turns brown, as well. Slowly stir in the puréed tomatoes. Add the onions, olives, broth, salt, and paprika. Stir and cook until the sauce is smooth and boiling.

OLIVE SAUCE–2

¼ c.	Green onions, sliced
¼ c.	Mushrooms, sliced
2 tsp.	Non-dairy margarine
1 c.	Black olives, sliced
2 T.	Liquid from the olives
1 c.	Cashew or Tofu Sour Cream
½ tsp.	Garlic powder
½ tsp.	Soy sauce

Sauté the onions and mushrooms in the margarine for 1 minute. Stir in the rest of the ingredients and heat just until hot–but not boiling.

ONION SAUCE–1

¾ c.	Onions, chopped
2 tsp.	Non-dairy margarine
1 tsp.	Soy sauce
½ tsp.	Sea salt
½ tsp.	Paprika

Sauté onions for 5 minutes in margarine. Add rest of ingredients.
Variation: Use chives instead of onions.

ONION SAUCE–2

3 c.	Onions, chopped
	Boiling water
2 c.	Boiling water
	UnBeef Broth
2 T.	Non-dairy margarine
3 T.	Unbleached white flour

Cover the onions with boiling water and cook for 5 minutes. Drain and cover with 2 more cups of boiling water. Boil them until they are soft. Rub through a sieve. Add enough broth to make 2 ½ cupfuls. Melt the margarine and stir in the flour until blended. Stir in the onion purée.

PIQUANTE SAUCE

2 T.	Non-dairy margarine
5 T.	Onions, sliced
½ tsp.	Garlic, minced
2 T.	Unbleached white flour
1 c.	Tomatoes, puréed
1 T.	Lemon juice
1 T.	Bell pepper, minced
⅛ tsp.	Cayenne
¼ tsp.	Sea salt
¼ tsp.	Paprika
¾ c.	UnBeef Broth

Melt the margarine and sauté the onions and garlic until the onions are light brown. Remove the onions and stir in the flour and cook until it turns brown, as well. Slowly stir in the puréed tomatoes. Add the onions, lemon juice, bell pepper, cayenne, salt, paprika, and broth. Stir and cook until the sauce is smooth and boiling.

SOUR CREAM AND CHIVE SAUCE

1 c.	Cashew or Tofu Sour Cream
4 tsp.	Chives
¼ tsp.	Louisiana Hot Sauce

Combine well.

SPANISH TOMATO SAUCE

Truly special!

½ tsp.	Garlic, minced
2 tsp.	Olive oil
1 qt.	Tomatoes, chopped
¾ c.	Tomato paste
1	Bay leaf
2 tsp.	Sea salt
½ tsp.	Oregano
½ tsp.	Basil
1 c.	Onions, chopped
½ c.	Bell pepper, chopped
½ tsp.	Cumin, ground

Sauté the garlic in the oil. Purée the tomatoes in a blender and add to the oil. Put all together, adding water if needed, and simmer until thick.

SPICY BARBECUE SAUCE–1

4 ½ c.	Tomato sauce
¾ c.	Tomato paste
⅓ c.	Barbados molasses
½ c.	Water
⅓ c.	White wine vinegar
2 T.	Lemon juice
2 T.	Prepared mustard
2 T.	Lea & Perrins Steak Sauce
2 tsp.	Hot pepper sauce
½ c.	Onions, finely chopped
1 tsp.	Garlic, minced
½ tsp.	Ground black pepper
½ tsp.	Ground cloves
½ tsp.	Allspice
¼ tsp.	Ground ginger
1 T.	Corn oil

Combine all the ingredients in a large saucepan. Cook over medium heat for about 30 minutes, stirring frequently to prevent sticking.

SPICY BARBECUE SAUCE–2

This is the sauce given for Barbecue "Spare Ribs," but it is good for everything.

½ c.	Onion, chopped
1 tsp.	Garlic, minced
1 T.	Corn oil
2 ½ c.	Tomato sauce
¼ c.	Water
1 c.	Sucanat
2 T.	Barbados molasses
½ c.	Prepared mustard
1 T. & 1 tsp.	Sea salt

1 tsp.	Allspice
1 ½ tsp.	Red pepper, crushed
1 ½ tsp.	Dried parsley or 1 sprig of fresh parsley
¼ c.	Water
2 T.	Lemon juice
1 tsp.	Liquid smoke
1 T.	Soy sauce

Sauté the onion and garlic in oil or margarine until the onions become clear and golden. Add tomato sauce, water, Sucanat, molasses, mustard, salt, allspice, pepper, and parsley. Bring to a boil, reduce heat, and let simmer for about an hour. Add water, lemon juice, liquid smoke, and soy sauce. Cook 10-15 minutes longer.

TACO SAUCE

5 c.	Tomatoes, chopped
2 ½ tsp.	Garlic, minced
1 tsp.	Crushed red pepper flakes
2 tsp.	Sea salt
1 T.	Bell pepper, minced
1 ½ c.	Onion, chopped fine
1 tsp.	Chili powder
1 tsp.	Oregano
1 tsp.	Thyme
1 T.	Sucanat
1 T.	Unbleached white flour
1 T.	Corn oil
1 T.	Wine vinegar

Blend in blender or food processor and cook for 1 hour.

TARTAR SAUCE

Never make UnFish without making some of this, too!

1 c.	Cashew or Tofu Mayonnaise, or Miraculous Whip
1 T.	Onions, minced
1 ½ tsp.	Prepared mustard
1 T.	Horseradish
¼ c.	Dill pickles (or sweet pickles, if you prefer)

Combine well and refrigerate for a while to let the flavor develop.

TOMATO SAUCE–1

⅓ c.	Onions, chopped
1 tsp.	Garlic, minced
2 tsp.	Corn oil
6 c.	Tomatoes, coarsely chopped

½ c. & 1 T.	Tomato paste
1 T.	Dried basil
1 ¼ tsp.	Sea salt
⅛ tsp.	Cayenne pepper
1 T.	Barbados molasses

Sauté the onions and garlic in the oil. Combine with rest of ingredients and cook.

TOMATO SAUCE–2

⅓ c.	Onions, chopped
1 tsp.	Garlic, minced
2 tsp.	Corn oil
6 c.	Tomatoes, coarsely chopped
½ c. & 1 T.	Tomato paste
1 ½ tsp.	Italian seasoning
1 ½ tsp.	Fennel seed
1 ¼ tsp.	Sea salt
⅛ tsp.	Cayenne
1 T.	Barbados molasses

Sauté the onions and garlic in the oil. Combine with rest of ingredients and cook.

TOMATO SAUCE–3

½ tsp.	Garlic, minced
1 tsp.	Olive oil
1 qt.	Tomatoes, chopped
¾ c.	Tomato paste
1	Bay leaf
2 tsp.	Sea salt
½ tsp.	Oregano
½ tsp.	Basil
1 tsp.	Sucanat (optional)

Sauté the garlic in the olive oil. Purée the tomatoes in a blender and add to the oil. Put all together, adding water if needed, and simmer until thick.

TOMATO AND CHEEZ SAUCE

2 tsp.	Non-dairy margarine
¾ c.	Onions, chopped
3 c.	Tomatoes, chopped
½ c.	Cashew Milk
¼ tsp.	Basil (or 1 tsp. fresh basil, finely chopped)
¼ tsp.	Oregano
Pinch	Cumin, ground
½ tsp.	Sea salt
¼ tsp.	Paprika
1 c.	Yeast, Pimento, or Notzarella Cheez

In a skillet heat the margarine over moderate heat. Sauté the onions until transparent, but not brown. Add everything else but the cheez and cook, stirring, for 5 minutes. Then, stirring constantly, add the cheez.

TOMATO AND ONION SAUCE

Once when there was a tremendous thunderstorm punctuated with hurricane-strength winds which kept me from going out to get anything to cook for several guests, I had to use what was at hand. That turned out to be tomatoes, onions, and rice. So this dish was born—to stay.
This is excellent over rice or pasta.

4 c.	Onions, chopped
1 T.	Garlic, minced
1 c.	Bell pepper, chopped
1 c.	Celery, chopped
1 T.	Jalapeño pepper, minced
3 T.	Corn oil
4 c.	Tomatoes, chopped
1 tsp.	Sea salt
½ tsp.	Cayenne pepper
3 T.	Soy sauce
1 c.	Water

Sauté the onions, garlic, bell pepper, celery, and jalapeños in the oil until the onions are soft and transparent, but not brown. Add the rest of the ingredients and cook with the onions thoroughly until the consistency is thick, but not dry.
Variation: Sauté 2 tablespoons of curry powder along with the onions, etc.

UNBEEF AND TOMATO SAUCE

1 ½ tsp.	Garlic, minced
1 c.	Onions, chopped
2 tsp.	Corn oil
2 c.	UnBeef, ground
3 c.	Tomatoes, finely chopped
⅔ c.	Tomato paste
2 T.	Sucanat
1 tsp.	Italian Herb Seasoning
1	Bay leaf
½ tsp.	Salt
⅛ tsp.	Black or cayenne pepper

Sauté the garlic and onion in the oil until the onions are soft. Add the gluten and sauté it well. Add the remaining ingredients. Simmer the sauce uncovered for about 20 to 30 minutes.

WHITE SAUCE

Thin:

2 tsp.	Non-dairy margarine
2 tsp.	Unbleached white flour
¼ tsp.	Sea salt
1 ½ c.	Cashew Milk

Medium:

1 T.	Non-dairy margarine
1 T.	Unbleached white flour
¼ tsp.	Sea salt
1 c.	Cashew Milk

Thick:

4 tsp.	Non-dairy margarine
2 T.	Unbleached white flour
¼ tsp.	Sea salt
1 c.	Cashew Milk

Melt the margarine in a saucepan over low heat. Blend in the flour and salt. Add the "milk" all at once. Cook quickly, stirring constantly, till the mixture thickens and bubbles. Remove the sauce from the heat when it bubbles. Add other flavorings—if any—at this point, stirring until smooth.
If sauce cooks too long, it becomes too thick and the margarine separates out. To correct this, stir in a little more "milk" and cook quickly, stirring constantly, until the sauce bubbles again.

Pasta Sauces

CREAM CHEEZ SPAGHETTI SAUCE

Forget modesty—this is another wonderful "invention" of mine!

4 c.	Tofu Cottage Cheez blended smooth
4 c.	Cashew Milk made with UnChicken Broth
1 tsp.	Non-dairy margarine
¼ tsp.	Garlic powder
¼ tsp.	Black pepper
¼ c.	Parmesan Cheez

Combine the cottage cheez and "milk" and heat in a double boiler. Combine the other ingredients and stir into the "milk" mixture. Cook for 30 minutes.

ITALIAN PASTA SAUCE

1 c.	Bell peppers, chopped
1 ½ c.	Onions, chopped
1 T.	Corn oil
6 c.	Tomatoes, chopped
½ tsp.	Sea salt
3 c.	Squash, chopped
½ tsp.	Basil
½ tsp.	Oregano
½ tsp.	Cayenne pepper
2 tsp.	Garlic, minced
3 c.	UnBeef Broth

Sauté the bell peppers and onions in the oil. Combine all ingredients and cook.

MARY KRIEGER'S SURE-TO-PLEASE SPAGHETTI SAUCE

This is heavenly simple and simply heavenly. It never fails. Thanks, Mary!

2 qts.	Canned tomato sauce
2 T.	Dried minced onion
1 tsp.	Dried minced garlic
½ tsp.	Black pepper
1 ½ tsp.	Italian seasoning
1 c.	Mushrooms, sliced or chopped
2 T.	Olive oil

Combine everything. Bring to a low boil, reduce the heat, and simmer 1 to 1 ½ hours, cooking until thickened, stirring occasionally.

ONION SAUCE FOR SPAGHETTI

Reliable!

2 c.	Onions, chopped
1 tsp.	Garlic, minced
1 ½ tsp.	Non-dairy margarine
1 ½ tsp.	Olive oil
½ tsp.	Sea salt
½ tsp.	Black or cayenne pepper
1 tsp.	Sucanat
2 c.	Tomato sauce
1 c.	UnBeef Broth

Sauté the onions and garlic in the margarine and oil until soft. Mix and simmer all ingredients for 30 minutes.

PASTA SAUCE NAPOLITANA

2 tsp.	Olive oil
2 T.	Garlic, minced

1 c. Black olives, sliced
¼ c. Fresh basil (firmly packed in the measure), chopped–or 1 T. dried
1 tsp. Hot pepper flakes
2 c. Canned tomato sauce
1 c. Yeast, Pimento, or Notzarella Cheez

Sauté the garlic in the oil slowly until it is softened but not browned. Add the olives, basil, pepper flakes, and tomato sauce. Heat through. Stir in the cheez and mix well until heated through. Serve over pasta. Sprinkle with Parmesan Cheez.

"SOUR CREAM" SPAGHETTI SAUCE

3 c. Cashew or Tofu Sour Cream
1 c. UnChicken Broth
2 tsp. Sea salt
2 4-oz. jars of pimentos
¼ c. Corn oil
3 T. Onions, minced

Put the "sour cream," broth, salt, and pimentos in a blender and blend until smooth. While the blender is still going, slowly add the corn oil. Put into a bowl and mix in the onions.

SPAGHETTI SAUCE

This never fails to please!

1 c. Onions, coarsely chopped
¾ c. Celery, chopped
¾ tsp. Garlic, minced
1 T. Olive oil
6 c. Tomatoes, chopped
1 ½ c. UnBeef or Soy Grits UnBeef
½ tsp. Hot pepper flakes
1 ½ tsp. Sea salt
1 ½ tsp. Italian seasoning
¼ c. UnBeef Broth
½ c. Tomato paste

Sauté the onion, celery, and garlic in the olive oil. Combine everything and cook for 1 hour or more.

TOMATO AND ONION SAUCE

Once when there was a tremendous thunderstorm punctuated with hurricane-strength winds which kept me from going out to get anything to cook for several guests, I had to use what was at hand. That turned out to be tomatoes, onions, and rice. So this dish was born– to stay.
This is excellent over rice or pasta.

4 c. Onions, chopped
1 T. Garlic, minced
1 c. Bell pepper, chopped
1 c. Celery, chopped
1 T. Jalapeño pepper, minced
3 T. Corn oil
4 c. Tomatoes, chopped
1 tsp. Sea salt
½ tsp. Cayenne pepper
3 T. Soy sauce
1 c. Water

Sauté the onions, garlic, bell pepper, celery, and jalapeños in the oil until the onions are soft and transparent, but not brown. Add the rest of the ingredients and cook with the onions thoroughly until the consistency is thick, but not dry.
Variation: Sauté 2 tablespoons of curry powder along with the onions, etc.

TOMATO-MUSHROOM MARINARA SAUCE

1 ½ c. Onion, coarsely chopped
1 ½ tsp. Garlic, minced
4 c. Mushrooms, sliced ¼-to-½-inch thick
2 T. Corn oil
5 c. Canned tomatoes, chopped, with their juice
1 tsp. Oregano
½ tsp. Fennel seed
2 T. Basil
¼ tsp. Hot pepper flakes
1 ¼ tsp. Sea salt

Sauté the onions, garlic, and mushrooms in the oil until the onion is soft. Combine everything and simmer for 1 hour, adding more water or tomato juice if it gets too thick.

UNBEEF AND TOMATO SAUCE

1 ½ tsp. Garlic, minced
1 c. Onions, chopped
2 tsp. Corn oil
2 c. UnBeef, ground
3 c. Tomatoes, finely chopped
⅔ c. Tomato paste
2 T. Sucanat
1 tsp. Italian Herb Seasoning
1 Bay leaf
½ tsp. Salt
⅛ tsp. Black or cayenne pepper

Sauté the garlic and onion in the oil until the

onions are soft. Add the gluten and sauté it well. Add the remaining ingredients. Simmer the sauce uncovered for about 20 to 30 minutes.

UNBEEF PASTA SAUCE

4 c.	UnBeef, cut into 1-inch cubes
4 T.	Olive oil
1 c.	Onion, chopped
2 ½ c.	UnChicken Broth
2	Bay leaves
⅓ c.	Celery, chopped fine
⅓ c.	Carrot, shredded
2 T.	Parsley, chopped fine
1 T.	Tomato paste
¼ tsp.	Sea salt
¼ tsp.	Pepper
1 c.	Canned tomatoes, drained and chopped
1 c.	Mushrooms, chopped

Brown the gluten in the oil. Add the onion and cook until golden. Add the broth, bay leaves, celery, carrot, parsley, tomato paste, salt, and pepper. Cook for 3 minutes. Stir in the tomatoes and mushrooms. Cover partially and cook, stirring occasionally, for 45 minutes.

UNCHICKEN PASTA SAUCE

½ c.	Onion (red preferred), minced
2 tsp.	Olive oil
1 tsp.	Garlic, minced
¼ c.	Bell pepper, cut into ¼-inch dice
½ tsp.	Chili powder
¼ tsp.	Ground cumin
⅛ tsp.	Cayenne
1 ½ c.	UnChicken, ground
2 c.	Canned tomatoes (Italian preferred) with the juice
¼ c.	Tomato paste
¼ tsp.	Basil
¼ tsp.	Oregano
¼ tsp.	Hot pepper flakes
¼ tsp.	Sea salt

Sauté the onion in the oil until soft. Add the garlic, bell pepper, chili powder, cumin, and cayenne, and cook, stirring, for 1 minutes. Add the gluten and cook, stirring, for 4 minutes. Stir in the tomatoes and juice, breaking them up, along with the tomato paste, basil, oregano, pepper flakes, and salt. Simmer, stirring occasionally, for 10 minutes or until thickened. *Variation:* Use another type of flavored gluten.

UNSHRIMP PASTA SAUCE

¾ tsp.	Garlic, minced
2	Green onions, minced
1 tsp.	Corn oil
1 ½ c.	Tomatoes, chopped
2 T.	Fresh basil, chopped
½ tsp.	Hot pepper flakes
½ tsp.	Sea salt
1 T.	Capers
1 c.	UnShrimp
2 tsp.	Non-dairy margarine
2 T.	UnShrimp Broth

Sauté the garlic and onions in the oil until the garlic is pale golden. Add the tomatoes, basil, pepper flakes, salt, and capers. Sauté the gluten in the margarine for 5 minutes, then add the broth and cook until most of the liquid is evaporated. Add the gluten to the sauce.

ZUCCHINI SPAGHETTI SAUCE

¾ c.	Onions, chopped
1 tsp.	Garlic, minced
2 c.	Zucchini, thinly sliced
1 ½ c.	Bell peppers, cut in julienne strips
2 T.	Corn oil
3 c.	Tomatoes, chopped
⅓ c.	UnChicken Broth
2 tsp.	Sea salt
⅛ tsp.	Paprika

Sauté the onions, garlic, squash, and bell pepper in the corn oil. Add rest of ingredients and cook for 15 minutes.
Variation: Use another type of squash—or even another type of vegetable.

Pasta

A NOTE ON MAKING AND COOKING PASTA

Although pasta can be made by simply mixing and rolling it out, a pasta machine is invaluable. If you have a hand-operated machine, when ready for the "rolling out" step put the dough through the machine at the thickest setting. Then narrow it down one point and run the dough through again. Keep repeating this until you run it through at the desired thickness (thinness, actually).

Whether you have a hand-operated or electric pasta maker, it will help keep your noodles from falling apart if you position an electric fan so it will blow on the noodles as they emerge from the machine.

If you will not be using the pasta completely, dry it out in a 200° oven. Then you can store it indefinitely in a sealed bag that is free from moisture.

Do not put oil in the water in which you cook pasta. It will make the pasta more likely to stick together and it will coat the pasta so seasonings and sauces will not adhere to it as they should.

BASIC PASTA

2 c.	Unbleached white flour
¼ c.	Gluten flour
½ tsp.	Sea salt
2 T.	Corn oil
½ c.	Water
½ c.	Nutritional Yeast

Mix all ingredients into a stiff dough, adding more water as needed. Knead briefly. Roll dough as thin as possible. Cut into size and shapes desired. Dry in the air overnight or in a 200° oven on cookie sheets until all moisture is gone.

BASIC N'EGG PASTA

Make the Basic Pasta recipe, given later, but add 3 n'eggs to the ingredients if you find that the Simple Pasta tends to fall apart.

BASIC SEMOLINA PASTA

Make the Basic Pasta recipe, given later, but in place of the 2 cups of unbleached white flour use 1 cup of flour and 1 cup of *white* semolina. And for any additional "flouring" use semolina instead of regular flour.

BAKED MACARONI WITH TOMATOES

4 c.	Macaroni, cooked
3 c.	Yeast, Pimento, or Notzarella Cheez
3 c.	Tomato juice
1 tsp.	Sea salt
¼ c.	Parsley, chopped
2 tsp.	Basil or thyme
½ c.	Yeast or Pimento Cheez
½ tsp.	Paprika
¼ tsp.	Onion powder
¼ tsp.	Garlic powder
1 c.	Bread crumbs

Mix the macaroni, cheez, tomato juice, salt, parsley, and basil in a casserole dish. Combine the ½ cup of cheez, paprika, onion powder, garlic powder, and bread crumbs. Spread this over all and bake at 350° for 30 minutes.

BAKED PASTA WITH UNBEEF

2 c.	UnBeef, ground
2 ½ tsp.	Garlic, crushed
¾ c.	Spaghetti sauce
¾ c.	UnBeef Gravy
½ c.	Cashew Cream
1 tsp.	Oregano
½ tsp.	Rosemary
	Cayenne pepper
¾ lb.	Pasta
1 c.	Yeast or Notzarella Cheez

Combine everything but the pasta and cup of cheez. Simmer this together, and at the same time cook the pasta and drain it well. Mix the pasta with the sauce. Put into a casserole and spread the cheez over the top. Bake, uncovered, at 350° for 25 minutes.

CALZONE

1 T.	Sucanat
1 c.	Water (lukewarm)
1 T.	Yeast (dry)
2 c.	Unbleached white flour
1 T.	Oil
½ tsp.	Sea salt
	Apple juice

Place the Sucanat, water, and yeast in a large bowl and stir until the yeast and Sucanat are dissolved. Let sit for 8 to 10 minutes or until it is foamy. Stir in 1 cup of flour and mix well. Let rise 20 minutes. Stir down and add remaining flour, oil, and salt. Knead 5 to 10 minutes or until pliable and not sticky, adding more flour as needed. Place dough on a floured board, cover with a towel and let it rise for 1 ½ hours. Divide the dough into 8 balls and roll each into an even circle. Place a filling–such as from the recipes found in the Casseroles, Dried Beans, Gravies and Sauces, Meat Substitutes, Pies, Square Meals, or Vegetables sections–in the center of each circle (if you like, include tomato sauce), spreading it to within 1 inch from the edge. Fold the circles into half-moon shapes and pinch the edges tightly closed. Pierce the tops three or four times with a fork to let out the steam. Brush the tops with apple juice. Place on an oiled baking sheet and bake at 400° for 25 minutes.

CHILI-MAC

This is great "kid food"–and am I ever a kid!

1 c.	Onions, chopped

1 tsp.	Garlic, minced
1 tsp.	Jalapeños, minced
2 tsp.	Corn oil
1 lb.	Macaroni, cooked in salted water and drained
¼ tsp.	Sea salt
6 c.	Chili recipe of choice

Sauté the onions, garlic, and jalapeños in the oil. Toss the macaroni with this along with the salt. Put the macaroni in a casserole, top with the chili, and bake at 350° for 30 minutes. (If you are using leftover chili that has gotten thick overnight, dilute it with 1 cup of tomato juice and heat.) *Variation:* Top with Yeast or Pimento Cheez before baking.

CREOLE SPAGHETTI

2 T.	Onions, chopped
½ c.	Bell pepper, chopped
2 tsp.	Corn oil
2 c.	Soy Grits Beef
2 c.	Stewed tomatoes
2 c.	Spaghetti, cooked and drained
½ tsp.	Sea salt
¼ tsp.	Cayenne pepper

Sauté the onions and bell pepper in the oil. Add soy grits, tomatoes, spaghetti, salt, and pepper. Cover and cook 15 to 20 minutes, stirring frequently.

DELICIOUS LASAGNA

The name tells it all!

½ lb.	Uncooked lasagna noodles
2 c.	UnBeef, ground
¼ c.	Onion, chopped
2 c.	Canned tomato sauce
3 ½ c.	Frozen spinach (2 10-oz. pkgs.), thawed and drained well
1 tsp.	Parsley flakes
½ tsp.	Oregano
1 tsp.	Basil
½ tsp.	Sea salt
¼ tsp.	Black pepper
2 c.	Tofu Ricotta Cheez
2 ½ c.	Notzarella Cheez

Cook the noodles and set aside. Combine the gluten, onion, tomato sauce, spinach, parsley, oregano, basil, salt, and pepper. Simmer, uncovered, for 10 minutes, stirring occasionally. Remove from heat and add the tofu ricotta. In a nonstick casserole layer half the noodles, half the gluten mixture, and half the notzarella. Repeat. Bake at 375° for 20 to 30 minutes–until the cheez starts to brown.

EGGPLANT LASAGNA

1	Medium eggplant, peeled and sliced ¼-inch thick
1 c.	Onions, chopped
1 ½ tsp.	Garlic, crushed
½ c.	Olive oil
3 c.	Tomatoes, chopped
½ c.	Tomato sauce
½ tsp.	Basil
½ tsp.	Oregano
½ tsp.	Parsley
2 T.	Unbleached white flour
Dash	Pepper
8 oz.	Lasagne noodles, cooked, drained, and set aside
1 lb.	Tofu, frozen, thawed, pressed, crumbled, and browned in olive oil
2 T.	Parmesan Cheez or soy parmesan

Salt both sides of the eggplant slices and let sit for 1 hour, then press out the moisture. Sauté the onions and garlic in 2 tablespoons of the oil until soft. Add the tomatoes, tomato sauce, basil, oregano, and parsley. Simmer 10 to 15 minutes. While the sauce is simmering, brown the eggplant in the oil and set aside. Put enough sauce into a baking dish to just cover the bottom. Put in a layer of eggplant slices. Add a layer of noodles, top with a layer of tofu, and cover with sauce. Repeat the layers ending with the sauce. Sprinkle the cheez over all. Cover and bake at 375° for 30 minutes.

FETTUCINI WITH SPINACH PESTO

12 oz.	Fettucini, uncooked
4 tsp.	Corn oil
¾ tsp.	Basil leaves
⅛ tsp.	Cayenne pepper
3 T.	Onions, chopped
1 tsp.	Garlic, minced
3 T.	Corn oil
2 c.	Fresh spinach
⅔ c.	Yeast, Pimento, or Notzarella Cheez
1 c.	Cashew or Tofu Sour Cream

Cook the fettucini. Put 2 teaspoons of corn oil, basil, cayenne, onions, and garlic in a blender and blend until smooth. Add the rest of the oil, then the spinach, cheez, and "sour cream," blending well and scraping down the sides of the blender when needed. Let sit a few minutes for the flavors to blend. Toss with the drained fettucini.

FRIED NOODLES

Make one of the Basic Pasta recipes, and cut into 1x¾-inch strips and deep-fry. These can be used in various recipes, including Chinese dishes, and can also be a snack for hungry children. These may be lightly salted or sprinkled with garlic salt, onion salt, or soy sauce for more flavor.

GNOCCHI

	UnBeef Broth
2 c.	Unbleached white flour
¼ tsp.	Sea salt
1 T.	Corn oil
4 c.	Potatoes, mashed with UnChicken or UnBeef Broth Spaghetti sauce of choice

Heat a large pot of UnBeef Broth. Meanwhile mix the flour and salt and shape into a mound in the center of a breadboard. Make a well in the center and pour in the oil and add the mashed potatoes. Knead the mixture with your hands (use extra flour if it gets sticky). Divide the dough into 4 balls and roll into long cylinders no more than an inch thick. Cut into 1-inch pieces. Rub fork tines over each piece of dough to make an impression. Drop the gnocchi into boiling broth. They will sink, then rise to the surface as they cook. Remove with a slotted spoon as soon as they rise. Toss with spaghetti sauce.

HERBED NOODLES

When you are in a hurry for something good—this is it!

12 oz.	Noodles of any type, cooked and tossed in ¼ cup of melted corn oil margarine
2 c.	Tofu Cottage Cheez
1 c.	Cashew or Tofu Sour Cream
⅓ c.	Onions, finely chopped
¼ tsp.	Garlic powder
¼ c.	Chopped parsley
½ tsp.	Italian Herb Seasoning
1 T.	Lemon juice
1 tsp.	Sea salt
⅛ tsp.	Cayenne pepper

Combine and let sit for a while to exchange flavors.

HERBED NOODLES WITH CHEEZ, LEMON, AND GREEN ONIONS

2 T.	Non-dairy margarine, melted
12 oz.	Noodles of any type, cooked
2 c.	Tofu, crumbled
¾ c.	Yeast, Pimento, or Notzarella Cheez
1 c.	Parmesan Cheez
½ c.	Green onion, finely chopped
¼ c.	Chopped parsley
1 ½ tsp.	Garlic, minced
½ tsp.	Italian Herb Seasoning
3 T.	Lemon juice
½ tsp.	Sea salt
⅛ tsp.	Cayenne pepper

In a 9x13-inch pan, toss the melted margarine with the cooked noodles. Beat together the remaining ingredients until thoroughly blended. Pour the mixture on the noodles and toss and turn until all is blended. Bake at 350° for about 20 minutes or until the top begins to brown. *Variation:* Add 10 oz. of chopped frozen spinach to the cheez mixture.

HUNGARIAN NOODLE BAKE

¼ lb.	Spaghetti, uncooked
¼ c.	Onions, finely chopped
½ tsp.	Garlic, minced
1 tsp.	Non-dairy margarine
1 ½ c.	Tofu Cottage Cheez
1 c.	Cashew or Tofu Sour Cream
Dash	Louisiana Hot Sauce
2 tsp.	Poppy seeds
½ tsp.	Sea salt
Dash	Paprika or cayenne pepper

Cook the spaghetti in boiling salted water till tender. Drain. Sauté onion and garlic in margarine till soft. Combine all together and put in an oiled baking dish. Bake at 350° for 25 minutes or until hot. Sprinkle with paprika. Serve with Parmesan Cheez.

LASAGNA

A leading favorite!

½ lb.	Lasagne noodles, uncooked
1 ½ c.	Mushrooms, sliced
1 ½ c.	Onions, chopped
2 tsp.	Garlic, minced
1 T.	Olive oil
3 c.	UnBeef, ground
4 tsp.	Parmesan Cheez
⅛ tsp.	Cayenne pepper
9 c.	Tomato Sauce–1
2 c.	Tofu Cottage Cheez
2-3 c.	Yeast, Pimento, or Notzarella Cheez

Cook the noodles, drain, and set aside. Sauté the mushrooms, onions, and garlic in the rest of the oil until the onions are soft. Combine with the gluten along with the "parmesan," cayenne, and 2 cups of the tomato sauce and cook for 5 more minutes. Layer a casserole dish or pan as follows:

> tomato sauce
> noodles
> cottage cheez
> gluten mixture
> a thin layer of the cheez
> tomato sauce
> noodles
> cottage cheez
> gluten mixture
> a thin layer of the cheez
> tomato sauce
> noodles
> cottage cheez
> tomato sauce

Bake at 375° 30-40 minutes.

LASAGNA NOODLES

Use Basic Pasta recipe. Roll out to ⅛-inch thickness. Cut into 1 ½-inch strips. Dry in the air overnight or in a 200° oven on cookie sheets until all moisture is gone.

LASAGNA ROLL-UPS

2 tsp.	Corn oil
1	10-oz. pkg. frozen chopped spinach, thawed and squeezed dry
2 T.	Green onions, minced
2 c.	Tofu Ricotta Cheez
¼ c.	Parmesan Cheez
5 ½ c.	Tomato Sauce-1 (recipe in this book)
½ tsp.	Sea salt
1	N'egg
12	Lasagna noodles, cooked and drained
½ c.	Water
2 c.	Notzarella Cheez

Cook the spinach and onions in the oil until tender, stirring frequently. Remove from heat and stir in the cheezes, 1 ½ c. of the tomato sauce, salt, and n'egg. Put the noodles in a single layer on waxed paper. Spread some of the cheez mixture on each noodle and roll up each one jelly-roll fashion. Combine the spaghetti sauce and water and put about ¾ of it into a casserole. Arrange the rolled noodles, seam side down, in the sauce. Top with the notzarella and rest of the sauce. Cover loosely with foil. Bake at 375° for 30 minutes or until hot and bubbly.

MACARONI AND CHEEZ

3 c.	Elbow macaroni, uncooked
2 T.	Non-dairy margarine
⅓ c.	Onions, chopped
⅓ c.	Unbleached white flour
3 c.	Cashew Milk
¾ tsp.	Sea salt
¼ tsp.	Cayenne pepper
3 c.	Pimento Cheez
	Sliced tomatoes

Cook the macaroni in boiling salted water as per package instructions. Drain and blanch. Set aside. In a saucepan melt the margarine and sauté the onions. Blend in the flour. While stirring, slowly add the "milk," salt, and pepper. Cook until thick and bubbly. Add the cheez and stir in well, being careful it does not burn. Pour this sauce into the macaroni and stir until all is well mixed. Put in a casserole and top with the tomatoes. Bake at 350° for about 30 minutes, until the top is slightly browned.
Variations: Use fettucini noodles instead of macaroni. Add 4 cups of a cooked vegetable, cut in small pieces, and 1 teaspoon of basil to the sauce while it is cooking.

MACARONI AND YEAST CHEEZ CASSEROLE

This is simple, but so flavorful that I could eat it just about every day.

¼ c.	Onions, chopped
2 T.	Non-dairy margarine
½ c.	Unbleached white flour
5 ¼ c.	Water
3 T.	Soy sauce
2 ¼ tsp.	Garlic powder
¼ tsp.	Tumeric
1 ½ tsp.	Sea salt
⅓ c.	Corn oil
1 ½ c.	Nutritional Yeast
8 ½ c.	Cooked macaroni

Sauté the onions in the margarine. Beat in the flour with a whisk, and continue to beat until the mixture is smooth and bubbly. Then whip in the water, soy sauce, garlic powder, tumeric, and salt, beating well until all is well mixed and smooth. Cook this until it thickens and bubbles. Finally whip in the corn oil and yeast flakes. Mix ¾ of the sauce with the macaroni and put in a casserole dish. Pour the rest of the sauce on top and sprinkle paprika over that. Bake at 350° for 15 minutes. Put under the broiler for a few minutes until the cheez is spotted brown.
Variations: Use fettucini noodles instead of macaroni. Add 4 cups of a cooked vegetable, cut in small pieces, and 1 teaspoon of basil to the sauce while it is cooking.

MACARONI DELIGHT

2 c.	Uncooked macaroni
2 c.	Cream of Mushroom Soup
1 c.	Cashew Milk
2 tsp.	Dijon-style mustard
¼ tsp.	Black pepper
2 c.	Broccoli flowerets
1 c.	Cauliflowerets
½ c.	Bell pepper (red preferred) cut into 1-inch squares
1 ½ c.	UnHam or UnTurkey, cubed
¾ c.	Yeast, Pimento, or Notzarella Cheez

Cook and drain the macaroni. Meanwhile heat the soup, "milk," mustard, and pepper to boiling. Add the vegetables, and bring back to the boil. Reduce the heat, cover, and simmer for 10 minutes or until the vegetables are tender–about 10 minutes–stirring occasionally. Stir in the gluten, cheez, and macaroni. Heat through.

MEXICAN BEAN AND PASTA DISH

⅓ c.	Bell pepper, chopped fine
⅓ c.	Onions, chopped
1 T.	Corn oil
6 c.	Tomatoes
½ tsp.	Cayenne pepper
½ tsp.	Oregano
1 tsp.	Sea salt
3 c.	UnBeef Broth
2 ½ c.	Pasta broken in small pieces and cooked
1 ½ c.	Corn
3 c.	Pinto or kidney beans–cooked

Sauté the bell pepper and onion in the corn oil.

Add to the tomatoes, cayenne, oregano, salt, and broth in a pot and bring to a boil. Simmer for 15 minutes. Add the pasta, corn, and beans and simmer, uncovered, for 10 more minutes.

MUSHROOM LASAGNA

1	Eggplant (about 1 ¼ lb.)
2 T.	Corn oil
1 ½ c.	Onions, minced fine
½ c.	Bell pepper
5 c.	Mushrooms, coarsely chopped
2 tsp.	Garlic, minced
5 c.	Canned crushed tomatoes with purée
2 T.	Parsley, chopped
¼ tsp.	Thyme
¼ tsp.	Nutmeg
¼ tsp.	Hot pepper flakes
1 tsp.	Sea salt
3 c.	UnBeef, ground
½ lb.	Lasagna noodles, cooked
1 c.	Tomato sauce
2 ½ c.	Tomatoes, sliced thin
3 c.	Notzarella Cheez

On a nonstick baking sheet roast the eggplant for 1 hour. Peel and finely chop the pulp. Set aside. In a large pan sauté the onions and bell pepper in the oil until just translucent. Add the mushrooms and sauté over medium heat for 15 minutes, or until all the liquid has evaporated. If you need, add some more oil for this. Stir in the eggplant, garlic, and crushed tomatoes. Cook until the eggplant is very soft and the liquid has evaporated. Add the parsley, thyme, ground nutmeg, and pepper flakes. Set aside. Spread ⅓ of the mushroom mixture over the bottom of a casserole. Cover with ⅓ of the notzarella. Cover with ⅓ of the UnBeef. Cover with a layer of noodles. Repeat layering with same proportions. Spread the tomato sauce over the top. Layer the sliced tomatoes over that. Sprinkle with salt and pepper. Bake at 350° for 40 minutes. Take from the oven and let sit 15 minutes before serving.

NOODLE BAKE

¼ lb.	Spaghetti, uncooked
¾ c.	Onions, chopped
½ tsp.	Garlic, minced
1 tsp.	Non-dairy margarine
2 c.	Yeast or Pimento Cheez
¼ tsp.	Sea salt
½ tsp.	Paprika

Cook and drain the spaghetti. Sauté the onions and garlic in the margarine. Combine everything. Put into a nonstick baking dish. Bake at 350° for 25 minutes. Sprinkle with paprika.

NOODLES ROMANO

2 T.	Dried parsley flakes
1 tsp.	Basil, dried
1 c.	Tofu Cottage Cheez, blended smooth
⅛ tsp.	Paprika
⅔ c.	Boiling water
8 oz.	Spaghetti, uncooked
1 tsp.	Garlic, minced
1 T.	Non-dairy margarine
½ c.	Pimento, Notzarella, or Yeast Cheez

Combine the parsley flakes, and basil, cottage cheez, and paprika. Stir in the boiling water. Blend the mixture well and keep warm over a pan of hot water or in a double boiler. Cook the spaghetti in salted water until just tender and drain. Sauté the garlic in the margarine for 1 to 2 minutes, then pour over the spaghetti and toss lightly and quickly to coat well. Sprinkle (or spread) the cheez over the spaghetti. Add the cottage cheez sauce and mix well.

NOODLES WITH UNBEEF SAUCE

4 tsp.	Garlic, minced
¼ tsp.	Ginger, powdered
¼ tsp.	Crushed hot pepper flakes
1 ½ c.	Onion, chopped
2 T.	Corn oil
2 c.	UnBeef, ground
½ c.	UnChicken Broth
⅓ c.	UnFish Broth
¼ c.	UnBeef Broth
¼ c.	Low sodium soy sauce
2 T.	Cornstarch
½ c.	Green onions, sliced diagonally
2 T.	Toasted sesame oil
16 oz.	Vermicelli noodles, cooked and drained
	Chopped green onions

Sauté the garlic, ginger, pepper flakes, and onion in the oil until the onion is transparent. Add the gluten and sauté until it is light brown. Combine ¼ cup of the UnChicken broth with the UnFish and UnBeef broths, and the soy sauce. Stir this into the gluten mixture. Cover, reduce the heat, and simmer for 10 minutes, stirring 1 or 2 times.

Dissolve the cornstarch in the rest of the UnChicken broth. Slowly stir this into the gluten mixture. Add the green onions. Cook, stirring, until the sauce is thick. Combine the cooked noodles and the sesame oil. Pour the gluten sauce over this and toss gently. Serve topped with chopped green onions.

PASTA PRIMAVERA–1

1 c.	Onions, cut into thin wedges
1 tsp.	Garlic, minced
1 c.	Mushrooms, sliced
1 T.	Non-dairy margarine
1 c.	Broccoli–flowerets and stem–sliced
⅔ c.	Carrots, cut in "matchsticks"
1 c.	Zucchini, sliced thin
¾ c.	UnChicken Broth
½ c.	Parsley, chopped
2 tsp.	Lemon juice
¾ tsp.	Basil, dried
¼ tsp.	Cayenne pepper
2 T.	Parmesan Cheez
8 oz.	Pasta, cooked

Sauté the onions, garlic, and mushrooms in the margarine for 2 minutes. Add the broccoli, carrots, zucchini, and broth. Simmer till the carrots are done. Add the remaining ingredients except the cheez and pasta, and cook for 1 minute. Toss everything together to mix well.

PASTA PRIMAVERA–2

1 T.	Olive oil
1 ¼ c.	Onion, diced
1 T.	Garlic, chopped
1 c.	Zucchini, sliced
1 c.	Yellow squash, sliced
1 c.	Bell pepper, cut into strips
1 ¾ c.	Canned tomatoes, chopped and drained (keeping the juice)
⅔ c.	Tomato paste
¾ c.	Warm water
½ tsp.	Sea salt
¼ tsp.	Black pepper
2 T.	Fresh basil, chopped, or 1 tsp. dried, crushed
1	9 oz. pkg. linguine

Heat the oil in a skillet and sauté the onion and garlic for 1 minute. Add the zucchini, squash, and bell pepper. Sauté 3 to 4 more minutes. Stir in the reserved tomato juice, tomato paste, water, salt, and pepper. Simmer until the vegetables are tender. Stir in the tomatoes and basil and simmer

20 more minutes. Prepare the pasta and serve the sauce over it.

PASTA SHELLS WITH BROCCOLI

3 T.	Onions
1 tsp.	Garlic, minced
1 tsp.	Olive oil
1 lb.	Small pasta shells, cooked and drained
1 head	Broccoli
1 c.	Tofu Cottage Cheez
⅛ tsp.	Cayenne pepper
½ tsp.	Basil
½ tsp.	Oregano
½ tsp.	Sea salt

Sauté the onions and garlic in the oil. Add the shells and set aside and keep warm. Cut the stems off the broccoli head and set aside. Cut the head into tiny flowerets and steam until just tender. Keep warm. Chop the broccoli stems into tiny pieces and cook until very tender. Cool and blend in a food processor or blender until smooth. Add the cottage cheez, cayenne, basil, oregano, onions, garlic, and salt. Combine well. Heat the cottage cheez mixture, *but do not cook or boil.* Pour over the warm pasta and toss till all is coated. Add the broccoli flowerets and toss lightly. Serve with "sour cream" on the side.

PASTA SNACKS

These can be made from leftover pasta, too.

After cooking the pasta, drain well, cool under cold running water, and pat dry. When pasta is dry, spray lightly with vegetable oil. Place on broiler trays and brown, turning a few times. These may be lightly salted or sprinkled with garlic salt, onion salt, or soy sauce for more flavor. This may also be done with leftover pasta.

PASTA WITH SPICY BROCCOLI

12 oz.	Pasta
1 lb.	Broccoli
½ tsp.	Hot pepper flakes
¼ tsp.	Garlic, minced
2 tsp.	Olive oil
3 ½ c.	Tomatoes, diced (or canned, diced, with ½ c. of the liquid)
½ tsp.	Sea salt

Cook the pasta in salted boiling water according to instructions. Cut broccoli into florets. Peel the stems and slice them into rounds. Steam the broccoli until tender-crisp (about 3 minutes), and set aside. Sauté the pepper flakes and garlic in the oil. Add the tomatoes and cook over medium heat for 5 to 10 minutes. Add to broccoli. Serve over cooked pasta.

PIROSHKIS

Follow the recipe for calzone, but roll out the entire dough as you would for a pie crust and then cut in rounds of the size you prefer. Bake at 400° until they start to brown.
Variation: Use pie crust dough instead of calzone dough.

QUICK CHEEZ DUMPLINGS IN TOMATO SAUCE

2 c.	Biscuit Mix
⅔ c.	Yeast or Pimento Cheez

Make biscuits with the mix, adding 2 tablespoons of the cheez to the biscuit dough. Pat or roll out the dough ⅛-inch thick. Cut into 3-inch rounds. Place 1 teaspoon of cheez in the center of each round. Wet the edges of the rounds with cold water. Gather up the edges to form a ball. Pinch them well. Drop the dumplings into thin tomato sauce, soup, or juice. Cover tightly and cook for 15 minutes. *Do not lift the lid until the time is up!*

SESAME NOODLES

3 T.	Low sodium soy sauce
2 T.	Rice vinegar and white wine vinegar
½ tsp.	Hot pepper flakes
2 T.	Sucanat
½ c.	Creamy peanut butter
1 T.	Oriental sesame oil
½ tsp.	Powdered ginger
½ c.	UnChicken Broth
8 oz.	Linguine or lomein noodles
	Green onion, chopped

In a saucepan combine the soy sauce, vinegar, pepper flakes, Sucanat, peanut butter, oil, ginger, and broth. Simmer, stirring, until thickened and smooth, and let cool slightly. Cook the noodles, drain them, rinse them under cold water, and drain again well. Put the noodles in a bowl and toss them well with the sauce. Serve at room temperature and garnish with the chopped green onions.

SIMPLE PASTA

½ c.	Onions, chopped
1 tsp.	Garlic, minced or sliced
1 ½ tsp.	Olive oil
6 c.	Pasta, cooked
1 tsp.	Total of herbs of choice, such as basil, oregano, rosemary, thyme, savory, bay leaf, dill weed, or Italian Seasoning
¼ tsp.	Cayenne pepper
½ tsp.	Paprika

Sauté the onion and garlic in the oil for 5 minutes. Combine all and heat through for 5 minutes, stirring occasionally. Nutritional yeast may be stirred in at the end for added flavor and nutrition.

SPAGHETTI AND SOY GRITS

⅔ c.	Onions, chopped
1 ½ tsp.	Garlic, minced
¼ c.	Black olives, chopped
½ c.	Bell pepper, chopped
1 c.	Squash, chopped
1 T.	Olive oil
2 c.	Soy Grits Beef
2 c.	Canned tomato paste
¼ c.	Low sodium soy sauce
½ tsp.	Oregano
1 tsp.	Paprika
¾ tsp.	Italian herbs
½ tsp.	Chili powder
1 tsp.	MSG
¼ tsp.	Sea salt
¼ tsp.	Black pepper
8 oz.	Spaghetti, cooked and drained

Sauté the onions, garlic, mushrooms, bell pepper, and squash in the oil until onions are clear. Add the grits and cook 5 minutes. Add the rest of the ingredients except the spaghetti. Cook slowly for 10 minutes. Mix sauce with the spaghetti.

SPAGHETTI BOLOGNESE

Top of the line!

2 ½ c.	Onions, chopped
2 ½ c.	Mushrooms, chopped
2 T.	Olive oil
1 ½ tsp.	Soy sauce
1 ½ tsp.	Sucanat
1 T.	Garlic, minced
1 ½ c.	Tomato paste
3 c.	Water

1 ½ tsp.	Basil
¼ tsp.	Fennel seed
¼ tsp.	Oregano
1 ½ tsp.	Sea salt
¾ tsp.	Black or cayenne pepper
½ lb.	Spaghetti, uncooked

Sauté the onions and mushrooms in the oil. Add the remaining ingredients–except the spaghetti–and cook for 30 minutes. Cook and drain the spaghetti. Combine with the sauce.

SPECIAL SPAGHETTI

6 oz.	Spaghetti, uncooked
½ c.	Yeast or Pimento Cheez
¼ c.	Onions, chopped
½ tsp.	Garlic, minced
2 T.	Mushrooms or black olives, chopped
2 tsp.	Corn oil
1 c.	Tomatoes, chopped
½ tsp.	Sea salt
¼ tsp.	Paprika

Cook the spaghetti in salted water. Drain, blanch, then rinse with hot water. Add the cheez and mix. Sauté the onions, garlic, and mushrooms (or olives) in the oil. Add the tomatoes, salt, and paprika, and cook for 10 minutes. Add the sauce to the spaghetti.

SPINACH LASAGNA

8 oz.	Lasagna noodles, uncooked (9 noodles)
1 ½ c.	Onions, chopped
2 ⅓ c.	Mushrooms, sliced
1 tsp.	Garlic, minced
1 T.	Corn or olive oil
2	10-oz. pkgs. frozen spinach, thawed and squeezed dry
1 tsp.	Dried oregano leaves
1 tsp.	Dried basil
¼ tsp.	Pepper
2 c.	Tofu Cottage Cheez or Tofu Ricotta Cheez
3 ½ c.	Notzarella Cheez
4 c.	Canned tomato sauce
¼ c.	Parmesan Cheez

Cook the noodles. While they are cooking, sauté the onions, mushrooms, and garlic in the oil for 5 minutes. Take from the heat and stir in the spinach, oregano, basil, and pepper. Set aside. Combine the tofu cheez with 2 cups of the notzarella. Line a nonstick baking dish with 3 noodles. Cover the noodles with half of the spinach mixture, half of the cheez mixture, and half of the tomato sauce. Cover this with 3 more noodles and repeat the layering. Top with the last 3 noodles and spread the 1 ½ cup of the notzarella over them. Sprinkle the parmesan over all. Bake at 375° for 45 minutes. Let stand 10 minutes before serving.

THAI-STYLE PASTA

Sesame oil can be used in this instead of corn oil, if you like.

1 c.	Onions, chopped
1 tsp.	Corn oil
1 lb.	Pasta, cooked and drained
1 tsp.	Sucanat
¼ c.	Soy sauce
3 T.	Fresh lemon juice
¼ tsp.	Crushed red pepper
⅔ c.	Unsalted roasted peanuts, chopped
½ c.	Water

Sauté the onions in the oil until transparent. Add rest of ingredients and sauté for 5 more minutes.

UNBEEF AND PASTA BAKE

4 oz.	Pasta
2 T.	Corn oil
1 c.	UnBeef, ground
½ c.	Onion, chopped
⅓ c.	Bell pepper, cut into strips
⅔ c.	Zucchini or yellow straightneck squash, sliced ¼-inch thick
1 tsp.	Garlic, minced
½ tsp.	Sea salt
¼ tsp.	Oregano
⅛ tsp.	Black pepper
2 c.	Spaghetti sauce of choice
¾ c.	Tomato, diced
1 c.	Notzarella Cheez

Cook the pasta. Meanwhile, heat the oil in a casserole and sauté the UnBeef, onion, bell pepper, zucchini, garlic, salt, oregano, and pepper until the onion is soft. Stir in the spaghetti sauce and cook, covered, until heated through well. Combine everything but the cheez in the casserole, spread the cheez over the top, and bake, uncovered, at 400° for 30 minutes.

UNBEEFY MACARONI AND CHEEZ

1 lb.	Uncooked macaroni

1 T.	Sea salt
½ c.	Onion, chopped
1 T.	Dried parsley flakes
¼ tsp.	Oregano
¼ tsp.	Black pepper
2 T.	Corn oil
2 c.	UnBeef, ground
3 c.	Cashew Milk
3 T.	Unbleached white flour
2 c.	Yeast or Notzarella Cheez
¾ c.	Tomatoes, diced

Cook the macaroni in water with the salt and drain. While the pasta is cooking, sauté the onion, parsley flakes, oregano, and pepper in the oil until the onion is soft. Add the UnBeef. Combine the "milk" and flour until smooth and stir into the UnBeef mixture. Cook over high heat, stirring, until the mixture boils and thickens slightly. Boil for 1 more minute. Reduce heat to low and stir in the cheez, tomatoes, and cooked macaroni. Bake uncovered at 400° for 20 minutes.

UNCHICKEN LASAGNA

1 ½ c.	Onion, diced
2 ½ tsp.	Corn oil
¼ c.	UnBacon, ground
4 c.	UnChicken, ground
¼ tsp.	Rosemary (dried)
1 tsp.	Sea salt
1 tps.	Cayenne
2 tsp.	Tomato paste
2 c.	UnChicken Broth
2	Bay leaves
2 c.	Mushrooms, sliced
1 lb.	Lasagna noodles, cooked
4 c.	White Sauce made with UnChicken Broth
3 c.	Yeast or Notzarella Cheez—or a combination

Sauté the onion in the oil until soft. Add the gluten and continue to sauté until it begins to brown. Combine everything but the noddles, white sauce, and cheez. Cook for 20 minutes. Line a nonstick casserole with some of the cooked noodles. Mix the white sauce thoroughly with the cheez. Combine 1 ⅓ cups of the white/cheez sauce and 3 tablespoons of the UnChicken sauce and set aside.

Layer in the following order:

¼ of the white/cheez sauce
noodles

⅓ of the UnChicken mixture
noodles
¼ of the white/cheez sauce
noodles
⅓ of the UnChicken mixture
noodles
¼ of the white/cheez sauce
noodles
⅓ of the UnChicken mixture
noodles
¼ of the white/cheez sauce

Cover with any remaining noodles (if there are none, it is all right). Top with the reserved sauce combination. Bake at 450° for 30 minutes.

WHITE LASAGNA

This is really special—I know you will agree!
It is also a gourmet's way to use up leftovers.

½ lb.	Lasagne noodles, uncooked
2 c.	Onions, chopped
2 c.	Mushrooms, sliced thick
1 T.	Garlic, minced
1 ½ c.	UnChicken, ground
2 c.	Broccoli, chopped fine, boiled, and drained
3 T.	Olive oil
2 c.	UnChicken Broth made with Cashew Milk
2 c.	Notzarella Cheez
⅛ tsp.	Cayenne pepper
⅛ tsp.	Black pepper
	Parmesan Cheez

Cook the noodles in salted water and set aside. Sauté the onions, mushrooms, garlic, gluten, and broccoli in the oil until the onions are soft. Combine the broth, cheez, and peppers, and heat until it becomes like a thick batter. In an oiled casserole put a layer of noodles. Spread half of the vegetable mixture over the noodles. Spread one third of the cheez sauce over the vegetables. Repeat these three layers. Make another layer of noodles. Spread the remaining third of the cheez sauce over the noodles. Sprinkle the "parmesan" over the sauce. Bake at 375° for 30 minutes or until light brown on top.
Variation: Instead of broccoli in the filling, use spinach or some other vegetables or beans (green or dried).

Pizza

BLENDER PIZZA SAUCE

I made this up in a pinch, and it was so good it became a permanent item in our cooking!

7 ½ c.	Canned tomatoes
½ c.	Tomato paste
2 tsp.	Onion powder
½ tsp.	Garlic powder
1 tsp.	Oregano
1 tsp.	Sea salt
½ tsp.	Cayenne
1 T.	Olive oil

Drain the tomatoes well in a colander, shaking them to drain fully. Put tomatoes into a blender and blend just until they are barely "scrambled." Pour them back into the colander and drain again, shaking to drain fully. Put the drained tomato pulp back into the blender and add the rest of the ingredients. Blend to mix everything well, but make sure the sauce does not become too liquid but remains thick and substantial.

CHEEZ-ONLY PIZZA

Make Quick Pizza, given later, but omit the tomato sauce. Omit the toppings, too, if you like.

EASY PIZZA CRUST

Make up the dough for the White Bread recipe, roll out, and use as crust for 2 pizzas.

"MEATZA" PIE

This is an adapted version of a Middle Eastern dish which does not have cheez—though it is good with cheez.

4 c.	Unbleached white flour

1 ½ c.	Warm water
2 tsp.	Yeast
1 T.	Olive oil
1 tsp.	Sea salt
2 c.	Onions, chopped
½ c.	Bell pepper, chopped
¼ c.	Olive oil
2 c.	Italian UnSausage, ground with 2 ½ tsp. of minced garlic
1 c.	Tomatoes, chopped
¼ c.	Tomato paste
¼ c.	Parsley, chopped
1 tsp.	Fresh mint or ¼ tsp. of dry mint Garlic Oil (see Seasonings section)
1 ½ c.	Notzarella Cheez Parmesan Cheez

Put the flour in a bowl and make a "well" in the center. Pour the water in the "well," spinkle the yeast on top of the water and stir it in lightly with your fingers. Let it rest for a few minutes until it becomes bubbly. Add the tablespoon of oil and the salt and mix it all together into a dough with your hands. Knead for a couple of minutes until you have a smooth dough. Let the dough rise for 1 to 1 ½ hours in a warm place. Sauté the onion and bell pepper in the ¼ cup of oil. When the onions become transparent, add the gluten and sauté until it starts to brown. Mix in the tomatoes, tomato paste, parsley, and mint and cook for 10 to 15 minutes. Roll out the dough to any shape you desire for the pizza, making sure it is thicker around the edges. Put the dough in a pan that has been dusted with corn meal. Wipe some garlic oil along the outer edges of the dough. Spread the notzarella over the dough. Put on the gluten topping. Sprinkle "parmesan" over the topping. Bake at 450° until the crust begins to brown. Take the pizza from the oven and brush more garlic oil around the edges of the crust. Continue to bake until the dough is golden brown and the bottom is brown (at least in spots) as well.

Variations: Use other types of UnSausage. Instead of gluten, use 4 cups of fresh mushrooms, and when sautéing them, add ¼ cup of soy sauce. Leave out the cheezes.

ONION-GARLIC PIZZA

This is an adaptation of the famous "Great White Pizza" that used to be made at Sadie's Saloon in Lincoln, Nebraska. Makes two 14-inch pizzas.

Crust:

3 T.	Yeast
1 ¾ c.	Water
1 ½ tsp.	Sucanat
5 ¼ c.	Unbleached white flour
1 ½ tsp.	Sea salt
2 T.	Oil

Dissolve yeast in the water with the Sucanat. Allow to froth. Sift the flour into a bowl, add the salt and oil, and stir. Add yeast mixture and combine thoroughly. Knead until smooth and elastic. Sprinkle 1 tablespoon of corn meal onto each pizza pan. Divide the dough into two equal parts. Roll out the dough and put it into the pizza pans, trimming off any excess dough.

Topping:

6 c.	Onions, sliced by being put through a food processor
2 T.	Garlic, minced
¼ c.	Non-dairy margarine
1 c.	Parsley, chopped
2 T.	Soy sauce

Sauté onions and garlic in melted margarine until soft. Add parsley and soy sauce and sauté 1-2 minutes. Spread evenly over two 14-inch pizzas. Bake at 350° for 15 minutes, then take out. Mix together:

2 tsp.	Rosemary, crushed
2 tsp.	Sage, rubbed
2 tsp.	Thyme, crushed

Sprinkle over the partially baked pizzas, along with salt and paprika. Top each pizza with Notzarella Cheez. Lightly sprinkle some of the herb mixture over the cheez. Return to the oven and continue to bake at 350° for fifteen minutes more.

PIZZA BREAD

2 ½ c.	Water
2 T.	Yeast
3 T. & 1 ½ tsp.	Sucanat
4 c.	Unbleached white flour
3 T.	Oil
1 T.	Sea salt

Make dough from the above ingredients. Spread out in a well-oiled casserole pan. Spread pizza sauce thickly over it. Bake at 500° until the sauce darkens.

PIZZA SAUCE–1

1 c.	Onions, chopped
1 T.	Garlic, minced
1 T.	Olive oil
6 c.	Tomatoes, chopped
1 tsp.	Sea salt
½ tsp.	Basil
½ tsp.	Oregano
½ tsp.	Hot pepper flakes
2 c.	Mushrooms, chopped
1 c.	Water

Sauté the onions and garlic in the oil. Combine with the rest of the ingredients and cook for 45 minutes, adding more water if it gets too thick.

PIZZA SAUCE–2

1 ½ c.	Onion, chopped
1 ½ c.	Mushrooms, thickly sliced
1 ½ tsp.	Garlic, minced or sliced
1 ½ tsp.	Jalapeños, minced or sliced
4 tsp.	Corn oil
4 c.	Canned tomatoes with juice
½ tsp.	Sea salt
½ tsp.	Basil
¼ tsp.	Oregano
¼ tsp.	Fennel seed

Sauté the onion, mushrooms, garlic, and jalapeños in the oil. Combine everything in a pot, bring to a boil, lower the heat, and simmer, uncovered, for 1 hour, adding more tomato juice if it gets too thick. Nutritional yeast may be stirred in at the end for added flavor and nutrition.

QUICK PIZZA

(Makes two 14-inch pizzas)

Make three cups of Notzarella Cheez. Make one time the Cracker recipe. Make one time the Blender Pizza Sauce recipe. Sprinkle 1 tablespoon of corn meal onto each pizza pan. Divide the dough into two equal parts. Roll out the dough and put it into the pizza pans, trimming off any excess. Bake at 550° for about 5 minutes. Spread the sauce on the crusts. Spread on the cheez. Sauté any topping such as ground gluten, onions, bell peppers, mushrooms, green olives, black olives, etc., in the smallest amount of oil and sprinkle over the pizzas. Bake until the crust lightly browns on the bottom–about 10 to 15 minutes.

TACO PIZZA

This makes 2 pizzas. Yum!
Since there are a lot of onions in the refried beans, none are put on the top, but if you are an onion lover, do so.

1	Times the Meatza Pie dough recipe
6 c.	Refried Beans (our recipe)
4 c.	Notzarella Cheez
4 c.	Lettuce, finely chopped
8 c.	Tomatoes, finely chopped
	Garlic Oil (see Etc. section)

Divide the dough in half and press it out on 2 sheet pans oiled with garlic oil. Coat the tops of the dough with garlic oil. Spread the refried beans over the dough. Put the pizzas in the oven and bake at 450° until the crust just begins to show color. Remove the pizzas from the oven and spread the cheez over the beans. Brush garlic oil around the outer edges of the pizza dough. Return to the oven and bake until the crust is golden brown. Take out of the oven and put the lettuce and tomatoes on top.
Variation: Put chopped black olives, pickled green tomatoes, pickled jalapeño slices, or Tomato Salsa

on top as well as lettuce and tomatoes.

TOMATO AND CHEEZ PIZZA

This is our version of the "Garden Pizza" that used to be available from Sadie's Saloon in Lincoln, Nebraska.

1	White Bread dough recipe
¼ c.	Mushrooms, chopped or sliced
¼ c.	Onions, chopped
1 tsp.	Garlic, minced
2 T.	Corn oil
2 c.	Tomatoes, chopped
¼ c.	Tomato paste
½ tsp.	Sage
½ tsp.	Basil
½ tsp.	Oregano
¼ tsp.	Sea salt
¼ tsp.	Paprika
12	Black olives, chopped
2 T.	Bell pepper, chopped
5	Tomatoes, in slices or wedges
2 c.	Notzarella Cheez

Knead the dough lightly, then–on a lightly floured surface–roll out to 12 inches in diameter, OR make 4 4-inch rounds. Place dough on an oiled baking sheet, cover with oiled plastic wrap, and leave in a warm place for 30 minutes to rise. Sauté the mushrooms, onions, and garlic in the oil until the onions are transparent. Add the chopped tomatoes, tomato paste, herbs, and seasonings. Simmer gently, stirring occasionally, until the mixture is pulpy. Spread the tomato mixture over the dough. Put the olives, bell pepper, and tomato slices (or wedges) over the top. Spread on the cheez. Bake at 425° for about 25 minutes (small pizzas will take about 15).

Focaccia

FOCACCIA

Focaccia is the granddaddy of pizza, and should not be neglected.
In Italy it is often eaten for breakfast.

3 ½ tsp.	Dry yeast
1 tsp.	Sucanat
1 ¾ c.	Lukewarm water
3 ½ c.	Unbleached white flour
1 tsp.	Sea salt
5 T.	Olive oil
	Coarse salt for sprinkling on top

Combine the yeast, Sucanat, and water, and let it sit for 5 minutes. During that time mix the flour and salt together. Add the yeast to the flour along with 3 T. of the oil and knead it until the dough is soft and slightly sticky. Form the dough into a ball and put it into an oiled bowl, turning it to coat it with the oil. Let the dough rise, covered with plastic wrap, in a warm place for 1½ hours, or until it is doubled in bulk. Press the dough evenly into a baking pan and let it rise, covered loosely, in a warm place for 1 hour, or until it is almost doubled in bulk. Dimple the dough, making ¼-inch deep indentations with your fingertips. Brush it with the remaining 2 T. of oil, and sprinkle it with coarse salt (omit this if you like). Bake in the lower part of the oven at 400° for 30 to 40 minutes, until it is golden brown. Let it cool in the pan on a rack. Serve either warm or at room temperature. You can split this for sandwiches.

ONION FOCACCIA

3 ½ tsp.	Dry yeast
½ tsp.	Sucanat

1 c.	Lukewarm water
3 ½ c.	Unbleached white flour
¾ tsp.	Sea salt
8 T.	Olive oil
3 c.	Onions, sliced thin
1	Large shallot, sliced thin
4	Green onions, chopped fine
¼ tsp.	Sage, crumbled
¼ tsp.	Cayenne pepper
2 T.	Parmesan Cheez

Combine the yeast, Sucanat, and water, and let it sit for 5 minutes. During that time mix the flour and salt together. Add the yeast to the flour mixture along with 3 T. of the oil and knead it until the dough is soft and slightly sticky. Form the dough into a ball and put it into an oiled bowl, turning it to coat it with the oil. Let the dough rise, covered with plastic wrap, in a warm place for 1 ½ hours, or until it is doubled in bulk. Press the dough evenly into a baking pan and let it rise, covered loosely, in a warm place for 1 hour, or until it is almost doubled in bulk. Stir together the remaining 5 T. of the oil with the onions, shallot, green onions, sage, and pepper. Sprinkle this evenly over the dough. Sprinkle the cheez over all. Bake in the lower part of the oven at 400° for 20 minutes. Remove from oven and brush some olive oil (use Garlic Oil if you have it) on the outer crust. Return to oven and bake 15 to 25 minutes, until it is golden brown. Let it cool in the pan on a rack. Serve either warm or at room temperature.
Variation: Include ½ to 1 cup of chopped or sliced black olives.

ROSEMARY FOCACCIA

3 ½ tsp.	Dry yeast
½ tsp.	Sucanat
1 c.	Lukewarm water
3 ½ c.	Unbleached white flour
1 tsp.	Sea salt
5 T.	Olive oil
½ tsp.	Garlic, minced
1 T.	Fresh rosemary, chopped fine, or 1 tsp. of dried, crumbled
	Coarse salt for sprinkling on top

Combine the yeast, Sucanat, and water, and let it sit for 5 minutes. During that time mix the flour and salt together. Add the yeast to the flour mixture along with 3 T. of the oil and knead it until the dough is soft and slightly sticky. Form the dough into a ball and put it into an oiled bowl, turning it to coat it with the oil. Let the dough rise, covered with plastic wrap, in a warm place for 1 ½ hours, or until it is doubled in bulk. Press the dough evenly into a baking pan and let it rise, covered loosely, in a warm place for 1 hour, or until it is almost doubled in bulk. Combine the remaining 2 T. of oil with the garlic and rosemary. Dimple the dough, making ¼-inch-deep indentations with your fingertips. Brush it with the oil mixture and sprinkle it with coarse salt (omit this if you like). Bake in the lower part of the oven at 400° for 35 to 45 minutes, until it is golden brown. Let it cool in the pan on a rack. Serve either warm or at room temperature.

UNSAUSAGE FOCACCIA

3 ½ tsp.	Dry yeast
½ tsp.	Sucanat
1 c.	Lukewarm water
3 ½ c.	Unbleached white flour
1 tsp.	Sea salt
8 T.	Olive oil
2 ¼ c.	UnSausage of choice
¼ tsp.	Black pepper
¼ tsp.	Dried oregano, crumbled
	Coarse salt for sprinkling on top

Combine the yeast, Sucanat, and water, and let it sit for 5 minutes. During that time mix the flour and salt together. Add the yeast to the flour mixture along with 3 T. of the oil and knead it until the dough is soft and slightly sticky. Transfer it to a lightly floured surface, and knead in the gluten, pepper, and oregano until they are incorporated completely. Form the dough into a ball and put it into an oiled bowl, turning it to coat it with the oil. Let the dough rise, covered with plastic wrap, in a warm place for 1 ½ hours, or until it is doubled in bulk. Press the dough evenly into a baking pan and let it rise, covered loosely, in a warm place for 1 hour, or until it is almost doubled in bulk. Dimple the dough, making ¼-inch-deep indentations with your fingertips. Brush it with the remaining 5 T. of the oil (use Garlic Oil if you have it), and sprinkle it with coarse salt (omit this if you like). Bake in the lower part of the oven at 400° for 35 to 40 minutes, until it is golden brown. Let it cool in the pan on a rack. Serve either warm or at room temperature.

Square Meals

REALLY A VARIATION on the piroshki (perogi) and calzone, these are marvelous. They are great to take along on trips or to "potluck." When we visit someone and want to bring along the food as well, these are the favorite for both ease and outright good eating.

Use other fillings than those given here, such as are in the Casseroles, Dried Beans, Sauces and Gravies, Meat Substitutes, or Vegetables sections. The possibilities for variety are limited only by your imagination.

Square meals freeze very well for future use.

HOW TO MAKE SQUARE MEALS

2 T.	Yeast
1 c.	Warm water
1 tsp.	Sucanat
3 T.	Corn oil
3 c.	Unbleached white flour
1 ½ tsp.	Sea salt
¼ c.	Nutritional Yeast
½ tsp.	Onion powder

Mix the yeast, water, and Sucanat. Let stand in a warm place for 10-15 minutes until risen and foamy. Whisk in the oil. In another bowl sift together the flour, salt, nutritional yeast, and onion powder, and mix well. Add this, small amounts at a time, with a whisk, to the yeast mixture. Continue to mix it with a spoon till it is smooth. Knead it for a while, just until it is a nice soft ball. Roll it out to ⅛-inch thickness. Cut into 4-inch squares. Moisten all 4 edges with water. Put ⅓ cup of filling (see recipes following)

in the center of each square. Bring the corners up over the filling and pinch together. Pinch the four seams closed as well. Put on a lightly oiled cookie sheet, seam side down. Poke holes in the top several times (at least 4) with a fork. Brush the tops with corn oil. Bake in a 400° oven for about 8 to 10 minutes, or until golden brown on top.

Variation: Add ¼ tsp. of garlic powder to the dough.

BARBECUE FILLING–1

1 ½ c.	Onions, chopped
2 tsp.	Garlic, minced
½ c.	Bell pepper, chopped
¼ c.	Celery, chopped
1 T.	Corn oil
2 c.	Tomato sauce
½ c.	Tomato paste
⅓ tsp.	Cayenne pepper
2 tsp.	Chili powder
½ tsp.	Sea salt
2 c.	UnBeef or Soy Grits UnBeef

Sauté the onions, garlic, bell pepper, and celery in the oil until soft. Add the tomato sauce, tomato paste, and spices, and cook for 5 minutes. Add the gluten and cook 5 more minutes.

BARBECUE FILLING–2

1 c.	Onions, chopped
1 tsp.	Garlic, minced
⅓ c.	Bell pepper
3 T.	Celery, chopped
¼ tsp.	Hot pepper flakes
2 tsp.	Corn oil

3 c.   UnBeef, sliced and chopped
1 ½ c.   Barbecue "Spare Rib" Sauce

Sauté the onion, garlic, bell pepper, celery, and pepper flakes in the oil until the bell pepper is soft. Add the gluten and barbecue sauce. Cook for 10 minutes. If it becomes too dry, add more barbecue sauce.

BROCCOLI & CHEEZ FILLING

2   16 oz. pkgs. frozen cut broccoli
1 c.   UnChicken Broth made with Cashew Milk
3 c.   Onions, chopped
1 T.   Corn oil
⅓ c.   Unbleached white flour
2 c.   Yeast or Pimento Cheez
1 tsp.   Sea salt
¼ tsp.   Cayenne

Thaw broccoli. Cook until tender in the broth. Sauté the onions in oil until transparent. Add flour, stirring until blended. Gradually add the broccoli, stirring constantly. Add cheez, salt, and cayenne and mix well.

BROCCOLI-MUSHROOM FILLING

1 c.   Green onions, sliced
¼ c.   Bell pepper, chopped
2 tsp.   Garlic, minced
2 T.   Corn oil
4 c.   Mushrooms, sliced
4 c.   Broccoli florets
2 c.   Yeast Cheez
3 T.   Soy sauce
¼ tsp.   Thyme
¼ tsp.   Cayenne
1 T.   Cornstarch dissolved in 2 T. cold water

While the dough is rising, sauté the onions, bell pepper, and garlic in the oil. Add the mushrooms and sauté 3 more minutes. Add the broccoli and sauté 2 more minutes. Add the cheez, soy sauce, thyme, and cayenne. Stir in the dissolved cornstarch and simmer until thickened–about 3 minutes. Let this cool some before filling the pastry.

CHEEZ AND ONION FILLING

2 ⅓ c.   Onions, coarsely chopped
4 tsp.   Corn oil
½ tsp.   Garlic, minced
3 ½ c.   Canned tomatoes, drained and chopped
½ tsp.   Oregano
¼ tsp.   Sea salt
⅛ tsp.   Black pepper
2 c.   Yeast Cheez

Sauté the onions in 3 teaspoons of the oil until soft. Set aside. Sauté the garlic in the remaining teaspoon oil until soft. Stir in the tomatoes, oregano, salt, and pepper. Cook for 10 minutes or until slightly thickened, stirring occasionally. Combine everything and heat through.

DAL FILLING

¾ c.   Red lentils
1 ½ c.   Flavoring Broth of choice
1 ¼ c.   Potato, peeled, cubed, and parboiled
¼ tsp.   Mustard seeds (black preferred)
¾ tsp.   Garlic, minced
½ tsp.   Ground ginger
⅓ tsp.   Tumeric
¼ tsp.   Cumin
¼ tsp.   Sea salt
1 T.   Corn oil
¼ tsp.   Ground coriander
¼ tsp.   Cayenne

Wash the lentils in a fine mesh colander several times with cold water and pick out debris. Bring to boil in a saucepan with the broth. Reduce heat and simmer 20 minutes, stirring frequently. Skim off the froth that rises to the top. Cook uncovered until the liquid is almost absorbed and the lentils have turned a golden color. Add the potatoes and stir well. Sauté the mustard seeds, garlic, ginger, tumeric, cumin, and salt in the oil for 1 minute. Add this mixture to the lentils along with the coriander and cayenne. Simmer for 10 minutes. Let this cool some before filling the pastry.

GLUTEN AND VEGETABLE FILLING

¼ tsp.   Crushed hot pepper flakes
2 T.   Corn oil
1 c.   Green onions, sliced
2 tsp.   Garlic, minced
½ c.   Bell pepper, chopped
2 c.   Carrots, grated
2 c.   Flavored gluten of choice, chopped
¾ c.   Potato, peeled and grated
2 tsp.   Dijon mustard
1 c.   Tomato sauce or mushroom gravy
3 T.   Dried parsley
½ tsp.   Sea salt

¼ tsp.   Cumin

Sauté the pepper flakes in the oil for 2 minutes. Add the onions, garlic, bell pepper, and carrots and sauté for 3 minutes. Stir in the gluten, potatoes, and mustard. Sauté for 5 more minutes. Add the rest of ingredients, reduce heat, and simmer 10 minutes. Let this cool some before filling the pastry.

HOT DOG AND BARBECUED BEAN FILLING

Baked beans:

½ c.	Bell peppers, chopped
2 tsp.	Garlic, minced
½ c.	Onions, chopped
1 T.	Corn oil
4 c.	Cooked dried beans, drained
½ tsp.	Cayenne pepper
3 c.	Tomato Sauce (one of the recipes from Gravies and Sauces)
¼ c.	Barbados molasses
¼ c.	Wine vinegar
1 T.	Sovex or Vegex (dissolve in the vinegar)
1 tsp.	Sea salt

Sauté the bell peppers, garlic, and onions in the corn oil. Combine all ingredients. Pour into a large oiled casserole. Add more tomato sauce if it is needed to cover the beans. Bake 40 minutes at 400°. *Refrigerate for one day before using. This is important.*

Hot dogs:

4 c.	Loma Linda "Big Franks," drained and ground

Sauté the Big Franks in a small amount of corn oil.

Assembly:
Mix the refrigerated beans and franks together.
Variation: Use 4 cups of ground UnHam or UnSausage instead of Big Franks.

HOT DOG AND SAUERKRAUT FILLING

2 c.	Onions, chopped
1 T.	Corn oil
4 c.	Sauerkraut, with juice *squeezed* out (not just drained)
½ tsp.	Caraway seeds
⅛ tsp.	Cayenne pepper
2 c.	Loma Linda "Big Franks," ground

Sauté the onions in the oil until soft. Put everything together and cook for 10 minutes.
Variation: Use 4 cups of ground UnSausage instead of Big Franks.

"MEAT PIE" FILLING

¼ c.	Bell peppers or pimentos, chopped
¼ c.	Onions, minced
⅛ tsp.	Cayenne pepper
1 T.	Non-dairy margarine
1 T.	Unbleached white flour
3 c.	Mixed vegetables, cooked
1 ½ c.	Medium White Sauce
1 ½ c.	UnBeef, UnChicken, UnPork, UnHam, or UnSausage, ground or chopped

Sauté the bell peppers (or pimentos), onions, and cayenne in the rest of the margarine. Stir in the the flour well. Add everything, including the gluten, and cook, stirring, until it is thick–about 10 minutes.
Variation: Make the white sauce with broth the flavor of the gluten.

MEXICAN FILLING–1

½ c.	Onions, coarsely chopped
2 tsp.	Garlic, minced
¼ c.	Bell pepper, chopped
1 T.	Corn oil
¾ c.	Tomatoes, coarsely chopped
1 ½ c.	Cooked pinto beans, drained and partially mashed
¼ tsp.	Cumin
1 ½ tsp.	Chili powder
½ tsp.	Black pepper
1 tsp.	Sea salt

Sauté the onion, garlic, and bell pepper in the oil until they begin to brown–about 5 minutes. Add the tomatoes and cook another 2 minutes. Stir in the rest of the ingredients, lower the heat, and simmer for 20 minutes.

MEXICAN FILLING–2

2 c.	Beef Gluten, chopped
1 c.	Onion, diced
1 ½ tsp.	Garlic, minced
1 ½ c.	Tomatoes, chopped
2	4-oz. cans of green chilies, chopped
1 ¼ c.	Potato, peeled, boiled, and diced
2 T.	Corn oil
1 tsp.	Sea salt

1 ½ tsp.   Oregano
2 tsp.   Chili powder
1 T.   Powdered coriander

Sauté the gluten, onion, garlic, tomatoes, chilis, and potatoes in the oil until the onions are soft. Add the salt, oregano, chili powder, and coriander. Simmer 2 to 3 minutes.

PIZZA FILLING

2 c.   Onions, chopped
2 c.   Mushrooms, chopped
2 tsp.   Garlic, minced
1 c.   Bell pepper, chopped
2 T.   Olive oil
2 c.   Tomato Sauce–2
¼ tsp.   Hot pepper flakes
¾ c.   Notzarella Cheez

Sauté the onions, mushrooms, garlic, and bell pepper in the oil until the onions and peppers are soft. Add the tomato sauce and pepper flakes and stir in the cheez. If this seems too dry, add some more tomato sauce; if too wet, let it cool down.

SPANAKOPITA FILLING

1 ½ c.   Onions, finely chopped
2 tsp.   Garlic powder
1 T.   Olive oil
1 ½ lb.   Frozen spinach, thawed and squeezed free of liquid
2 tsp.   Sea salt
2 tsp.   Oregano
1 ½ tsp.   Black pepper
2 ½ c.   Tofu Cottage Cheez, crumbled

Sauté the onion and garlic in the olive oil for 5 minutes, or until the onion begins to brown. Add the spinach and the spices, and cook, stirring frequently, for 5 minutes. Let it cool and add the cottage cheez.

SPICY GARBANZO FILLING

½ c.   Onions, finely chopped
1 tsp.   Garlic, minced
2 tsp.   Olive oil
¾ c.   Tomatoes, chopped
1 ⅓ c.   Cooked garbanzos
¼ c.   Parsley, chopped
2 tsp.   Lemon juice
¾ tsp.   Cumin, ground
¾ tsp.   Coriander, ground
1 ½ tsp.   Tumeric

⅛ tsp.   Cayenne pepper
½ tsp.   Sea salt

Sauté the onions and garlic in the oil until the onion begins to brown. Add the tomatoes and sauté for 2 or 3 minutes more. Add the rest of the ingredients, and cook together for 20 minutes.

HOW TO MAKE SWEET SQUARE MEALS

⅔ c.   Cashew Milk
½ c.   Sucanat
⅓ c.   Non-dairy margarine
2 T.   Yeast
¼ c.   Lukewarm water
1 tsp.   Sucanat
1   N'egg
4 ½ c.   Unbleached white flour
1 tsp.   Lemon rind, grated
½ tsp.   Mace

Heat the cashew milk with the Sucanat and margarine until the margarine melts. Allow this mixture to cool to lukewarm. Combine the yeast, water, and 1 teaspoon of Sucanat until dissolved. Add the n'egg and the yeast mixture to the cashew milk mixture. Combine half the flour with lemon rind and mace, then add the liquid, beating until smooth. Mix in the remaining flour. Let it stand for 10 minutes. Knead for 5 minutes on a lightly-floured board. Place dough in a lightly-greased bowl, turning once to bring the greased side up. Cover with a damp cloth and let rise in a warm place until double. Punch down, turn over, cover, and let rise until double again. Punch down, shape into a ball, and put on a lightly-floured surface. Cover with a bowl and let it rest 10 minutes. Roll it out to ⅛-inch thickness. Cut into 4-inch squares. Put ⅓ cup of filling (see recipes following) in the center of each square. Bring the corners up over the filling and pinch together. Pinch the four seams closed as well. Put on a lightly oiled cookie sheet, seam side down. Poke holes in the top several times (at least 4) with a fork. Brush the tops with corn oil. Bake in a 400° oven for about 8 to 10 minutes, or until golden brown on top.

APPLE FILLING–1

2 ½ c.   Apples, peeled, cored, and sliced
1 T.   Water
2 c.   Sucanat
2 T.   Barbados molasses

Half   Lemon rind, grated
¼ tsp. Cinnamon

Put the apples, water, Sucanat, molasses, lemon rind, and cinnamon in a saucepan. Simmer 10 minutes, stirring occasionally. Do not allow the apple to become mushy. Cool.
Variation: For a "Mincemeat" flavor, use ground cloves instead of cinnamon.

APPLE FILLING–2

6 c.	Apples, peeled, cored, and cut up small
1 ¼ c.	Sucanat
½ tsp.	Cinnamon
Dash	Nutmeg
4 tsp.	Non-dairy margarine
2 T.	Unbleached white flour

Mix all ingredients together and simmer for 10 to 15 minutes, or until the apples are soft.

BLUEBERRY FILLING

1 ¾ c.	Canned blueberries
⅓ c.	Sucanat
¼ c. & 2 T.	Unbleached white flour
¾ tsp.	Sea salt
¾ tsp.	Cinnamon
2 T.	Non-dairy margarine

Drain berries and save liquid. Combine Sucanat, flour, salt and cinnamon, and stir into the liquid saved from the berries. Heat, stirring constantly, until thick and smooth. Add the margarine and berries.

CHERRY FILLING

1 ⅓ c.	Liquid from canned cherries, or water if they are fresh
½ c.	Cornstarch
1 ⅓ c.	Sucanat
1 T.	Non-dairy margarine
¼ tsp.	Sea salt
4 c.	Cherries, pitted (if canned, save liquid and use in recipe)

Mix some of the liquid with the cornstarch. Heat rest of liquid to boiling. Add cornstarch mixture, stirring with a wire whisk. Cook until thick and clear. Stir in the Sucanat, margarine, and salt. Bring to a boil, stirring. Remove from heat. Add cherries and mix gently. Cool thoroughly.

DRIED FRUIT FILLING

1 c.	Mixed dried fruit, coarsely chopped
1 c.	Apple juice, unsweetened
¼ c.	Walnuts, chopped
½ c.	Sucanat
1 ¼ tsp.	Cinnamon
⅛ tsp.	Brandy or rum extract

Put dried fruit and apple juice in a saucepan. Let it soak for 1 hour. Bring to a boil, partially covered, and simmer for 10 minutes or until the liquid is absorbed and the fruit is soft. Add the walnuts, Sucanat, cinnamon, and extract (if used). Combine.

PEACH FILLING

1 T.	Non-dairy margarine
2 T.	Unbleached white flour
4 c.	Peaches, sliced
1 c.	Sucanat
⅛ tsp.	Cinnamon
⅛ tsp.	Sea salt

Melt the margarine. Stir in the flour well. Add the rest of the ingredients and keep stirring until the Sucanat liquefies. Cook until the peaches turn darker.

STRAWBERRY FILLING

4 c.	Frozen strawberries
1 c.	Sucanat
3 T.	Unbleached white flour
½ tsp.	Sea salt

Thaw and drain the berries and save the liquid. Combine the Sucanat, flour and salt, and stir into the liquid. Heat, stirring constantly, until thick and smooth. Add berries.

Pickles, Relishes, Salsa, Etc.

ANNE GOLDSTEIN'S MARINATED MUSHROOMS

1 c.	Olive oil (or ½ c. olive oil and ½ c. corn oil)
¾ c.	Balsamic vinegar
½ c.	Onion (red preferred), chopped
⅓ c.	Parsley, chopped
1 ½ tsp.	Garlic, sliced
1 tsp.	Sucanat
	Sea salt
	Pepper
2 lb.	White mushrooms, with the stems cut off to under the tops
½ c.	Bell pepper (red preferred), cut into strips

Combine everything and marinate in the refrigerator for at least a full day–2 or 3 days are even better.

ANNE GOLDSTEIN'S CAPONATA

This is a must!

1	Large eggplant
1	Large bell pepper
⅓ c.	Olive oil
1	Large onion, cut into ½-inch squares
3	Celery ribs, diced
2 tsp.	Garlic, minced
3 ½ c.	Canned tomatoes, coarsely chopped
2 T.	Tomato paste
¼ c.	Brine-cured olives
2 ½ T.	Capers
2 T.	Balsamic vinegar
2 tsp.	Sucanat
2 tsp.	Sea salt
¾ tsp.	Oregano
¼ tsp.	Hot pepper flakes
1 T.	Parsley, chopped
½ tsp.	Black pepper

Broil or grill the eggplant and bell pepper. Put them into a paper bag so the gathered moisture will soften them. Peel and cube the eggplant. Dice the bell pepper or cut it into strips. Heat the oil and sauté the onion in it for 3 to 5 minutes. Add the celery and sauté 5 more minutes. Add half of the garlic and sauté another minute. Add the eggplant, pepper, tomatoes, tomato paste, olives, capers, vinegar, Sucanat, salt, oregano, and pepper flakes. Cook, partially covered, for 20 minutes until most of the liquid is evaporated. Stir in the parsley, black pepper, and the rest of the garlic.

ANNE GOLDSTEIN'S CORN RELISH

2 lb.	Frozen or fresh corn
1 ½ c.	Onion (red preferred), chopped
½ c.	Green bell pepper, chopped
½ c.	Red bell pepper, chopped
3 c.	Balsamic vinegar
½ c.	Sucanat
1 tsp.	Mustard seed
1 tsp.	Celery seed
1 T.	Sea salt
1 T.	Black pepper

Combine everything in a saucepan and bring to a boil. Reduce heat and cook until it thickens slightly–about 40 minutes. Cool.

AUNT LOU MAXEY'S TOMATO RELISH

My great-aunt Lou Maxey could not cook to save her soul. But she sure could make relish!

7 ½ lbs.	Tomatoes
1 ½ c.	Onions, coarsely chopped
1 c.	Bell pepper, coarsely chopped
3 T.	Sucanat
1 T.	Sea salt
3 T.	Cider vinegar
1 ½ tsp.	Cinnamon, ground
½ tsp.	Allspice, ground
½ tsp.	Nutmeg, ground (fresh preferred)
½ tsp.	Cloves, ground

Put the tomatoes, onions, and bell peppers in a food processor and chop to medium coarseness. Transfer to a heavy cooking vessel and stir in the Sucanat and salt. Bring to a boil over high heat. Stirring frequently, cook briskly, uncovered, until the mixture is reduced to about half its original volume and is thick enough to hold its shape almost solidly in a spoon. Add the vinegar, cinnamon, allspice, nutmeg, and cloves. Reduce the heat to low, partially cover, and simmer for 1 hour. Immediately ladle the relish into hot sterilized jars, filling them to within ⅛ inch of the tops. Seal the jars at once.

AUNT MAY'S PEPPER RELISH

The mildness of this is its virtue!

½ c.	Red bell pepper, chopped fine
½ c.	Green bell pepper, chopped fine
½ c.	Yellow bell pepper, chopped fine
¼ c.	Onion
2 T.	Garlic, minced
3 T.	Parsley, chopped
3 T.	Balsamic vinegar
3 T.	Olive oil
1 tsp.	Sea salt
1 tsp.	White pepper
½ tsp.	Cayenne pepper

Whisk everything together in a bowl to combine thoroughly. Chill, covered, for at least 2 hours and up to 2 days. Stir before serving.

BREAD AND BUTTER ZUCCHINI

12 c.	Zucchini, sliced ¼-inch thick
1 ½ c.	Onions, thinly sliced
2	Large garlic cloves
⅓ c.	Sea salt
2 qts.	Crushed ice
4 c.	Sucanat
1 ½ tsp.	Tumeric
1 ½ tsp.	Celery seed
2 T.	Mustard seed
3 c.	White vinegar

Combine the zucchini, onions, and garlic. Add the salt and mix thoroughly. Cover with crushed ice or ice cubes. Let stand for 3 hours. Drain thoroughly. Remove garlic cloves. Combine Sucanat, spices, and vinegar. Heat just to boiling. Add the drained zucchini and onion slices and heat for 5 minutes. Pack hot pickles loosely into sterilized, hot pint jars to ½ inch of the top. Seal and process in a boiling water bath for 5 minutes.

CAJUN CATSUP

This am delighteous, I garontee!

4 c.	Onion, chopped
1 c.	Celery, chopped
1 c.	Bell pepper, chopped
1 c.	Parsley, chopped
3 T.	Corn oil
2 T.	Garlic, chopped
3 c.	Lea & Perrins Steak Sauce
½ c.	Louisiana Hot Sauce
3 c.	Tomato sauce
3 tsp.	Sea salt

In a large skillet, sauté the onions, celery, bell pepper, and parsley in the oil until the onions are soft and transparent. Add the garlic and cook a little longer. Add the steak sauce, hot sauce, tomato sauce, and salt, and bring to a boil. Lower the heat and cover, and cook for 2 to 3 hours. This can be kept refrigerated for a few weeks.

CAPONATA

Always!

6 T.	Olive oil
1 tsp.	Hot pepper flakes
2 c.	Celery, coarsely chopped
3 c.	Onion, coarsely chopped
1 T.	Garlic, minced
⅔ c.	Bell pepper (red preferred), coarsely chopped
3 ½ c.	Canned tomatoes with juice
8 c.	Eggplant, cut into ½-inch dice and deep-fried
10	Black olives, chopped fine
5	Green olives, chopped fine
2 T.	Capers, rinsed and minced

⅓ c. Parsley, minced
¼ c. Balsamic vinegar
2 T. Sucanat
½ tsp. Sea salt
¼ tsp. Black pepper

Heat the oil in a large saucepan. Stir in the pepper flakes and celery, and cook, stirring occasionally, for 5 minutes. Add the onion, garlic, and bell pepper. Sauté for 5 more minutes, or until the onion is soft. Add the tomatoes and liquid, breaking up the tomatoes. Reduce heat, cover, and simmer 10 minutes. Add the eggplant, olives, and capers, stir in well, cover, and simmer for 15 more minutes. Stir in the parsley, vinegar, and Sucanat. Cook just until the Sucanat is dissolved. Add the salt and pepper.

CHILI MACHO

Go ahead—I dare you!

3 c. Canned tomatoes
1 c. Onions, chopped
1 Garlic clove, minced
1 c. Jalapeño peppers
1 ½ tsp. Sea salt

Blend all in the blender, but only until coarsely chopped. Let sit until the flavors are well blended.

CHILIPETIN SAUCE

Whew!

1 c. Green chili peppers, chopped
1 c. Onions, chopped
1 Garlic clove
1 Green tomato
1 tsp. Flour
1 c. Vinegar
2 T. Sucanat
1 tsp. Sea salt

Grind fine or chop the peppers, onion, garlic and tomato. Put in a saucepan with the flour and stir well. Bring the vinegar, Sucanat and salt to a boil. Pour into the pepper mixture. Stirring occasionally, boil, uncovered, for about 30 minutes, or until it thickens slightly. Seal while hot in sterilized jars. The sauce will be thin, but it thickens with age.

DILL PICKLES

If the angels in heaven make dill pickles they use this recipe!

4 lb. Cucumbers
3 c. White vinegar
3 c. Water
⅓ c. Sea salt

For each pint jar:

2 T. Dill seed
3 Peppercorns
1 or 2 Dried chili peppers
1 Garlic clove

Wash the cucumbers. Either leave them whole or cut them in half or into spears. Combine the vinegar, water, and salt, and heat to the boiling point. Pack the cucumbers into hot, sterilized jars. Add the dill seed, peppercorns, peppers, and garlic. Fill the jars up to the mark (molded in the glass) with the boiling hot vinegar mixture. Seal the jars and process in a boiling water bath for 10 minutes. Makes 6 to 8 pints.

DILLED GREEN BEANS

8 c. Whole green beans

For each pint jar:

¼ tsp. Crushed hot pepper flakes
½ tsp. Mustard seed
½ tsp. Dill seed (or 1 dill head)
1 Garlic clove
5 c. Vinegar
5 c. Water
½ c. Sea salt

Wash beans thoroughly. Drain and cut into lengths that will fit into pint jars. Pack the beans in sterilized, hot jars. Add the hot pepper flakes, mustard seed, dill seed and garlic. Combine the vinegar, water and salt; heat to boiling. Pour boiling liquid over the beans. Seal and process in a boiling water bath for 5 minutes.

GREEN TOMATO PICKLES

Simply beyond description. The tomatoes are exquisitely flavorful with a texture like butter.
This recipe can be used to pickle any vegetables you wish— alone or in combination—including cucumbers.
For a stronger dill taste, use fresh dill weed instead of seeds.

Wash the tomatoes well. Sterilize the quart jars

and lids. Combine and bring to a boil:

9 c.	Water
6 c.	Cider vinegar
¾ c.	Sea salt

In each quart jar put enough green tomatoes cut in halves or quarters to fill the jar to its neck. As you are filling each jar with the tomatoes, intersperse among them:

3	Garlic cloves, peeled and cut in half
1 tsp.	Dill seed
3	Red chili peppers, stemmed

Pour the boiling brine into the jars, making sure the tomatoes are completely covered. Seal and process in a boiling water bath for 20 minutes.

GREEN TOMATO SALSA

This sneaks up on you and is HOT!!! But is worth it!

2 c.	Hot peppers, chopped fine
1 ½ c.	Red onions, chopped fine
¼ c.	Bell pepper, chopped fine
2 ½ c.	Green tomatoes, chopped fine
2 ½ c.	Water
4 c.	Ripe tomatoes, chopped, (or canned tomatoes, drained and chopped–use juice for liquid, replacing some or all of the water)
1 T. & 1 tsp.	Sea salt
2 T.	Balsamic vinegar

Combine all and bring to a boil. Simmer for 1 ½ to 2 hours. For a bit more tang you can add 1 more tablespoon of vinegar.

HOT HERBED CARROTS

4	Hot peppers
4	Garlic cloves
1 tsp.	Rosemary
4 c.	Baby carrots, or 2 lbs. larger carrots cut in 4-inch lengths
2 c.	Water
2 c.	White vinegar
3 T.	Sucanat
3 T.	Sea salt

Halve the peppers lengthwise. In each of 4 pint jars, put 1 pepper (2 halves), 1 garlic clove, and ¼ tsp. of rosemary. Pack the jars full of carrots. Combine the water, vinegar, Sucanat, and salt, and bring to a boil. Reduce the heat and simmer for 5 minutes. Pour the liquid over the carrots. Seal and process in a boiling water bath for 10

minutes.

HOT STUFF

This is half-way between a simple salsa and a relish. It brings out the flavor of dishes that are bland in both flavor and texture.

2 c.	Onions, chopped fine
2 c.	Hot peppers, stemmed, seeded, and chopped
	Sea salt
¾ c.	White vinegar
¼ c.	Water

Combine the onions and peppers in a bowl. Spoon into sterilized canning jars and add the salt–1 teaspoon per quart jar, or ½ teaspoon per pint jar. In a small saucepan, heat the vinegar and water together, but do not bring it to a boil. When the liquid is too hot to stir with your finger, it is ready. Pour it into the jars, making sure to cover the peppers and onions. Seal, and let it sit for 3 to 4 days before using it.

JALAPEÑO AND BELL PEPPER CHUTNEY

I can eat this by the spoon!

3	Red bell peppers, chopped
3	Green bell peppers, chopped
3	Jalapeños, seeded and minced
1 c.	Onion, chopped
1 ½ c.	Sucanat
1 ½ c.	Cider vinegar
1 tsp.	Sea salt

Combine everything in a heavy saucepan. Bring to a boil and simmer, stirring occasionally, for 1½ hours or until the liquid is syrupy. Transfer to a bowl and chill, covered, overnight.

LOUISIANA HOT SAUCE

This has the zing of the commercial version, yet is somehow milder.
Because of the garlic it has more flavor, too.

3 c.	Hot peppers, stemmed and finely chopped
1 c.	White vinegar
½ c.	Water
1 T.	Garlic, chopped fine
1 T.	Sea salt

Combine all the ingredients in a saucepan and simmer, covered, until the peppers are very soft, stirring occasionally. Take from the heat and mash with a potato masher. Press the mixture through a sieve so that only the skins and seeds remain in the sieve. Discard them. If the mixture is too thick to pour, add more salt and vinegar. Pour into sterilized jars and seal.

MARINATED MUSHROOMS

Simply Miraculous! And simply a Must!

12 oz.	Mushrooms
½ c.	Green onions, sliced
¼ c.	Bell pepper, chopped
2 T.	Parsley, minced
½ c.	Italian salad dressing (Wishbone brand recommended if you don't make your own)

Combine everything in a glass bowl and marinate several hours or overnight.

MARINATED TOMATOES

Taste-full!

3 c.	Tomatoes, sliced thick
⅓ c.	Olive oil
¼ c.	Red wine vinegar
1 tsp.	Sea salt
¼ tsp.	Black pepper
½ tsp.	Garlic, minced
2 T.	Onion, chopped
1 T.	Parsley, chopped
1 T.	Fresh basil, chopped, or 1 tsp. dried

Put the tomato slices in a large shallow dish. Combine the rest of the ingredients in a blender and blend well. Pour over the tomato slices. Cover and refrigerate a few hours.

MEAN GREEN

For those with the moxie!

3 c.	Green tomatoes, or tomatillos, very coarsely chopped
¾ c.	Onion, chopped
1 c.	Jalapeños (*with* seeds), coarsely chopped
1 ½ tsp.	Garlic, put through a press
2 tsp.	Sea salt
¼ tsp.	Dried oregano (crushed leaves)
⅛ tsp.	Coriander
⅛ tsp.	Sucanat

Process everything in a food processor using the metal chopping blade. Cook, stirring, for 5

minutes.

PICKLED BEANS AND ONIONS

6 c.	Green beans
2 c.	Vinegar
2 c.	Sucanat
1 ½ c.	Water
1 T.	Pickling spice
1 T.	Mustard seed
2 c.	Pearl onions, peeled

Wash beans and trim the ends. Parboil in salted water about 5 or 6 minutes and drain well. Combine vinegar, Sucanat, water, and spices in a large saucepan. Simmer about 15 minutes. Pack the beans and onions into sterilized hot jars, leaving ¼-inch head space. Remove any air bubbles with a non-metallic spatula. Adjust the caps. Seal and process for 10 minutes in a boiling water bath canner. Makes four 1-pint jars.

PICKLED CALICO VEGETABLES

6 c.	Cauliflower flowerets (1 large head)
1 c.	Onions, cut in chunks
2	Bell peppers, chopped into ½-inch pieces
2 c.	Carrots, sliced
¼ c.	Pickling salt
	Crushed ice
1 qt.	White vinegar
1 ½ c.	Sucanat
2 tsp.	Mustard seed
2 tsp.	Celery seed
2 tsp.	Louisiana Hot Sauce

Combine the vegetables and salt in a large mixing bowl. Cover with crushed ice and let it stand for 3 hours. Drain the vegetables. Rinse them well. Combine the vinegar, Sucanat, mustard seed, celery seed, and hot sauce in a large saucepan or pot. Bring to a boil. Add the vegetables and simmer 5 to 7 minutes. Carefully pack into sterilized hot jars, leaving ¼-inch head space. Remove any air bubbles with a non-metallic spatula. Seal and process 10 minutes in a boiling water bath canner. Makes 5 1-pint jars.

QUICK TOMATO RELISH

3 c.	Tomatoes, diced
2 c.	Bell pepper, chopped
¼ c.	Italian Dressing

Combine and refrigerate so flavor can develop.

SWEET TOMATO RELISH

12 c.	Tomatoes, seeded and chopped
1 c.	Celery, sliced thin
1 ½ c.	Bell pepper, chopped
3 c.	Onion, sliced thin
2 T.	Prepared horseradish, drained
3 T.	Sea salt
1 c.	Sucanat
¼ tsp.	Black pepper
¼ tsp.	Cloves, ground
1 T.	Mustard seeds
1 tsp.	Cinnamon
1 c.	Cider vinegar

Thoroughly combine the tomatoes, celery, bell pepper, onion, horseradish, and salt. Chill, covered, overnight. Drain. Add the rest of the ingredients. Cover and chill, stirring occasionally, for at least 3 hours before serving.

TOMATO RELISH

Zesty!

1 qt.	Tomatoes, finely chopped
⅓ c.	Onions, finely chopped
½ c.	Celery, finely chopped
¼ c.	Bell pepper, finely chopped
1 tsp.	Sea salt
⅓ c.	Lemon juice
2 T.	Olive oil

Combine and refrigerate so flavor can develop.

TOMATO SALSA

This is a staple for us. Unbeatable!

1 c.	Bell pepper, chopped
¼ c.	Onions, chopped
1 T.	Corn oil
1 c.	Jalapeños, chopped, or 2 tsp. of hot pepper flakes
4 c.	Tomatoes, chopped
1 tsp.	Garlic powder
1 ½ tsp.	Sea salt
1 T.	Vinegar

Sauté the bell peppers and onions in the corn oil. Combine with rest of ingredients and cook. *Variation:* Instead of fresh tomatoes, use 2 cups of canned tomato sauce.
Note: When made with jalapeños, this gets hotter in a few days, so you might want to use only ½ cup of jalapeños the first time around.

TOMATO SALSA CRUDA

Nothing crude about this sophisticated relish!

2 c.	Canned tomatoes
2 T.	Onions, minced
1 tsp.	Hot pepper flakes
1 T.	Parsley, minced
1 tsp.	Lemon or lime juice
1 T.	Olive oil
¼ tsp.	Sea salt

Purée the tomatoes in a blender or processor until fairly smooth. Combine the purée with the remaining ingredients and let them stand for at least 15 minutes to flavor. Use as soon as possible.

TOMATO SALSA FRESCA

2 c.	Canned tomatoes, chopped well
3 T.	Onions, minced
½ c.	Bell pepper, minced
1 tsp.	Hot pepper flakes
1 T.	Lemon or lime juice
1 T.	Olive oil
1 tsp.	Sea salt

Combine and let stand for 30 minutes to blend.

ZUCCHINI PICKLES

Try it and like it!

8 c.	Zucchini, thinly sliced
2 c.	Onions, thinly sliced
½ c.	Coarse salt
	Water
1 qt.	White vinegar
2 c.	Sucanat
2 tsp.	Celery seeds
2 tsp.	Mustard seeds
2 tsp.	Dill seeds
1 tsp.	Dry mustard

In a large bowl, combine the zucchini, onions, and salt with enough water to cover. Let it stand 1 hour. In a saucepan, combine the vinegar, Sucanat, celery seeds, mustard seeds, dill seeds, and the dry mustard. Bring to a boil and boil for 3 minutes. Drain the zucchini and onions. Pour the hot vinegar mixture over the zucchini and onions. Let stand 1 hour. Transfer to the large saucepan, bring to a boil, and boil for 3 minutes. Pack into sterilized jars, seal, and process in boiling water, enough to cover the jars, from 10 to 15 minutes, according to the jar manufacturer's instructions. Cool and store in a cool, dry place.

ZUCCHINI–RED PEPPER RELISH

2 c.	Zucchini, cut in ½-inch cubes
2 c.	Sweet red pepper, cut in ¼-inch squares
2 T.	Sea salt
2 ½ c.	Water
1 ½ c.	White vinegar
1 ¼ c.	Sucanat
2 T.	Instant minced onion
1 tsp.	Cumin seed
1 tsp.	Instant minced garlic
½ tsp.	Hot pepper flakes

In a large bowl, place zucchini, peppers, and salt. Mix well. Cover and refrigerate 12 to 15 hours. Take from the refrigerator, drain off liquid, rinse vegetables well, and drain thoroughly. In a large saucepan, place the water, vinegar, Sucanat, onion, cumin, garlic, and pepper flakes. Bring to a boil. Reduce the heat and simmer, covered, for 10 minutes. Add the zucchini and peppers. Simmer, covered, stirring occasionally until the vegetables are tender, about 15 minutes. Ladle into 8 (½-pint) sterilized hot canning jars, leaving ¼-inch head space. Cover, following manufacturer's directions. Process for 10 minutes in a boiling water bath according to the jar manufacturer's directions.

ZUCCHINI RELISH

This is worth its weight in gold!

5 c.	Zucchini, minced
½ c.	Sea salt
2 ½ c.	Onions, minced
½ c.	Celery, diced
¾ c.	Bell pepper, diced
1 tsp.	Tumeric
1 ½ tsp.	Dry mustard
4 ½ tsp.	Celery seed
3 c.	Sucanat
2 ½ c.	White vinegar
1 ½ T.	Cornstarch

Combine the zucchini, salt, onions, celery, and bell pepper. Allow this to stand overnight to draw out the juices. Drain and rinse thoroughly. Drain again in a colander. While the vegetables are still in the colander, press out as much liquid as possible. Combine the pressed vegetables with the rest of the ingredients in a pot and bring it to a rolling boil. Reduce the heat and simmer for 20 minutes. Ladle the relish into hot sterilized jars and seal, or put in refrigerator and keep.

Sandwiches and Spreads

APPLE BUTTER

1 gal.	Puréed fruit
3 c.	Sucanat (4 cups for peach butter)
1	Orange, peeled and diced with all the juice
2 T.	Lemon or lime juice
1 Pinch	Sea salt

Combine and cook on low heat (simmer) for six hours, or till it turns dark brown and is thick. This keeps very long in the refrigerator.

BARBECUE BEAN SANDWICH SPREAD

Mix together 1 part of Barbecue Beans and 1 part of Cheez Spread.

BEAN SANDWICH SPREAD

8 c.	Cooked dried beans, mashed
½ c.	Bell pepper, chopped fine
2 c.	Tomatoes, chopped
½ c.	Onions, minced
2 T.	Lemon juice
1 T.	Corn oil
1 ½ tsp.	Sea salt

CHEEZ SPREAD–1

6 c.	Yeast or Pimento Cheez
⅓ c.	Onions, chopped
1 c.	Black olives, chopped
1 c.	Bell pepper, finely chopped
1 ½ c.	Cashew or Tofu Mayonnaise, or Miraculous Whip
¼ tsp.	Cayenne pepper
½ tsp.	Basil

| ⅛ tsp. | Dill weed |
| 1 ½ tsp. | Sea salt |

Variation: If this seems a bit too bland, put in a little wine vinegar or lemon juice.

CHEEZ SPREAD–2

6 c.	Yeast or Pimento Cheez
½ c.	Onions, chopped
1 c.	Dill pickles or green olives, chopped fine
¼ c.	Pimento, chopped fine
1 ½ c.	Cashew or Tofu Mayonnaise, or Miraculous Whip
1 T.	Prepared mustard
2 tsp.	Louisiana Hot Sauce
½ tsp.	Sea salt

CHEEZ TOAST

Spread slices of bread with non-dairy margarine—better yet, with melted margarine that has been mixed with onion or garlic powder. Bake on high, or broil until toasted. Take from oven. Lightly sprinkle each slice with finely chopped UnBacon. Cover each slice with Yeast or Pimento Cheez. Replace in oven and broil or bake until brown spots appear.

"EGG" SALAD

½ c.	Onion, chopped fine
¼ tsp.	Tumeric
¼ tsp.	Dill weed
¼ tsp.	Sea salt
1 ½ tsp.	Olive oil
1 c.	Firm tofu, crushed
½ c.	Cashew or Tofu Mayonnaise, or

Miraculous Whip
2 T. Green onion tops, chopped
½ tsp. Louisiana Hot Sauce
1 tsp. Nutritional Yeast

Sauté the onions, tumeric, dill, and salt in the oil till the onions are soft, and set aside. When cool, combine with the rest of the ingredients.
Variations: Add ¼ tsp. garlic powder. Add 1 T. jalapeños, minced. Add sliced lettuce and tomatoes (in making the sandwiches).

EGGPLANT APPETIZER SPREAD

¼ c. Corn oil
6 c. Eggplant, peeled and cut into ½-inch cubes
1 tsp. Cornstarch
⅔ c. UnChicken Broth
1 tsp. Garlic, minced
½ tsp. Powdered ginger
3 tsp. Red chili paste
1 T. White wine vinegar or rice vinegar
3 Green onions, sliced thin
2 T. Soy sauce
2 tsp. Sucanat
1 Bell pepper (red preferred), minced

In the corn oil sauté the eggplant until it is tender and browned. Transfer with a slotted spoon to paper towels to drain. Dissolve the cornstarch in the broth. In the oil sauté the garlic, ginger, chili paste, and vinegar for 30 seconds. Add the onions and sauté for 30 more seconds. Add the soy sauce, Sucanat, cornstarch mixture, bell pepper, and eggplant, and sauté for 1 minute, or until the eggplant has absorbed most of the liquid.

EGGPLANT "CAVIAR"

2 Large eggplants, baked at 400° for 45 minutes (should yield about 3 cups of pulp)
¾ c. Tomato paste
¾ c. UnBeef Broth
2 tsp. Corn oil
1 tsp. Sea salt
½ tsp. Onion powder
¼ tsp. Garlic powder

Blend everything in a food processor and cook until most of the liquid evaporates. Refrigerate. Best served cold or at room temperature–not warm or hot.

GRILLED CHEEZ SANDWICHES

Not really the same, but plenty good!

2 ½ c. Tofu, lightly salted and crumbled
3 c. Yeast or Pimento Cheez

Stir the crumbled tofu into the cheez. Spread between two slices of bread. Put non-dairy margarine on the outsides of the bread and grill. Chopped onions, chopped bell pepper, chopped UnBacon, or slices or pieces of tomato can also be added to the cheez before grilling.

FRUIT BUTTER

This makes about 6 cups of "butter"–which will go quickly once you taste it!

1 gal. Puréed fruit
3 c. Sucanat (4 cups for peach butter)
1 Orange, peeled and diced with all the juice
Pinch Sea salt

Combine and cook on low heat (simmer) for six hours, or till it turns dark brown and is thick. This keeps very long in the refrigerator.

GLUTEN SANDWICH SPREAD

Try it and like it!

3 c. Flavored gluten, coarsely ground
¾ c. Tofu Cream Cheez, 1 or 2
1 tsp. Lemon juice
10 Green onions, minced
1 c. Miraculous Whip
4 tsp. Louisiana Hot Sauce
3 T. Lea & Perrins Steak Sauce

Combine everything.

PIMENTO CHEEZ SPREAD

⅓ c. Cashew or Tofu Mayonnaise, or Miraculous Whip
¼ c. Pimentos, drained
1 tsp. Prepared mustard
1 c. Yeast Cheez or Pimento Cheez
1 tsp. Soy sauce

Process in a blender until smooth and creamy. Or: Chop the pimentos and mix with the rest of the ingredients by hand.

REUBEN SANDWICHES

Reliable goodness!

In a wok put ½ c. water and bring it to a boil.
Add:

4 c.	Cabbage, shredded
¾ c.	Bell pepper, chopped

Stir well, cover and let steam until tender–about
1 or 2 minutes. Remove the cabbage and peppers
from the wok and put in a bowl. Add:

½ tsp.	Dill weed
½ tsp.	Sea salt
¾ c.	Cashew or Tofu Sour Cream

Spread a slice of bread with Italian Dressing. Put
½ c. of cabbage mixture on the bread. Put tomato
slices on the cabbage. Top with Yeast or Pimento
Cheez and broil until spotted brown.

Variation: Try Quick Sauerkraut instead of the
cabbage-bell pepper mixture.

SATURDAY NIGHT SPECIALS

Special is the word!

2 c.	Pimento, Yeast, or Notzarella Cheez
½ c.	Onions, finely chopped
¼ c.	Bell pepper, finely chopped
½ c.	Green or black olives, sliced or chopped
⅛ tsp.	Cayenne pepper
⅛ tsp.	Garlic powder
¼ c.	Catsup
1 T.	Prepared mustard
3 T.	UnBacon, finely chopped

Mix all ingredients. Spread ¼-inch thick over
bread. Broil until the cheez gets brown spots.

SLOPPY JOES

Not just for kids!

1 c.	Soy grits
2 c.	UnBeef Broth
1 ½ c.	Onions, chopped
½ c.	Bell pepper, chopped fine
¼ c.	Celery, chopped fine
4 tsp.	Corn oil
2 c.	Tomato sauce
¼ tsp.	Cayenne pepper
1 ½ tsp.	Chili powder
¼ tsp.	Sea salt

Soak the grits in one cup of the broth. Sauté the
onions, bell pepper, and celery in the oil until
the onions are transparent. Add the grits and sauté
for 10 minutes. Add the rest of the ingredients–
including the second cup of broth–and stir
around, sautéing for another 10 minutes, adding
more tomato sauce if needed.

Variation: Instead of the soy grits, use 2 cups of
ground UnBeef, leaving out the second cup of
the UnBeef Broth. At the end, mix in 3 cups of
Yeast, Pimento, or Notzarella Cheez.

SUPER CHEEZ SANDWICHES

Garlic "butter" made with non-
  dairy margarine
Parmesan Cheez
Pimento Cheez
Notzarella Cheez
Shredded lettuce
Chopped black olives
Sliced onions
Sliced tomatoes
Dill pickles, sliced
Pickled jalapeño slices
Prepared mustard
Hamburger buns (or something
  like)

Spread halves of the buns with garlic butter and
sprinkle with Parmesan Cheez. Spread ½ of the
halves with Pimento Cheez. Spread the rest of
the halves with Notzarella. Bake at 550° until the
cheez starts to brown in spots. Take out of oven
and top with mustard, lettuce, onions, tomatoes,
olives, pickles, and pickled jalapeños. Join
together and serve.

Variation: Use a salad dressing, such as Thousand
Island, instead of mustard. Use guacamole instead
of mustard.

N'Eggs

I N MANY recipes from ordinary cookbooks, eggs are called for when the dish will come out just fine without them as you adapt them for vegetarian use. However this is not always so, therefore you will sometimes find that you need a "N'egg," the formulas for which are given in this section.

These two formulas—whose name is an abbreviation of "No egg"—can be used whenever an egg is called for in a recipe.

One is specifically for use in baked goods–pastries. The other is for everything else.

PASTRY N'EGG

1/3 cup of this formula equals one egg.

  ¼ c.   Flax seeds
  ¾ c.   Water

Grind the seeds to a powder. Mix in a blender with the water. As said above, ⅓ cup of this equals one egg. Refrigerate what you don't use, but use it within 24 hours, for it does not keep well.

ALL-PURPOSE N'EGG

This formula equals one egg.

  2 T.   Gluten flour, or unbleached white
          flour
  1 ½ tsp. Corn oil
  ½ tsp. Baking powder
  2 T.   Water

Combine thoroughly. Use right away, because the baking powder loses its effectiveness within 2 hours.

Seasonings

ALL-PURPOSE SEASONING

Make this up, taste it, and decide in what ways you can use it.

¼ tsp.	Hot pepper flakes
2 ½ tsp.	Sage, rubbed
½ tsp.	Nutmeg, ground
½ tsp.	Dry mustard
½ tsp.	Black pepper
4 tsp.	Paprika
1 ½ tsp.	Sea salt

Put everything in a blender and blend on high until all is ground fine. Do not take the mixture out of the blender but let it sit 3 minutes. Remove it and store it in a covered container.

FINES HERBES

1 part	Rosemary
1 part	Thyme
½ part	Oregano or Summer Savory
3 parts	Basil

Combine and store in an airtight container.

GARAM MASALA–1

This is one formula for the Garam Masala (Hot Mixture) that is used in Indian cooking. You might like to try it also in other dishes, as in Anandamayi Kitchuri, or try substituting it for curry powder or even for black or cayenne pepper.

3 T.	Coriander seed
2 tsp.	Cumin seed
8	Whole cloves
1	2-inch stick cinnamon
½ tsp.	Black pepper

4	Bay leaves

Roast the coriander and cumin seeds in a dry frying pan over medium heat, shaking often, for 4 minutes or until they are lightly browned. In a blender or nut grinder grind all the ingredients together to a fine powder. Store in an airtight container.

GARAM MASALA–2

This is far more complex than the first formula, but well worth the making.

1 T. & 1 ½ tsp.	Cayenne pepper
2 T.	Paprika
1 T.	Onion salt
1 tsp.	Garlic powder
1 tsp.	Basil, dried
½ tsp.	Ginger, powdered
¼ tsp.	Black pepper
⅛ tsp.	Cloves, ground
⅛ tsp.	Cinnamon, ground
⅛ tsp.	Cardamon
⅛ tsp.	Nutmeg
⅛ tsp.	Allspice
⅛ tsp.	Cumin
⅛ tsp.	Fenugreek
⅛ tsp.	Tumeric

Grind everything together in a blender or nut grinder to a fine powder and store in an airtight container.

HOT OIL

An ideal way to spice up food! Add some to cooking oil—even popcorn oil—for real effect!

2 c. Corn oil

½ c.   Hot pepper flakes

Combine the oil and pepper flakes in a small heavy saucepan. Warm it until the oil almost begins to bubble, then reduce the heat. Cook over low heat until the chilis darken but do not turn black. Let cool overnight at room temperature. Strain through cheesecloth. Store, tightly covered, in the refrigerator, and this will keep indefinitely. Serve at room temperature.

Note: Asian cooks prefer to cook over the low heat until the chilis blacken in the oil. You can try both ways and see which you like best. The first way produces a beautiful red oil that is plenty hot. The second will be quite a bit darker and somewhat heavier in taste.

GARLIC OIL

Keep this always on hand. It has many uses, such as spreading on pizza or bread dough, sautéing vegetables, or mixing in with other oils to give a subtle garlic taste to dishes.

4 ½ tsp.   Garlic, crushed
1 c.   Olive oil

Stir the crushed garlic into the oil, and let it sit overnight in the refrigerator before using. Keep in refrigerator.

SPECIAL SEASONING

Make this up, taste it, and decide in what ways you can use it.

1 ⅓ c.   Nutritional Yeast
1 T.   Onion powder
2 tsp.   Garlic powder
1 T.   Paprika
½ tsp.   Celery seed, ground
½ tsp.   Tumeric
1 tsp.   Dried parsley
1 T.   Barley malt powder
3 T.   Sea salt

Put everything in a blender and blend on high until all is ground fine. Do not take the mixture out of the blender but let it sit 3 minutes. Remove it and store it in a covered container.

Desserts

APPLE CRISP

Fit for a king!

8 c.	Apples, sliced
½ c.	Cashew Milk
⅓ c.	Non-dairy margarine
¾ c.	Rolled oats
½ c.	Unbleached white flour
2 tsp.	Cinnamon
½ tsp.	Sea salt
2 ½ c.	Sucanat

Grease a casserole dish with some non-dairy margarine. Put in the apples and pour in the "milk" on top. Melt the ½ cup of margarine. As margarine is melting, mix all the other ingredients together. Add margarine and stir with a fork until all is moistened. Spread (crumble) this mixture over the apples. Bake at 350° for about 45 minutes until the apples are done and topping is brown.
Variation: Use other kinds of fruit.

APPLE SQUARES

Filling:

½ c.	Sucanat
4 T.	Cornstarch
2 c.	Water
10 c.	Apples, thinly sliced
1 tsp.	Cinnamon
½ tsp.	Nutmeg
2 T.	Lemon juice

Combine the Sucanat, cornstarch, and water in a saucepan, mixing until well blended. Add the apples and heat to boiling, stirring constantly. Reduce the heat, and simmer 5 minutes, stirring

frequently. Remove from the heat. Stir in the spices and lemon juice. Set aside.

Pastry:

2 c.	Unbleached white flour
½ tsp.	Sea salt
⅔ c.	Non-dairy margarine, chilled
2	N'eggs
¼ c.	Cold water
1 T.	Lemon juice

Combine the flour and salt. Cut in the margarine until the mixture is crumbly. Combine the n'eggs, water, and lemon juice. Blend into the flour mixture, which will form a ball. Divide this in half. On a lightly floured surface roll half of the dough between two pieces of waxed paper so it will fit into a 13x9x2-inch baking pan. Put into the pan and spread the filling over it. Roll the rest of the dough out to fit over the pan, and put it on top. Fold the bottom pastry over the top and press to seal. Cut a few small slits in the top crust. Bake at 400° for 40 minutes or until lightly browned.

Glaze:

½ c.	Sucanat
1 T.	Cashew Milk
1 T.	Non-dairy margarine
½ tsp.	Vanilla

Combine everything and drizzle over the warm pastry.

BANANA PUDDING

Luscious is the word for this!

4 c.	Cashew Milk
1 c.	Sucanat

½ c.   Coconut
½ c.   Cornstarch
¼ tsp. Sea salt
2 tsp. Vanilla
4   Ripe bananas
1 ½ c. Tofu Whipped Cream

Put the "milk," Sucanat, coconut, cornstarch, salt, and vanilla in a saucepan and stir constantly while cooking until thick. Mash 2 bananas and add to mixture. *Do not cook.* Slice the other bananas and add. Pour into a dish and chill until set. Top with tofu whipped cream.

BLUEBERRY CHEEZ CAKE

So virtuous it's positively sinful!

1 c.   Tofu Cream Cheez
1 c.   Sucanat
1 tsp. Vanilla
1 c.   Soy Whipped Cream or Tofu
        Whipped Cream
1   Recipe of Graham Cracker Crust
1   Recipe of Blueberry Pie Filling

Beat together the cream cheez, Sucanat, and vanilla until smooth. Fold in "whipped cream." Spoon into graham cracker crust. Spoon blueberry filling on top. Chill to set.

CAROB CUSTARD

½ c.   Pecans
¼ tsp. Vanilla
3 ¼ c. Water
½ tsp. Salt
¼ c.   Carob powder
1 ½ c. Sucanat
6 T.   Cornstarch
        Shredded dried coconut

Blend ingredients together in a blender until the nuts are smooth. Heat until thick, stirring constantly. Pour into custard cups. Sprinkle with the coconut.

CAROB PUDDING

3 T.   Cornstarch
2 T.   Soy flour
3 T.   Carob powder
¼ tsp. Salt
½ c.   Sucanat
2 c.   Cashew Milk
2 tsp. Vanilla
1 c.   Whole, lightly toasted peanuts

Mix all ingredients except the vanilla and the peanuts. Cook for 5 minutes, stirring constantly. Add the vanilla and peanuts. Pour into molds to cool.

CHERRY COBBLER

You won't be sorry!

4 c.   Cherries, pitted
2 T.   Cornstarch
⅔ c.   Sucanat
2 T.   Lemon juice
¼ tsp. Almond extract
1 c.   Unbleached white flour
¼ c.   Non-dairy margarine
1 tsp. Baking powder
½ tsp. Sea salt
2 T.   Sucanat
7 T.   Water
¼ c.   Boiling water

Into the cherries stir the cornstarch, ⅔ cup of the Sucanat, lemon juice, and almond extract. Combine the flour, margarine, baking powder, salt, Sucanat, and water, blending them until all resembles coarse meal. Stir in the boiling water, stirring only until the batter is just combined. In an 8-inch skillet or a baking dish bring the cherry mixture to a boil. Drop the batter by heaping tablespoons onto it. Bake at 350° for 45 to 50 minutes, until the top is golden.

COCONUT RICE PUDDING

You will remember this long and lovingly!

2 c.   Cashew Milk
6   Sticks cinnamon
1 tsp. Whole cloves
¼ tsp. Powdered ginger
1 qt.   Water
1 c.   Rice, uncooked
2 c.   Coconut milk
1 c.   Sucanat
1 tsp. Sea salt
½ c.   Raisins

Put the "milk," cinnamon sticks, cloves, and ginger in a saucepan. Bring to a boil over high heat, then lower the heat and simmer, uncovered, for 5 minutes. Remove from heat and set aside for at least 1 hour. Strain the "milk" through a fine sieve. Discard the cinnamon, cloves, and ginger. If there is less than 2 cups of "milk," add more to make 2 cups. Bring the water to a boil and drop in the rice. Cook, uncovered, for 5 minutes, then drain the rice in a sieve and wash it under cold water. In a saucepan, combine the coconut milk, strained spiced "milk," Sucanat, and salt. Bring to a boil over high heat, then stir in the rice, cover the pan, and reduce the heat. Simmer for 30 minutes, then stir in the raisins, recover the pan, and cook for 10 minutes longer, or until the liquid is completely absorbed and the rice is tender. Sprinkle with cinnamon and serve at room temperature.

DATE AND APPLE SQUARES

2 c.	Apples, chopped
1 ½ c.	Pitted dates, chopped
1 c.	Unbleached white flour
1 ½ tsp.	Baking powder
½ c.	Sucanat
⅓ c.	Barbados molasses
2 T.	Non-dairy margarine, melted
1	N'egg
Pinch	Salt

Mix all together well to combine evenly. Spread mixture into a lightly oiled square cake pan. Bake at 400° about 30 minutes, or until golden brown and risen. Cut into squares.

FRENCH SILK PIE

There is a frozen commercial version of this that gave us a real sugar blitz! But what a way to go! Still, good sense prevailed and we worked out our own that is truly even better...
Bliss without blitz!

Cookie crust:

3	Sticks of non-dairy margarine, cold
2 ½ c.	Sucanat
1 ½ tsp.	Vanilla
3 c.	Unbleached white flour
¾ c.	Unsweetened cocoa powder
½ tsp.	Sea salt
½ tsp.	Baking soda
1 ½ c.	Semi-sweet chocolate chopped into ⅛-inch bits

Cream the margarine and Sucanat together until smooth and light. Add everything else and mix well. Gather the dough into a ball. On a floured surface roll out the dough to ¼-inch thickness and cut out desired shapes. Put on greased cookie sheets and bake—one sheet at a time in the middle of the oven—at 350° for 12 to 15 minutes. When cool, put the cookies in a food processor or blender and blend until they reach crumb consistency. You will have enough cookies for 6 crusts.

For each crust, cut 3 tablespoons more of margarine into ⅓ cup of cookie crumbs. Press this into a 9-inch pie pan or dish and bake at 375° for 8 minutes.

Filling for one pie:

1	Stick of non-dairy margarine
1 c.	Sucanat
1 ½	Squares of unsweetened chocolate
2 tsp.	Vanilla
1 c.	Cashew Milk
2 tsp.	Agar flakes

Cream the margarine and Sucanat together until smooth. Add the vanilla. Melt the chocolate and beat it into the margarine mixture. Stir the agar flakes into the "milk" and bring to a boil, lower heat, and simmer 1 to 2 minutes, then beat into the margarine mixture. Pour into a cooled cookie crust and let sit and come to room temperature. Chill for several hours, then top with Cool Whip non-dairy topping and semi-sweet chocolate shavings.

FRUIT AND ALMOND CREAM TART

1	Recipe of Convent Pie Crust
2 c.	Fruit, sliced or chopped
⅓ c.	Sucanat
¼ tsp.	Cinnamon
⅛ tsp.	Nutmeg
2 T.	Non-dairy margarine in bits
2	N'eggs
½ c.	Sucanat
¼ c. & 1 T.	Unbleached white flour
1 c.	Cashew Milk, hot
3 T.	Non-dairy margarine
½ tsp.	Vanilla
¼ tsp.	Almond extract
¼ tsp.	Rum flavoring
⅓ c.	Blanched almonds, ground

Roll out the pie dough ⅛-inch thick on a floured surface and fit it into a 10-inch round tart pan with a removable bottom. Trim the dough, leaving a 1-inch overhang, and fold the overhang over the rim, pressing it onto and ¼-inch above the rim of the pan. Prick the shell lightly with a fork and chill it for 30 minutes. Line the shell with wax paper, and fill the paper with uncooked rice to weight it, and bake the shell at 425° for 10 minutes. Remove the rice and paper carefully, and bake for 5 to 10 more minutes, or until it is pale golden. Cool in the pan or on a rack.

Put the fruit in a single layer in a baking dish, sprinkle with the ⅓ c. of Sucanat, cinnamon, and nutmeg, and dot with the 2 T. of margarine. Bake the fruit at 350° for 20 to 30 minutes, or until the fruit is just tender and has given off its juice. Let the fruit cool completely, strain the cooking juice through a sieve into a small saucepan, and reserve it.

Beat the ½ c. of Sucanat and n'eggs together well. Sift in the flour and beat until smooth. Add the hot "milk" in a stream, beating, and beat until all is well combined. Transfer this to a heavy saucepan, bring it to a boil while stirring and simmer, stirring, for 3 minutes until it thickens. Take from the heat and stir in the 3 T. of margarine, vanilla, almond extract, and rum flavor. Strain this through a sieve set over another bowl.

Into the sieved mixture fold the almonds, and chill, covered with a "buttered" round of wax paper, for 1 hour. Spoon the almond cream into the shell and top with the fruit. Boil the reserved juice until it is reduced to a glaze, and spoon this over the fruit. Chill the tart for 1 to 3 hours.

FRUIT COCKTAIL BREAD PUDDING

When you've got to—you've got to!

10	Slices of stale bread
3	N'eggs
2 ¾ c.	Sucanat
¼ c.	Non-dairy margarine
1 c.	Raisins
1 c.	Pecans, chopped
1	16-oz. can of low calorie fruit cocktail sweetened with fruit juice
2 ½ c.	Cashew Milk
2 T.	Vanilla

Mix all ingredients together in a large bowl, blending well. Turn into an oiled 9x13-inch pan. Bake at 400° for 55 minutes or until it gets brown on top.

FRUIT SHORTCAKE

This gives a whole new meaning to "heavenly"!

Filling:

1	3-inch cinnamon stick, crushed
4	Whole cloves
2 c.	Fruit, sliced
1 c.	Water
1 c.	Sucanat

Tie the cinnamon and cloves into a small piece of cheesecloth. Put the fruit, water, Sucanat, and spice bag into a saucepan and simmer 5 to 7 minutes—until the fruit is just tender. Transfer the fruit with a slotted spoon to a bowl. Boil the cooking liquid until it is reduced by half. Add any fruit juice that may have accumulated in the bowl. Let the syrup cool to room temperature and discard the spice bag. Add the syrup to the fruit and chill, covered, for at least 1 hour, or until it is cold.

Shortcakes:

2 c.	Unbleached white flour
2 T.	Sucanat
1 T.	Baking powder
½ tsp.	Sea salt
¼ c.	Non-dairy margarine
½ c.	Cashew Cream
2	N'eggs
1 tsp.	Vanilla
	Apple juice
2 c.	Soy Whipped Cream or Tofu Whipped Cream, well chilled

Sift the flour, Sucanat, baking powder, and salt together into a bowl. Blend in the margarine until the mixture resembles coarse meal. Whisk together the "cream," n'eggs, and vanilla, and add this to the flour mixture, stirring with a fork just until a soft dough is formed. Turn the dough out onto a floured surface and knead it gently for 20 seconds. Pat the dough into an 8-inch round, transfer it to a "buttered" baking sheet, and cut it into 6 equal wedges without cutting all the way through. Brush the wedges with apple juice, and bake at 425° for 15 to 20 minutes, or until it is golden. Transfer to a rack, cool, and separate the wedges. Split each wedge horizontally with a fork, arrange the bottom halves on 6 plates, and spoon the filling over them. Top the filling with the "whipped cream" and then put on the top half of the wedge.

FRUIT SQUARES

Crumble:

2 T.	Vegetable oil
½ c.	Sucanat
⅓ c.	Water
1 c.	Unbleached white flour
1 tsp.	Salt
1 ½ c.	Quick oats
½ c.	Oat flour (make by grinding rolled oats in a blender)

In a bowl mix the oil, Sucanat, and water. In another bowl, mix the flour, salt, quick oats, and oat flour. Combine both bowls, and crumble together.

Filling:

1 c.	Dates or Raisins
1 c.	Water
1 tsp.	Lemon juice
½ tsp.	Vanilla
⅛ tsp.	Salt
2 T.	Cornstarch

Mix the fruit, water, lemon juice, vanilla, salt, and cornstarch. Boil until the fruit is soft. Press half of the crumble on the bottom of a greased pan. Spread the filling over it. Cover with the rest of the crumble. Bake at 375° for 40 minutes, until browned. Cool. Wet the top layer by spooning ¾ cup of pineapple juice over it. Cover the pan and keep in the refrigerator overnight. Cut into squares.

Variation: Instead of dates (or raisins) and water, prepare the filling from 2 cups of crushed, unsweetened pineapple, canned pears, or apples.

LEMON CHEEZCAKE

1 c.	Very fine graham cracker crumbs
3 T.	Non-dairy margarine
3 ½ c.	Tofu Cottage Cheez, made without garlic power
2	Lemons–juice and grated rind
1 ⅓ c.	Powdered Sucanat

Stir the crumbs into the margarine and press into the base of a round cake pan. Run the cottage cheez through blender until it is perfectly smooth. Beat the lemon juice and rind together with the Sucanat. Slowly add the blended cottage cheez, beating, until all is smooth. Spread the mixture in the cake pan and smooth surface. Cover and refrigerate for several hours.

LEMON CHEEZCAKE DELUXE

For the sophisticate in you!

2 ½ c.	Graham cracker crumbs
¼ c.	Sucanat
10 T.	Non-dairy margarine, melted
3 c.	Tofu Cream Cheez, made without onion powder
3	N'eggs
1 ½ c.	Powdered Sucanat
3 T.	Lemon juice
1 tsp.	Vanilla

1 T.	Grated lemon peel
1	Lemon, sliced paper-thin
3 c.	Water
1 ½ c.	Sucanat
2 T. & 2 tsp.	Cornstarch
⅓ c.	Lemon juice

Combine the graham cracker crumbs, Sucanat, and margarine, and press into the bottom and 2 inches up the sides of a 9-inch springform pan. Bake at 350° for 5 minutes and cool. Beat together the cream cheez and n'eggs. Gradually add in the Sucanat, lemon juice, and vanilla, and mix well. Fold in the lemon peel. Pour into the crust. Bake at 350° for 40 minutes. Cool to room temperature and refrigerate at least 4 hours. Remove any seeds from the lemon slices, reserve 1 slice for garnish, and coarsely chop the rest of the slices. Place these in a saucepan with 2 cups of the water, bring to a boil, reduce the heat, and simmer, uncovered, for 15 minutes. Drain and discard the liquid. In a saucepan combine the Sucanant and cornstarch, stir in the remaining water, lemon juice, and cooked slices, bring to a boil, stirring constantly, and boil for 3 minutes. Chill until cool, stirring occasionally. Pour over the cheezcake and garnish with the lemon slice. Chill until ready to serve.

LEMON CUSTARD

1	Lemon, quartered, seeds removed
½ c.	Water
2 c.	Orange juice
2 T.	Oil
1 ¼ c.	Sucanat
¼ c.	Cornstarch

Place the lemon in a blender–peel and all–with all the other ingredients and blend until it is finely ground. Place in a saucepan and bring to a boil. Simmer about 2 minutes, stirring constantly. Pour into serving dishes. Put a few pecans, a few raisins, or a date on top.

Use also as a pie filling.

Variation: Use 3 oranges, peeled and with seeds removed, instead of the orange juice. They should be blended with the lemon until fine.

MAPLE PECAN CHEEZCAKE

A triumph!

2 c.	Ginger Snaps (see Cookies section), crushed into fine crumbs
6 T.	Non-dairy margarine, melted

4 c.	Tofu Cream Cheez, made without onion powder
1 c.	Powdered Sucanat
½ c.	Genuine maple syrup
3	N'eggs
½ c.	Tofu Sour Cream or Cashew Sour Cream
½ tsp.	Sea salt
1 tsp.	Vanilla
¾ tsp.	Maple flavoring
1 c.	Pecans, toasted lightly and chopped fine

Make the crust by stirring together the gingersnap crumbs and margarine until well combined, and press this onto the bottom and halfway up the side of a 9-inch springform pan. With an electric mixer cream the cream cheez and Sucanat together until light and fluffy. Beat in the syrup, n'eggs, "sour cream," salt, vanilla, maple flavoring, and pecans. Put the filling into the crust, and bake at 350° for 1 hour. Turn off the heat and let the cake cool down thoroughly in the oven with the door slightly open, and then chill, covered, overnight.

PEARS IN "CUSTARD"

An Attention-Getter!

4 c.	Pears, sliced thin
⅓ c.	Sucanat
1 T.	Lemon juice
2 T.	Unbleached white flour
¾ tsp.	Cinnamon
½ tsp.	Ginger, ground
¼ tsp.	Sea salt
⅓ c.	Orange juice concentrate
12 oz.	Tofu
¼ c.	Cashew Milk
½ c.	Sucanat
1 tsp.	Vanilla
1 tsp.	Lemon peel, grated
½ tsp.	Cinnamon
¼ tsp.	Ginger, ground

Combine the pears, Sucanat (⅓ cup), lemon juice, flour, cinnamon, ginger, and salt, and put into a baking dish or pan. Put the rest of the ingredients into a blender and purée until smooth. Pour the purée over the pears and bake at 350° for 40 to 50 minutes. Serve warm or cold.

PEARS IN MUSTARD SYRUP

This goes with gluten!

4 c.	Pears, peeled, cored, and cut into ⅓-inch dice
⅓ c.	Sucanat
1 T.	Lemon peel, grated fine
¼ c.	Water
1 c.	Fresh or frozen (not thawed) cranberries
1 tsp.	Candied ginger, minced
1 T.	Dry mustard

In a saucepan combine the pears, Sucanat, lemon peel, and water. Stir to mix well, bring to a boil, and simmer until the pears are just tender–about 8 minutes. Stir in the cranberries and ginger and cook until the cranberries pop–about 4 more minutes. With a slotted spoon transfer the fruits to a bowl. Boil the liquid in the saucepan over high heat until syrupy–about 2 minutes. Stir the syrup into the fruit and set it aside to cool for 15 minutes. Stir in the mustard until thoroughly combined. Serve at room temperature. (This can be made as much as 2 days ahead and kept, covered, in the refrigerator.)

PINEAPPLE PUDDING

4 c.	Unsweetened pineapple juice
1 ½ c.	Sucanat
⅓ c.	Cornstarch
½ tsp.	Mint flavoring
1 c.	Crushed unsweetened pineapple, drained
½ tsp.	Salt

Bring 3 cups of the juice and Sucanat to a rolling boil. Mix the cornstarch with the other 1 cup of the juice and add gradually to the rest, stirring constantly. Add the remaining ingredients. Pour into dessert cups. Chill. May serve with "whipped cream," if desired.

SPICED BREAD PUDDING

8	Slices of bread
1 ½ c.	Cashew Milk
⅔ c.	Raisins, soaked in 1 cup of hot water and drained
2 T.	Non-dairy margarine
⅓ c.	Sucanat
⅓ c.	Barbados molasses
1 T.	Allspice
1	N'egg
Pinch	Nutmeg

Break up the bread and place it in a mixing bowl with the "milk." Let soak. Add the raisins, margarine, Sucanat, molasses, allspice, and n'egg. Beat well. Put in an oiled casserole dish, level the surface, sprinkle with nutmeg, and bake at 350° about 45 minutes or until "set." Serve hot or cold.

STEAMED IRISH RAISIN PUDDING

1 ¾ c.	Cashew Milk
½ c.	Sucanat
1 ½ c.	Plumped raisins
1 ½ c.	Unbleached wheat flour
½ tsp.	Salt
¼ tsp.	Coriander
1 T.	Lemon rind, grated
1 ½ c.	Bread crumbs
1 c.	Apples–peeled and grated

"Plump" the raisins by putting them loosely in a container and covering them with hot water. Let them sit overnight or until soft as fresh prunes. (May be stored in the refrigerator until you need them.) Blend the "milk" and Sucanat together. Combine all the ingredients and turn into a well-greased 2-quart tube mold or large can. Steam for 2 hours. Cool and unmold. Slice and serve with a dessert sauce.

SUMMER FRUIT TERRINE

When you care enough to fix the very berry best!

Terrine:

1 c.	White grape juice
¾ c.	Sucanat
3 T.	Lemon juice
¼ tsp.	Almond extract
4	Large peaches
2 T.	Agar flakes
⅓ c.	Water
18	Strawberries, hulled and halved lengthwise
½ c.	Raspberries (fresh only)
½ c.	Blueberries
¾ c.	Seedless white (green) grapes, halved lengthwise

In a saucepan combine the grape juice, Sucanat, lemon juice, and almond extract. Bring to a boil, stirring, until the Sucanat is dissolved. Add 2 of the peaches, peeled, pitted, and coarsely chopped. Simmer the peaches for 10 to 15 minutes, or until they are very tender, and transfer them with a slotted spoon to a blender. Add 1 cup of the cooking liquid and blend until smooth.

In a small saucepan sprinkle the agar flakes over ⅓ cup of water and let it soften for 5 minutes. Heat this over low heat, stirring, until the gelatin is dissolved. With the blender running, add the gelatin mixture in a stream to the peach mixture and blend until it is combined well. (There will be about 2 ½ cups of purée.)

Line a terrine or loaf pan with plastic wrap and pour into it about ¼ cup of the purée, or enough to just cover the bottom. Arrange half the strawberries, cut sides down, in one layer on the peach purée. Pour enough of the peach purée over the strawberry layer to just cover it.

Peel, halve, and pit the remaining 2 peaches, slice them thin, and in a bowl toss them with ¼ cup of the peach purée. Arrange half of the peach slices, overlapping them slightly, over the strawberry layer and pour enough of the remaining peach purée over the peach layer to just cover it.

Toss the raspberries and blueberries with the ¼ cup of the peach purée. Arrange the berries in one layer over the peaches. Pour enough of the remaining peach purée into the terrine to just cover the berries.

Toss the grapes with about 2 tablespoons of the remaining purée, and arrange them in one layer over the berries. Pour enough of the remaining purée into the terrine to just cover the grape layer.

Arrange the remaining peaches in one layer, overlapping them slightly, over the grapes and pour enough the purée over them to just cover them.

Arrange the remaining strawberries, cut sides up, in one layer over the peaches and cover them with the rest of the purée.

Chill the terrine for 1 hour or until it is just set. Cover it with plastic wrap and chill it overnight.

Remove the plastic wrap from the top of the terrine, invert the terrine onto a serving plate, and peel off the plastic wrap carefully. Cut the terrine into ¾-inch slices with a serrated knife and serve it with the sauce.

Sauce:

½ c.	Sucanat
3 T.	Lemon juice
¼ c.	Water
¼ tsp.	Almond extract
2	Large peaches, peeled, pitted, and chopped
1 ½ c.	Fresh raspberries, or 10 oz. frozen in light syrup, drained

In a saucepan combine the Sucanat, lemon juice, and ¼ cup of water. Bring this to a boil, stirring until the Sucanat is dissolved. In a blender purée the peaches and the raspberries with the syrup until smooth. Force the mixture through a fine sieve set over a bowl. Discard the solids. Chill the sauce, covered, for at least 1 hour or overnight.

Note: If fresh raspberries are not available for the terrine, omit them and add ½ cup *more* blueberries instead.

VANILLA PUDDING–1

2 ¼ c.	Cashew Milk
½ c.	Sucanat
⅛ tsp.	Salt
2 tsp.	Agar flakes
2 T.	Arrowroot powder
1 tsp.	Vanilla extract
1 T.	Non-dairy margarine

Combine 1 ¾ cup of the "milk" with the Sucanat and salt in a small saucepan. Sprinkle in the agar flakes and bring to a simmer over medium heat without stirring. Simmer for one minute. Thoroughly dissolve the arrowroot in the remaining ¼ cup of cashew milk and add it to the pudding while stirring briskly. Return to a simmer and cook for 1 to 2 minutes. Remove from heat and mix in the vanilla and margarine. Chill.

VANILLA PUDDING–2

3 T.	Cornstarch
⅓ c.	Sucanat
¼ tsp.	Salt
2 c.	Cashew Milk
2 tsp.	Vanilla

Mix cornstarch, Sucanat, and salt in top of a double boiler. Gradually add "milk" until smooth. Place over boiling water and cook, stirring constantly, until mixture thickens. Cover and continue cooking 10 minutes. Stir in vanilla and chill.

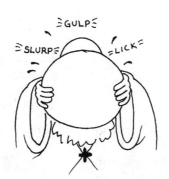

N'Ice Cream

F ROM THE HEALTH standpoint, the major reason we "went vegan" was our realization that every bout of 'flu that swept through the monastery occurred the day after a big ice cream bash. (I had once had a private 'flu epidemic on my own when travelling that was also preceded by an ice cream orgy.) What, then, to do? And here is the answer. Freeze and enjoy!

BANANA N'ICE CREAM

Simple and heavenly!

4	Large *frozen* bananas
1 tsp.	Sucanat

Cut the frozen bananas into chunks. Place them in a food processor fitted with a steel blade. Pulse until chopped. Add the Sucanat. Process until the bananas are smooth and creamy. Serve immediately.
Variation: Add one cup of frozen fruit when processing.

COCONUT N'ICE CREAM

Better than You-Know-Who's!

2 c.	Coconut, shredded
3 c.	Coconut milk
1 c.	Raw cashew pieces
2 tsp.	Vanilla
2 ½ c.	Tofu
1 ½ c.	Bananas
1 c.	Genuine maple syrup
⅔ c.	Coconut oil

¼ tsp. Sea salt

Put everything in a food processor in batches and purée until creamy and smooth. Freeze in an ice cream freezer.

TAHINI N'ICE CREAM

A character all its own!

1 ⅓ c.	Fruit purée
⅔ c.	Tahini
2 T.	Sucanat
½ tsp.	Almond or vanilla extract

Mix fruit purée with tahini until smooth, stir in the remaining ingredients, and freeze.

TOFU N'ICE CREAM-1

You won't regret it!

2 ¼ c.	Tofu, well chilled
6 T.	Genuine maple syrup
1 T.	Corn oil
2 tsp.	Vanilla
⅛ tsp.	Salt

Combine 1 ½ cups of the tofu with the syrup, oil, vanilla, and salt in a blender and purée for 1 minute. Put in a covered container and put in the freezer overnight. Purée the other ¾ cup of tofu in a blender until smooth. Cut the frozen tofu into small chunks. While puréeing at high speed, add a few chunks of the frozen tofu at a time to the tofu in the blender until all has been added and the mixture is smooth and thick. Serve immediately.
Variations: Toward the end of the puréeing add ½ cup (well packed) of frozen fruit. Instead of 2

teaspoons of vanilla, use 1 teaspoon of vanilla and 1 teaspoon of almond extract. Instead of 2 teaspoons of vanilla, use 1 teaspoon of vanilla and 1 teaspoon of rum extract and at the end add ½ cup of chopped pecans. Add 2 teaspoons of peppermint or other extract.

TOFU N'ICE CREAM–2

This is the deluxe model!

4 c.	Fruit
1 c.	Pineapple juice
1 c.	Raw cashews, ground very fine
2 tsp.	Vanilla
2 ½ c.	Tofu
1 ½ c.	Bananas
1 c.	Genuine maple syrup
⅔ c.	Corn oil
3 T.	Lemon juice
¼ tsp.	Sea salt

Put everything in a food processor in batches and purée until creamy and smooth. Freeze in an ice cream freezer.

Note: When making peach or mango n'ice cream, use ½ teaspoon of almond extract and ½ teaspoon of vanilla.

Cake

CAROB CAKE

1 ½ c.	Unbleached white flour
3 T.	Carob powder
½ tsp.	Sea salt
2 tsp.	Baking powder
⅓ c.	Sucanat
⅓ c.	Barbados molasses
1 tsp.	Vanilla
6 T.	Non-dairy margarine, melted
¾ c.	Water

Sift the dry ingredients into a bowl. Mix the liquid ingredients–including the melted margarine–in a separate bowl. Pour the liquid ingredients into the dry, and stir until the batter is smooth. Pour the batter into an oiled, floured pan. Bake in a preheated 350° oven for 35 to 45 minutes.

Variation: Leave out the carob powder for a white cake.

CHRISTMAS FRUITCAKE

⅓ c.	Crystallized ginger, coarsely chopped
1 c.	Walnuts, coarsely chopped
½ c.	Almonds, coarsely chopped
¾ c.	Golden raisins
⅓ c.	Currants
½ c.	Dried prunes, quartered
¾ c.	Dried apricots, quartered
1	Orange peel, grated
1	Lemon peel, grated
1 tsp.	Brandy extract in ⅓ c. water
1 ¼ c.	Sucanat
½ c.	Non-dairy margarine
2	N'eggs

1 c.	Flour
1 ½ tsp.	Baking powder
¼ tsp.	Baking soda
1 tsp.	Cinnamon
½ tsp.	Nutmeg

Combine the first 10 ingredients. Stir well. Cover and let rest for 30 to 60 minutes. Cream the Sucanat and margarine. Beat in the n'eggs. Sift the flour, baking powder, soda, cinnamon, and nutmeg, and add to the margarine mixture and beat until smooth. Combine with the fruit. Mix thoroughly by hand. Spoon into an oiled ½-quart cake pan that has been lined with waxed paper. Bake at 275° for 2 hours. Remove and let rest for 5 minutes. Unmold. Decorate top with nuts and apricot halves. Cool.

COTTAGE PUDDING

Simply indescribable as a "shortcake."

¼ c.	Corn oil
1 ¾ c.	Unbleached white flour
2 tsp.	Baking powder
½ tsp.	Sea salt
¾ c.	Sucanat
¾ c.	Cashew Milk
1	N'egg
1 tsp.	Vanilla

Mix the oil, flour, baking powder, salt, and Sucanat. Add the "milk," n'egg, and vanilla and beat until smooth. Pour into an oiled and floured baking pan, cover and bake at 350° for 45 to 60 minutes. Let stand 5 minutes before removing from pan.

CRAZY CAKE

3 c.	Unbleached white flour
2 c.	Sucanat
½ c.	Carob powder
1 tsp.	Sea salt
2 tsp.	Baking soda
2 T.	White vinegar
2 tsp.	Vanilla
2 c.	Water
¾ c.	Corn oil

Sift the dry ingredients together. Add the vinegar, vanilla, water, and oil. Bake at 350° for 50 minutes, or until a toothpick inserted comes out clean.

DATE-NUT CAKE

Quietly good.

2 ¾ c.	Sucanat
1 c.	Non-dairy margarine
2	N'eggs
1 c.	Walnuts, chopped
2 c.	Dates, chopped
1 tsp.	Cinnamon
½ tsp.	Allspice
½ tsp.	Cloves
3 c.	Unbleached white flour, sifted
2 tsp.	Baking soda
½ tsp.	Sea salt
1 ½ c.	Water
½ c.	Liquid barley malt

Cream the Sucanat and margarine. Sir in the n'eggs, nuts, dates, and spices. In another bowl sift the flour, baking soda, and salt together and stir in the water and malt. Combine the mixture with the margarine-Sucanat and mix until well blended. Bake in a casserole pan at 350° for 1 hour and 15 minutes.

DEVON APPLE CAKE

2 c.	Unbleached white flour
3 tsp.	Baking powder
¼ tsp.	Sea salt
½ tsp.	Cinnamon, ground
½ tsp.	Allspice, ground
⅓ c.	Sucanat
⅓ c.	Barbados molasses
½ c.	Non-dairy margarine
2 c.	Apples, peeled, cored, and coarsely chopped
1	N'egg

Oil and flour the base of a square cake pan. In a bowl combine the flour, baking powder, salt, cinnamon, allspice, Sucanat, and molasses. Rub in the margarine until the mixture resembles fine crumbs. Add apples and n'egg to mixture and stir quickly to combine. Spread evenly in the pan and bake at 375° about 30 minutes, or until risen and firm to the touch. Allow to cool in pan before cutting into squares.

FRUIT CAKE–1

For me this is REAL fruit cake!

1 ½ c.	Dried apricots, chopped
1 ½ c.	Dates, chopped
1 ½ c.	Golden raisins
1 c.	Water
1 c.	Orange juice
½ c.	Corn oil
3 c.	Unbleached white flour
4 ½ tsp.	Baking powder
1 c.	Pecans, broken
1 T.	Barbados molasses
1 T.	Finely grated lemon rind
2 tsp.	Allspice, ground
1 ½ c.	Sucanat
3 T.	Rum flavor (*not* extract)

Line 2 9x5x3 loaf pans with waxed paper. Place all the ingredients in a bowl and beat well until evenly mixed. Pour into the pans and bake at 300° about 1 ½ to 2 hours or until they test done.

FRUIT CAKE–2

1 ½ c.	Non-dairy margarine
3 c.	Sucanat
6	N'eggs
1 c.	Cashew Milk
1 tsp.	Brandy extract
1 tsp.	Vanilla
½ tsp.	Sea salt
½ tsp.	Cream of tartar
1 c.	Water
3 ½ c.	Unbleached white flour
1 c.	Raisins
1 c.	Dry apricots, chopped and soaked
½ c.	Dried cherries, chopped and soaked
½ c.	Dried orange, chopped (you may have to make this yourself by chopping up an orange and letting it dry)
½ c.	Dried lemon, chopped (ditto)
1 c.	Pecans, chopped

Cream the margarine and Sucanat together. Add the n'eggs, "milk," brandy extract, vanilla, salt, cream of tartar, and water. Add the flour slowly and mix while doing so. Fold in the fruits and nuts. The batter should be stiff but not dry. If needed, add more water. Divide in half and place in two oiled loaf pans. Bake at 275° for 2 to 2 ½ hours. Use a toothpick to tell if the cake is done. Also, the sides of the cake should not adhere to the pan when it is done.

GINGERBREAD

If the old witch had known this recipe the kids would have truly eaten her out of house and home!

½ c.	Non-dairy margarine
½ c.	Sucanat
1 c.	Barbados molasses
2 ½ c.	Unbleached white flour
2 ½ tsp.	Baking soda
1 tsp.	Cinnamon
2 tsp.	Ginger, ground
½ tsp.	Cloves, ground
½ tsp.	Sea salt
1 c.	Boiling water

Cream margarine and Sucanat. Add molasses and dry ingredients. Blend well. Add boiling water and beat well. Pour batter into a well-greased and floured baking pan. Bake at 350° for 30 to 35 minutes or until it passes the "toothpick test."

LEMON CAKE

8 T.	Non-dairy margarine
¾ c.	Sucanat
1	Lemon–its juice and its rind, grated
1	N'egg
1 c.	Unbleached white flour
1 ½ tsp.	Baking powder

Oil and flour a square cake pan. Heat margarine and ½ cup of the Sucanat over low heat until the margarine is melted. Take off the heat and stir in the lemon rind. Beat the n'egg into the Sucanat mixture. Fold in the flour and baking powder and turn the mixture into the pan. Bake at 350° about 30 minutes or until it is just firm to the touch. Warm the lemon juice and ¼ c. of Sucanat and mix together. Prick the cake all over with a fork or toothpick, and spoon the syrup over it. Leave in the pan to cool.
Variation: Use a small orange–juice and rind–instead of lemon.

MEXICAN FRUITCAKE

2 c.	Unbleached white flour
2 c.	Sucanat
1	20-oz. can of unsweetened crushed pineapple with the juice
2	N'eggs
2 ½ tsp.	Baking soda
⅔ c.	Shredded coconut
⅔ c.	Pecans, coarsely chopped

Mix all together. Put in an oiled 9x13 pan (or in two 8x8 pans). Bake at 350° for 40 minutes (if in the two pans–for 30 minutes). Top with "whipped cream."

MOLASSES CAKE

¾ c.	Barbados molasses
2 T.	Non-dairy margarine
1 ½ c.	Unbleached white flour
Pinch	Sea salt
½ tsp.	Allspice, ground
¼ tsp.	Nutmeg, ground
¼ tsp.	Cinnamon, ground
1	N'egg
¾ tsp.	Baking soda
3 T.	Cashew Milk

Heat the molasses and margarine together until the margarine has melted. Remove from heat and beat in the flour, salt, spices, and n'egg. Blend the baking soda and "milk" together and stir into mixture. Put in an oiled cake pan. Bake at 350° for 25 to 30 minutes, or until golden brown and firm to the touch. Cool slightly before turning out onto a wire rack.

ORANGE GINGERCAKE

2 c.	Unbleached white flour
1 ½ tsp.	Ginger, ground
1 ½ tsp.	Baking powder
½ tsp.	Baking soda
½ tsp.	Sea salt
1 ⅓ c.	Sucanat
2 T.	Barbados molasses
6 T.	Non-dairy margarine
4 T.	Cashew Milk
1	N'egg
1	Orange–grated rind
2 T.	Orange juice

Oil and flour a cake pan. Put the flour, ginger, baking powder, baking soda, and salt in a mixing bowl. Heat together the Sucanat, molasses, and margarine until the margarine is melted.

Combine all ingredients, beat well, and pour into the pan. Bake at 325° about ½ hour, or until just firm to the touch. Cool in the pan. Cut into squares.

PINEAPPLE UPSIDE-DOWN CAKE

This truly bears repeating!

2 T.	Non-dairy margarine
1 c.	Sucanat
2 ½ c.	Crushed pineapple, drained well
1 ½ c.	Unbleached white flour
2 tsp.	Baking powder
½ tsp.	Salt
¾ c.	Sucanat
1	N'egg
½ c.	Water
½ c.	Non-dairy margarine

Melt the 2 tablespoons of margarine. Add the 1 cup of Sucanat and mix well. Put this in the bottom of a cake pan. Cover this with the pineapple and set aside. Sift the flour, baking powder, salt, and ¾ cup of Sucanat together. Mix the n'egg, water and ½ cup of margarine together. Mix this into the flour mixture well until it is smooth. Spread this over the pineapple. Bake at 400° for about 35 minutes until brown and crusty. Let cool for 30 minutes and then turn out of the pan, fruit side up, onto a serving tray or platter.
Variation: At the beginning mix in 1 cup of pecan pieces with the margarine and Sucanat.

SHORTCAKE

2 ⅓ c.	Biscuit Mix
½ c.	Cashew Milk or water
3 T.	Sucanat
3 T.	Non-dairy margarine, melted

Mix all together until a soft dough forms. Spread in an ungreased pan. Bake at 425° for 15 to 20 minutes until golden brown. Cool for 10 minutes, cut into pieces, and split each horizontally.

SYRUP CAKE

2 ½ c.	Unbleached white flour
1 ½ tsp.	Baking powder
½ tsp.	Baking soda
1 tsp.	Ground ginger
1 tsp.	Cinnamon
¼ tsp.	Nutmeg (fresh preferred)
¼ tsp.	Ground cloves
½ tsp.	Sea salt
¾ c.	Pecans, coarsely chopped
½ c.	Raisins
1 T.	Unbleached white flour
⅔ c.	Sucanat
⅓ c.	Barbados molasses
1 ¼ c.	Boiling water
⅔ c.	Non-dairy margarine, softened
½ c.	Sucanat
2	N'eggs

Grease and flour a 9x13 cake pan. Combine the flour, baking powder, baking soda, ginger, cinnamon, nutmeg, cloves, and salt, and sift them together into a mixing bowl. In a separate bowl, mix the pecans, raisins, and flour. Combine the Sucanat, molasses, and boiling water. Cream the margarine and ½ cup of Sucanat. Beat in the n'eggs. Add about ⅔ cup of the flour and spice mixture and, when it is well incorporated, beat in ½ cup of the syrup mixture. Repeat three more times, alternating about ⅔ cup of the flour and spice mixture with ½ cup of the syrup mixture, beating well after each addition. Add the floured pecans and raisins, folding them in gently but thoroughly with a rubber spatula. Pour the batter into the pan, spreading it evenly and smoothing the top with the spatula. Bake at 350° for 35 to 45 minutes, or until a toothpick or cake tester inserted in the center comes out clean.

UNCOOKED FRUIT CAKE

1 c.	Raisins, ground
1 c.	Dates, chopped
2 c.	Dried fruit (any kind), chopped
¾ c.	Water
1 c.	Fruit juice or nectar
1 c.	Bread crumbs
1 c.	Sunflower seeds, or other nuts broken small

Soak the dried fruits in the water and fruit juice for 2 hours. Add the crumbs and seeds, pack into an oiled mold and set for one or more days in the refrigerator. Unmold, slice, and serve.

VANILLA CAKE-1

1 ¾ c.	Unbleached white flour
1 tsp.	Baking powder
½ tsp.	Sea salt
¾ c.	Sucanat
⅓ c.	Non-dairy margarine, melted
⅔ c.	Water
2 tsp.	Vanilla

1 T.   Wine vinegar

Sift the dry ingredients in a mixing bowl. Whip together the liquid ingredients and pour them into the dry. Stir with a wooden spoon until smooth, with no lumps remaining. Pour the batter into an oiled cake pan or muffin tin (for cupcakes). Bake at 375° for 30 to 40 minutes.

VANILLA CAKE-2

3 ½ c.	Unbleached white flour
2 c.	Sucanat
1 tsp.	Sea salt
2 tsp.	Baking soda
2 T.	White vinegar
4 tsp.	Vanilla
2 c.	Water
¾ c.	Corn oil

Sift the dry ingredients together. Add the vinegar, vanilla, water, and oil. Bake at 350° for 50 minutes, or until a toothpick inserted comes out clean.

VELVET CRUMB CAKE

1 ½ c.	Biscuit Mix
½ c.	Sucanat
1	N'egg
½ c.	Cashew milk or water
2 T.	Non-dairy margarine
1 tsp.	Vanilla
½ c.	Flaked coconut
⅓ c.	Powdered Sucanat (packed in well)
¼ c.	Chopped nuts
3 T.	Non-dairy margarine, softened
2 T.	Cashew Milk or water

Beat the first six ingredients together, at low speed, stirring constantly, for 30 seconds, then beat at medium speed, scraping the bowl occasionally, for 4 minutes. Pour into a greased and floured baking pan and bake at 350° for 30 to 35 minutes until a wooden pick inserted in center comes out clean. Cool slightly and spread with topping made by combining the rest of the ingredients. Broil 3 inches from the heat for 3 minutes until the topping is golden brown.

Cookies

APPLE CAKES

A perfect soft cookie-cake.

2 c.	Unbleached white flour
Pinch	Sea salt
½ tsp.	Cinnamon, ground
1 tsp.	Baking powder
¾ c.	Non-dairy margarine
2	Apples, peeled, cored, and diced
1 c.	Sucanat
1	N'egg

In a bowl combine flour, salt, cinnamon, and baking powder. Rub in the margarine until the mixture resembles fine crumbs. Add remaining ingredients and combine well together. Place heaped spoonfuls on a lightly oiled baking sheet and bake at 375° for 20 to 25 minutes or until golden brown. Cool slightly before transferring to a wire rack.

BUTTERSCOTCH SHORTBREAD

1 c.	Non-dairy margarine
½ c.	Sucanat
¼ c.	Barbados molasses
2 ¼ c.	Unbleached white flour
¾ tsp.	Sea salt

Beat the margarine, Sucanat, and molasses together. Mix all ingredients together well. Roll out ¼-inch thick. Cut into rounds or shapes. Bake on an ungreased baking sheet at 300° for 20 to 25 minutes.

CANADIAN SHORTBREAD

1 c.	Non-dairy margarine
½ c.	Sucanat

1 tsp.	Vanilla
1 c.	Unbleached white flour
½ tsp.	Baking soda
2 c.	Rolled oats

Beat the margarine, Sucanat, and vanilla until fluffy. Combine the flour, baking soda, and oats. Add to margarine mixture and mix well. Chill an hour or more (or freeze for later use). Roll out to ¼-inch thick. Cut into rounds. Bake on an ungreased baking sheet at 350° for 10 to 12 minutes.
Variation: Form dough into 1 ½-inch balls and flatten them rather than roll out and cut out rounds.

CAROB CHIP COOKIES

Now THIS has enough chips to satisfy!

½ c.	Non-dairy margarine
¾ c.	Sucanat
1	N'egg
1 tsp.	Vanilla
1 c.	Unbleached white flour
½ tsp.	Baking soda
¼ tsp.	Sea salt
1 ½ c.	Carob chips

Let margarine stand at room temperature until soft. In a bowl, cream together the softened margarine, Sucanat, n'egg, and vanilla. In a separate bowl stir the flour, baking soda, and salt together. Add to creamed mixture and stir well. Stir in carob chips. Drop from a teaspoon 2 inches apart onto a greased cookie sheet. Bake at 375° for 10 to 12 minutes, or until golden brown.

COCONUT COOKIES

These are excellent for those who do not like overly sweet goodies.
If Red Riding Hood had some of these in her basket the wolf might have taken them and been satisfied!

½ c.	Non-dairy margarine
½ c.	Corn oil
⅓ c.	Water
¾ c.	Sucanat
¼ tsp.	Sea salt
½ tsp.	Vanilla
⅔ c.	Coconut
1 tsp.	Baking powder
1 T.	Cornstarch
2 c.	Unbleached white flour

Whip together the margarine, oil, water, and Sucanat until creamy. Beat in the salt, vanilla and coconut. Mix the baking powder, cornstarch, and flour and add to the creamed mixture to make a smooth drop batter. Drop the batter by heaping teaspoonfuls onto an oiled baking sheet. Bake at 350° for 10 to 12 minutes, until set. Remove immediately from the sheet and cool on a rack.

COLOSSAL COOKIES

The name says it all!

⅔ c.	Non-dairy margarine
5 c.	Sucanat
⅔ c.	Tofu Mayonnaisc, Cashcw Mayonnaise, or Miraculous Whip
1 ½ tsp.	Vanilla
2 ½ c.	Chunky peanut butter
7 ½ c.	Rolled oats
1 ¼ c.	Carob chips
1 T.	Baking soda

Cream the margarine and Sucanat. Add "mayonnaise" and vanilla. Add rest of ingredients. Drop by 2 tablespoonfuls on an oiled baking sheet. Bake at 375° in the middle of the oven until golden brown.

CRUNCHIES

8 T.	Non-dairy margarine
⅔ c.	Sucanat
1 ½ c.	Unbleached white flour
1 ¾ tsp.	Baking powder
½ c.	Oatmeal
2 T.	Currants
1 T.	Barbados molasses
½ tsp.	Allspice, ground

Melt the margarine in a saucepan. Remove from heat and stir in all the ingredients until evenly blended. Roll mixture into balls about the size of a walnut. Place well apart on a lightly greased baking sheet. Bake at 350° 12 to 15 minutes. Allow to cool slightly on the baking sheet before transferring to a wire rack.

FIERY GINGER SNAPS

Please Do!

¾ c.	Non-dairy margarine
1 ¾ c.	Sucanat
¼ c.	Barbados molasses
1	N'egg
2 ¼ c.	Unbleached white flour
2 tsp.	Baking soda
½ tsp.	Sea salt
1 T.	Powdered ginger
1 ¼ tsp.	Cinnamon
⅔ tsp.	Ground cloves
½ tsp.	Cayenne pepper

Cream together the margarine, Sucanat, molasses, and n'egg till light and fluffy. Sift together the other ingredients and stir into the molasses mixture till blended. Form into small balls. Roll heavily in powdered Sucanat and place 2 inches apart on an oiled cookie sheet. Flatten the cookies with the bottom of a glass. Bake at 375° for about 10 minutes. Remove from the pan immediately. Makes about 5 dozen cookies.

FIG BARS

Filling:

2 c.	Dried figs
2 tsp.	Lemon peel, grated
Pinch	Sea salt
1 ½ c.	Apple juice or cider

Crust:

½ c.	Non-dairy margarine
⅔ c.	Sucanat
1 c.	Unbleached white flour
1 c.	Rolled oats
1 tsp.	Baking powder
¼ tsp.	Sea salt

Bring figs, lemon peel, salt, and juice (or cider) to a boil. Simmer, covered, about 15 minutes, until the figs are fairly tender. Mash figs thoroughly with a potato masher. If necessary, simmer 10 more minutes and mash again until the mixture is smooth.

In a mixing bowl, combine the margarine and

Sucanat. Add the flour, oats, baking powder, and salt, and mix well. Crust should be crumbly. Press half the crust in the bottom of an 8-inch square baking pan. Spread the fig mixture evenly over it. Press the remaining crust mixture evenly on top. Bake for 40 minutes or until the topping is lightly browned.

Variation: Use other kinds of dried fruit.

FROSTED APPLE-DATE BITS

Cookies:

¾ c.	Non-dairy margarine
1 c.	Sucanat
1 tsp.	Vanilla
⅔ c.	Cashew Milk
2 c.	Unbleached white flour
½ tsp.	Baking soda
½ tsp.	Sea salt
1 tsp.	Cinnamon
¼ tsp.	Nutmeg
1 c.	Apples, very finely chopped
1 c.	Dates, finely chopped

In a large bowl, cream together margarine and Sucanat. Add vanilla and "milk" and mix well. Separately, mix the flour, baking soda, salt and spices. Add flour mixture to creamed mixture. Stir until well blended. Stir in chopped apples and dates. Drop by large tablespoonfuls onto greased cookie sheet. Bake at 375° for 8 to 10 minutes or until done. Cool.

Frosting:

2 T.	Non-dairy margarine
¼ c.	Water
1 tsp.	Cinnamon
1 ½ c.	Powdered Sucanat

Heat together the margarine and water over low heat until the margarine melts. Transfer to a mixing bowl. Add cinnamon and Sucanat. Blend well. Let set until thickened, then spread on cooled cookies.

FRUIT BARS

Truly elegant.

3 T.	Corn oil
1 T.	Barbados molasses
⅔ c.	Sucanat
¾ c.	Dates, chopped, or raisins
1	N'egg
2 tsp.	Vanilla
1 ½ c.	Unbleached white flour
¼ tsp.	Sea salt

½ tsp.	Baking powder
⅓ c.	Water

Beat together the first 8 ingredients. Stir in the baking powder and water. Beat well, then pour into a greased and floured cake pan. Bake at 350° for 25 to 30 minutes, or until just firm to the touch. Cut into bars while still warm.

GINGER SNAPS

Yes, they do!

¾ c.	Non-dairy margarine
1 ½ c.	Sucanat
¼ c.	Barbados molasses
1	N'egg
2 ¼ c.	Unbleached white flour, sifted
2 tsp.	Baking soda
½ tsp.	Sea salt
1 tsp.	Ginger
1 tsp.	Cinnamon
½ tsp.	Cloves

Cream together the margarine, Sucanat, molasses, and n'egg till light and fluffy. Sift together the other ingredients and stir into the molasses mixture till blended. Form into small balls. Roll in powdered Sucanat and place 2 inches apart on an oiled cookie sheet. Bake at 375° for about 10 minutes. Remove from the pan immediately. Makes about 5 dozen cookies.

GINGERNUTS

If you've read about these in Jane Eyre—here they are. And if you haven't, cook a batch and read the book as you eat them!

5 T.	Non-dairy margarine
1 ½ c.	Unbleached white flour
1 ¾ tsp.	Baking powder
⅓ c.	Sucanat
4 T.	Barbados molasses
¾ tsp.	Baking soda
2 tsp.	Ginger, ground

Rub margarine into flour and baking powder until mixture resembles fine crumbs. Stir in Sucanat. Warm molasses in a saucepan and stir in baking soda and ginger. Add ginger mixture to dry ingredients, and knead well to form a soft dough. Roll mixture into balls about the size of a walnut. Place well apart on oiled baking sheets and flatten slightly. Bake at 350° about 15 minutes. Allow to cool slightly on the baking sheet before transferring to a wire rack.

MAPLE NUT CHEWS

These have real style and rich flavor.

½ c.	Golden raisins
	Apple juice
3 T.	Non-dairy margarine
½ c.	Sucanat
½ tsp.	Maple flavoring
1	N'egg
½ c.	Unbleached white flour, sifted
¼ tsp.	Sea salt
¼ tsp.	Baking powder
½ c.	Pecans or walnuts, chopped

In a small saucepan, put the raisins and cover them with apple juice. Bring to a boil, turn off the heat, and let the raisins sit for 10 minutes. Drain the raisins and reserve the apple juice. In a saucepan, melt margarine and Sucanat, then cool slightly. Beat in the maple flavoring and n'egg. Sift flour, salt, and baking powder. Stir in the margarine mixture and 3 tablespoons of the reserved apple juice. Stir in the raisins and nuts. Spread ½ to ¾-inch thick in a greased pan. Bake at 350° for 25 to 30 minutes. Cool slightly and cut in bars. (The flavor is markedly better the next day.)

MOLASSES COOKIES–1

A favorite cookie, one to which we often turn whenever the cookie hunger strikes.

¾ c.	Non-dairy margarine
1 c.	Sucanat
1	N'egg
¼ c.	Barbados molasses
2 ¼ c.	Unbleached white flour
2 tsp.	Baking soda
¼ tsp.	Sea salt
1 tsp.	Ginger, ground
1 tsp.	Cinnamon, ground
½ tsp.	Cloves, ground
¼ c.	Powdered Sucanat for rolling

Cream together the margarine and Sucanat. Add n'egg and molasses and mix well. Separately combine the flour, baking soda, salt, and spices. Add flour mixture to creamed ingredients and blend well. Form dough into small or medium balls. Roll in powdered Sucanat and place 2 inches apart on a greased cookie sheet. Bake at 375° for 6 to 8 minutes.

MOLASSES COOKIES–2

6 c.	Unbleached white flour
¾ c.	Sucanat
1 ½ tsp.	Sea salt
4 ½ tsp.	Baking powder
¾ tsp.	Baking soda
2 ¼ c.	Barbados molasses
1 ½ tsp.	Wine vinegar
1 c.	Corn oil

Sift the dry ingredients together. Blend the liquid ingredients. Slowly add the dry into the wet ingredients while mixing with an electric hand mixer. Spoon out onto oiled cookie sheets. Bake at 350° for 10 minutes.

MOLASSES COOKIES–3

1 ¼ c.	Sucanat
¼ c.	Water
1 tsp.	White vinegar
1 c.	Non-dairy margarine
1 ¾ c.	Barbados molasses
3 c.	Unbleached white flour
2 tsp.	Ginger
2 tsp.	Cinnamon
1 tsp.	Salt
1 T.	Baking powder
½ tsp.	Baking soda

Blend Sucanat, water, vinegar, margarine, and molasses together. Sift together all remaining ingredients. Combine blended and sifted ingredients, and mix together well. Roll into balls, each about 2 tablespoons. Place on greased cookie sheet. Bake at 350° for about 10 minutes.

MONASTERY SHORTBREAD

We serve this to every one of our visitors.
Many have asked for the recipe but we have kept it as a trade secret. Now I give it to you!

3 c.	Unbleached white flour
¼ tsp.	Sea salt
¾ c.	Non-dairy margarine
½ c.	Genuine maple syrup
1 tsp.	Vanilla

Combine the flour and salt. Beat the margarine, syrup, and vanilla until smooth. Mix this into the flour, using your hands if necessary, until the dough is uniform and holds together. Pat into an oiled 9x13 pan. Bake at 350° 8 to 12 minutes until the edges are lightly browned. While still warm, cut into 2-inch squares. Cool completely in the pan and then remove.

OATMEAL CHEWIES

6 c.	Rolled oats
2 c.	Unbleached white flour
4 tsp.	Soy flour
1 tsp.	Baking soda
½ tsp.	Sea salt
2 dashes	Cinnamon
⅔ c.	Corn oil
⅔ c.	Water
2 c.	Barbados molasses
2 tsp.	Vanilla
1 c.	Raisins

Sift the dry ingredients together. Add rest of ingredients and mix together. Place on an oiled cookie sheet –2 tablespoons per cookie. Bake at 375° until light brown on the bottom.

OATMEAL-RAISIN COOKIES

If you missed these in childhood, then make up for it by eating plenty throughout your adulthood!

¾ c.	Non-dairy margarine
¾ c.	Sucanat
¼ c.	Barbados molasses
2 tsp.	Vanilla
1 ½ c.	Unbleached white flour
1 tsp.	Baking soda
1 ½ c.	Rolled oats
1 c.	Raisins

Cream together the margarine, Sucanat, and molasses. Stir in vanilla. Separately, combine the flour and baking soda. Combine flour mixture and creamed mixture and blend thoroughly. Add oats and raisins and mix well. Drop by large spoonfuls onto greased cookie sheet. Bake at 375° for 10 to 12 minutes or until done.

PEANUT BUTTER COOKIES–1

I think that peanut butter cookies—not apple pie—have become the standard of Americanism!
And these can set the standard!

1 ¼ c.	Unbleached white flour
¾ tsp.	Baking soda
¼ tsp.	Sea salt
½ c.	Non-dairy margarine
1 c.	Sucanat
½ c.	Peanut butter
1	N'egg
½ tsp.	Vanilla
½ tsp.	Water
	Powdered Sucanat

Combine the flour, soda, and salt. Separately combine the margarine and Sucanat. Combine everything and mix thoroughly, adding more water if necessary to get a moist–but not sticky– consistency. Shape in 1-inch balls. Roll in powdered Sucanat and place on a cookie sheet. Press on the tops of the balls in a crisscross pattern with a fork. Bake at 375° for 15 minutes.

PEANUT BUTTER COOKIES–2

These are not gourmet food, but although you CAN eat just one, you cannot eat just two or three!

1	N'egg
1 c.	Sucanat
1 c.	Smooth peanut butter

Mix all together. Scoop out level tablespoonfuls and roll into balls. Put on an unoiled baking sheet and flatten with a fork. Bake at 350° for 18 minutes. Cool on a wire rack.

SPICY HERMITS

Not quickly forgotten!

½ c.	Non-dairy margarine
1 ½ c.	Sucanat
¼ c.	Barbados molasses
1	N'egg
1 ½ c.	Unbleached white flour
1 T.	Instant coffee powder
½ tsp.	Baking soda
½ tsp.	Cinnamon
¼ tsp.	Sea salt
¼ tsp.	Nutmeg
¼ tsp.	Cloves
¾ c.	Raisins
½ c.	Walnuts, broken

Cream the margarine, Sucanat, molasses, and n'egg together. Sift the dry ingredients together and add to the creamed mixture. Stir in the raisins and nuts. Drop from a teaspoon 2 inches apart on a lightly oiled cookie sheet. Bake at 375° for 10 minutes. Makes about 3 ½ dozen cookies.

SUCANAT HEALTH COOKIES

1 ½ c.	Sucanat
½ c.	Corn oil
1 c.	Cashew Milk
2	N'eggs
1 T.	Vanilla
1 tsp.	Almond extract
½ tsp.	Sea salt

2 tsp.   Cinnamon
2 c.   Rolled oats
1 ½ c.   Unbleached white flour
2 tsp.   Baking powder
½ c.   Sunflower seeds
½ c.   Almonds, chopped
½ c.   Walnuts or pecans, chopped
1 c.   Raisins

Combine the Sucanat, "milk," and n'eggs. Stir in the vanilla, salt, and cinnamon. Then the oats, flour, baking powder, nuts, and raisins. Drop by tablespoons on a cookie sheet and flatten with fingers. Bake 12 to 15 minutes at 350°.

Pies

BASIC PIE CRUST

The secret of this is for the margarine and water to be as cold as possible.

- 6 c. Unbleached white flour
- 1 T. Sea salt
- 1 ½ c. Non-dairy margarine, cold, and cut into bits
- 1 c. Ice water

Sift the flour and salt together. Add the margarine and stir with a fork until all is crumbly. Add the water slowly, kneading it at the same time until all holds together–then stop. Divide into balls. Roll out about ⅛-inch thick. Put in a pie pan or dish. Bake at 350° for 35 minutes.

CONVENT PIE CRUST

- 1 ½ c. Unbleached white flour
- ⅛ tsp. Sea salt
- 2 T. Sucanat
- 6 T. Non-dairy margarine
- ½ tsp. Vanilla
- 3-4 T. Cold water

Put the flour, salt, and Sucanat is a food processor and process with the standard cutting blade for 1 minute. Add the margarine and process 30 more seconds. Add the vanilla and water through the tube and process until the dough forms into a ball. (If you do not have a processor, just combine the first three ingredients, cut in the margarine, add the vanilla and water, and stir to form a ball.) Wrap in wax paper and chill at least 30 minutes. Roll out the dough and put into a 9-inch pie pan. *Note:* For non-sweet dishes, omit the Sucanat and vanilla and increase the salt to ¼ tsp.

GRAHAM CRACKER CRUST

- 1 ¼ c. Graham crackers, ground
- ¼ c. Sucanat
- ¼ c. Non-dairy margarine
- Pinch Cinnamon
- Pinch Nutmeg

Combine all ingredients and press into a pie pan and bake at 375° for 6 to 8 minutes or until browned.

GRAHAM CRACKER-WALNUT CRUST

- 1 ½ c. Graham cracker crumbs–very fine
- 1 c. Walnuts, chopped
- 3 T. Non-dairy margarine, softened

Mix everything together well and press into a pie pan.

GRAPE-NUTS PIE CRUST

- 2 c. Grape-Nuts
- ⅓ c. Apple juice concentrate, thawed
- 3 T. Water
- 1 tsp. Cinnamon
- 1 tsp. Dried lemon peel

Put the Grape-Nuts into a blender or food processor and process briefly until crushed, or put them in a plastic bag and crush with a rolling pin. Put everything in a bowl and combine thoroughly, adding more water if needed to make the Grape-Nuts come together. Press into a nonstick pie pan or dish.

APPLE PIE

4 c.	Apples
1 T.	Water
3 c.	Sucanat
2 T.	Barbados molasses
½	Lemon rind, grated
¼ tsp.	Cinnamon
	Pie crust dough

Peel, core, and slice the apples. Put apples, water, Sucanat, molasses, lemon rind, and cinnamon in a saucepan. Simmer 10 minutes, stirring occasionally. Do not allow the apples to become mushy. Cool. Line a 9-inch pie pan with dough. Fill with the apples. Top with pie crust and seal edges well. Make a hole in the center of the top crust. Bake at 400° about 25 minutes, or until golden brown.

Variation: For a "mincemeat" flavor, use ground cloves instead of cinnamon.

BANANA CREAM PIE

Luscious is the word for this!

4 c.	Cashew Milk
1 c.	Sucanat
½ c.	Coconut
½ c.	Cornstarch
¼ tsp.	Sea salt
2 tsp.	Vanilla
4	Ripe bananas
1 ½ c.	Soy Whipped Cream or Tofu Whipped Cream

Put the "milk," Sucanat, coconut, cornstarch, salt and vanilla in a saucepan and stir constantly while cooking until thick. Mash 2 bananas and add to mixture. DO NOT COOK. Slice the other bananas and add. Pour into a baked pie crust and chill until set. Top with whipped cream.

Variation: Use a graham cracker crust.

BERRY CREAM PIE

Crust:

1 ½ c.	Graham cracker crumbs
2 T.	Sucanat
¼ c.	Almonds, ground to a meal in a blender
1 tsp.	Cinnamon
½ tsp.	Ground ginger
3 T.	Oil

Combine the cracker crumbs, Sucanat, almonds, cinnamon, and ginger in a medium-sized mixing bowl. Add the oil and mix well. Press the mixture on the bottom and sides of an 8 or 9-inch pie pan. Bake at 375° for 10 minutes. Cool before filling.

Glaze:

1 c.	Apple juice or white grape juice
1	Heaping tablespoon of agar flakes or 1 ½ T. arrowroot powder dissolved in 1 ½ tablespoons of cold water

Pour the juice into a small saucepan and bring it to a simmer. *If using agar:* sprinkle the flakes over the juice without stirring and simmer gently 3 to 5 minutes, stirring if necessary to completely dissolve the agar. *If using arrowroot:* add the dissolved powder to the simmering juice while stirring briskly. Continue stirring until the mixture thickens–1 to 2 minutes. Cool to lukewarm before using.

Filling:

1 recipe	Vanilla Pudding
2 c.	Blueberries
1 ½ c.	Peaches or strawberries, sliced

Prepare the vanilla pudding and allow it to cool to lukewarm. Pour it into the prebaked shell. Cover with 1 ½ cups of the blueberries. Neatly arrange the sliced peaches or strawberries on top. Add the remaining ½ cup of blueberries. Spoon the glaze over the berries.

BLUEBERRY COBBLER

2 c.	Fresh or canned blueberries
1 ½ c.	Sucanat
1 c.	Unbleached white flour
1 ½ tsp.	Baking powder
¼ tsp.	Salt
1	N'egg
1 c.	Cashew Milk
2 T.	Non-dairy margarine, melted

Place the berries in a buttered 9x9-inch baking pan. Sprinkle a little less than half the Sucanat over them evenly. In a bowl, mix together the flour, baking powder, and salt. Mix the rest of the Sucanat and the n'egg and stir it into the flour. Slowly add the "milk." Then add the melted margarine. Stir vigorously until it is smoothly blended. Pour this batter evenly over the berries. Bake at 400° for 30 to 35 minutes, or until the batter is golden brown.

BLUEBERRY PIE FILLING

1 ¾ c.	Canned blueberries
⅓ c.	Sucanat
¼ c. & 2 T.	Unbleached white flour
¾ tsp.	Sea salt
¾ tsp.	Cinnamon
¼ c. & 2 T.	Non-dairy margarine

Drain berries and save liquid. Combine Sucanat, flour, salt, and cinnamon, and stir into the liquid saved from the berries. Heat, stirring constantly, until thick and smooth. Add margarine and berries.

CATHERINE XENIA'S PUMPKIN PIE FILLING

Those who love pumpkin pie will love this even more!

1	16-oz. can pumpkin
1 c. & 2 T.	Sucanat
¼ c.	Tapioca
1 ½ tsp.	Cinnamon
½ tsp.	Powdered ginger
¼ tsp.	Ground cloves
½ tsp.	Sea salt
1 ¾ c.	Cashew Milk
¼ c.	Genuine maple syrup
1	9-inch unbaked pie crust (Convent Pie Crust)

Mix pumpkin and the dry ingredients. Add the "milk" and syrup and heat. Pour into the pie shell. Bake at 400° for 15 minutes. Turn down to 300° and bake for 55 more minutes. Cover the edges of the crust with foil after 35 minutes to prevent overbaking. Let the pie cool completely. Then combine:

¾ c.	Chopped walnuts
6 T.	Sucanat
3 T.	Genuine maple syrup
2 T.	Non-dairy margarine, melted

Spread this over the top of the pie. Broil about 5 inches from the heat source for 3 minutes or until the topping is bubbly.

CHERRY COBBLER

You won't be sorry!

4 c.	Cherries
2 T.	Cornstarch
⅔ c.	Sucanat
2 T.	Lemon juice
¼ tsp.	Almond extract

1 c.	Unbleached white flour
1 tsp.	Baking powder
½ tsp.	Sea salt
2 T.	Sucanat
1 T.	Water
6 T.	Non-dairy margarine, cold and cut into bits
¼ c.	Boiling water

Pit the cherries. Into the cherries stir the cornstarch, ⅔ cup of Sucanat, lemon juice, and almond extract. Combine the flour, baking powder, salt, Sucanat, tablespoon of water, and margarine, blending them until all resembles coarse meal. Stir in the boiling water, stirring only until the batter is just combined. In an 8-inch skillet or baking dish bring the cherry mixture to a boil. Drop the batter by heaping tablespoons onto it. Bake at 350° for 45 to 50 minutes, until the top is golden.

CHERRY PIE

1 ⅓ c.	Liquid from canned cherries, or water if they are fresh
½ c.	Cornstarch
1 ⅓ c.	Sucanat
¼ tsp.	Sea salt
4 c.	Cherries, pitted (if canned, save liquid and use in recipe)
2 T.	Non-dairy margarine

Mix some of the liquid with the cornstarch. Heat rest of liquid to boiling. Add cornstarch mixture, stirring with a wire whip. Cook until thick and clear. Stir in the Sucanat and salt. Bring to a boil, stirring. Remove from heat. Add cherries, mixing gently. Cool thoroughly. Put in unbaked pie shell. Dot the top with the margarine and put on the top crust, cutting ventilation slits in it. Bake at 425° for 1 hour or until well browned.

CONVENT CARAMEL APPLE PIE

Proof that you can always make a good thing better!

½ c.	Sucanat
½ c.	Genuine maple syrup
2 T.	Unbleached white flour
1 ½ tsp.	Lemon juice
½ tsp.	Lemon peel, grated
⅓ c.	Cashew Milk
½ tsp.	Cinnamon
½ tsp.	Vanilla
5 ½ c.	Apples, peeled and cut into about 16 slices per apple

1 9-inch unbaked pie shell

Combine all the filling ingredients except the apples, and stir to combine well. Add the apples and stir well again. Pour into the pie shell. Cover entire pie lightly with foil. Bake at 375° for 1 hour or until the apples are soft. Remove the foil, bake 10 to 15 more minutes—enough to brown the crust. Take from the oven. Spoon the liquid that has settled at the bottom over the apples to coat them. Cool on a rack.

FRUIT PIE–1

4 c.	Fruit
1 ½ c.	Sucanat
3 T.	Cornstarch
⅛ tsp.	Sea salt
⅓ c.	Water for blending–only if needed
2 T.	Lemon juice (*only* if fruit is not naturally tart)
1	Baked pie crust

Chop 1 cup of the fruit–not too fine. Blend the rest of the fruit with the Sucanat, cornstarch, salt, and water (if needed). Boil until thickened. Add the lemon juice, if needed. Cool slightly and mix in the whole fruit. Pour into the baked pie crust and let cool.

FRUIT PIE–2

4 c.	Fruit
1 ½ c.	Sucanat
3 T.	Cornstarch
⅛ tsp.	Sea salt
⅓ c.	Water for blender, only if needed
2 T.	Lemon juice (ONLY if fruit is not naturally tart)

Set aside 3 cups of fruit . Blend 1 cup of the fruit with the Sucanat, cornstarch, salt and water (if needed). Add the 3 cups of whole fruit to mixture. Boil until thickened. Add the lemon juice, if needed. Pour into an unbaked pie crust. Cover with top crust that has slits in it to let out the steam. Bake at 400° about 30 minutes until brown.

LEMON CUSTARD PIE

1	Lemon, quartered, seeds removed
½ c.	Water
2 c.	Orange juice
1 T.	Oil
1 ¼ c.	Sucanat
¼ c.	Cornstarch

Place the lemon in a blender–peel and all–with all the other ingredients and blend until it is finely ground. Place in a saucepan and bring to a boil. Simmer about 2 minutes, stirring constantly. Pour into a baked pie shell and chill.
Variation: Use 3 oranges, peeled and with seeds removed, instead of the orange juice. They should be blended until fine with the lemon.

PEACH PIE

4 c.	Peaches, sliced
1 c.	Sucanat
2 T.	Unbleached white flour
⅛ tsp.	Cinnamon
⅛ tsp.	Sea salt
2 T.	Non-dairy margarine

Combine the ingredients except for the margarine. Put in unbaked pie shell. Dot the top with the margarine and put on the top crust, cutting ventilation slits in it. Bake at 425° for 1 hour or until well browned.

PECAN PIE

How I used to yearn for pecan pie–but since eggs seemed a necessary ingredient I had to keep on yearning! But now I can have all I want–and so can you!

¼ c.	Non-dairy margarine, melted
¼ c.	Cornstarch or arrowroot
2 c.	Cashew Milk
½ c.	Genuine maple syrup
½ c.	Sucanat
2 tsp.	Vanilla
1 c.	Chopped pecans, toasted in 4 teaspoons of margarine
½ c.	Pecan halves, toasted in 2 teaspoons of margarine
1	10-inch baked pie shell

Combine the margarine, cornstarch (or arrowroot), "milk," syrup, Sucanat, and vanilla in a blender and blend until smooth. Cook in a saucepan until thickened, stirring constantly–5 minutes. Stir in the chopped pecans. Pour into the pie shell and top with the pecan halves. Let cool.

PINEAPPLE PIE

2 c.	Crushed, unsweetened pineapple
⅓ c.	Cornstarch
1 tsp.	Lemon or orange peel, grated
¾ c.	Sucanat
⅛ tsp.	Salt

Drain off the pineapple juice and mix the cornstarch into it. Combine all the ingredients and cook until thick. Pour into a baked pie crust.

SHOOFLY PIE

1 c.	Unbleached white flour
¾ c.	Sucanat
1 tsp.	Cinnamon
¼ tsp.	Ginger, powdered
¼ tsp.	Cloves, ground
¼ tsp.	Sea salt
3 T.	Non-dairy margarine, softened and cut into bits
½ c.	Barbados molasses
½ c.	Boiling water
½ tsp.	Baking soda
1	Pie crust

In a mixing bowl, combine flour, Sucanat, spices, and salt. With a fork, work the margarine into the dry ingredients until the mixture resembles a coarse meal. In another bowl, dissolve the molasses in the boiling water. Sprinkle in the baking soda and stir until it dissolves. Add about two-thirds of the crumb mixture and stir together until the crumbs are moistened, but the mixture need not be smooth. Pour into the pie crust and top with the remaining crumbs. Bake at 375° for 30 to 35 minutes, or until the crust and crumbs are golden and the filling is set. Serve warm or at room temperature.

SISTER MARY MICHAEL'S MINCEMEAT PIE

Truly worth it!

1 ½ c.	Granny Smith apples, peeled, cored, and chopped fine
1 c.	Golden raisins, chopped
½ c.	Prunes, chopped
½ c.	Apple juice
¼ c.	Orange juice
3 T.	Lemon juice
2 tsp.	Lemon rind, grated
2 tsp.	Orange rind, grated
1 c.	Sucanat
½ tsp.	Sea salt
1 tsp.	Cinnamon
¼ tsp.	Cloves
3 T.	Unbleached white flour
½ tsp.	Vanilla

Combine all the ingredients and put into a pie shell. Cover the outer edges of the crust with foil. Bake at 350° for 45 minutes. Remove the foil and bake 15 more minutes. Cool to room temperature before serving.
Note: If the lemon or orange peel is dyed, you should lightly shave off the outermost layer with a potato peeler before grating.

STRAWBERRY PIE FILLING

4 c.	Frozen strawberries
½ c.	Sucanat
3 T.	Unbleached white flour
½ tsp.	Sea salt

Drain berries and save liquid. Combine the Sucanat, flour and salt, and stir into the liquid. Heat, stirring constantly, until thick and smooth. Add berries.

Sweet Pastry

CINNAMON ROLLS

Why comment? Enjoy!

4 tsp.	Cinnamon
½ c.	Powdered Sucanat
1	Sweet Roll Dough recipe
½ c.	Non-dairy margarine, melted
1 c.	Raisins or thick fruit jam

Combine the cinnamon and Sucanat. Make the Sweet Roll Dough recipe. Roll out the dough into a 8x14-inch rectangle. Brush with melted margarine. Sprinkle with cinnamon-Sucanat, and then the raisins or jam. Roll up like a jelly roll, starting at the wide end. Cut into 1-inch "slices." Place close together in an oiled pan and brush with melted margarine. Cover and let rise in a warm place until one-half again as big. Bake at 375° for 20 to 30 minutes. Let cool, then spread Confectioner's Icing (2 times the recipe) over the rolls.

CONFECTIONER'S ICING

3 T.	Water
1 tsp.	Non-dairy margarine
1 ⅔ c.	Powdered Sucanat
Pinch	Sea salt
1 tsp.	Vanilla

Bring the water to a boil and immediately add the margarine, stirring. When the margarine is melted, add the Sucanat, salt, and vanilla. Stir until the Sucanat is melted. Add more boiling water drop by drop if necessary to produce a smooth-spreading consistency. Beat 2 or 3 minutes until very creamy, keeping the sides scraped down. Drizzle immediately on slightly warm baked goods.

Variation: Add ⅓ cup of carob powder. Lemon or other fresh (strained) fruit juice may be substituted for the water and vanilla, if desired.

DOUGHNUT SQUARES

¼ c.	Lukewarm water
1 pkg.	Dry yeast
¼ c.	Sucanat
2 T.	Non-dairy margarine
½ tsp.	Sea salt
½ c.	Boiling water
½ c.	Cashew Cream
1	N'egg
4 ½ c.	Unbleached white flour

Pour the water in a small bowl and sprinkle the yeast over it. Let it rest for 2 or 3 minutes, then mix well. Set in a warm, draft-free place for about 10 minutes, or until the yeast bubbles up and the mixture almost doubles in bulk.

Meanwhile combine the Sucanat, margarine, and salt in another bowl. Pour in the boiling water and stir with a wooden spoon until the ingredients are thoroughly blended and the mixture has cooled to lukewarm. Stir in the "cream," yeast mixture, and n'egg. Add 2 cups of the flour and, when it is completely incorporated, beat in up to 2 ½ more cups of flour, ¼ cup at a time. Add only enough flour to make the dough smooth and not sticky.

When the dough becomes too stiff to stir easily with the spoon, work in the additional flour with your fingers. Gather the dough into a ball, place it on a lightly floured surface and pat it into a rectangle about 1 inch thick. Dust a little flour over and under the dough and roll it out from the center to within an inch of the far edge (of the *dough*, that is, not the floured surface!). Lift the dough and turn it at right angles, then roll again from the center as before.

Repeat–lifting, turning, rolling–until the rectangle is about ¼-inch thick and at least 25 inches long by 10 inches wide. (If the dough sticks to the surface, lift it with a wide metal spatula and sprinkle a little flour under it.)

With a pastry wheel or sharp knife, cut the dough into 10 5-inch squares. Immediately deep-fry them in 350° oil, two or three at a time. Turn them over with a slotted spoon as they rise to the surface. Continue deep-frying, turning frequently, for about 3 to 5 minutes, or until they are crisp and golden brown on all sides. Transfer to paper towel.

When lukewarm, glaze with Confectioner's Icing.

DOUGHNUTS

Make Sweet Roll Dough recipe. Roll out to ½-inch thickness. Let rest five minutes. Dip a 3-inch doughnut cutter into flour and cut out doughnuts. Let rise, uncovered, on floured pans in a warm place until light (about 45 minutes). Fry in deep fryer at 370° for about 3 minutes, turning once. (They should be golden brown on each side.) Drain on paper towels. Glaze with Confectioner's Icing.

FRUIT SCONES

2 c.	Unbleached white flour
3 tsp.	Baking powder
	Pinch of salt
6 T.	Non-dairy margarine
3 T.	Sucanat
½ c.	Golden seedless raisins, soaked in warm water 30 minutes and drained
½ c.	Cashew Milk

Put flour, baking powder, and salt in a bowl. Rub in the margarine until mixture resembles fine crumbs. Stir in Sucanat and raisins, then add enough "milk" for a soft, manageable dough. Knead gently on a lightly floured surface, then roll out about ¾-inch thick. Cut out 3-inch rounds. Place fairly close together on a lightly greased baking sheet and bake at 425° for 10 to 15 minutes, or until golden brown. Cool on a wire rack. Best to eat these the day they are made.

JELLY-FILLED DOUGHNUTS

Make as above, except cut into 2 ½-inch rounds. After draining on paper towels, inject fruit filling. Glaze with Confectioner's Icing.

RAISIN DUNKERS

A treasure! We have relied on these through the years!

2 ⅓ c.	Unbleached white flour
¼ c.	Sucanat
1 T.	Baking powder
1 tsp.	Sea salt
¼ tsp.	Cinnamon
⅓ c.	Non-dairy margarine
¾ c.	Cashew Milk
⅔ c.	Raisins, chopped
1 c.	Non-dairy margarine, melted
¾ tsp.	Cinnamon
¾ c.	Powdered Sucanat (see the Etc. section)

Sift the flour with the Sucanat, baking powder, salt and cinnamon. Cut in the ⅓ cup of margarine. Add the "milk" and raisins, stirring to a soft dough (add more cashew milk if necessary). Turn onto a lightly floured board. Roll out to ½-inch thickness. Cut into strips 2 inches wide and 5 inches long. Dip in the melted margarine and place on a baking sheet. Bake at 425° for about 15 minutes, until lightly browned. Mix the cinnamon and Sucanat together. Dip the dunker strips again in melted margarine and roll in the cinnamon-Sucanat. One times this recipe makes about one dozen dunkers.

RAISIN-ORANGE COFFEE CAKE

2 T.	Unbleached white flour
3 T.	Sucanat
1 T.	Non-dairy margarine, softened
1 c.	Unbleached white flour
2 tsp.	Baking powder
½ tsp.	Sea salt
¼ c.	Non-dairy margarine
⅓ c.	Sucanat
2 tsp.	Grated orange peel
⅓ c.	Orange juice
¼ c.	Cashew Milk
½ c.	Raisins

Mix together the first three ingredients until crumbly and set aside for topping. Stir together the 1 cup of flour, baking powder, and salt, and set aside. In a small mixing bowl beat the margarine and Sucanat until well combined. Add orange peel and beat well. Stir in orange juice, "milk," and raisins. Add flour mixture, stirring until just moistened. Spread batter evenly in a greased baking pan. Sprinkle with topping. Bake at 350° about 25 minutes or until it tests done. Drizzle with a glaze made of Powdered Sucanat and hot water.

SWEET ROLL DOUGH

⅔ c.	Cashew Milk
Pinch	Sea salt
½ c.	Sucanat
½ c.	Non-dairy margarine
2 T.	Yeast
¼ c.	Lukewarm water
1 tsp.	Sucanat
1	N'egg
4 ½ c.	Unbleached white flour
1 tsp.	Lemon rind, grated
½ tsp.	Mace

Heat the "milk" with salt, ½ cup of Sucanat, and margarine until the margarine melts. Allow to cool to lukewarm. Combine yeast, water, and teaspoon of Sucanat, and allow to dissolve. Add the n'egg and the yeast mixture to the cashew milk solution. Combine half the flour with lemon rind and mace, then add the liquid, beating until smooth. Mix in the remaining flour. Let it stand for 10 minutes. Knead for 5 minutes on a lightly floured board. Place dough in a lightly greased bowl, turning once to bring the greased side up. Cover with a damp cloth and let rise in a warm place until double. Punch down, turn over, cover, and let rise until double again. Punch down, shape into 2 balls on a lightly floured surface. Cover with a bowl and let rest 10 minutes. Dough is then ready for use in doughnuts, cinnamon rolls, or other pastries.

Etc.

BAKED SPRING ROLLS

2 oz.	Rice vermicelli
½ tsp.	Sesame oil
¾ c.	Carrots, coarsely grated
½ c.	Green onions, thinly sliced
½ c.	Water chestnuts, cut into matchstick pieces
½ c.	Bamboo shoots, cut into matchstick pieces
½ c.	Snow peas, thinly sliced
½ c.	Savoy cabbage, very finely shredded
¼ c.	Sunflower seeds
1 T.	Sesame seeds, toasted
1 tsp.	Soy sauce
4 tsp.	Corn oil
8	Sheets (8 ½-inch diameter) of rice paper

Cook the rice vermicelli in boiling water for 3 minutes, and drain. Place in a large bowl and toss with the sesame oil. Add the vegetables, sunflower seeds, sesame seeds, and soy sauce. Toss again and set aside. Place the oil in a small dish. Dip 1 sheet of the rice paper into warm water for 15 to 30 seconds, until soft. Place on a dish towel. Brush the surface lightly with oil. Spoon ⅛ of the filling onto the bottom half of the rice paper. Fold the bottom edge of the rice paper to just cover the filling. Brush the surface lightly with oil. Fold in the edges, then roll up, brushing the surfaces with oil as you roll. Repeat with the remaining rice paper sheets and filling. Place each roll seam-side down on a foil-lined cookie sheet. Bake at 450° on the lowest oven rack for 15 to 20 minutes, turning once, until lightly browned.

BREAD CRUMB TOPPING

2 c.	Bread crumbs
1 ½ tsp.	Garlic cloves, minced
2 T.	Parsley, chopped
2 T.	Corn oil
	Black pepper
	Tomato purée or paste

Toss the crumbs, garlic, parsley, oil, and pepper together in a bowl. Mix in just enough tomato purée or paste to add a touch of color.

BREADING FOOD FOR FRYING

The breading material may be cracker crumbs, bread crumbs, corn meal, or any "crunchy" form of grain. They may be used plain or combined with seasonings. Roll the food to be breaded in the crumbs, then dip them in n'egg and again roll them in the crumbs. To avoid sticky hands, bread with one hand and dip with the other. If breading is done half an hour before the food is fried, the crumbs will have a better chance to adhere. It is important to cover the entire surface of the food with n'egg–or dip in "milk"–before the second "crumbing."

CAROB FUDGE

How sweet it really is!

3 T.	Non-dairy margarine
½ c.	Carob powder
¼ c.	Powdered Sucanat
⅔ c.	Ground almonds
1 tsp.	Vanilla extract
3 T.	Almonds, ground or finely chopped

Blend margarine and carob powder thoroughly. Add the Sucanat, almonds, and vanilla, and mix thoroughly. Sprinkle ground almonds on a clean dry surface and shape the fudge into a roll, coating it with almonds. Cut into bite-size pieces. Keep in refrigerator until needed.

CINNAMON TOAST

Mix one part cinnamon with three parts of Powdered Sucanat. Sprinkle on buttered toast. Place toast slices in a moderate oven or under a broiler to crisp them.

Variation: Instead of 1 part cinnamon, use half nutmeg and half cinnamon.

COCONUT MILK

After breaking the shell and removing the meat, pare off the brown skin. Chop or break the meat into small chunks. Measure the meat and put it and an equal measure of hot (not boiling) water into a blender and blend at high speed for 1 minute. Stop the machine and scrape down the sides with a rubber spatula. Blend again until the coconut is reduced to a thick, fibrous liquid. Scrape the entire contents of the blender into a fine sieve lined with a double thickness of dampened cheesecloth and set over a deep bowl. With a wooden spoon, press down hard on the coconut to extract as much liquid as possible. Bring the ends of the cheesecloth together to enclose the pulp and wring the ends vigorously to squeeze out the remaining liquid. Discard the pulp.

DEEP-FRYING BATTER

This is excellent for frying gluten, but works for vegetables, too.

1 tsp.	Basil, powdered
1 tsp.	Black pepper
½ tsp.	Garlic salt
3 c.	Unbleached white flour
2 T.	Baking powder
2-3 c.	Club soda

Combine the basil, pepper, garlic salt, flour, and baking powder. Add the soda until you have a batter of the desired consistency. Dip whatever you wish to fry into the batter and then deep-fry at 400°.

FRENCH TOAST

1 ½ c.	Water

3 T.	Soy flour
1 T.	Cornstarch
1 T.	Sucanat
¼ tsp.	Vanilla
Pinch	Sea salt
Pinch	Cinnamon
2 T.	Non-dairy margarine, melted
¼ tsp.	Tumeric

Blend everything in a blender until perfectly combined and smooth. Heat together until it thickens into a "batter." Soak bread slices in the batter and then fry to golden brown on both sides.

FRIED CHEEZ BALLS

1 c.	Biscuit Mix
⅓ c.	Water
1 ½ c.	Yeast or Pimento Cheez
⅓ c.	Onions, chopped

Mix everything together, form into 1-inch balls, and fry in oil.

FRUIT JAM

¾ c. & 2 T.	Cornstarch
6 c.	Sucanat
6 c.	Fruit, mashed well

Mix the cornstarch with the Sucanat, and add to the fruit. Cook for 20 minutes. Allow to cool, and can or refrigerate.

GARLIC BREAD

½ c.	Non-dairy margarine
1 T.	Garlic, put through a garlic press
¼ c.	Parmesan Cheez
⅛ tsp.	Black pepper

Melt the margarine, add the garlic, and let it "steep" at very low heat for 2 minutes. Mix in the cheez and pepper, and stir well. Spread generously on bread and toast it in the oven.

GARLIC OLIVES

Oh, my, oh, my!

⅔ c.	Olive oil
⅓ c.	Lemon juice or vinegar
1 T.	Garlic, minced
1 ¼ c.	Ripe olives

Combine everything and refrigerate overnight or at least for several hours. Use whenever ripe olives are called for. Improves with age.

HOT CHEEZ AND CIDER DIP

Now this is really different!

½ c.	Apple cider
1 c.	Yeast or Pimento Cheez
½ tsp.	Sea salt
⅛ tsp.	Cayenne pepper
¼ tsp.	Parsley or chives, finely chopped
Pinch	Garlic salt

Heat the cider to the boiling point, then reduce to a simmer. Stir the cheez gradually into the cider until all is well blended. Add the seasonings.

INSTANT TOMATO JUICE

1 c.	Tomato paste
4 c.	Water
1 tsp.	Sea salt

Mix together thoroughly. You can put it through a blender, but will have to wait until the bubbles and froth subside.
Note: For a tomato juice cocktail, add pepper (or hot sauce), garlic powder, and a little lemon juice to this.

INSTANT TOMATO PURÉE

1 c.	Tomato paste
1 c.	Water
1 tsp.	Sea salt

Mix together thoroughly. You can put it through a blender, but will have to wait until the bubbles and froth subside.

INSTANT TOMATO SAUCE

1 c.	Tomato paste
2 c.	Water
1 tsp.	Sea salt

Mix together thoroughly. You can put it through a blender, but will have to wait until the bubbles and froth subside.

"MAPLE" SYRUP

2 c.	Sucanat
1 c.	Water
½ tsp.	Cream of tartar
½ tsp.	Maple flavoring

Boil the Sucanat, water, and cream of tartar for 3 minutes. Remove from heat and add maple flavoring.

MULLED CIDER

1 qt.	Cider
3	Whole cloves
3	Whole allspice
1	3-inch stick of cinnamon
¼	Lemon, unpeeled, thinly sliced
¼ c.	Sucanat

Boil together for 10 minutes. Strain and serve hot.

ORANGE-GRAPE JUICE

Equal parts of white grape juice and orange juice.

PANCAKE SYRUP–1

1 c.	Water
2 c.	Sucanat
1 ½ tsp.	Maple flavor

Combine all ingredients, bring to a boil, and immediately take off the heat and set to cool.

PANCAKE SYRUP–2

1 c.	Barbados molasses
2 c.	Sucanat
½ c.	Water
1 ½ tsp.	Maple flavor

Combine all ingredients, bring to a boil, and immediately take off the heat and set to cool.

PANCAKES–1

2 c.	Biscuit mix
1 c.	Cashew Milk or water
2	N'eggs

Beat the ingredients until smooth and pour by scant ¼ cupfuls onto a hot griddle (oiled if necessary). Cook until the edges are dry, then turn over and cook until golden brown.

PANCAKES–2

1 ¼ c.	Flour
2 T.	Sucanat
2 tsp.	Baking powder
½ tsp.	Sea salt
2 T.	Corn oil
1 ¼ c.	Water (or ½ cup of Cashew Milk plus ¾ cup of water)

Combine the dry ingredients. Pour the liquids into a "well" in the center of the dry ingredients. Stir together until just blended–the batter will be lumpy. (Do not overmix.) Cook on oiled griddle or skillet.

PARTY CHEEZ DIP

2 c.   Tofu Cream Cheez
1 c.   Pimento or Notzarella Cheez
1 T.   Pimento, chopped
1 T.   Bell pepper, chopped
1 T.   Onion, chopped fine
1 T.   Lemon juice
4 tsp.   Lea & Perrins Steak Sauce
2 T.   Louisiana Hot Sauce
⅛ tsp.   Sea salt

Combine all and let sit for a while to develop flavor.

PECAN PATTIES

1 c.   Pecans, ground to a cornmeal-like consistency
1 c.   Rice, cooked
1 c.   Cashew Milk
1 T.   Soy flour
1 tsp.   Sea salt
1 T.   Dried parsley flakes
1 c.   Bread crumbs
1 T.   Dried minced onion
¼ tsp.   Garlic powder

Combine all ingredients and shape into patties. Place on an oiled cookie sheet. Brush the tops with corn oil. Bake at 350° until brown–about 30 minutes.

POWDERED SUCANAT

½ c.   Sucanat
2 T.   Cornstarch

Combine and powder at high speed in a blender.

SELF-RISING FLOUR

1 c.   Unbleached white flour with 2 tsp. taken out
1 ½ tsp. Baking powder
½ tsp.   Sea salt

Combine well.

SPICY TOMATO JUICE

7 c.   Tomato juice, made from fresh tomatoes
1 tsp.   Sea salt
⅛ tsp.   Cayenne pepper

Simmer together for 15 minutes. Cool and refrigerate.

UNSHRIMP DIP

Don't dilute the soup but use it direct from the can.

1 can   Campbell's Tomato Soup
½ c.   Catsup
4 tsp.   Louisiana Hot Sauce or 2 tsp. Tabasco
½ tsp.   Onion juice
¼ tsp.   Garlic salt
½ tsp.   Celery, minced
Dash   Paprika
Dash   Cayenne pepper
1 T.   Non-dairy margarine

Combine everything except the margarine, and beat together well. Chill. Just before serving, blend in the margarine until the mixture becomes smooth.

UNCOOKED APPLESAUCE

This is a wonderful surprise! Having tried it, you will never want the canned goop!

8 c.   Granny Smith apples, peeled, cored, and quartered
2 T.   Lemon juice
1 c.   Sucanat
½ tsp.   Cinnamon
⅛ tsp.   Nutmeg

Purée the apples in a blender until just smooth. Add rest of ingredients, mix well, and chill.

VEGETARIAN DOG FOOD

This was formulated by a veterinarian for his dogs, and we have raised several healthy dogs using it as their basic food. However, you should obtain Dogs and Cats Go Vegetarian, *by Barbara Lynn Peden, for a full picture on vegetarian dogs and cats and their nutritional requirements.*

1 gal.   Leftover vegetables, peels, ends, etc.
          Water to cover
2 T.   Baking yeast
4 c.   Soybeans
6 c.   Rolled oats

Save the peels, ends, etc., from vegetables when you prepare your food, and keep them refrigerated, *uncooked*, until you have 1 gallon, or just put in what extra vegetables you may have to make up the amount. If need be, cut the vegetables into chunks. The night before you are going to make the dog food, put the soybeans in water and let them soak overnight. The next day grind them in either a food mill or a blender. (If there is any corn among the vegetables, that should be ground, as well.) When ready to cook, put the vegetables, soybeans, and yeast in a large pot and cover with water. Bring to a boil and simmer/low boil for about 2 hours. Add the rolled oats and cook until they are done.

WAFFLES

2 c.   Biscuit Mix
1 ½ c.   Cashew Milk
1   N'egg

Beat the ingredients until smooth. Pour onto center of hot waffle iron. Bake until steaming stops. Remove carefully.

Index